D0908867

VOLUME TWO

The Illustrated History of Humankind

GREAT CIVILIZATIONS

SOCIETY AND CULTURE IN THE ANCIENT WORLD

VOLUME TWO

The Illustrated History of Humankind

GREAT CIVILIZATIONS

SOCIETY AND CULTURE IN THE ANCIENT WORLD

GENERAL EDITOR GÖRAN BURENHULT

FOG CITY PRESS

Published by Fog City Press
814 Montgomery Street
San Francisco CA 94133 USA

Chief Executive Officer: John Owen
President: Terry Newell
Publisher: Lynn Humphries
Editorial Coordinator: Jessica Cox
Production Manager: Caroline Webber
Production Coordinator: James Blackman
Sales Manager: Emily Jahn
Vice President, International Sales: Stuart Laurence

Project Coordinators: Julia Cain, Annette Carter, Dawn Titmus
Copy Editors: Glenda Downing, Rosemary Harrington, Jacqueline Hochmuth, Margaret McPhee, Margaret Olds, Bruce Semler, Fiona Sim
Picture Editors: Karen Burgess, Annette Crueger, Kathy Gerrard, Jenny Mills
Art Director: Sue Burk
Design: Denese Cunningham, David Roffey

ISBN: 1 877019 29 1

Color reproduction by Colourscan Co Pty Ltd
Printed by Kyodo Printing (Singapore) Co Pty Ltd
Printed in Singapore

A WELDON OWEN PRODUCTION

Page 1
This gold death-mask of a king from Mycenae, thought by German archaeologist Heinrich Schliemann to be Agamemnon, dates from the sixteenth century BC.
C.M. DIXON/PHOTO RESOURCES

Pages 2–3
A view of the fifteenth-century Inka fortress of Saqsawaman, at Cuzco, in Peru.
ROBERT FRERCK/ROBERT HARDING PICTURE LIBRARY

→ The famous "lost city of the Inkas", Macchu Picchu, is situated on a ridge overlooking the Urubamba River valley, in Peru.

LOREN MCINTYRE

General Editor

Editorial Board

Contributors

Dr Atholl Anderson
Professor of Prehistory
Australian National University
Canberra, Australia

Dr Frances F. Berdan
Professor of Anthropology
California State University, USA

Dr Richard E. Blanton
Professor of Anthropology
Purdue University, USA

Wendy J. Bustard
Postgraduate student
Department of Archaeology
University of New Mexico, USA

P.J. Casey
Reader in Archaeology
Department of Archaeology
University of Durham, UK

Dr Terence N. D'Altroy
Associate Professor
Department of Anthropology
Columbia University, USA

Dr Peter Damerow
Center for Development and Socialization,
Max Planck Institute for Human Development and Education
Berlin, Germany

Dr Henry F. Dobyns
Adjunct Professor
Department of Anthropology
University of Oklahoma, USA

Dr Christopher B. Donnan
Professor, Department of Anthropology, University of California, USA

Corinne Duhig
Research student
Faculty of Oriental Studies
University of Cambridge, UK

Dr William L. Fash
Professor of Anthropology
Northern Illinois University, USA

Dr Ben Finney
Professor of Anthropology
University of Hawaii, Hawaii, USA

Dr Christopher Fyfe
Former Reader in African History
Centre of African Studies
University of Edinburgh, UK

Dr José Garanger
Professor of Archaeology
Sorbonne University, Paris, France

Dr Ian C. Glover
Senior Lecturer, Department of Prehistoric Archaeology, University College London, UK

Dr Helena F. Hamerow
Lecturer in Early Medieval Archaeology, Department of Archaeology, University of Durham, UK

Dr Richard J. Harrison
Reader in Archaeology
Department of Classics and Archaeology, University of Bristol, UK

Dr Pontus Hellström
Professor of Classical Archaeology and Ancient History
University of Uppsala, Sweden

Dr Mary G. Hodge
Associate Professor of Anthropology, School of Human Sciences and Humanities
University of Houston, USA

Dr Cho-yun Hsu
University Professor of History
University of Pittsburgh, USA

Mark J. Hudson
Postgraduate student
Department of Archaeology and Anthropology, Australian National University,Canberra, Australia

Dr John Hyslop
Research Fellow, Institute of Andean Research, New York, USA

Graham Joyner
Lecturer in History, School of History, Philosophy, and Politics, Macquarie University, Sydney, Australia

Barry Kemp
Reader in Egyptology
Faculty of Oriental Studies
University of Cambridge, UK

Dr Foss Leach
Honorary Curator of Archaeological Fauna, Museum of New Zealand
Te Papa Tongarewa
Wellington, New Zealand

Dr Katheryn M. Linduff
Professor, Department of Fine Arts
Department of Anthropology
University of Pittsburgh, USA

J.G. Macqueen
Former Reader in Classics and Ancient Middle Eastern Studies
Department of Classics and Archaeology, University of Bristol, UK

Dr Joyce Marcus
Professor of Anthropology and Curator of Latin American Archaeology,
University of Michigan, USA

Akira Matsui
Senior Officer
Nara National Cultural Properties,
Research Institute, Nara, Japan

Dr Patrick C. McCoy
Archaeologist State Historic Preservation Division
Hawaii Department of Land and Natural Resources, Hawaii, USA

Dr Mary Ellen Miller
Professor, History of Art Department
Yale University, USA

Dr Elizabeth H. Moore
Lecturer, Department of Art and Archaeology, School of Oriental and African Studies, University of London, UK

Dr Robert G. Morkot
Department of Egyptology
University College London, UK

Dr Craig Morris
Curator of Anthropology
(for South American Archaeology)
American Museum of Natural History
New York, USA

Dr Boyo G. Ockinga
Senior Lecturer in History
School of History, Philosophy, and Politics, Macquarie University
Sydney, Australia

Dr Susan Pollock
Assistant Professor of Anthropology
State University of New York at Binghamton, USA

Dr Ann F. Ramenofsky
Associate Professor
Department of Anthropology
University of New Mexico, USA

Dr Himanshu Prabha Ray
Assistant Professor
Centre for Historical Studies
Jawaharlal Nehru University
New Delhi, India

Dr Charles L. Redman
Professor of Anthropology
Arizona State University, USA

Dr John W. Rick
Associate Professor
Department of Anthropology
Stanford University, USA

David Ridgway
Reader, Department of Classics
University of Edinburgh, UK

Dr Vuka Roussakis
Textile Conservator
Department of Anthropology
American Museum of Natural History
New York, USA

Dr Charlotte Scheffer
Senior Lecturer
Department of Classical Archaeology and Ancient History
University of Stockholm, Sweden

Dr Izumi Shimada
Professor of Anthropology
Southern Illinois University at Carbondale, USA

Dr Katherine A. Spielmann
Associate Professor
Department of Anthropology
Arizona State University, USA

Dr I.M. Stead
Deputy Keeper
Department of Prehistoric and Romano-British Antiquities
British Museum, London, UK

David Stuart
Lecturer in Anthropology
Harvard University, USA

Dr John R. Topic
Professor of Anthropology
Trent University, Ontario, Canada

Emily Umberger
Associate Professor
School of Art
Arizona State University, USA

Håkan Wahlquist
Curator of Asian Anthropology
National Museum of Ethnography
Stockholm, Sweden

Dr Peter Warren
Professor of Ancient History and Classical Archaeology
University of Bristol, UK

Dr Charlotte Wikander
Lecturer
Department of Classical Archaeology and Ancient History
University of Gothenburg, Sweden

Dr Örjan Wikander
Associate Professor
Department of Classics
Lund University, Sweden

⇐ A Viking Age silver hoard from Cuerdale, in Lancashire, England, dating from the beginning of the tenth century AD.
BRITISH MUSEUM

C o n t e n t s

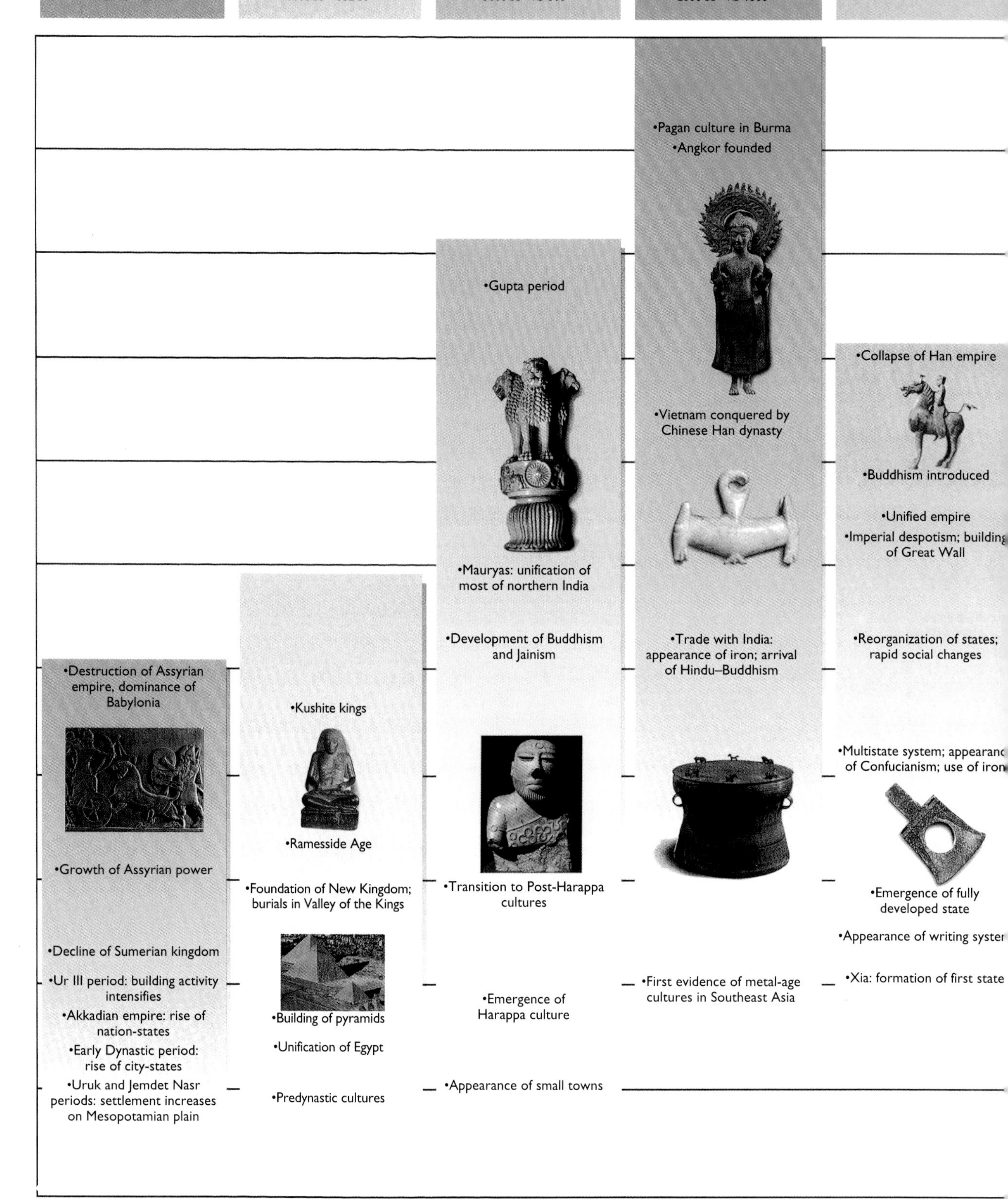
MESOPOTAMIA AND THE FIRST CITIES
4000 BC – 539 BC
•Destruction of Assyrian empire, dominance of Babylonia
•Growth of Assyrian power
•Decline of Sumerian kingdom
•Ur III period: building activity intensifies
•Akkadian empire: rise of nation-states
•Early Dynastic period: rise of city-states
•Uruk and Jemdet Nasr periods: settlement increases on Mesopotamian plain
THE CIVILIZATION OF ANCIENT EGYPT
5000 BC – 332 BC
•Kushite kings
•Ramesside Age
•Foundation of New Kingdom; burials in Valley of the Kings
•Building of pyramids
•Unification of Egypt
•Predynastic cultures
CIVILIZATIONS IN SOUTHERN ASIA
3000 BC – AD 500
•Gupta period
•Mauryas: unification of most of northern India
•Development of Buddhism and Jainism
•Transition to Post-Harappa cultures
•Emergence of Harappa culture
•Appearance of small towns
CIVILIZATIONS OF SOUTHEAST ASIA
2000 BC – AD 1500
•Pagan culture in Burma
•Angkor founded
•Vietnam conquered by Chinese Han dynasty
•Trade with India: appearance of iron; arrival of Hindu–Buddhism
•First evidence of metal-age cultures in Southeast Asia
DYNASTIES IN CHINA
2000 BC – AD 220
•Collapse of Han empire
•Buddhism introduced
•Unified empire
•Imperial despotism; building of Great Wall
•Reorganization of states; rapid social changes
•Multistate system; appearance of Confucianism; use of iron
•Emergence of fully developed state
•Appearance of writing system
•Xia: formation of first state

	EMERGING MEDITERRANEAN CIVILIZATIONS 3200 BC – 800 BC	THE AGE OF ANCIENT GREECE 1100 BC – 31 BC	THE RISE AND FALL OF ROME 900 BC – AD 500	THE IRON AGE IN EUROPE 800 BC – AD 1050	THE DEVELOPMENT OF AFRICAN STATES 3000 BC – AD 1500
AD 1500					•Muslim states in North Africa, Great Zimbabwe in south
AD 800				•Viking Age	•Kingdoms emerge in western Sudan and West Africa: Ghana, Igbo-Ukwu, Ife, Benin, Mali, and Songhai
AD 450			•Disintegration, last emperor of western empire dethroned •Division of the empire •Economic instability and military anarchy	•Collapse of Roman Empire: start of migration period	
AD 200					
0			•Octavian Augustus becomes emperor; empire reorganized •First triumvirate; Caesar becomes dictator	•Celtic power crushed by Rome	
300 BC		•Hellenistic Age •Alexander the Great •Ionian renaissance •Fighting between cities; dominance of Sparta •Classical period; dominance of Athens •Archaic period; war with Persia	•Beginning of Punic wars •Rome in possession of entire Italic peninsula • Last Etruscan king overthrown; Temple of Jupiter on Capitoline Hill inaugurated		•Meroë kingdom in the Sudan
600 BC			•Etruscan urbanization spreads southwards: Rome emerges as a city; Tarquin dynasty	•Contacts with Mediterranean world and Scythians: emergence and spread of Celtic tradition •Hallstatt C phase: princely burials	•Kingdom of Aksum created on Red Sea coast
900 BC	•Destruction of Mycenaean and Hittite civilizations	•Overseas trade; Greek colonies; population growth; appearance of Greek alphabet; rise of city-states			
1400 BC	•Emergence of Mycenaean civilization in Greece and Hittite civilization in Anatolia •Emergence of Minoan palatial civilization in Crete				
2000 BC	•Small, planned towns founded in eastern Mediterranean region				•Emergence of Kush kingdom in the Sudan •Loosely structured indigenous societies
3500 BC					
5000 BC					

THE EMERGENCE OF CIVILIZATION IN MESOAMERICA
1500 BC – AD 1521

- •Spanish conquest of Mesoamerica
- •Aztecs rule Valley of Mexico
- •Postclassic period: decline of dominant major centers
- •Toltec empire in Tula

- •Classic period: grid layout city of Teotihuacan rules the region
- •Monte Albán: first capital city
- •Formation of states
- •Formative period: first settled agricultural villages; pottery
- •Earliest Mesoamerican writing: Zapotec glyphs
- •Elaborate monumental constructions
- •Olmec culture

THE MAYA
2000 BC – THE PRESENT

- •Spanish conquest of Maya
- •Period of political fragmentation

- •Overpopulation and environmental depletion
- •Period of war and conquest
- •End of Classic period
- •Classic center of Copán

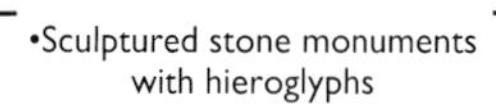

- •Classic centers under rule of hereditary elite
- •Hieroglyphic text and dates in southern lowlands area
- •Tikal and El Mirador: urban centers Mesoamerica
- •Sculptured stone monuments with hieroglyphs

THE RISE OF THE AZTECS
AD 1200 – AD 1521

- •Spanish conquer Tenochtitlan: Aztec capital
- •Late Aztec phase
- •Triple Alliance
- •Early Aztec phase
- •*Chinampa* system of agriculture in Valley of Mexico
- •Mexica tribe arrives in Valley of Mexico

CIVILIZATIONS IN THE ANDES
3000 BC – AD 1470

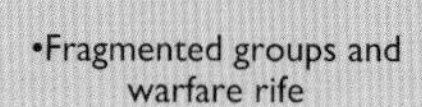

- •Inka conquer empire of Chimor
- •Demise of capital Chan Chan

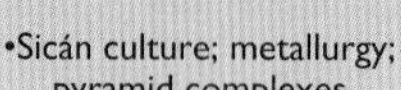

- •Fragmented groups and warfare rife
- •Sicán culture; metallurgy; pyramid complexes

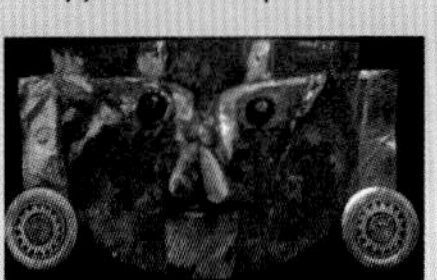

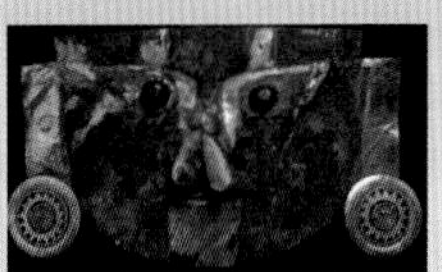

- •Rise of highland states
- •Moche culture: first Andean state
- •Nasca lines: geoglyphs
- •Chavín style of art
- •Ceramic vessels; monumental ceremonial complexes; agriculture: move inland from coast; irrigation canals
- •Valdivia culture: beginnings of complex Andean society and settled village life

THE INKA STATE
AD 1400 – AD 1532

- •Inka conquered by Spanish
- •Inka state Tawantinsuyu
- •Building of roads, bridges
- •Cuzco: capital city
- •Period of rapid Inka expansic
- •Inka conquer Andean peopl

Date	CONSTRUCTING JAPAN 400 BC – AD 1600	THE OCCUPATION OF THE PACIFIC ISLANDS 50,000 BC – AD 1500	STONE-BUILT MONUMENTS OF THE SOUTH PACIFIC AD 1 – THE PRESENT	PREHISTORIC WAYS OF LIFE OF NATIVE AMERICANS 10,000 BC – AD 1850	THE CLASH OF CULTURES AD 620 – THE PRESENT
AD 2000 – AD 1750			•Recent megalith-building societies in Melanesia	•Great Plains American Indians •Spanish explorers introduce horses to the Plains; Plains people become mobile	•Christian missionaries in Africa •European discoveries in Australia and the Pacific
AD 1750 – AD 1500	•Political unification of central islands under Tokugawa shogunate •Trading with Europeans begins			•Rapid decline of Native American population owing to European-introduced diseases	•Natives of Canary Islands become extinct •Spanish conquer Inka, Maya, and Aztecs
AD 1500 – AD 1250	•Warlords rule; castletown settlements •Interaction of Japanese state with Ainu culture	•Construction of hill-forts (*pa*) in New Zealand	•Stone-built temples (*marae*) with altar platforms (*ahu*) in Polynesia		•African-European trade in goods and slaves begins •Portuguese reach India •Spanish begin to colonize Americas; "Columbian Exchange" begins •Mongols dominate China-Russia-India
AD 1250 – AD 1000		•Settlement of New Zealand •Settlement of Micronesian islands by Polynesians	•Construction of Nan Madol, Pohnpei	•Agriculture-based Plains Village tradition •Mississippian settlements: social hierarchy; agricultural base	•First Crusade begins
AD 1000 – AD 750	•Rise of samurai; warrior elite		•*Moai* statues on Easter Island	•Maize becomes staple food	
AD 750 – AD 500	•Fujiwara: first capital city with grid layout •Buddhism and Confucianism arrive from China		•Earliest *ahu* platforms on Easter Island		•Beginning of Islamic expansion; Muslims v. Christians
AD 500 – AD 250	•Large regional chiefdoms •Complex social structures; tomb mounds	•Settlement of East Polynesia		•Classic Northwest Coast culture: dense populations and lavish ceremonies •California Archaic: social development without agriculture •Desert Archaic: pinyon nuts staple; seasonal migrations	
AD 250 – 0			•Earliest known megaliths in Melanesia: Otuyam, Trobriand Islands		
0 – 3500 BC		•Beginning of occupation of Remote Oceania •Lapita culture in Bismarcks		•Massive earthworks construction in lower Mississippi Valley •Northwest Coast culture •Simple pottery first appears in North America	
3500 BC – 7000 BC				•Bison hunting on Great Plains •Boreal and Maritime Archaic traditions: early adaptation to forest traditions in subarctic regions; more permanent settlements	
7000 BC – 10,500 BC				•Paleoindian tradition: highly developed food-gathering techniques	

GEORG GERSTER/RAPHO

MESOPOTAMIA AND THE FIRST CITIES

4000 BC – 539 BC

On the Pathway to Urban Society

CHARLES L. REDMAN

ONE OF THE MOST significant milestones in the development of human societies was the growth of the first cities on the Mesopotamian plain. This process, often called "The Urban Revolution", involved much more than just an increase in the size of settlements: it included fundamental changes in the way people interacted, in their relationship to the environment, and in the very way they structured their communities. Processes and institutions that began at this time have continued to evolve, forming the basic structure of urban society today.

Writing, legal codes, the wheel, the plow, metallurgy, mathematics, and engineering principles—all commonplace in our modern world—were first developed in the cities of Sumer (present-day southern Iraq). Despite the vast scope of these technical developments, the most significant changes were those of social organization. There was a quantum leap in the number of inhabitants living in the largest settlements.

The ziggurat of Choga Zambil, on the plain of Khuzistan, in present-day southwestern Iran, dates from about 1250 BC. Ziggurats have a long tradition in Mesopotamia, serving both as raised platforms for important temples and as the focus of public ceremonies.

This clay figurine of a woman holding an infant was excavated in the pre-urban levels of Ur, and dates from about 4000 BC.
THE IRAQ MUSEUM, BAGDAD/SCALA

A Babylonian boundary stone, from about 1120 BC, records a gift of land near Edina, in southern Babylonia.
C.M. DIXON/PHOTO RESOURCES

As some groups of people acquired access to sources of production—for example, better farmland, more irrigation water, and rare goods traded from other regions—social class became one of the main structures within communities. These communities were organized according to the emerging hierarchical political and administrative systems, which often used written legal codes.

Craft specialization, mass-production industries, and large-scale trade characterized the new economy. Organized warfare, with both massive defensive works and long-distance offensive campaigns, played an increasing role in the survival of societies.

Cities and Their Surrounds

The physical environment of Mesopotamia (present-day Iraq and part of southwestern Iran) and the surrounding regions provided suitable ecological conditions for the early introduction of agriculture and the subsequent growth of the first urban society. An awareness of these conditions is essential to an understanding of the changes that took place.

Mesopotamia is a large, alluvial plain created by two major rivers—the Tigris and the Euphrates—and is surrounded on two sides by better-watered mountainous zones. The climatic pattern is one of summer drought and winter rainfall, although the lowland plain receives minimal rainfall.

In the south, where the Tigris and Euphrates rivers join and eventually empty into the Persian Gulf, the land is almost flat, and there are many

JONATHON T. WRIGHT/BRUCE COLEMAN LTD

The Tigris and Euphrates rivers and their tributaries provided the water essential to Mesopotamian agriculture.

To the north and east of Mesopotamia, many of the mountain river valleys were the scene of early agricultural experiments, and they continued to be important resource zones for the city-states of Mesopotamia.

ROBERT HARDING PICTURE LIBRARY

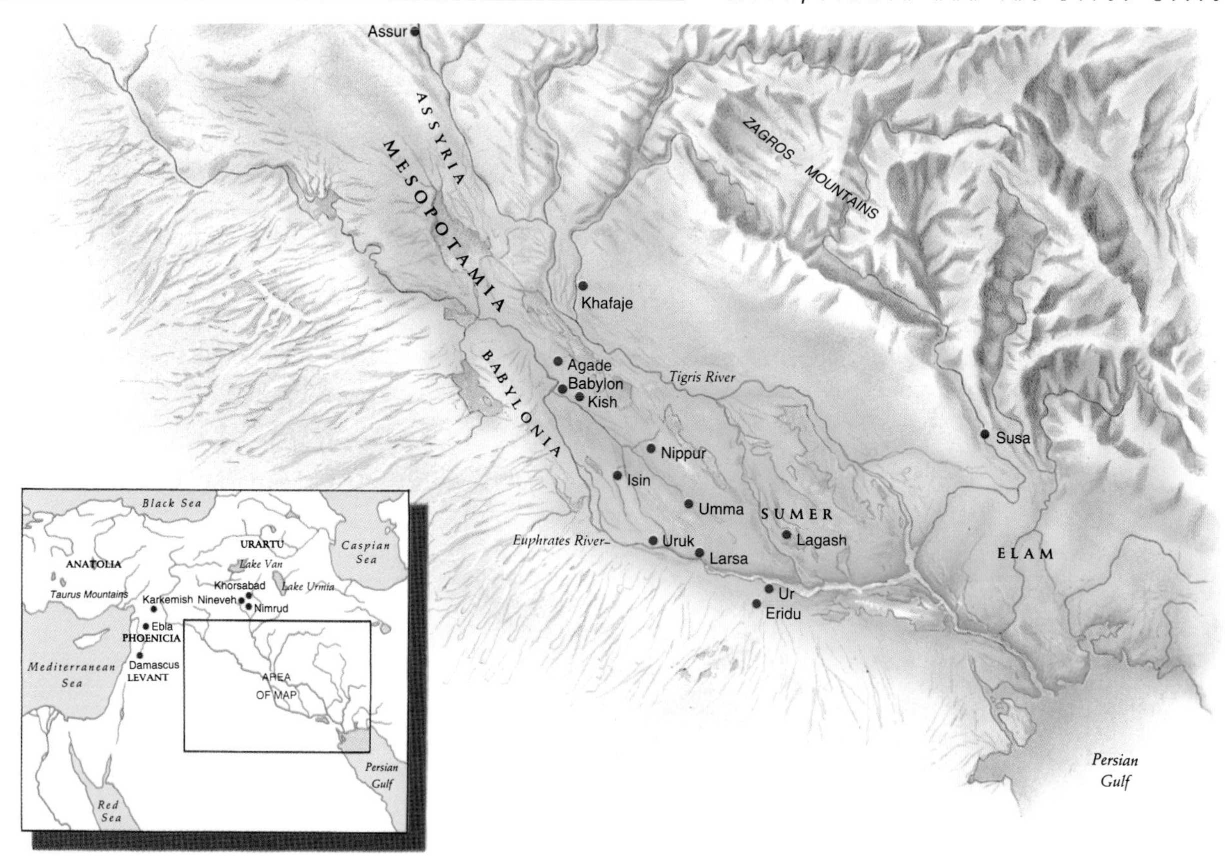

marshy areas. Moving upstream, to the northwest, the slope is small, but it increases perceptibly, giving rise to more clearly defined watercourses surrounded by arid plains. Effective natural levee formation in the southern reaches of the Mesopotamian plain strongly influenced the selection of settlement locations.

Furthest from the rivers were lowland areas that were marshes during the flood season and dry the rest of the year. Some of these lowland areas were saline; others supported natural grasses, which made them useful for grazing animals. Nearer the rivers were farmlands, which, though low-lying, were protected from marshiness by their height above the river. They were within reach of irrigation water, and the closer they were to the river, the greater their productivity. Along the river banks were the levees, which were higher and better drained than the surrounding plain. These were the best locations for intensive cultivation and settlement. The levees had several natural advantages: they were fertile, quickly drained, and least vulnerable to winter frosts. Equally important, as the population density of farmers increased, the levees gave access to river water during years in which the river level was low and all fields could not be adequately watered.

Moving further upstream, to the more northerly areas of the Mesopotamian plain, the gradient increases, the landscape becomes undulating, and the rivers cut into the landscape, making irrigation more difficult. Continuing to the north, the major rivers and their tributaries cut across a series of increasingly high ridges and ultimately reach the Taurus Mountains, to the north, and the Zagros Mountains, to the northeast. Proximity to the uplands and the large tributary rivers provided natural advantages to settlement in the north, such as access to stone and timber for building, while the vast stretches of relatively easily irrigated land facilitated growth in the south.

MESOPOTAMIA

Mesopotamia is a broad, alluvial plain that slopes gently to the southeast, and the Tigris and Euphrates rivers wind their way to the Persian Gulf. To the north and east, the plain steps up into the successively higher, intermontane valleys of the Taurus and Zagros mountains.

CARTOGRAPHY: RAY SIM

ROBERT HARDING PICTURE LIBRARY

⇐ Sheep, seen here grazing near the Euphrates River, were among the key resources of the early Mesopotamian cities. They provided meat and milk and their wool was essential to the development of textile production and trade.

GEORG GERSTER/JOHN HILLELSON AGENCY

Intensively irrigated farmlands along the Shatt-al-Arab River, in extreme southern Mesopotamia (present-day southeastern Iraq). Although this area may not have been farmed in antiquity, it is thought that the areas near the ancient cities of Eridu and Ur that are now desert may have looked like this in the third millennium BC.

A village along the upper Euphrates River in southeastern Anatolia (Turkey). The stone foundations, mudbrick walls, and timber and mud roofs of this village are similar to those of prehistoric villages that have been found all along the upland fringes of Mesopotamia.

Neolithic settlement (8000 BC to 5000 BC) of Southwest Asia had concentrated on the uplands, with only a few settlements around the margin of Mesopotamia in southeastern Turkey, on the Irano-Iraqi borderlands, or along the upper reaches of the major rivers. Researchers have not yet found evidence of any substantial settlement in southern Mesopotamia before about 5500 BC. Between 6000 BC and 4000 BC, however, the area of settlement expanded from the uplands to include more and more of the Mesopotamian plain. This was not a rapid expansion in terms of a single lifetime; it took many generations to learn ways to manage crops and animals in the heat and aridity of the lowlands. At first, expansion was limited to areas of possible, although unreliable, rainfall. Subsequently, with the aid of primitive irrigation systems, settlers moved into areas that previously could not be cultivated.

Why Did Cities Arise?

The formation of cities and their linking together as one civilization on the Mesopotamian plain was relatively rapid, considering the scope of the social and technological changes involved. Only 2,000 years after the earliest-known occupation of this region, about 5500 BC, cities emerged, and writing and such other traits of urbanism as monumental buildings and craft specialization had appeared. The question of what led to this all-important transformation has challenged scholars for decades. A variety of theories has been advanced to account for the rise of cities, most of which rely on Mesopotamia as their main source of evidence. The rise of cities is not simply the growth of large collections of people—rather, it involves communities that are far more diverse than their predecessors and more interdependent. Specialization in the production of various goods and complex exchange networks are typical of urban societies. Cities are also interdependent with their hinterlands of towns and villages.

Theorists have suggested a variety of factors that could have prompted the growth of cities and the reorganization of society. One of the earliest explanations for the growth of complex society in Mesopotamia and elsewhere, put forward by Karl Wittfogel in the 1950s, was the social reorganization required by large-scale irrigation works. The proposition was that arid alluvial valleys, such as Mesopotamia, would need irrigation to support significant populations, and that the construction, maintenance, and allocation of irrigation works would require a managerial elite. The elite, in turn, would form the core of the complex society.

Another theory, developed by American anthropologist Robert Carneiro in the 1970s, was based on the processes set in motion by an increasing population density. Arable land would "fill up", and conflict would then develop among the settlers and their neighbors. One group would be subdued, forming the lower class for the conquerors, who would assume the role of the elite.

CHARLES L. REDMAN

EARLY MESOPOTAMIAN CITIES AND THE ENVIRONMENT

CHARLES L. REDMAN

Vast stretches of the rich and productive landscape of early Mesopotamia are now unfarmable desert. The conclusion drawn by many is that the climate must have changed dramatically between then and today. Careful research has shown, however, that the climate has changed very little over the past 5,000 years, and so we must look for another cause of this environmental degradation. A comparison of the dissolution of the Ur III state about 2000 BC with the later demise of the Sasanian empire of the early Middle Ages (AD 226 to AD 637), which covered the area of present-day Iran and Iraq, suggests some possible causes.

A view of the mound of Tell Drahem, in southern Mesopotamia. About 2000 BC, according to texts found there, this was an important center for cattle-raising and for preparing meat for shipment to the nearby city of Nippur. Today, the once productive region is largely desert because of the extreme salinization of the soil.

Centralized Control and Environmental Damage

Paradoxically, it seems that the rapid rise of centralized political control within Ur III society contributed to an era of declining agricultural productivity and environmental damage. Centralized control of the once independent city-states was a logical objective for the Ur III rulers. It gave them access to larger pools of workers, military conscripts, trade goods, and agricultural produce. And, significantly, it helped to maximize the production of food and other goods.

Some of this increased productivity was achieved through increased specialization, but most resulted from the centralized management of the construction and maintenance of the growing irrigation network that fed the Mesopotamian fields and of the allocation of water within it. It was, therefore, a logical decision for Ur III rulers to try to extend the area served by irrigation and to increase the capacity of the existing canal system to carry water to the fields. But the very decisions that brought short-term increases in production—as evidenced by the high population density and the great construction projects of the Ur III period—seem to have rapidly undermined the region's agricultural base.

The people of Ur III appear to have caused their own ultimate downfall through the salinization of their soils. Salinization occurs when salt accumulates near the surface of the soil. In this case, salt from the sedimentary rocks in the mountains was carried by rivers and deposited on the Mesopotamian fields during natural flooding or planned irrigation. In southern Mesopotamia, the natural water table comes to within roughly 2 meters (6 feet) of the surface. Excessive irrigation brings the water table up to within 50 centimeters (18 inches) of the surface. In waterlogged situations, the salt is then carried to the surface, where it kills most plants.

Written records of temple storehouses from the time of the Ur III empire have allowed scholars to reconstruct the relative productivity of fields and the crops planted. There was a long-term decrease in productivity between 2400 BC and 1700 BC. About 2400 BC, wheat was an important crop, accounting for at least 16 percent of the cereals produced. As salinization increased, however, the emphasis gradually shifted to barley, a more salt-tolerant crop. By the end of the Ur III dynasty, wheat accounted for only 2 percent of the cereals grown. By 1700 BC, wheat seems to have been totally abandoned as a crop in southern Mesopotamia. The tail end of this process coincided with a long period without centralized political control. Many cities were abandoned or reduced to villages, and the emphasis shifted from producing as much as possible for the central rulers to just satisfying the needs of the local populations.

The Sasanian Empire

The decline of the Sasanian empire brings some of these issues into clearer focus. The Sasanians had assembled a truly great "world" empire, spanning most of Iraq and much of Iran. They built large cities and had a very strong central government. Even more than the people of Ur III, they relied on cereal cultivation in irrigated fields and had built a massive system of canals and other facilities to bring water to an ever-increasing area of land. Although it is hard to know for certain, one scholar has estimated that three to four times as much land was farmed during the Sasanian period as in the Ur III epoch. But, as within the Ur III empire, this attempt to maximize production had wide-ranging repercussions. First, the amount of water being brought to the land increased the risk of salinization, even though the Sasanians tried hard to combat this process. Second, the enormous scale of the Sasanian irrigation systems required more comprehensive and more effective management to be successful, allowing little room for errors of judgment. Third, extending cultivation to more marginal lands used yet more water and also swallowed up the fallow lands that had formerly been used for herding. This third point is particularly important, in that herd-raising had always provided a buffer against bad agricultural years and was also a means of diversifying the diet.

Even the great Sasanian empire could not hold together under these pressures. Scholars believe that diminished productivity was already taking its toll on central control when the region was hit by the plague several times in the sixth and early seventh centuries AD. This further debilitated the system, so that when Muslim armies entered Sasanian territory in AD 637, they were able to topple the Sasanians with surprisingly little resistance.

The Costs of Growth

In these periods of Mesopotamia's past, political stability and economic growth were achieved by centralizing political control and maximizing agricultural production. In fact, this weakened the ability of the agricultural system to react to problems and led ultimately to a decline in productivity.

State ideologies at that time, and probably now as well, assumed that everyone's interests converged in the objectives of a central authority. Yet the objectives may not have been shared by all members of a society, and, indeed, may not have been to the benefit of all. What is less obvious is that the objectives of such ideologies may not even be in the best interests of the central authority in the long term.

C.M. DIXON/PHOTO RESOURCES

⊖ Copper tools and weapons from Tell Sifr, dating from about 1900 BC to 1750 BC. Although all metal ore had to be imported to Mesopotamia, the production of metal implements became quite important in the economy of early cities.

D. BOURBONNAIS/EXPLORER/AUSCAPE

⊕ Although they often focus on the activities of royal personages, later Assyrian bas-reliefs provide graphic illustrations of daily life in Mesopotamia. Hairstyles and dress were often used to portray different ethnic groups, and size was usually employed to denote the importance of the individual.

BAGHDAD MUSEUM/PICTUREPOINT LTD

⊖ A ritual cart in terracotta, found at Khafaje, in northeastern Mesopotamia, dating from about 2600 BC. By Early Dynastic times, it appears that wheeled carts were in use throughout Mesopotamia.

Other theories, including those of Australian prehistorian Vere Gordon Childe and American archaeologist Henry Wright, point towards craft production and exchange as the primary factors in developing the complex Mesopotamian society. With the invention of metallurgy and the various applications for the newly developed wheel, among other technological breakthroughs, it is clear that new industries with specialized workers would emerge. Also, Mesopotamia lacked many natural resources for daily life and some industries, while it appeared to be able to produce surplus goods in other categories. Thus, the efficient organization of manufacturing and the large-scale exchange of products both inside and outside Mesopotamia would promote the rise of a managerial class and specialized producers, both key elements in an urban society.

We know from archaeological findings and somewhat later written records that each of these factors—irrigation, population growth, warfare, specialized production, and large-scale trade—existed in early Mesopotamia, but the actual order of their development is not clear. The key question is whether advances in one or more of these areas preceded cities and were instrumental in leading to urban growth, or whether they followed the formation of cities as a natural outcome of the newly formed urban society. A careful examination of the archaeological evidence by scholars has led to a number of theories that rely on a combination of these and other factors working together to bring about the fundamental changes the urban society implies. In these theories, the importance of irrigation, agriculture, and the exchange of goods is acknowledged as forming the necessary foundation on which a Mesopotamian civilization could be built. But theories such as the multivariate approach of American cultural ecologist Robert McC. Adams look to the changing social relations caused by the increasing numbers of settlements in the Mesopotamian environment. The ideas of the original theorists have not been entirely rejected, but parts of them are used in current theories that focus on the close interrelationship of environment, economics, technology, and changes in social relations.

The Threshold of Civilization

Because of the natural aridity of the lowland parts of the Mesopotamian plain, few people lived there before 5500 BC, when the necessary farming and irrigation techniques were developed. During the next 2,000 years, in a broad period archaeologists have termed the 'Ubaid, advances were slow, but together they laid the foundation for Mesopotamian civilization. Many scholars suggest that the people we now call the Sumerians came to Mesopotamia at this time. During this long period, many of the characteristics of civilization and the Sumerian society itself emerged. However, it was to be another thousand years before true cities and a sophisticated urban network developed.

Sites that date to the 'Ubaid period, and that share many cultural traits, have been discovered throughout Mesopotamia and in the surrounding foothills, on both the Iraqi and Iranian sides of the border. While each site has contributed new detail to the increasingly clear picture of 'Ubaid life, it is one of the first excavated, Eridu, that still seems most informative. Located in the extreme south of the Mesopotamian plain, Eridu, in some ways, may have attained the highest level of development. The original settlement here was probably not much larger than the villages that had dotted the upland mountain valleys for several thousand years, but the people obviously understood the principles of irrigation, and their wheat, barley, sheep, goats, and cattle must have suited the extremes of the Mesopotamian climate. Because there were no natural stands of timber and outcrops of rock, the people relied heavily on clay, not only to make their pots, but to construct their buildings and even to fashion tools, such as sickles and axes, that were made of stone in other regions.

Perhaps the find in Eridu most indicative of things to come was a series of buildings that the excavators interpreted as temples. This inference was based on the layout of the buildings, which had three-part arrangements with exterior buttressing, characteristics duplicated in later Sumerian buildings and identified by written sources as temples. By the time these buildings were being constructed at Eridu, about 3500 BC, the community had grown to cover 10 hectares (about 25 acres) and probably housed at least 2,000 people. The existence of so many people in one settlement implies the evolution of social relations to a new level of integration within the community and a potential reliance on surrounding settlements for some subsistence goods.

ERICH LESSING/MAGNUM

This find of a clay model shows that two-story houses were built in Mesopotamia..

CIVILIZATIONS IN MESOPOTAMIA: 5500 BC – 2000 BC

BC	CULTURES OF MESOPOTAMIA	SOCIAL AND POLITICAL EVENTS	CULTURE AND TECHNOLOGY
2000	Ur III state 2111 BC – 2005 BC	Shift in focus of growth and power to central and northern Mesopotamia	Serious salinization in southern Mesopotamia Ur-Nammu began impressive building program 2111 BC
2500	Akkadian state 2350 BC – 2150 BC	First nation-state 2350 BC – 2150 BC Promulgation of earliest legal codes 2350 BC Major period of Ur burials 2600 BC – 2100 BC	New language for official business Cuneiform writing adopted
3000	Early Dynastic city-states 2900 BC – 2350 BC	Earliest Ur burials Era of the city-state Major military campaigns	Building of palaces Temple ovals built at some cities
3500	Uruk and Jemdet Nasr period 3500 BC – 2900 BC		Monumental art Sculptures in the round Earliest written script Construction of first ziggurats for temples
4000			Use of the wheel
4500			Development of copper/bronze metallurgy Use of the plow
5000			
5500	'Ubaid period 5500 BC – 3500 BC	First settled villages	Small-scale irrigation

An aerial view of the central part of the great, early city of Uruk (biblical Erech), in southern Mesopotamia. By the end of the Early Dynastic period, Uruk was enclosed by a massive defensive wall, and at its center, there were large temples built atop ziggurats.

This libation jug of stone, with inlaid mosaic, was found at the site of Uruk. It dates from the Jemdet Nasr period, about 3200 BC.

THE IRAQ MUSEUM, BAGHDAD/SCALA

The City Takes Form

During the following period, the signs of civilization are more abundant, and settlement in the Mesopotamian plain increased significantly. Called the Uruk and Jemdet Nasr periods by archaeologists, this epoch spans roughly 3500 BC to 2900 BC. By then, there were many settlements that probably housed more than a thousand people, both in southern Mesopotamia and also in the north, where recent archaeological research is uncovering large communities along the upper Euphrates and its tributaries. Despite the impressive developments in the north, the focus of urban development appears to have been concentrated in the southern reaches of the Mesopotamian plain.

There was not a revolutionary change in the ways of life of the people of Mesopotamia, but with the growth in community size, agricultural

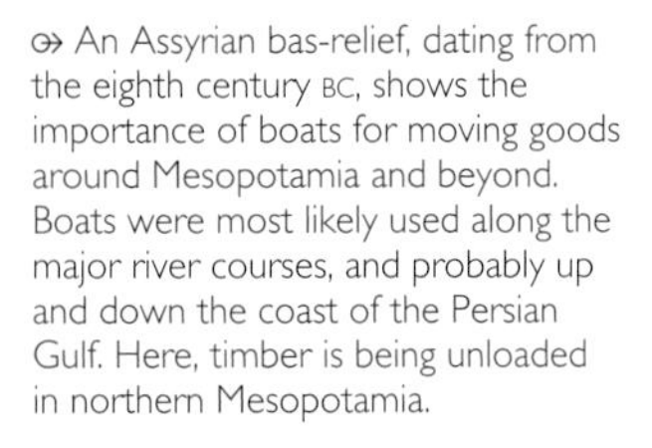

An Assyrian bas-relief, dating from the eighth century BC, shows the importance of boats for moving goods around Mesopotamia and beyond. Boats were most likely used along the major river courses, and probably up and down the coast of the Persian Gulf. Here, timber is being unloaded in northern Mesopotamia.

B. BOURBONNAIS/EXPLORER/AUSCAPE

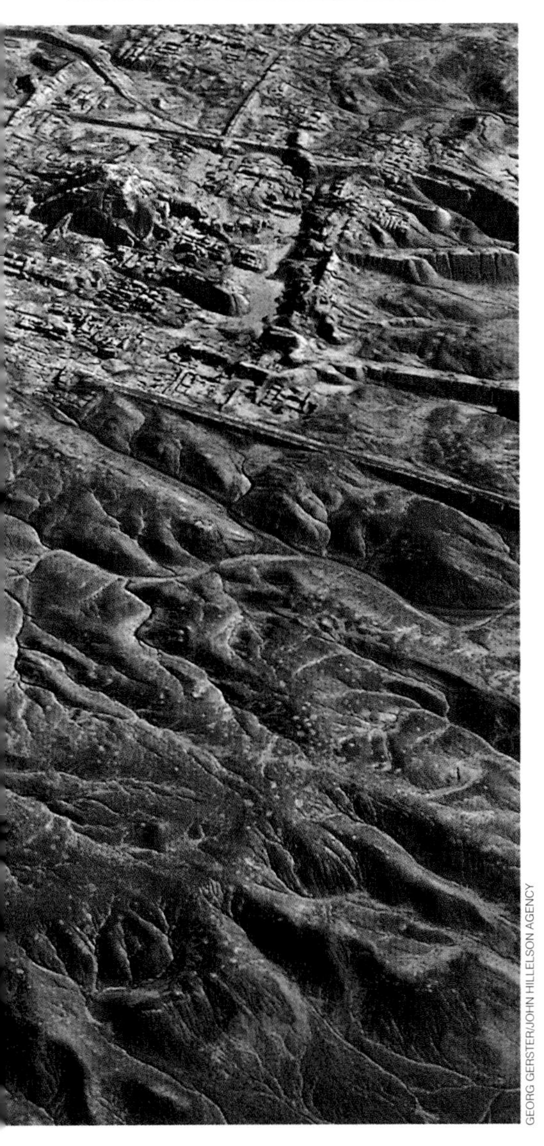
GEORG GERSTER/JOHN HILLELSON AGENCY

The most impressive developments in the south are known from the long-term German excavations at the site of Warka (ancient Uruk), not far upstream from Eridu. Here, in a settlement several times the size of the largest of its predecessors from the 'Ubaid period, is evidence of what were clearly temples in the Sumerian tradition. Whereas the largest 'Ubaid period temples at Eridu were only 20 meters by 10 meters (66 feet by 33 feet), several Uruk period temples at Warka were 80 meters by 30 meters (263 feet by 100 feet). Moreover, at Warka, there appears to have been at least one precinct where several temples were adjacent. Some of these impressive structures were built on top of a large platform, or ziggurat, to make them seem even grander. Ziggurats have been uncovered at several sites in southern Mesopotamia from levels dating to the Uruk and Jemdet Nasr periods. These raised temple platforms are the largest examples of Sumerian architectural skill, growing in size and complexity over the next thousand years until they came to dominate the cities.

The following epoch, from 2900 BC to 2350 BC, is now called the Early Dynastic, because we have written records, and actual kings and queens are identified. It is in this period that the cultural identity and language of the Sumerians became distinct and coherently structured.

Whereas in the preceding period there had been a major growth in villages and towns, during the Early Dynastic, much of the population moved into about two dozen cities, a few of which certainly housed tens of thousands of people. More productive farming methods developed to support this population. Although communities still seem to have been established near the banks of the natural watercourses, there is evidence of some major canal construction. Other seed crops were added to the staples of barley and wheat, and orchard fruits, especially dates, became a regular part of the diet.

The ziggurat at Uruk. It is believed that its now-eroded ramps and stairways were the scene of major rituals, witnessed by the population of the early city.

and craft production appear to have become more organized. Most pottery vessels were made on a wheel or in molds, both processes that allow greater output and standardization of vessels. It has even been suggested that some of these vessels were used to measure standard quantities in a complex trading economy. Metal was more commonly being used to make artifacts, and most important, there is evidence of early efforts at writing on stone and clay. (See the feature *Our Oldest Written Documents*.) Much of this early writing was used for record-keeping, further evidence of the growing sophistication of the Mesopotamian economy. Although not yet completely deciphered, the bulk of the material indicates a continuity with later Sumerian writing and language, and points to the presence of the Sumerians in Mesopotamia during this period, if not earlier.

ROBERT HARDING PICTURE LIBRARY

OUR OLDEST WRITTEN DOCUMENTS

PETER DAMEROW

MESOPOTAMIA WAS THE CENTER of cuneiform writing, a system that was used for about 3,000 years. Usually, the Mesopotamians wrote on tablets of clay, and the signs of the script were produced by impressing a stylus into the smooth surface of the wet clay. This left the wedge-shaped markings typical of the writing system. Cuneiform writing was used in many languages, most of which are now well understood, as the cuneiform script was deciphered in the middle of the nineteenth century.

Archaic Texts

The oldest clay tablets displaying the developed system of cuneiform writing were written about 2500 BC. At the end of the nineteenth century, some older texts were excavated that seemed then to be the precursors of the cuneiform writing system. These were found in Susa, the urban center of a region east of southern Babylonia known in the third millennium as Elam. This pictographic system of writing was thus called "proto-elamite". Drawings of more than 200 of these texts were published in 1905. This system seemed to have many similarities to later cuneiform writing. In particular, it displayed the same kind of number notations impressed vertically or obliquely into the clay using a round stylus.

Only a short time later, however, it was discovered that proto-elamite writing was not the direct precursor of the cuneiform writing systems. Beginning with some tablets unearthed before 1915, more and more clay tablets excavated in the center of southern Mesopotamia showed another system of pictographic writing. It was immediately obvious that this system was the true precursor of the cuneiform script. It is called "proto-cuneiform" writing, and proto-cuneiform and proto-elamite texts are grouped together as "archaic texts".

Archaic writing in this sense covers the period from about 3100 BC to 2800 BC. So far, about 4,500 proto-cuneiform and 1,500 proto-elamite texts or text fragments have been excavated, at several sites in southern Mesopotamia and the highland area of Persia (Iran). They represent our oldest-known writing system. The oldest of these texts are proto-cuneiform texts from Uruk, archaic level 4, where the majority of proto-cuneiform texts have been found. It seems well established now that the proto-elamite writing system, which was used for only a short time, was influenced by this proto-cuneiform script.

Deciphering the Texts

The archaic texts are still only poorly understood, but substantial progress has been made in recent years by the Uruk project in Berlin. Deciphering the texts is mainly based on relationships between the archaic signs and corresponding signs in the developed cuneiform writing system. Cuneiform signs were used both as syllabic signs with phonetic values and as ideograms (pictures that express concepts or objects). As yet, researchers have not been able to identify any archaic signs that were used with phonetic values, but the meaning of several cuneiform ideograms is obviously derived from the meaning of their archaic precursors. Although in most cases the meaning of the cuneiform ideograms had shifted away from the original meaning of the archaic signs, they nevertheless provide valuable hints for reading the archaic signs.

In addition to this, a new technique of analysis has been developed recently, giving a better understanding of the archaic texts. Most of these texts are administrative documents. They record economic activity controlled by the ancient urban centers, such as the allocation of labor, the distribution of rations, and the production of consumables. Most of the texts contain quantitative information arranged in a sophisticated book-keeping system. Hence, by investigating the arithmetic and the system of weights and measures, and the way they are combined, researchers are able to reconstruct the texts.

The Puzzle of Numbers

A major result of this structural analysis is the clarification of the puzzling nature of the numerical notations in the texts. Former attempts to understand these notations were aimed mainly at finding the numerical values of the different signs. The results were contradictory, because they were based on the assumption that these signs represented numbers in the modern sense. But a careful study of the numerical notations has now established beyond doubt that they do not represent anything like abstract numbers. Rather, they predate arithmetic, and their meaning is dependent on the context. Such constructs are well known from preliterate cultures.

The archaic numerical signs were used in different contexts with different meanings and differing numerical values. Fifteen different numerical notation systems have been identified so far. They consist partly of the same signs, but each system has particular numerical relations between the units and a specific area of application. The values of the numerical signs changed with each system, probably because the counting technique suitable in one context needed to be changed for another context. For example, the signs that later assumed the values of 1 and 10 were used in the archaic texts with these values when they were applied to count beer jugs. But the same signs assumed the values 1 and 6 when they were applied to barley measures, and took the values 1 and 18 when they were applied to measures of field areas.

The deciphering of the archaic texts, scanty as it still is, has provided us with the insight that writing was invented to maintain political power and to control property. Some of the most fundamental ideas of humankind, such as the concept of numbers, emerged as a by-product of archaic book-keeping. At the dawn of literacy, humans did not write down their history, their myths, or their religious beliefs. It was another century before people realized that writing could also be used for a purpose quite different from economic control: namely, to represent spoken language in an enduring medium.

⊛ A protocuneiform text showing the calculated quantities of raw materials required for several consignments of grain products and beer. This extraordinarily well-preserved tablet is a key document for our understanding of archaic numerical notation systems. Entries relating to various barley products are recorded, followed by figures showing the required quantities of barley groats and malt. Five different numerical notation systems were used to match the different measurement and counting systems applied to different types of goods. A sexagesimal system was used for counting beer jars, a bisexagesimal system for counting barley products and workers' barley rations. There were also three different notation systems for grain measures. The abstract symbols of cuneiform script developed after the scribes had changed the orientation of such tablets by turning them 90 degrees to the left so that the pictographs appeared sideways (as here). This then became the standard way of writing the symbols. It is not known when this change took place, and so assyriologists orient all tablets to match the way cuneiform script was written in its developed form.
M. NISSEN, BERLIN

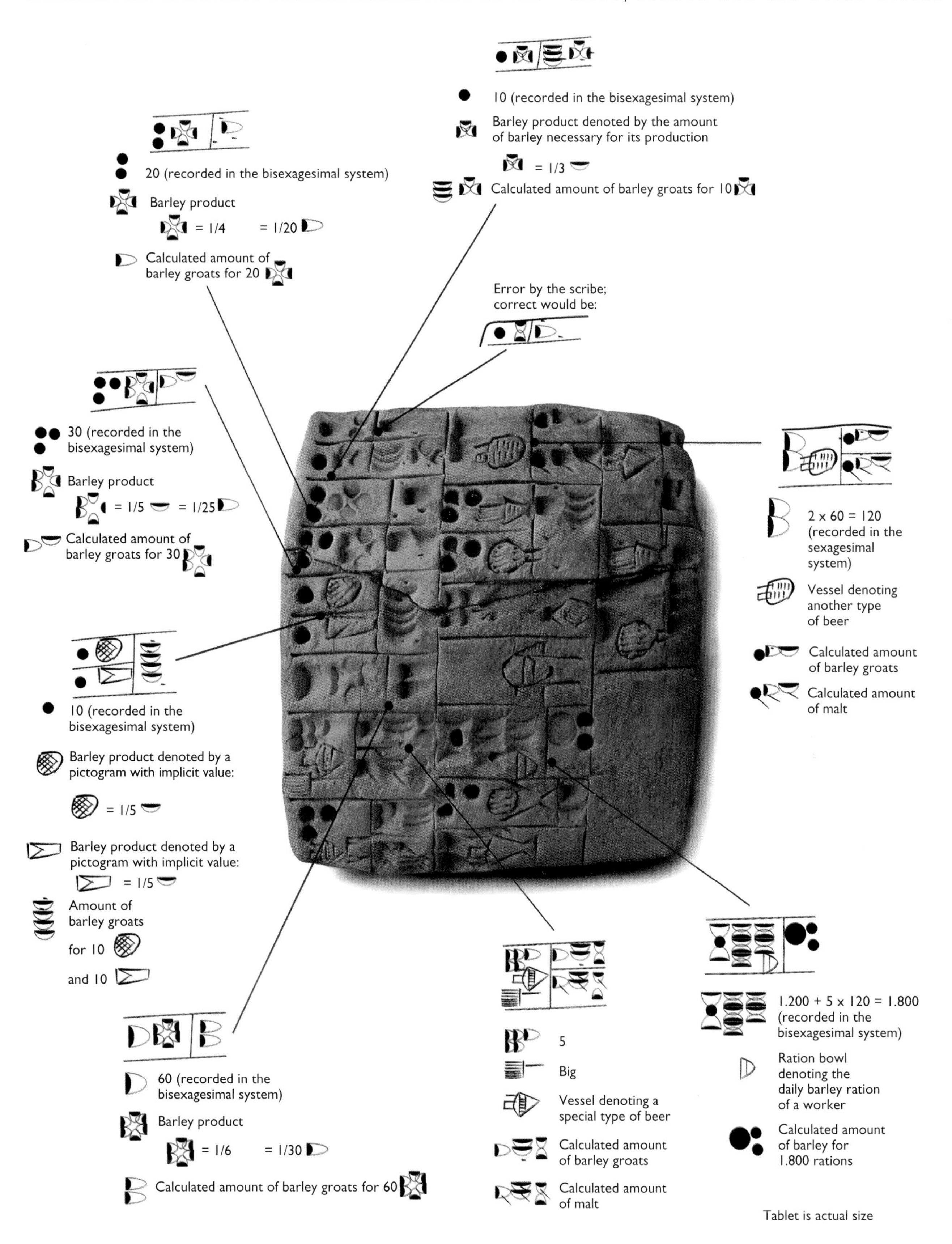
10 (recorded in the bisexagesimal system)
Barley product denoted by the amount of barley necessary for its production
= 1/3
Calculated amount of barley groats for 10
20 (recorded in the bisexagesimal system)
Barley product
= 1/4
= 1/20
Calculated amount of barley groats for 20
Error by the scribe; correct would be:
30 (recorded in the bisexagesimal system)
Barley product
= 1/5
= 1/25
Calculated amount of barley groats for 30
2 x 60 = 120 (recorded in the sexagesimal system)
Vessel denoting another type of beer
Calculated amount of barley groats
Calculated amount of malt
10 (recorded in the bisexagesimal system)
Barley product denoted by a pictogram with implicit value:
= 1/5
Barley product denoted by a pictogram with implicit value:
= 1/5
Amount of barley groats
for 10
and 10
60 (recorded in the bisexagesimal system)
Barley product
= 1/6
= 1/30
Calculated amount of barley groats for 60
5
Big
Vessel denoting a special type of beer
Calculated amount of barley groats
Calculated amount of malt
1.200 + 5 x 120 = 1.800 (recorded in the bisexagesimal system)
Ration bowl denoting the daily barley ration of a worker
Calculated amount of barley for 1.800 rations

Tablet is actual size

Urban Society in Sumer

Within the new cities, the production of ceramic vessels, metal, and woven goods became more organized, being handled by specialists arranged into industry groups. Stone, wood, metal, ores, and other exotic materials were brought into the lowland cities in ever-increasing quantities. Some of the raw materials were fashioned into goods for the local elites, while other materials and materials were transported back as payment to people in the source areas.

Newly developed products formed an increasingly important part of the local economy. Stone bowls, metal tools and weapons, bitumen for boats, cut stone for temples, and precious metals and gems for ornaments all became essential elements of elite life in the Mesopotamian city. Traders organized by the dynastic leader of the city, and perhaps others operating on their own account, set off in all directions carrying manufactured goods from Mesopotamia to exchange for raw materials from other areas. From written and archaeological evidence, we know that these trade routes extended to the east across the Iranian plateau, to the southeast by boat down the Persian Gulf, and to the northwest to the Anatolian highlands, Syria, and the Levant.

By about 2500 BC, writing had become standardized across the entire Mesopotamian plain, and the variety of texts extended well beyond economic data to more literary, religious, and historical records. Moreover, the original ideographic symbol system, where pictures represented objects or quantities, had evolved into a script where the symbols represented phonetic elements. This greatly simplified Sumerian writing, reducing an original 2,000 symbols to a script with about 600 symbols by

ERICH LESSING/MAGNUM

A necklace of gold wire, lapis lazuli, and other semiprecious stones, and a pendant depicting a nude goddess. Dating from the thirteenth century BC, these pieces are an example of the elaborate jewelry that was prized by the elite of the time.

ERICH LESSING/MAGNUM

A bronze figurine of a man on a crouching camel, found at Nineveh, in Mesopotamia. Camels had been domesticated by the middle of the second millennium BC, and it is likely that they expanded the possibility of long-distance trade across the dry regions that border Mesopotamia.

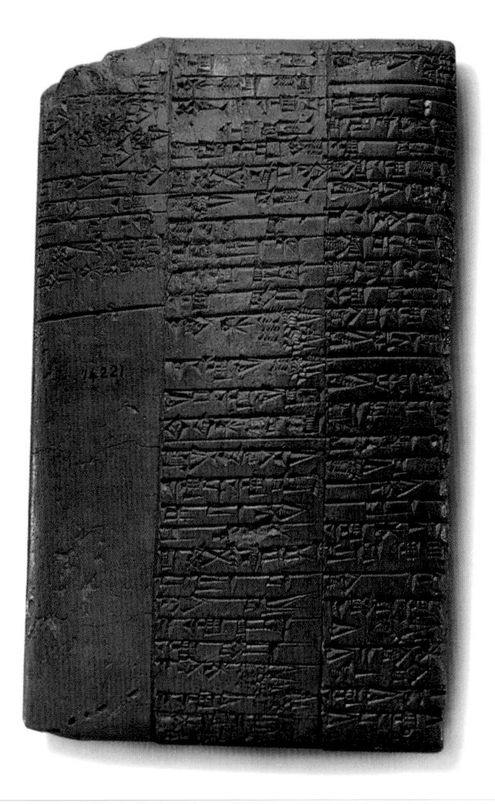

By the end of the third millennium BC, texts were being used to record a wide variety of information. This detailed medical text in cuneiform comes from Nippur.
THE UNIVERSITY MUSEUM, UNIVERSITY OF PENNSYLVANIA

the end of the Early Dynastic period. The precisely drawn symbols, too, were simplified by using a stylus that produced wedge-shaped marks (or cuneiforms) on the wet clay tablets, replacing actual drawings, and thus making writing and reading less difficult. Hundreds of thousands of tablets of Sumerian texts—perhaps even more—were written in cuneiform. This widely used cuneiform script was so efficient that ultimately it was adopted for use with several later languages, such as the Akkadian and Assyrian languages—distant ancestors of contemporary Semitic tongues—after Sumerian had gone out of common usage.

The cities of the Early Dynastic period began to take on the appearance of ancient urbanism. Dense residential areas made up much of the settlement. Short, twisting streets with multiroomed houses created what must have been a labyrinth for the uninformed visitor. Many of the cities were surrounded by enormous defensive walls. Major areas near the centers of the cities were devoted to massive civic buildings or temples. All of these were made primarily of sun-dried clay, fired bricks, and wood. Occasionally, stones were used as well.

As was the case throughout most of early Mesopotamian history, the buildings identified as temples and their ziggurat platforms were the largest structures in the cities. Because of this, and evidence from written records, it is now widely believed that much of the political and centralized economic control was associated with the temples. Although it appears that there were city lords and even some who called themselves kings, they seem to have been strongly reliant upon the temple community, at least during the first centuries of the Early Dynastic period. Textual records point towards the association of the temple with long-distance trade and manufacturing as well. A physical sign of this integration of religious, political, and economic activities is the architectural complex called the Temple Oval, which has been excavated in several Early Dynastic cities. The best-known example is from the northern Mesopotamian town of Khafaje. Here, the complex was made up of two

A cylinder seal and the impression of its design in clay. Termed the "brocade" style by art historians, this is typical of stamps and cylinders used to seal vessels or clay envelopes for texts during the Early Dynastic and later periods.
THE IRAQ MUSEUM, BAGHDAD/SCALA

The so-called Standard of Ur is one of the magnificent examples of craftsmanship found in the Royal Cemetery at Ur. It demonstrates the way in which representational art was used to portray the social order of the times. The lower register shows goods being transported to the city, while the middle register depicts local people with domestic animals and food in vessels, presumably destined for the elite people shown in the top register (note the larger size), who are seated and being served drinks.
BRITISH MUSEUM/ROBERT HARDING PICTURE LIBRARY

ROBERT HARDING PICTURE LIBRARY

A view of the partially restored ziggurat of the city of Ur from the site of the earlier Royal Cemetery precinct.

An alabaster statuette of a Sumerian man. His clean-shaven head and suppliant hand gestures are two typically Sumerian features.
THE LOUVRE/GIRAUDON

concentric ovals of mudbrick walls, enclosing at their center a modestly sized ziggurat surmounted by a temple. Also within the ovals was a series of buildings believed by the excavators to have housed the ruling family, priests, and workers. Outside the oval, the buildings were all of a smaller, more domestic, size and were arranged in what appears to be a labyrinth of twisting alleyways.

A very different building form from the second half of the Early Dynastic period has been excavated at several other, and larger, Early Dynastic sites. Because of their more residential design and massive enclosure walls, they have been identified as palaces. Some scholars have interpreted the palaces as evidence of the growing influence of a secular authority semi-independent of the temple community. Clearly, however, such a dramatic shift in the nature of control in the earliest cities cannot be inferred from the partial excavation of only a fraction of the known cities of the period.

Other evidence of the possible shift in political control comes from the change in distribution of settlements across the landscape from the earliest 'Ubaid settlement through to the end of the Early Dynastic period. In a 1972 survey, Robert McC. Adams and Hans J. Nissen found many communities from each of these periods in the region surrounding the key southern Mesopotamian city of Uurk. Interestingly, during the first half of the Early Dynastic period, and even before this, there were many settlements scattered along the ancient river courses and in the countryside. Larger centers, such as Uruk, were already apparent, but a significant proportion of the population lived in smaller villages. At least in this region, however, the settlement pattern changed dramatically in the last part of the Early Dynastic period, many of the smaller settlements disappearing and the cities growing rapidly.

The implication is that many rural people moved into the large, and newly fortified, cities such as Uruk. On the evidence of numerous written references and the building of massive city walls, Adams and Nissen have suggested that this may have occurred in response to an increased frequency of intercity warfare, which, in turn, may have been related to the new dominance of a secular-based ruling elite. Although Adams has not found similar settlement shifts in all of the subregions of Mesopotamia he has examined, it seems plausible that the growing power of a militarily based authority could have been a crucial factor in the rise of cities and of state society.

The Growth of City-states

During the Early Dynastic period, these cities continued to grow in number and size as irrigation spread over much of the plain. It is likely that the political entity expanded in many instances to include not just individual cities, but the towns, villages, and countryside immediately around the city. These city-states may still have been ruled in much the same way as in earlier times, but the scale and complexity of political matters must have increased significantly.

By the later part of the Early Dynastic period, there were city-state rulers who identified themselves in texts as kings and warlords. These texts also indicate that some of these warlords were able to conquer several other city-states. For example, Lugalzagesi, ruler of the city of Umma, assumed the title of king of the land and claimed to have ruled a confederation of 50 city-states. Whatever the truth of these claims, political developments during the Early Dynastic period laid the foundation for the subsequent growth of nation-states.

The last Early Dynastic period king of Lagash, a city of growing importance, was Urukagina. About 2350 BC, Urukagina promulgated legal reforms that are preserved in inscriptions on buildings of his time. This code is the earliest-known formal attempt at creating a legal system. It explicitly established rights, delegated authority, and defined punishments. Urukagina claimed that he had a covenant with Ningirsu, the city-god of Lagash, whereby "he would not deliver up the weak and the widowed to the powerful man". Urukagina's intent was to lighten the burdens imposed on the general population by governors and priests, but it may, in fact, also have been an effort to strengthen his position as king. Working-class people were freed from certain taxes and from supervision by an over-expanded officialdom. Protection against the stealing of property and unfair business transactions also benefited the ordinary population. Social injustices involving marriage, divorce, and personal property were corrected. It is interesting to note that efforts to solidify the power of the newly emerged kings were already necessary. The establishment of legal codes, and their enforcement through military might, set the pattern for many episodes in later Mesopotamian history.

By the end of the Early Dynastic period, it is also clear that the more or less egalitarian villages of earlier periods—run primarily along kinship lines—had developed into a hierarchy of towns and cities, with sharply defined social classes among various task-oriented groups, as well as kinship groups. Much of this social stratification was related to the growing specialization of production and the differing access to resources that it entailed.

Sargon and the Rise of Nation-states

The Early Dynastic period came to an end with the ascendancy of Sargon of Agade, a military ruler from central Mesopotamia. Myth surrounds the early years of Sargon, but it is clear that he was a member of a Semitic group, ethnically distinct from the Sumerians. Apparently, Semites had populated much of central Mesopotamia for some time, settling especially in the countryside. Sargon's conquests began with the city of Kish, and spread to the south from there. With him went Semitic culture and language. His successes led to the fall of the last Sumerian rulers and the amalgamation of their cities into the Akkadian empire, centered on the city of Agade. This empire was so integrated that many scholars consider it the first nation-state in world history. The empire lasted from about 2350 BC to 2150 BC.

Although the Akkadian empire seems to have been largely a conglomeration of different groups under a military power, important achievements in the development of state administration are evident. A new language was used for official business, and it gradually became the language of international affairs in ancient Southwest Asia for the next thousand years. Sargon installed local rulers or agents to oversee his interests in newly conquered territories. The appointed officials were supported by military garrisons within the conquered cities. A more integrated system of trade developed, controlled by the palace. There is evidence that

A stone bas-relief from the reign of Ur-Nanshe, during the Early Dynastic period, found at the site of Tello. It apparently depicts a ruler, and perhaps a deity, being attended by less important (smaller) people.
THE LOUVRE/SCALA

This Early Dynastic bas-relief, known as the Stele of the Vultures, provides a detailed illustration of armaments and military formations of the period.
THE LOUVRE/GIRAUDON

A stone statue of Gudea, priest-king of Lagash, dating from about 2150 BC. Gudea is well known from his ambitious construction campaign, and many statues of him have been found in southern Mesopotamia.
THE LOUVRE/ROBERT HARDING PICTURE LIBRARY

The excavations area at the ancient site of Nippur. In Sumerian times, the city had great importance as a ritual center located midway between Sumer and Akkad. It continued to be used as a center periodically for the next 3,000 years.

trade extended as far as the Indus Valley, in present-day Pakistan, both overland and by sea.

The extent of Sargon's empire and the huge scale of his military successes were without precedent. The scribes of his period and those of later times extolled the Akkadian state and held it up as a model for later dynasties. Tribute flowed from the provinces to central Mesopotamia, but, perhaps more important, Sargon had gained control over the sources of raw materials that were sorely needed in the lowland cities: wood was imported from Lebanon, the Taurus Mountains, and the Zagros Mountains; metal (mainly copper) came from Anatolia and Iran; bitumen was obtained from the middle Euphrates; and stone was brought from surrounding upland areas.

In Southwest Asia, there were other important cities and states, which traded with, but were not under the direct control of, Akkad. One of these, Tell Mardikh, identified as ancient Ebla, was a major center on the trade route from the Euphrates to the Mediterranean.

Sargon supported an enormous number of people to carry out the administration of tribute, trade, and militarism in the newly assembled empire. He boasted of feeding 5,400 men at his table every day. The scale of society and administration required a large and growing bureaucracy. The increasing number of functionaries of various kinds itself affected the development of Mesopotamian civilization.

But despite the accomplishments of the Akkadian state, it did not create either a political or an economic system that was to be long-lived. In 2159 BC, less than two centuries after it was founded, the city of Agade was sacked. A series of local revolts culminated in the dissolution of the Akkadian empire nine years later.

GEORG GERSTER/COMSTOCK

Ur III and the Resurgence of Sumer

In the wake of these events, individual city-states re-emerged, each vying with its neighbors for control of more irrigated farmland and traded products. The city of Lagash became very successful, extending its control over an area that included many of its rivals. This was not primarily the re-emergence of a powerful military state, but the growth of an economic empire. The rulers of Lagash attempted to monopolize trade in certain commodities, but this time without a massive military commitment. Their agents traveled throughout Southwest Asia, securing supplies and raw materials. The prosperity of these rulers is amply documented by the number of buildings and works of art they commissioned. Their architectural and artistic legacy shows Akkadian influence, but it can be better understood as a revival of Sumerian ideas and authority.

This revival of Sumerian dominance can be clearly seen in the establishment of the Third Dynasty of Ur, by Ur-Nammu, in 2111 BC. This dynasty was soon to control all of Mesopotamia. The main motivation for this growing empire was, once again, economic, and great strides were made in improving administrative techniques. Legal codes giving clear definitions of authority and appropriate conduct, and written boundary markers showing clearer lines of political control, typified the Ur III state.

The impressive building program carried out by Ur-Nammu and his successors shows their resourcefulness. The canal system was extended, both to increase the amount of farmland that could be irrigated and to improve intercity water transport, which became essential to bring food to the city dwellers. Temples were repaired, and new ones erected. The greatest intensity of building was at Ur, Uruk, and Nippur. The ziggurat of the moon-god Nanna, at Ur, was given its final form by Ur-Nammu. In earlier periods, it had been conceived as a platform for a temple, but it was now transformed into a monument made up of superimposed platforms topped by a shrine. Its design was perfected by Ur III architects. Today, it remains the characteristic building of ancient Mesopotamian civilization.

During the Early Dynastic period, urbanization, especially around Uruk, depopulated the rural countryside. This was not so with the growth of the cities of the Ur III dynasty. Rather, the cities and rural towns and villages all grew at the same rate. This probably reflected an explicit attempt by the rulers to increase the efficiency and total agricultural yield of their lands. The exact extent of the Ur III domain, or that of any other early Mesopotamian state, is difficult to determine with certainty. It is likely that most, if not all, of the Mesopotamian plain and some of the uplands to the north were controlled by the rulers of the Ur III dynasty. The territories were divided into approximately 40 administrative districts. Each district was ruled by an *ensi* (city lord), who conducted local business but was responsible to the king. Certain important or troublesome districts were run by *shagins* (military governors). The king took precautions to make certain that local *ensis* did not establish hereditary succession. *Ensis* were transferred to unfamiliar districts, and even whole populations are known to have been relocated by the rulers. These early attempts at reducing the potential power of local authorities and groups in order to maintain the strong centralized government increased in subsequent dynasties.

The two major centers of administrative activity in each city were the palace and the temples. The largely autonomous communities of the palace and temples held land, traded, and produced goods. The palace of the king was the main administrative authority, but other productive units existed, although they frequently took orders from the central authority. The palace and temple officials kept detailed written accounts, including daily records of goods brought in by individuals and balance-sheet tallies of receipts and payments. Silver was used as a standard of exchange, although much of the exchange was for other materials. A system of dry volume and weight measures was also employed.

A well-organized transport system overcame the great distances within the realm of Ur III, and kept it closely tied together. River and canal transport was highly developed and tightly controlled. This was especially important for the movement of foodstuffs from the countryside into the large cities, because city dwellers depended on these imports for a large part of their food.

The legal system was another mechanism that held the society together. Legal codes, such as the one established by Ur-Nammu, set standards of behavior and generally upheld the rights of the poorer classes. Courts were established to settle disputes.

A combination of factors seems to have led to the downfall of the Ur III dynasty—the last period of Sumerian dominance. The continual influx of less sedentary groups from the surrounding uplands provided a temporary labor force at some times, but proved to be a threat at others. Local rulers, particularly of the cities of Isin and Larsa, established their own power bases and challenged the central authority in Ur. In addition, the fertility of much of the Mesopotamian plain gradually decreased as a result of intensive irrigation. (See the feature *Early Mesopotamian Cities and the Environment*.) Taken together, these factors created an unstable situation, where even the relatively strong central administrative system of Ur III could not hold the empire together or even defend the capital. It appears that the final blow came during a period of general famine—probably in 2005 BC—when Ishbi-Erra, the local governor of the city of Isin, refused to send needed food to the king and the city of Ur. This led to the break-up of central control. The isolated and weakened city of Ur was unable to resist an invasion from its former subjects in Elam, to the east, who sacked the city. The great Sumerian empire—the model state for the later ages—came to a tragic end.

A stone head of Gudea, the priest-king of Lagash.
MUSEUM OF FINE ARTS, BOSTON

The Legacy of the Earliest Cities

What is the legacy of the Sumerians and other gifted people who banded together to create the world's earliest cities? Many of their innovations have evolved and become central to modern life. In the realm of technology, the people of Mesopotamia and their neighbors in Southwest Asia appear to have been the first to employ the wheel, the plow, irrigation for agriculture, metallurgy, and a variety of engineering principles. They were also masters of food production, expanding and making more productive the wheat–barley and sheep–goat–cattle farming mix. They also introduced dates, figs, grapes, olives, flax, oats, and a variety of other crops to farming. Equally important, they developed the use of secondary products from domestic animals, such as milk and wool, and began to use animals to pull carts and plows. The manufacturing of textiles, ceramics, and metals developed within the Mesopotamian cities. Trading networks stretched across Southwest Asia and to the further reaches of the known world. Much of this trade was centrally organized for the benefit of the state; by the time of Ur III, and perhaps earlier, there was a class of entrepreneurs who traded on their own behalf as well as for the king.

Dating from about 2100 BC, this bronze statue was used as a votive offering in the foundation of a temple at Nippur, during the reign of Ur-Nammu.
THE IRAQ MUSEUM, BAGDAD/SCALA

THE ROYAL CEMETERY OF UR

SUSAN POLLOCK

SIR LEONARD WOOLLEY'S excavation of the Royal Cemetery of Ur ranks among the most spectacular archaeological discoveries of this century. In five seasons, from 1927 to 1932, he and his co-workers unearthed approximately 2,000 graves, revealing extraordinary wealth and supposed evidence of human sacrifice. Despite more than a century of archaeological work in Mesopotamia, the Royal Cemetery remains in many ways a unique discovery.

This unique gold helmet comes from the richly furnished "private grave" of Meskalamdug. A seal of "Meskalamdug the king" was found in a Royal Tomb, but this may not refer to the same person.
THE IRAQ MUSEUM, BAGHDAD/SCALA

The cemetery was used continuously from approximately 2600 BC to 2100 BC. The earliest graves date to the Early Dynastic period (from 2900 BC to 2350 BC) and include the 16 known as the Royal Tombs. One distinctive characteristic of the tombs is that they include brick or stone-walled chambers with vaulted roofs. In contrast, all other interments—the so-called "private graves"—consisted of simple earthen pits into which the body was placed, occasionally in a coffin, but most commonly wrapped in a reed mat. In addition, most graves in the cemetery were the burial place of a single person. All the Royal Tombs, however, contained multiple burials, ranging from 4 to as many as 75 individuals. Woolley convincingly argued that these did not represent reuse of the tombs but, rather, the burial of a principal person accompanied by a variety of retainers. He considered this to be evidence of human sacrifice.

The Royal Tombs revealed a wealth of grave goods, including elaborate jewelry of gold, silver, copper, lapis lazuli, and carnelian; stone and metal vessels; elaborately decorated musical instruments; and tools and weapons of precious metals. As Woolley was quick to point out, however, great wealth was not exclusive to the occupants of the Royal Tombs: a number of private graves also had rich and abundant grave goods. Indeed, the cemetery included a wide range of burials, from those with no accompanying goods or just a couple of clay pots, to those containing vast wealth and the ultimate offering—other human beings.

BRITISH MUSEUM

Many female retainers in the Royal Tombs were lavishly adorned with necklaces of gold, silver, and semiprecious stone beads, heavy gold earrings, and headdresses of gold ribbon and gold leaves strung on beads, as shown in this reconstruction.

THE IRAQ MUSEUM, BAGHDAD/SCALA

The crushed head of a female retainer from a Royal Tomb, with jewelry in place. Gold ribbon, gold leaves, and beads form a headdress, and strings of lapis lazuli and gold beads were worn around the neck.

One of two similar goat statues found together in a Royal Tomb. The pair may have been part of a larger composition. Goats were among the animals that figured frequently in Sumerian art.

BRITISH MUSEUM/ADAM WOOLFITT/ROBERT HARDING PICTURE LIBRARY

This lapis lazuli mosaic inlaid with shell and red limestone is part of the Standard of Ur. It depicts people at a banquet, including a musician with an instrument similar to those found in the Royal Tombs.
ANCIENT ART & ARCHITECTURE COLLECTION

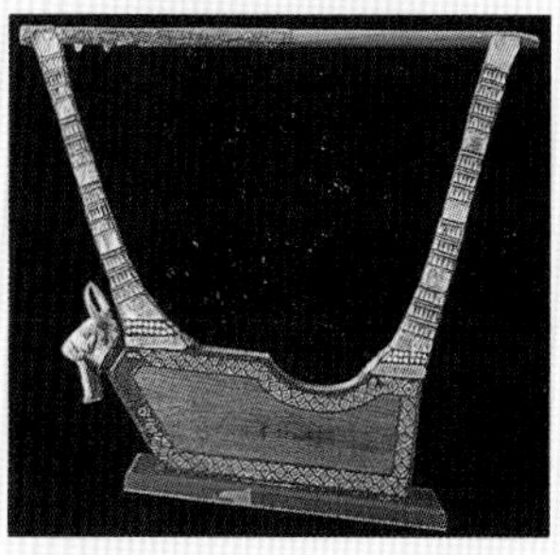

THE IRAQ MUSEUM, BAGHDAD/SCALA

Several Royal Tombs contained musical instruments such as this lyre. Their recovery was one of Woolley's excavation triumphs, since the wooden frames had long since decayed.

Who, then, were the people buried in the Royal Cemetery? What entitled some to burial in the Royal Tombs? Why did the practice of burying additional people in tombs—"human sacrifice"—die out, and why is there no evidence of similar practices elsewhere in Mesopotamia at this time? These and many other questions have continued to intrigue archaeologists up to the present day.

Woolley identified the people buried in the Royal Tombs as kings and queens, accompanied by members of their courts. He based his argument on finds of inscribed artifacts in some of the tombs that named individuals and also bore the designation "LUGAL", the Sumerian word for king. He believed that the other graves in the cemetery were those of private citizens, some of whom were very wealthy, but none of whom was royalty.

Some scholars, however, have disputed this claim. One difficulty is that none of the inscribed artifacts was found in direct association with the principal occupant of a tomb. The artifacts might, therefore, represent gifts from mourners rather than a possession of the dead person. Second, if all the Royal Tombs were graves of royalty, how do we explain the variation in their size, architecture, and number of occupants? This variation might suggest that there were significant differences among the people buried in the tombs.

Another interpretation of both the Royal Tombs and the private graves is possible if we consider them in a broader context. Documentary sources indicate that the Early Dynastic palaces and temples competed with each other for power and wealth, as well as working to erode the traditional power base of wealthy families. From other sites, we know that Early Dynastic mortuary practices included burial in both cemeteries and houses. The placement of the dead below the house floor implies a close connection to the domestic, family unit. By contrast, burial in a cemetery, removed from direct association with the house, may imply that family ties were weaker. People buried in cemeteries may have been those whose principal ties were to the temples or palace.

According to this interpretation, the people buried in the Royal Cemetery were those whose livelihood was closely tied to the temples and palace of Ur, from those in the highest positions—the high priestesses and priests, kings and queens—to the most menial laborers and the full range of people in between. The variation among the Royal Tombs might, then, be related to the differences between temples and palaces and their personnel.

Reference to the tensions and power struggles in Early Dynastic society may also help to explain the spectacular wealth of some of the burials. Following the argument of prehistorian Vere Gordon Childe, conspicuous consumption in burial practices may characterize periods of great sociopolitical competition. On this view, burial practices are one arena in which competition is played out, with each party vying to mount a more lavish spectacle than anyone else. The vast material wealth and unprecedented evidence for the burial of human retainers in the Royal Cemetery might be just such an indication of competitive display. Whether the competition declined or mortuary practices were no longer part of the struggle for power, the practice of building Royal Tombs and furnishing them with human retainers ceased before the end of the Early Dynastic period, about 2500 BC.

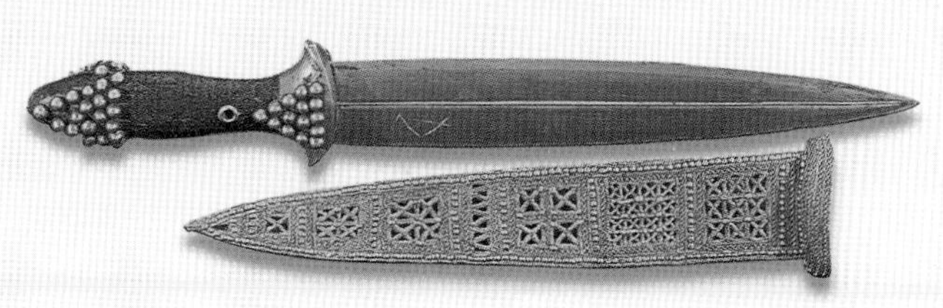

This gold dagger with a lapis lazuli hilt and an intricately worked gold sheath was found in one of the most badly disturbed of the Royal Tombs. The design of the sheath resembles that of sheaths made of plaited reeds or rushes found in less wealthy graves.
THE IRAQ MUSEUM, BAGHDAD/SCALA

The Uruk Vase, a stone beaker with three registers that portray a similar set of activities to the Standard of Ur.
HIRMER FOTOARCHIVE, MUNICH

Early Mesopotamian society also set the stage for many later developments in religion, law, and ethics. Two major ways of maintaining order in the growing cities of Mesopotamia were organized religion (rituals and sacred beliefs) and legal codes as put forward by secular leaders. According to texts of the time, Sumerian religion was based on a fatalistic theology. The gods established laws that were unchanging. People did not have free will but were governed by the decisions of both the major gods and their own personal intermediary gods. The gods were lords of each of the temples and their estates. In addition, certain gods and goddesses were closely associated with each city. The Sumerian gods were related to life-giving powers in nature, such as water, earth, and air. Humans had been created specifically to relieve the gods of the tedium of work, and the gods appointed human representatives to direct day-to-day activities. At first, these must have been priests within the temple. But with the ascendancy of a secular power base within Sumerian city-states, the gods became associated with the validation of the king's authority as well. Further validation of the superiority of the kings and the relative inferiority of other powers, such as the priests and the landed elite (farm owners), came from the legal codes issued by Sumerian and later kings.

A less obvious, but perhaps an equally powerful, means of expressing and reinforcing the social order comes from the representational art of the early cities. During the Uruk and Jemdet Nasr periods, there was a significant increase in large-scale representational art, and some of it is explicit in its portrayal of what must have been the hierarchical relationships within early Sumerian society. Not surprisingly, this is exactly when writing was developing and moving through its highly representational stage, about 3000 BC. During the following Early Dynastic period, art flourished in many media, and among the many astonishing pieces are some that once again appear to portray a social order and appropriate modes of behavior, such as on the Royal Standard from Ur or the Uruk Vase.

Not all of the developments that accompanied the growth of early cities in Mesopotamia were necessarily good for the majority in all respects. With the growth of social complexity and the need to maintain order, access to productive resources became restricted and was allocated on the basis of class. Instead of being temporary, family or individual wealth became institutionalized into a permanent difference, and an early form of class society developed. Along with these formalized differences between families and broader kin groups, it is likely that the roles of males and females within society further diverged, leading to less social and geographical mobility for women and less access to the centers of civic authority. The factors that caused this process of increased inequality are not clear, but the resulting restrictions placed on females became institutionalized and still affect the choices available to many women.

In the Early Dynastic period, warfare became more frequent and involved larger, more organized groups. It may have been a combination of conflicts over land, irrigation-water access, or outright seeking of booty that began the series of intercity campaigns. These are chronicled in some of the earliest written texts and also attested by the construction of massive defensive walls around most cities.

The formation of the world's first cities on the broad alluvial plain of Mesopotamia initiated one of the great transformations of human history: people learning to live together in large groups for long periods of time. Even as early as about 2000 BC, as much as half the population of lowland Mesopotamia lived in cities, where previously the peoples of the world had known life only in villages and small bands. The concept and development of urbanism swept across the world. Something about urbanism—either its attractions or the coercion of its leaders—was so powerful that today the vast majority of all people throughout the world live in cities that bear a striking resemblance to those of early Mesopotamia.

An inlaid table found in the Royal Cemetery at Ur, dating from about 2600 BC. This table and associated pieces are believed to have been used as a board game. Pictorial representations of animals and mythical figures are characteristic of many of the pieces found in the cemetery.
THE IRAQ MUSEUM, BAGHDAD/SCALA

THE IRAQ MUSEUM, BAGHDAD/SCALA

Early Dynastic alabaster statuettes from Tell Asmar, in northeastern Mesopotamia. The woman's dress and the man's curly hair and beard have been interpreted as reflecting the characteristics of a distinctive group that may have populated Akkad (north of Sumer).

BABYLONIANS AND ASSYRIANS: STRUGGLING POWERS IN MESOPOTAMIA

GÖRAN BURENHULT

After the decline of the Sumerian kingdom, about 1800 BC, the people of Elam—the Elamites—occupied Mesopotamia, and at the same time, a new Semitic people arrived from the west: the Amorites. The Sumerian cities fell into disrepair, and the Sumerian language became extinct. The subsequent history of the Mesopotamian plain is characterized by a continuous struggle for supremacy between two centers of power: the Babylonian kingdom, in the south, and the Assyrian kingdom, in the north.

An Amorite dynasty made Babylon its capital, and under King Hammurabi (1728 BC to 1686 BC), the old Babylonian kingdom flourished and conquered Assyria, in the north. However, Hammurabi's fame rests mainly on his law-making and organizational skills, such as the large-scale irrigation projects he organized, which created opportunities for a rich material culture to develop. The power of Babylon was crushed about 1530 BC, when the Hittites, from present-day Turkey, conquered and plundered the city.

Towards the middle of the second millennium BC, not only Babylon, but also other early powers of the Near East—such as Egypt and the Hittite empire—collapsed and left behind a vacuum that soon made way for a patch-work of smaller states. Most important of these were Phoenicia, on the Mediterranean coast; Urartu, in present-day Armenia; Karkemish and other Hittite–Hurrite cities, in northern Syria; Damascus, in southern Syria; and the Jewish kingdom, in Palestine.

Between about 1300 BC and 1100 BC, Assyrian power grew rapidly, and from time to time, the country even controlled its arch enemy, the Babylonian kingdom. During this period, nomadic Jewish tribes migrated into Palestine—according to legend, after the exodus from Pharaoh Ramses II's Egypt. Assyria's first true emperor, Tiglat Pilesar I, ascended the throne about 1100 BC, but soon after, a decline occurred, the reasons for which are not known in detail. It was not until the beginning of the eighth century BC that Assyria, under the ruthless King Assurnasirpal (883 BC to 859 BC), regained its powerful position. His successor, Salamanassar III (858 BC to 824 BC), defeated Damascus and received tribute from King Jehu of Israel.

BRITISH MUSEUM/ERICH LESSING/ARCHIV FÜR KUNST UND GESCHICHTE, BERLIN

A scene from the reliefs at the Assyrian king Assurnasirpal II's palace at Nimrud, showing the king on a lion hunt. It dates from the ninth century BC.

The Rise of Assyria

However, Assyria was still surrounded by rebel vassal states, such as Babylon, Elam, and Urartu, but under Tiglat Pilesar III (745 BC to 727 BC), the country's powerful military forces conquered large areas, among them Urartu. Large-scale deportations were part of the Assyrian rulers' strategy, and the deported populations were replaced by colonists from other countries. Samaria was conquered by Sargon in 722 BC, and the 10 tribes of Israel were exiled. Sargon crushed Urartu once and for all, and the road now lay open for advancing nomadic horsemen, such as the Kimmerians, and later, the Scythians, which was to prove disastrous for Assyria in 612 BC, when Scythians are thought to have taken part in the destruction of Nineveh. Sargon's son Sanherib (704 BC to 681 BC) leveled Babylon to the ground, and Assarhaddon (680 BC to 669 BC) turned Egypt into an Assyrian vassal state. The Assyrian empire now reached its high point and was the sole ruler of the Near East. Its domains stretched from Egypt and the Mediterranean, in the west, and from Anatolia, in the north, to the Persian Gulf, in the southeast.

Assyria has been called the world's first military power, and rightly so. The strength of the Assyrian war machinery was based partly on the education of an extremely effective organization under well-educated commanders in special branches of the army, and partly on advanced techno-logical knowledge including engineers who constructed roads, bridges, and new weapons, such as battering-rams and catapults. The cavalry was swift and very mobile, and it was supported by both light and heavy infantry, with lances and bows and arrows as the main weapons. Two-wheeled war carts, drawn by two or more horses, were also part of the military forces. In addition, the development of the siege strategy is attributed to the Assyrians.

The Assyrian empire, one of the world's first imperial structures, was based on an organization of provinces, ruled by powerful governors in local palaces. The royal palaces in the Assyrian capitals, first in Assur and later in Nimrud, Khorsabad, and Nineveh, were filled with detailed reliefs of war and hunting scenes. These are our primary source of knowlege about certain aspects of everyday life in Assyria.

The decline of the Assyrian power had already begun during the reign of the famous emperor Assurbanipal (668 BC to 625 BC). Egypt was abandoned, and the advancing Persians conquered large parts of the country. Nevertheless, it is thanks to Assurbanipal's great interest in art and culture that important information has survived for posterity. For instance, in Babylon, he had copies made of old Babylonian scripts, as well as scientific and religious works, and thereby created the famous library of Nineveh, which, to a great extent, has been recovered.

Babylonia Regains Power

Following the death of Assurbanipal, Babylonia regained its independence under King Nabopalassar, who attacked and destroyed the Assyrian capital, Nineveh, in 612 BC. The Assyrian empire was totally destroyed, and once again, southern Mesopotamia became the center of power. Under Nebuchadnezzar, Babylonia flourished and became great, and the magnificent city of Babylon—with its splendid temples, great ziggurat, and famous hanging gardens—is, essentially, his work. It was not until the Persian invasion of Babylonia when the Persian king Kyros stood outside the town wall of Babylon, in 539 BC, that the cultural hegemony of Mesopotamia came to an end.

THE CIVILIZATION OF ANCIENT EGYPT

5000 BC – 332 BC

Life along the Nile

Boyo G. Ockinga

Few cultures have been so dependent upon and influenced by their natural environment as ancient Egypt. This was already recognized in the fifth century BC by the Greek historian Herodotus, who called Egypt the gift of the Nile. Although there is evidence that Egypt's climate may have been wetter in prehistoric times, from about 3000 BC, it was characterized by excessive aridity, making life totally dependent upon the waters of the Nile. The Egyptians recognized their reliance on the great river, which distinguished them from other peoples; in his hymn to the sun-god Aten, King Akhenaten praises the god for creating the Nile to keep "humankind" (the Egyptians) alive, and for creating a Nile in the heavens (rain) for foreigners.

A Middle Kingdom hymn calls the Nile: "Bringer of food, rich in provisions, creator of all good things, Lord of awe, sweet of perfume, who satisfies when he comes. Maker of herbage for the cattle, who gives sacrifice for every god. He is in the netherworld, but Heaven and Earth are in his charge, the one who takes possession of the two lands; who fills storerooms, enlarges granaries, and gives goods to the poor."

About 2000 BC, the first hints of a general judgment of the dead appear, involving weighing the heart before the lords of the netherworld. In this eighteenth-dynasty *Book of the Dead* vignette, Khai and his wife, Merit, having passed the test, approach Osiris, king of the netherworld. The papyrus is from their tomb at Deir el-Medina.

Already in predynastic times, Egypt had trade and cultural ties with western Asia. The ivory handle of this finely worked, ripple-flaked, flint knife, found at Gebel el-Arak, near Nag Hammadi, in Upper Egypt, is decorated with a combat scene, and includes two high-prowed boats thought to be of Mesopotamian origin.

THE LOUVRE/ERICH LESSING/MAGNUM

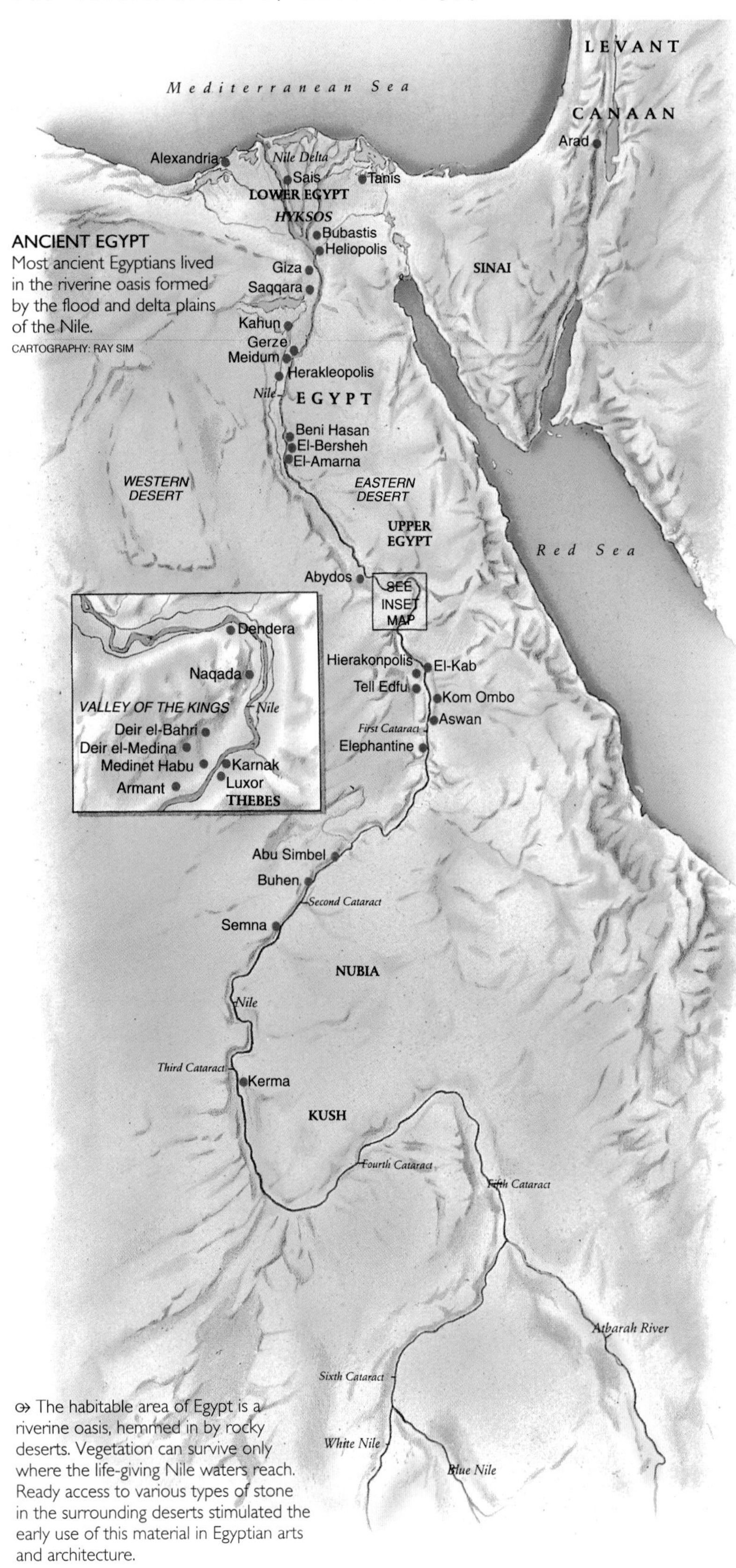

ANCIENT EGYPT
Most ancient Egyptians lived in the riverine oasis formed by the flood and delta plains of the Nile.
CARTOGRAPHY: RAY SIM

The oases in the western desert were clearly part of Egypt from at least the Old Kingdom (about 2640 BC to 2135 BC) onwards, and as recent archaeological work has shown, they played a significant role in the country's history and economy. The deserts that flank the Nile Valley were important sources of raw materials, particularly minerals and stone. Nevertheless, home for the vast majority of ancient Egyptians was the riverine oasis formed by the flood and delta plains of the Nile.

The cultivable part of Egypt is formed by a deep layer of silt that began to be deposited in significant quantities some 24,000 years ago, by the annual flooding of the Nile. The silt-bearing waters, which stem from the summer rains in the Ethiopian highlands and tropical Africa, covered the Nile Valley from August to November. The Egyptian year revolved around the Nile; its rise began about the middle of July, more or less coinciding with the rising of the star Sirius (to the Egyptians, Sothis), marking the start of the year and its seasons—*akhet*, inundation, *peret*, sprouting of the seed, and *shemu*, summer.

The physical geography of Egypt not only governed the material aspects of the life of its people, it also had a fundamental influence on their world view, which was dominated by cyclical patterns and the principle of duality. A cyclical movement was observed in such natural phenomena as the regular, predictable rising and falling of the Nile and the rhythmic movements of the stars and planets. These cyclical processes in nature corresponded with an understanding of history in which events were seen in a renewable cycle rather than as part of a linear progression. The principle of duality is obvious in such geographical features as the arid desert and the fertile valley, the broad expanse of the delta and the narrow ribbon of the Nile Valley, and the two banks of the great river. Together with more universal examples of duality in nature—heaven and earth, sun and moon, night and day, male and female—this is reflected in the concept of the

GUIDO ALBERTO ROSSI/THE IMAGE BANK

→ The habitable area of Egypt is a riverine oasis, hemmed in by rocky deserts. Vegetation can survive only where the life-giving Nile waters reach. Ready access to various types of stone in the surrounding deserts stimulated the early use of this material in Egyptian arts and architecture.

whole as made up of two complementary parts. It is mirrored in such things as the institution of dual kingship; the king was styled "King of Upper and Lower Egypt". The principle of duality in the structure of the state emerges in such administrative titles as "Overseer of the two treasuries" and "Overseer of the two granaries". When texts speak of the whole of the population, they refer to the *pat* and *rekhit* (nobles and commoners), or "the great and the small". Duality and symmetry are also very obvious elements of Egyptian religion and art.

The regularity and dependability of nature, believed to result from the activity of the gods, gave rise to the concept of a divine cosmic principle, behind the operation of the universe. The Egyptians called this power *maat*; it not only determined the functioning of the universe at large, but also governed the behavior of society at all levels. In the context of human relationships and behavior, it denotes what we call justice.

The ancient Egyptians were a Mediterranean people who spoke an Afro-Asiatic language. They referred to themselves by a number of terms such as *remetch*, people, or *Kemet* or *Kemtiu*, "People of the black land" (people of the fertile Nile Valley). Since men were more exposed to the sun, their skin is conventionally brown in artistic representations, while that of women is light yellow. Careful distinctions are made between the various races in tomb and temple reliefs and paintings; Asiatics and Libyans, who have the same skin hues as the Egyptians, are distinguished mainly by costume; Nubians and southerners by darker skins and distinctive facial features.

Historical Beginnings

The basic structures of later Egyptian civilization were formed in prehistoric times, from about 5500 BC to 3050 BC. During this period, there is evidence of distinct cultures in Upper and Lower Egypt, which did not merge until late predynastic times. Generally named after the sites where they were first discovered, the Badarian, Amratian (or Naqada I), and Gerzean (Naqada II and III) cultures succeeded one another in Upper Egypt. Parallel Lower Egyptian cultures are those of Merimda, Omari, and Maadi. The period is not renowned for its great monuments, but its artisans achieved a high degree of sophistication and skill in the minor arts, particularly in the production of fine stone vessels and pottery decorated with animal and geometric motifs.

Egyptian history is described according to its dynasties of rulers, a practice that goes back to Manetho, an Egyptian priest who wrote a history of Egypt for Ptolemy I Soter early in the third century BC.

For later Egyptians, what we call the Predynastic period (about 5000 BC to 3000 BC) was a time when the gods ruled on Earth; later, they handed over the kingship to earthly rulers. The earliest rulers were the anonymous "Followers of Horus". The legendary Menes is the first named king in Egyptian tradition, but whether he was a historical figure is disputed. Some scholars regard him as a later "founder hero", but others identify him with the historic King Aha. Although tradition

ARCHAEOLOGICAL MUSEUM, FLORENCE/SCALA

The goddess Maat—in mythology, the daughter of the sun-god Re—was the personification of a concept that embraces truth, justice, and cosmic and social order. Her symbol is the feather, against which the heart of the deceased was weighed at the judgment of the dead.

BOYO G. OCKINGA

The dominant place agriculture held in the life of ancient Egypt is illustrated by this representation of King Ramses III in his funerary temple at Medinet Habu. The king is shown plowing and reaping in the fields of the hereafter, like the humblest of his subjects.

King Narmer dominates this scene on the Narmer palette. He is depicted smiting a defeated enemy. The falcon-god, Horus, holds the symbol of the defeated marsh region by a leash, and below the king are two other prostrate enemies: the left one represents town-dwellers; the other, nomadic hunters.
THE EGYPTIAN MUSEUM, CAIRO/ WERNER FORMAN ARCHIVE

attributes the initial unification of Egypt to Menes/ Aha, this distinction more rightly belongs to another historical figure, King Narmer. On his famous palette in the Cairo Museum, he is depicted wearing the two crowns of Upper and Lower Egypt, triumphing over his enemies. Archaeology has shown that soon after the end of the Predynastic period, an advanced culture had emerged with fully developed forms of kingship, religion, art, and script that are distinctly Egyptian in character.

The development of writing in Egypt is a controversial issue. It is generally held that, as in many other cultures, it was connected with the development of administration that occurred here in the Early Dynastic period (2950 BC to 2640 BC). There are, however, indications that it may have come considerably earlier. In the tomb of Hemka, at Saqqara, dated to the reign of Den early in the first dynasty (2950 BC to 2770 BC), a roll of blank, uninscribed papyrus was discovered, and the book roll as a hieroglyphic sign is also known from the first dynasty onwards. Given that papyrus was produced then, writing must have been in wide use considerably earlier in order to stimulate the development of such a sophisticated writing material. It has been suggested that ritual scenes, such as the goddess of writing, Seshat, recording the length of the king's reign on the leaves of the sacred ished-tree of Heliopolis, may reflect an early use of leaves as a writing material. Once the script

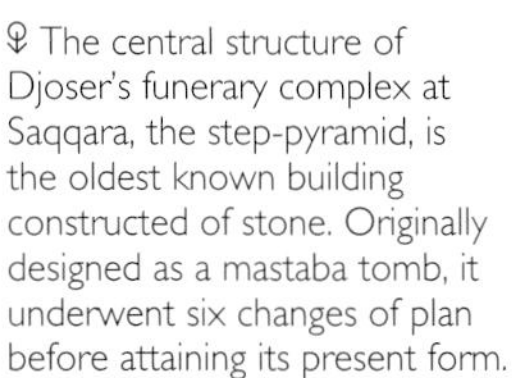

The central structure of Djoser's funerary complex at Saqqara, the step-pyramid, is the oldest known building constructed of stone. Originally designed as a mastaba tomb, it underwent six changes of plan before attaining its present form.

ALAIN CHOISNET/THE IMAGE BANK

had been developed and was widely used, its practitioners, the scribes, enjoyed a greatly increased social standing, and the profession became a coveted one. Even the sons of kings were not averse to depicting themselves in the posture of a scribe, and in tomb and later temple reliefs, the scribe is a ubiquitous figure, depicted recording and controlling the activity of others.

Very few written records survive from the Early Dynastic period, but the cultural achievements of this period are considerable, particularly in the minor arts and the development of a central administration. The Old Kingdom began with the third dynasty (about 2640 BC to 2575 BC), and already the second ruler of this period, Djoser, had built a magnificent funerary complex in stone, including the famous step-pyramid at Saqqara. (See the feature *The Quest for Eternity: Temples and Tombs*.) This is the earliest stone building known to history, yet it displays a perfection in skill and form that matches the best that ancient Egypt was to produce. An achievement of this dimension is possible only if a solid cultural base exists upon which its creators can draw.

The Pyramid Builders

The fourth dynasty (2575 BC to 2465 BC) is the age of the great pyramid builders—Snefru, Khufu (Cheops), Khafra (Chephren), and Men-kau-re (Mycerinus). Their massive structures are apt symbols of the Egyptian state, with the king at its apex, his officials (drawn mainly from members of his family) at the higher levels, and the mass of the people forming the bulk of the pyramid.

The fourth dynasty saw a rise in the prominence of the sun-god Re, with the king adopting the title "Son of Re", and the successors of Khufu often including the name of Re in their names. In the fifth dynasty (2465 BC to 2325 BC), most monarchs built a temple in honor of the god. (See the feature *The Sons of Re: The Kings of Egypt*.)

The Old Kingdom is generally held to come to a close shortly after the end of the sixth dynasty (2155 BC). According to Manetho, its last effective ruler, Pepi II, reigned for 94 years; the dynasty ended with a woman, the shadowy Nitocris, who is known only from later records. The reasons for the fall of the Old Kingdom are probably connected with decline in the effectiveness of the administration. There is evidence to show that the size of the bureaucracy continually grew until the state could no longer afford adequately to pay its officials, which no doubt led to inefficiency and corruption, and subsequent collapse under the pressure of a series of low Niles and poor harvests.

During the period of instability known as the First Intermediate period (2135 BC to 2040 BC), a number of rival kingdoms vied for supremacy. Thebes finally won out in Upper Egypt, while Lower Egypt was held by the Herakleopolitans. The movement for reunification emerged from the

ANCIENT EGYPT: 4000 BC – AD 1

	DYNASTIES	RULERS	SIGNIFICANT EVENTS
AD 1	Romans	Augustus Cleopatra	
	Ptolemies	Ptolemy I	Manetho's history of Egypt
	30th	Alexander the Great	
500	27th	Persian domination	Herodotus in Egypt
	26th	Necho II	Circumnavigation of Africa by Egyptian expedition
	25th	Piankhi	Greek and Carian mercenaries in Egypt Assyrian occupation Kushite rule
		Sheshonk I	Egypt invades Israel and Judea
1000	21st		Libyan dynasty The *Story of Wenamun*
	20th	Ramses III	Battle against Sea Peoples
	19th	Ramses II Tutankhamun	Egyptian–Hittite treaty Battle of Kadesh
	18th	Akhenaten Amenhotep II Thutmosis III Hatshepsut	Amarna period Consolidation of empire Deir el-Bahri temple
1500	Hyksos Second Intermediate period	Kamose Seqenenre Apophis	Wars of independence; reunification under Thebes Hyksos control Egypt
	12th	Amenemhet III Sesostris I Amenemhet I	The *Story of Sinuhe* Reunification under Thebans
2000	11th First Intermediate period	Mentuhotep III	
	6th	Pepi II Unas	Collapse of Old Kingdom Pyramid texts
2500	5th		Rise of cult of Re, construction of sun-temples
	4th	Khufu	Giza pyramids
	3rd	Djoser	Stone architecture: step-pyramid at Saqqara
	2nd		
	1st		
3000		Aha (Menes?)	Unification of Egypt Narmer palette
		King "Scorpion" Narmer	
		Naqada III Protodynastic cultures	
3500		Naqada II	
		Naqada I	
4000 BC		Predynastic cultures	

In her temple at Deir el-Bahri, Hatshepsut depicts herself as a traditional Egyptian king. Here, wearing the double crown of Upper and Lower Egypt, she appears in the form of Osiris, god of the dead.

A wooden statue of Sesostris I. It is one of a pair depicting the king wearing the red crown of Lower and (here) the white crown of Upper Egypt.
JUERGEN LIEPE, BERLIN

This ceremonial axe of Ahmose, founder of the eighteenth dynasty, was found in the tomb of his influential mother, Queen Ahhotep.
JUERGEN LIEPE, BERLIN

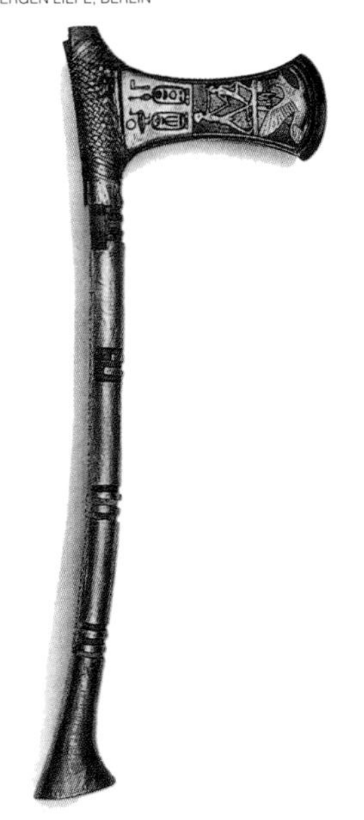

south, and the energetic Thebans under their king Nebhepetre Mentuhotep II of the eleventh dynasty (2134 BC to 1991 BC) succeeded in gaining control over the north.

During the First Intermediate period, arts and learning declined considerably in the south, which was cut off from the schools of the old royal residence. When the Thebans brought back experts from the north, there was a gradual return to the old standards.

Mentuhotep II built himself a splendid funerary temple and tomb of truly royal quality at Deir el-Bahri, in western Thebes, a building that was to inspire the architect of Hatshepsut's better-known temple. The last king of the eleventh dynasty, Mentuhotep IV, does not seem to have been a legitimate heir to the throne, for he is omitted in later king-lists.

The Feudal Age

Egypt's next ruler was Amenemhet I (1991 BC to 1962 BC), perhaps the vizier (chief minister) of the last king of the eleventh dynasty, although this is not certain. The *Prophecy of Neferti*, a text fictitiously set in the fourth dynasty in the time of Snefru, purports to record a prophecy that, after a period of chaos, the "son of a woman of Nubia", called Ameni, would become king and bring stability back to the land. This was to usher in the Middle Kingdom (2040 BC to 1650 BC), the classical period in Egypt's history. In spite of their southern origins, the rulers of the twelfth dynasty moved their capital to the north, the natural center of gravity of Egypt, at the apex of the delta and the head of the long, narrow Nile Valley.

The Middle Kingdom was a period when the pen was put to work to support the new state. The *Prophecy of Neferti* was clearly propaganda intended to attract support for the new government. The famous *Story of Sinuhe* also belongs to this period. Other texts were specially composed for use in the schools to win young men for the administration, which had to be rebuilt after the First Intermediate period, and to inculcate in them a sense of loyalty towards the new dynasty.

The Middle Kingdom is also known as Egypt's "feudal age", for the provincial overlords held great power. Some even dated events according to their period of office, and they built themselves great tombs, such as those at Beni Hasan. Elements of the old royal funerary practices were adopted—for example, the construction of valley temples. One nomarch, or provincial governor, Djehutihotep of el-Bersheh, proudly records how he had constructed for himself a statue of truly royal proportions; it was more than 6 meters (20 feet) in height, and in his tomb, he depicts how it was transported.

Not until the energetic Sesostris III (1878 BC to 1841 BC) came to the throne was the power of the nomarchs curbed, so strong was the tradition of independence established in the First Intermediate period.

The last ruler of the twelfth dynasty, as of the sixth, was a woman, Sobekneferu. The thirteenth dynasty (1785 BC to 1650 BC) shows the same characteristics as followed the sixth; there was a rapid succession of rulers and a weakening of central authority, ushering in the Second Intermediate period (1650 BC to 1540 BC). In the eastern delta region, the Asiatic Hyksos, called "rulers of foreign lands" by the Egyptians, took advantage of this situation to wrest control of the area and set up their own kingdom. Although the Hyksos gained influence over most of Egypt, it seems they were content to allow Egyptian dynasts to keep control of their local princedoms as feudal dependencies.

Again, it was from Thebes and the south that the movement for reunification sprang. Sekenenre Ta'a II and his son Kamose, the last two kings of the seventeenth dynasty (about 1650 BC to 1551 BC), began the war of independence against Apophis, the last of the Hyksos. Kamose set up a pair of stelae in Karnak, telling of his glorious deeds of battle. His reign was short, and it was left to Ahmose, his brother and successor, to complete the expulsion of the Hyksos from Egypt.

The Warrior Ethos in the New Kingdom

Ahmose founded a new dynasty, the eighteenth (1540 BC to 1295 BC), and a new age—the New Kingdom (1540 BC to 1070 BC). The warlike events that ushered in the New Kingdom saw the rise of a new warrior ethos in Egypt, and brought about the establishment of a well-organized standing army. Innovations in warfare, influenced by the Hyksos, also appeared: in particular, the use of the horse-drawn chariot as a fighting platform, and new types of weapons, such as the powerful

GUIDO ALBERTO ROSSI/THE IMAGE BANK

The *Story of Sinuhe* was a biography, probably fictitious, of an official who fled Egypt at the death of Amenemhet I, but was encouraged to return by Sesostris I.

I reached the Walls of the Ruler that were built to ward off the Asiatics, to control the Sand-farers. I crouched in a bush for fear of being spotted by the guards on duty at the walls. At night, I set out. By daybreak, I had reached Peten. I rested at the island of Kemwer. Thirst overtook me: I was parched, my throat was dry. I said, 'This is the taste of death.' My spirits lifted, and I pulled myself together when I heard the sound of lowing cattle. I saw Asiatics, and a scout among them—who had been in Egypt—recognized me.

From the *Story of Sinuhe*, translated by Boyo G. Ockinga

composite bow. In the Old Kingdom, armies were raised as required. Since the First Intermediate period, small bands of professional soldiers had been kept by the provincial governors or the king, and these were supplemented by enlistment when needed. In the New Kingdom, a large army of infantry and chariot forces was maintained.

With a few notable exceptions, most rulers of the New Kingdom led their troops into battle, and placed great emphasis on their personal prowess and feats of arms. The most famous of these kings is doubtless Thutmosis III, often called the Napoleon of Egypt. In the course of countless campaigns, he established Egypt's empire in western Asia. His son, Amenhotep II, was an avid sportsman and soldier, who proudly boasted of his martial and sporting achievements. In one of his inscriptions, his outlook on life is succinctly summed up by the description of himself that he places in the mouth of his father, Thutmosis III.

Hatshepsut placed her funerary temple (in the foreground) to the south of that of her predecessor, Mentuhotep II, using the backdrop of the cliffs of western Thebes to spectacular effect. The now-ruined structure on the platform of Mentuhotep's temple may originally have incorporated a pyramid.

THE ARCHAEOLOGY OF DEATH

CORINNE DUHIG

THE ANCIENT EGYPTIANS typically used many methods in an attempt to ensure life after death. Perhaps the best-known is mummification, which aimed to preserve the body as an enduring home for the soul.

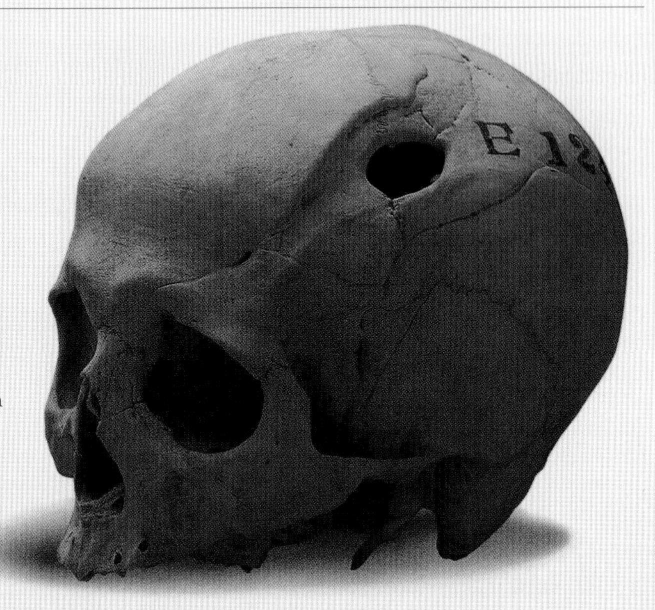

This skull from Giza (about the sixth century BC) is of a man who had survived a disabling head wound.
G.J. OWEN/DUCKWORTH COLLECTION, CAMBRIDGE UNIVERSITY

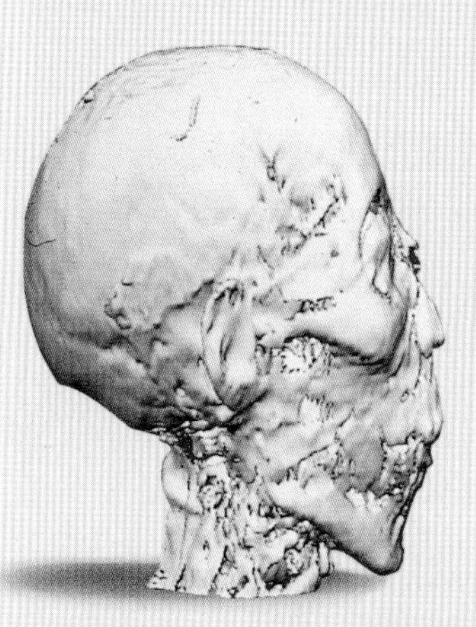

A reconstruction of the priestess Tjentmutengebtiu's head inside its bandages was made using multiple X-ray slices processed by a computer to form a three-dimensional image. Images of the skull revealed that the priestess's brain had been removed, and the chamber stuffed with linen. She died about 900 BC.
ST THOMAS' HOSPITAL (MEDICAL PHYSICS), LONDON

The excavation or plundering of innumerable Egyptian tombs has uncovered huge quantities of human remains. A great deal is poorly preserved, of unknown origin, or even unrecovered—some of the ancient grave-fields are scattered with human bones, mummy fragments, and pieces of bandage. But much is housed in museum collections throughout the world, providing a valuable research resource.

Almost every type of human tissue can be recovered for examination. In special cases, scientific autopsies have been carried out, but the days of "unrolling" mummies from their bandages are now past, and nondestructive methods are preferred. Ingenuity is needed to investigate intact specimens: the use of conventional radiology is a long-established method, but recently, flexible endoscopes have allowed the inside of body cavities to be viewed, and CAT scans have been used to obtain a three-dimensional image of the body.

Marc Armand Ruffer pioneered human paleopathology (the study of ancient diseases) in the nineteenth century. He found bilharzia flatworms (which cause bladder disease) in mummies, examined hardened arteries, and produced a classic description and illustration of spinal tuberculosis. Modern research—using methods including histology (the microscopic study of tissue structure), serology (the study of serums), and various types of electron microscopy—has revealed the disease experience of ancient Egyptians, from pharaohs to commoners. Diseases included parasite infestation, degenerative arthritis, and the most worn and abscessed teeth in the ancient world. Wounds healed well, however, probably because the climate was dry and most people were basically healthy. Syphilis, the scourge of later times, seems to have been absent. Tuberculosis was present from the Predynastic period, but the only evidence for leprosy is from two bodies from a late Nubian cemetery.

Knowledge of ancient diseases is only one aspect, albeit morbidly fascinating, of the study of human remains. Bones and bodies record many aspects of human inheritance and experience. An X-ray survey of the royal mummies in Cairo revealed the skull and facial morphology of several pharaohs from the eighteenth dynasty, revising the identifications made by priests of the twenty-first dynasty. DNA analysis can establish familial relationships: for example, it has confirmed the genetic similarity of Tutankhamun to his supposed grandmother Queen Tiye. Broader projects, using modern measurement and statistical methods, attempt to describe and explain genetic variation in the ancient Nile Valley. Lively academic argument continues as to the composition of the population, and the roles played by migration and interbreeding.

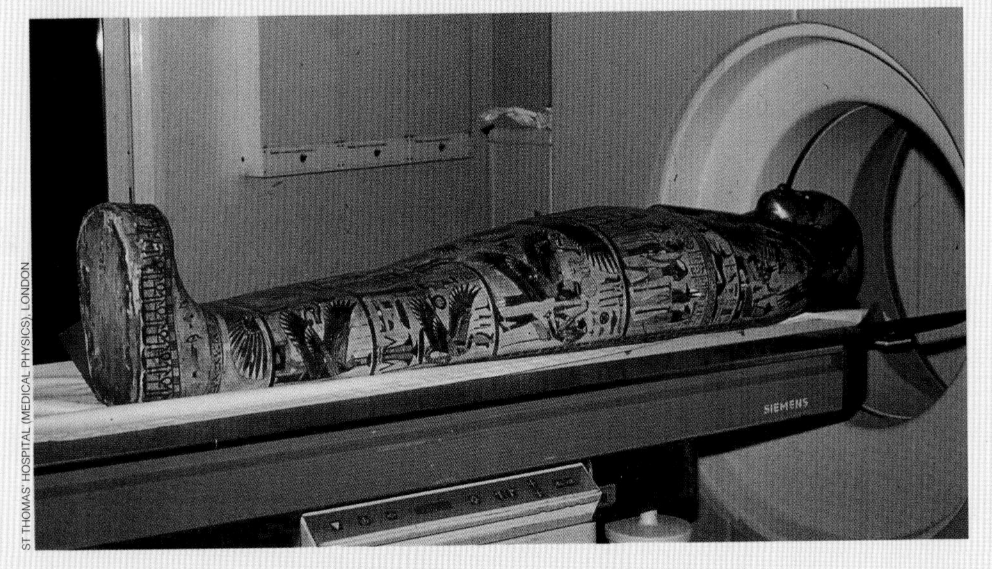

ST THOMAS' HOSPITAL (MEDICAL PHYSICS), LONDON

The priestess Tjentmutengebtiu about to undergo a CAT scan.

"He is not even of an age to engage in military activity and look, he has turned his back on the pleasures of the flesh and chooses strength!"

The famed Queen Hatshepsut (1479 BC to 1457 BC) is best known for her works of peace—her obelisks in Karnak, her funerary temple at Deir el-Bahri, and her expedition to the land of Punt, on the coast of present-day Sudan—but even she kept up the warrior tradition, and depicted herself as a ferocious sphinx trampling down her enemies. Similarly, Amenhotep III, who typifies the pleasure-loving oriental monarch, paid lip service to the warrior ideal. His commemorative scarabs record his hunts against wild bulls and lions, and an inscription reports his campaign in Nubia. His son, the famous Akhenaten, who for so long was idealized as the first pacifist pharaoh, was in fact very traditional in this respect. He, too, set up inscriptions recording his campaign into Nubia and describing himself as a warrior king.

Although the warrior tradition was dominant, New Kingdom Egypt was no Egyptian Sparta. Egypt reached the zenith of material prosperity and imperial power in this period, and art and architecture flourished. In the reign of Hatshepsut, the classical standards of the Middle Kingdom in art, architecture, and the language of royal inscriptions were taken as models. In the age of Amenhotep III (1391 BC to 1353 BC), the art of the New Kingdom reached a climax of sophistication and refinement, exemplified in the reliefs of such tombs as those of Ramose and Kheruef, at Thebes, and the older parts of the temple of Amun, at Luxor. The second king of the eighteenth dynasty, Amenhotep I, established the royal cemetery in the Valley of the Kings, at Thebes.

ROBERT HARDING PICTURE LIBRARY

BOYO G. OCKINGA

Almost all that remains of Amenhotep III's once massive funerary temple are these two colossal statues, mistakenly identified by early Greek travelers as belonging to their legendary hero Memnon. The statues flanked the entrance to the temple.

This relief from Ramses II's temple at Abydos shows the Egyptian infantry and chariotry that formed part of the army he led against the Hittites at Kadesh. Four of the divisions of the army were named after the gods Amun, Re, Seth, and Ptah. A fifth was formed of fresh recruits, the Na'arin, whose timely arrival at Kadesh saved the day for Ramses.

One of the 401 *ushabti* (worker) figures from the tomb of Tutankhamun, who were to carry out tasks for the king in the other world. He wears the nemes headdress and a diadem with protective vulture and cobra goddesses on his brow, and holds one of the royal insignia, a flywhisk, in his right hand.
SCALA

An unfinished quarzite head of Akhenaten's queen, Nefertiti. The piece is an exquisite example of late Amarna art, and was found in the workshop of the sculptor Thutmosis, at el-Amarna.
STAATLICHE MUSEEN, AEGYPTISCHES MUSEUM, BERLIN/ ERICH LESSING/MAGNUM

It is also in the New Kingdom that probably the most enigmatic personality of Egyptian history ascended the throne of the pharaohs: Amenhotep IV, better known as Akhenaten, the son of Amenhotep III and his nonroyal queen, Tiye. Akhenaten (1353 BC TO 1338 BC) attempted to introduce a genuine monotheism in Egypt. The old gods, particularly Amun, were mercilessly eradicated. So thorough were the king's servants in their attempt to obliterate the memory of Amun that they climbed to the tops of lofty obelisks to erase his images there, even though they could not be seen from the ground. One of the surest indicators of date in an inscription is the erasure of the name Amun, which proves that it predates the establishment of Akhenaten's new capital at el-Amarna.

Akhenaten's reform naturally failed; his religion was too other-worldly and could not meet the needs of the ordinary people. Its greatest deficiency was probably in the area of funerary practice, where it offered almost nothing compared to the rich traditional rituals.

Akhenaten's two successors, Semenkhkare (1338 BC to 1336 BC) and Tutankhamun (1336 BC to 1327 BC), were short-lived. With the early death, at about eighteen, of Tutankhamun, who restored the old faith, and won immortality through the chance survival intact of his tomb with its magnificent burial equipment, the royal family of the eighteenth dynasty died out. In the following period, it was the military that was to win control of the country. The immediate successors of Tutankhamun, Ay and Horemheb, were both army commanders, as was the founder of the nineteenth dynasty (1295 BC to 1188 BC), the general Paramessu, who was to become Ramses I.

The military pharaohs were able to stem the tide that was advancing against Egypt in Syria, and reassert Egypt's position there against the encroachments of the Hittites of Asia Minor (present-day Turkey). The most famous Ramesside king is doubtless Ramses II (1279 BC to 1213 BC), whose memorials the traveler to Egypt meets at every step. His monuments fill the land—no previous king left so many temples and other works. After a great battle against the Hittites at Kadesh, on the Orontes River, in the fifth year of his rule, the king just escaped with his life, and

ALAIN CHOISNET/THE IMAGE BANK

A view from the second courtyard of the Ramesseum. Ramses II was the most prolific builder of Egypt's kings. His funerary temple in western Thebes, named after his throne name, Usermaatre, was known in classical antiquity as the "tomb of Ozymandias". A painting of the ruins of the temple inspired Percy Bysshe Shelley's poem "Ozymandias".

only staved off a complete rout thanks to the timely arrival of reinforcements. The Hittites and Egyptians then came to an accommodation in Syria, and eventually formed an alliance that was sealed by the marriage of Ramses with a Hittite princess, given the Egyptian name of Maat-Hor-Neterure. Egypt then enjoyed its last long period of peace and prosperity in the remaining 45 or so years of Ramses's reign.

The last of the strong Ramesside kings was Ramses III, the second ruler of the twentieth dynasty (1186 BC to 1070 BC). He warded off attacks from the Libyans in 1180 BC, and three years later, from the coalition of Sea Peoples, who originated on the east coast of Asia Minor and the Aegean islands. His great funerary temple at Medinet Habu preserves the record of these impressive achievements.

Empire-building in Western Asia

The New Kingdom saw a change in Egypt's relationship with its northern, Asiatic neighbors. Trade contacts had already existed in predynastic times; western Sinai was a coveted source of copper and turquoise, energetically exploited by the Egyptians, who asserted their interests by force of arms when necessary. The coastal city of Byblos (in present-day Lebanon) was also an important trading partner of Egypt in the early period; coniferous timbers, the so-called cedars of Lebanon, were used in first-dynasty tomb construction. The sea route to Byblos was already well established in the Old Kingdom, when the term "Byblos ship" for an ocean-going vessel first appears. The nature of Egypt's relationships with the Levant and Canaan in the Middle Kingdom is disputed. The *Story of Sinuhe*, which speaks of royal messengers regularly traveling through the land, and the numerous finds of Egyptian objects make it clear that they were close. Although it seems unlikely that there was any permanent Egyptian presence in the area, the Egyptians were not averse to using force to exert their will, and mining and trading expeditions were regularly accompanied by soldiers. Yet, on the whole, they relied on trade and the common Bronze Age practice of exchange of gifts between rulers to obtain what they wanted.

In the New Kingdom, the situation changed dramatically. Through the energy of a number of warrior pharaohs—in particular, Thutmosis III—Egypt was able to establish an Asiatic empire in northern Syria and Palestine, organized into three provinces. Imperial rule was loose; each province had an Egyptian governor, and small detachments of troops were stationed in various centers. Day-to-day government was exercised by native city rulers, who were left to their own devices so long as they remained loyal to Egypt and regularly delivered their tribute.

G. COLLIVA/THE IMAGE BANK

Two of the four colossal, seated, royal statues that flank the entrance to Ramses II's rock-temple at Abu Simbel, in Nubia. Abu Simbel is one of many Egyptian temples built in Nubia to serve as both religious and economic centers.

RIJKSMUSEUM VAN OUDHEDEN, LEIDEN/ERICH LESSING/MAGNUM

A detail of a relief in the Saqqara tomb of the general (later king) Horemheb. It depicts Asiatic captives in wooden manacles being led by Egyptian soldiers into the presence of Tutankhamun.

THE QUEST FOR ETERNITY: TEMPLES AND TOMBS

Boyo G. Ockinga

Ancient Egypt is best known for the brilliance and impressiveness of its monumental art and architecture, which expresses its people's love of life and their search for eternity. The link between monumental architecture and the consciousness of eternity is illustrated by the oldest surviving monumental structures. These are the great mudbrick mastaba tombs and other funerary monuments built at Abydos, in the Early Dynastic period, by the kings for themselves, their families, and retainers, where they were buried, and at Saqqara, where they constructed cenotaphs. The early temples and shrines are smaller and were often built of perishable materials, such as reed and matting. The early tombs were undecorated, for the needs of their occupants were provided for by the institution of a funerary cult conducted by their descendants.

But such cults eventually discontinued, and they were supplemented by inscriptions and reliefs within the tomb showing the requirements of the dead. At first, simple stelae were erected at the offering place, but eventually, the tombs were provided with chapels, whose walls were decorated with scenes of offerings and depictions of the dead ones involved in their favorite activities, showing in fascinating detail the production of the things required for the afterlife.

The earliest stone monument is also a funerary complex, that of King Djoser (2624 BC to 2605 BC) of the third dynasty, at Saqqara, with its dominating step-pyramid. This remarkable group of buildings incorporates the king's tomb, his cenotaph, and his Sed-festival complex. The monument was built by his famous architect, Imhotep, a man later revered as a sage and patron of doctors, and identified by the Greeks with Asclepius.

Djoser's step-pyramid combines two potent symbols—the primeval hill that rose from the waters, the site of the creator god's act of creation; and the pyramidal form, symbol of the greatest of the creator gods, Re, the sun-god of Heliopolis. From the fourth dynasty onwards, the pyramid was to dominate royal funerary architecture, although not all pyramids are as massively built of solid stone as those of Khufu, Khafra, and Men-kau-re, at Giza.

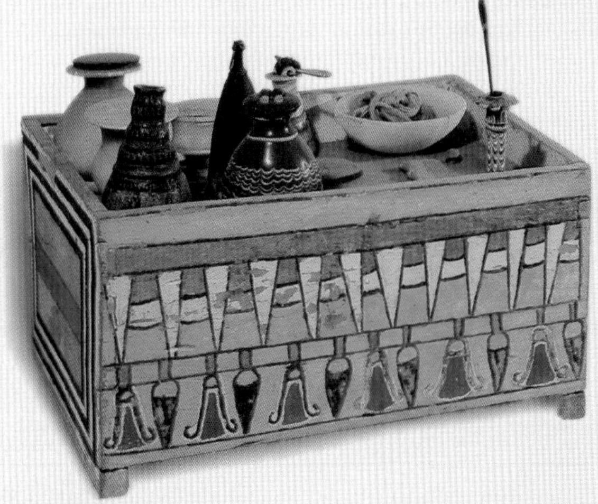

Not only were tombs decorated with depictions of the daily needs of the deceased, but models of objects used in daily life, or the actual objects themselves, were also placed inside them. This cosmetic chest, with jars of alabaster and colored glass, which belonged to a lady of the eighteenth dynasty named Merit, wife of Khai, was found in the couple's tomb at Deir-el-Medina.
PICTUREPOINT LTD

Unlike the tombs of officials, royal pyramids were undecorated until the reign of Unas (2355 BC to 2325 BC), the last ruler of the fifth dynasty. Later Old Kingdom rulers decorated the walls and ceilings of their burial chambers with texts designed to ensure their continued life after death.

Eventually, stone was widely used for temples and tombs, but the dwellings of living mortals continued to be built of less durable mudbrick and wood, for they were needed for only a limited time, whereas the temples and tombs were to last for eternity.

Temples in the New Kingdom

While funerary cults fell into abeyance and the monuments themselves gradually deteriorated, the cults of the gods seemed to endure, and funerary cults became linked with temple organizations and the setting up of statues or stelae in the temples of the gods. A commoner could obtain this only as a favor granted by the monarch, but the monarchs were responsible for building the temples and maintaining their cults, which offered them the opportunity to leave monuments to themselves while gaining the favor of the gods. The result was an explosion of building activity in the New Kingdom. Not only were old mudbrick temples rebuilt in stone, but older structures were expanded. In particular, the temple of Amun, the great state-god of the empire, was added to, resulting in the vast complex that has survived to the present day. With its numerous chapels, halls, pylons, and courts, it was surrounded by a massive wall of mudbrick and covered an area 500 meters by 500 meters (1,640 feet by 1,640 feet).

Plant forms are typical adornments of Egyptian architecture of all periods; in particular, stone columns often represented such plants as papyrus stalks and palms. They had special significance from at least the New Kingdom onwards, when temples had a religious, symbolic significance and represented the cosmos. The floor—which the texts say was covered with silver—represented water from which papyrus plants, the columns, grew. The ceiling, painted blue and decorated with stars and birds, represented the sky. The innermost sanctuary, where the image of the god resided, was the primeval hill on which the creator god stood and performed his act of creation.

A statue of Amenophis, son of Hapu, an influential official of Amenhotep III, depicts him as a scribe with a roll of papyrus on his lap and a scribe's palette—a holder for brush and ink—slung over his left shoulder. The statue stood in the temple of Amun at Karnak, and its inscription addresses visitors, proposing that he act as an intermediary between them and the god in return for an offering.
SCALA

In the New Kingdom, the increasing importance of the temples for ensuring the immortality of the ruler led to the separation of the royal tomb and the funerary temple. Earlier, the royal funerary temple was attached to the pyramid tomb, but now the tombs were built in the Valley of the Kings, in Thebes. The symbol of the pyramid maintained its significance, however, and chapels of the tombs of commoners

PHILIPPE ROY/EXPLORER/AUSCAPE

Two statues of Thutmosis III, later usurped by Ramses II, standing in front of the seventh pylon at Karnak. These are two of the countless royal and nonroyal statues set up in the temple. After the second century BC, there were so many that some 800 were cleared from the temple and buried in the courtyard in front of the seventh pylon.

were usually topped with a small pyramid. It may well be more than coincidence that from certain viewpoints, the highest peak of the mountains in which the royal tombs were excavated has the appearance of a pyramid.

The royal tombs were now also decorated, but not with scenes of daily life. Instead, the walls were covered with the texts and illustrations of various books that describe the netherworld, veritable guidebooks to the hereafter. The central theme of these compositions is the nightly journey of the sun-god through the netherworld. The royal tomb was to be a realization of the underworld, where the dead monarch mystically united with the sun-god and shared his immortality.

Tutankhamun's Tomb of Gold

Although the tombs were built in a well-guarded and secluded valley in the western mountains, already, in antiquity, they were plundered, leaving little of their original movable contents for the modern archaeologist to discover. The great exception to this is the tomb of the young king Tutankhamun. The sensational discovery of his intact tomb, in 1922, by Howard Carter and Lord Carnarvon, made world headlines and captured the imagination of all, even influencing fashions in clothing, furniture, and architecture at the time. Tutankhamun died unexpectedly, before his royal tomb had been completed, and the body was placed in a smaller tomb intended for another person. But no cost was spared with the equipment that accompanied him into the next world. The tomb was filled to overflowing with objects the king had used in his lifetime—clothing, jewelry, weapons, chariots—as well as things he would need in the afterlife. Many of the items were of gilt or solid gold, and the quantity of gold in the tomb showed the wealth of Egypt at the time, a land where, in the words of the king of Mitanni, Tushratta, gold was as plentiful as the dirt on the ground.

The funerary temples were built where everyone could see them, on the edge of the cultivated land. In fact, they were shrines of the state-god, Amun, incorporating the funerary cult of the ruler, who was also worshiped as a form of the god. Here, just as in the main temples, the deeds of the rulers were recorded in word and image for future generations, thereby securing the rulers' immortality.

The tradition of the ruler as temple builder continued into the Greco-Roman period (332 BC to AD 395); the Ptolemys, in particular, instigated an extensive temple-building program, but the role of the ruler became fossilized. Admittedly, the monarch is still omnipresent, but he or she appears only in the standard religious scenes, performing the temple rituals. No longer do we find anything like the expansive reliefs of the New Kingdom depicting the ruler in a historical situation, doing battle with those symbols of the chaotic, threatening forces of the universe, the foreign foes of Egypt. The individuality of architecture that some of the older temples display is also absent in those of the Greco-Roman period, which are all built to a standard plan.

What particularly impresses the modern visitor is how completely preserved many of the later temples are, with their numerous rooms, lofty ceilings, stairways leading to the roof, and mysterious subterranean chambers. Some of the Ptolemaic temples, such as the temple of Isis, in its beautiful setting on the island of Philae, capture our imagination, and their architectural detail—in particular, the capitals of columns—is impressive. Although they give a measure of eternity to the rulers who built them, it is the gods who were worshiped in them who are immortalized. The countless inscriptions that cover the walls and pillars preserve for future generations myths about the gods, as well as the words of the sacred rituals that once echoed around their halls.

This funerary mask of Tutankhamun is of solid gold, beaten and burnished, and is inlaid with semiprecious and glass-paste imitation stones. It weighs 11 kilograms (24 pounds) and originally covered the head and shoulders of the king's mummy.

EGYPTIAN MUSEUM, CAIRO/PICTUREPOINT LTD

GUIDO ALBERTO ROSSI/THE IMAGE BANK

The three pyramids of Giza belonging to Khufu, Khafra, and Menkau-re. Just as their houses were built around the royal palace, the tombs of the king's officials were built around the royal pyramid. This can be clearly seen in the case of Khufu's tomb, at the top of the photograph.

BOYO G. OCKINGA

On the outer face of the east wall connecting the seventh and eighth pylons at Karnak, the high priest of Amun presents himself before a statue of Ramses IX. That his figure is on the same scale as that of the king is indicative of the growing influence of the high priests of Amun in the face of the weakness of the later Ramesside rulers.

Egypt's new policy in Nubia, the less-developed region to the south, was a continuation of the old. Nubia was of great interest to Egypt as a source of gold, copper, semiprecious stones, and stone for building and statuary, and as a corridor along which the exotic goods of tropical Africa—ivory, ebony, incense, slaves, and animals—passed to reach the Mediterranean. Whereas, in late predynastic times, relations with Nubia appear to have been cordial and based on trade, soon after unification (about 3050 BC), Egypt seems to have decided to eliminate the Nubian intermediaries and establish its own presence there. Raids were conducted into Nubia, and there was an Egyptian settlement near Buhen, just north of the second cataract, from at least the fourth dynasty (about 2500 BC). In the sixth dynasty, a new cultural group appeared in Nubia, and Egypt's direct control was lost.

In the Middle Kingdom, Egypt's presence was reasserted through the building of a series of great fortresses that controlled the Nile as far south as Semna, below the second cataract. Control was interrupted in the Second Intermediate period, when an independent kingdom of Kush controlled the south as far north as Elephantine, and maintained trade and diplomatic contacts with the Hyksos rulers of the north. After the expulsion of the Hyksos, however, Egypt regained Nubia, and extended its influence down to the fourth cataract, inaugurating a long period of imperial control. Nubia was ruled directly by an Egyptian viceroy, the King's Son of Kush, and the natural resources of the region were exploited to the full. In the tombs of a number of New Kingdom officials, depictions of the presentation of Nubian tribute appear, giving a vivid insight into the richness and variety of the raw materials Egypt acquired there.

The Years of Decline

The Ramesside age after Ramses II (1213 BC to 1070 BC) is a story of gradual, steady decline, ushered in by the assassination of Ramses III in 1153 BC. Surviving records tell of corruption in high places, and the famous tomb robberies, which we know about from the court records of the trial of the culprits, also took place at the end of this period. The kings resided in the north of the country, while in the south, the high priests of Amun grew steadily in power. A relief at Karnak shows the high priest Amenhotep being rewarded by Ramses IX; not only is it unprecedented for a high priest to be represented in a temple relief, he is also depicted the same size as the king. The temple of Khons is another witness to this process. It was completed by the high priest Herihor, who depicts himself as a king. The process led eventually to the establishment of a theocracy of Amun in Thebes, more or less independent of the twenty-first dynasty (1070 BC to 945 BC), founded at Tanis by Smendes, husband of a Ramesside princess, on the death of Ramses XI.

A gold pectoral (breast pendant) from the tomb of the twenty-first-dynasty king Amenemope depicts him offering incense to the funerary god, Osiris. Like those of the other kings of the dynasty, Amenemope's tomb was built, for security reasons, inside the wall of the Amun temple complex at Tanis.

ANCIENT ART & ARCHITECTURE COLLECTION

The twenty-first dynasty begins what is generally termed the Third Intermediate period (1070 BC to 712 BC), but as the chaos associated with the First and Second Intermediate periods was not repeated, the suggested alternative, the Post-imperial period, is probably more apt. The twenty-first dynasty was succeeded by the Bubastide kings of the twenty-second dynasty (945 BC to 722 BC), who were descended from Libyan mercenaries settled in the delta. The founder of the line, Sheshonk I, is the king who, in 926 BC, conducted a campaign in Palestine and sacked the temple of Jerusalem, as recorded in the Old Testament (I Kings 14.25ff.). The twenty-third and twenty-fourth dynasties are other minor Libyan dynasties that existed concurrently at various times with the twenty-second.

THE EGYPTIAN MUSEUM, CAIRO/E.T. ARCHIVE/AUSTRALIAN PICTURE LIBRARY

⇧ The head on the silver coffin of the twenty-first-dynasty ruler Psusennes I is detailed in gold. In the Old Kingdom, silver was more valuable than gold, but by the time of the New Kingdom, gold was twice as costly as silver. In Egyptian mythology, the flesh of the gods was said to be of gold and their bones of silver, so it was more usual for face masks to be made of gold.

G. COLLIVA/THE IMAGE BANK

⇦ The gateway leading from the first court into the hypostyle hall at Karnak. Flanking the gateway are statues of Ramses II, who completed the decoration of this hall. The large column in the foreground is one of 10 belonging to the colonnade built during the reign of the Nubian king Taharka, of the twenty-fifth dynasty.

A new phase of Egypt's history begins with the twenty-fifth dynasty (712 BC to 664 BC): the so-called Ethiopian or, more accurately, Kushite kings. As the name implies, this line of kings originated in Nubia—the old colonial territory, which had won its independence from the motherland. The second ruler of the dynasty, Piankhi, conquered the whole of Egypt, once again forming a united kingdom.

In 671 BC, Egypt was occupied by the Assyrians for some seven years before the twenty-sixth (Saite) dynasty (664 BC to 525 BC) regained the nation's independence. This was a period of renaissance, when an attempt was made to return to the "golden age", the "first time"—that is, the beginning of civilization. For the Saites, this golden age was the Old Kingdom, and we find the art and religious texts as well as the administrative titles of that period being adopted. So skillful were the Saite artists in copying early reliefs that many have been mistaken for genuine works of the Old Kingdom.

With the end of the Saite dynasty and the invasion of the Persians in 525 BC, Egypt lost its independence for ever, apart from a short interlude from 404 BC to 343 BC. The second period of Persian domination was ended by the conquest of Egypt by Alexander the Great, in 332 BC. The Romans, in their turn, then ruled Egypt from 30 BC to AD 642, when the country was conquered by the Arabs. The next Egyptian to govern Egypt was Nasser, who ousted King Farouk, an Albanian who was the last of the dynasty of Mehemet Ali, in 1952.

THE SONS OF RE: THE KINGS OF EGYPT

BOYO G. OCKINGA

The institution of kingship was central to ancient Egyptian civilization, and although it sometimes failed, it was never replaced by another form of government. It is not known just how it emerged from the Predynastic period, but it no doubt developed from the position of chieftain of a small group, who was chosen largely on the basis of physical strength and ability. (All four of the female rulers we know of acted out a male role.) Traces of this custom can be seen in the Sed festival, celebrated after the first 30 years of a monarch's reign. On this occasion in the historic period, the powers of the ruler were ritually renewed by the gods, but the ceremonies also included tests of the king's physical powers. Perhaps the ceremony originated in a test of the king's strength, and if found wanting, he was ritually killed and replaced by a fitter man.

Defender of the People

It was the duty of the ruler to protect his people from danger, particularly foreign enemies, and the image of the king smiting the foreign foe became a classic icon from Early Dynastic to Greco-Roman times. The importance given the king's physical prowess as late as the twentieth dynasty is illustrated in reliefs on the outer walls of the temple of Ramses III at Medinet Habu, which depict him defeating chaotic human and animal forces threatening Egypt.

A king was customarily succeeded by his eldest son by his chief wife, but if the chief wife did not produce a son, then a son by one of his secondary wives was chosen. In the latter situation, if the chief wife had a daughter, the heir could be married to his half-sister. Power politics and intrigue doubtless often played an important part in the selection of the king, and although we only rarely have glimpses into the actual historical events, there are documented cases of palace intrigues, one of which resulted in the assassination of Ramses III in 1153 BC.

Although human agents and actions were involved in the selection of a king, the choice was considered to be divinely sanctioned. Kingship was closely linked with divinity, and the ancient Egyptian king-lists record the gods as having once ruled on Earth. The concept of kingship was not necessarily static over the course of the millennia, however. The king shared in the divinity of the gods to a greater or lesser degree, depending on the period. His divinity was expressed in terms of his relationship to the chief of the pantheon. Initially, the king was seen as the earthly incarnation of the falcon-god, Horus, but from the fourth dynasty onwards, the title "Son of Re" appears, proclaiming the king as the son rather than the incarnation of the sun-god.

Here begins a gradual decline in the status of the king's relationship to the god. In the Middle Kingdom, no new titles are introduced, and royal inscriptions make it clear that the king is seen as being his divine father's junior. In the Old Kingdom, the ruler independently exercised his father's reign on Earth; in the Middle Kingdom, he is at pains to emphasize that his deeds are in accordance with his father's commands. The change is reflected in royal statuary. In the reign of Sesostris III, the king's features lose the serene, self-confident expression typical of the Old Kingdom, and now express the burden and responsibility that rest upon the king. From the end of the Middle Kingdom, the change in the king's position also finds its expression in a new term, the "image of the sun-god", which proclaims him to be the god's representative on Earth.

The "heretic" pharaoh Akhenaten attempted to reassert the king's divinity by reverting to the kingship concept of the Middle Kingdom, but his reform was not to outlast his reign. The concept of the king as the image, the earthly representative, of the god is still found as late as the reign of the Persian king Darius I (522 BC to 468 BC), who ruled Egypt as part of the Persian empire. On a royal statue found at Susa, in Persia, but made in Egypt, an inscription calls the king: "Progeny of Amun, living image of Re, who placed him upon the throne in order to bring to a good end that which he [Re] had

⇧ A black granite statue of Sesostris III. The large ears are typical of royal statuary of the reign, as is the care-worn facial expression, perhaps reflecting the concept of the king as the all-hearing monarch, who is conscious of the great responsibilities of his office.
BRITISH MUSEUM

⇦ The painted chest from the tomb of Tutankhamun. The six scenes depicted on the lid and sides all have the same theme—the king, as upholder of *maat*, triumphing over the forces of chaos, be they human (here, the Nubians) or animal (gazelles). The contrast between the orderly Egyptian forces and the chaotic enemies is sharply drawn.
PIERRE TETQEL/EXPLORER/AUSCAPE

PICTUREPOINT LTD

⟲ In his temple at Abu Simbel, Ramses II is shown smiting his northern enemies with a curved sword in a posture that goes back to prehistoric times. Behind the king is the symbol of the royal *ka*, the life-force that was infused with divine power at his coronation.

begun on Earth." Here, the king was placed upon the throne by the sun-god, and it is the king's status as the sun-god's chosen one that is the basis of his legitimacy. According to an inscription of Hatshepsut, the foreign Hyksos rulers lacked legitimacy, because "they ruled without Re". Darius's text also mentions the purpose of kingship—to continue and complete what the god began on Earth; that is, to maintain the god's creative activity, bringing order out of chaos.

The concept of the divine duty, rather than right, of the king is expressed in a number of texts from as early as the Middle Kingdom. It is easy to dismiss the official theological view of kingship as empty propaganda, designed to hoodwink the masses and keep them submissive to the ruling elite. But this interpretation is problematical, imposing the prevalent skeptical, cynical view of religion of our own time on a society that genuinely believed in the divine and in the intervention of the gods in human affairs.

THE EGYPTIAN MUSEUM, CAIRO/WERNER FORMAN ARCHIVE

⟲ The serene facial expression of this statue of Khafra, from the valley temple of his pyramid at Giza, well illustrates the confident, god-like character of kingship in the Old Kingdom. The falcon-god, Horus, of whom the ruler is the earthly representative, spreads his wings protectively behind the king's head.

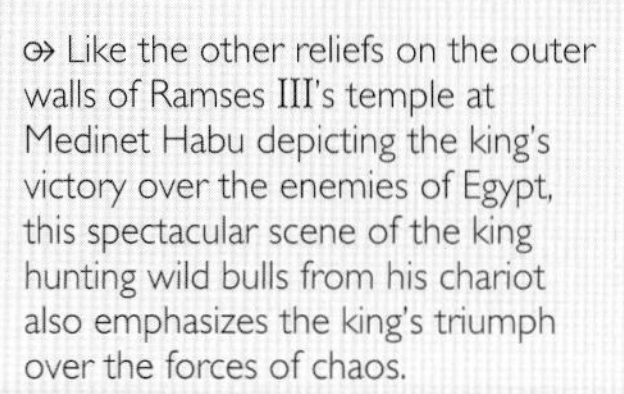

⟳ Like the other reliefs on the outer walls of Ramses III's temple at Medinet Habu depicting the king's victory over the enemies of Egypt, this spectacular scene of the king hunting wild bulls from his chariot also emphasizes the king's triumph over the forces of chaos.

BOYO G. OCKINGA

The Legacy of Egypt

A number of phenomena appearing in the late New Kingdom probably contributed to Egypt's decline. There were indications of widespread corruption and maladministration, with failures in the redistribution system, and consequent economic difficulties. Internal security was weak, and the country was plagued by incursions of marauding Libyans, who penetrated as far south as Thebes. The "warrior ethos" of the early New Kingdom was lost; so, too, it would seem, was the will to defend oneself. Early in the Ramesside period, foreign mercenaries were already being conscripted into the Egyptian army, and their numbers grew after Ramses III, who was followed by a succession of weak kings. The Libyans, who formed the greater proportion of the mercenaries, eventually established their own, the twenty-second, dynasty.

Today, when Tutankhamun is a household name, it is difficult for us to imagine a time when the only thing most people knew about ancient Egypt was what they read in the Bible. The gradual fading of ancient Egypt from the consciousness of the West began with the early Christianization of the country, in the second and third centuries AD, and was sealed by the fall of Alexandria to the Arabs, in AD 642. The final stage of the language of ancient Egypt survived in the form of the Coptic of Christian Egypt, but since this was written in an alphabet based on the Greek, knowledge of the hieroglyphic script was lost.

In the Renaissance of the fifteenth and sixteenth centuries, when scholars were driven by the desire to return to ancient wisdom, Egypt and its legendary Hermes Trismegistos (the Egyptian god Thoth) were held to be the founts of knowledge. The idea was expressed in the floor mosaic of the cathedral in Siena, in Italy, which depicts the god presenting Egypt with the art of writing and law. Giovanni Bernini's design for the erection of the obelisk in the Piazza della Minerva, in Rome, in 1667, symbolizes the belief in the wisdom of the Egyptians: wisdom, the obelisk, is supported by strength, the elephant.

Not until the eighteenth century did people set about rediscovering ancient Egypt in a spirit of scientific inquiry. Only after Jean-François Champollion succeeded in deciphering the hieroglyphic script, in the first quarter of the nineteenth century, could the ancient inscriptions and writings once again be read. Yet although ancient Egypt had had little direct influence on Western culture before that time, its indirect influence was more significant than is often realized, since it was filtered through the two traditions from which Western culture has largely sprung: the Greco-Roman and the Judeo-Christian. To cite just two examples, Proverbs 22.17–24 parallels the Egyptian *Teaching of Amenemope*, and through such works as Plutarch's *On Isis and Osiris*, Egyptian ideas found their way, via Freemasonry, into Schikaneder's libretto for Mozart's *The Magic Flute*.

Egyptian cultural influence spread far beyond Egypt's borders, as shown by this eighth-century BC Phoenician carving in ivory, found at Nimrud, in Mesopotamia. It depicts a winged Egyptian sphinx wearing the royal headdress and the double crown.
BRITISH MUSEUM/E.T. ARCHIVE/ AUSTRALIAN PICTURE LIBRARY

Opposite page: This linen mummy shroud, dating from 180 BC, depicts the deceased standing between the jackal-headed Anubis, god of embalming, and Osiris, lord of the netherworld, who receive him into the next life. The scene well illustrates the symbiosis of Hellenistic and Egyptian culture of the time. Anubis is represented according to the conventions of Egyptian art, with his head shown in profile; while Osiris's iconography is less conventional: he wears an adaptation of his traditional crown, his face is shown frontally, which is very unusual for Egyptian art, and he does not wear his customary ceremonial beard. In contrast, the deceased, who wears a Roman toga, is depicted according to Greco-Roman artistic conventions.
AEGYPTISCHES MUSEUM, BERLIN/ERICH LESSING/MAGNUM

THE FUTURE OF EGYPT'S HERITAGE

BARRY KEMP

THE DECAY OF THE GREAT SPHINX, publicized when a lump from one shoulder fell off in 1988, has turned what was once a symbol of the enigmatic wisdom of the past into a symbol of its vulnerability. This is, however, only the most public aspect of the dubious future of Egypt's archaeological heritage.

The first detailed European accounts of Egypt, in the late eighteenth and early nineteenth centuries, show the survival of a rich archaeological landscape. This included standing monuments—largely the tombs and temples of Upper Egypt—and mounds representative of ancient settlements spread along the Nile Valley and across the Nile delta alike: a detailed record, spanning thousands of years, of one of humankind's oldest civilizations. The last two centuries have witnessed the devastation of that haunting landscape on a scale that is scarcely believable. No one has tried to measure the loss, but perhaps about 80 percent is not far from the truth.

Three influences from the modern world have largely determined ancient Egypt's fate: economic modernization, population pressure, and the outside world's fascination with pharaonic Egypt. Economic modernization began early in the nineteenth century and quickly hit hard at archaeological sites. A number of lesser ruins became building-stone, but the main damage came through a nationwide move to quarry ancient settlement mounds for agricultural fertilizer, sometimes on an industrial scale. In this way, countless sites were razed. An Egyptian government department to protect antiquities (the Service des Antiquités) was created in 1858, but its vision was long restricted to art treasures and monuments. At the same time, a lust for buried treasure amongst the local population was inflamed by the European passion for collecting Egyptian antiquities. Official agreements led to a number of conspicuous monuments (including three obelisks) being exported to Europe and North America, but their loss was as nothing compared to the methodical looting of sites, sometimes under official license. Desert cemeteries, where ancient artifacts were often remarkably well preserved, were the prime target.

The theft and export of antiquities, although by no means suppressed, is today no longer a scandal—there is much less to steal. The assault on the ravaged archaeological landscape continues, however, as towns, factories, and farmland expand during the current rapid economic growth and modernization essential for a population that is estimated to double in the next 20 years. A landmark of change was the final step in the total regulation of the waters of the Nile, which came with the completion of the Aswan High Dam in 1971. This hugely increased the volume of water available for agricultural reclamation, which continues relentlessly to eat away the archaeologically rich desert margins. Ground water now stands constantly at a higher level than in the past, impeding archaeological excavation and concentrating salt in the soil, with highly destructive effects as it crystallizes on exposed surfaces of ancient stonework.

Archaeologists, too, play a part in the destruction of ancient sites by removing ancient deposits, and the buildings covered by such deposits are frequently left exposed to decay. This is especially the case with buildings of sun-dried mudbrick—the usual building material in ancient Egypt—which tends to disintegrate after exposure to the elements. At many of the less spectacular but still important sites (including Akhenaten's short-lived capital city at el-Amarna and the court cemeteries of the first dynasty at Abydos and Saqqara), mudbrick ruins are almost all that survive. Preservation requires not only painstaking work on a large scale, but also permanent maintenance. Modern remedies only delay disintegration; they do not stop it.

Certain sites, being the focus of mass tourism, face particular problems. Because they are prominent in the public eye, they are safeguarded from outright destruction. Some of them are on so large a scale that they can absorb the daily visits of thousands of people without sustaining damage.

A detail of an image of Queen Nefertari from her burial chamber, showing detachment of the plaster layer and damage from surface salts. Recently, the paintings have been cleaned and conserved by the joint efforts of the Getty Conservation Institute and the Egyptian Antiquities Organization.

BILL PIERCE/SYGMA/AUSTRAL

The requirement then is for imaginative policies to control tourist access and tourist trade, and for modern facilities to harmonize with the setting. The temples at Karnak and Luxor and the Giza pyramid plateau are sites where successful schemes have been, or are being, introduced. Many tombs, however, including the royal tombs in the Valley of the Kings, are too small to admit the present numbers of tourists without suffering serious deterioration. The painted walls are constantly touched or brushed against, and humidity—up to 9 liters (two gallons) of perspiration per day in the tomb of Tutankhamun —invades the naturally dry air that preserved the paintings for so long. The threat is sufficiently serious to prompt suggestions that replicas of the most visited tombs be made in the vicinity of the real ones. In the meantime, the tomb of Tutankhamun and several other famous tombs remain closed.

Egypt has comprehensive legislation covering all aspects of its ancient heritage, and has, in the Egyptian Antiquities Organization (successor to the Service des Antiquités), a large official agency charged with managing it. All archaeologists, whether Egyptian or foreign, work under its control, and one condition is that all finds remain in the country. Tourism is a key source of revenue for Egypt, and the condition of major monuments is a matter of political concern. For these reasons, it is likely that the principal monuments will be looked after in ways that will ensure their long-term survival as objects of admiration. It may be, however, that a time will come when these are the only ancient sites left. The real reservoir of future knowledge are the less spectacular archaeological sites away from the main centers. They have become an endangered resource, but, unlike species of wildlife, their stock cannot be replenished.

BARRY KEMP

The temple of Ptah, at Memphis, dates from the nineteenth dynasty. The floor is beneath the water table, and salts are forming on the stone surface.

A limestone temple of the nineteenth dynasty at Hermopolis (Ashmunein). The building is suffering badly from salts forming on the stone surface.

BARRY KEMP

BARRY KEMP

The ancient city of el-Amarna, showing the Nile, cultivated land, and the remains of ancient walls from the city on the desert land. Cultivated land watered by the Nile is steadily encroaching on ancient desert ruins, such as the city walls of el-Amarna, shown here.

PICTUREPOINT LTD

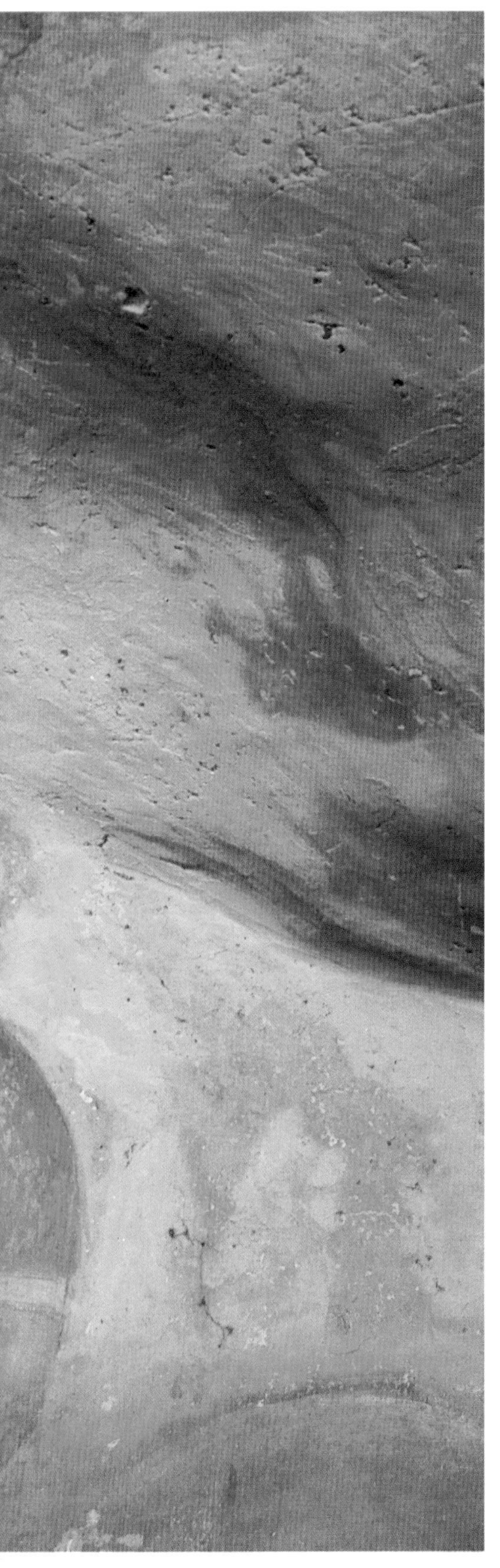

CIVILIZATIONS IN SOUTHERN ASIA

3000 BC – AD 500

The Rise of Kingdoms on the Indian Subcontinent

IAN C. GLOVER AND HIMANSHU PRABHA RAY

The great geographical and ecological variation found over the Indian subcontinent—with its deserts and lofty mountains, the fertile plains of the Indus and Ganges rivers, eroded hills and plateaus, as well as deep forests—has fostered the rich regional and cultural diversity that distinguishes this part of the world.

When the ruins of Mohenjodaro and Harappa were first uncovered in the 1920s, it was believed that they were simply extensions of the Bronze Age urban civilizations of Mesopotamia. At that stage, there was little evidence of any village or town life on the Indian subcontinent during the preceding Neolithic and Copper ages. Now, some 70 years later, we can see that these first cities of South Asia were the product of some 4,000 years of local cultural development. They owed little to Mesopotamian civilizations, and were quite different in their formal structure and organizational principles. The collapse of the Indus civilization and the later appearance of new ethnic groups from the north paved the way for the growth of a series of lavishly wealthy kingdoms, whose art, architecture, and religion formed the basis of the splendor that was to become India's.

The Sigiriya frescoes are the earliest examples of the Sri Lankan school of painting often described as classical realism. The beauty and elegance of these "celestial maidens" is eulogized in graffiti left by visitors to the site from the sixth to the thirteenth centuries AD.

A game board (a type of chessboard) found in the excavations at Harappa. Similar specimens made of pottery fragments, brick, and stone have been found at other sites of the Harappan culture, together with a variety of gaming pieces, some with heads of animals.

ROBERT HARDING PICTURE LIBRARY

The foothills of the Afghan-Iranian Plateau, in present-day Afghanistan, were the home of South Asia's first villages. It was from these that the civilizations of the Indus Valley later arose.

THE MACQUITTY COLLECTION

This skull was found in a grave at Mehrgarh, on the Kachi Plain. Large cemeteries from the Aceramic Neolithic phase have been found within the habitation area, some burials containing baskets coated with bitumen and also cakes of red ocher.

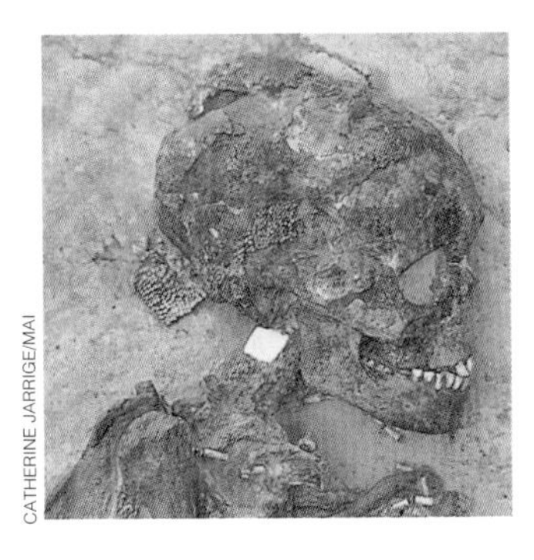

CATHERINE JARRIGE/MAI

Ornaments of local and imported stone, shell, and bone were the other grave goods found during excavations at Mehrgarh. The fine workmanship of many of these beads shows the use of stone microdrills and bow-drills.

THE INDUS CIVILIZATION: 6000 BC TO 2400 BC

To understand the civilizations of the Indus Valley, we must look at the settlements from which they arose. The first villages of South Asia appeared in the foothills of the Afghan-Iranian Plateau and on the western margins of tributaries of the Indus River. The earliest and best studied is Mehrgarh, on the Kachi Plain, where the Bolan River has cut 9 meters (30 feet) through the layers of a village known as MR3. Established before 6000 BC and lasting until about 2000 BC, Mehrgarh started out as a collection of small, rectangular, multiroom houses. Stone tools, and grains preserved in mudbricks, indicate that agriculture formed the basis of the villagers' livelihood. In the early levels, the remains of wild beasts outnumber those of domesticated animals, but later, domesticated sheep, goats, and cattle came to dominate.

The people of Mehrgarh buried their dead with beads made from bone, shell, local stones, and imported turquoise, and sometimes with young goats. The turquoise and shell ornaments show that they participated in exchange networks extending from the coast of the Arabian Sea to the edges of central Asia. We call this phase the "Aceramic Neolithic", since neither pottery nor metal tools supplement the numerous finds of chert knives, arrowheads, bone awls, and polished stone axes. The inhabitants must have known the value of copper, however, for a single bead of rolled native copper was found among the grave goods. Small figurines of unfired clay, resembling finds in western Iran, represent the earliest human images so far known from South Asia.

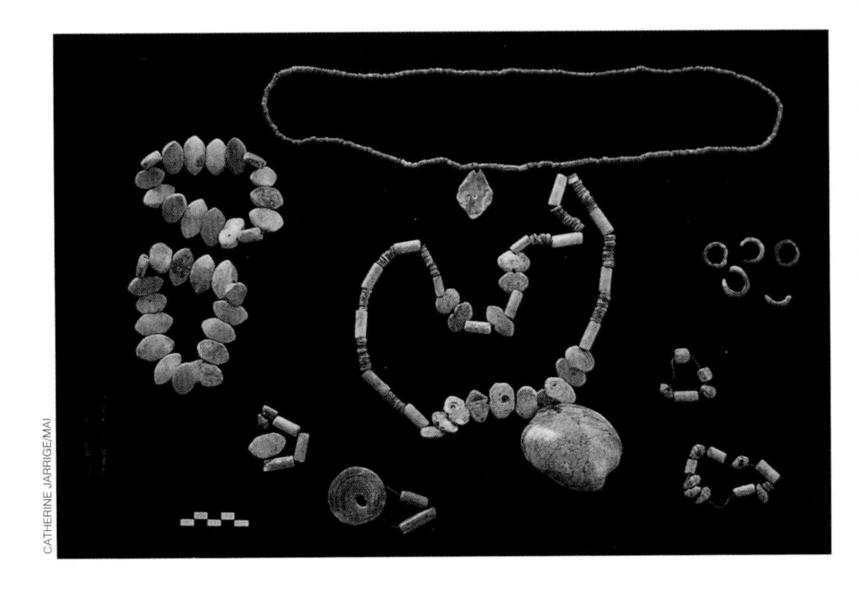

CATHERINE JARRIGE/MAI

Small settlements of up to a few hundred people, like Mehrgarh, have been discovered all along the margins of the plateau and in the well-watered valleys that feed the Indus River following the snow-melt in spring. But most sites are deeply buried under later occupation, and have allowed only small excavations. At Mehrgarh, the focus of settlement regularly moved along the banks of the Bolan River; and since the later Neolithic and Copper Age settlements were located a little downstream, quite extensive excavations of the first phase of settled village life in the region have been possible.

Small Neolithic and Copper Age villages proliferated over the next 2,000 years throughout the Indo-Iranian borderlands. The people kept sheep, goats, and humped zebu cattle, and cultivated barley, wheat, cotton, and, possibly, date palms. About 4000 BC, settlements appeared on the plains of the Indus Valley. If any earlier aceramic villages existed near the great river, they

The changing course of the Bolan River has eroded a natural section about 9 meters (30 feet) deep through the pre-pottery layers of the earliest village settlement at Mehrgarh.

would have been deeply buried under the silt brought down by the summer floodwaters. Sites such as Amri, where occupation continued after 3000 BC as part of the Indus civilization, were probably founded by migrants from the borderlands moving on to the fertile plains, where there were greater agricultural rewards but also the constant threat of unpredictable floods. Pottery was being made in a variety of local styles, and although flint tools remain in evidence, copper came into regular use in the third millennium BC for simple knives, projectile points, and even axes.

By 3500 BC, some sites had grown into small towns, which were occasionally fortified with stone walls (as at Kot Diji) or mudbrick defenses (as at Mundigak Period 4, and Rachman Dheri, on the Gomal Plain of northern Pakistan). Rachman Dheri, a huge settlement measuring some 22 hectares (54 acres), was laid out on a grid pattern of streets and enclosed by massive walls. With a population of several thousand, its three major periods of occupation are identified by changing ceramic styles. Rachman Dheri was inhabited for at least a thousand years, from 3500 BC to 2500 BC. Although it is clearly contemporary with Mohenjodaro, Harappa, and the other great settlements of the Indus civilization, the city and its surrounding territory seem always to have stayed outside the "Indus system". Perhaps it was the capital of another Bronze Age polity, contemporary with and rivaling the better-known Indus civilization.

CIVILIZATIONS IN SOUTHERN ASIA: 6000 BC – AD 500

	CULTURES AND CIVILIZATIONS	CULTURAL AND POLITICAL EVENTS	CRAFT AND TECHNOLOGY
500	The imperial Guptas AD 319 – AD 450	Hindu religion receives support Sanskrit as the written language of the elite	Large bronze religious images cast
AD 1			Trade with the Mediterranean and Southeast Asia
200		Buddhism emerges as dominant religion	
500	The Mauryas 321 BC – 185 BC First historic state of northern India	Mauryan administrative system detailed in the *Arthasastra* New trade routes opened	Iron Age flourishes in the south Northern Black Polished Ware (NBPW)
1000		Development of Buddhism and Jainism Introduction of the horse in battle Vedic epic poetry	Black and Red Pottery Painted Gray Ware (PGW)
1500	Post-Harappan cultures in western India and Pakistan 1500 BC – 200 BC	Communities from Iran migrate into far northwest	Ocher-colored Pottery (OCP) Widespread use of copper
2000	Late Indus civilization 2000 BC – 1500 BC	Decline in social and political control Major Harappan sites abandoned	Light yellow or gray pottery Introduction of iron Cemetery H ware
2500	Mature Indus civilization Harappa culture 2400 BC – 2000 BC	Development of Harappan script	Square, inscribed seals and baked bricks
3000			Faience articles, soapstone seals Terracotta figurines New ceramic styles in the Indus Valley: Kot Diji
3500		Development of small towns	Beginning of copper metallurgy
4000		Settlement on plains of the Indus Valley	Earliest pottery cultures
5000			
6000 BC	Emergence of the Indus civilization 6000 BC – 2400 BC		Aceramic Neolithic period

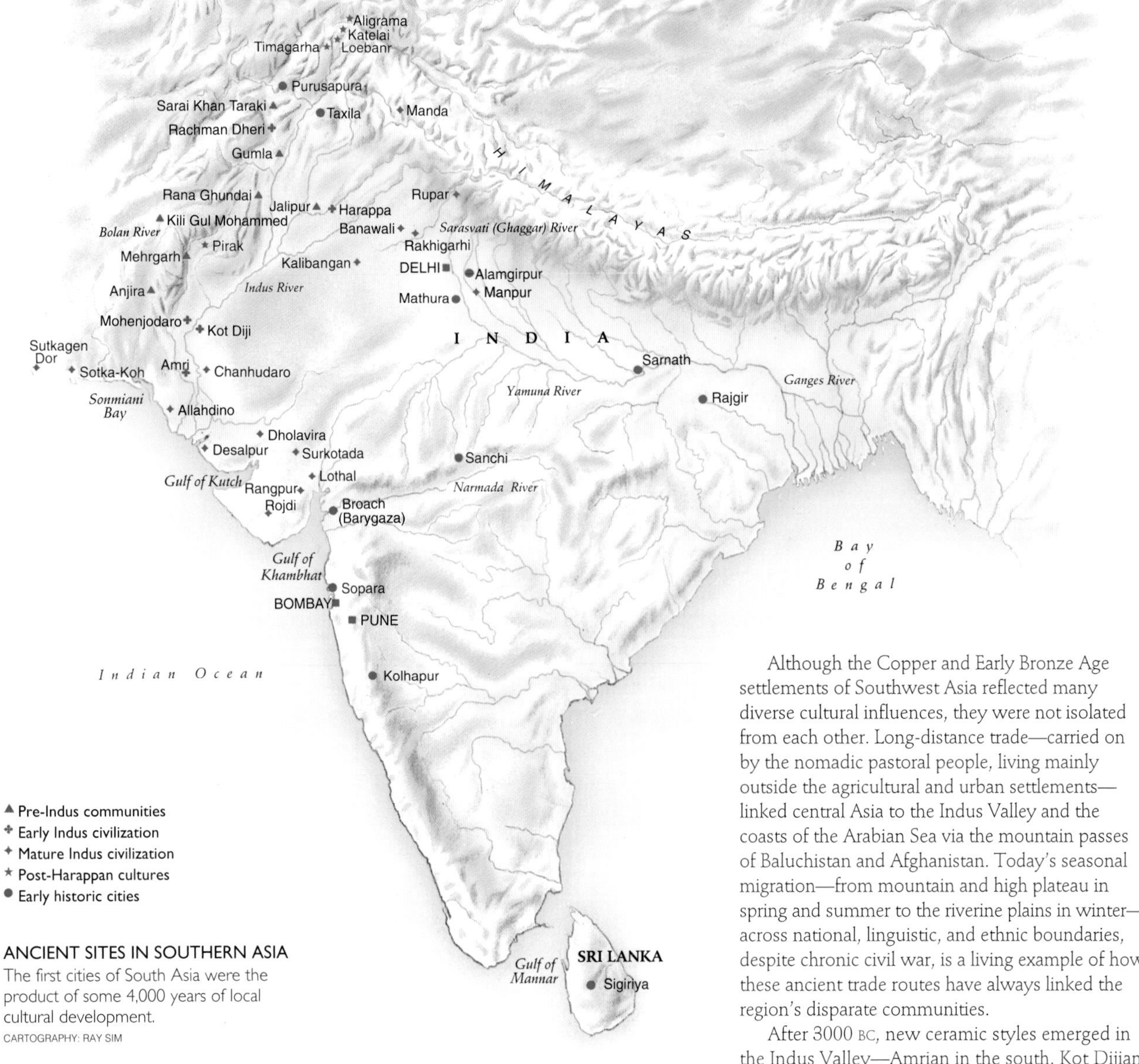

ANCIENT SITES IN SOUTHERN ASIA
The first cities of South Asia were the product of some 4,000 years of local cultural development.
CARTOGRAPHY: RAY SIM

EARLY TRADE ROUTES

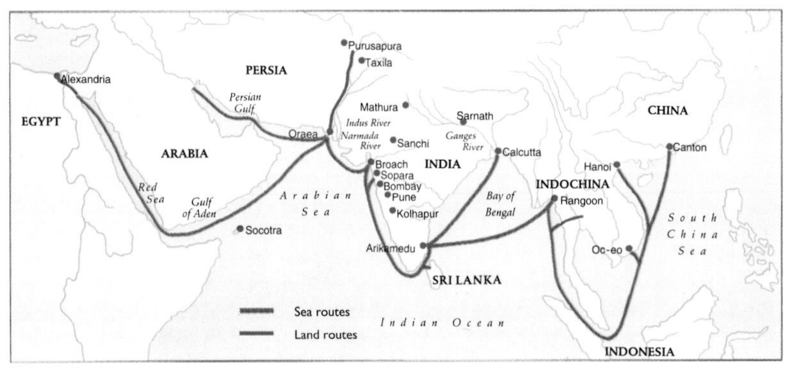

Although the Copper and Early Bronze Age settlements of Southwest Asia reflected many diverse cultural influences, they were not isolated from each other. Long-distance trade—carried on by the nomadic pastoral people, living mainly outside the agricultural and urban settlements—linked central Asia to the Indus Valley and the coasts of the Arabian Sea via the mountain passes of Baluchistan and Afghanistan. Today's seasonal migration—from mountain and high plateau in spring and summer to the riverine plains in winter—across national, linguistic, and ethnic boundaries, despite chronic civil war, is a living example of how these ancient trade routes have always linked the region's disparate communities.

After 3000 BC, new ceramic styles emerged in the Indus Valley—Amrian in the south, Kot Dijian in the north, and Sothian in the east. All are marked by strong horizontal bands of black paint alternating with rows of linked triangles, chevrons, hatched squares and leaves, or stylized animal horns. At Kot Diji, a distinctive "fish-scale" motif anticipated a design associated with the Mature Indus culture of a few hundred years later; at Kot Diji and Kalibangan, stylized buffalo heads prefigured the *Pasupati* icon (the Hindu god Siva as "Lord of the Animals") found on some Indus seals. Male and female terracotta figurines found at many sites throughout the region suggest the existence of common beliefs and ritual practices. Despite their regional differences, these cultures shared enough common elements to be grouped together as the Early Indus period.

THE HARAPPA CULTURE: 2400 BC TO 2000 BC

About 2400 BC, the diverse cultures of the Early Indus period merged in a distinctive new phase known as the Mature Indus civilization or the Harappa culture. Its emergence was apparently quite sudden, although features such as the mass production of pottery in a few standardized designs, terracotta figurines, and simple metal tools were all associated with some of the Early Indus cultures. What is new in the Harappa culture is the use of writing, particularly on square inscribed seals, and some copperplate inscriptions and graffiti on pottery fragments. Other novel elements include the extensive use of baked bricks for ordinary houses as well as public buildings, and careful architectural planning. Many sites appear to have been divided into two major areas: a lower, usually eastern, section of domestic buildings, craft workshops, and private shrines; and an elevated, sometimes fortified, area to the west, containing public buildings.

While not all sites within the Greater Indus Valley exhibit the distinctive elements of the Harappa style, there is evidence of some form of central administrative control and trade within the Indus Valley linking the region to Mesopotamia, via the Makran coast of Baluchistan, and to sites in Oman and Bahrain. Nearly a thousand Harappan sites have been identified in Pakistan, India, and Afghanistan within a territory of 1.25 million square kilometers (485,000 square miles)—more

More than 2,500 soapstone seals have been found at Harappa culture sites, the majority of which have an animal engraved on them and a short inscription. The animal most frequently represented is a humpless bull, earlier referred to as a "unicorn", since only one horn is shown in profile.
KARACHI MUSEUM/THE MACQUITTY COLLECTION

Terracotta models of bullock carts from Harappa culture sites are similar to carts still used in the region. Cart-tracks found during the excavation of the cities indicate that the wheelspan of the Indus carts has changed little.
KARACHI MUSEUM/ROBERT HARDING PICTURE LIBRARY

NATIONAL MUSEUM OF INDIA, NEW DELHI/THE BRIDGEMAN ART LIBRARY

A terracotta figurine of the mother-goddess, excavated at Mohenjodaro and dating from 2300 BC to 1750 BC.

The pottery from Harappa culture sites is frequently plain, but a substantial part is decorated with a red slip and black-painted designs. The painting often has a utilitarian quality, although some pieces show remarkable delicacy of line and artistic freedom. This fragment of a terracotta vase from Mohenjodaro depicts an ibex (wild goat).
KARACHI MUSEUM/SCALA

GEORG HELMES

⇧ An aerial view of the citadel mound at Mohenjodaro. On the right can be seen the Great Bath, which was probably used for ritual bathing. On the left is the granary.

than for any comparable Old World civilization. The Harappa culture only partly penetrated the northern part of the Indus Valley, and although it had some influence on the Kot Diji and Rachman Dheri cultures, the latter seems to have retained its cultural, and perhaps political, independence for an extensive period. Some Harappan sites have been found in the area, however, notably at Harappa itself (once a Kot Dijian settlement, which was possibly colonized by migrants from the south) and at Shortugai, some 500 kilometers (300 miles) northwest of Harappa on the Oxus River, where a colony was established to keep open the trade routes from central Asia to the Arabian Sea.

East of the Indus River, the Harappa civilization expanded rapidly into present-day India; some 300 sites have been identified along the now-dry bed of the Ghaggar River. Before the headwaters were captured by the Yamuna about 2000 BC, this was a flourishing, well-watered area, and one major site, Kalibangan, has been excavated on a large scale. Harappan settlements, such as Banawali, Rupar, and Rakhigarhi, were founded in the eastern Punjab, and the culture reached as far as Alamgirpur and Manpur, east of present-day Delhi.

In the south, Harappan settlements spread westwards along the Makran coast towards the Persian border, and the fortified site of Sutkagen Dor provided a staging post for coastal trade to the Persian Gulf. Settlements also extended southeast into the Kutch peninsula, which was probably an offshore island in Harappan times, and south along the Gujarat coast towards Bombay. Two major sites in this region, Lothal and Dholavira, and a fortified village at Rojdi, in Saurashtra, have provided a revealing picture of provincial Harappan society.

Harappan Architecture

Although Harappa was the first site to be excavated, extensive brick robbing by nearby villagers (to build houses and, in the mid-nineteenth century, to provide ballast for the Multan Lahore railway) has destroyed many of the buildings. Harappan architecture is best preserved at Mohenjodaro, which was excavated on

Marshall's team excavated a series of public buildings, the most spectacular of which is the Great Bath. This measures 12 meters by 9 meters (40 feet by 30 feet) and is sunk 2.5 meters (8 feet) below the surrounding pavement. The bath was built from meticulously laid bricks set in gypsum plaster over a waterproof bitumen layer. A nearby well supplied water, which was emptied through a massive corbeled drain.

The lower, eastern part of the city had a grid of streets and lanes roughly oriented north-south and east-west, with blocks of houses entered through narrow lanes. Although the houses varied in size, they all had rooms arranged around a central courtyard, usually with a well in a small room off the court and a bathroom and latrine draining through the wall, either into a soak pit or a covered drain under the street surface. Some houses were of two stories, with brick stairs and tubular drainpipes extending from the upper story. Plumbing installations for the provision of water, bathrooms with polished brick floors, and exterior drains are some of the most remarkable features of the cities of the Indus civilization, and are without parallel in any other prehistoric society.

Although there are public buildings on the citadel mound, no obvious large public temple has been found at either Mohenjodaro or Harappa. Recent architectural analysis of earlier excavations has, however, confirmed a house in the lower town at Mohenjodaro as the possible site of a "Tree Temple". At Kalibangan and Lothal, fire altars were excavated both in private houses and on the "citadel" areas of those towns, which provided space for congregations to assemble. The emphasis on fire and water in ritual activity is central to the two major religions to emerge in this region in historic times—Vedic Hinduism and Zoroastrianism.

ROBERT HARDING PICTURE LIBRARY

A public drain in a street at Mohenjodaro. Among the most remarkable features of cities of the Indus civilization are plumbing systems for supplying water, bathrooms with polished brick floors, and exterior drains.

There is no exact parallel for the Great Bath at Mohenjodaro, with its polished floor tiles sealed with bitumen and its corbeled brick drain to carry the water outside the town walls. It is generally thought to have been used for bathing before worship, a custom found in later Indian religions. Many of the other, larger Harappan towns were equipped with washing facilities in the ceremonial areas. At Lothal, there were 12 bathing places on the highest part of the mound, and Allahdino and Dholavira had large water tanks in the center of the citadel areas.

a large scale from 1922 to 1927 under Sir John Marshall, of the Archaeological Survey of India. Since 1931, a number of archaeological teams have excavated the site. The most recent work has concentrated on completing and correcting the documentation of earlier researchers, and conserving the previously excavated brick buildings, which were suffering badly from salt encrustation caused by the rising water table around Mohenjodaro.

The highest part of the western mound at Mohenjodaro rises 12 meters (40 feet) above the surrounding plain. The earliest and deepest levels of settlement have never been reached, since the Indus floods have raised the plain at least 10 meters (33 feet) over the last 5,000 years. Recently constructed dams and canals have also contributed to raising the water table. It is believed, however, that there are about 30 meters (100 feet) of stratified settlement debris on the site and that the mound was sometimes raised artificially to counter periodic floods. The citadel mound rests on an artificial platform of mud and mudbricks, and is topped by a later Buddhist stupa from the third century AD.

TETTONI, CASSIO, & ASSOC./PHOTOBANK

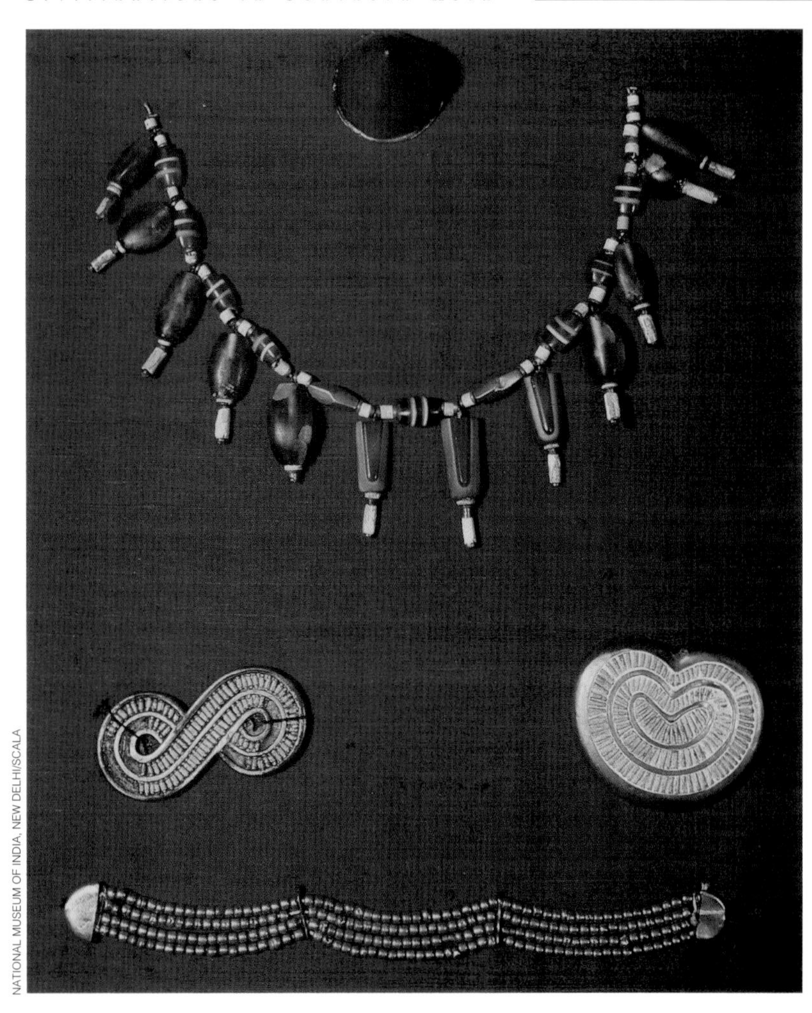

NATIONAL MUSEUM OF INDIA, NEW DELHI/SCALA

These examples of jewelry from the Harappa culture were clearly made with superb skill. The necklaces of ground and polished beads of stone (top) and of gold (bottom) show considerable sophistication. The figure-of-eight-shaped piece was perhaps used as a hair ornament, while the round ornament was tied to a fillet worn on the forehead.

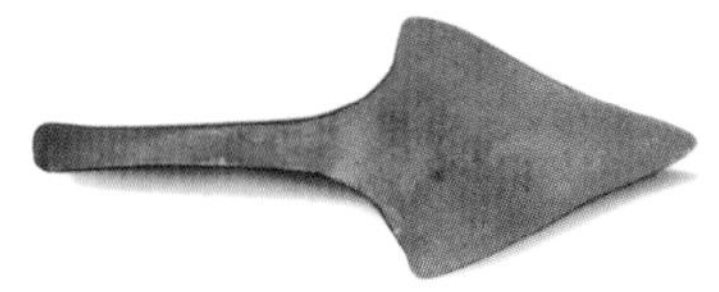

A copper spearhead from the Harappa culture with a tang for hafting on a wooden shaft. Although the Indus civilization was a Bronze Age culture, most artifacts were made of copper, because of the scarcity of tin to make bronze.

NATIONAL MUSEUM OF INDIA, NEW DELHI/ THE BRIDGEMAN ART LIBRARY

Craft Industries

Although we refer to the Indus civilization as a Bronze Age culture, unalloyed copper was used for most artifacts, and only rarely was enough tin available to make bronze. Tools and weapons were simple in form, showing little skill in design or manufacture. They include flat-cast axes and chisels, arrows and small spearheads, small knives, saws and razors, and fishhooks. Nonetheless, craft industries were organized through guilds or associations, and certain areas specialized in specific crafts. Harappan metalworkers were skilled in making beaten copper and silverware. They used modern brassware techniques, such as riveting, and lapped and soldered joints; and made small plates and weights of lead, and gold and silver jewelry of considerable sophistication. Examples of the latter rarely survive, since the Harappans did not bury their dead with the sort of spectacular grave goods found in contemporary Egyptian and Sumerian burials. However, terracotta figurines give some idea of their use of beads, bangles, and necklaces.

As copper knives were rare, and probably not very effective, the Harappans continued to use chert blades for reaping crops and probably for most other tasks requiring sharp-edged knives. Chert was quarried from nearby limestone outcrops, and Harappan craftworkers produced some of the finest knapped blades known from any early culture. The same skill was applied to making superb beads from imported agate and carnelian. Indus Valley etched beads provide some of the best evidence we have for long-distance trade between 3000 BC and 2000 BC.

Pottery technology was very advanced, with utilitarian wheel-thrown forms being made at most sites and fired in large kilns. Massive storage jars were also produced, splendidly painted in black on a bright red surface, with parallel designs depicting plants and birds. Pottery sherds of these enable archaeological surveyors to identify Mature Harappan sites with relative ease. Other distinctive pottery forms include tall, cylindrical, pierced strainers and enigmatic triangular pieces of terracotta, which have variously been interpreted as being pot-boilers, sling stones, hearth liners, and abraders for rubbing callouses from workers' feet!

Other significant Harappan crafts include the manufacture of faience (a form of glass) for small ornaments and figurines, and microbeads molded from soapstone paste, a specialty of Chanhudaro. Soapstone, in block form, was also used for making distinctive and beautiful seals, more than 2,500 of which have been found, nearly half at Mohenjodaro. They generally conform to a highly standardized design: square, from 1 to 3 centimeters (three-eighths of an inch to one and a quarter inches) in diameter, with a perforated boss at the back for suspension. The blocks were sawn and polished before being carved with metal or chert gravers, and the finished seals then heated to harden the stone. The surface always bears some characters of the still undeciphered script, above either a single, highly naturalistic animal or, more rarely, a scene depicting animals and people, or semihuman figures, participating in a ceremony.

This copper vase from the Harappa culture, dating from about 2300 BC to 1750 BC, is of simple design, like many of the artifacts found from the Indus civilization.

NATIONAL MUSEUM OF INDIA, NEW DELHI/THE BRIDGEMAN ART LIBRARY

The Harappan Script

The language and writing system of the Harappans still defy translation. Although nearly 4,000 inscriptions have now been found, most are very short, with a maximum of 21 characters out of the 419 known to exist. Furthermore, there are no bilingual inscriptions of the sort that enabled scholars to translate Near Eastern cuneiform writing and Egyptian hieroglyphs. Some scholars believe that the Harappan language belonged to the Dravidian family, now found mostly in South India. Others think it is an early Indo-European language and a forerunner of Sanskrit. We do know, however, that both seals and script were used for such administrative purposes as sealing bales of merchandise and even "authenticating" the manufacture of stoneware bangles by sealing shut the saggers, the fireclay boxes that protected them from the great heat of the furnace. It seems likely that the script refers to personal names and official administrative titles.

If writing was widespread—and the occasional graffiti on potsherds, ivories, and bronzes suggests that it was—then it was probably done on some common perishable material such as cloth or palm leaves. This being the case, only the excavation of a waterlogged site with substantial archives will enable the writing system to be definitively translated. In a recent excavation by an Indian archaeologist, R.S. Bisht, at Dholavira, in Gujarat, an inscription 2.8 meters (about 9 feet) long consisting of gypsum characters, 10 centimeters (4 inches) high, was found on a partly preserved wooden board below the main gate to the town. It may have indicated the name of the ancient settlement.

A Classless and Clean Society

We know quite a lot about the Harappans' way of life, trade, craft industries, and religious symbolism, but next to nothing about their social and political system. Unlike contemporary societies in Egypt and Mesopotamia, Harappan culture lacks royal burials, great funerary structures, monumental art, and other symbols of royal or priestly authority. So it would seem that the usual model of a kingdom or empire, headed by a "priest-king" and supported by a royal clan holding authority through dynastic succession, does not apply in this case. There is also little evidence of the strong military influence usually found in Old World empires. The "fortifications" at Harappa, Mohenjodaro, Kalibangan, and some other sites seem to have been intended as much to define social and functional spaces as to protect the citizens from external enemies. The gateways at Harappa show no sign of planning for military defense. However, consistency in the layout of settlements, the use of modular sizes of bricks, and widespread similarities in metal and chert tools, pottery styles, and systems of weights and measures provide strong evidence of firm administrative control over the production and distribution of goods and services.

The pattern of foreign trade also reveals many anomalies when compared with that of other societies. There is evidence for the import of raw materials, exotic stones, gold, copper, tin, and silver, but very few manufactured or prestige goods from outside the Indus culture area have been found. The absence of larger and more ornate houses, exotic luxury goods, and richer than usual burials suggests there was no clearly wealthy class. All these factors suggest the Indus civilization emphasized conformity, lack of personal display, efficient organization of manufacturing and trade, and a concern for sanitation and health without parallel in the past. If we seek a model for the social and political order of the Harappans, it is to be found in the later, Buddhist monasteries of India, or in the Christian West, rather than in the palace and temple society of Ancient Egypt or Mesopotamia.

Few stone sculptures survive from the Harappan period, and they are usually small, crudely made, and badly damaged. An exception is this soapstone image of a bearded man wearing a decorated cloak over one shoulder; a diadem, perhaps once inlaid with a jewel, to tie back his hair; and a similarly decorated armband. Only 18 centimeters (7 inches) high, this powerful but anonymous sculpture from Mohenjodaro is usually called "The Priest King", but this identification is no more than guesswork.

⇧ Iron tools and weapons are abundant in South Indian megalithic graves. Shown clockwise from top left are a spearhead, a sickle, and an adze or hoe with iron fastening bands.
C.M. DIXON/PHOTO RESOURCES

⇩ The stylized humped bull and peacocks painted on this pottery sherd are characteristic of the so-called Cemetery H culture, which coincided with the end of the Indus civilization at Harappa. Apart from its pottery, we have almost no sources of information about this culture.
C.M. DIXON/PHOTO RESOURCES

The Harappans in Decline: 2000 BC to 1500 BC

In the central part of the Indus Valley, the Harappa culture seems to have come to a rather abrupt end, although the timing and causes of this are poorly understood and frequently disputed. At Mohenjodaro, administrative control was relaxed after 2000 BC; seals and inscriptions are no longer found in this period, and by about 1800 BC, much of the city seems to have been deserted. Kot Diji, Allahdino, Kalibangan, Rupar, Surkotada, Desalpur, and other Harappan settlements were also virtually deserted at this time. Either the population of the Indus Valley had declined, or the people had returned to a more nomadic pastoral way of life, leaving few traces of this transition for today's archaeologists to find.

Several excavators at Mohenjodaro have reported finding groups of bodies hastily buried or even lying in the streets or where they had tumbled down staircases—evidence of a "final massacre" of the last inhabitants of the once great city. Certainly, natural events had much to do with the end of the Harappan civilization. For instance, there is widespread evidence of earthquake activity, including tectonic uplift along the Makran coast and dramatic changes in the course of the Indus River, resulting in the drying up of the ancient Sarasvati (Ghaggar) river system. It is possible that the Indus totally deserted its ancient riverbed, and with it, the city of Mohenjodaro, which was so dependent on it.

At some sites, such as Chanhudaro, life continued, although building standards declined, as did the manufacture of high-quality soapstone and carnelian beads for export. A range of local pottery styles replaced the relative uniformity typical of Mature Harappan ceramics. At Harappa, too, the later period is typified by flimsy buildings made of reused bricks and a new ceramic style known as Cemetery H ware. Typical Harappan funeral customs changed, from simple burials, sometimes in brick-lined pits, to the placement of bones with other offerings inside large funerary urns. The evidence clearly points to both a complete breakdown of the regional civic administration and the arrival of new ethnic and cultural groups in various parts of the Indus Valley.

Despite the collapse of the Indus civilization, not all was lost. Although the disciplined urban culture of Mohenjodaro, with its sophisticated plumbing, vanished entirely, the traditions and symbols of its religious cults—purification by water and fire, reverence for cattle, tree cults, and the horned deity flanked by animals—were handed on to become integral parts of Brahmanism, Zoroastrianism, and Buddhism.

Post-Harappa Cultures: 1500 BC to 200 BC

Little is known about events in the western part of the Indian subcontinent from 1500 BC. Many villages and towns that had been inhabited over the previous thousand years were deserted, or housed only temporary buildings. After about 1800 BC, communities from Iran migrated into the valleys of the far northwest. Because almost everything known about them is based upon their burial customs, they are called the Gandhara Grave culture.

The main Gandhara sites so far excavated are Katelai, Loebanr, Aligrama, and Timagarha, all situated in the Swat Valley. Their graves usually consist of oblong pits, with dry stone walls covered by roof slabs. The bodies were accompanied by plain, light yellow or gray pottery, highly stylized terracotta figurines, and occasional bronze pins and iron tools. Cremation also became common for the first time in South Asia, the ashes being deposited in urns decorated with carved faces. The discovery of iron artifacts and two horse burials, together with a bronze model horse at Katelai and an iron horse harness at Timagarha, strongly suggests that the Gandhara people were descendants of the iron-using, largely pastoral Indo-European speakers who migrated to northern India from the west in the post-Harappan period. These people are also known to have cultivated wheat, barley, rice, and grapes.

Many settlements in the valleys of Baluchistan also seem to have been deserted. From about 1300 BC, footed goblets and bowls, painted gray, replaced the elaborate Harappan wares, and weapons such as short swords and shaft-hole axes are found in graves at many sites from the Makran coast of Pakistan to northern Afghanistan. In some places, however, settled life continued throughout the period. At Pirak, on the Kachi Plain, after a short break following the Harappan occupation, the village was regularly rebuilt in a consistent style with thick-walled houses incorporating massive wall niches. The inhabitants cultivated rice and sorghum, in addition to wheat and barley, and produced beautiful, multicolored pottery with designs resembling woven textiles.

Ceramic Traditions

In the eastern Punjab and the region of the Yamuna-Ganges Doab, around present-day Delhi, the earliest villages show many elements of the Mature and Late Harappan style. In the southern part of this region, where there are rich copper deposits, we find a ceramic tradition called "Ocher-colored Pottery" (OCP), after the distinctive rusty-red color of its painted surface. This pottery has been found in the earliest levels of village mounds, sometimes associated with hoards of massive, cast-copper tools and weapons. OCP is often discovered in waterlogged deposits or shows evidence of having been immersed in moving water, giving support to ancient Indian traditions of massive flooding in the Doab and the Yamuna River's capture of the waters that once flowed southwest through the ancient Sarasvati (Ghaggar) River into the Arabian Sea. At one time, OCP and its associated copper hoards were regarded as a purely post-Harappan phenomenon. Indian archaeologists now believe, however, that the beginnings of this tradition go back beyond 2000 BC. OCP communities in the Rajasthan copper belt may have provided much of the copper for Harappan metalwork.

About 1200 BC, new ceramic traditions appeared in the Punjab and Rajasthan in the form of Black and Red Pottery, and Painted Gray Ware (PGW). At some sites, PGW is clearly stratified above OCP. In most places, however, the makers of PGW founded new settlements along the rivers flowing east into the Ganges system. It is fairly clear that these new settlements represent the eastward migration of the Gandhara Grave people, encountered a few hundred years earlier in the northwestern valleys of Pakistan. They brought with them iron tools and weapons, the practice of riding horses in battle, prestige exchange, and even sacrifice. This is the period of the later Vedic epic poetry, which, although written down much later, recounts stories of the wars and alliances of the Indo-European tribes, particularly their struggles with the Dasas, the native peoples of the Indus Valley and the Punjab. The Dasas were gradually overwhelmed and reduced to the status of slaves and laborers, the ancestors of the "untouchables" of recent times.

Vedic literature, although difficult to link directly to archaeological evidence, provides a mass of information about the daily life and culture of the times. Ironsmiths rivaled copper workers in importance; wheat, barley, millet, and rice were cultivated; and forests and swamps were cleared for farmland. Houses were simple, circular structures of timber and thatch, with wattle-and-daub walls and partitions, not unlike the dwellings of many present-day tribal peoples of India.

The center of gravity of Indian civilization moved steadily eastwards down the Ganges Valley. By 500 BC, the fertile lands of the areas known today as the states of Uttar Pradesh and Bihar were wealthy enough to support the first historic state of northern India, the Kingdom of Magadha, established in the sixth century BC at the fortified hilltop site of Rajgir. At this time, PGW, which was already wheel-made from fine clay and fired at high temperatures, was developed into a luxury ware, sometimes painted white, sometimes with metallic crystals on the lustrous, thick black surface. Known as "Northern Black Polished Ware" (NBPW), this pottery matches, both in appearance and technical skill, the contemporary Greek black-painted pottery of the Mediterranean.

THE MACQUITTY COLLECTION

⊕ Rice was not cultivated by the Harappans, except in Gujarat, wheat and barley being the main crops in the Harappan period. It was later introduced to the northwestern part of the Indian subcontinent from the Ganges plain.

Trade and the Spread of Religion

This period, at first dominated by Brahmanical Hinduism, saw the development of two great reforming religions, Buddhism and Jainism, which spread as interregional trade became increasingly more important than agriculture. The NBPW culture moved south along the trade routes linking the upper Ganges to the Narmada Valley and the Arabian coast, where maritime trade linked India to communities in Egypt and the Mediterranean. Money, in the form of silver coins struck by several kingdoms in northern and central India, facilitated this commerce. In the fourth century BC, much of northern India was united into the Mauryan empire by Chandragupta Maurya. At this point, India entered the Western historical tradition when the Macedonian Alexander the Great led his army through the passes of the northwest to confront the Mauryan army on the banks of the Indus. Although victorious, the Greeks withdrew to Bactria, where Alexander's successors maintained trade, cultural, and diplomatic relations with the Mauryan kings, providing the first detailed written accounts of the wealth and brilliant achievements of historical Indian civilization.

Ian C. Glover

⊕ This gold coin of the horseman type dates from the time of Chandragupta II, about AD 380 to AD 415. It was under the Guptas that Brahmanical Hinduism re-established itself in South Asia, coinciding with the gradual decline of Buddhism on the Indian subcontinent.
C.M. DIXON/PHOTO RESOURCES

THE MAURYAS: 321 BC TO 185 BC

Until the rise of the Mauryas in 321 BC, the Ganges plain was divided into a patchwork of republics and monarchies. It was the Mauryas who unified most of northern India for the first time, establishing themselves in parts of the Deccan peninsula. In the northwest, their domain was bordered by the Seleucid Empire and the Indo-Greek kingdoms; in the south flourished the Iron Age megalithic communities and chiefdoms of the Colas, Ceras, and Pandyas. The most famous Mauryan ruler was Asoka, renowned for his policy of tolerance and *ahimsa*, or nonviolence, by which he renounced all forms of killing, including war and conquest.

By the third century BC, agriculture had become the mainstay of the economy in the north and land tax was the primary source of state income, supplemented by trade revenues and levies on manufactured items. Details of the Mauryan administrative system are contained in the *Arthasastra*, a contemporary treatise on polity and economics. A recurring theme is that the king should take active steps to increase state revenue. The area under cultivation should be increased, either by expanding irrigation facilities or by encouraging peasants living in overpopulated regions to migrate to new areas. Several categories of taxes and land tenures are mentioned: the state-owned, or crown, lands supervised by employees of the king; private land worked by peasants; and communally owned land—a common feature of erstwhile republics.

Asoka publicized his laws throughout the four corners of his empire, having them inscribed on rocks and placed in market centers, at crossroads, and in the cities. His edicts were based on his concept of *dharma*, or piety, a unique idea that the king's duty was to promulgate measures for his subjects' welfare.

While Asoka is credited with the construction of many Buddhist monasteries, or stupas, most of these were enlarged and embellished by later rulers. The finest specimens of Mauryan art are the monolithic stone columns, cut and polished to a shining finish and with finely modeled column heads. The four-lion head of the Asokan column at Sarnath, near Varanasi, has been adopted as the emblem of the present-day Indian republic.

Many historians have associated the policy of nonviolence with the decline of the empire's military strength and its eventual break-up. More recent research indicates that it was rather the Mauryas' failure to expand their resource base that contributed to their decline. Being reliant on localized systems of revenue collection, the empire was ultimately destabilized by regional shortfalls in income.

⊕ The capital of an Asokan pillar from Sarnath, near Varanasi, where the Buddha preached his first sermon. The pillar bore an edict of Asoka, warning Buddhist monks against creating dissension within the Sangha (monastic order).
TETTONI, CASSIO, & ASSOC./PHOTOBANK

HIMANSHU PRABHA RAY

⊕ An elephant carved out of rock at Dhauli, near Bhubaneshwar, dated to the Mauryan period. Dhauli is also the site of an Asokan inscription.

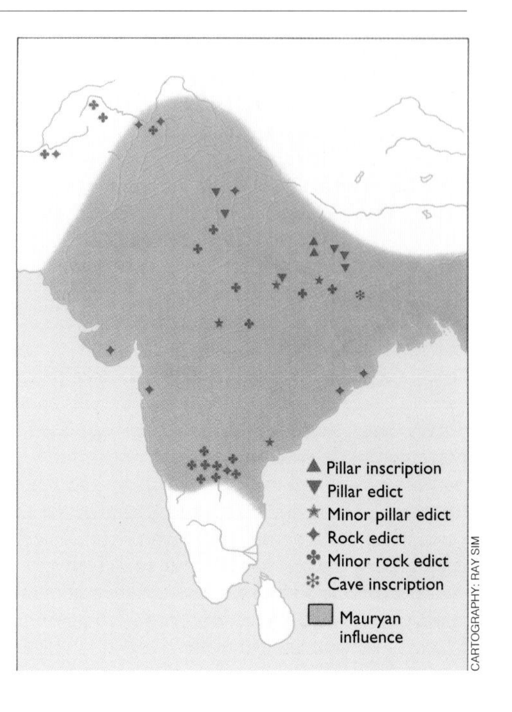

CARTOGRAPHY: RAY SIM

THE EXTENT OF MAURYAN INFLUENCE, SHOWING THE LOCATION OF ASOKAN INSCRIPTIONS
Asokan inscriptions were placed in highly visible locations, such as at the entrances to towns, crossroads, and frontier posts. Before being engraved on rocks and pillars, they were orally proclaimed in front of an audience.

The Satavahanas and the Expansion of Trade

The opening up of new routes under the Mauryas, and official patronage of Buddhism and Jainism, led to an unprecedented expansion of cities and trade networks during the last two centuries BC. Buddhism emerged as the dominant religion of the ruling elite as well as of merchants, traders, and craftspeople.

The northwestern part of the Indian subcontinent faced constant challenges, with frequent incursions of nomadic tribes from central Asia. The first of these were the Sakas, who moved down the Indus Valley and settled in western India. But the most successful were the Yueh-chi tribes, who rose to power in Afghanistan and a large part of northern India, and started the line of Kusana kings. Purusapura, near modern-day Peshawar, in Pakistan, was the capital of the Kusanas, while Mathura, near Delhi, had the status of a secondary capital.

While tribal chiefs continued to rule in the far south and in isolated enclaves in the north, one of the local tribal groups in the Deccan peninsula established the Satavahana dynasty. Land routes through the peninsula were established, and the region was opened up to coastal traffic. Coastal maritime routes linked the west coast port of Broach (Barygaza) to settlements in Sri Lanka and

↪ This ivory plaque found during archaeological excavations at Begram, near Kabul, formed part of a palace treasure that included Indian ivories, glass and bronze objects of Hellenistic origin, and Chinese lacquer of the early centuries AD.

MUSÉE GUIMET/RMN

↑ A relief from the Buddhist stupa at Goli, in Andhra Pradesh, depicting a cart used for transportation in early India. Bronze models of similar carts have also been found.
HIMANSHU PRABHA RAY

the Persian Gulf. Another prominent destination of transoceanic trading voyages was Suvarnabhumi, the land of gold, sometimes identified with lower Burma (Myanmar).

One of the significant characteristics of this period was the development and spread of an urban way of life. New settlements were planned and constructed, and the quality of life improved. Baked brick and stone were widely used to build fortifications, houses, and large water tanks. Consumer items such as jewelry, ivory objects, fabrics, perfumes, and wine were also in demand. A variety of crafts sprang up, and long-distance trade routes expanded over land and sea.

Broach (Barygaza) and Sopara were only two of a series of ports along the west coast. Commodities such as wheat, rice, cloth, and clarified butter were brought to these ports from centers far inland and exported from them to trading communities on the island of Socotra, at the mouth of the Red Sea. Timber was also exported for shipbuilding in the Persian Gulf. To Alexandria and other towns in Egypt went aromatics, spices, fine cottons, Chinese silk, pearls, diamonds, gems, and pepper. In return, Indian communities received imports of wine, glass,

↑ Gold jewelry found in a hoard near Madras that also contained Roman coins and carnelian intaglios.
HIMANSHU PRABHA RAY

HIMANSHU PRABHA RAY

A typical Satavahana terracotta figure from Ter, in Maharashtra, made in a double mold. The use of a double mold for the production of terracottas is typical of the Satavahana period.

frankincense, dates, coral, metals, and Roman money that had been exchanged at a profit for local currency. While comparatively few Roman coins have been recovered in the Deccan peninsula, they are more common further south.

Archaeological and literary evidence reveals that many nationalities were involved in this maritime trade network, including Arabs and Egyptian Greeks, as well as Indian seafarers. The trade with Southeast Asia is not nearly so well documented, although objects of Indian origin have frequently been found in archaeological excavations in this region. Findings include beads, pendants, carnelian seals with inscriptions in Brahmi (an ancient Indian script), ivory objects, and Indian pottery. These clay vessels were either used as containers or traded as such, and some sherds carry the owners' names, indicating the place of origin. Commodities from Southeast Asia and the Indonesian archipelago that were in demand in India included cinnamon, cassia, cloves, sandalwood, and, perhaps, tin. Many of these items were shipped on from Indian ports to Roman Egypt.

Buddhism and Trade

Historians have debated whether trading links in antiquity helped to spread cultural influences, especially between India and Southeast Asia. Trade was conducted by peddlers with low caste status in Brahmanical society. Such people, it was argued, could hardly be regarded as likely carriers of cultural change. However, recent research shows that until the Gupta period, Buddhism was the paramount religion on the Indian subcontinent, and it actively promoted trading activities.

Writing was used to record the many donations made to Buddhist monasteries by the ruling elite, traders, and craftspeople. Monasteries were the most significant monuments of the period. They consisted of *viharas*, or residences for the monks, and *caityas*, or places of congregation and worship. The image of the Buddha developed along the lines of two distinct schools of art: the Gandhara, in the northwest, which was influenced by the Hellenistic tradition, and the local Mathura style.

Some Buddhist monuments, such as those at Taxila or Sanchi, in central India, were embellished with stone railings depicting scenes from the life of the Buddha and incidents from his previous births. Others were carved out of rock, and more than 800 of these caves survive in the hills of western India. The construction of these monuments was supported by donations from the ruling elite and other devotees drawn from trades such as jewelers, ironsmiths, merchants, and gardeners. One of the reasons for Buddhism's wide appeal among these occupational groups was its tolerant view of society. While Buddhism did not oppose the Brahmanical caste system, it promoted the concept of a social hierarchy determined by moral values rather than caste.

HIMANSHU PRABHA RAY

The interior of a rock-cut *caitya* at Bedsa, near Bombay. The resources for the construction of these Buddhist monuments were donated by traders, merchants, and *yavanas* (foreigners).

An image of the Buddha of the Mathura school of art, carved in red sandstone, with an inscription on the pedestal dated to the thirty-second year of the Kusana era, corresponding to the first century AD.

NATIONAL MUSEUM OF INDIA, NEW DELHI/ THE BRIDGEMAN ART LIBRARY

TETTONI, CASSIO, & ASSOC./PHOTOBANK

The original stupa at Sanchi, built on a hill by Asoka, is the sole surviving example from that period. The brick structure was later enlarged and enclosed by a stone railing, to which richly carved stone gateways were added in the first century BC.

J.L. NOU/EXPLORER/AUSCAPE

This exquisite metal sculpture depicting the marriage of the god Siva with Parvati was made during the Cola period (AD 900 to AD 1300), well known for the development of the lost-wax method of bronze casting.

A head of the Buddha carved in the Gandharan style, the characteristic features being wavy hair and a moustache.
NATIONAL MUSEUM OF ORIENTAL ART, ROME/SCALA

The ascendancy of Buddhism did not continue unchallenged for long. Strong contenders emerged from among the different sects of the Brahmanical religion, including Saivism and Vaisnavism. Images of Hindu gods such as Siva and Vishnu were worshiped in simple shrines and received patronage and support from the later Gupta dynasty. It was, however, from the seventh and eighth centuries AD onwards that the Brahmanical temple attained monumental proportions and emerged as the religious focal point of society.

One group that sought acceptance within the Buddhist trading network was the *yavanas*, or foreigners. The term *yavana* initially referred to an Ionian Greek, but by the beginning of the Christian era, it was used to refer to any alien. Gifts from *yavanas* are recorded in the Buddhist monasteries of central India and the Deccan. Many *yavanas* adopted Buddhist names, and according to early Tamil sources, those living further south took up other occupations as well as trade, some working as royal palace guards.

of the fifth century AD, the Huns had broken into northern India, and the rule of the Guptas had given way to fragmented principalities and kingdoms.

Land grants to *brahmanas*, as members of the Brahman caste were known, were common practice under the Guptas. A way of ensuring that land under cultivation increased, the practice can be traced back to the Satavahanas, who donated land and villages both to Buddhist monasteries and to *brahmanas*. From the Gupta period onwards, these grants included inhabited villages, with rulers waiving their right to governance and revenue. This led to the growth of *brahmana* feudal territories that were autonomously administered.

Under the Guptas, fine arts and literature reached their peak. Specialized treatises on mathematics, astronomy, law, medicine, and philosophy were written in Sanskrit, the language of the elite.

Images of the deity evolved as the focus of devotional worship among the Hindus, and began to take the form of gods in human form with multiple arms. The symbols held in each of these arms represented the god's diverse powers. Buddhism maintained its position, although it was gradually losing its distinct identity from Brahmanism. This was one of the factors that led to its eventual decline in India, even though it continued to flourish unchallenged in other parts of Asia.

Himanshu Prabha Ray

This stone sculpture of Skanda, son of Siva and Parvati, dates to the Gupta period, when the proportions of images and their attributes were fixed in accordance with the Brahmanical tradition.
C.M. DIXON/PHOTO RESOURCES

A silver coin cast by the Huns in imitation of those of the Guptas, whom they defeated in the fifth century AD.
C.M. DIXON/PHOTO RESOURCES

THE IMPERIAL GUPTAS: AD 319 TO AD 450

The Gupta period has often been referred to as the "golden age" of Indian history. It was during this time that Brahmanical social and religious values and culture were firmly established. However, this was true only in the northern part of India. In the Deccan peninsula and in the south, civilization reached its high-water mark about AD 800. Unlike the vast plains of the north, peninsular India was handicapped by the scattered nature of its agricultural lands. Rival groups were constantly at loggerheads for control of fertile tracts of land.

Although the Gupta era is generally dated from the accession of Chandragupta I, about AD 319, to AD 320, the origins of the Guptas are obscure. The dynasty continued its rule until the fifth century AD, when the first invasions of the Huns threatened the Guptas' hold on the north-western part of the subcontinent. By the end

TETTONI, CASSIO, & ASSOC./PHOTOBANK

An image of Vishnu from Udaigiri, 7 kilometers (4 miles) northeast of Sanchi. Twenty Brahmanical caves were carved in these sandstone hills, not far from the ancient city of Vidisa, during the reign of the Gupta dynasty.

THE PALACE-FORTRESS OF SIGIRIYA

Himanshu Prabha Ray

Sigiriya is an outstanding example of the planned, moated, and walled urban centers found in South and Southeast Asia. It was the political capital of Sri Lanka for a brief period of about 15 years from AD 477, when Kasyapa I, who believed he was a god-king, moved his court and administration to Sigiriya from Anuradhapura, having seized power from his father. Sigiriya is renowned for the paintings on the west face of the rock, the surviving examples consisting of female figures. Their identity is uncertain, although they have often been described as ladies of Kasyapa's court, or *apsaras,* meaning heavenly maidens.

TETTONI, CASSIO, & ASSOC./PHOTOBANK

Flanked by the head, chest, and forepaws of a colossal sphinx-like lion made of timber, brick, and plaster, the lion staircase was a magnificent sight to pilgrims in antiquity, who inscribed poems in praise of it on the so-called "mirror wall".

C.M. DIXON/PHOTO RESOURCES

Located on top of the rock are the remains of the fifth-century AD palace, which extends over almost 3 hectares (about 7 acres), while on the plain below are two fortified precincts surrounded by successive earthen ramparts and moats.

C.M. DIXON/PHOTO RESOURCES

The royal pleasure gardens of Sigiriya are unique in being the earliest landscaped gardens in Asia with an elaborate drainage system. Marble slabs from the nearby quarries were hauled to the summit of the precipitous rock for the construction of tanks and drainage pipes.

ROBERT HARDING PICTURE LIBRARY

Massive natural outcrops were the favored building sites of ancient architects, but the fortified capital of Sigiriya remains unsurpassed for its location on a spectacular natural rock formation 200 meters (650 feet) above the surrounding plain.

MICHAEL FREEMAN

CIVILIZATIONS OF SOUTHEAST ASIA

2000 BC – AD 1500

A Blend of Traditions

Ian C. Glover and Elizabeth H. Moore

THE CULTURAL DEVELOPMENT of Southeast Asia after the time of the rice-growing Stone Age communities was characterized by an extraordinarily strong regional diversity, unparalleled elsewhere in the world. The region became a melting pot of cultural impulses from other parts of Asia (mainly India, to the west, and China, to the north)—including technology, art, religion, trade, and politics—which were assimilated by the indigenous cultures. These influences soon triggered the growth of cities and, in time, whole nations. The area also saw large-scale migrations of people. The result of this flourishing cultural exchange and development, which were often intimately linked to Hinduism and Buddhism, is still evident in Southeast Asia today.

The first metal cultures emerged during the earliest phases of the Bronze Age, about 2000 BC, and were almost certainly developed locally. Iron first came into use about 700 BC. The technique of iron-working may have been developed locally, but probably came from India.

Each of the perforated stupas on the summit of Borobudur houses an image of the Buddha. The Buddha's tranquil expression reflects the serenity that awaits the pilgrims who reach the monument's upper levels.

A bronze axehead and its casting mold from a grave of the Ban Chiang culture, in northeastern Thailand, dating from about 1500 BC.
TETTONI, CASSIO, & ASSOC./PHOTOBANK

CIVILIZATIONS OF SOUTHEAST ASIA: 2000 BC – AD 1800

	BURMA, THAILAND, AND NORTH VIETNAM	SOUTH VIETNAM AND CAMBODIA	INDONESIA
1800	Buddhist kingdom of Bangkok founded		
1600	Burmese–Thai wars	Christianity introduced to Vietnam	Islam replaces Hinduism and Buddhism in Java "Religion of the Hindu doctrine" (Bali) developed
1400			
	Buddhist kingdom of Ayutthaya (Thailand) AD 1300 – AD 1700		Bali colonized
1200			
	Kingdom of Pagan (central Burma) AD 1000 – AD 1200		Hindu temple of Prambanan (Java) built
1000	Mon combined with Pyu and Burmese cultures Stone Buddhas in form of *sema* (boundary) stones		Buddhist temple of Borobudur (Java) built
800		Khmer kings of Angkor (Cambodia) AD 800 – AD 1200 Stone temples	
	Mon "kingdom" of Dvaravati AD 600 – AD 1000		Monumental architecture AD 700 – AD 1300 (Java)
600	Massive stone *cakra*	Kingdom of Champa (South Vietnam) AD 600 – AD 900 Kingdom of Chenla (Cambodia) AD 500 – AD 800	
400		Hindu–Buddhist influences	
	Intensification of trade with India		
200			
AD 1	Pyu (Burma) AD 100 – AD 900 Tibeto-Burman group	Kingdom of Funan (South Vietnam) AD 100 – AD 500	Indo-Roman pottery and glass found in Java and Bali
	Late Bronze Age to Iron Age Dongson culture 500 BC – AD 200		Spread of metallurgy from the mainland
500	Lost-wax casting of large, bronze kettledrums throughout Southeast Asia. Iron appears in certain areas of Southeast Asia. Iron artifacts are made by the "direct" process.		
1000	Middle Bronze Age Go Mun culture 1100 BC – 500 BC	Use of iron in later period of Sa-Huynh culture 1000 BC – AD 100	Megalithic structures at Cipari, in Java
1500	Early Bronze Age Dong Dau culture 1500 BC – 1100 BC		
2000 BC	Use of bronze in Late Neolithic Phung Nguyen culture 2300 BC – 1500 BC		Expansion of Austronesian-speaking agriculturalists

THE BRONZE AGE AND IRON AGE IN SOUTHEAST ASIA: 2000 BC TO AD 400

The first bronze artifacts discovered by Western archaeologists in Southeast Asia are large kettledrums, found from South China to eastern Indonesia. In 1705, naturalist G.E. Rumpf gave a detailed description of a drum from Pejeng, in Bali, and sent another to Europe. Many more drums were discovered in the nineteenth and early twentieth centuries. Where the drums came from was not known until the 1920s, when French customs official Emile Pajot excavated some on the banks of the Ma River, at Dongson, near Than Hoa, in Vietnam.

↑ Dongson drums, such as the one shown here, were classified in 1902 by the German ethnographer Franz Heger into four main types, now known as Heger types I to IV. This is a Heger type I drum.
RIJKSMUSEUM VOOR VOLKENKUNDE

Origins of Bronze in Southeast Asia

Archaeologists long believed that all bronze artifacts found in Southeast Asia came from a "Dongson civilization", centered on South China and Vietnam, which was thought to have traded drums and other bronze ritual vessels throughout the area. Until the mid-1960s, it was thought that bronze came into use in Southeast Asia between 700 BC and 500 BC, probably through the spread of metallurgical techniques from China, or even from southeastern Europe. Recent excavations, however, have caused this belief to be abandoned: Vietnamese excavations at Dongson and elsewhere show continuity from earlier Neolithic cultures.

In the 1960s, a modern phase of excavation began in Thailand, and in 1966, excavations at Non Nok Tha ("Partridge Mound"), in Northeast Thailand, uncovered a burial ground that included numerous bronze axes, ornaments, and projectile points. More important were casting molds, crucibles, and casting spillage, indicating that the artifacts were manufactured locally.

At about the same time as the Non Nok Tha excavations, rich Bronze Age burials and superbly painted pottery were dug from graves by the villagers of Ban Chiang, just south of the Mekong River and nearly 125 kilometers (80 miles) north of Non Nok Tha. Excavations by Thai archaeologists in 1967 and 1972, and by a joint Thai–American team from 1974 to 1975, yielded a wealth of bronze and pottery provisionally dated to various phases from about 3600 BC to AD 200.

This site was extensively looted by villagers, who readily sold the decorated pottery, bronzes, and stone and glass jewelry for which Ban Chiang is famous. Public and private collections in Thailand and overseas benefited, but the context of the finds was ignored, and much of the evidence of burial and occupation was destroyed.

Later reassessments caused revision of the date for the first appearance of bronze at Non Nok Tha and Ban Chiang to about 2000 BC, roughly contemporary with its earliest use in North China. Virtually all specialists now reject the notion that metallurgical knowledge was introduced into Southeast Asia from outside, thinking it more probable that the indigenous peoples, with abundant and easily accessible copper and tin, developed their own methods of smelting and casting.

Since then, other Bronze Age cemeteries have been excavated, notably at Ban Na Di, 25 kilometers (15 miles) south of Ban Chiang; Non Pa Kluay, near Non Nok Tha; Tha Kae, near Lopburi, in central Thailand; and most recently, at Non Nor, on the eastern side of the Gulf of Thailand. The Bronze Age soil strata at all of these sites can be dated to about 2000 BC to 800 BC.

Since the mid-1980s, investigation has shifted to ancient mines and metal-smelting sites, especially around Phu Lon, on the northern end of the Petchabuan Mountains and just south of the Mekong River, and in the Wong Prachan Valley, in central Thailand. The evidence reveals intensive mining and smelting of both surface and deeper copper ores from just after 2000 BC. An unusual technique of crucible smelting produced copper ingots for transport to the village bronze casters of the Khorat Plateau.

This drum top found in Indonesia is decorated with frogs. It is thought that drums were used in rain-making ceremonies to summon the frogs that appear in the rice fields just before the monsoon rains begin.
RIJKSMUSEUM VOOR VOLKENKUNDE

A pedestal bowl from the Late period at Ban Chiang, a site famous for its decorated pottery, bronzes, and stone and glass jewelry.
TETTONI, CASSIO, & ASSOC./PHOTOBANK

A bronze bracelet, dating from the first millennium BC, excavated in the Ban Chiang region, in northeastern Thailand.
LUCA INVERNIZZI TETTONI/GIRAUDON

Copper ingots from the Wong Prachan Valley, in central Thailand, dating from the Late Bronze to Early Iron Age.
IAN C. GLOVER

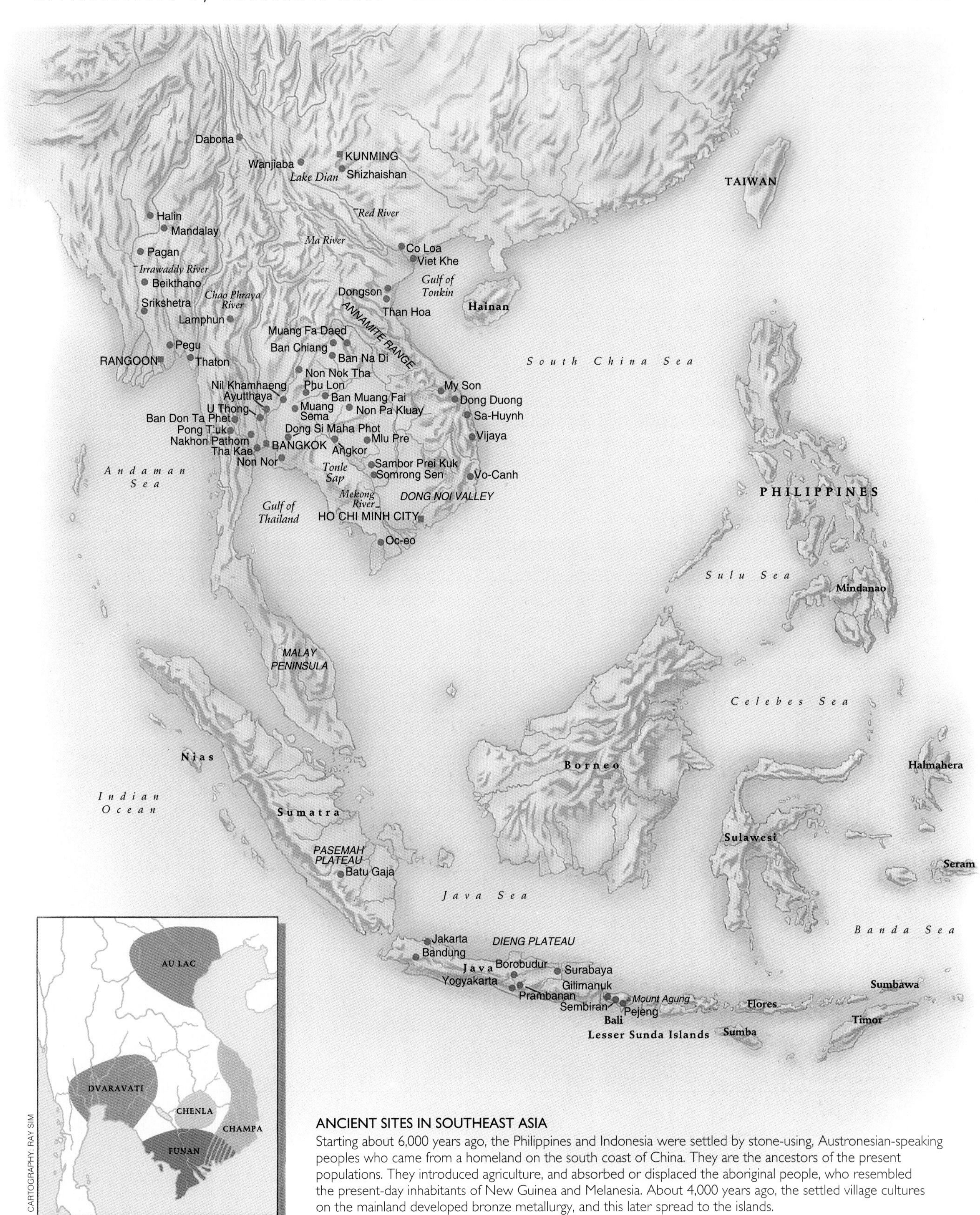

ANCIENT SITES IN SOUTHEAST ASIA
Starting about 6,000 years ago, the Philippines and Indonesia were settled by stone-using, Austronesian-speaking peoples who came from a homeland on the south coast of China. They are the ancestors of the present populations. They introduced agriculture, and absorbed or displaced the aboriginal people, who resembled the present-day inhabitants of New Guinea and Melanesia. About 4,000 years ago, the settled village cultures on the mainland developed bronze metallurgy, and this later spread to the islands.

Trade and Exchange in the Bronze Age

During this period, copper–tin alloys (bronzes) were extensively used in northeastern Thailand and central Thailand east of the Chao Phraya River. In the west, northwest, and south of that country, and throughout the Malay peninsula into Indonesia, there is little evidence of the production and use of metals until much later. Occasional finds of bronze artifacts can better be accounted for by exchange networks along the rivers and coasts, which also carried marine shells and ornaments inland to villages in the far northwest and to the Khorat Plateau.

No doubt, most trade was in organic materials that have not survived in the archaeological record, but enough stone axes from igneous rock deposits, chert and quartz for flaked cutting tools, shells and bronze axes and ornaments have been found to give some indication of Neolithic exchange systems. From about 500 BC, these carried iron, semiprecious stones, and glass jewelry from the west. Later, they carried Indian Hindu–Buddhist ideology and statehood concepts to the most inland parts.

Bronze Metallurgy in Northern Vietnam

With independence in North Vietnam in 1954, and despite war with the French, Americans, and South Vietnamese, numerous surveys and excavations were undertaken in the northern and central provinces. Special attention has been given to the Dongson culture of the Late Bronze to Early Iron Age (about 700 BC to AD 100), which the Vietnamese see as the finest expression of their native genius, before they came under Chinese influence during Vietnam's 900 years as a province of the Chinese Empire.

Vietnamese archaeologists have established a sequence of cultures in the central Red River valley. There, the Late Neolithic Phung Nguyen culture (about 2300 BC to 1500 BC) employed bronze in its final stages. In the Early Bronze Age Dong Dau culture (about 1500 BC to 1100 BC), bronze replaced stone for about 40 percent of edged tools and weapons, rising to about 60 percent in the Middle Bronze Age Go Mun culture (about 1100 BC to 500 BC). Here, there are not only bronze weapons, axes, and personal ornaments, but also sickles and other agricultural tools. In the Late Bronze Age–Iron Age Dongson culture (500 BC to AD 200), bronze accounts for more than 90 percent of tools and weapons, and there are exceptionally rich graves such as that at Viet Khe, where a hollowed log coffin more than 4.5 meters (15 feet) long contained some hundred bronzes, including small drums.

In the Dongson period, a few exceptionally rich cemeteries—the burial places of powerful chiefdoms—contain ritual and personal artifacts such as drums, bucket-shaped ladles, musical instruments, buckles, and ornamented daggers. Towards the end of the period, from about 200 BC, there is an increasing range of imported Han Chinese mirrors, wine vessels, coins, halberds (*ge*), and even a seal such as the Han emperors gave to dependent principalities outside the empire.

Here, Chinese historical texts (the *Shu shu*) and Vietnamese legendary histories come together. Vietnamese scholars identify the Dongson culture in its later stages with Van Lang/Au Lac, traditionally the first unified kingdom of Vietnam, with a ruling royal dynasty, a professional administrative class, and its capital at Co Loa. This fortress, on the northern edge of modern Hanoi, bounded by ramparts extending more than 600 hectares (1,500 acres), was conquered by the Chinese in the first century AD. Much Dongson material has been found around Co Loa, including a huge bronze drum weighing some 70 kilograms (160 pounds) and containing more than 100 socketed bronze hoes or plow shares. Nevertheless, the identification of Co Loa as the capital of an indigenous kingdom remains uncertain.

Dongson bronze weapons and tools, from central Vietnam. Excavations by Vietnamese archaeologists at Dongson and many other sites in the Red and Ma River valleys show continuity between this culture and the earlier Neolithic cultures.
IAN C. GLOVER

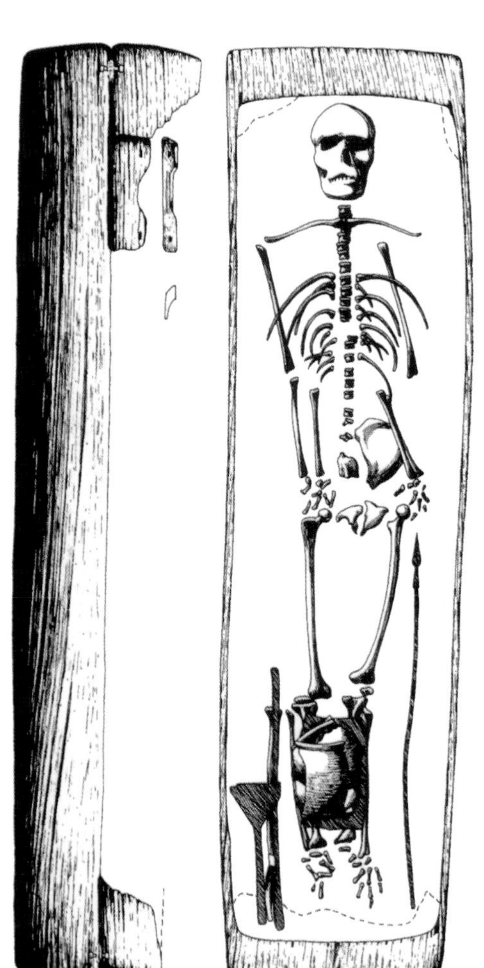

This hollowed log coffin excavated at Chau Can is similar to one found at Viet Khe, in northern Vietnam, dating from the Dongson period. The Viet Khe coffin contained some hundred bronzes, including small drums.
CHARLES HIGHAM

Designs on Dongson bronze drums depict details of daily and ceremonial life. The upper panel shows armed warriors with a drum on a boat, and the lower panel shows people playing drums in front of a house with outswept gables that is similar to the modern-day houses of the Toraja people, of Sulawesi, in Indonesia.
IAN C. GLOVER

A Dongson-style drum, from Thailand. Although some Chinese scholars believe that these drums originated in South China from more utilitarian containers, the Vietnamese remain convinced that they developed first in the lower Red River valley and spread northwestwards into China.
TETTONI, CASSIO, & ASSOC./PHOTOBANK

The Drums of Dongson

Several hundred of the great bronze kettledrums of the Dongson culture have been reported; some 150 from Vietnam, 50 from Indonesia, 20 to 30 in Thailand, and many more in South and Southwest China, particularly from Yunnan, Guangxi, Guizhou, and Guangdong provinces. The drums exhibit great skill in the lost-wax casting of large objects—the Co Loa drum would have required the smelting of between 1 and 7 tonnes (1 and 7 tons) of copper ore and the use of up to 10 large casting crucibles at the one time. The pictorial information on the drums' sides illustrates vivid details of daily and ceremonial life. Armed warriors in boats can be seen carrying the very drums on which they are portrayed; there are domestic tasks such as food preparation and the feeding of animals; and music, dance, and religious ceremonies are depicted.

Scholars have argued as to whether the drums were made for religious ceremonies, to rally men for war, or for another secular role. They have been found from China to the borders of Burma (Myanmar) and east to the islands of eastern Indonesia, and it is unlikely that they had the same functions in all communities. Most drums were made in Vietnam and South China, but they were traded to the south and west, and were valued by people with very different cultures. In eastern Java and Bali, a distinctive style of drum developed, taller and narrower with an overhanging tympanum. This is the Pejeng type, first described by Rumpf in 1705, and still in its temple tower at Bedulu, in central Bali.

The Pejeng drums, probably made in the early centuries AD, gave rise to the later and smaller *moko* drums, which were still made in the late nineteenth century. They served as a form of money among certain peoples of eastern Indonesia. In mainland Southeast Asia, too, the early drums were modified and remained in production up to the twentieth century, serving to communicate with the spirit world, for rain-making and shamanist rituals. They were used by many of the mountain hill tribespeoples of Yunnan, in China; Laos; the Annamite Range of Indochina; Northeast Thailand; Burma; and as far west as the northeast frontier provinces of India. They are still made in Laos and Thailand for the tourist trade.

The Dongson drums date to at least the seventh century BC, and probably come from the mountains of far west Yunnan. The earliest known were found at Wanjiba, in a huge wooden tomb from about 600 BC. At Dabona, the "drums", if that is what they are, have a convex end, resembling large cooking cauldrons.

Bronze drums in many shapes and sizes as late as the first century BC have been found among the spectacular royal regalia of the Kingdom of Dian, a powerful multi-ethnic state centered around Lake Dian—south of present-day Kunming, in Yunnan—and outside the Han empire until about 115 BC. Shizhaishan, the royal burial ground on a hill, once an island in the lake, has produced some of the most striking remains in the whole of East Asia. Some drums are clearly of the Dongson style, others are unique to Yunnan; yet others have been adapted as containers for vast numbers of cowrie shells. These have separate lids bearing extraordinary images of war, ritual, musical performances, human sacrifice, and serpent worship, as well as weaving, cooking, and feasting, and village elders in conference with their chiefs.

The Bronze Age in Vietnam and Cambodia

South of the Dongson area, the later prehistory of Vietnam and Cambodia is very poorly known. However, several regionally distinct Bronze Age cultures have been identified, with their own styles of axes, daggers, and ornaments.

The Sa-Huynh culture, for example, is a late prehistoric metal age society on the central coast of the old kingdom of Annam. In 1909, about 200 jar burials were uncovered at Sa-Huynh. Since then, many more have been found, at some 50 sites. Because of the acid soils, these jars seldom contain human bones, but incised pottery, glass and carnelian beads, bronze ornaments, and iron tools and weapons are common. More than 100 examples of a jade ear pendant representing a mythical two-headed beast have been found in Vietnam, with some others in Thailand, the

Philippines, and Taiwan—evidence of the widespread trading of the Sa-Huynh people.

An early stage of the Sa-Huynh culture, the Long Thanh, is dated a little before 1000 BC. The jars at these sites are egg-shaped; they contain stone tools and ornaments, but no metal. Bronze tools appear in the Binh Chau stage, just after 1000 BC, followed by iron in the Sa-Huynh stage, about 500 BC. Bronze thus appears rather late in central Vietnam, partly perhaps because of the distance from ore sources. As in western Thailand, iron is rather early, quickly replacing bronze.

From about AD 500, the central coast of Vietnam was dominated by the Chams, an Austronesian-speaking people who adopted elements of Indian political and religious culture. Although the first French studies of the Chams did not connect them with earlier cultures, recent Vietnamese work has shown that they are linguistic and cultural descendants of the Sa-Huynh people. There are also many early traces of contact with the west. Indian glass and semiprecious stone beads are abundant, and iron seems to have been used by the Sa-Huynh peoples when their Dongson neighbors were still mostly using bronze.

In Cambodia, rich Bronze Age sites have long been known at Somrong Sen, on the branch of the Mekong River that flows into the "great lake", Tonle Sap, and at Mlu Pre, in the northeast. Conflict in that country stopped all recent archaeological work, and although the prehistoric Cambodian cultures were probably related to those of Thailand and Vietnam, details and chronology before the emergence of the great Khmer towns and temples remain obscure.

Cham architecture at the Mison temple complex, in central Vietnam, dating from the ninth to eleventh centuries AD. The Chams were an Austronesian-speaking people who have recently been shown to be the linguistic and cultural descendants of the Sa-Huynh people.

A jade and glass ear pendant from the Sa-Huynh culture, representing a mythical, two-headed beast.
IAN C. GLOVER

This decorated Cham tile end was excavated from Bui Chau hill, Tra Kieu, in central Vietnam.
IAN C. GLOVER

⇧ An iron spear from Ban Don Ta Phet, in western Thailand, dating from the fourth century BC.
IAN C. GLOVER

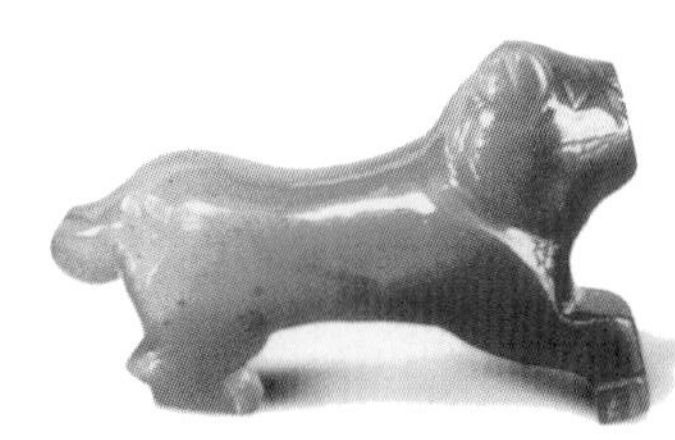

⇧ A carnelian lion from Ban Don Ta Phet, a site rich in significant burial deposits.
IAN C. GLOVER

The Arrival of Iron, and Trade with India

Iron appears in certain areas of Southeast Asia between 700 BC and 500 BC. The earliest evidence comes from copper-mining and smelting sites in the Wong Prachan Valley of central Thailand, especially Nil Khamhaeng, where burials of metalworkers with iron tools and bangles have been dated to 700 BC. By about 500 BC, iron appears in central and northeastern Thailand and the Sa-Huynh sites of central Vietnam. By the early fourth century BC, iron completely replaced bronze for edged weapons and tools at Ban Don Ta Phet, on the western edge of Thailand's central plains.

It was once argued that the technique of manufacturing iron was introduced into Southeast Asia from China. Annals of the Han empire mention that iron was little known there, and specifically forbade its export to the "Southern Barbarians". But recent archaeological work has shown that iron came into use in Southeast Asia as early as in northern and central China, but was made by the "direct" process. Chinese iron-making was dominated by the "indirect" manufacture from cast iron —a technique not adopted in Thailand until the arrival of Chinese iron masters in the eighteenth century AD.

Archaeologists working in Thailand tend to see the development of iron as a local process arising out of the use of iron-rich copper ores. Its early occurrence at the copper-smelting site of Nil Khamhaeng supports this view. On the other hand, we start to get abundant evidence of trade with India in the form of glass, agate, and carnelian beads, including the etched variety, from about 500 BC. Since we know that iron-working spread throughout India from 1000 BC to 700 BC, it is likely that its appearance in Southeast Asia was a consequence of trade.

In Indonesia, too, we find at this time many sites with evidence of exchange with India. The cist (slab) graves of Sumatra and Java also contain Indian glass and semiprecious stone beads. (See the feature *Southeast Asian Megaliths*.) Even the form of some of these burial structures may have been influenced by South Indian tombs. In Bali, the Gilimanuk site, from the first century AD, is rich in glass and stone. At the newly discovered trading port of Sembiran, on the north coast of Bali, pieces of Indo-Roman Rouletted Ware occur. This ceramic type of the second century BC to the first century AD is well known from sites in the eastern states of India. One Sembiran fragment has characters in the Indian *Karoshti* script.

Ban Don Ta Phet in Western Thailand

Excavations between 1975 and 1985 at Iron Age Ban Don Ta Phet give the best evidence of the earliest "Indianization". About 100 burial deposits, dated between 390 BC and 360 BC, were found. They contained only a few fragmentary bones, but numerous pottery vessels, and iron tools and weapons; high-tin bronze vessels and ornaments; and more than 3,000 glass beads, and some 500 of agate, carnelian, jade, and rock crystal, including about 50 etched beads of types well known from early Buddhist sites in North and northwestern India. Although the pottery is a locally made low-

TETTONI, CASSIO, & ASSOC./PHOTOBANK

⇦ Carnelian and agate necklaces from Ban Don Ta Phet, in western Thailand. From about 500 BC, there is abundant evidence of trade with India in the form of glass, agate, and carnelian beads.

⟲ These bronze bowls and bracelets from Ban Don Ta Phet, in western Thailand, date from the fourth century BC. By this time, iron was used for tools and weapons, but high-tin bronzes were valued for their golden color and as prestigious, nontoxic food containers.
TETTONI, CASSIO, & ASSOC./PHOTOBANK

fired earthenware, and the iron tools are quite different from forms known at contemporary Indian sites, the bronzes, and glass and stone ornaments can be widely matched in India, and provide evidence not only for trade, but also for the penetration of Indian Buddhism. A conical boss surrounded by inscribed circles appears in the base of some bronze vessels. The symbol is well known on pottery from Indian Buddhist towns such as Sisulpalgarh, in Orissa; on rare high-tin bronze vessels from the Nilgiri Hills and Coimbatore, in southern India; and from a superb carved and polished granite vessel found in an early stupa at Taxila. The date of Ban Don Ta Phet shows that long-held views that Hindu–Buddhist ideas and symbolism affected Southeast Asia only from the second to third centuries AD must now be abandoned.

The Arrival of Hindu–Buddhism in Southeast Asia

By about AD 500, much of Southeast Asia—from central Indonesia to the Sa-Huynh culture of Vietnam—had come under the influence of Hindu–Buddhist civilizations of eastern and southern India. Traditional South Asian histories, such as the *Mahavamsa* of Sri Lanka, record that in the late third century BC to the early second century BC, the Mauryan Emperor Asoka sent three missionaries—Son, Uttara, and Gavtampti—to spread Buddhism in the countries of *Suvanabhumi* (the "Lands of Gold"), in Southeast Asia. From this beginning, the Indianization of Southeast Asia continued.

But, as with St Augustine's mission to the court of King Ethelbert of Kent, England, in AD 597, the official religious conversion followed long-popular routes of communication and exchange. Its success depended on a prior knowledge of the great wealth, prestige, and power of the metropolitan states. Just as archaeological evidence in the form of the cross and fish symbols on the personal jewelry, wall paintings, and mosaics of late Roman Britain testify to the widespread knowledge and partial acceptance of Christianity 400 years before St Augustine's evangelical mission to Britain, so new archaeological data from Southeast Asia are beginning to show that some populations there were familiar with Indian religious ideas long before official Indianization.

Ian C. Glover

⚲ The stone reliefs of Brahma at Pagan, in central Burma, are unique. Shown here are his three faces depicted at Nanpaya temple. Evidence of Hindu worship, however, along with Mahayana Buddhism, is mixed with the predominating Theravadan Buddhism.

TETTONI, CASSIO, & ASSOC./PHOTOBANK

⊖ This detail of a relief from Borobudur, in Java, Indonesia, shows the type of boat that may have been in use during the ninth century AD. The story is from the *avadanas*, or heroic tales, and recounts the voyage of Hiru to found a new city.

THE RISE OF HINDU AND BUDDHIST STATES IN SOUTHEAST ASIA

During the rise of the Hindu and Buddhist states, foreign and indigenous styles blended to transform Southeast Asian art. For about the first 12 centuries AD, the Indian religions provided a common iconography, but the architecture and sculpture are unique. The impact of Indian culture was profound, and from it stemmed concepts of state and kingship, writing, and legal systems.

A Blending of Styles

Contact with China was the other major influence on Southeast Asia, whose position gave rise to the traditional name "Indochina". Northern Vietnam was conquered by the Chinese Han dynasty in 111 BC, marking the beginning of some 900 years of Chinese rule. Tribute missions to the Chinese court were recorded over many centuries, but it was Indian ideas that were assimilated into Southeast Asian culture, as indicated by the use of Indian-based terms. For example, inscriptions of the Khmer kings of Angkor, in Cambodia, about AD 800 to AD 1200, adopted the suffix *varman*, meaning "protector". The first such uses are much earlier: a Cham inscription at Vo-Canh, Vietnam, has been dated to AD 300, and others in Vietnam go back to the late fourth century AD.

TETTONI, CASSIO, & ASSOC./PHOTOBANK

Religion and Trade

Despite the evidence of Indian culture, how it was introduced to Southeast Asia remains a mystery. The archaeological record points to trade. By the first century AD, demand in the West, particularly from Rome, stimulated Indian trade. Voyages from India to Southeast Asian ports were made in accordance with the seasonal monsoons, and ships would often wait many months in port for winds to change. At least 18 months commonly passed between outward and return trips, and traders may well have married locally. Others exploited overland routes, from relatively short distances across the Malay peninsula to longer circuits from Burma into China, or across northeastern Thailand to the valley of the Mekong River.

Scholars have argued that Indian Buddhist missionary activities resulted in Buddhist monasteries and communities being established in Southeast Asia. But peaceful coexistence is characteristic of Hinduism and Buddhism there, as is the blending of both religions with pre-existing ancestral cults.

Indian concepts of state and kingship in Southeast Asia reflect the political power held by religious figures. Native rulers may often have invited Hindus or Buddhists to take positions of power in their courts, where Indian ideas of royalty legitimated the rulers' positions.

In the Hindu periods of the kingdom of Angkor, the essence of kingship was expressed in the *devaraja*, a Sanskrit word meaning "god who is king", which consecrated a ruler as an incarnation of a Hindu god such as Vishnu or Siva. Temples and statues dedicated to these and other deities embodied the ruler and expressed his power. On Earth, the *devaraja* established harmony in the human world, between subterranean chaos and the realm of the gods.

The ideal ruler of the Buddhist state was the *cakravartin*. The *cakra*—"disk" or "wheel" in Sanskrit—was set in motion by the Buddha in preaching his first sermon, but it may also be an attribute of the Hindu god Vishnu, and can also symbolize the sun. The *cakravartin* is a righteous and universal emperor whose chariot can roll anywhere without hindrance.

⊕ A pre-Angkorean image of the Buddha, 1.5 meters (5 feet) high, probably dating from the sixth to seventh centuries AD. The iconography of this image is strongly influenced by the art of Gupta India, but the symmetry of the arms and the front fold of the robe are also akin to the art of the Dvaravati, in Thailand. Although Angkor was predominantly a Hindu city, Buddhist sects continued to practice. This was particularly true in the pre-Angkorean period (pre-ninth century AD), and again during the reign of Jayavarman VII, at the end of the twelfth century. This second period of Buddhism was Mahayanist, however, whereas pre-Angkorean Buddhism was mostly Theravadan.

TETTONI, CASSIO, & ASSOC./PHOTOBANK

TETTONI, CASSIO, & ASSOC./PHOTOBANK

A stone statue of Vishnu, measuring 1.7 meters (5 feet, 8 inches) high, from Surat Thani, in southern Thailand. Somewhat similar statues have been found to the north, including one near Ayutthaya. The dating of all these images is uncertain.

This *dharmacakra*, or "wheel of law", was found near Prachinburi, in south-central Thailand. Other examples have been found in the northeastern part of the country, illustrating the wide geographical area over which sculpture of the Dvaravati style is found.

TETTONI, CASSIO, & ASSOC./PHOTOBANK

Protohistoric Southeast Asia: The Mon of Dvaravati

The Mon "kingdom" of Dvaravati, one of many small polities, was probably located in central and northeastern Thailand, from about AD 600 to AD 1000. Its culture is characterized by massive stone *cakra*, 1 to 2 meters (3 to 6 feet) in diameter. The Indian ruler Asoka is believed to have originated the placing of *cakra* on tall pillars, which may also have occurred in Thailand.

The Thai *cakra* has a central socket, and some scholars suggest that carved stone bas-reliefs—the *panaspati*—were fixed there. The *panaspati* is a mythical creature not seen outside the Dvaravati period. It is a composite of the vehicles of the principal Hindu deities, with the body of Siva's bull Nandi, the beak of Vishnu's Garuda bird, and the wings of Brahma's *hamsa* or goose. The Buddha riding on the *panaspati* signifies the triumph of Buddhism over Hinduism.

⊕ Dating from the eighth to ninth centuries AD, this *panaspati* is 37 centimeters (15 inches) high.
TETTONI, CASSIO, & ASSOC./PHOTOBANK

⊕ Although the *vitarka*, or "teaching mudra" (symbolic gesture), of the Buddha's hands is known in India, the double *vitarka* of the Dvaravati style is unique.
TETTONI, CASSIO, & ASSOC./PHOTOBANK

⊕ *Opposite page*: The fluidity of Dvaravati stucco work can be seen in this detail of a relief from Chula Pathom Chedi, thought to date from the seventh to ninth centuries AD.

The blending of Hinduism and Buddhism in the *panaspati* typifies Southeast Asia's assimilation of Indian religions. Beikthano, the name of the first to fifth-century AD Buddhist site in central Burma, means "City of Vishnu". In Burma, today renamed Myanmar, spirit worship remains closely interwoven with veneration of the Buddha. This blending of religious ideas and iconographies began during the protohistoric period (the last centuries BC and the early centuries AD).

Written evidence from this period is scant: brief inscriptions on upright stone slabs or columns, references in Chinese dynastic accounts, and inscribed coins. It is from these coins that the name "Dvaravati" was confirmed. A seventh-century AD Chinese traveler referred to a kingdom east of Burma and west of Cambodia as "T'o-lo-po-ti", which in Sanskrit is "Dvaravati". The name is also part of the official titles of two later Thai Buddhist kingdoms: Ayutthaya, AD 1300 to AD 1700; and Bangkok, the present capital, founded in the late eighteenth century AD after the Burmese sacked Ayutthaya. In 1963, the name was firmly substantiated when two silver coins inscribed in Sanskrit with Indian characters, dateable to the seventh-century AD Indian Pallava dynasty, were unearthed at Nakhon Pathom. The characters were translated as "meritorious work of the King of Dvaravati".

Many inscriptions from these sites are in the Mon language rather than Sanskrit, which has led to the identification of Dvaravati with the Mon peoples. The Mon, dating from about AD 500, were found from Burma to the eastern shore of the Gulf of Thailand, across present-day Cambodia, and northeast towards Laos.

The historical record of Dvaravati barely justifies referring to it as a kingdom. It probably included a number of city-states, one of which was Dvaravati. Other sites where Dvaravati objects have been found were U Thong, Pong T'uk, Ku Bua, Dong Si Maha Phot, Muang Fa Daed, Muang Sema, and Ban Muang Fai. Many of these were enclosed by an earthen wall, and sometimes one or several moats. Plans are irregular, each city differing from the others, and there is no obvious religious significance to the shape. Images of the Buddha occur at these and other sites in materials including stone, terracotta, and stucco, and are strikingly similar. Some very fine images are fully rounded, others are bas-reliefs.

The stone Buddhas are in the form of *sema* (boundary) stones. Dated between AD 800 and AD 900, in Thailand, they have been found only in the northeast. The slabs are as much as 2 meters (6 feet) high, carved with scenes from the life of the historical Buddha, as well as with *jatakas*—tales of the Buddha's former lives. The largest collection comes from Muang Fa Daed. Bas-reliefs from the central region of Thailand have been dated as from the seventh to ninth centuries AD. Generally in stucco or terracotta, they are softly modeled and have great charm.

Mon Culture in Buddhist Burma

The kingdom of Pagan, in central Burma, dating from the tenth to the twelfth centuries AD, combined Mon with Pyu and Burmese cultures. The Mon heartland was some 500 kilometers (300 miles) south of Pagan. Many early Mon cities there, such as Thaton and Pegu, have been occupied for more than a thousand years, and dating is difficult, for sacred sites have remained consecrated places. Tantalizing links exist between Thaton and Mon sites in Thailand. A Thai chronicle states that in the eleventh century AD, Mon people migrated to Thaton to escape cholera in their town of Lamphun. At Thaton, they are said to have established Buddhism, displacing Hinduism. Several *sema* stones of that period are still in the Kalyani Sima Pagoda in Thaton. Like the *sema* from northeastern Thailand, they bear scenes from the Buddha's former lives.

From Thaton, the Mon heritage reached Pagan, on the central reaches of the Irrawaddy River. There, the supreme achievement of Buddhist art is found. In Pali, the sacred language of the Theravada ("Way of the Elders") Buddhists, Pagan was "Arimaddanapura", "City of the Enemy Crushers"; the Mons called it "Tattadesa", "Parched

TETTONI, CASSIO, & ASSOC./PHOTOBANK

⊕ Many features of this Buddha are typical of Dvaravati images: the downcast eyes, thick lips, large hair-curls, and joined eyebrows. This is a detail of a limestone image, 1.5 meters (4 feet, 10 inches) tall, now in the Bangkok National Museum, in Thailand.

MICHAEL FREEMAN

The massive Dhammayangyi temple, at Pagan, in central Burma, dates from the twelfth century AD. The graceful tiers of the upper terraces balance the horizontal and vertical elements of the structure.

Opposite page: A detail of a mural painting in the Myinkaba Kubyauk-gyi temple, at Pagan, in central Burma, dated to the early twelfth century AD. This guardian figure of a Bodhisattva (savior) protects the entry to the temple. The style is quite different from the *jataka* mural paintings further inside the temple.

Country". Within the region, remains of nearly 5,000 stupas and temples cover an area of about 40 square kilometers (16 square miles). The foundation of Pagan as a cluster of villages is traditionally attributed to the Pyu king Thamudrit. The present moated and walled city was established much later, in AD 849; the kingdom lasted only until AD 1287, when it was sacked by the Mongols.

In AD 1057, King Anawrahta of Pagan invaded Thaton in search of sacred scriptures to purify the religion of Pagan, then said to be in the hands of the Ari, Mahayana Buddhists who worshiped snakes. Thaton also gave access to the sea, vital for trade and contact with Theravadan communities in Sri Lanka. Anawrahta returned to Pagan with 30 elephant-loads of the Tripitaka ("the Three Baskets"), the sacred writings of Theravada Buddhism.

The extent of Mon influence at Pagan is uncertain. Many depictions of *jataka* tales on the temples are bas-reliefs, generally glazed terracotta plaques. These are similar to the bas-reliefs of the Dvaravati Mon. Below each scene, a phrase identifies the life of the Buddha that is pictured. At the earlier temples, these phrases are in Old Mon, and these, according to some, are the only elements at Pagan that are proper to Mon culture. Other authorities describe the temples, single-story and dimly lit, as Mon.

The use of ethnic and linguistic labels for kingdoms and styles makes identification of Pagan's artistic elements difficult. A similar problem surrounds Dvaravati, where the wide distribution of similarly carved Buddhas has led to the conclusion that the artistic spread defined a Buddhist kingdom. At Pagan, the capture of Buddhist scriptures from Thaton resulted in their known dissemination, and analysis has seized upon this to locate elements that may be labeled Mon. The confusion increases when many of the elements called "Mon" in Thailand are called "Pyu" in Burma.

Pyu Culture in Burma

Three major Pyu urban sites are Beikthano (Vishnu City), Srikshetra (Thayekhittaya, near Prome), and Halin (near Shwebo), ranging from about the first to the ninth centuries AD. The Pyu people came from the same Tibeto-Burman group as the Burmese; earlier immigrants than the Burmese, they gradually merged with them. Many Pyu cities were deserted long ago, and have thus preserved some of the earliest Burmese Buddhist remains. Like the Mon, Pyu culture was a crucial model for much classical Pagan architecture.

Buddhist remains at Beikthano include a brick monastery close to two dome-like structures. The building rests on a plinth, measuring 35 meters by

12.5 meters (115 feet by 40 feet); its eight small cells are laid out similarly to contemporary monasteries in South India. The remains at Srikshetra are more complete, including bulbous domes and hollow temples thought to have been prototypes for structures at Pagan. The brick dome of the Bawbawgyi Pagoda, outside the city walls of Srikshetra, rises some 45 meters (150 feet).

The brick wall of Srikshetra is said to have been drawn by Sakra, lord of the devas (gods), using a rope pulled by a serpent, or *naga*. Although the *naga* sheltered the Buddha after his enlightenment, it is rarely seen in the later iconography of Buddhist Burma. One reason may be King Anawrahta's elimination, in the eleventh century AD, of the Ari sect's *naga* worship from Pagan's Buddhist symbolism.

The finds from Srikshetra are primarily Theravadan, but several Mahayanist figures have been recovered, as well as images of Vishnu. The blending of Hindu and Buddhist styles endured at Pagan, and is particularly apparent in the mural paintings.

Technical harmony in royal and religious architecture was achieved at Pagan by the use of brick, stucco, and wood. Stone inscriptions there recount that royal devotees donated palaces for religious use. The combination of the royal and the religious dates back to the historical Gautama Buddha, in the sixth century BC. Born into a royal family, Gautama married but then renounced his princely life. The future incarnation, the Buddha-to-be, can be seen at Pagan in a series of plaques on the Ananda temple, built in AD 1090, where he sits at ease in front of one of the pavilions with roofs of five, seven, and nine tiers.

The Burmese Pyatthat

The tiered roof is known in Burma as a *pyatthat*, from the Sanskrit *prasada*. The word originally referred to any lofty palatial building. The *prasada*, in a Hindu context, is seen in the towering spires of Angkor, in Cambodia; in Burma, it came to denote the multiple roofs of religious or royal buildings. *Pyatthats* were originally constructed in wood, and in Burma, this continued over centuries. Graceful wooden *pyatthats* crown the many entrances of the nineteenth-century AD palace at Mandalay, the last of the Burmese royal capitals before British colonial rule began in 1885.

The wooden *pyatthats* are long gone, but their translation into brick is widely visible in Pagan's architecture. Receding roofs grace the city's temples, from the eleventh-century AD Ananda to later structures, such as the Thatbyinnyu. Another variation crowns the library built by King Anawrahta to house the Buddhist scriptures, the Pitakat-taik; a result of restorations by later Burmese kings, it is further evidence of the continuity of the form. Finally, the tiered roofs of the *pyatthat* appear as decorative window architraves—for example, at the twelfth-century AD Myinkaba Kubyauk-gyi.

Further evidence of combined religious and royal architecture may soon come to light as a result of current excavations at the presumed site of King Kyanzittha's (AD 1084 to AD 1113) palace. An inscription found near the city gates describes the palace as a *pancaprasada*, or "five-fold pavilion"—a central building surrounded by four corner structures. The massive *prasada*, presumably, was once crowned with wooden *pyatthat*.

TETTONI, CASSIO, & ASSOC./PHOTOBANK

The Buhpaya temple, at Pagan, has been rebuilt many times, most recently after an earthquake in 1975. Although the present structure is new, its general form dates from about the ninth century AD.

TETTONI, CASSIO, & ASSOC./PHOTOBANK

JENNY MILLS

Four "perfume chambers", or *gandhakuti*, are found on the four sides of the Shwezigon stupa, at Pagan. In the background, the tower, or *sikhara*, can be seen. The tiered roof of the rest house in front displays the fine woodworking typical of the Burmese *pyatthat*.

The twelfth-century AD temple of Angkor Wat, in Cambodia, seen from the summit of the nearby hill of Phnom Bakheng.

Cultural Influences at Angkor

Pagan and Angkor have many common architectural elements, including the royal and religious use of the multitiered roof. But although wooden forms certainly existed, all the surviving structures at Angkor are in stone, and for the most part, they crown Hindu temples. The towering roofs are commonly called *prasats*, again from Sanskrit *prasada*.

Angkor was founded north of the "great lake", Tonle Sap, in AD 802, when a Hindu priest consecrated the local ruler King Jayavarman II as "victorious protector". Jayavarman became the first *devaraja*, "god who is king", of Angkor. A settlement already existed, and the natural ecology provided an ideal environment for wet-rice agriculture, the economic basis of the Angkorean empire.

Other kingdoms existed in the region before Angkor, and the Mon Dvaravati certainly played a cultural role in them, but distinguishing Mon elements in Khmer art has proved difficult. For example, of several bronzes cast in the same workshop, one is a Theravadan image considered to be in Mon Dvaravati style, whereas the other is a Mahayana piece thought to be early Angkorean Khmer. They originate from Buri Ram, in northeastern Thailand. Inscriptions indicate this may have been a Buddhist kingdom known as Sri Canasa about the ninth century AD.

Chinese Tribute Missions

The names given by the Chinese to tribute missions from Southeast Asia refer to many small realms in southern Vietnam, Cambodia, and northeastern Thailand early in the first 1,000 years AD. One of these, Funan, was in present-day South Vietnam, on the eastern shore of the Gulf of Thailand; another, Chenla, was probably in northern Cambodia and northeastern Thailand. Some scholars suggest Funan is a Chinese transcription of the Khmer word for mountain, and that the rulers of Funan were "kings of the mountain". Funan's heyday, about the first four centuries AD, appears to precede that of Chenla, from about AD 500 to AD 800.

The enormous moat that surrounds the temple of Angkor Wat symbolizes the cosmic ocean surrounding the sacred temple mountain. The five peaks of the shrine can be seen in the distance, across the 200 meter (650 foot) wide expanse of the moat.

MICHAEL FREEMAN

During the period, China received tribute from all the Southeast Asian kingdoms, and Chinese Buddhist scholars traveled there. In the seventh and eighth centuries AD, particularly, there was considerable Chinese trade along the route to India. Abundant evidence has come from excavations at Oc-eo. Foreign finds were mostly small, highly portable objects, including Indian and Roman medallions, coins, seals, and jewelry.

Chenla was an inland kingdom, the direct predecessor of Angkor, and undoubtedly established many of Angkor's agricultural practices. The irregular moated sites of northeastern Thailand and northern Cambodia exemplify the land and water management that exploited the terrain.

Champa, in Vietnam, was also important in the history of Angkor. Remains at the temple complex of Mison, central Vietnam, date from AD 600 to AD 900, and at Dong Duang is a large Cham Buddhist complex, Quang nam. After the Vietnamese takeover of the north at the end of the tenth century AD, the Cham moved their capital south to Vijaya, in the province of Binh Dinh.

MICHAEL FREEMAN

ELIZABETH H. MOORE

A detail of a window of the Myinkaba Kubyauk-gyi temple, at Pagan, showing a tiered *pyatthat* roof in relief.

The Khmer Temple: Angkor Wat

The cultures of all the region's kingdoms are blended in the art and architecture of Angkor. Few pre-Angkorean remains are earlier than AD 802, but the prototype of Angkor's temple may be seen at Sambor Prei Kuk, the seventh-century AD capital of Isanavarman I of Chenla. The stone temples were simple cells crowned with a multitiered tower, the *prasat*—often likened to a lotus bud or the summit of a mountain. Interior space gave room only for the priest and an image of the god.

Although Khmer temples of Angkor became highly elaborate, the small interior remained constant. What developed in the ninth to thirteenth centuries AD was the cosmological aspect. The enclosure symbolized the Hindu cosmos, and the temple itself stood for the five peaks of Mount Meru, abode of the gods. The wall and surrounding moat recalled the six concentric rings of land and seven oceans that circled the mountain, the pivot of the world.

The culminating expression of these elements came in Angkor Wat, built by King Suryavarman II (AD 1113 to AD 1150). Although most Khmer Hindu temples are dedicated to Siva, the king chose Vishnu; most Khmer temples face east, but Angkor Wat faces west, Vishnu's direction. The temple was not completed until after Suryavarman's death, perhaps serving as his tomb. The reliefs on the walls of Angkor Wat read counterclockwise, which is often taken to mean that the temple is a tomb.

Architecturally, Angkor Wat is considered the most harmonious of all the Khmer temples. The Khmer did not develop vaulting, which allowed the Burmese at Pagan to erect their towering temples, and this lack meant that large areas could not be roofed. But the Khmers wanted multiple chapels with tiered roofs, and joined tower units with galleries around the central spire of Mount Meru. Overlapping roofs on the galleries and the spire create a sense of scale; the stone roofs are carved to resemble tiles. The three terraces of the temple rise successively: the first is 3.2 meters (11 feet); the next, 6.4 meters (21 feet); and the third, 12.8 meters (42 feet). These vertical units are balanced by the massive horizontal enclosure; the moat is 4 kilometers (2 ½ miles) in circumference. Despite the gargantuan scale, the interior cell is only 4.6 meters by 4.7 meters (15 feet by 16 feet). The power of the temple lies not in its interior space, but in its re-creation of the universe in microcosm.

Hindu cosmology and architecture blended with pre-existing Khmer beliefs. Local ancestral and fertility gods were easily admitted into the new pantheon. Royal power was certainly augmented by the temples, but for the people, they were an expression of long-held beliefs.

MICHAEL FREEMAN

The exquisite temple of Banteay Srei, in Cambodia, was built in the tenth century AD. With its diminutive proportions and detailed carvings in deep-pink sandstone, the temple represents a unique moment in Khmer art.

TETTONI, CASSIO, & ASSOC./PHOTOBANK

↑ The overall plan of the ninth-century AD monument of Borobudur, in Java, is best seen from the air: the basement or "hidden foot", the square terraces, and the upper, rounded—but not quite circular—terraces.

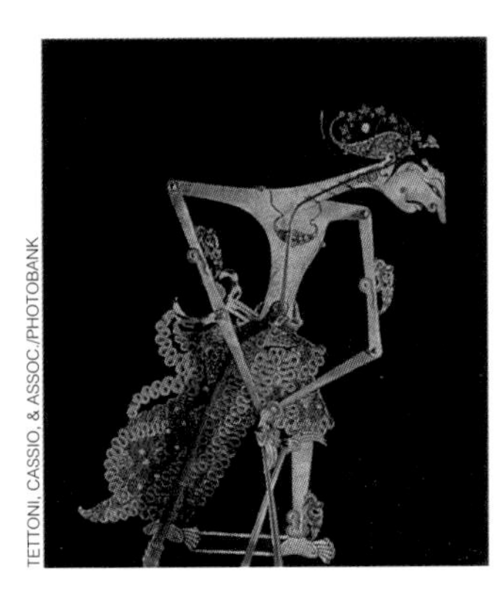
TETTONI, CASSIO, & ASSOC./PHOTOBANK

↑ The *wayang*, or shadow puppets, of central Java are used in a wide variety of performances, and continue to be popular today. Although the puppets are highly decorated, lights behind them are used to cast their images upon a screen: it is these shadows that the audience sees during the play.

→ One of the tiered structures of the tenth-century AD Hindu temple of Prambanan, in Java, known locally as Lara Jonggrang.

Java and Bali

The date and manner in which Hinduism and Buddhism arrived in Indonesia remain uncertain. From the seventh to the thirteenth centuries AD, Java was the center of monumental architecture; as on the mainland, this was a unique adaption of Indian elements. The earliest remains are found on the isolated, volcanic Dieng Plateau. The small shrines there, dedicated to the Hindu god Siva, are called *candi* in Indonesian; the word broadly means any Indianized stone structure with a tower of receding tiers.

The major Buddhist and Hindu remains of Java—Borobudur and Prambanan—are east of the Dieng Plateau, at the foot of the mountain chain forming the island's central spine. Borobudur, the master work of the Mahayana Buddhist Sailendra dynasty, is dated to the ninth century AD. During reconstruction of the temple in the 1970s to 1980s, much was learned about its evolution. The temple may have begun as a Hindu stepped pyramid, similar to temples at Angkor, but doctrinal changes during its construction have resulted in one of Southeast Asia's most complex monuments. (See the feature *Interpretations of Borobudur: Mountain, Stupa, or Mandala?*)

Near Borobudur is Prambanan, known locally as Lara Jonggrang. It is Hindu rather than Buddhist, and was completed later than Borobudur, about AD 900. Whereas Borobudur's cosmic mountain is softly rounded, here the central tower, dedicated to Siva, is more than 40 meters (130 feet) high. It is flanked by buildings dedicated to Brahma and Vishnu, and remains of more than 200 small *candi* surround the central group. The carving on the temple is among the most animated of the classical Javanese period.

Java's most important later monuments are on the eastern end of the island; none of these is on the scale of Borobudur or Prambanan. Developments in sculpture and architecture are reflected today in the arts of the island of Bali, just off the east coast of Java. The naturalistic contours of central Javanese figures became sinuous and elongated, emphasizing silhouettes rather than volumes, in the manner of the popular *wayang* puppet figures. The other major development was in temple plinths and roofs, which became highly elaborated and enlarged.

By the sixteenth century AD, Islam had replaced Hinduism and Buddhism in Java, and ultimately became the religion of all Indonesia except Bali. Bali is thought to have had contact with the central Javanese kingdoms of the eighth to tenth centuries AD, and after the court moved to East Java in the tenth century, links increased. In the fourteenth century, Bali was colonized. When Java became Muslim, Javanese nobles are thought to have fled to Bali, and indigenous ancestor cults blended there with Hinduism, creating *Agama Hindu Dharma* or "Religion of the Hindu doctrine". This unique religion of Bali has continued until today.

Foremost among the symbols of Balinese architecture is the tiered roof, or *meru*. As elsewhere, the tiers are uneven in number; they may honor gods or ancestors within the complex hierarchy of Balinese temples. The largest of these is the great "Mother Temple" of Besakih, on the slopes of Mount Agung—the high mountain that is the center of the Balinese system of orientation. The tiered *meru* are found even in the smallest shrines, living testimony of a 2,000-year-old tradition of religious blending in the far-flung and varied countries of Southeast Asia.

Elizabeth H. Moore

TETTONI, CASSIO, & ASSOC./PHOTOBANK

SOUTHEAST ASIAN MEGALITHS

IAN C. GLOVER

Megalithic cist (slab) graves from the Pasemah Plateau, in Sumatra.
PETER BELLWOOD/AUSTRALIAN NATIONAL UNIVERSITY

BELINDA SYME

In the highlands of central Sulawesi, in Indonesia, large, enigmatic stone statues stand on the edges of the rice fields, sometimes with huge stone jars, such as those shown below from Laos. Archaeologists believe that they date from the early centuries of the Christian era. This example is one of 14 megalithic statues from the Bada Valley.

These huge stone jars were found at the site of Ban Xieng Di, in Xieng Khouang province, Laos, near the better-known site of Ban Ang, also known as the Plain of Jars.
VÉRONIQUE DAUGE/UNESCO, CAMBODIA

A decorated stone in the late "megalithic" tradition, in honor of the women of the village of Botohosi, in the Nias Islands, off the west coast of Sumatra, Indonesia.
W. MARSCHALL/UNIVERSITÄT BERN

Megaliths are among the most imposing prehistoric structures. Built from massive, largely unshaped stones by people in different parts of the world—who had few or no links with each other—megaliths are particularly common in Atlantic Europe, around the Mediterranean basin, in northern Africa, peninsular India, Indonesia, Melanesia, Korea, Japan, and in parts of South America.

Originally, it was believed that all megaliths were historically related, having been erected by a "megalithic people" who took the building tradition to other parts of the world in their search for metal ores. This simplistic view of megaliths has been discarded, although megaliths found in adjacent regions are sometimes historically related. For example, the great megalithic Iron Age stone circles and graves of peninsular India may be culturally linked with those of Sumatra and Java, in Indonesia.

In the islands of Southeast Asia, megaliths are found principally in south central Sumatra; Java; on the Lesser Sunda Islands east to Timor; in Sarawak and Sabah, in Borneo; in the central highlands of Sulawesi; and in Mindanao, in the southern Philippines. On the mainland, megaliths occur in peninsular Malaya and in the Annamite Mountains of Vietnam; and north to the Plain of Jars, in central Laos. In Thailand and Burma, only one or two megalithic structures have been reported.

To date, no megalith in Southeast Asia has been definitely shown to predate the Iron Age, although a date of about 1000 BC has been claimed for the megalithic structures at Cipari, Java. Appearing about 700 BC, the great megalithic grave structures in South India are the most obvious source of inspiration for megaliths and burial traditions in Southeast Asia, particularly in Sumatra and Java: many details of the design and structure are similar.

Sumatra and Java have the most megaliths and the greatest range. They include dolmens (capped standing stones), menhirs (standing stones), stone cist (slab) graves, stone sarcophagi, troughs, mortars, cairns, stone seats, terraced structures, and large statues. In peninsular Malaya, menhirs are most commonly found (singly and aligned in groups), along with cist graves. In Borneo, dolmens as well as menhirs and cist graves predominate. In central Sulawesi, some huge stone urns have been discovered that are remarkably similar to those found in the Plain of Jars, Laos, as well as stone statues and circles. In the Lesser Sunda Islands, stone assembly places, tables, statues, and dolmens are particularly common, some having been built in very recent times.

There have been few technically competent archaeological investigations of Southeast Asian megaliths. Although no single structure has been unequivocally dated, artifacts found with the megaliths suggest that some of them may have been built in the last five centuries BC. For example, iron tools, semiprecious stones, and glass beads were found in cist graves in Java and Sumatra; and glass, iron, bronze, and, occasionally, gold ornaments were found in stone sarcophagi in Java and Bali. Carvings of helmeted warriors, some riding elephants and carrying Dongson-style bronze drums, were found at Batu Gajah (Elephant Rock) and Airpurah, in South Sumatra. These finds provide evidence of wide-ranging cultural connections: with India in the case of glass and stone jewelry; and with northern Vietnam or South China in the case of the bronze drums.

Recently, Indonesian prehistorians have shown a renewed interest in excavating ancient megalithic sites, and in documenting contemporary megalithic traditions. The most notable recent find has been a series of splendid wall paintings inside cist graves in South Sumatra. These paintings of a tiger, a buffalo, and people carrying Dongson-style drums were discovered in 1990, and are clearly related to those reported in a 1932 study in South Sumatra.

INTERPRETATIONS OF BOROBUDUR: MOUNTAIN, STUPA, OR MANDALA?

Elizabeth H. Moore

Borobudur is a unique Buddhist temple that rises serenely above the Kedu Plain, on the island of Java, in Indonesia. Dated to between about AD 835 and AD 860, it is thought to have been built by the obscure Sailendra dynasty. This area favored settlement, and labor must have been plentiful, for more than a million blocks of stone were cut nearby and transported to the site.

The basement of Borobudur is carved with 160 relief panels. Each panel is 2 meters (6 feet, 6 inches) wide and more than half a meter (1 foot, 8 inches) high. Their motifs are taken from Buddhist ethical texts. During construction, the monument threatened to collapse. The basement was later shored up with a second layer of stone, a wide terrace measuring 113 meters (370 feet) on each side. This covered the reliefs, and even today, only a few, specially uncovered, are exposed for viewing.

From the basement, five square terraces rise in balustraded galleries, representing the world of form above the world of desire. The inner and outer walls at each level are covered with beautifully carved panels, illustrating the path of enlightenment.

The first gallery is 360 meters (1,180 feet) in perimeter; above it, the others progressively diminish in size. The panels are 1 to 2 meters (3 feet, 3 inches to 6 feet, 6 inches) wide by 0.5 to 1 meter (1 foot, 8 inches to 3 feet, 3 inches) high.

Three circular terraces surmount the squares. These are open and simple, representing the realm of formlessness. Seventy-two stone stupas, 3.5 to 3.75 meters (11 feet, 6 inches to 12 feet, 4 inches) high, stand here, all carved in open lattices. The perforations on the first two circles are diamond-shaped, a form said to express change and movement. On the last terrace, they are square, expressing calm stillness. Each stupa shelters a Buddha, which becomes apparent only as the monument is ascended. From a distance, the stupas appear solid.

The temple is crowned with an enormous stupa, some 16 meters (52 feet) in diameter, containing an unfinished Buddha. Some scholars see the Buddha's incomplete state as symbolic of his formlessness;

⊖ The wide, lower terrace of Borobudur represents the earthly realm of desire. The reliefs of the square terraces represent the world of form. No reliefs are seen in the formless world of the upper, rounded terraces—only the many images of the Buddha.

GEORG GERSTER

On each of the four sides of Borobudur, the images of the Buddha display the same symbolic gesture, or "mudra". In combination with the Buddhas on the uppermost level, these represent the five celestial Buddhas. They were originally set in niches, like those seen in the upper row and in the photograph on the right.

TETTONI, CASSIO, & ASSOC./PHOTOBANK

An image of the Buddha on one of the middle terraces. In the center of the niche's arch can be seen the lion-like face of the mythical demon creature known as the *kala*, or *kirtimukha* ("face of glory"), his fearsome expression repelling all evil.

DAVID NICHOLAS GREEN/THE PHOTO LIBRARY, SYDNEY

others take the view that the original statue was stolen and the incomplete one is a replacement.

Borobudur is thought to have served a variety of purposes, being at once a visualization of doctrine for the initiate; a mandala, a design symbolizing the universe and used in meditation; and a sacred and ordered world, a center of ritual activity.

A mandala requires perfect placement of all its elements. The form most commonly identified with Borobudur is the Diamond World mandala, often associated with the Tantric Buddhism practiced in Tibet and Nepal. This interpretation depends largely on the arrangement of the smaller stupas, and the gestures of the Bodhisattva (Buddhist savior) images, but the lack of complete evidence leaves it open to question.

It is more convincing to see Borobudur as a symbolic stupa or mountain. Seen as a stupa, Borobudur represents a continuation of local custom. Stupas were originally earthen mounds topped by pillars of wood. The ashes of the Buddha were later buried under eight such stupas, built in eight of the places important in his life. As a result, the stupa has come to signify any structure that contains relics. It is also credible to interpret Borobudur as a symbolic mountain. The mountain as a sacred place occurs throughout Southeast Asian religious architecture. It may be an expression of Hinduism or Buddhism, or apply to objects of local veneration. The construction of Borobudur on a natural hill, and its blending with the surrounding landscape, confirm this.

Although the precise significance of Borobudur may never be known, some understanding of it comes from seeing the temple itself as the doctrine: Borobudur combines elements of the mountain, the mandala, and the stupa. It is these that comprise the "text".

TETTONI, CASSIO, & ASSOC./PHOTOBANK

This detail from the side of the panel at left shows three courtiers, each with a slightly different, elaborate coiffeur. The wealth of detail on the reliefs of Borobudur provides an excellent source of information about the customs of Java in the ninth century AD. The soft, naturalistic style of carving is unique to Borobudur. The faces are somewhat rounded, the eyes downcast, and the lips form a slight and gentle smile.

TETTONI, CASSIO, & ASSOC./PHOTOBANK

The majority of the relief panels of Borobudur portray episodes from the *Gandhavyuha*, an epic tale of the young Prince Sudhana's search for enlightenment. In this detail, the figure of the prince is sheltered by a royal umbrella. His elaborate headdress also sets him apart from the other figures.

LEO MEIER/AUSTRALIAN PICTURE LIBRARY

DYNASTIES IN CHINA

2000 BC – AD 220

From Early States to Nationhood

CHO-YUN HSU

THE XIA "DYNASTY" is regarded in Chinese legend as the first in a long series of "royal dynasties". In ancient times, the Xia, the Shang and the Zhou were called the Three Dynasties. Together, they are considered to be the fountainhead of Chinese culture known from later history.

In modern archaeology, the Xia period is located at the junction of the Late Neolithic period and the Early Bronze Age, about the end of the third millennium BC. Until now, the Xia have not been definitely identified among the numerous Neolithic cultures of the middle reaches of the Yellow River. Since the Xia period is mentioned in the ancient classics so frequently and so consistently, however, it is generally assumed that the Xia people lived along the middle and lower reaches of the Yellow River, especially on the northern bank. This area is a part of the great plain and plateau formed by a thick loess—a fine-grained, fertile soil deposited by wind and water. In this vast stretch of the yellow-earth plain, Neolithic people settled in farming villages. Hundreds of these sites have been excavated, yielding such items as pottery, stone artifacts, and remnants of dwellings and burials.

Fields of crops, with the Chola Mountains, in western Sichuan province, in the background. Numerous Late Neolithic cultures existed in the Sichuan basin, west of the yellow-earth plain.

This bronze wine vessel (*jue*), excavated at Erlitou, in Henan province, was cast in the Yellow River basin in the first half of the second millennium BC for members of a powerful family. Such vessels were used in sacrificial rituals that paid homage to the ancestors, and were then buried with a family member.
METROPOLITAN MUSEUM OF ART

CHINA TOURISM PHOTO LIBRARY

↑ The Yellow River winds through a heavily eroded desert landmark in Ningxia region, in northern China.

↓ A ritual bronze axe (*yue*) dating from the middle Shang period. It was found at Panlongcheng, in Hubei province, far south of the dynastic capital, and was used in the burial ceremony as a beheading instrument.
METROPOLITAN MUSEUM OF ART

The Xia culture, represented in archaeology by the Erlitou culture in Henan province, was only one of the Late Neolithic cultures that spread into the Yellow River floodplain. Beyond the yellow-earth plain, there were other cultures in the coastal area of the east, the Yangtze Valley and the Han River valley in the south, and the Sichuan basin in the west. Further afield were the Neolithic cultures in Manchuria—in the north-east highland regions below the steppe land in the north—and in the vast territory of mountainous regions in the far south and the southwest.

These cultures shared some features with the floodplain cultures, and the speed of cultural evolution was generally consistent across all cultures. Thus, it is quite possible that in a number of regions of China at that time, clusters of villages were being organized into states. However, the best records, both legendary and archaeological, of such organization are found in the middle and lower valleys of the Yellow River. Thus, from what we know, the Xia probably formed the earliest state in China.

The Formation of the First State under the Xia

According to legend, the pre-Xia male leaders were the predominant power and were regarded as "sage-kings" of the ancient "royal court", each one being chosen by his predecessor to succeed to the throne through merit. Once the new king had been installed, his predecessor voluntarily abdicated. Although there are vague references to power struggles among these sage-kings, detailed information is too meager for any conclusion to be drawn about the precise nature of this leadership. However, it is thought that a loose federation of tribes or "nations" was formed by passing the leadership from one individual to another, or from the chiefs of one participating group to those of another.

Legendary sources tell us that the Xia people changed this process. A cultural hero named Yu restored the course of the Yellow River, which had flooded, and was thus chosen to succeed to the throne of the sage-king Shun. Yu then successfully organized a rather more solid confederation of numerous "states". It is said that as many as 800 lords attended great assemblies periodically convened by Yu in various places. Yu's authority was so unchallenged that he could (and did) depose some of these lords, and even occasionally executed the most unruly ones. After Yu died, the successor he had chosen failed to command the lords' support, and the people preferred to make Yu's son the successor to the throne. This was the first "royal dynasty", so it is said, whose ruling house was made up of several generations of father–son successions.

In the case of the Xia, there was, according to legend, a change from the loose federation of participating groups to a state possessing stable and institutionalized authority. The precise extent of Xia territory, however, remains uncertain. Later traditional Chinese history projected a large, unified Chinese empire from the Xia state, and referred to the Xia as overlord of at least the entire northern part of China proper. Modern historical research and archaeology, on the other hand, place the Xia on a much more modest scale, located in the present-day provinces of southern Shanxi and western Henan.

The Xia's heyday would have been from about the end of the third millennium BC to the middle of the second millennium BC. Archaeological research has uncovered bronze tools and artifacts in the Erlitou culture sites in Henan province. Although tools and implements made of bone and shell were more commonly found than bronze pieces, the bronze culture had definitely emerged. The Erlitou culture sites have also yielded remains of large buildings on platformed foundations, and a number of such sites were partly walled in. This indicates that there was some form of urban center with public buildings, which is consistent with the existence of a state.

Cultural Advancement in the Shang Period: 1600 BC to 1100 BC

The Shang, who were part of the Xia federation of ancient "states", were originally located on the lower yellow-earth plain, east of the Xia. A large, dense distribution of Neolithic villages indicates that this area had a substantial population in the Late Neolithic period. The Shang probably founded a state not much later than the Xia,

⊖› An oracle bone from the Shang dynasty. Bones of oxen and sheep were used to communicate with the spirits of the ancestors. After a question was asked of the spirits, a hot rod was placed onto the surface of the bone and cracks appeared. These signs were "read" by the ritual leader as the answer from the gods.
BRITISH MUSEUM/ THE BRIDGEMAN ART LIBRARY

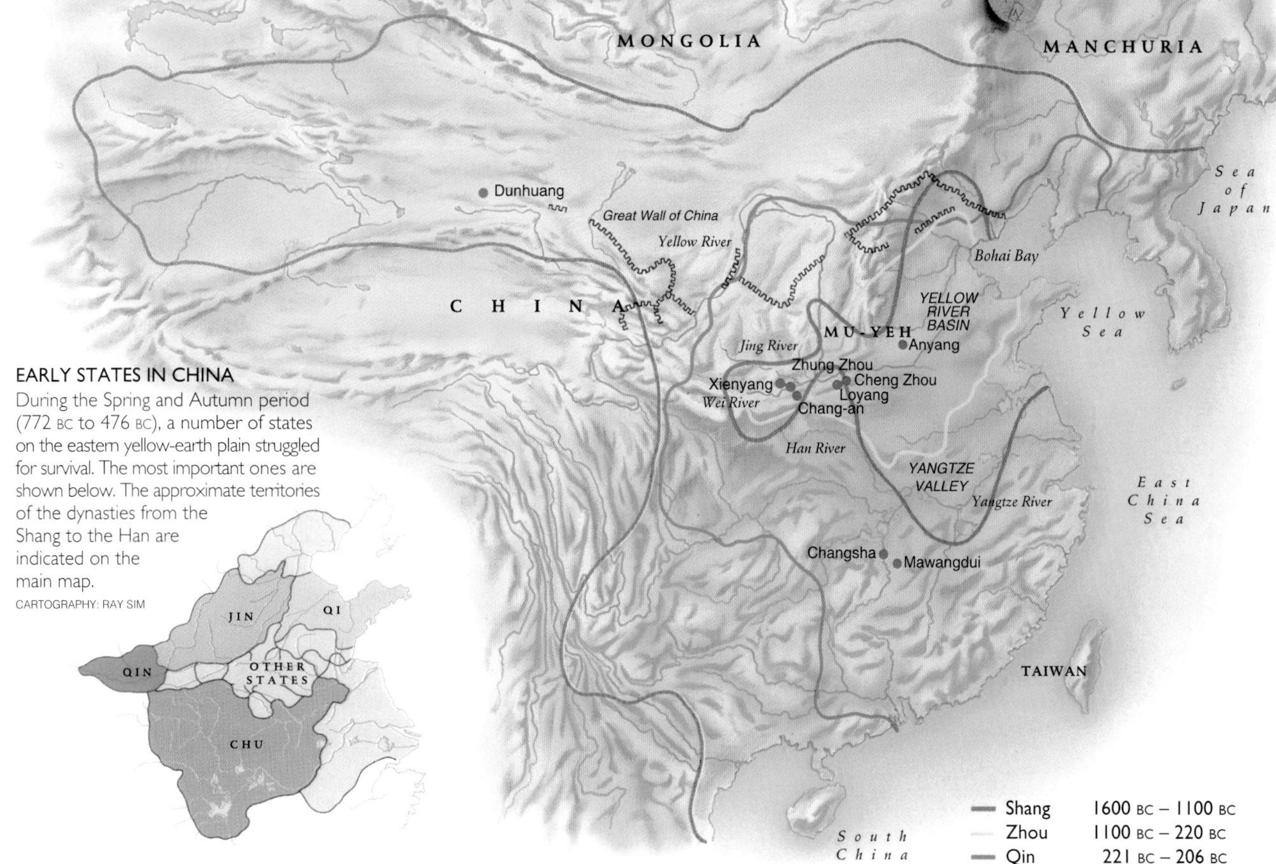

EARLY STATES IN CHINA
During the Spring and Autumn period (772 BC to 476 BC), a number of states on the eastern yellow-earth plain struggled for survival. The most important ones are shown below. The approximate territories of the dynasties from the Shang to the Han are indicated on the main map.
CARTOGRAPHY: RAY SIM

DYNASTIC CHINA: 2500 BC – AD 200

	STATE SOCIETY	INTELLECTUAL ACTIVITIES	CULTURE AND TECHNOLOGY
200	Three kingdoms Development of the South Invasion of foreign tribes	Taoist religion Spread of Buddhism	Advancement of sciences
AD 1	Eastern Han	Imperial Academy established Confucianism challenged Buddhism introduced	Invention of paper
200	Western Han Unified empire Consolidation of China Qin unification	Confucianism as orthodoxy	Civil examinations Silk Road Great Wall built
250	Bureaucratic government Imperial despotism		Highway network constructed
500	Warring States period Reorganization of states	Major schools of thought develop	Rapid social changes: commercialization and urbanization; development of free private land tenure; metal coins appear
800	Eastern Zhou Spring and Autumn period Multistate system	Confucianism Concept of mandate of heaven	Technological improvements in agriculture, irrigation, and manufacturing Use of iron
1000	Feudalism Western Zhou		
1500	Fully developed state Shang		Development of metallurgy Oracle-bone inscriptions Writing system appears Bronze culture War chariot appears
2000	Xia Formation of state		
BC 2500			Late Neolithic cultures

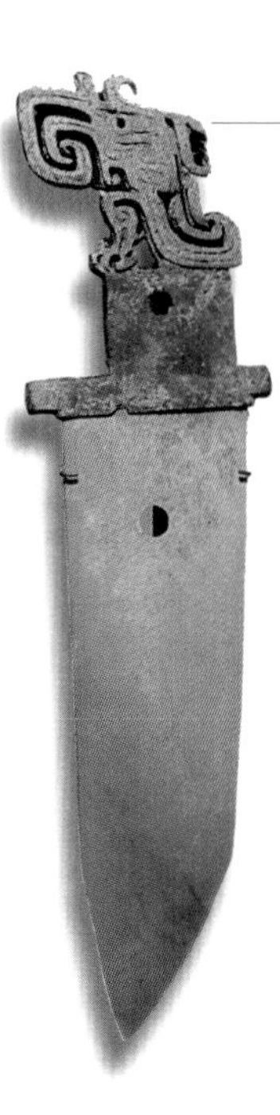

A jade and bronze halberd (ge) from the mid-second millennium BC, excavated in 1974 at Panlongchen, in Hubei province. This type of weapon, cast in bronze, was the most characteristic weapon of the Bronze Age. The blade in this example was delicately carved from a single piece of jade, and was too large and fragile for practical use. It was probably used only as a burial object.
RONALD SHERIDAN/ANCIENT ART & ARCHITECTURE COLLECTION

and had been an important power dominating the eastern plain ever since the Xia established their overlordship.

Since the 1920s, archaeologists have excavated several Shang city sites—including one of the capitals, Anyang—and hundreds of settlements and burial sites. The Shang sites were often located in the river valleys on the floodplain. Thanks to abundant archaeological finds from the Shang period—particularly some especially revealing written records from Anyang—we have much more material on the Shang culture than on the Xia. Not only do these records provide more information about Shang life than is available from conventional historical sources; they also confirm many of the legends about Shang history.

The appearance of a developed writing system, by about the seventeenth century BC, is of great historical significance. The Shang records, called oracle-bone inscriptions, consist of predictions about future events recorded on turtle shells or animal bones. The writing system was a prototype of modern written Chinese. The basic units are characters formed from a combination of ideograms (pictures that depict an object or concept) and phonetic elements. There are about 5,000 such characters in the Shang texts, a large number of which can be transcribed into present-day forms and deciphered. The sentence structure found in the Shang texts resembles that of classical Chinese, and is slightly different from the modern structure.

The oracle-bone inscriptions contain a variety of information about the life of the Shang ruling class, including details of ceremonies, rituals, warfare, administration, weather, disease and medicine, hunting, and routine predictions of fortunes every 10 days.

The Shang Take Power

The Shang took over from the Xia as the leading power on the yellow-earth plain in the second millennium BC. The core area of the Shang's dominance seems to have been in the eastern part of today's Henan province and in the southwest of Hebei province. Until the fifteenth century BC, the Shang capital, for some unknown reason, moved from one place to another four times. Finally, Anyang seems to have been the Shang capital for about two centuries. Anyang was certainly the center of the Shang's activities, even though its function was possibly ceremonial and ritualistic rather than political and military.

The Shang state structure appears to have been more complicated than the Xia model. The Shang ruling house was surnamed Zi, and used as its emblem a character resembling an infant with raised arms. There were several branches on the Zi family tree, all of which used a modified version of the principal ruling house's emblem. Thus, the Shang ruling class probably regarded themselves as members of a hierarchically arranged kinship network, sharing the same ancestry and therefore the same identity. The non-Zi people were perhaps subjects of the Zi groups or may even have been in servitude to them. There were also less important lineages, which bore other surnames, and it seems likely that some of these were associated with the Zi through alliances, marriages, or conquest. The Shang state was, therefore, organized by means of a network of various lineages. This type of social structure is characteristic of a chiefdom, consisting of one dominant tribe and a number of lesser groups.

Apart from the fact that their royal authority had yet to be firmly consolidated, the early history of the Shang is by no means clear. After they had settled at Anyang, the state continued to be governed by a hierarchy of social networks. The king and his court resided in the Great City of Shang (Anyang), while other members of the Zi family—headed by generals, princes, or even queens—were scattered within the kingdom of the Shang. As the Shang expanded the territory under their control, other subordinate groups—known as *hou* states (marquisates)—were formed around the Shang people. These groups would respond to the Shang's call for support in their military campaigns against unfriendly states beyond the *hou* territory. Some of these states may have become the Shang's satellites, while others may have continued to resist Shang dominance. Some would no doubt have alternated between these two responses. The Shang retained their supremacy only by periodic displays of force. Their sphere of influence seems to have extended as far as the present-day Shanxi province in the west, the coastal region around Bohai Bay in the east, and the transitional zone between the steppe land in the north and China proper.

Shang royal authority appears to have evolved gradually towards a strong monarchy. By about 1200 BC, the last king of the Shang had even proclaimed himself to be the human counterpart of a supreme god. The kings—who had once been served by royal relatives and domestic servants—now had a government consisting of departments with separate functions, and the former *hou* states were turned into provinces supervised by personnel dispatched from the royal court.

Shang Social Structure

The Shang possessed a sizeable army of archer-warriors, who rode in war chariots accompanied by foot soldiers armed with halberds. The foot soldiers were recruited in the thousands or five thousands from provinces governed by princes and royal agents. It appears that these soldiers were also the farmers who were the mainstay of the Shang farming population. At the lower end of the social scale were the slaves, most likely captured in war from tribes known to the Shang by such descriptions as "the numerous shepherds" and "the numerous horse-breeders".

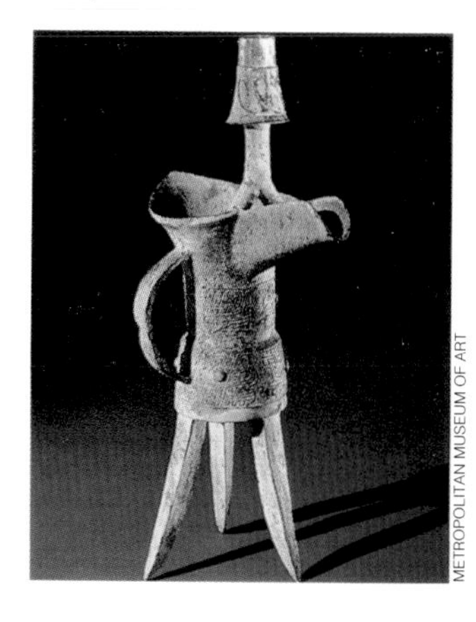

METROPOLITAN MUSEUM OF ART

↑ A Shang bronze ritual wine vessel (*jue*) dating from the fifteenth to fourteenth centuries BC, found in Anhui province.

↓ This square bronze wine vessel (*fang lei*) from the Anyang period (about 1300 BC to 1100 BC) was cast for the Shang aristocracy. It is decorated with a large *taotie*, or animal mask, on the center of each side, which may signify the Shang clan.

METROPOLITAN MUSEUM OF ART

E.T. ARCHIVE

A ritual bronze vessel (*ding*) from the Anyang period. This vessel, which is very typical of the period, was used for storing sacrificial meat.

The arrangement of royal tombs vividly reveals the relative status of the various groups. Around the royal coffin, in the central burial chamber, are women and men who were to be the royal companions in the other world. Along the steps of a long ramp is a line of fully armed warriors in a half-kneeling position. Each royal tomb was built upon tightly pounded earthen foundations in which were buried several hundred beheaded bodies of people who had perhaps been used as slaves to build the mausoleum. The entire mausoleum area is surrounded by burial pits in each of which are 10 soldiers and a sergeant. There are also numerous war chariots buried in the pits with horses. Thus, Shang kings obviously had the power of life and death over their subjects.

Shang State Religion

The Shang's faith was shamanism. The *Wu*—who were seers, medicine men, and sorcerers—and their associates—the diviners (people who told fortunes or predicted the future)—were the mediums between the supernatural world and the human world. They also served as scribes and clerks, ceremonial dancers, musicians, and even high-ranking officials. Moreover, they were prototype intellectuals, who could not only write and keep accounts, but who were also archivists and historians. Because the cosmos of shamans is full of spirits of all kinds, the Shang state religion was mainly concerned with offering food and entertainment to male and female ancestors of the ruling house; to deceased great men; and to the deities of the mountains, water, rivers, wind, and stars. Since the ceremonies and rituals were of great significance to Shang life, the archaeological finds excavated at the capital at Anyang reflect these functions, rather than administrative ones.

Material Culture

The sophistication of Shang material culture is quite impressive. The long tradition of Neolithic pottery provided the Shang with the foundation for producing pottery fired in kilns. And it was upon that same foundation that the Shang bronze culture was developed. West Asian bronze culture antedates the Shang bronze culture by at least a thousand years, and it may reasonably be assumed that the ancient peoples of China learned

A bronze ritual vessel, called the Fu Hao *fang ding*, from a tomb of the Anyang period. The deceased was Fu Hao, a consort of the third king at Anyang. Her name is inscribed inside on the base of the vessel.
METROPOLITAN MUSEUM OF ART

A bronze axe (*yue*) from the late Shang period. This kind of weapon was used for beheading at burial ceremonies.
ART RESOURCE

about making bronze alloy in the vast trans-Asian steppe land in North and central Asia. It was there that the technology of the ancient Chinese bronze industry was later developed. Shang bronze vessels are fine, ritualistic pieces that symbolize the authority of the Shang state. The abundance of bronze weapons, tools, and other artifacts discovered in various Shang sites indicates that the Shang had control of, and created, great wealth.

Shang cultural influences seem to have extended far more widely than Shang political power, to areas as far south as the provinces of Guangxi and Guangdong; and Shang-styled pottery and bronzes have been found as far north as western Manchuria.

To their successors, the Zhou, the Shang bequeathed a solid cultural foundation in northern China and political experience that would consolidate the structure of an effective state.

The Zhou Period: 1100 BC to 220 BC

The Zhou were one of the satellite states in the Shang sphere of influence, although the Zhou people were perhaps originally related to the Xia ethnically and culturally. They may have lived initially in the southwest of present-day Shanxi province, the old home of the Xia. Following a rather winding path of migration, the Zhou seem to have been in contact with peoples in the northern steppe land until they finally settled in the valley of the Jing-Wei River, in present-day Shanxi province. In their new home, they established a close relationship with the Chiang people to the west.

From the Jing-Wei River valley, the Zhou gradually expanded eastwards towards the yellow-earth plain, and came into contact with the Shang. The relationship between the two fluctuated between friendly relations and war. The Shang were a major power, and the Zhou were caught in their network of states. During the last 50 years of Shang domination, however, the Zhou maneuvered to build an alliance of lesser states that half surrounded the Shang in the south and the west. In the meantime, the last kings of the Shang had exhausted their resources by engaging in costly foreign wars and expeditions. Their armies no longer had the morale to fight, and they were finally defeated by the Zhou in a showdown at Mu-yeh to which the Zhou had committed their full military might. Thus did a minor neighbor state succeed in destroying the most powerful state in ancient China.

Having inherited the Shang's network of states, the Zhou organized a new interstate order. Princes of the Zhou royal house and their close allies, particularly leaders of the Chiang, were dispatched to set up garrison states on the eastern plain. An eastern capital, Cheng Zhou, was established in Shang territory. Because of a shortage of labor, the Zhou had to seek the collaboration of the Shang people. Consequently, a Shang prince continued to rule part of the original Shang kingdom, and the Shang troops who had surrendered to the Zhou were stationed alongside the Zhou forces to guard the garrison states. The Zhou feudalistic network was reinforced by matrimonial ties between Zhou–Chiang feudal lords, Shang leaders, and native leaders of the newly conquered land. Similarly, Zhou children were linked together by a bond of kinship that formed a gigantic Zhou lineage system.

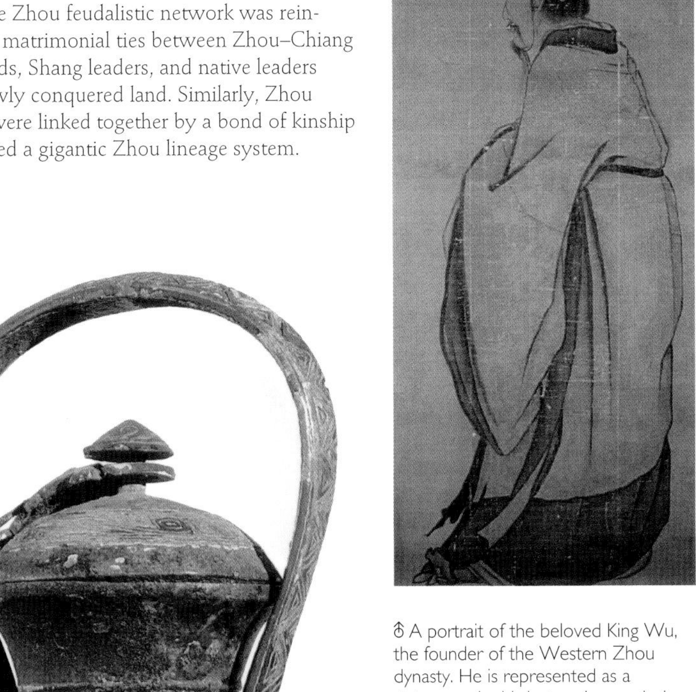

E.T. ARCHIVE

A portrait of the beloved King Wu, the founder of the Western Zhou dynasty. He is represented as a statesman, by his hat, and as a scholar, by his robe, denoting the high esteem in which he was held in the early nineteenth century, when this portrait was painted.

The bronze lid of a ritual wine vessel, from the early Western Zhou dynasty (tenth to eleventh centuries BC). On the surface of this piece is the *taotie*, or animal mask—used here, presumably, to pay homage to the already defeated, but honorable, Shang people.

C.M. DIXON

A bronze ritual vessel called a *you*, from the royal tomb at Anyang. This type of wine bucket appeared in the late Shang dynasty and had disappeared by 900 BC. Its tall and slender form suggests that it dates from about 1100 BC.

GIRAUDON/ART RESOURCE

Kinship Networks and Religion

The Zhou thus forged a dual network of both kinship and feudal ties, which encompassed the vast territory of the Yellow River floodplain and formed a much stronger political bloc than the Shang had ever formed. It was the Zhou's open-mindedness, evidenced by a willingness to accept and share power with non-Zhou leaders—even those of their former enemies—that allowed such a network to function. The garrison states became vassal states, and in a typical one, there were often three ethnic and cultural groups—the Zhou nobility, the Shang elites, and the leaders of the people subjugated by the Zhou—all of whom were bound to each other by a network of matrimonial and kinship ties. The Zhou king, with his supremacy as patriarch of the Zhou kinship network and overlord of the feudal pyramid, occupied a pivotal position.

In the Zhou state religion, with its worship of ancestors and a multitude of natural forces, the heavenly god was regarded as the supreme deity. The Zhou believed that they had received the heavenly mandate to rule the world "under heaven", and that this mandate was bestowed upon them—and upon them alone—because they were worthy, the Shang leaders having lost the mandate through their failure to lead a decent life and to behave morally. This was the first time in Chinese history that a supreme god was believed to have passed judgment on human conduct explicitly in accordance with a moral criterion. The Zhou concept of a moral god was a major departure from the notion of a tribal god, and represents a breakthrough that paved the way for the development of the concept of universal moral standards. This new consciousness of a moral god probably provided the Zhou with the legitimacy necessary for developing a claim for universalism; while the coexistence of various groups within the Zhou feudal network helped to create the common identity that was the foundation of a Chinese nation.

The Zhou Are Weakened

In the reigns of at least the first three kings, further feudalization consolidated the Zhou system, and the Zhou continued to expand towards the Yangtze Valley. Their confrontations with northern neighbors along the steppe land, however, were far from successful. Finally, the kingdom of the Zhou, which was directly exposed to the pressure of tribes in the north and the northwest, was lost to the mostly peaceful penetration of non-Zhou peoples, who for several generations had migrated into the core royal domain. The Zhou were weakened not only by defeat in military campaigns against the northern tribes, but also by the heavy burden of maintaining a large defense force recruited from the eastern vassal states, and by the depletion of resources caused by the royal court's continuous parceling out of land to create new vassal states for royal relatives. In 773 BC, the last Zhou king was killed by a coalition of Zhou rebels and non-Zhou tribes within the royal domain. However, the so-called Zhou period proper lasted until 220 BC.

The crown prince of the Zhou fled to Cheng Zhou, the eastern capital, where a new court was established. However, the Eastern Zhou—so named to distinguish them from the court that had reigned in the old royal capital in the west, Zhung Zhou—were never able to hold the original Zhou system together. The Zhou elements of the vassal states, having been localized to their assigned land for centuries, had their own interests to look after. From then on, they merely accorded the Eastern Zhou court nominal recognition of its royal status, while they strove to shape a new multistate system. The centuries that witnessed such a transition are known as the Spring and Autumn period (from 772 BC to 476 BC)—which is named after a chronicle of the early period of the Eastern Zhou—and the Warring States period (from 475 BC to 220 BC)—collectively known as the Eastern Zhou period.

The Spring and Autumn Period

During the Spring and Autumn period, the former vassal states on the eastern yellow-earth plain struggled for survival. Often one state established dominance over the others. The pretext for doing so was to enable the Eastern Zhou states to form an alliance to ward off the threat from the non-Zhou peoples, among whom the most noteworthy was a southern state, Chu, which had developed in the Yangtze Valley during the early Spring and Autumn period. The struggles for supremacy among the states first took place in the central part of the eastern yellow-earth plain. No sooner had the central states exhausted each other, than neighboring states that had much land in which to expand entered the fray. The number of contending states was reduced to no more than four or five major ones, plus a dozen or so minor ones. The most important states were Jin in the north and the central area; Qi on the east coast; Chu in the south—that is, the Yangtze Valley—and Qin in the west, the former Zhou western domain. Cultural exchanges blurred the differences between the Zhou and the non-Zhou: the Chu and Qin became part of the world of Zhou China, while Jin and Qi substantially absorbed non-Zhou elements in the north and east respectively.

Opposite: A bronze ritual vessel called the Qi Hou *yu*, from the Eastern Zhou period (sixth century BC). This large food container bears an inscription inside, suggesting that it was made on the occasion of a marriage contract between Qi and the royal Zhou clan.

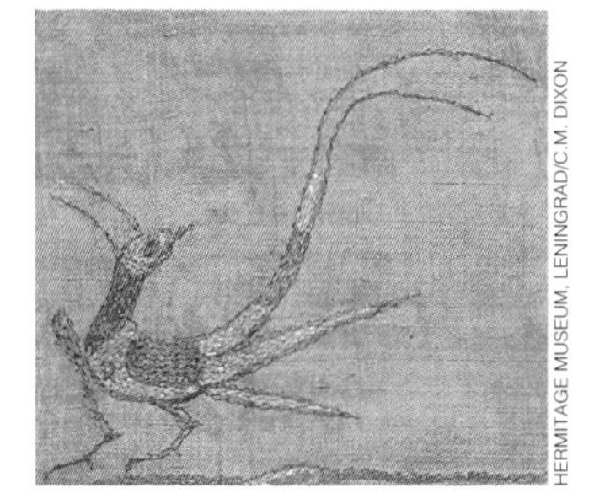

HERMITAGE MUSEUM, LENINGRAD/C.M. DIXON

A detail of an embroidered tussah silk representing a phoenix, dated to between the fifth and sixth centuries BC.

This terracotta figure of a kneeling woman from the Qin dynasty was found near the outer wall of the mausoleum of the First Emperor of Qin.

NATIONAL MUSEUM, BEIJING/ERIC LESSING/ART RESOURCE

THE TOMB OF THE FIRST EMPEROR OF THE QIN EMPIRE

KATHERYN M. LINDUFF

The imperial tomb of Qin Shi Huang (259 BC to 210 BC), the first emperor of China and founder of the short-lived Qin dynasty (221 BC to 206 BC), lies 35 kilometers (20 miles) east of the city of Xi'an, in Shaanxi province. The tomb took 36 years to build, and the mausoleum was part of the lavish construction program that characterized the emperor's reign.

Emperor Qin Shi Huang was a man of remarkable talents and achievements. His military conquests were partly the result of a superb mastery of the newest arts of war, such as the use of chariots and mounted soldiers and long spears and swords. He abolished the feudal system, and created a form of centralized, autocratic government, which was essentially maintained until the fall of the last Chinese dynasty in the twentieth century AD. He promulgated a uniform law code. He standardized currency, weights, and measures; the written language; and the axle length of wagons and chariots. He built a vast network of tree-lined roads, 50 paces (about 15 meters/50 feet) wide, radiating from the Qin capital at Xianyang, 30 kilometers (18 miles) northwest of Xi'an. He joined the separate walls created by the earlier northern states, built to deter raiding tribes from the north, into a single 3,000 kilometer (1,850 mile) "Great Wall".

He had a number of elaborate palaces constructed for his own glorification. Although the entire mausoleum is still to be explored and excavated, we know from written records that it was an underground palace complex—the tomb chamber ceiling was a model of the heavens, and the floor was a map of the empire.

In March 1974, the first fragments of what turned out to be terracotta warriors and horses were identified as dating from the Qin dynasty. Three large pits have been excavated to date, and thousands of life-sized clay figures and horses have been unearthed. In December 1980, a pair of bronze four-horse chariots, each with a charioteer, was found at the same site.

METROPOLITAN MUSEUM OF ART

A painted terracotta warrior from the tomb-pit of the First Emperor of the Qin dynasty, in Lintong, Shaanxi province, dating from about 210 BC. It formed part of the battalion guarding the emperor after his death.

A painted terracotta charioteer from the area of the tomb of the First Qin Emperor. This life-sized standing figure was found with a total of about 6,000 figures of men and horses, with their chariots, in a pit to the east of the emperor's tomb.

METROPOLITAN MUSEUM OF ART

JOHN LEE/STOCK HOUSE

Rows of life-sized, terracotta warriors flanking the tomb of the emperor were revealed in the course of excavations in Lintong, Shaanxi province.

CULTURAL RELICS PUBLISHING HOUSE

An excavation pit at the tomb of the First Emperor, which contained thousands of terracotta warriors dating from about 210 BC.

The great underground terrcotta army represents the First Emperor's imperial guard, which was stationed to the east of the capital during his lifetime. The entire pit evokes the military might and spirit that secured Qin authority to rule a unified China. The practice of placing clay figures in the tomb replaced the habit of sacrificing people and animals.

There is great variety in the terracotta warriors' dress, facial expressions, hairstyles, headgear, armor, weapons, and vehicles. These detailed, realistic renderings of the military offer graphic evidence of the might and majesty of imperial life in the third century BC, as well as being the first examples of the artistic and cultural values of the emperor.

One of a pair of chariots and charioteers discovered in 1980 in a pit to the west of the tomb of the First Emperor. Made of gilded cast-bronze with silver inlay, they are one-third life size.
CULTURAL RELICS PUBLISHING HOUSE

Life-sized pottery figures of a horse and cavalryman from the tomb-pit of the First Emperor of Qin. Each figure is individually fashioned. The figures and horses were originally painted and outfitted with metal weapons or trappings.

METROPOLITAN MUSEUM OF ART

PHOTOGRAPHIE GIRAUDON

This early nineteenth-century engraving depicts a scene from the life of Confucius (Kung Fu-tzu) and his disciples.

Bronze coins in the shape of a knife (top) from the state of Qi, and a hoe from the state of Zhao, in North China, from the Warring States period. During this period, states developed independently, and coined their own money.

C.M. DIXON

The Warring States Period

The Warring States period witnessed the second phase of the struggle for a new order. The Jin was broken up into three states, while most of the leaders of the other major states were overthrown and replaced by new rulers. None of these states paid even lip service to the remnant of the Zhou royal court, and each of the ruling houses of the principal contending states proclaimed itself the titular king. The major states had by now increased in number, and at least seven engaged in ceaseless wars, forming alliances and counter-alliances. Finally, in the third century BC, the Qin, the least wealthy and least civilized of the seven states, spent about 50 years (the reigns of three kings) defeating the six other states. The king of Qin proclaimed himself emperor in 222 BC.

Although the Spring and Autumn period and the Warring States period were marked by constant warfare, China experienced changes in every aspect of life. The Zhou feudal structure was gradually destroyed. For the purpose of mobilizing resources effectively, the Qin states and the former vassal states were transformed into monarchical states, served by a civilian government bureaucracy and an army of professional soldiers. The aristocracy gave way to bureaucrats recruited from among intellectuals who had been educated by members of the former elite. These intellectuals—among whom were Confucius (Kung Fu-tzu), Mencius (Meng-tzu), Laotzu, Mo-tzu, Chuang-tzu, and Hsun-tzu—not only trained other intellectuals, but, what is more significant, also developed schools of thought that redefined the fundamental premises of Chinese culture. The most important ones were Confucianism, which taught humanism, and Taoism, which taught individualism. Debates on politics and social relationships were common among many intellectuals, and thus, these issues, which had existed since the time of the Eastern Zhou, remained central to Chinese civilization.

During these two periods, bronze was gradually replaced by iron for tools, implements, and weapons. Technological improvements took place in agriculture, irrigation, and manufacturing. A trend towards commercialization and urbanization was evident throughout the Spring and Autumn period and accelerated in the Warring States period, perhaps because of the increasingly frequent communication, and exchange of ideas and materials among the various regions. Free, private land tenure and a monetary economy resulted from all these changes.

The Eastern Zhou period was characterized by dramatic changes, being marked by political turmoil, social mobility—both for members of the feudal system and for commoners—and economic revolution. All these changes occurred rapidly and simultaneously, at a pace that accelerated throughout the 500 years or so of the period. It was a time during which people suffered war and upheaval, yet it also witnessed the most important cultural breakthroughs in Chinese history.

The Rise of the Ancient Empire: 221 BC to AD 220

The Qin's unification of China ushered in a long line of imperial dynasties. The multistate system of the Eastern Zhou period was over, and a single empire, held together by one culture, prevailed for more than 2,000 years. From the Qin, China acquired its name in Western languages.

Under the energetic leadership of the First Emperor of Qin, all the states that existed during the Warring States period were turned into provinces ruled by governors dispatched from the imperial court. A military commandant and an imperial inspector, who supervised officials, were also assigned to each province. Consequently, it was not possible at the provincial level to challenge the supremacy of imperial authority. Laws and writing systems were standardized, and intellectuals were forbidden to criticize policies or to discuss theoretical issues. Only matters of practical value, such as agriculture, horticulture, and medicine, were allowed to be taught by experts; otherwise, the local bureaucrats provided students with the skills and knowledge needed for the civil service.

A jade statuette of Laotzu, the reputed founder of Taoism, sitting on a water buffalo.
ANCIENT ART & ARCHITECTURE COLLECTION

The Great Wall Is Built

To keep China secure from foreign invasion, the First Emperor ordered the defensive networks built by the individual states in the Warring States period to be linked together into a Great Wall—a long stretch of walls and forts, guarded by 500,000 soldiers. Large numbers of troops were deployed along routes and canals leading to the mountainous region in the south. In addition, a network of highways was built to link all parts of China to the capital, Xianyang, in present-day Shaanxi province, and to each other in order to facilitate deployment of the imperial army. The First Emperor also had an imperial mausoleum built for himself near the capital. It is said that 700,000 conscripted laborers were put to work on making a mound that was filled with treasures guarded by terracotta soldiers. (See the feature *The Tomb of the First Emperor of the Qin Empire.*) All these costly projects demanded enormous labor power, and the whole country was subjected to heavy demands for unpaid vassal labor. To make matters worse, harsh punishment was meted out to those who failed to report for work or who were late in doing so.

In 210 BC, the First Emperor died. There were rebellions throughout the empire, and after about five years of civil war, the Qin were overthrown. Liu Ban, a commoner who had led peasant rebels against the Qin, then established a new dynasty, the Han, which lasted 400 years.

BRITISH MUSEUM/E.T. ARCHIVE

The Han Empire: 206 BC to AD 220

The Han inherited from the Qin their basic government structure, although they partly restored feudalism by setting up vassal states scattered in the provinces. After rebellions by some of these states, the Han required all vassal states to be governed by appointed officials, and thus, China was once again an empire ruled by one monarch.

In the early Han period, there was a general attitude of laissez-faire, which was a reaction against Qin despotism. As a result, productivity was rapidly restored, the population increased, and China experienced unprecedented prosperity. In early Han burials, as archaeological discoveries testify, even minor aristocrats had astonishingly rich treasures. (See the feature *The Tomb of Lady Dai.*)

The Han not only inherited the Qin government structure, but also made significant adjustments to it. The upper echelons of the Qin government had been an efficient civil service staffed by professional bureaucrats, but there was no mechanism for the recruitment of talent, or for the exchange of information between state and society. Beginning in the second century BC,

Ritual jade items. From the top: a fish pendant; a *bi*, or ring, symbolizing heaven; a scabbard chape; and a pair of ornaments in the shape of cicadas, which symbolized immortality.
ART RESOURCE

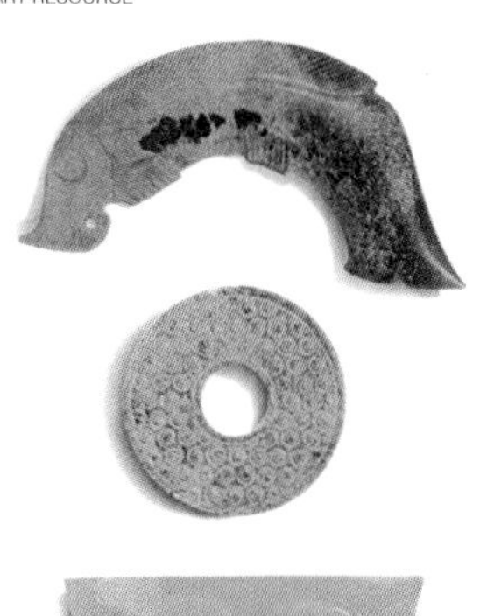

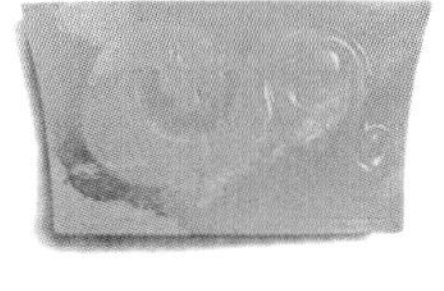

This ceramic model of a sheep pen dates from the late Eastern Han dynasty. Models of painted clay were often buried with landowners to provide the deceased with wealth beyond death.

D. & J. HEATON/STOCK HOUSE

therefore, the Han gradually developed a system for recruiting intellectuals from the local grass roots into government service. Usually, the role of these recruits was to report to the government on local conditions and to explain government policies to their compatriots.

Meanwhile, Confucianism was made an orthodoxy. Since it was the only subject taught in the Imperial Academy, Confucian ideology dominated the Han bureaucracy. Confucianism is not a religion, however, and so a church–state division did not exist. The Confucian emphasis on humanism, meritocracy, the individual's social responsibility, and collective security—especially solidarity with kinship groups—stabilized the relationship between state and society, and struck a balance between an absolute monarchy and the welfare of the people, while providing a check against wrongdoing by the monarchy.

A ceramic jar from the Eastern Han dynasty. The ceramic industry greatly expanded and diversified during the Han period. This example is of protoporcelain, and prefigures the sophistication of later potters in producing fine, thin-walled porcelains.
SOTHEBY'S LONDON/THE BRIDGEMAN ART LIBRARY

A gilt-bronze lamp from the Western Han dynasty, excavated from the tomb of Empress Dowager Dou, in Mancheng, Hebei province.
METROPOLITAN MUSEUM OF ART

Part of the Great Wall at Baodeling. Long sections of the wall were constructed during the reign of the First Emperor of Qin, in the third century BC. The Qin emperor built the wall in order to set the boundaries of China and to keep the nomads out.

THE TOMB OF LADY DAI

Katheryn M. Linduff

Four kilometers (about 2 miles) east of the city of Changsha, a major city in the central Yangtze Valley, lies a small hill known as Mawangdui. Excavation work at this site began in 1972, when construction of a hospital on the adjacent land revealed evidence of ancient ruins. These were thoroughly investigated, and in what turned out to be a burial ground, archaeologists made some of the most spectacular finds seen in the People's Republic of China in recent years.

The first tomb opened at Mawangdui, now known as Han Tomb no. 1, contained the well-preserved remains of a noblewoman who died some time after the middle of the second century BC, during the period of the Western Han dynasty (from 206 BC to 8 AD). In addition to the corpse, the tomb chamber contained more than a thousand objects, including a large funerary banner of silk painted with multicolored scenes; clothing; food; a large amount of lacquerware retaining its original brilliant coloring; 4 unusually decorated coffins; and more than 100 wooden tomb figures. The identity of the woman is still somewhat uncertain, but she is probably the wife of Li Cang, known as Xin or Xinzhiou, the first Marquis of Dai. Sima Qian, the great historian of the Han dynasty, placed the death of Li Cang at 186 BC. Since Lady Dai's tomb is later than his, she must have died in about 150 BC. Two other tombs have been excavated at the same mound: those of her husband (Tomb no. 2) and her son (Tomb no. 3). All were richly furnished with goods appropriate to a family of noble rank.

CULTURAL RELICS PUBLISHING HOUSE

A detail from the funerary banner, or *feiyi*, from Tomb no. I at Mawangdui, depicting the land of the immortals. The banner is the earliest polychrome painting on silk known from China. The elaborate design is still quite well preserved.

Two painted and lacquered wooden coffins from Tomb no. I at Mawangdui. Four coffins were nested inside the tomb of Lady Dai, the wife of the last Chu governor of the region, Li Cang.
CULTURAL RELICS PUBLISHING HOUSE

Tomb Construction

Tomb no. 1 is located in an oblong pit measuring 20 meters (65 feet) from north to south, and 17.5 meters (about 60 feet) from east to west. The tomb extends for 20 meters (65 feet) from the top of the covering mound to the bottom of the shaft. The excavators built four steps to access the crypt; a slanted wall led to the tomb chamber itself. The tomb was oriented towards the north, and arranged so that the corpse would lie with its head to the north.

The crypt contained a tomb chamber constructed of large cypress planks, the largest of which are 5 meters (about 16 feet) long and weigh almost 1,500 kilograms (more than 3 tons). Mortise and tenon construction was used throughout the chamber. Inside lay four coffins, snugly fitted one inside the other. The compartments between the tomb chamber and the outer wall of the crypt are divided into four sections, and contain most of the tomb furnishings.

The large northern section was draped with silk cloth and contained a considerable number of wooden figures—including several fully attired in ceremonial dress—as well as platters of food. When it was opened, this northern section was found to contain a liquid consisting of mercury and various acidic organic compounds. The purpose of these substances is not clear.

In the western section were plaited bamboo boxes and baskets—containing food, many kinds of herbs, clothing, and bolts of silk and cotton—and musical instruments. The instruments included a type of zither with 25 strings (*sê*); a type of mouth organ with 22 pipes in 2 rows (*yü*); and 12 pitch pipes (*yü lü*), inscribed with the names of the scales of ancient Chinese music.

The eastern section contained more figurines and a complete inventory of the tomb contents written on bamboo strips.

The southern section was filled with lacquer vessels, and the northern section also contained utilitarian implements of all sorts, such as chopsticks and eating bowls, as well as figurines. Some implements were cast-bronze copies of official ritual vessels from previous periods, which were dedicated to ancestors or to officials in commemoration of deeds well done. In accordance with the decrees of Emperor Wen, who reigned from 179 BC to 156 BC, the tomb contained no precious metals, jade, or jewelry.

A layer of charcoal 1.4 to 1.5 meters (4 feet, 7 inches to 5 feet) thick was placed outside the tomb chamber, and the space between the charcoal and the crypt wall was filled with a layer of fine white clay at least a meter (about 3 feet) wide. The marvelous preservation of the tomb and its contents can be attributed to this combination of materials, which kept out moisture and oxygen. The practice of using white clay and charcoal to surround a burial chamber is associated with the local Chu culture. In other parts of China during the Han dynasty, tombs were constructed in a different way. The tombs at Mawangdui clearly point to the continuation of the strong cultural tradition of the Chu state, which had ceased to be a political entity in 223 BC. The early part of the Western Han dynasty was obviously a period when accepted practice in such matters as burial regulations varied widely.

A Flying Garment

The large silk banner found in Tomb no. 1 (a similar example was found in Tomb no. 3) is described in the inventory as a "flying garment" *(feiyi)*. Its placement in the tomb corresponds to the prescribed location for funerary banners *(ming-ching)* displayed during funeral ceremonies and carried in the funeral procession, as described in classical literary sources from the Han period.

The banner from Tomb no. 1 has a painted red field on which an elaborate design was painted in heavy colors, which are still quite well preserved. The cross arm of the T-shaped banner is just under a meter (3 feet) long, the overall height is just over 2 meters (6 feet, 8 inches), and the width at the bottom is 48 centimeters (just under 2 feet). Tassels extend from the four lower corners.

Numerous scholars have tried to decipher the iconography of the scenes depicted on the *feiyi*. It is generally agreed that the scenes represent the conducting of the souls of the dead to the realm of the immortals. The search for immortality was of the utmost concern during the Han dynasty, and this funerary banner is the first example found that illustrates visually, and quite literally, the route of the soul (or souls).

The painting on the banner is divided into three sections. The lower section represents the subterranean region; the middle section, the largest, represents the habitat of human beings on Earth; and the upper section represents the land of the immortals, including the sun and moon. The guiding principles for understanding the painting seem to come from a genuine piece of Chu literature called the *Chuji*, or the *Songs of the South*, which says that the voyage of the souls after death leads in all directions to the four quarters of the universe, as well as above and below. The banner charts that voyage.

At the bottom is the land of the netherworld, a place of water creatures and of darkness below the surface of the Earth, where souls undergo their first metamorphosis. This is the place that the Taoists call the cosmic womb, where the spirit represented by the *yin* symbols of female creation dwells. It is a place of eternal darkness, with water in its deepest section.

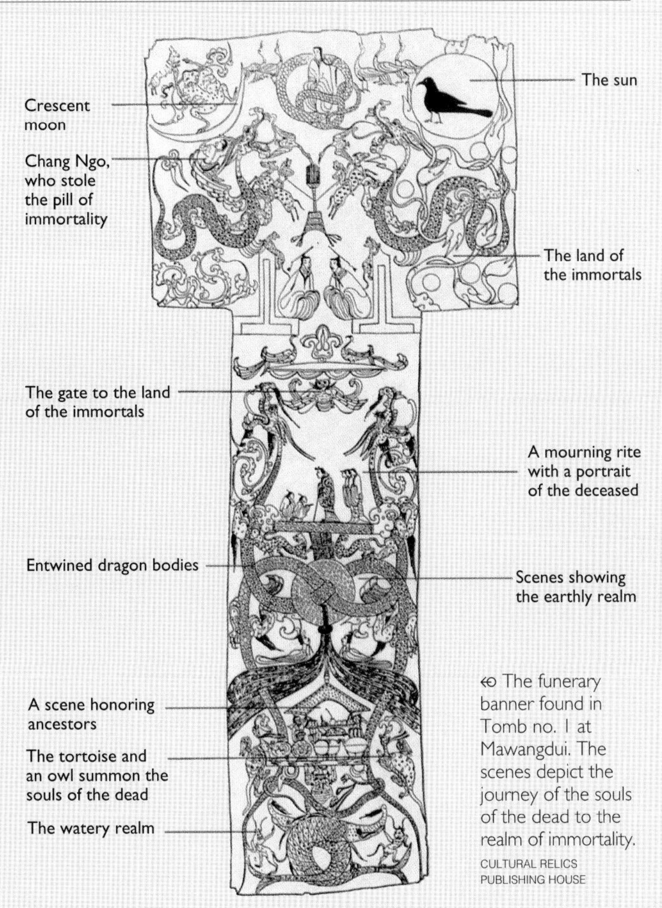

⇐ The funerary banner found in Tomb no. 1 at Mawangdui. The scenes depict the journey of the souls of the dead to the realm of immortality.
CULTURAL RELICS PUBLISHING HOUSE

Above the watery realm are depicted two scenes that take place on Earth, both showing mortals acting out their parts in mourning rites. The lower scene depicts a shaman, or holy person, to the left, and a group of attendants seated behind ritual vessels used at sacrifices dedicated to honoring ancestors. Many wooden, lacquered *hu* and *ting* (copies of official vessels cast in bronze in the Shang and Zhou dynasties) were found in the side chambers of the tomb. The shaman's duty was to contact the soul from "below". The upper scene shows another mourning rite, that of welcoming home the soul. The large figure standing in profile in the center is thought to be a portrait of the deceased, and she is shown as if crossing to the "other" world. These two terrestrial scenes represent ritual activities performed after death. Above and below, the deceased proceeds towards immortality.

The horizontal section at the top of the banner represents the land of the immortals and depicts legendary subjects. The gatekeepers and the bell (whose sound is thought to "penetrate the beyond") are transitional images, standing between heaven and Earth. Above and to the left is the crescent moon, the toad (the symbol of the moon's waxing), and the hare (a symbol of the full moon). The female figure is probably that of Chang Ngo, who stole the pill of immortality from Hou Yi, the archer, and flew off to the moon and caused it to wane. When the pill was returned, the moon waxed. In the center of this section is the figure of Fu Xi, an ancient clan god regarded as the first in the line of legendary rulers—he was the progenitor of the race and the symbol of the essence of everything under heaven. He was thought to be the point from which *yin* and *yang*, the sun and moon, and heaven and Earth emerged.

The journey of the souls proceeds from death, when the souls separate (one going to the underworld, the other remaining on Earth), through the rites carried out in the earthly realm to "re-join" the souls, to return to the first ancestor of the race and to immortality. The three sections are arranged to correspond to the structure of the cosmos. Upon death, the path of the souls reflects the birth, life, and rebirth as embodied in the nature of ancestor worship, which was already well established in the Han period.

Chu Culture

The tomb of Lady Dai belongs to the Chu cultural tradition. The Chu people inhabited an area southwest of the great north Yellow River basin, and, in historical times, expanded their power into the central Yangtze Valley, encompassing the present-day provinces of Hunan and Hubei. The Chu became one of the largest and strongest contenders for power in the third century BC. They were conquered and destroyed in 223 BC by the generals of the Qin, who went on to unify China in 221 BC. After the fall of the Qin, the Chu again became a very powerful and vigorous group with their own identity. The revival (or continuation) of their own local tomb customs found at Mawangdui is evidence of their pride in their ethnic heritage.

The Western Han period is one of the great formative periods of Chinese history. It took more than a century to reunify China after the fall of Qin. The burials at Mawangdui show that in the kingdom of Changsha in the first half of the second century BC, the requirements of Han rule were not inimical to the continued existence of the Chu cultural tradition. This changed in the time of Emperor Wu (who reigned from 140 BC to 87 BC), but these tombs offer no clues to those later events. They remain as a monument to the complexity and high degree of skill achieved in the craftwork of the Chu people.

BIBLIOTHÈQUE NATIONALE/THE BRIDGEMAN ART LIBRARY

An emperor of the Han dynasty with scholars translating classical texts. With the establishment of the Han dynasty, classical texts were rewritten from memory by court scholars, the texts in the royal library having been destroyed during the previous period of the Qin dynasty.

Painted pottery jars in the shape known as *hu*, recovered from burials dating from the Eastern Han dynasty. Vessels of this type were often made of clay rather than the more expensive bronze.

Trade Networks and Technological Advances

During the Han period, a nationwide trade network was formed to distribute commodities produced by intensive farming and by the cottage industry. The cottage industry, which had developed as a way of absorbing the excess labor generated seasonally by intensive farming, produced such commodities as clothing, craftworks, and furniture. The network gradually emerged as population pressure made intensive farming a necessity and, according to some scholars, technological advancement a possibility. The trade network reinforced the stability of the unified empire, and, together with Confucian ideology and the imperial bureaucracy, helped China develop a self-sufficient economic system. Thanks to this system, China has remained unified throughout most of the last 2,000 years.

Han territory expanded considerably beyond the Yellow River and Yangtze River floodplains, reaching the mountainous and coastal areas in the south. The most significant development during this time was the conflict with the Xiongnu nomadic empire in the steppe land in central Asia and Mongolia. After suffering repeated defeats, the Han finally managed to drive out some of the Xiongnu, and established their hegemony in East Asia. Contact with peoples in central Asia resulted in the appearance of a trading route for silk, which was also a communication corridor between China and the European world, via the many peoples through whose territory the route passed. (See the feature *The Silk Road*.)

In the Han period, technological advances were made in many fields. The Han Chinese were the first to make paper, to construct machinery driven by water power, and to develop the science of metallurgy for the production of steel. Moreover, their mathematics, astronomy, and chemistry were the most advanced in the world. At the same time, Taoism and other schools of thought took their place alongside Confucianism, which had become a highly sophisticated system of thought, as part of the Chinese frame of reference.

An enameled ritual vessel in the shape known as *fang ding*. This ancient style was revived during the Han dynasty to pay homage to traditions of the past.
C.M. DIXON

ART RESOURCE

THE IMAGE BANK

Fishing in Guilin, Guangxi province. With the famous limestone outcroppings that dot the countryside throughout South China, this is a typical southern scene.

The Collapse of the Han Empire

The Han dynasty was interrupted briefly by the reign of Wang Mang (from AD 8 to AD 23), after which a member of the Han imperial family succeeded in restoring the Han. The dynasty that resulted is known as the Late Han (or the Eastern Han), while the Han rule ended by Wang Mang is called the Former Han (or the Western Han). By about AD 170, foreign wars, power struggles at the court, and peasant rebellions led by the followers of folk religions had brought about the collapse of the Han. In AD 189, the Han capital, Chang-an, was sacked by mercenaries, and the Han empire was torn by wars among local warlords. Although the last Han emperor continued to reign over the empire—divided by warlords—until AD 220, Han rule effectively ended in AD 189.

During the Han period, China was consolidated into a state that spanned four centuries, and the Chinese established an identity as a nation. It is for this reason that speakers of the predominant language group in China—Mandarin, which is spoken by 85 percent of the population—including Chinese speakers in Taiwan, Hong Kong, and Hainan, still call themselves the Han people.

A bronze horse and rider from the Eastern Han dynasty. This piece is part of a set of cast-bronze horses and horsemen found in a tomb at Lingtai, in Gansu province. Horses were very highly regarded at this time—the emperor even sent abroad for his saddle and parade horses.

GIRAUDON/ART RESOURCE

THE SILK ROAD

HÅKAN WAHLQUIST

ARCHAEOLOGICAL TREASURES and written documents clearly show that, from the earliest times, different regions of the "Old World" were connected by routes along which contacts were made—contacts of war and of military acquisition and defense, but also of peace, trade, and cultural expansion. The first contacts were between neighboring nations; later, more distant nations were linked. From Greek historians, including Herodotus in the fifth century BC, we know that extensive networks of routes stretched eastwards, and from those who recorded the official annals of the Han dynasty (from 206 BC to AD 220), we know about Chinese penetration to the west. It was by interlocking emerging regional trading systems that political and cultural centers as far apart as China and Rome were connected to one another.

ROLAND & SABRINA MICHAUD/THE JOHN HILLELSON AGENCY

↑ The overland routes, connecting the Mediterranean region to China, crossed high mountains and wide deserts through the interior of Asia. Bactrian camels, commonly used to carry people and cargo, are here negotiating the Pamir mountains.

WERNER FORMAN ARCHIVE

↓ Nowadays, only ruins remain of Bezcklik, once a flourishing settlement on the northern branch of the Silk Road. It was a major Buddhist center east of the Turfan depression, noted for its extensive monasteries and beautiful murals.

When these systems were tied up, there came into existence the long-distance trading routes that the German geographer von Richthofen (1833–1905) called the "Silk Road", because silk played such a vital role in the commercial transactions along the "road". It is useful, however, to think of the Silk Road not as a single "road", but as a network of routes that, because of political and economic changes in the areas that it linked over the centuries, varied in extent and structure. Certain routes were important during certain periods, with the flow of commerce being diverted to alternative routes during other periods. Two kinds of routes were followed: by sea and by land.

The Sea Route

India and Arabia played valuable intermediary roles in the emerging long-distance maritime trade. For several centuries BC, India and China had already been trading, partly via Burma, but, more importantly, by small ships around Southeast Asia. From India, merchandise was carried by Arab ships to the Red Sea or the Persian Gulf, overland to the Mediterranean, and then to European markets.

The sea routes became more significant as maritime knowledge increased and larger ships were built. With the break-up of the Roman Empire and growing Arab expansion towards central and South Asia, access to traditional caravan routes was upset, and trade tilted even more in favor of the sea passage. The final transfer from caravans to ships, however, did not occur until the end of the fifteenth century AD, when Portuguese explorers gave Europe direct access to South and East Asia by ship around Africa. By then, the ancient overland Silk Road, which had existed for at least 1,500 years, had already lost its dominance. When the Ming dynasty came to power in AD 1368, China entered a period of relative isolation. Moreover, political developments in West Asia severely hampered transit trade.

Routes through Asia

The most important early Western move towards the East was undoubtedly Alexander the Great's "invasion" of Asia in 334 BC, a remarkable undertaking that brought European culture and influence far into the continent. A few centuries later, the Chinese moved westwards in earnest. The Han emperors, worried about their nomadic enemies in the west, expanded across what is today Gansu, and consolidated their empire by extending the Great Wall. A new element was introduced into Han policy after 139 BC, when emissaries were sent far beyond the borders of the empire into the land of potential enemies and allies. As the commercial advantages of establishing contact with these areas became evident, envoys were sent yearly to places such as Parthia (Iran) and India. Diplomatic missions also arrived in the Han capital, bringing tribute and goods for trade. The Silk Road as an artery for commerce had been established.

The old Han capital, Chang-an (today's Xi'an), was the easternmost town along the Silk Road. From there, the road ran westwards via Lanzhou, towards the rim of the Lop and Taklimakan deserts. At Dunhuang and Anxi, it split into several alternative routes. One went north of the deserts, another to the south. A third route went west through the Lop Desert, skirting the Lop Nur lake, to the garrison town of Loulan, from where it joined either the northern or the southern trade roads. This desert route was abandoned in the fourth century AD, when Lop Nur changed its position, or dried up, and Loulan was abandoned.

At Kashgar, at the western end of the Taklimakan Desert, the routes met, only to divide again. One went south into the Indus Valley. From there, travelers either turned west through Afghanistan towards Iran, or continued southeast into the heartland of northern India. The other route carried travelers across the Alai Mountains into West Turkestan and on to Iran. In Mashad, it reunited with the desert route that had come from Afghanistan through eastern Iran. The caravans could then move on through Mesopotamia, passing Baghdad before turning south towards Alexandria, west towards the Mediterranean, or north towards Turkey and Byzantium. Eventually, the westernmost extensions of the Silk Road reached the major cities of Europe.

ROLAND & SABRINA MICHAUD/THE JOHN HILLELSON AGENCY

The oasis of Dunhuang is fabled for its caves. These caves were once inhabited by Buddhist monks and pilgrims, such as the one depicted with a tiger on this mural.

Well-preserved and superbly painted and glazed figurines from the Tang dynasty (AD 618 to AD 907) have been found in China. Among other things, they show us that foreign merchants, like this distinctly non-Chinese man, probably from western Asia, frequented the markets in China at that time.

WERNER FORMAN ARCHIVE/IDEMITSU MUSEUM OF ARTS, TOKYO

CARTOGRAPHY: RAY SIM

THE SILK ROAD
The Silk Road was a network of caravan routes crisscrossing the continent and sea routes connecting the shores of the Yellow Sea with the Indian Ocean and the Mediterranean Sea.

Travelers and Goods

The people who traveled along these routes were from all the nations and cultures that the Silk Road touched during the several thousand years of its existence: Roman, Greek, and Slavonic; Arabic, Iranian, Turkic, Mongolian, Tibetan, Chinese, and Indian. They were soldiers and robbers; emigrants and refugees; merchants, missionaries, and monks; administrators, artisans, and scholars. They left evidence of their lives in the form of chronicles; accounts of trading trips and pilgrimages; administrative and commercial records; religious texts; merchandise taken from one place to another; secular and sacred monuments, and works of art; and land broken and worked.

Along the Silk Road, people carried ideas, knowledge, and skills, as well as artifacts and trading goods. They spread political ideologies, religious faiths, techniques of production, arts, fashions, and material goods. Buddhism was taken from India to central Asia. There, as in China, Korea, Japan, and Mongolia, it was to exert great influence, in confrontation, but also in harmony, with indigenous Chinese philosophies such as Confucianism and Taoism. Islam, emerging in the mid-seventh century AD, spread from Arabia to East Turkestan, taking firm root along the way.

Horses were the first "merchandise" the Chinese desired. Later, when trade extended all the way to Rome, other goods began to arrive: gold, silver, and coins; glassware; textiles; bronze vessels; wine; and papyrus. To the west flowed silk and other luxury goods: skins and furs, household slaves, jewelry, ivory, pearls, tortoise shells, and lacquer. In addition, Europeans developed a taste for a host of new spices and dyes: pepper, cinnamon, cardamom, ginger, cloves, indigo, and cochineal.

NATIONAL MUSEUM, ATHENS/SCALA

EMERGING MEDITERRANEAN CIVILIZATIONS

3200 BC – 800 BC

Warlords, Palace Cultures, and the First States in Europe

PETER WARREN, J.G. MACQUEEN, AND RICHARD J. HARRISON

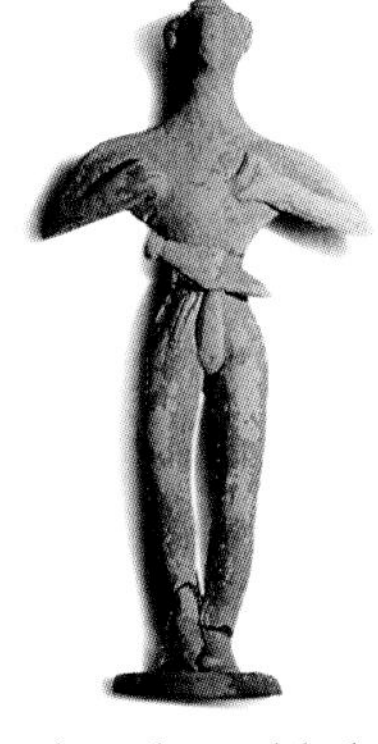

DURING THE SECOND MILLENNIUM BC, Europe's first civilizations developed in the eastern Mediterranean region. The period is characterized by a marked stability, and the rich societies of the Middle Bronze Age were soon transformed into distinctive palace cultures—first came the Minoan culture, on Crete; and later, the Mycenaean culture, on the Greek mainland. These important cultural worlds had complex bureaucratic systems, and developed important trading connections with the central Mediterranean region, with occasional links north of the Alps and to eastern Europe. Europe's first states had been established, and the first writing systems, known as Linear A and Linear B, were developed.

At the same time, an Indo-European-speaking people known as the Hittites established a powerful kingdom in Anatolia (present-day Turkey)—a kingdom that soon expanded in all directions. The Hittites were the first to master the technique of iron-smelting, and they thus began the first Iron Age culture in the world. In contrast to the societies in Crete, mainland Greece, and Anatolia, the local bronze-producing cultures in the Iberian peninsula never developed into true civilizations.

Part of a wall painting from the West House at Akrotiri, on Thera, dating from the sixteenth century BC. Shown here is the end of the "Fresco of the Ships". At what is probably the home port of the approaching fleet, crowds of men and women of different social ranks are looking out towards the ships.

A votive figure from the Peak Sanctuary at Petsofa, in Palaikastro, Crete, dating from about 2000 BC to 1700 BC.

RONALD SHERIDAN/ANCIENT ART & ARCHITECTURE COLLECTION

An embossed gold pendant of a deity holding two waterbirds. Probably made in Crete, it dates from the seventeenth century BC and shows both Cretan and Egyptian influences.
BRITISH MUSEUM/C.M. DIXON/PHOTO RESOURCES

These pottery vessels from Cyprus, dating from the fourteenth century BC, were found in a Bronze Age wreck off Kas (Ulu Burun), in Turkey.

EARLY AEGEAN CIVILIZATIONS

The Aegean region has been the scene of more than 50,000 years of human development. A high point was reached between 3000 BC and 1000 BC in the sophisticated and splendid civilizations of Crete, the Cyclades, and the Greek mainland. The region is small by global standards: just 600 kilometers (360 miles) from the northern Aegean coast to Crete in the south, and 700 kilometers (420 miles) from the western Ionian islands eastwards to Rhodes. To the west, the Ionian and Adriatic seas offered access to the central Mediterranean, while contacts northwards were made possible by the Axios and Vardar rivers and the Macedonian plains. Although the Rhodope Mountains formed a barrier to the northeast, the Anatolian coastlands (in present-day Turkey) were a critical bridge between the Anatolian plateau and its civilizations, and those of the Aegean island communities. East of Crete lay Cyprus and the Levant, south lay Egypt—all distant enough to allow Crete a measure of protection from attack, but not so far distant as to prevent the flow of goods and secular and spiritual ideas.

BILL CURTSINGER

The Aegean is a region of sharp contrasts: the remote mountains and steep, wooded glens of northwestern Greece and Albania, and the fertile plains of eastern Greece, watered in the north by the Balkan mountain rivers. Then there are the islands, located off Greece's western coast; in the northern Aegean Sea; in the central Aegean (the Cyclades); to the south (Crete); and off the Anatolian coast (Lesbos, Chios, Samos, Kos, and Rhodes).

Natural resources were plentiful throughout the region. Timber, limestones, and sandstones for building; clays; and potentially good agricultural land, pasture, edible herbs, and aromatic plants were widely available. But it was the localized concentrations of the raw materials necessary for higher civilization that promoted complex exchange networks and simple strategies of acquisition. Some Cycladic islands and southern Attica had supplies of copper, silver, and lead; gold occurred on Siphnos and in the northern Aegean. Several islands possessed fine white marble. Red marble and porphyritic rock (*lapis Lacedaemonius*) existed only in the southern Peloponnese; black obsidian for tools was acquired from Melos; and volcanic rocks for mortars were available from Melos as well as from Thera and Aigina. Tin, ivory, and exotics such as glass, gemstones, ostrich eggs, alabaster, and rock crystal, and also fine woods and copper, came from bordering regions to the east and south. Interestingly, the major centers of civilization—Crete, Mycenae, and Thebes—had no abundant natural resources of their own, other than fertile land. Like Troy and Poliochni, in the northeastern Aegean, their geographical position was highly significant, and the popularity of their exports ensured a strong supply of further raw materials.

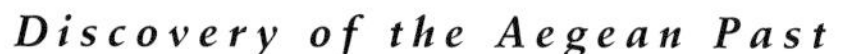

Discovery of the Aegean Past

Our knowledge of early Aegean society and civilization has been gained from archaeological excavations and surveys conducted for just over a hundred years. Heinrich Schliemann cleared the shaft graves of Mycenae, packed with warrior wealth, in 1876, and he uncovered the remains of Troy during the following years. Tombs at Mycenae, at Vapheio, and whole cemeteries in the Cyclades were excavated in the later part of the nineteenth century. From 1896 to 1899, a British team on Melos revealed a major settlement at Phylakope. This was followed by the richest era of discovery in Crete when Arthur Evans, assisted by Duncan Mackenzie, began to uncover the Palace of Knossos on 23 March 1900. American, Italian, and British teams excavated other Cretan sites, and the great Cretan scholar and archaeologist Stephanos Xanthoudides cleared a series of communal tombs dated to before 2000 BC.

While valuable finds were made in the 1920s and 1930s, the most significant discoveries have been made only since the Second World War. Probably the most important of all was the decipherment of the Mycenaean Linear B tablets (a script developed from the Minoan Linear A to write an early form of Greek) by Michael Ventris in 1952. This had immense implications for the understanding of the Mycenaean economy and the structure of the state. Meanwhile, the Neolithic tells (mounds) of Thessaly and Macedonia; the palaces of Pylos and Phaistos; the town of Akrotiri, on Thera (the Pompeii of the Aegean); and the finds from the fourteenth-century BC shipwreck off Kas (Ulu Burun), in southern Turkey, all came to light.

Accompanying these and other discoveries at scores of sites explored in recent years have been fundamental, new, scientific approaches to archaeology. Powerful techniques, such as chemical element analyses, enable the origins of objects, chiefly pottery, to be determined. High-resolution microscopy has revealed details of the technology and structures of metalwork. The application of resistivity techniques (an electromagnetic means of showing horizontal planes of structures below ground), ground-penetrating radar (which gives vertical profiles of remains below ground), and digitized computer mapping systems is transforming the recording of sites and terrains in archaeological surveys. Paleobotany has created entirely new levels of understanding of the ancient environment and of food plants; archaeozoology has identified wild and domesticated fauna. Radiocarbon dating has enabled the chronological sequences and time scales of all Aegean societies before about 2000 BC to be determined. After this date, evidence derived from Aegean pottery in Egypt and western Asia, and Egyptian finds in the Aegean, provide the basis for dating periods and developments. Radiocarbon dating offers general confirmation of the sequence of events, although views are divided as to how accurate it is for dating single events such as the Late Bronze Age eruption of the volcano of Thera.

The Beginnings of Aegean Civilization

Aegean society, economy, and culture developed in a series of stages. The idea that historical processes operate at the same time, but at different levels and paces, is useful for understanding the early Aegean in terms of its social, economic, technological, political, and spiritual development. The different levels are: long-term, almost imperceptible human change in relation to the environment; the history of groups, which is measurable across time, as in the rise and maintenance of stable states; and short-term events, such as sudden collapses of stable states or the impact of natural events. There are, of course, constant interactions between these concurrent levels.

ERICH LESSING/MAGNUM

↑ This section of a wall painting from Akrotiri, on Thera, dating from the sixteenth century BC, depicts a coastal town surrounded by rivers and mountains (with deer being pursued by a lion). Standing on the mountains, men and a woman watch departing ships.

Middle Paleolithic stone artifacts found on the Ionian island of Kephallenia, dated to about 50,000 years ago, provide evidence that sea voyages of at least 20 kilometers (12 miles) between shorelines were made at that time. In nearby Epirus, on the mainland, excavations at cave sites indicate the existence of small groups who migrated according to the seasons along established land routes. They hunted a wide range of animals, including ibex, chamois, beaver, red deer, cave lion, lynx, wolf, pine marten, and badger, according to findings at Klithi (from 17,000 to 10,000 years ago). Mining for red ocher is reported from Thasos at the end of the Paleolithic, when the island formed part of the Thracian plain.

During the final stages of the Paleolithic, continuing through the Mesolithic and Early Neolithic periods, profound developments occurred. At Franchthi, on the Argolid coast, obsidian was being brought a considerable distance by sea from the island of Melos as early as 12,000 years ago. This mastery of land and sea distances by the people of the Paleolithic is the background to the first Neolithic colonies, very probably from Anatolia, between 7000 BC and 6000 BC. Settlements were established on the plains and beside the rivers of Macedonia and Thessaly. The colonization of Crete, however, was their most astonishing achievement, requiring a long sea voyage from southern Anatolia to Knossos, with one or more vessels transporting people, livestock (notably cattle), cereals (especially breadwheat), and provisions such as fresh water.

During this period, agriculture and the domestication of sheep, goats, cattle, and pigs were introduced into mainland Greece and, at a slower pace, into Crete. Exchange networks had also been developed within the Aegean region, since Melian obsidian is found at many sites, and pottery was

↑ An early Cycladic folded-arm figurine made of white marble, from Naxos, dating from about 2500 BC.
NATIONAL MUSEUM, ATHENS/SCALA

An early Cycladic pottery "frying pan" figure from Syros. It dates from between about 2500 BC and 2200 BC, and shows a longboat with paddles.
NATIONAL MUSEUM, ATHENS/ C.M. DIXON/PHOTO RESOURCES

Part of the frieze from the north wall of room 5 of the West House at Akrotiri, on Thera, dating from about 1530 BC. It depicts a seaborne attack and drowning defenders.

circulated in northern Greece. After 4000 BC, objects of copper, silver, and gold were used in a minor way.

About 3000 BC, further profound social and economic changes occurred. Small, planned towns were founded in the northeastern Aegean region and in northwestern Anatolia, at Besik Tepe, Troy, Poliochni, and Thermi. There is evidence for social ranking and the display of wealth in finds of rich collections of gold jewelry and metal vessels. In Thessaly, the town of Pefkakia had developed as a thriving coastal center with links around the northern Aegean, in contrast with inland Thessalian and Macedonian towns, which were in decline after the richness of their Late Neolithic period. Further south, large settlements were established on virgin ground in Boeotia and Euboea. By 2500 BC, Lerna, on the Argolid coast, once a fortified settlement, had crossed a significant political threshold in becoming an administrative center. Seal impressions on clay found in its main building indicate a system of organized storage.

Meanwhile, on the islands, the farming and maritime villages of the Cyclades reached the zenith of independent achievement. Their production of slender figurines and vessels of finest white marble, and a wide range of copper and bronze tools and silver jewelry, was outstanding. Cultural artifacts found in Lefkas, in the Ionian islands to the west, have distinct Cycladic links, and island longboats, of which lead models and depictions on pottery survive, prove that sea voyages were undertaken. So, too, does a shipwreck full of pottery at Dhokos, near the island of Hydra. Nearby, mainland Attica had a material culture that was very similar to that of the Cyclades.

The basic food supply, determined by careful investigation at Lerna, comprised einkorn and emmer wheat, barley, oats, brome grass, broad beans, lentils, peas, vetches, figs, grapes, and strawberry tree fruit. This diet may have been typical of the Aegean region, although the absence of olives is a striking exception. The local animals included red fox, hare, boar, red and roe deer, ox, badger, beech marten, otter, and wolf; and domestic cattle, sheep, goats, pigs, dogs, and asses.

On Crete, settlements ranged from small agricultural villages, such as Myrtos (Phournou Koryphe), to coastal sites with Cycladic and Southwest Asian connections, such as Mochlos. The major town of Knossos, with links extending as far as the Greek mainland and Egypt, grew.

Greek mainland and Cycladic island communities suffered severe disruption in the late third millennium BC, probably as a result of migrations from West Anatolia. The impact of these new groups is seen in their architecture, wheel-made pottery, and metalwork, which appeared at several places, from Pefkakia, in Thessaly, to Kastri, on Syros.

Crete, in sharp contrast, maintained its development within a framework of strong cultural continuity. Out of this framework emerged the first monumental buildings or palaces, Phaistos (about 1800 BC) providing the best example. A recently discovered building at Aghia Photia, in eastern Crete, comprises a single small structure of about 500 square meters (600 square yards), with more than 30 rooms arranged around a rectangular court. The monumental approach to architecture probably arrived from western Asia, along with imports of tin and copper. This form of architecture probably coincided with the emergence of a ruling elite.

NATIONAL ARCHAEOLOGICAL MUSEUM, ATHENS/THE BRIDGEMAN ART LIBRARY

Early State Society in Crete: 2000 BC to 1500 BC

This was the great age of Minoan palatial civilization (named after the legendary King Minos), with an administration supported by documents in the Cretan hieroglyphic and Linear A scripts (a form of writing using signs for syllables, together with numerals and symbols). Major regional centers, with administrative buildings and storage and production facilities, stood at the head of a network of lesser towns, large country estates, farms, and ports. They also served religious sites on mountain tops, in rural settings, and in caves. Economic links with the mainland, the Cyclades (and as far north as Samothrace), western Anatolia, Cyprus, the Levant, and Egypt were highly developed. At the same time, Minoan settlements were founded in the southern Aegean region (or Minoan elements were added to local cultures).

It is clear that the Minoan rulers exerted control over the import of valuable raw materials—notably, metals, fine stones, and ivory. The distribution of imported goods, however, suggests the existence of at least semi-independent merchants.

In the absence of social information in the written records, the excavated sites themselves can throw some light on Minoan society of this period. Knossos was the largest center (estimated at 75 hectares/ 185 acres), with a population of between 9,000 and 12,000 people. Most other towns had populations of only a few hundred. Taking into account the small population and a short life expectancy (35 years for men, 28 years for women), which allows but a few years for individual achievement, the scale of the total Minoan palatial complex appears all the more remarkable.

The structure of Minoan society remains a mystery, with only a few clues left behind. Collective burials and the compact, cellular settlement plans of the prepalatial period suggest a communal social system. The presence of defined living areas could well indicate the existence of nuclear families or extended family groups. Economic prosperity brought with it differences in status, perhaps already showing up in the Early Bronze Age harbor town of Mochlos, with its very rich communal tombs contrasting with much simpler burials. It has been suggested that powerful families probably occupied the first monumental buildings about 1900 BC to 1800 BC. Soon afterwards, specialized workshops, such as those found at Mallia, could well have been family-based. House sizes in the neopalatial towns suggest that they were family residences, housing about 10 people. The palaces, at least in their final form, were planned on a regular measurement unit, and were divided into functional areas around a great central court. This layout implies a sophisticated organization and administration, but who made the decisions is unknown. A single "ruler" seems likely. In Minoan Crete, as good a case for a female as for a male ruler can be made. Iconography suggests that a female sat on the throne at Knossos—as priestess, ruler, or both. Women were certainly prominent in religion.

The Minoan economy was based on a diversified system of agriculture: different types of wheat and barley, probably oats, pulses, olive oil, wine, figs, honey, edible plants, spices, beef, pork, mutton, venison, and fish, and probably game, milk, and cheese, were staples.

The level of technological achievement across a huge range of activities was astonishing. Buildings were constructed with ashlar masonry (finely dressed on the front face) and large beams of Cretan cypress. Two of the finest examples of construction are the five-story Grand Staircase, in the East Wing of the Knossian palace, and the 35 meter (100 foot) long buildings at the port of Kommos. (See the feature *The Minoan Palace of Knossos*.) Craft products were worked in brilliant stones, including imported speckled obsidian and rock crystal, ivory, faience, gold, silver, and terracotta (including a multitude of brilliantly painted, sometimes eggshell-thin pots). Bronzework sometimes featured the fusion of different metals by heat and pressure, similar to modern-day "Sheffield plate". Delicate, multicolored wall paintings sympathetically depicting the natural environment were created. Many such crafted items were used in religious rituals or left as offerings in shrines. Others were exported.

Artifacts, excavated sites, and scenes carved in relief on stone vessels or engraved on gold rings and sealstones all demonstrate that religious belief and cult practice played a major role in Minoan life. Rituals included animal and occasionally human sacrifice, food and floral offerings, and the dedication of small votive human and animal figures. Shrines were places where the divine and human worlds interacted. Music, dance, invocation, ecstatic actions with cult stones and trees were the means of attracting the divinity's presence. The purpose of religious activity was to promote the fertility and renewal of the whole environment, including humans and animals, and to avert disease or natural disaster. Whether the Minoans worshiped many divinities equally or a single great female divinity manifesting different aspects, with an entourage of lesser divinities, remains a matter for debate.

At their highest stage of development, in the later fifteenth century BC, the centers of Minoan civilization suffered sudden destruction. Most excavated settlements and estate centers show evidence of fire. The eruption of Thera, the volcano 110 kilometers (65 miles) to the north of Crete, occurred too early to be the cause of the Minoan disaster. Since there is no sign of internal stress in Minoan society (in fact, the opposite is the case), discussion now centers on two possibilities: an invasion by Mycenaean warriors from the Greek mainland; or, with Crete being on the boundary of the African and Aegean tectonic plates, a severe earthquake.

The Emergence of Mycenaean Civilization

After several centuries of peace in the Aegean region, there is evidence that a military elite had begun to emerge about 1600 BC. At Mycenae, quantities of swords have been found in shaft graves, along with pottery, exotic objects from Crete, and about 200 vessels, many of them made of gold. Tombs elsewhere, mostly long since plundered, indicate the growth of wealth and status: at Eleusis, in Attica; at Dendra (Midea), Lerna, and Vapheio; and at Peristeria, in Messenia. It was one or more of these warrior-led communities that either conquered

A dagger of inlaid gold, silver, and copper from Shaft Grave IV at Mycenae. Dating from the sixteenth century BC, it depicts a lion hunt.
RONALD SHERIDAN/ANCIENT ART & ARCHITECTURE COLLECTION

Knossos in the later fifteenth century BC or filled the vacuum left by natural disaster. This was a pivotal moment in the history of Aegean civilization, as the less sophisticated but powerful and adaptive Mycenaeans quickly learned the structure and centralized administration of a high civilization established centuries earlier by the Minoans.

The Mycenaeans ruled Crete from Knossos for less than a hundred years, before the capital was itself destroyed forever as a palace center (probably no later than about 1350 BC). From this time, palaces were also established on the mainland, at Mycenae, Pylos, Tiryns, Thebes, and, almost certainly, Athens. They were based on the old megaron, or longhouse, plan, incorporating a porch that led to an anteroom and main room. Long side corridors gave access to smaller rooms and courts. Palaces at Pylos and Tiryns also had secondary, smaller, megaron suites. In addition to their palaces, the Mycenaeans achieved remarkable feats of hydraulic engineering: a dam near Tiryns; an aqueduct to supply Pylos with water; and drainage of the Kopais basin through channels and tunnels, to convert the area surrounding Gla into good agricultural land.

Pylos, Mycenae, Thebes, and Tiryns, the four main palace complexes, were the capitals of their states, and were each headquarters of a centralized,

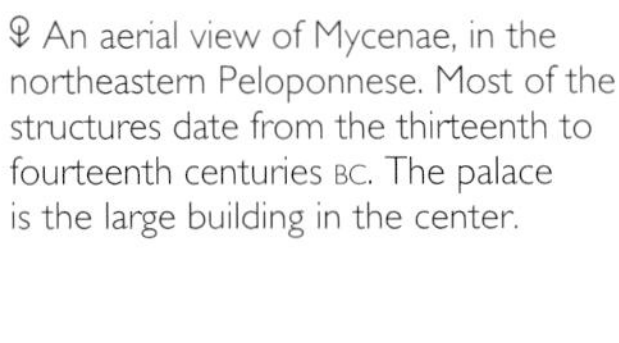

An aerial view of Mycenae, in the northeastern Peloponnese. Most of the structures date from the thirteenth to fourteenth centuries BC. The palace is the large building in the center.

IRA BLOCK/THE IMAGE BANK

very tightly controlled economy. We know this from translations of contemporary Linear B tablet records, which deal primarily with fiscal matters, including taxation in kind. Raw materials and rations were distributed, and finished products, including agricultural and animal produce, were allocated quotas. Some tablets record contracts of sale of slaves. Large and small estates were owned by individuals, perhaps in return for military service. Some tablets are specifically concerned with military equipment, including armor and weapons. Countless details of technical production, ranging from elaborate inlaid furniture and textiles to chariot parts and scented oils and spices are listed by practitioner or product.

As might be expected from such a controlled economy, society was elaborately ranked, with the king (*wanax*) at the top. Under the king, ranked approximately in the following order, were: the *lawagetas* (second only to the king); *equetai*, or followers; *telestai*, or major landholders; governors and deputy governors of towns or subregions; leaders of craft groups; religious dignitaries; craftspeople; and shepherds and workers (some of whom were slaves), including female textile workers employed in the palace. Farmers are not mentioned, nor are merchants, although the former must have comprised the majority of the population.

As well as the palaces, a number of settlement sites and dozens of cemeteries have been found, including tholos (domed) tombs and chamber tombs. Excavation of palaces or other buildings in palatial towns has yielded inscribed tablets, wall paintings, tens of thousands of pots, carved ivories, stone and metalwork (including multicolored inlaid weapons and cups), and jewelry. Mycenae was an important cult center. Tiryns and the major Cycladic town of Phylakope, on Melos, had shrines that continued to be used after 1200 BC, their location suggesting that their purpose was to ensure divine protection for the walled city.

While most of our information about economic, social, and political matters comes from tablets, these make no mention of trade. The status of trade within the Mycenaean economy is a matter of debate. Although the economy was essentially agricultural, the archaeological evidence is clear: trade (or rather, exchange in its many forms) existed, although it may have involved only the upper ranks of society. Traded items included the fine Mycenaean pottery and the scented oils that originally filled many of the pots found in southern Italy, Sicily, Sardinia, and Spain and at more than a hundred sites from Syria to Egypt. A ship wrecked

C.M. DIXON/PHOTO RESOURCES

The entrance to the "Treasury of Atreus", a tholos tomb at Mycenae dating from the fourteenth century BC. The triangular space and the door surrounds were decorated with carved slabs and columns in colored marble.

These items were among those retrieved from a Bronze Age wreck off Kas (Ulu Burun), in Turkey, dating from the fourteenth century BC. As well as a consignment of more than 100 amphoras, the cargo included gold pendants, gold roundels with embossed decoration, and artifacts made of bronze.

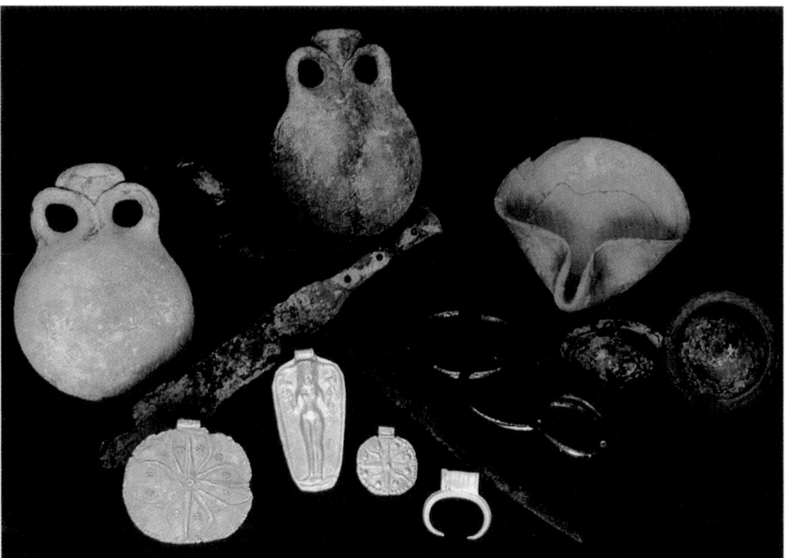

BILL CURTSINGER

THE DEVELOPMENT OF MEDITERRANEAN CIVILIZATIONS

BC	ANATOLIA	AEGEAN REGION	WEST MEDITERRANEAN REGION
1000			
	Destruction of Hattusas	Mycenaean destructions	
	Battle of Qadesh	Mycenaean palaces	
		Fall of Knossos Linear B script developed	
	Reign of Suppiluliumas	Destructions in Crete	Atlantic Late Bronze Age: contacts with Britain and France
1500			
	Hittite capture of Babylon	Volcano of Thera erupts Mycenaean shaft graves	Bronze Age expansion in central Spain
	Foundation of Hittite kingdom	Linear A script developed	
		Minoan trade to Egypt, the Near East, and Anatolia	
2000	Assyrian merchant colonies	Cretan palaces	Single graves and citadels at Fuente Alamo and El Oficio Early Bronze Age
	Troy II and Alaca treasures	Movement from Anatolia to Cycladic islands and Greek mainland	
2500		Lerna: early Helladic administration center	Construction of Los Millares and Almizaraque
	Developments in metallurgy	Cretan round tombs	
		Cycladic marble figures	Bell beaker pottery Collective tombs and fortified sites
3000	First city of Troy	Early Bronze Age	Copper Age

off Kas (Ulu Burun), in southern Turkey, carried a cargo of some 357 copper ingots, tin, ivory, cobalt blue glass ingots, spices, ebony, and more than a hundred Canaanite amphoras (two-handled vessels), with nearly 1 tonne (1 ton) of terebinth resin suitable for use in perfumes and incense. In the fourteenth century BC, such a cargo must surely have been destined for a Mycenaean palatial center.

In postpalatial Crete, during the fourteenth and thirteenth centuries BC, Khania, on the north coast, and Kommos, on the south, flourished as port towns with links to western Asia and Italy.

The civilization of the Mycenaeans lasted 200 years at most. In the thirteenth century BC, some rulers built great defensive walls around their citadels and, in some cases, passages beneath the walls to protect water supplies. Athens, Gla, Dendra, Mycenae, and Tiryns are outstanding examples of defensive architecture. A strong wall was built across the Isthmus of Corinth, while Pylos and the Menelaion remained unwalled. All this activity must mean that there was fear of attack by neighbors. The citadels were, in fact, destroyed over a period from about 1250 BC to 1200 BC. Explanations differ: some argue that there were internal conflicts within individual states, as marginal lands and food supplies became scarce; others believe that there was conflict between states (the isthmus wall supporting this view). It must be noted, however, that recent excavators have independently argued that Mycenae, the Menelaion, and Tiryns were destroyed by earthquake.

Mycenaean armor from Dendra, in the Peloponnese, dating from the fourteenth century BC. This unique find of a bronze cuirass (a piece of armor that protected the torso) and a boar's-tusk helmet has been restored.
NAUPLION MUSEUM/C.M. DIXON/PHOTO RESOURCES

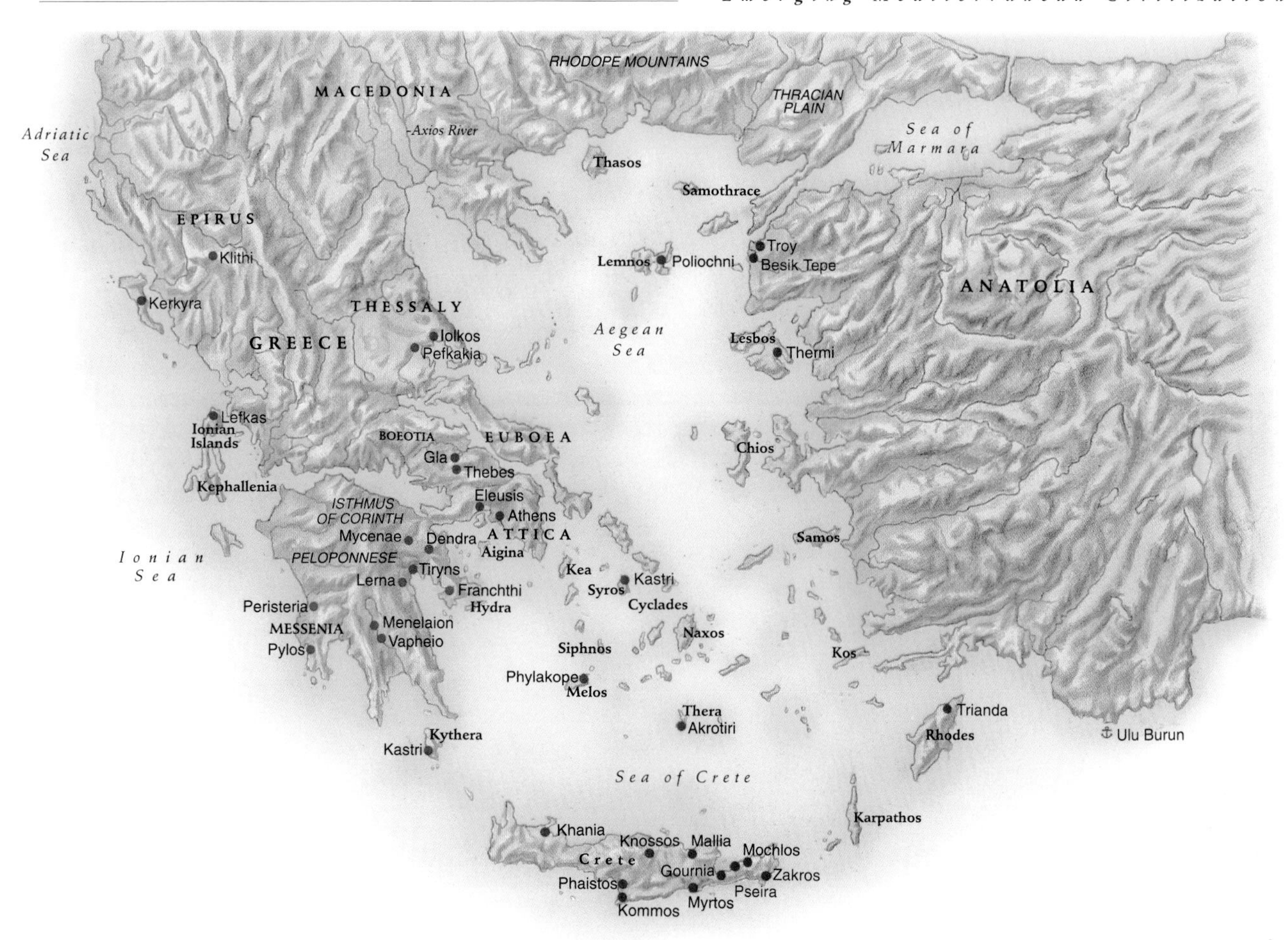

THE AEGEAN REGION

Europe's first civilizations developed in the eastern Mediterranean region during the second millennium BC. The map shows most of the important sites mentioned in the text.

CARTOGRAPHY: RAY SIM

⚓ Shipwreck

Discontinuities, Survivals, and Continuities

The destructions that culminated about 1200 BC swept away the centralized economies, along with the politically defined kingdoms and complex social systems. Exchange systems, insofar as they were controlled by, and for, the palace rulers, must also have changed radically. Writing stopped. After 1200 BC, there was considerable migration to less densely populated areas—the northwestern Peloponnese and the Ionian islands, in western Greece, and eastern Attica, Euboea, and the Cyclades. There was renewed Mycenaean activity on Crete, and a population shift to naturally defended locations. Mycenaean communities also moved to Tarsus, in southern Anatolia, and to Cyprus and the West Anatolian coast. Iolkos, on the coast of Thessaly, appears to have escaped destruction, and tradition had it that Athens did likewise.

Until recently, it was thought that the migration from the core areas of the northeastern Peloponnese and Boeotia had left these areas severely underpopulated. But discoveries at Mycenae, and especially Tiryns, show that these places remained inhabited, Tiryns being a major town in the twelfth century BC. Its excavator, the late Klaus Kilian, even speculated that the origins of the later Greek polis (city-state) might lie in the twelfth century. New forms of political organization were necessary. Later Greek sources indicate that communities were ruled by kings, or *basileis* (a title that had existed in Mycenaean times, but was then relatively insignificant).

In Crete, new excavation has shown twelfth-century settlement at lowland Knossos, as well as at inaccessible hill sites. Mountain and cave sanctuaries continued to be inhabited, and it was here that much of the religious inheritance of the Bronze Age was preserved and developed in an unbroken line.

Since the tablets of the Mycenaean palaces had already listed many of the later Greek gods and goddesses, continuity of belief was also likely on the mainland. The Greek language also survived. Land use remained the same as it had been for thousands of years, although the control and organization of land, like the political structures, must have changed radically. Although the Homeric poems—largely completed by about 700 BC—might reflect the new social world of the Iron Age, they are even more significant as a record of the Mycenaean Bronze Age past.

Peter Warren

THE MINOAN PALACE OF KNOSSOS

GRAHAM JOYNER

THE PALACE OF KNOSSOS was a social, economic, administrative, and religious center for a large local population. The original palace, dating from about 1900 BC, probably began as a series of separate buildings with different functions, grouped around a central courtyard. After an earthquake about 1700 BC, these separate, specialized units were rebuilt into one complex structure on several levels, linked by corridors, staircases, and light wells. The palace had a sophisticated plumbing and drainage system and was decorated with frescoes depicting activities of the time. It included storerooms, workrooms, a domestic area, and a multitude of ceremonial rooms, some identified as shrines. Occupied by Mycenaeans about 1450 BC, the palace was destroyed by fire about 1375 BC.

This fresco fragment, dating from about 1400 BC, belongs to a frieze showing at least two large-scale women with several smaller men. Wearing long robes, the men are seated on folding stools and sharing cups. The loop at the back of her neck suggests that the figure known as "La Parisienne" is a goddess or priestess. A ritual is probably in progress, possibly connected with the west side of the palace, where the fresco was found.

ALEX STARKEY/CAMERA PRESS/AUSTRAL INTERNATIONAL

The light well next to the Grand Staircase, on the east side of the courtyard, provides light and access to the domestic area. The left corridor leads to a large hall; on the right are the living quarters. The quality of craftsmanship is revealed in the finely dressed stone, painted cypress beams and columns, and walls decorated with a shield fresco.

ALEX STARKEY/CAMERA PRESS/AUSTRAL INTERNATIONAL

F.H.C. BIRCH/SONIA HALLIDAY PHOTOGRAPHS

AUSTRAL INTERNATIONAL

A suite of rooms near the Grand Staircase identifies the palace's living quarters. They include a "sitting room" looking onto a light well, this bathroom, with its clay tub (emptied by hand), and a flushing lavatory.

When storerooms were excavated, they were found to contain food storage vessels still in place. Up to 2 meters (7 feet) high, the vessels were hand-formed and decorated with many handles.

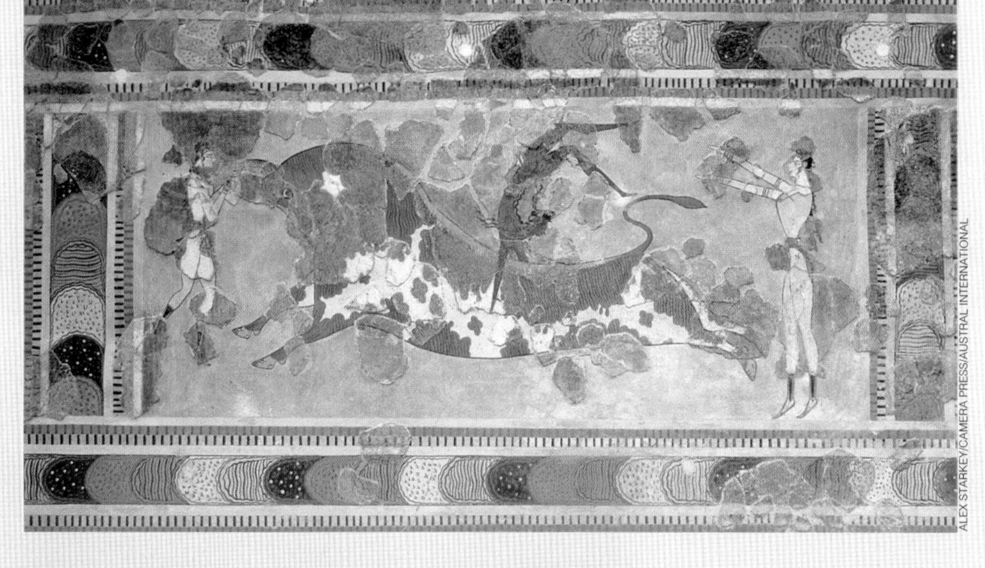

ALEX STARKEY/CAMERA PRESS/AUSTRAL INTERNATIONAL

A man vaults over a bull's back, and a woman stands behind with outstretched arms. (The woman in front probably does not belong to this scene.) Dating from about 1450 BC, this frieze probably came from public rooms on the east side of the courtyard. Bull-jumping may have been an activity performed in the courtyard, with spectators watching safely from balconies and windows. It remains uncertain whether it was a ritual or a sport.

GIRAUDON/THE BRIDGEMAN ART LIBRARY

The ruins of the North Pillar Hall, the palace's northern entrance. An open-air ramp leads up to the courtyard. The galleries above the ramp (shown in a restoration by Sir Arthur Evans) were decorated with relief frescoes. This approach contrasts with the main, formal entrance at the south, whose long, winding corridors were decorated with frescoes showing several hundred large figures in procession.

THE HITTITES: A POWERFUL AND PRACTICAL PEOPLE

CHRIS HELLIER/ANCIENT ART & ARCHITECTURE COLLECTION

A view over the temple area in the lower city of Hattusas. The principal building (the central courtyard of which is clearly visible) contained shrines dedicated to the sun-goddess of Arinna and the weather-god of Hatti. It was surrounded by rows of long storerooms.

Few people visiting the arid steppe country of what is now central Turkey would guess that the area was once the center of one of the ancient world's great powers. Yet the impressive remains found near the village of Boğazkale (formerly Boğazköy), about 160 kilometers (100 miles) east of Ankara, show that between 1650 BC and 1180 BC, this was Hattusas, the capital of the Hittites. These were a people whose power and influence were at the time equal to those of the better-known kingdoms of Babylon, Assyria, and Egypt.

Dramatic Monuments

The royal palace of Hattusas was built on a great outcrop that juts from the north-facing slope of a rocky ridge, with an almost vertical drop on the northern and eastern sides to a stream bed far below. On the level ground at the foot of the slope, to the west and northwest, lay a "lower city", the site of the principal temple. To the south, a great city wall rose to the top of the ridge, enclosing several lesser "castles" on smaller outcrops, an artificial lake some 90 meters by 60 meters (300 feet by 200 feet) in size, and no fewer than 31 temples. Several surviving gateways are flanked by impressive guardian figures. The total area enclosed within the city wall is more than 160 hectares (400 acres).

Not far from Hattusas, at Yazilikaya, to the northeast, is another dramatic Hittite monument. Here, worn by time and weathering into yet another rocky outcrop, are two natural rock chambers, the walls of which are adorned with low-relief carvings of more than 60 figures. Those in the larger chamber form two processions, one of male and one of female deities, which converge at the inner end, where the principal deities come face to face. Watching the scene from behind the female procession is the figure of a Hittite king. The same king can be seen in the smaller chamber in the protective embrace of his guardian-god. In front of him is carved a huge 3 meter (9 foot) sword, its pommel, or knob, in the form of a god's head, its hilt formed of lions' bodies, and its blade plunged into the rock. On the opposite wall is a frieze of 12 warrior-gods (who also appear at the rear of the male procession in the larger chamber),

GIRAUDON

The guardian figure of the King's Gate at Hattusas. He wears only a short kilt and a helmet with flaps to protect his ears and neck, and is armed with a short, curved sword and an elaborate battle-axe.

SCALA

The King's Gate in the city wall of Hattusas. The double gateway, of characteristic pointed shape, was flanked by strong towers. Further protection was provided by the carved figure of an armed deity (illustrated above) set against the inner gate-jamb.

moving in menacing formation with their curved swords over their shoulders.

About 35 kilometers (20 miles) to the north of Boğazkale, at the site of Alaca Hüyük, there is further evidence of Hittite architecture and sculpture. Here, the main gate of a small but strongly fortified settlement was guarded by two large sphinxes. The outer walls of the towers flanking the gate were decorated with low reliefs of sacrificial, festive, and hunting scenes.

Who, then, were the Hittites, who left behind these impressive remains? Fortunately for us, their capital has yielded ample documentary evidence that enables us, to a great extent, to reconstruct their history and assess their achievements. They appeared on the political scene about 1650 BC, when their first monarch, Hattusilis I, chose to rebuild Hattusas, which had been destroyed in a local conflict about a century earlier. Intending to use it as a base from which to expand his territory, he eventually controlled central Anatolia, reaching the Mediterranean coast and gaining access to northern Syria, the most important center of trade routes in the ancient Middle East. By about 1600 BC, Aleppo, the main power center of the area, was in Hittite hands, and in 1595 BC, a Hittite army swept far down the Euphrates River to capture Babylon, bringing the dynasty of Hammurabi to an inglorious end.

The Hittites demonstrated both military strength and ambition to achieve status as an international power. But such ambitions are not easily sustained, and it was soon clear that the Anatolian newcomers had overreached themselves. A speedy withdrawal from conquered territories was followed by a series of coups d'etat that quickly reduced the emergent power to its former provincial status. Partial revivals in about 1500 BC, and again in about 1450 BC, promised much, but in the end, achieved little.

The Rise to Power

It was not until about 1380 BC that a young and vigorous king, called Suppiluliumas, was able to re-establish Hittite power on a firm basis throughout central Anatolia. Once again, he conquered northern Syria, thus gaining what was to be lasting control of the vital area between the Euphrates River and the Mediterranean Sea. Final confirmation of Hittite international importance came in about 1352 BC, when the widow of Tutankhamun, the recently deceased pharaoh of Egypt, wrote a passionate letter to Suppiluliumas begging him to save her from being overthrown by sending one of his sons to be her husband and ruler of Egypt. Unfortunately, the king hesitated, giving her opponents time to consolidate their position. When the son was finally dispatched to Egypt, he was murdered before he could be installed as pharaoh. Despite this setback, the Hittites remained one of the major powers of the ancient world, and a series of strong and capable rulers ensured that their power would not be easily lost.

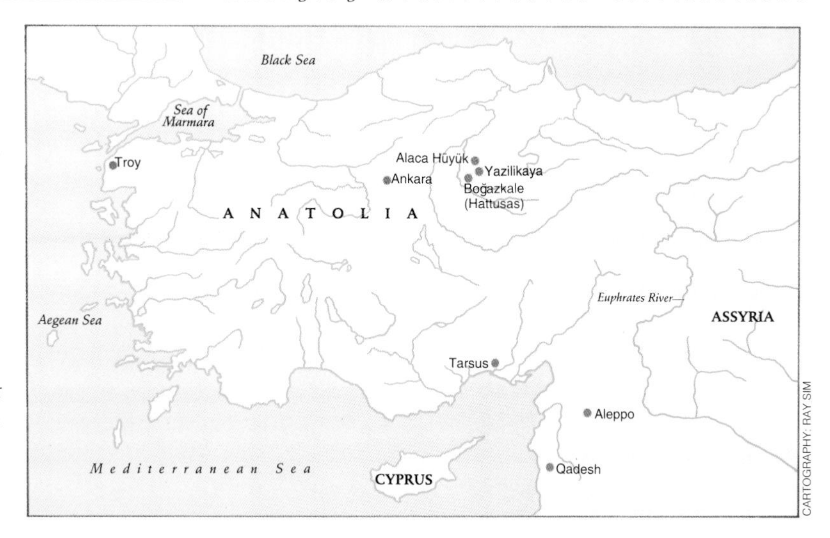

HITTITE SITES IN ASIA MINOR
Hattusas, the Hittite capital, in central Anatolia, became the center of a feudal state of considerable power.

Mursilis II (about 1340 BC to 1306 BC) turned his attention to the west, and successfully extended Hittite control to the Aegean Sea. His successor, Muwatallis (about 1306 BC to 1282 BC), had to face a renewed challenge from Egypt, but when the two powers met in 1286 BC, near the North Syrian town of Qadesh, the Egyptian advance was halted, leaving the Hittites in firm control of this vital area. Even the emergence of a new danger, Assyria, which took advantage of Hittite–Egyptian rivalry to extend its boundaries as far as the eastern bank of the Euphrates and make raids into Hittite territory, did little to diminish Hittite power. Instead, it brought the Hittites and Egyptians into alliance in the face of mutual danger from the east. For 75 years, under Hattusilis III, Tudhaliyas IV, and Suppiluliumas II, the Hittites played an important part in maintaining an international balance of power that provided a period of stability for an insecure world.

At the height of its power, the Hittite state was ruled on feudal lines, with the king at the peak of the social pyramid, supported (or often, not

The 12 warrior-gods from the smaller rock chamber at Yazilikaya, kilted and with sickle-shaped swords at the ready. The sculpture gives a strong impression of relentless, forward movement.

↑ A small gold figurine of a Hittite god. Objects such as this were presumably personal possessions, and had the same protective function as large-scale sculptures such as that on the King's Gate.

RONALD SHERIDAN/ANCIENT ART & ARCHITECTURE COLLECTION

supported!) by aristocratic "barons", who swore an oath of loyalty to him and were rewarded by grants of land. Towards the bottom of the pyramid were the free citizens, most of whom worked either on the land or as craftworkers. The bottom level consisted of slaves, who belonged to individual owners, and deportees from conquered territories, who remained under the control of the state.

The basis of the economy was agriculture, but trade and industry were also important; bronze for weapons and tools, for instance, was vital, and control of metal sources, or of routes that led to them, played a large part in imperial policy.

Local religion was primarily concerned with people's relationship to the great powers of nature. Under the empire, the many local deities were, with difficulty, organized into a state pantheon headed by the sun-goddess of Arinna (who, despite her title, seems to have been a deity of the "mother-goddess" type), and, in a rather subordinate position, the weather-god of Hatti. The king had extensive religious duties, which were regarded as being so vital to the welfare of the state that he sometimes had to return from military campaigns to ensure that the duties were performed at the proper time.

Towards 1200 BC, the situation began to deteriorate. Assyria was becoming increasingly aggressive, while throughout Hittite territory, it became more and more difficult for the king to control his unruly nobles and vassals. About 1235 BC, the Hittite capital itself was temporarily seized by a rival claimant to the throne. Crop failures brought famine conditions in some areas, increasing social instability. In other circumstances, the Hittite kingdom might well have survived this crisis. But far to the west, in the Aegean, and even possibly in the Balkans, a situation was developing over which the Hittites had no control.

→ A pair of ritual pottery vessels excavated at Hattusas. They represent the two sacred bulls of the weather-god of Hatti, and are about 1 meter (3 feet) tall. Liquid can be poured in through the funnel-like opening on their backs, flowing through their nostrils when the bulls are tilted.

THE HITTITE MUSEUM, ANKARA/SONIA HALLIDAY PHOTOGRAPHS

Upheaval and Decline

The course of events is impossible to reconstruct with any accuracy. This was a time of social and political upheaval, which resulted in the uprooting of entire communities, and their enforced migration along the coasts of Anatolia and through Syria and Palestine towards the borders of Egypt. Although there is little evidence to suggest that these developments directly affected Hattusas itself, it is clear that the pressure on the western and southern periphery of the already weakened realm was so great that a total collapse followed. Hittite power disintegrated, and the capital was sacked, probably by long-standing enemies from the north. Soon, the very existence of the Hittite Empire was forgotten.

The main area of Hittite interest and influence outside their central Anatolian homeland was, as we have seen, towards the southeast, in northern Syria, where so many of the region's most important trade routes converged. In this area, they must have made contact not only with the other powers of the Middle Eastern world, but also with the Mycenaean Greeks, whose presence is firmly attested to by the abundance of Mycenaean pottery discovered at many coastal sites. It is likely that contacts were also made along the Aegean coast, when Hittite power extended far to the west. Surprisingly, little archaeological evidence for this contact has been discovered in the form of Mycenaean artifacts in central Anatolia or Hittite artifacts at Mycenaean sites. But Hittite texts give ample evidence for relations, both friendly and hostile, with a land known to them as Ahhiyawa. Ahhiyawa can plausibly be equated with the land of the Akhai(w)oi or Achaeans, one of the Homeric names for the Greeks who fought in the Trojan War.

The Hittite Achievement

If we attempt to sum up the Hittite achievement, we have to admit that there were few, if any, ways in which they made a permanent impact on later periods. But while they were at the height of their power, they provided secure and stable government, backed by a humane legal system and a disciplined and efficient army, which never descended to the bloodthirsty ruthlessness displayed by the Assyrian army during the following centuries. If, in comparison to their contemporaries in Egypt, Crete, and Greece, they were lacking in artistic inspiration and achievement, they could at least claim a mastery of large-scale practical architecture, and their sculpture, conventional and repetitive though it is, often has a sense of lively vigor that is in itself attractive. On the whole, however, their achievements were practical rather than intellectual. In that sense, they might be described as the Romans of their age.

J.G. Macqueen

FROM BRONZE TO IRON IN THE MEDITERRANEAN REGION

GÖRAN BURENHULT

THE ADVENT OF the Iron Age is closely connected to a period of great economic, social, and political turmoil, and violent changes in the history of southeastern Europe and Southwest Asia. It entailed one of the major technical innovations in the history of humankind, with far-reaching and revolutionary economic, social, and political consequences. One of these consequences was the rapid collapse of Europe's social systems, which had developed in the Stone Age. Iron was accessible to everyone, and power could no longer be based on the control of trade routes for precious materials.

A Villanovan burial urn of clay, together with a fibula and a razor.
ARCHAEOLOGICAL MUSEUM, FLORENCE/SCALA

The invention of iron-working has often been attributed to the Hittites of Asia Minor (present-day Turkey), who were thought to have guarded the secrets of this technology for a long time. This, however, is most probably a misinterpretation of Hittite manuscripts, and the identity of the first ironworkers remains uncertain. We do know, however, that the Hittites were the first to master iron-smelting, and thus began the first true Iron Age culture in the world. Although iron objects appeared as early as about 5000 BC, it was not until about 900 BC that the new metal became the dominant raw material for toolmaking and weaponry.

Iron technology depends on the knowledge of two processes: carburization (the absorption of carbon by iron to produce steel) and quenching (the rapid cooling of hot metal to produce a much harder final product). Shortage of metal supplies for bronze has been put forward as one of the reasons for the development of iron-working, but this explanation does not apply to most regions in the eastern Mediterranean and Anatolia. An increasing overall demand for metal is more likely to be the main reason for the accelerating use of iron. Furthermore, unlike copper, tin, and zinc, iron was available practically everywhere, a fact that soon led to a rapid change from bronze to iron technology.

A proto-Geometric vase, probably manufactured in Athens during the eleventh century BC. The checkered pattern is typical of the period, whereas the wavy lines may be a remnant of Mycenaean artistic traditions.
BRITISH MUSEUM

After the collapse of the Mycenaean palace societies in Greece, the archaeological record reveals a period of extensive depopulation and complete lack of centralized political power. The time between 1300 BC and 900 BC, called the Submycenaean and the proto-Geometric phases by archaeologists, has been referred to as a period of cultural darkness—the Dark Ages. But it was during this period, from about 1100 BC, that iron became increasingly common in the area. And, successively, archaeological research has bridged the cultural gap between the downfall of the Mycenaean world, about 1300 BC, and the rise of the Greek city-states, in the seventh century BC.

The Geometric period, between 900 BC and 700 BC, got its name from the range of motifs on the pottery—meandering lines, zigzags, and rhombic shapes. About 800 BC, human figures also appear as decoration, and the high-water mark of Geometric art appears somewhat later with the so-called Dipylon style, manufactured in Athens about 750 BC. Dipylon vases often show burial scenes or processions with chariots and armed warriors—the first depictions of what would become mythological representation in Greek art.

The Villanova Culture

In Italy—mainly in Etruria, the Po Plain, and parts of Campania—the Early Iron Age is called Villanova, after a site outside Bologna. Villanova had its roots in the Urnfield tradition of the Late Bronze Age—the proto-Villanova phase—with close connections to central Europe. Characteristic of this period are fortified settlements, built on the top of high ground. At the beginning of the eighth century BC, the Villanova culture was to develop into the Etruscan civilization under strong influence from Greek and Phoenician seafarers.

The Villanova cemeteries were really urnfields, and the tombs were often pit tombs, dug into the soft, tuffaceous rock. Cremation was practiced, and the burned bones were deposited in biconical urns or in characteristic hut-urns—clay model replicas of the real houses for the living. The graves contain bronze objects, often richly decorated, such as helmets, situlas (bucket-shaped vessels), drinking vessels, and a series of elegant fibulas (brooches and clasps).

Many of the Villanovan settlements show a gradual development into what later were to become Etruscan cities—for example, Tárchuna (Tarquinia), Caere (Cerveteri), Veii (Veio), Felsina (Bologna), Pupluna (Populonia), and Klevsin (Chiusi)—and the same continuity can be shown in the large cemeteries attached to these settlements.

A shallow clay bowl with interior decoration from a collective tomb at Los Millares. Ritual objects frequently accompanied richer burials in the third millennium BC.
ARCHAEOLOGICAL MUSEUM, MADRID/SCALA

A BRONZE AGE MOSAIC IN THE IBERIAN PENINSULA

Village life emerged in the Iberian peninsula (present-day Spain and Portugal) about 3200 BC, the same time as the people began to work with copper. The uneven distribution of natural resources and arable land, and big variations in population, meant that different areas of the region developed at different rates—some did not progress at all, while others became centers of innovation. The latter growth was concentrated around the southern and southwestern coasts of Iberia. A major settlement at Los Millares (Almería), in the southeast, extended over 2 hectares (5 acres), and was protected by triple walls of stone and reinforced with towers. An imposing barbican (outer defense) with guard chambers and arrow slits projected from the gateway. Stretching more than 300 meters (980 feet) high above the River Andarax, these defensive ramparts straddle a cemetery containing more than 70 collective tombs. On the nearby hills, 10 or 15 smaller citadels guard the approaches to the village. Inside the walls are a number of modest, round dwellings and a large workshop in which copper was smelted and objects cast in simple molds. Contemporary mines and copper-smelting slags have been found in the Sierra de Alhamilla, less than 20 kilometers (12 miles) to the east.

BRONZE AGE SITES IN THE IBERIAN PENINSULA
Parts of the region developed at different rates: the centers of innovation were clustered around the southern and southwestern coasts of the peninsula.
CARTOGRAPHY: RAY SIM

The Bronze Age farmstead of El Castillo (center) commands wide views over the fertile valley below. Defense from enemy attacks was an important consideration when selecting places for permanent settlement.
RICHARD J. HARRISON

Metallurgical Knowledge

Advanced metalworking techniques, so widely used throughout southern Iberia, may have been locally developed. However, it is possible that metallurgical know-how circulated quite freely in the prehistoric Mediterranean region, and that the Iberians learned skills discovered elsewhere. The economy was totally based on agriculture; wheat and barley were grown and a range of domestic animals were kept, including cattle, pigs, sheep, and goats. Floodwater was probably all that was available to irrigate river-bottom land in this arid region.

The various objects found in graves at Los Millares, such as cosmetic or perfume vases, copper implements, personal ornaments, and decorated beaker pottery for drinking and feasting, indicate this was a stratified society with marked inequality of wealth. The defensive walls surrounding the settlement and the number of forts suggest the existence of social instability, as well as the raiding and fighting that went with it. This picture is reinforced by similar defended villages found in the western outskirts of Seville and at the Cabezo del Plomo (Murcia), in the east. But it is only in central Portugal that the size of Los Millares can be matched—at Vila Nova de São Pedro and Zambujal. Many Copper Age villages shrank in size or were abandoned by 2000 BC, as Bronze Age settlement shifted to new sites, sometimes only a few hundred meters away. In southeastern Spain, steep hilltops were favored for their inaccessibility.

Social Differences

Meanwhile, the custom of burying people below the floors of their houses replaced the collective burial practices of the Copper Age societies. Evidence of differences in social standing is very marked at grave sites at settlements such as El Argar and El Oficio (Almería), where the richest women were adorned with a silver diadem or a gold bracelet, while important men were equipped with a bronze sword, axe, and polished pottery. At Fuente Alamo (Almería), the elite lived apart from the rest of the village, in square stone houses with round granaries and a water cistern nearby. Such customs were reflected on a lesser scale in the southern Meseta, where fortified hamlets, known as *motillas,* dominated a flat landscape. In eastern and northern Spain, people did not live in villages at all, but in hamlets such as Moncín, in Zaragoza, or on family farms such as El Castillo (Frías de Albarracin, Teruel). Several hundred of these have been discovered in the mountains behind Valencia. On the other hand, metalworking was in evidence everywhere—first in copper, then in bronze. Metals were obtained through regional exchanges.

Domestic horses became important for the greater mobility they provided, both for riding to distant hunting grounds in search of pelts and furs —for example, at Moncín—or for raiding neighbors. A greater emphasis on hunting as well as dairying meant that small communities could maintain their independence, free from external domination.

In the wetter regions, along the Atlantic coast and Bay of Biscay, small settlements fortified by deep ditches, called *castros,* were established. Here, a flourishing bronze industry developed links with southern Britain and France. The people practiced the same customs of burying hoards of metal tools and weapons. In fact, hoarding metal implements, especially axes, reached a peak in Galicia and northern Portugal between 1000 BC and 700 BC, mirroring similar practices in Brittany and, to a lesser degree, in Britain and Ireland. Scrap was collected for recycling. Deep mining for copper minerals was practiced widely. At El Milagro, Aramo (Asturias), and Riner (Lérida), antler picks and levers abandoned by miners have been found in the underground galleries.

Deer antler was often selected to haft stone and metal tools, because it absorbed the shocks from heavy blows.
NATIONAL MUSEUM OF ANTIQUITIES, EDINBURGH/ADAM WOOLFITT/ ROBERT HARDING PICTURE LIBRARY

P. WITTE/DEUTSCHES ARCHÄOLOGISCHES INSTITUT

These decorated gold bracelets from the hoard of Villena were made between 900 BC and 800 BC, probably in southwestern Spain.

P. WITTE/DEUTSCHES ARCHÄOLOGISCHES INSTITUT

Two gold bowls with punched geometric decoration from a dinner service buried in the hoard of Villena. They show the wealth and taste for conspicuous luxury among the ruling aristocracies of the early first millennium BC.

Gold Treasures

Western Iberia has gold treasures, too, such as the ornaments, comb, and cups found at Caldas de Reyes (Pontevedra). Gold became more common after 1100 BC, and a series of massive ornaments has been discovered. Two neckrings from Berzocana (Cáceres) were buried in a bronze bowl made in the eastern Mediterranean about 1100 BC; a collar from Sintra (Portugal) was crafted from three neckrings attached to a base plate; and a 9.75 kilogram (20 pound) treasure from Villena (Alicante) includes a decorated tableware service, and 28 massive gold bracelets, which may have been loot from a raid.

The variety of ways of life and burial customs indicates that Bronze Age Spain formed a social mosaic ranging from tribal villages to much looser associations based on dispersed dwellings. Societies like these were prospering when Phoenician sailors reached southern Spain about 800 BC, opening up a new era of cultural exchange within the Mediterranean region.

Richard J. Harrison

GREEK AND PHOENICIAN COLONIZATION: 800 BC TO 500 BC

GÖRAN BURENHULT

BETWEEN THE SEVENTH and fifth centuries BC, the Mediterranean world was dominated by two far-reaching events that had considerable impact on subsequent cultural developments in the area: Greek and Phoenician colonization. There were several reasons behind this expansion, such as the need for new settlement areas for the rapidly growing populations in the homelands—in Greece, the time of colonization coincides with a period of marked overpopulation—and the ever-increasing need for raw materials and other necessities. To a great extent, both Greece and Phoenicia lacked metal-ore resources, as well as wood for shipbuilding. Later, grain and other foodstuffs played a significant part in the growing trade.

With the exception of parts of present-day Egypt and Libya, Greek expansion largely followed the northern shores of the Mediterranean—the coasts of the Aegean and Adriatic seas, southern Italy, Corsica, southern France, and eastern Spain—as well as the shores of the Black Sea. In contrast, the Phoenicians founded their trading colonies in the south—in North Africa, western Sicily, Sardinia, and southern Spain. The earliest Phoenician colonies were founded in the metal-rich Tartessa region of southern Spain; while the earliest Greek one has been found at Pithekoussai, on the island of Ischia, in Italy. Many trading colonies evolved into important seaports that exist to this day, including Massilia (Marseilles), in France; Neapolis (Naples), in Italy; Carthage (Tunis), in Tunisia; and Syracuse, in Sicily.

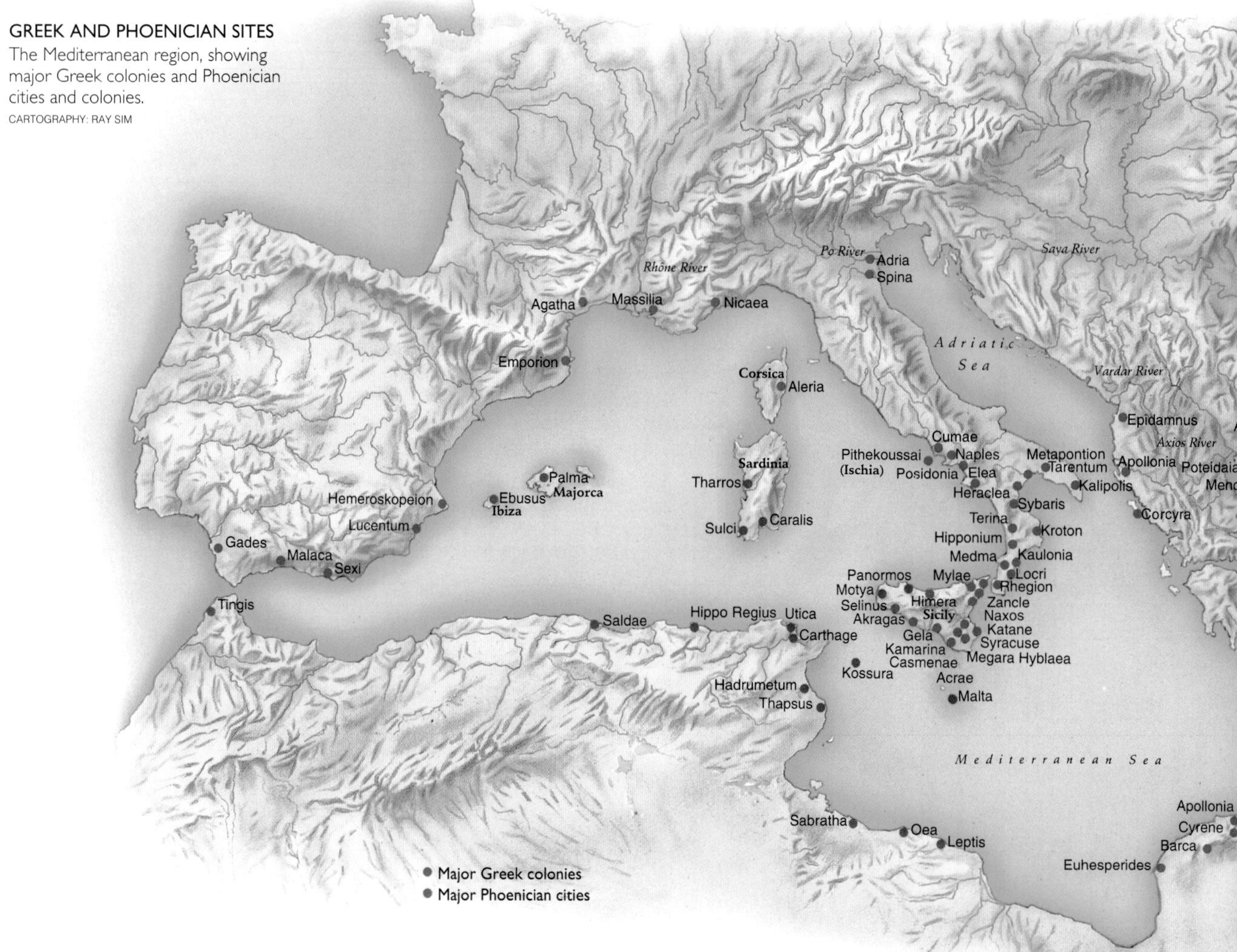

GREEK AND PHOENICIAN SITES
The Mediterranean region, showing major Greek colonies and Phoenician cities and colonies.
CARTOGRAPHY: RAY SIM

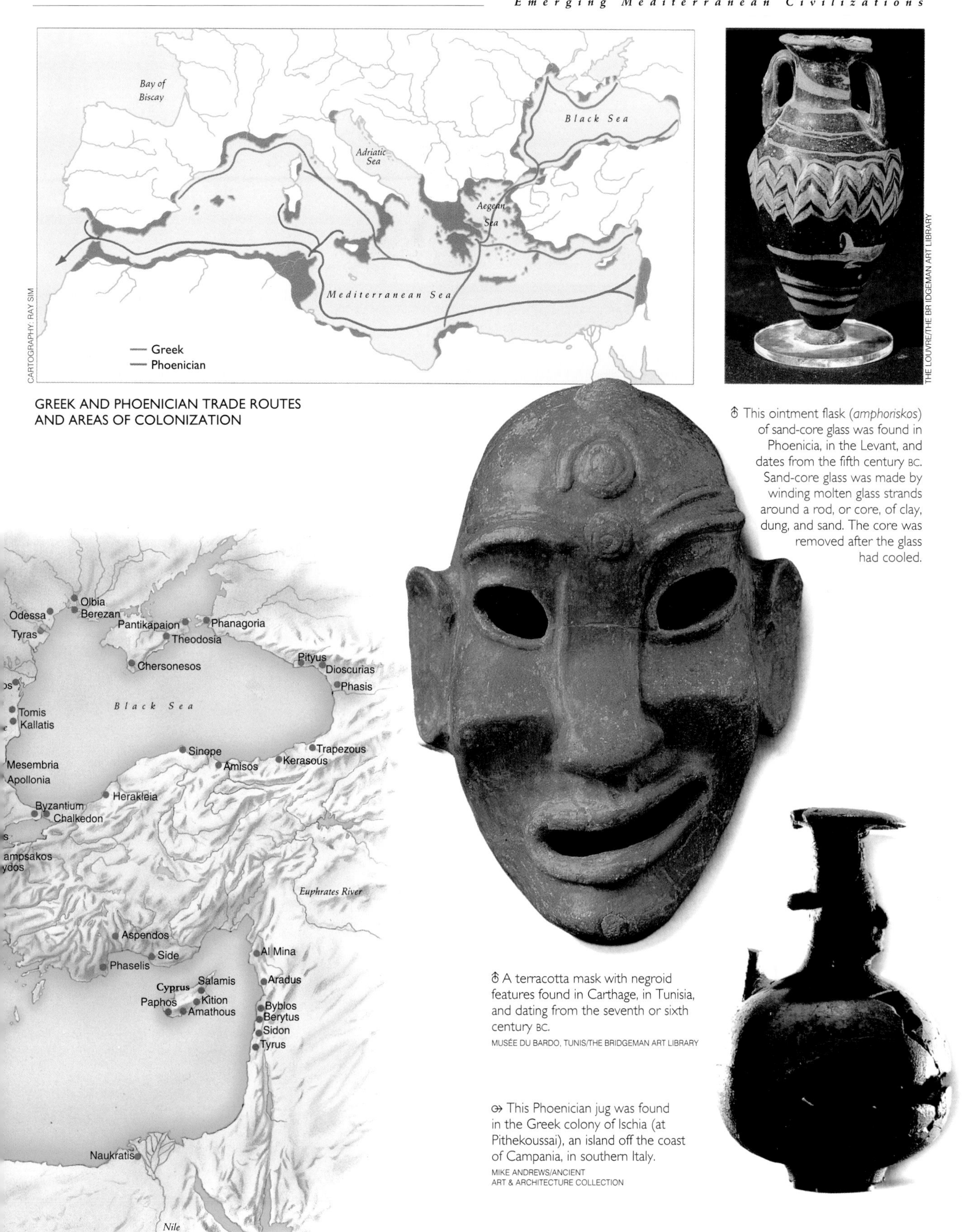

GREEK AND PHOENICIAN TRADE ROUTES AND AREAS OF COLONIZATION

This ointment flask (*amphoriskos*) of sand-core glass was found in Phoenicia, in the Levant, and dates from the fifth century BC. Sand-core glass was made by winding molten glass strands around a rod, or core, of clay, dung, and sand. The core was removed after the glass had cooled.

THE LOUVRE/THE BRIDGEMAN ART LIBRARY

A terracotta mask with negroid features found in Carthage, in Tunisia, and dating from the seventh or sixth century BC.

MUSÉE DU BARDO, TUNIS/THE BRIDGEMAN ART LIBRARY

This Phoenician jug was found in the Greek colony of Ischia (at Pithekoussai), an island off the coast of Campania, in southern Italy.

MIKE ANDREWS/ANCIENT ART & ARCHITECTURE COLLECTION

AUSTRALIAN PICTURE LIBRARY

THE AGE OF ANCIENT GREECE

1100 BC – 31 BC

The Birth of Modern Europe

Pontus Hellström

WILD AND FORBIDDING mountains made land contact difficult between settlements in ancient Greece. People living on the numerous coastal or inland plains found waterways the most important means of communication and transport. Overseas connections were common, and not only for those Greeks who had settled on the islands and on the eastern shore of the Aegean Sea.

It is therefore understandable that the ancient Greeks never managed by themselves to form a political unit; the only serious attempt in this direction was the fifth-century BC naval confederacy called the Delian League, led by Athens. Ultimately, unification was imposed on the Greeks, first by Macedonia and later by Rome, but by then, Greece was no longer its own master.

So long as Greece remained independent, it consisted of a large number of separate, self-governing cities, each forming its own city-state. Most of the city-states were small, and consisted of a single settlement surrounded by farmland. The few notable exceptions, such as Athens, Sparta, and Thessaly, were on wide plains, which made larger political units possible.

In ancient Greece, the building of marble temples to the gods gave cities prestige. Dating from 447 BC to 438 BC, the Parthenon temple on the Acropolis of Athens is the most perfect of them all. It was built with the use of such subtle refinements as a very slight inwards inclination of the columns, to give an unusual impression of harmony and strength.

A large number of painted marble statues of girls stood on the Acropolis of Athens as gifts to the goddess. This lovely Athenian maiden was one of them. Dating from about 500 BC, she was found by archaeologists a hundred years ago.
ACROPOLIS MUSEUM/SCALA

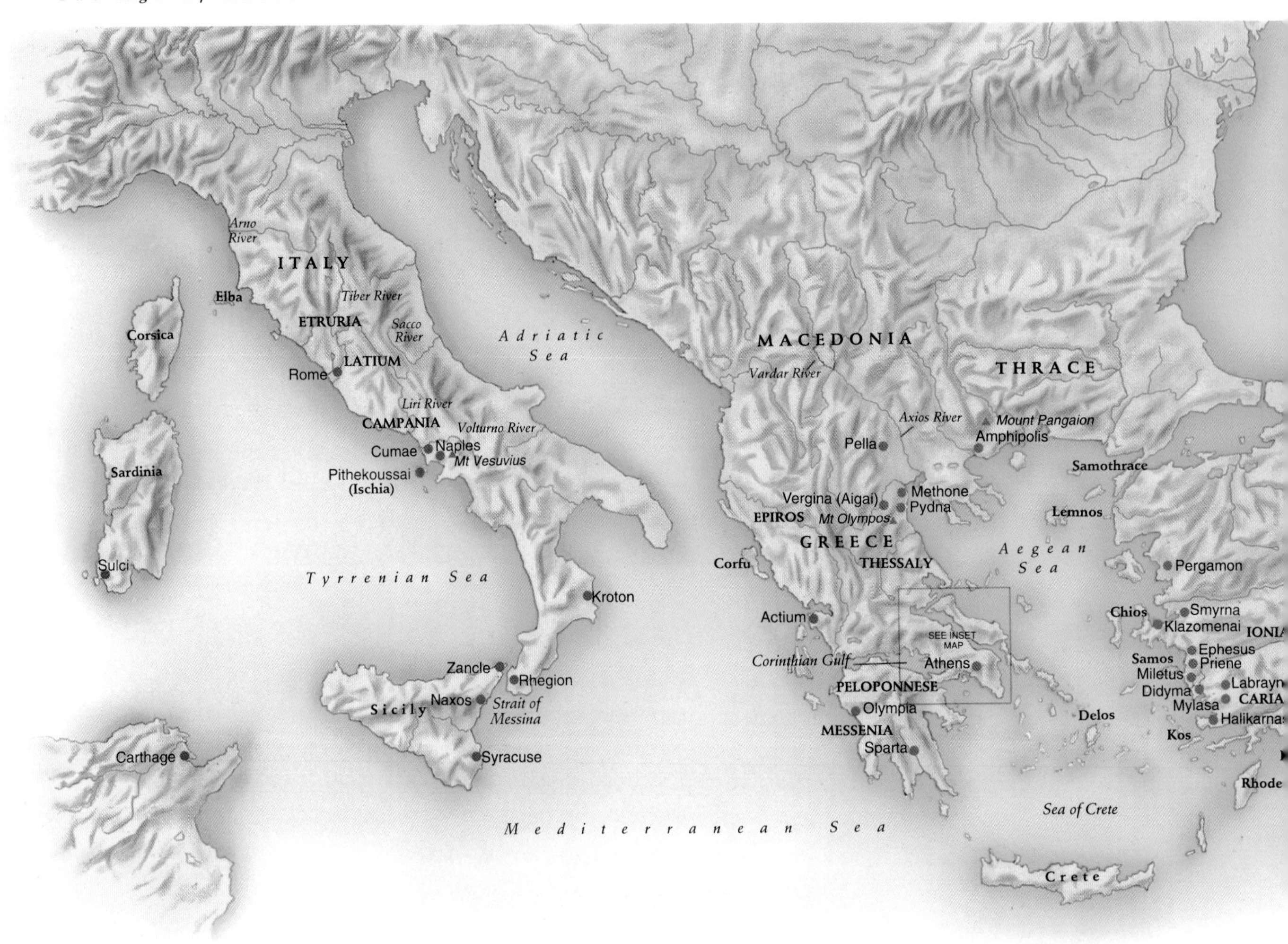

THE ANCIENT GREEK WORLD
The ancient Greek world included Sicily and southern Italy, to the west, and western Asia Minor and Cyprus, to the east.
CARTOGRAPHY: RAY SIM

After the collapse of the Mycenaean Bronze Age civilization, about 1100 BC, Greece was rather sparsely populated for some centuries. This coincides to a large extent with the so-called Dark Age, which lasted until about 700 BC. Our knowledge of the history of these non-literate centuries is comparatively limited, and is based largely on archaeological finds. For the later history of Greece, we have a literature rich in information of many kinds.

THE AGE OF EXPLORATION: 800 BC TO 600 BC

Greek culture did not regain momentum until about 750 BC. With a fresh interest in overseas trade, Greek colonies were founded both in the west (in Italy) and in the east (on the Levantine coast). (See the features *The Trading Port of Pithekoussai* and *The Greeks in the West.*) In the homeland, there are signs of a growth in population. Overseas connections brought a wide spectrum of cultural influences and foreign inspiration.

This was a time of creativity and invention, in which the Greeks showed themselves to be a highly talented people. In the late eighth century BC, the Greek alphabet came into use, and the oldest preserved Greek literature, by Homer and Hesiod, was written. We also see the beginnings of columnar architecture and sculpture in the round. In vase painting, a number of local schools appeared in various parts of Greece, sometimes showing their apparent pleasure in figured scenes.

Greek society, in this period, was feudal, and we can learn much about it from the works of Homer and Hesiod. Cities were small, and ruled by local aristocracies and chieftains. A new era was rapidly taking over, however—that of the Greek "polis" or city-state.

The Rise of the City-state

A polis can roughly be defined as a small, independent community, with a constitution—either formal or informal—and consisting of male citizens, their families, immigrants, and slaves. It occupied a central

city surrounded by farmland. It was ruled by its male citizens, who met in assembly in the marketplace and elected their own officials—although sometimes the supreme power lay with an unconstitutional ruler. Its army consisted of citizens equipped as foot soldiers (called hoplites), fighting in close formation. Their equipment was cheap enough to be within the means of ordinary citizens, and consisted of corselet, greaves, and helmet; a round shield; a thrusting spear; and a sword.

The Greek city-states were not only on the Greek mainland and Greek islands of today, but also on the eastern coast of the Aegean Sea, in what today is Turkey. By means of colonization, Greek cities were established across the Mediterranean, notably on the coasts of Sicily and southern Italy and on the shores of the Black Sea.

In Dark Age Greece, the cities of Chalkis and Eretria (on Euboea, an island north of Attica) played an important role in overseas trade and colonization. In the late eighth century BC, probably about 720 BC, legend has it that a devastating war broke out between Chalkis and Eretria over the Lelantine plain. If so, this was probably the reason for the end of Euboean supremacy. In the following century, trade was taken over to a large extent by Corinth, which had two excellent harbors: Lechaion, on the Corinthian Gulf, for trade to the west; and Kenchreai, on the east coast of the Peloponnese, for the eastern trade. During the seventh century BC, small Corinthian decorated pottery flasks—containers for perfumed oil—were exported throughout the Mediterranean.

In this formative period for Classical Greek civilization, however, the Greek cities in Ionia, on the eastern coast of the Aegean Sea (now Turkey), played an important role. The poet Homer lived on this coast, which was also the home of the earliest Greek philosophy, mathematics, and science. Most of the Greek cities on the northern coast of the Aegean Sea and on the coasts of the Black Sea were founded by colonists sent out from Ionia. Miletus, one of the most important Greek cities in Ionia, allegedly founded 90 colonies.

A so-called *aryballos*, a little pottery bottle produced at Corinth between about 600 BC and 575 BC for the export of perfumed oil. The motifs are of Near Eastern origin, and were probably inspired by imported textiles from the Levant.
MIKE ANDREWS/ANCIENT ART & ARCHITECTURE COLLECTION

This huge clay vase dating from about 750 BC was used as a grave-marker in the cemetery of Athens. It stands 1.55 meters (5 feet) tall. The central part of the painting shows a funeral scene, with the dead lying on a bier, surrounded by mourners.
NATIONAL MUSEUM ATHENS/SCALA

The first beauty contest in world history, painted on an Athenian vase. To the left is a procession of the three contestants: Aphrodite, the goddess of love; Athena, goddess of the arts and of orderly warfare, identified by her helmet; and Hera, Mother of the Gods. At the head of the procession is Hermes, the messenger god, and to the right sits the judge, Prince Paris of Troy. Aphrodite won by bribing the judge. In Greek legend, this contest was the origin of the Trojan War. In return for his favorable decision, Paris won the love of Helen, the most beautiful woman on Earth. She followed him to Troy, thereby causing the Greek war of revenge that ended with the destruction of Troy.

ANCIENT ART & ARCHITECTURE COLLECTION

Athena, goddess of the arts and of orderly warfare. This ancient copy of Phidias's famous gold-and-ivory statue in the Parthenon temple on the Acropolis of Athens, which stood 11 meters (36 feet) tall, dates from the period of emperor Hadrian (AD 117 to AD 138).

RONALD SHERIDAN/ANCIENT ART & ARCHITECTURE COLLECTION

Gods and Heroes

The Greeks had many gods. Their gods had human form, and each had his or her own sphere of influence. Seen from the outside, with Homer as our guide, the gods seem a rather frivolous crowd. This gives an impression that Greek religion was not a very serious matter—a feeling expressed by philosophers of the time.

Homer's stories about immoral behavior among the gods, however, have no connection with the common people's respect for their local deities. By age-old tradition, every village had its own guardian god or goddess. There were also cults of other gods directing specific aspects of life. Thus, cults of Dionysus, for instance, connected with fertility, took place in the appropriate season.

Another characteristic of Greek religion is the hero cult. Many Greek myths are about half-gods, who had a partly human origin. The most famous of these heroes was Hercules, who was worshiped in many places and was of national importance. Other heroes were worshiped only locally—for example, Theseus (worshiped mainly in Attica) and Bellerophon (worshiped at Corinth). The cult of local heroes took its most important step forward in the later Dark Age, when hero cults were created at Bronze Age tombs in the countryside. This can be at least partly explained as a cult of invented ancestors, whereby the landed aristocracy confirmed inherited rights.

The cult of gods of human origin paved the way for a cult of rulers. Such cults had, in a way, begun in the colonization period, when overseas leaders of city-state colonial enterprises received a hero's burial and cult worship in city centers. We also hear of a hero's cult of the still-living Spartan admiral Lysander, which was created in Samos, in the fifth century BC, in gratitude for his having saved the island. This led to a feature of Hellenistic and Roman times, when kings and emperors were the subject of heroic cult worship in their lifetime.

The cult of the gods differed from the heroic cult in the way sacrifices were made. To the gods fell only a part of the sacrifice, and the rest was distributed to those taking part in the rite. The sacrifice to heroes, like that to gods of the underworld, was not to be shared by others; the sacrificed animal was either thrown into a sacrificial pit or completely burned.

The recording in writing of Greek myths was undertaken by the earliest Greek poets, Homer and Hesiod. Homer's *Iliad* and Hesiod's *Theogony* were, however, not holy books like the Bible. The details of the myths could be changed at will, and the texts were not inviolable. When tragedians in the fifth century BC gave alternative versions of older myths, and partly invented new ones according to their dramatic needs, it caused no concern to the audience.

Sacrifice, Creed, and Mystery Cults

The relationship between the Greeks and their gods did not require creed; it required only that proper actions should be taken at the proper times. Taking part in the sacrificial feasts of the gods was one such proper action. It was also important that the sacrifice be performed according to the rules. No creed was involved in the cult of oracular gods—the gods, such as Apollo, who were credited with the power of divine revelation at such sanctuaries as Delphi and Didyma.

It was in the mystery cults that the Greeks came closest to religious feeling and creed. The most sacred mystery cults were those of Demeter and Persephone, at Eleusis, near Athens. There were other famous mystery cults on the islands of Samothrace and Lemnos.

Loosely connected to the mystery cults were some sects based on philosophical ideology. One was founded by the sixth-century BC Samian philosopher Pythagoras, who emigrated to Kroton, in southern Italy, to found a school of philosophy that exerted great influence on philosophical and religious thinking for many centuries. Pythagoras is especially known for his ingenious discovery of the relationship between mathematics and musical harmony, and the consequent theory of the harmony of the spheres. The Pythagoreans believed in reincarnation, and were therefore vegetarians, a custom that brought them into conflict with traditional cult practice requiring citizens to take part in the killing and eating of animals.

A cult-image of Dionysos, god of wine and fertility, surrounded by women celebrating at the festival of flowers known as Anthesteria, held in the month of February, when the new wine was ready for drinking.
NATIONAL MUSEUM, NAPLES/SCALA

ANCIENT GREECE: 1100 BC – 31 BC

BC	AGE	THE GREEK WEST	MAINLAND AND ISLAND GREECE	THE GREEK EAST
31	HELLENISTIC AGE 323 BC – 31 BC		Battle of Actium 31 BC	End of Ptolemaic rule in Egypt 31 BC
100–200		Rise of Roman Empire	Romans sack Corinth 146 BC Rome defeats Macedonia at Pydna 168 BC	Great altar of Zeus and Athena built at Pergamon c. 180 BC
300–400	CLASSICAL GREECE 480 BC – 323 BC		Alexander the Great 356 BC – 323 BC Demosthenes 384 BC – 322 BC Philip II 382 BC – 336 BC Peloponnesian War 431 BC – 404 BC	Alexandria library built 300 BC Ptolemy I rules Egypt c. 320 BC – 283 BC Alexander conquers the Near and Middle East 334 BC – 325 BC Maussollos governs Caria 377 BC – 352 BC
500	ARCHAIC GREECE 700 BC – 480 BC		Delian League 478 BC Persian War 499 BC – 479 BC Peisistratos rules Athens 546 BC – 528 BC	
600–700		Greek colonization in Sicily and southern Italy c. 750 BC – 580 BC	Draco promulgates legal code in Athens c. 620 BC Corinth in the lead c. 725 BC – c. 575 BC Lelantine War c. 720 BC	Sciences and culture flourish in Ionia 700 BC – 500 BC Homer c. 700 BC
800	DARK AGE 1100 BC – 700 BC	Euboeans found Pithekoussai c. 750 BC	Euboean expansion c. 750 BC Rise of the city-state 800 BC – 750 BC Feudal society c. 840 BC	
900–1000				
1100 BC			Collapse of Mycenaean Bronze Age civilization c. 1100 BC	

THE TRADING PORT OF PITHEKOUSSAI

David Ridgway

According to the Greek geographer Strabo (63 BC to AD 21), the trading port of Pithekoussai was established by Greeks from Euboea, the large island off the east coast of mainland Greece. At the end of the eighteenth century AD, the site was identified with the modern resort of Lacco Ameno, on the island of Ischia, in the Bay of Naples. It has emerged from Giorgio Buchner's excavations (from 1952 onwards) as the western Greeks' first and most northerly base in Italy, in full working order by about 750 BC. For the next 50 years or so, it seems to have functioned as a major international trading center, of a kind then unique in the west and thus attractive to a wide variety of foreign entrepreneurs. Unlike Euboean Cumae (Kyme), its immediate successor on the adjacent Campanian mainland, Pithekoussai was not a Greek colony in the strict sense.

Craftsmen Welcomed

From the outset, the finds from the well-defined family plots in the Pithekoussai cemetery indicated that the Euboeans welcomed merchants and craftsmen, not only from many other parts of Greece, but also from the Levant, where there is good evidence for a Euboean presence in the multinational "emporium" of Al Mina, at the mouth of the Orontes, in present-day Turkey.

Indeed, knowledge of the potentially profitable sea routes to the west might well have been one of the more valuable commodities acquired in the ninth century BC, when the Euboeans became the first Greeks since the Mycenaeans to establish direct contact with the Cypro-Levantine world. By then, Cyprus, in particular, had long had a special relationship with Sardinia, which, in turn, was already involved in commercial and other exchanges with the area centered on the Colline Metallifere ("metal-bearing hills") in Tuscany.

Buchner's excavations in the cemetery (Valle di San Montano), on the acropolis (Monte di Vico), and in the suburban industrial quarter (Mezzavia) of Pithekoussai have revealed a wide range of activities in the second half of the eighth century BC. Iron (identified as originating from the island of Elba) and the constituent elements of bronze were imported and worked. Bronze was extensively used to make Italian types of fibulas (dress pins)—which suggests interaction, and probably intermarriage, with the native Iron Age communities on the mainland.

Precious metals seem to have been worked, too, perhaps by resident Levantine specialists. If so, a weight from the industrial quarter suggests that the value of the resulting jewelry was assessed on the standard later used for Euboean coinage.

The first Euboean settlers clearly included a number of accomplished potters. They exploited the island's clay beds to produce excellent painted wares in a recognizably Euboean style for local domestic and funerary purposes. Some Pithekoussan ceramic products soon found their way to Sulci, in Sardinia, and to Carthage, in North Africa, while towards the end of the eighth century BC, a few *aryballoi* (small perfume jars) made at Pithekoussai by expatriate Corinthian potters were exported to the Italian mainland.

A locally made crater (wine bowl) from the Pithekoussai cemetery bears a shipwreck scene, and is the oldest-known piece of narrative figured art ever found on Italian soil. A fragment of another example of the same shape from the industrial quarter preserves the earliest-known potter's signature using the *m'epoiese* ("X made me") formula—a kind of advertisement that became familiar throughout the Greek world in later centuries. It was used, for example, on the vases made by the master potters of Classical Athens.

Prosperous People

Pithekoussan literacy is further attested by three lines of verse inscribed (in a Euboean version of the Greek alphabet) on a cup imported from Rhodes and interred in the cemetery about 720 BC: "Nestor had a fine cup, but anyone who drinks from this one will soon be struck with desire for fair-crowned Aphrodite." This witty challenge to King Nestor's drinking cup, a magnificent artifact described in Homer's *Iliad*, is one of the earliest surviving examples of post-Mycenaean Greek writing. Its appearance at Pithekoussai shows that the prosperous community there was cultured enough to produce Europe's first literary allusion.

With the rise of Cumae from the beginning of the seventh century BC, the importance of Pithekoussai inevitably declined. At the same time, it seems that events in Greece blocked continued Euboean participation in east–west commerce.

Other Greeks, especially those from Corinth, were better able to build on the foundations laid by the nameless pioneers from Euboea, and soon established colonies of their own elsewhere in South Italy and in Sicily. Meanwhile, Cumae shrewdly directed the manufacturing skills it had inherited from Pithekoussai towards the lucrative markets offered by the increasingly sophisticated native aristocracies of Campania, Latium, and, above all, Etruria.

DAVID RIDGWAY

The Baia di San Montano, at Lacco Ameno, a small town on the island of Ischia, in the Bay of Naples. This is a perfect natural harbor, and the Euboean pioneers who arrived here, about 750 BC, would have been glad of the shelter it provided for their boats. The beach (left) is at the end of the valley that served as their cemetery. This view is taken from the summit of their acropolis, Monte di Vico, the lower flank of which can be seen on the right.

C.M. DIXON

The temple of the god Apollo at Corinth. Dating from about 540 BC, this early temple is of limestone, and was originally coated with white stucco to make it look like marble. With their muscular, swelling form, its columns are typical of the early period of Greek architecture.

ARCHAIC GREECE: 600 BC TO 480 BC

The need for formal constitutions followed the rise of the city-state. The motor for change in Greek political life was perhaps the advent of foot-soldier tactics in battle, which required all citizens to fight together in close formation to defend the city. Citizens thus had equal responsibility in battle, and equal expenses for armor. This may have led to a quest for political equality as well. In many cities, the old ruling aristocratic families were overthrown, and new leaders took power. These leaders were called tyrants, a word for "unconstitutional ruler" that carried no connotation of cruelty.

In spite of the rule of tyrants in many city-states, more power came to lie with a widened circle of male citizens, who met in assemblies to elect their magistrates and for other matters. The constitutions created at this time responded, of course, to needs of the day, but they also helped to shape the future. The never-resolved conflict between Athens and Sparta was, to a great extent, caused by their different constitutions. Sparta clung to its old-fashioned, never-changing constitution, whereas the Athenian constitution was repeatedly modernized to meet needs.

Sparta drew up its constitution in the early seventh century BC. Its regulations made Sparta the efficient military machine that, step by step, by force and by diplomacy, subjugated the entire Peloponnese. The heads of state were two kings, one from each of two old families. There were also 5 annually elected ephors (magistrates) and a council of 25 elders, all of whom were ex-ephors. All major decisions of the state were made by these 32 people. There was an assembly, but it had little real power. It consisted of some 9,000 male members of the aristocracy. Some of the remaining inhabitants were *perioikoi*, "those living around", who were free citizens of surrounding villages with no political rights. The others were helots, the state-owned serfs, who were the indigenous population of the conquered area of Messenia. Helots worked the farms, and presented a constant threat of revolution.

The most important rule in the constitution was that the sons of aristocratic families were taken from their mothers at the age of 5 to begin a training that continued until they turned 30, making them the most professional soldiers Greece ever saw.

The first law code of Athens was drafted by Draco in about 620 BC. We know little more about its rules than that they were severe—"draconian", as we say. Presumably, power lay within a narrow circle of aristocratic families, who elected magistrates and a council of ex-magistrates, called the Areopagus, among themselves. In the early sixth century BC, many farmers had become serfs because of debts to the big landowners. The Athenian politician and poet Solon was assigned to modernize the constitution. The farmers were absolved from their old debts, and a new council was introduced beside the old Areopagus, which thereby lost much of its power. Solon also gave to the assembly the power of a supreme court. These changes sound far from radical, but for the time being, they saved the state from revolution. Solon's was probably the optimum solution—it gave a wider circle of citizens extended power, but not more than would be yielded by the ruling families.

Feud of the Families

Sixth-century BC Athens was politically dominated by the conflict between two families—the old, Athenian Alcmaeonid family, and the Peisistratid family from Brauron, on the east coast of Attica. Peisistratos ruled as tyrant for several decades, at first intermittently from the late 560s BC, then continuously from 546 BC to 528 BC. After his death, his son Hippias took over. Hippias fell in 510 BC, because of Spartan help to the Alcmaeonids. Athens received a new constitution in 507 BC, drawn up by Kleisthenes, head of the Alcmaeonid family.

The most important innovations in this constitution were a widely extended citizenship and a new administrative grouping of Attica's 139 *demes*, or villages, into 30 blocks: 10 each from the City, the Coast, and the Plain. These were, in turn, grouped into 10 administrative units, called Tribes, each consisting of 3 blocks, one from the City, one from the Coast, and one from the Plain. Each Tribe elected 50 members to the council, and these groups took turns at governing the state, each exercising power for one-tenth of the year. Ten generals were also elected, one by each Tribe. They were military leaders, and were also entrusted with power in certain administrative and financial matters.

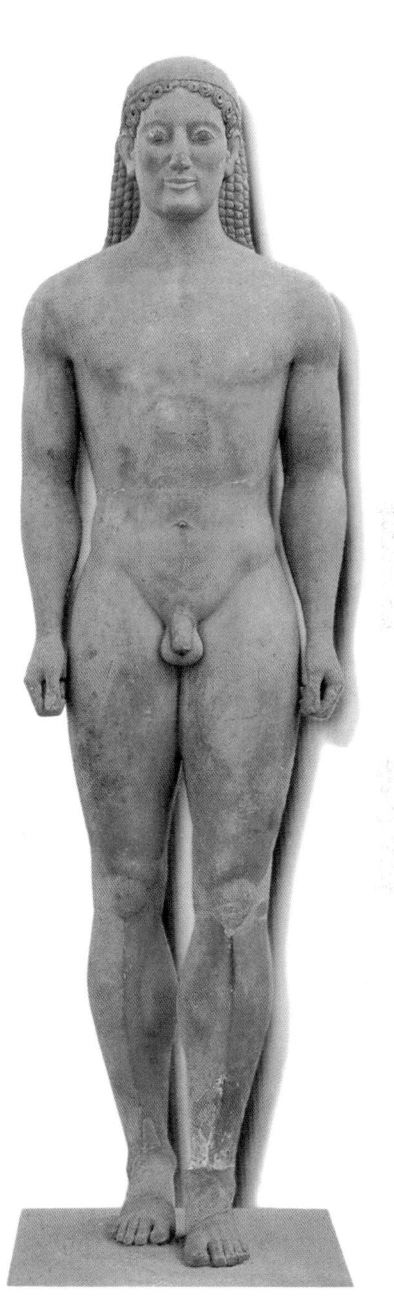

This marble statue dating from about 530 BC comes from the tomb of Kroisos, a young Athenian who fell in battle. An inscription on the base reads: "Stop and grieve at the tomb of the dead Kroisos, slain by wild Ares in the front rank of the battle."
NATIONAL MUSEUM, ATHENS/SCALA

THE GREEKS IN THE WEST

CHARLOTTE WIKANDER

In the *Odyssey*, Homer depicts Sicily as the pastures for the flocks of the sun-god Helios: a wonderful land of plenty, empty of people. The south of Italy and Sicily became an important and well-exploited part of the Greek world, and this mythical imagery of a bountiful nature and a land of plenty played a large part in the Greek view of the west.

From Greek literature, we know of the political and economic prominence of colonial cities such as Syracuse, in Sicily. The impressive ruins of these cities—especially their great temples—have been landmarks for centuries and have attracted travelers from the eighteenth century to our day. But it is only since the Second World War that archaeology has provided more systematic insights into the origins of the colonial enterprises, the life of the Greek colonials, and the relationship between the colonies and the indigenous inhabitants in Italy.

The earliest cities in the west were founded about the middle of the eighth century BC. The first colony was Cumae (Kyme), on the Bay of Naples, shortly before 750 BC. It was followed by the earliest Sicilian colony, Naxos, in 735 BC, and in the following year, by what became the mightiest city in Sicily, Syracuse.

Archaeologists have been able to shed light on the speed of colonization. The presence of Mycenaean Greeks in Italy during the Bronze Age has been shown to be much more extensive than was hitherto believed, and excavations at Pithekoussai, on the island of Ischia, in the Bay of Naples, have proved that a group of settled Greeks and Phoenicians was already trading from there to Etruria by 750 BC. (See the feature *The Trading Port of Pithekoussai.*) Cumae lies on the mainland directly opposite Ischia, and was thus an extension of an already existing settlement. This early Greek presence in Italy also explains some of the rapidity with which the colonies spread. This was not completely unknown land; it had been explored for at least a generation.

DENNIS STOCK/MAGNUM

A view of the volcano Etna from the Roman theater of Taormina, on Sicily. Taormina is the site of the original Greek colony, called Tauromenion by the Greeks.

Trade and Farming

What, then, motivated this massive colonial expansion? Two reasons seem obvious from our sources: trade and farming. Of these, trade was the earlier motivation. Greece is notoriously poor in natural resources, particularly metal, and the magnet that attracted traders to Italy was the rich ores of copper and iron in Tuscany, Etruria. The inhabitants of Iron Age Etruria were, however, obviously able to defend their resources. No Greek colonies were founded north of the Bay of Naples, and the archaeological finds in Etruria amply demonstrate the enormous quantities of goods traded by the Greeks and Phoenicians in exchange for the coveted metals.

In keeping with their trading concerns, the earliest colonies were established at good and easily defended harbor sites, Syracuse being a prime example. Two protected harbors and an island, Ortygia—offering a settlement site for the arrivals—made this a perfect location for such an enterprise.

Syracuse's mother city, Corinth, became the dominant trading power with Italy in the seventh century BC. The main trading competitors were at first Chalcidians (inhabitants of Chalcis) from Euboea, the island just off the coast of Attica. They took control of the trade passages by founding twin cities on each side of the Strait of Messina: Rhegion and Zancle.

Greece was also poor in arable land. According to various commentators, including the Greek historian Herodotus and the Greek poet Hesiod, there was increasing social tension and conflict during the late eighth and the seventh century BC, one reason apparently being overcrowding and competition for farmland. The extensive areas available for farming in the west were an obvious remedy to the situation. Colonial cities based on agriculture were founded along the coastline of southern Italy and on the southern seaboard of Sicily.

A Community Enterprise

A colonial venture was not conceived as an individual enterprise. A Greek city-state let it be known that it intended to found a colony. In some cases, we know that citizen families were required to send one adult son; otherwise, impoverished farmers, whose lots were no longer adequate to support them, set out together under the aegis of the mother city. A leader for the project, the *oikist*, was appointed by the mother city, and the site was chosen in advance with the approval of Apollo's oracle at Delphi.

When the settlers arrived, the new town and its hinterland were carefully divided into lots for habitation and cultivation, with space allotted for public use: the marketplace (*agora*) and buildings functioned as the venue for political organization and religious life. The colonies' prosperity is nowhere so clearly shown as in the massive resources put into the building of sanctuaries, which were obviously a source of civic pride as well as serving a religious function.

Indigenous People

Nevertheless, the areas occupied by Greeks were not empty on their arrival. What of the indigenous people? Did they accept this massive influx of strangers, dividing the land between them? Seemingly, they did, to a surprising extent. Mentions of conflict are practically nonexistent in the early colonial period. The archaeological evidence suggests some of the reasons behind this quiet: excavation of indigenous tombs and sites has shown how extensively native populations took advantage of Greek technology and raised their own standard of living through imports of such foreign luxuries as high-quality pottery and perfumed oils.

Only after about 300 years is there evidence of a changed attitude. The local people of southern Italy—Messapians, Lucanians, and, most of all, the Samnites—put the Greek cities under increasing military pressure from the late fifth century BC onwards. In the end, the proud colonial cities had to apply to the motherland for help, but to little avail: the greediest Italic state, Rome, finally subdued them all. Nevertheless, the colonial cities kept their Greek cultural identity for a long time, and by their profound influence on the culture of Rome, contributed towards the creation of a Hellenized culture throughout western Europe.

In this way, all parts of Attica, however distant from Athens, received equal political rights, and at the same time, the old groupings based on loyalties and geographical proximity lost much of their influence. By creating a completely new administrative structure and giving all Athenian male citizens equal rights, Kleisthenes united Attica, and gave it a modern constitution that was the most democratic of its time. That this constitution excluded women, immigrants, and slaves is only a reflection of the age in which it was created.

Greek Architecture

Greek monumental architecture, in the form of temples surrounded by wooden colonnades, was born about 650 BC. The transformation into stone followed by the end of the century. The temples' columns were of two kinds, or "orders"—the Doric, on the mainland, and the Ionic, on the eastern Aegean coast and the Aegean islands. The most obvious difference between the orders lay in the shape of their capitals, or column heads, but each order also had its own set of proportions and details, especially for the superstructure, or entablature.

Ancient theoreticians compared the Doric column to the male form because of its stout, muscular proportions and severe shape. The Ionic, with its more slender proportions and floral style, was likened to the female form—indeed, the spiral coils of the Ionic scrolled column head do resemble a coiffure.

The earliest Doric temples, surrounded by columns on all sides, were built in the northeastern Peloponnese. The earliest Ionic temples were erected on the island of Samos and at Ephesus, on the eastern Aegean coast. These were big temples, built to glorify the ruling tyrants in these cities.

War with Persia

The Archaic period ended with the Great War against Persia (from 499 BC to 479 BC), which was a successful defensive war, and which brought Greece, and especially Athens, enormous confidence. Between 550 BC and 500 BC, the Persian empire had been steadily growing, and everything indicated that the future would bring either a confrontation with Greek city-states or an unconditional Greek surrender. By the end of the century, all of Asia Minor (present-day Turkey) and Cyprus; all of the eastern and northern Aegean coasts; the entire eastern coast of the Mediterranean; Egypt; and Libya, as far as Cyrenaica, were under Persian rule.

In 499 BC, the Ionian city of Miletus asked the Greek mainland to support an uprising of many Greek cities on the eastern Aegean coast, but the reaction was hesitant. In the end, only Athens and Eretria sent a small force each, 25 ships in all. The Persians crushed the revolt in 494 BC, and turned for revenge on the two Greek cities. The Greek response was prodigious: 10,000 Athenians, with only 192 casualties, crushed a vastly larger Persian army on the plain of Marathon in 490 BC. The Greek navy of 280 ships, led by Athens, outdid a Persian navy three times as big at Salamis in 480 BC; and the Spartans defeated the Persians on the battlefield of Plataiai, in 479 BC, with some 35,000 to 40,000 troops against a far greater army.

The Greeks' strength was partly psychological. The very idea of trying to stop a Persian army perhaps 200,000 strong with a force of only 7,000 (as the Greeks nearly succeeded in doing at Thermopylae in 480 BC) is against all reason. But, of course, the final Greek victory depended very much on superior strategy, on making fewer mistakes than the enemy, and on the efficiency of foot-soldier warfare.

The heroic general Leonidas, commemorated in this statue in the acropolis of Sparta, fell in battle against the Persians at the mountain pass of Thermopylae in 480 BC, but succeeded in securing the safe retreat of his fellow Greeks.
SPARTA MUSEUM/SONIA HALLIDAY PHOTOGRAPHS

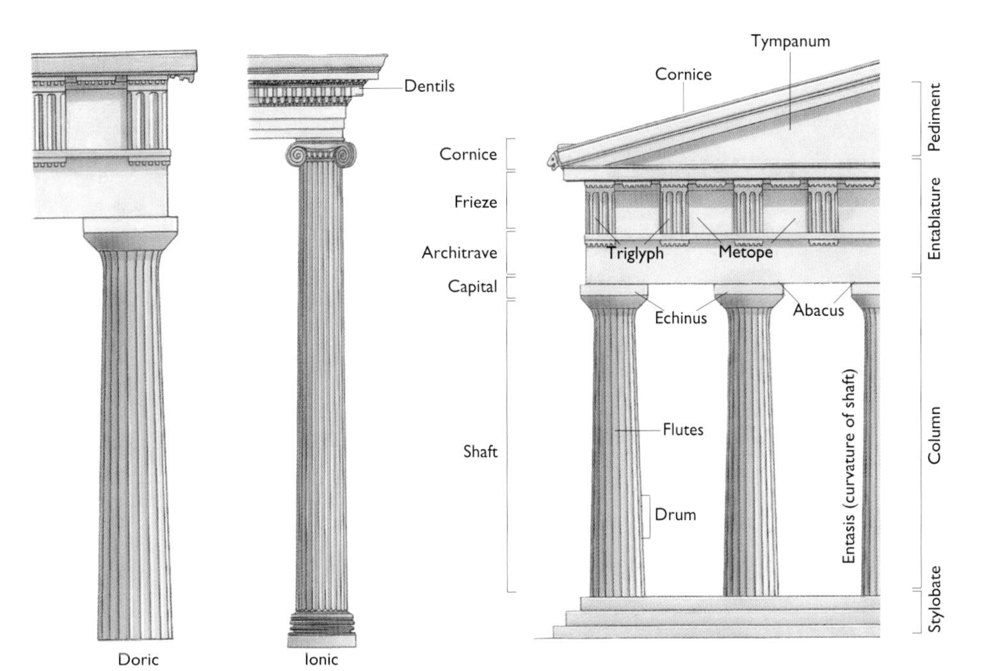

The Doric capital (column head) was quite simple, and consisted of a circular cushion (the echinus), under a square plinth (the abacus). In the Doric entablature, the most conspicuous detail was the frieze with alternating triglyphs and metopes. The Ionic column had more elegant proportions than the Doric, and was set on a molded base. The capital had its origin in plant forms, and consisted of a scroll-like member rolling into a spiral on each side of the column top. Above the architrave beam were the so-called dentils, which imitated the ends of close-set rafters. In later Ionic, the dentils were sometimes exchanged for a figured continuous frieze running round the building on all sides.
ILLUSTRATION: MIKE LAMBLE

MICHAEL FREEMAN/BRUCE COLEMAN LTD

The Acropolis of Athens was the religious center of the Athenian empire in the fifth century BC. To the left is the Parthenon, the largest building of the sanctuary, built between 447 BC and 438 BC and richly decorated with marble sculptures. To the right is the Erechtheion, the main cult building, with its old wooden statue of Athena, the city goddess. In the background is the Propylaia, the monumental entrance building of the Acropolis.

CLASSICAL GREECE: 480 BC TO 323 BC

If our sources for reconstructing the history of Greece in the fifth century BC had been purely archaeological, one of the two main military powers would easily have escaped notice. Thanks to our rich literary sources, however, we know that the fifth century saw constant confrontation between Athens and Sparta. Sparta won in the end, but its triumph is not archaeologically visible, because it did not use its resources to erect lasting monuments, like the temples on the Athenian Acropolis.

After the Persian War, which ended with Greek victories on land and at sea, there was relative peace in Greece for almost 50 years. This brought population growth, and by the middle of the century, Athens, the largest city of the world, and the countryside of Attica surrounding it, had about 250,000 inhabitants. Some 75,000 of these lived within the city walls. The male citizens may have numbered about 40,000; the slaves, 100,000. The rest were women, children, and immigrants.

Athens had taken the lead both politically and culturally. Politically, Athens had, in 478 BC, created a naval confederacy as a defense against Persian threats. This was the Delian League, which consisted of some 170 Greek city-states, almost all of them situated on the islands and the coast of the Aegean Sea. The formal seat of the league was the sanctuary of Apollo, on the island of Delos. The league's treasury was kept there until 454 BC, when it was moved to the Athenian Acropolis, ostensibly for safety, but actually to be within easy reach when needed by Athens. In reality, the league was an Athenian empire, with all power centered in the capital of Athens. On several occasions, member-states that wanted to quit the league were brutally forced by Athens to remain in it.

In this period, Athenian democracy saw some small but important adjustments. In 462 BC, jury members in the courts were selected by lot and paid for their work, which made even male citizens who were not very rich eligible. Pay for council members on active duty and for participation in the festivals followed. In the last years of the century came pay for attending the assembly. Thus, there were no economic restrictions on any male citizen wishing to take an active part in politics. That magistrates should be selected by lot and paid was a basic principle of fifth-century BC Athenian democracy. However, the 10 generals remained elected to their position, and since there was a certain doubt about the ability of citizens chosen by lot, the generals came to be the most powerful magistrates of the city. Pericles, who in reality was the ruler of Athens from 451 BC until his death in 429 BC, held the position of one of the 10 annually elected generals for 15 consecutive years.

Athens at Its Peak

Athenian culture was at its height in the fifth century BC. It was created not only by Athenians, but also by intellectuals from other cities, especially from Ionia, where the political climate had changed for the worse after the Persian War. Among such immigrants were the town planner Hippodamos of Miletus; the Ionian philosophers Anaxagoras of Klazomenai and Aspasia of Miletus; and the historian Herodotus of Halikarnassos.

Thanks to its military successes, the young democracy of Athens was enormously confident, and its confidence was reflected in literature, philosophy, art, and architecture. It is still manifest in the remains of the huge building project on the Acropolis, which used the resources of the Delian League, and was under the supervision of Phidias, the most famous sculptor of antiquity, and Pericles, the great statesman and orator. It is also reflected in the painted vases produced in the flourishing pottery district of Kerameikos, in Athens, that can now be seen in major museums. (See the feature *Vase Painting of Ancient Greece.*)

Athens' confidence is even more manifest in literature. This was the period of the great tragedians Aeschylus, Sophocles, and Euripides; of the comedy writer Aristophanes; and of the historians Herodotus and Thucydides. The writings of such philosophers as Plato and Aristotle came in the next century, but followed on from the intellectual climate of fifth-century BC Athens.

In architecture, the Doric and Ionic orders had from the beginning been geographically separated: Ionic on the Aegean islands and eastern Aegean coast, Doric on the mainland. In the fifth century BC, the two orders were used side by side in the great Acropolis project—both within the same buildings and as the orders of different buildings. We can assume that they were seen as representative of their respective cultural districts. Their mixture in the most important and central sanctuary of the empire had seemingly political overtones.

Ever since the Persian War, a cold war had been going on between Athens and Sparta, with their respective allies. There were minor conflicts, but as yet, no major conflict had erupted. Now and then, a truce was declared to give peace a better chance. In the late 430s BC, however, an acute conflict between Athens and Corinth prompted Corinth to appeal to Sparta to put a stop to Athenian oppression. Finally, Sparta decided to take action, and from this evolved the great Peloponnesian War, which lasted from 431 BC to 404 BC, and in which almost all Greek states took part. Sparta emerged victorious, but both sides were so exhausted by the fighting that neither ever completely recovered.

THE FOURTH CENTURY BC

The political history of Greece in the fourth century BC, after the Peloponnesian War, is a story of fighting between cities now weaker than ever—a situation that invited foreign powers to enter the scene. Sparta dominated Greece, and Athens played a secondary role. Athens recovered enough to create a new naval league in 377 BC, but it lasted only until 355 BC.

In the last years of the fifth century BC, an expeditionary force of 10,000 foot soldiers, mostly Spartan mercenaries, was hired by Prince Kyros of Persia to help in overthrowing his brother, the king of the Persian Empire, Artaxerxes. The Greeks did not succeed, but managed to return (the famous "retreat of the ten thousand") with the lesson that Persia was not invincible. Nor was Sparta, as it turned out: in the 370s BC, Thebes, under the general Epaminondas, managed briefly to become the strongest military power in Greece, inflicting a heavy defeat on Sparta at Leuktra, in central Greece, in 371 BC. With the death of Epaminondas in 362 BC, at the battle of Mantineia, in the Peloponnese, the dominance of Thebes came to an abrupt end.

BRACCIO NUOVO, VATICANO/SCALA

Athenian lawyer and politician Demosthenes (384 BC to 322 BC), the most famous orator of antiquity. He desperately but in vain tried to stop Philip II of Macedonia from conquering the rest of Greece.

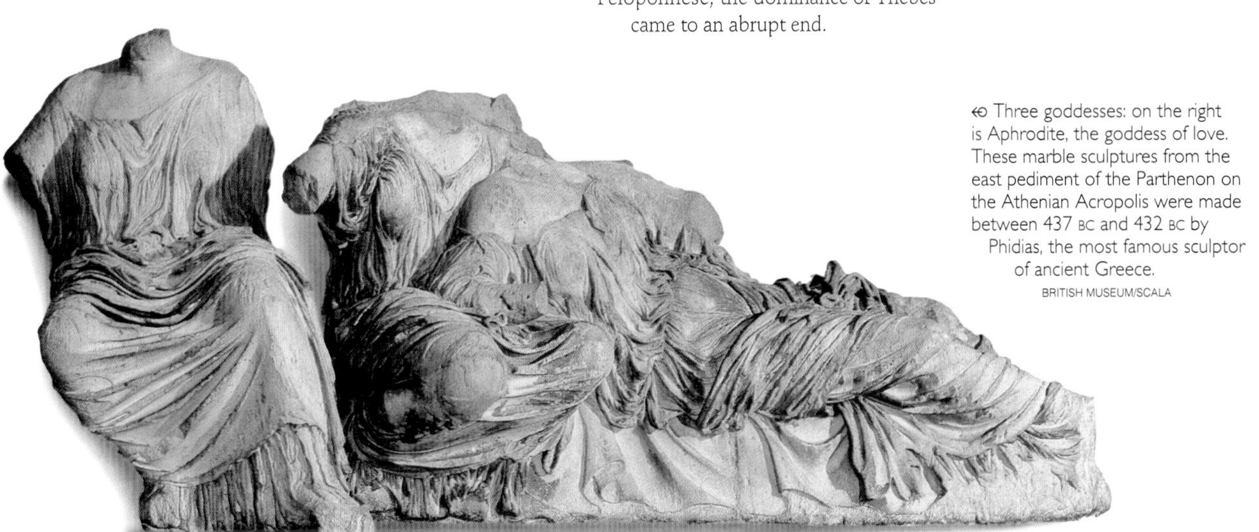

Three goddesses: on the right is Aphrodite, the goddess of love. These marble sculptures from the east pediment of the Parthenon on the Athenian Acropolis were made between 437 BC and 432 BC by Phidias, the most famous sculptor of ancient Greece.

BRITISH MUSEUM/SCALA

THE RIDDLE OF "PHILIP'S TOMB"

PONTUS HELLSTRÖM

IN NOVEMBER 1977, Manolis Andronikos, of the University of Thessaloniki, made the extraordinary find of an unlooted, very rich, fourth-century BC tomb at Vergina, in Macedonia. The discovery was the most widely publicized archaeological find in Greece in the 1970s, and is a strong candidate to be named the find of the century in Classical archaeology. Its importance lies primarily in the identification of the tomb as that of Philip II. This gives it a very special historical interest, not only because Philip was the father of Alexander the Great, but also because he was a powerful ruler, without whose conquest of Greece Alexander could not have conquered the East.

A waxwork reconstruction of the skull found in the tomb, made by a new technique using surviving cranial bones. The eye wound appears to confirm the identification with Philip II, who lost an eye in battle. More recent research by the British team, however, indicates that Philip's eye injury was well treated and left little scarring. If this were Philip's head, and not that of an unknown, one-eyed Macedonian prince, the wound would have looked less nasty. The question then remains: how many one-eyed noblemen were there in warlike Macedonia in the fourth century BC?
UNIVERSITY OF MANCHESTER/LAMBRAKIS PRESS

Vergina is doubtless the ancient Macedonian capital Aigai, where the royal cemetery was situated. Since the tomb was in the biggest mound on the site, it seemed probable that the occupant was a Macedonian king. The tomb contained the cremated remains of two people, each deposited in a heavy, beautifully worked golden chest. In the main chamber, a man aged 40 to 50 years was buried with a rich assortment of weapons and other prestigious grave goods. In the anteroom were the remains of a woman aged 20 to 30 years.

The approximate date of the tomb was established via pottery vases dating from about 350 BC to 325 BC. The only two Macedonian kings from this time and shortly afterwards were Philip II, who died in 336 BC, and Philip III Arrhidaios, Alexander's half-brother and successor, who died in 317 BC and was not a very famous king. Alexander himself was excluded, because we know that he was buried at Alexandria, in Egypt, having died at Persepolis in 323 BC.

All kinds of evidence indicated to Andronikos that the man buried in the main chamber was Philip II, but none of the evidence was conclusive. Other scholars were skeptical and argued for a different interpretation. They asked, for example, who the woman in the anteroom was, and why Philip III should be ruled out.

ARCHAEOLOGICAL MUSEUM OF THESSALONIKI/EKDOTIKE ATHENON SA

The front of the unlooted tomb at Vergina, which contained about 20 kilograms (45 pounds) of gold objects. If the tomb belonged to Philip II, the grave goods were only a small part of his wealth: he received more than 20 tonnes (20 tons) of gold annually from the gold mines of Mount Pangaion, in Macedonia, alone.

The debate was not resolved until 1983, when surprising evidence emerged from scientific research on the cremated remains. A British team consisting of specialists in archaeology, osteology, and criminology—John Prag, Jonathan Musgrave, and Richard Neave—produced a reconstruction of the dead man's head, using cranial bones that had escaped destruction in the funeral pyre. The reconstruction revealed a serious injury to one eye. Since it is known from literary sources that Philip II lost an eye during the siege of Methone, in Macedonia, some years before he was assassinated, the new evidence made many skeptics change their mind and consider the case proved in favor of Philip II.

Moreover, the evidence against Philip III Arrhidaios is overwhelming. In particular, there is evidence that the bodies in the tomb were buried at different times. This is apparent from the fact that the wall plastering in the main chamber was unfinished—indicating that the burial was performed in haste—whereas the plastering in the anteroom, containing the second burial, was finished. We know from written sources, however, that Philip III and his queen, Eurydice, were buried together.

But there is another possibility: the body in the main chamber may have belonged to some other member of the Macedonian royal family. The only evidence that the tomb is a king's, apart from the royal splendor of the grave goods, is the presence of a royal diadem, which, it is thought, could not have been part of a prince's grave goods. Such diadems were, however, used not only by kings, but also by poets and priests.

Philip II of Macedonia then entered the scene. In 359 BC, at the age of 24, he became the ruler of Macedonia. Step by step, he expanded Macedonian territory in all directions. In the west, he reached the Adriatic at Epiros. To the east, he took Amphipolis from Athens in 357 BC, and with it, the very rich gold mines of Pangaion, on the northern shore of the Aegean. He continued east and north, conquered Thrace in a series of campaigns, held all the north coast of the Aegean, and seized a large part of what is now Bulgaria, reaching the shore of the Black Sea.

To the south, he conquered Thessaly in 352 BC, and so acquired a seat in the Delphic council of Greek states. On the pretext of defending the rights of the Delphic council, he took part, with his army, in Greek internal affairs. After having infiltrated territory further south, he was opposed by Athens and Thebes, but it was too late. At the final battle at Chaironeia, in 338 BC, all remaining Greek opposition was decisively defeated, and Greece became part of Macedonia. In 337 BC, Philip declared war on Persia, a war of revenge for the Persian devastation of Greece in 480 BC, but in the following year, before the war had started, Philip was assassinated.

Considering this gloomy background of fourth-century BC political history, it is understandable that art, architecture, and cultural life did not reach the same level of splendor as in the preceding century. The main exception was philosophy, with its giants Plato and Aristotle. Aristotle introduced true scientific inquiry, which was the basis of Hellenistic scholarship and science, as in Alexandria. From the fourth century BC, the center of cultural life started moving away from mainland Greece.

The Ionian Renaissance: 360 BC to 330 BC

Before the Persian War, architecture, sculpture, philosophy, and the sciences had flourished in the Greek cities on the eastern shore of the Aegean. This era ended abruptly with the unsuccessful revolt against the Persians from 499 BC to 494 BC. The succeeding fifth century was a dark age for culture and the arts in Ionia. In architecture, it is a blank: official building all but ceased.

A new era opened in the fourth century BC. Mainland Greece and the Persian Empire were in decline, but the climate improved along the eastern Aegean. In 377 BC, a local prince named Maussollos succeeded his father, Hekatomnos, as satrap (governor) in the new Persian province of Caria, in present-day Turkey. He was the oldest of three brothers and two sisters, the so-called Hekatomnids, who were all to succeed him in turn. Maussollos remained in power for almost 25 years, until 352 BC. From his actions, we can conclude that he was actively working towards the establishment of a kingdom of his own, and like his contemporary Philip II, he apparently had far-reaching ambitions.

Maussollos and His Ambitions

Maussollos's old capital was Mylasa, in the Carian inland. Soon after his ascension to power, in the year the second Athenian confederacy was formed, Maussollos moved his capital to Halikarnassos (present-day Bodrum), a city with an important strategic position on the seafront and an excellent double harbor. There, he kept a fleet of 100 ships, which was put to good use. His policy, unlike the Persians', was anti-Athenian, and he managed to install garrisons in some Greek cities previously belonging to the Athenian confederacy, such as Kos, Chios, and Klazomenai. He systematically enlarged the area over which he ruled on the Asiatic mainland to include Lycia, to the east, and perhaps as far as Smyrna, to the north. His ambitions may have extended even further. He took part in the great satraps' revolt against the king of the Persian Empire, Artaxerxes II, and escaped unhurt.

The temple of Athena at Priene was built after 350 BC by the architect Pytheos, who also wrote a book about its architecture. According to an inscription on the temple, Alexander the Great gave the temple to the goddess (meaning that he paid for it).

ADAM WOOLFITT/ROBERT HARDING PICTURE LIBRARY

⊖ The sanctuary of Labraynda, in Caria, Southwest Asia Minor, as it would have looked in the middle of the fourth century BC. On the upper terrace is the temple of Zeus, surrounded by columns. To the left and on the terrace below are two banqueting halls, with two columns at the front.
ILLUSTRATION: OLIVER RENNERT

⊙ Maussollos, the ruler of Caria (377 BC to 352 BC). This portrait comes from his tomb, the huge mausoleum at Halikarnassos, one of the seven wonders of the ancient world.
RONALD SHERIDAN/ANCIENT ART & ARCHITECTURE COLLECTION

Maussollos used the best available Greek architects and artists to work on his most famous building project—his own tomb, the mausoleum at Halikarnassos—which had a podium base, a colonnade, and a pyramidal roof. Because of its sheer size—it was some 50 meters (165 feet) high—and its unusually rich sculptural decoration, it became known as one of the seven wonders of the world. It was in the heart of the city, and was obviously intended to be seen as a monument to a city founder, which means that Maussollos planned for himself the status, and no doubt the sacrifices, of a hero or demigod.

In this period, beginning with the reign of Maussollos, a score of temples and other sacred buildings were built at Carian sanctuaries. The biggest building project apart from the mausoleum was at the mountain sanctuary of Labraynda. Several temples were also built in Ionian cities under Hekatomnid influence. One of them was the temple of Athena, at Priene, which Alexander the Great paid for, but which was begun before his conquest of the district in 334 BC. Another is the huge temple of Artemis, at Ephesus, another of the seven wonders of the world.

These buildings reveal a common source of inspiration in the forms of the Archaic Ionic temples. This architectural style is, therefore, called the "Ionic Renaissance". Considering Maussollos's fight against the Athenian empire, it was natural that his architects should return to old local Ionic forms, rather than use the more recent Athenian style. This was a means of expressing cultural identity against the political power of Athens.

Glorifying the Ruler

At the main Carian sanctuary of Labraynda, in the solitary mountains of the inland, Maussollos launched a major architectural project, which was finished by his brother and successor, Idrieus, who ruled from 351 BC to 344 BC. Swedish excavations at the site since 1948 have revealed an Ionic temple dedicated

to Zeus, the father of the gods, and a number of other buildings with marble fronts, all erected within some 15 years in the middle of the fourth century.

The first structure to be built was a monumental, temple-like banqueting hall (called an *andron*, or "men's hall"), intended to be used for ritual meals during an annual five-day sacrificial feast. At the back of the main room was a large rectangular niche for statues of the rulers. This type of building was a new architectural creation, inspired by the urge to glorify the Hekatomnid dynasty. Its combination of ritual banqueting and glorification of the ruler makes it a forerunner of Hellenistic and Roman rulers' cult buildings.

It is generally considered that the Hellenistic period began with Alexander the Great, and his conquest of the East to the Indus River (in present-day Pakistan), which opened up the East to Greek cultural influence. Hellenism by conquest was, however, preceded by a Hellenism by peaceful contacts along the border between East and West. Perhaps the most notable example of such pre-Alexander Hellenism can be seen in the architecture of Hekatomnid Caria of the mid-fourth century BC, especially at the sanctuary of Labraynda. Maussollos and the Hekatomnids did not reach their political goals, but their buildings made a lasting contribution to the history of architecture.

Alexander the Great

When his father, Philip II, was assassinated in 336 BC, Alexander was 19 years old and full of energy and ambition. As soon as it was feasible, he launched the great campaign against Persia that Philip had planned. In 334 BC, he pushed into Asia Minor (present-day Turkey), most of which he subdued, twice defeating the Persian army. After a time-consuming but strategically necessary siege of Tyre, on the Levantine coast, he advanced to Egypt, where he founded the metropolis-to-be Alexandria, one of the many cities that were to carry his name.

In 331 BC, after turning east again, he decisively defeated the Persian king at Gaugamela, on the Tigris, in what today is northern Iraq. After this victory, the Persian Empire fell into his hands. He continued eastwards to India, and by 325 BC, had overcome all resistance up to the Indus River. In 323 BC, only two years after returning to Mesopotamia, he died of a fever. He was 33 years old.

Alexander's military genius brought him a series of astonishing victories on the battlefield. His conquests would probably have had little impact on history, however, had he not founded a large number of cities with Greek and Macedonian settlers. As it was, his empire split into several smaller kingdoms almost immediately after his death. The same fate would no doubt have fallen upon the Hellenistic culture had Alexander not seen how to consolidate his victories. One wonders how much this degree of foresight came from the early training he received from Aristotle. We can probably see Aristotle's influence behind Alexander's decision to include scholars and scientists on his staff. That later conquerors have done the same is no doubt due to Alexander's influence.

This marble portrait of Alexander the Great was found at Pergamon, in present-day Turkey. Born in 356 BC, he was the king of Macedonia from 336 BC until 323 BC, when he died at the young age of 33.

THE EMPIRE OF ALEXANDER THE GREAT

In 334 BC, Alexander started the great war against the Persian Empire. The route of his army is shown in red. By 325 BC, he had conquered not only Persia but all of the Near and Middle East, as far as the Indus River.

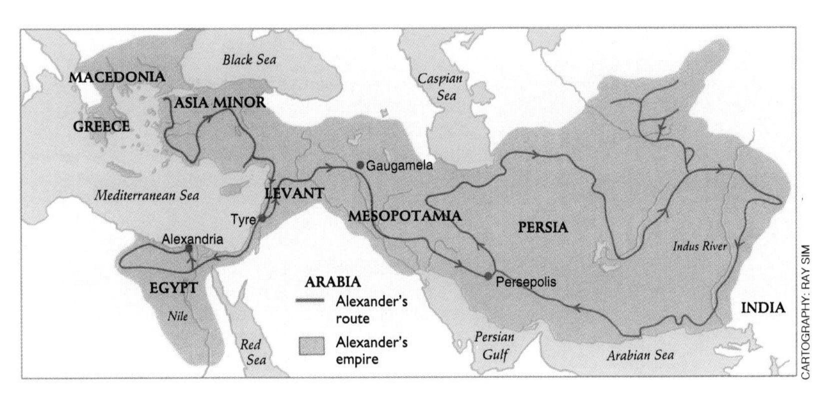

VASE PAINTING OF ANCIENT GREECE

CHARLOTTE SCHEFFER

GRECIAN URNS ARE indeed things of beauty, but they are also practical articles of long durability and transmitters of meaning from times long past. The technique—black figures on a red background from the seventh century BC, replaced in the late sixth century BC by red figures surrounded by black—consisted of "painting" the vases with different kinds of clay, and firing them in three stages with varying levels of oxygen in the kiln. Corinth and, from the sixth century BC, Athens were the leading places of manufacture.

Many different painters have been distinguished, some of them known by name from their signatures. The motifs are at the same time pure decoration, pious stories from the myths, pictures of reality, and ideological statements on the proper behavior of Greek men and women.

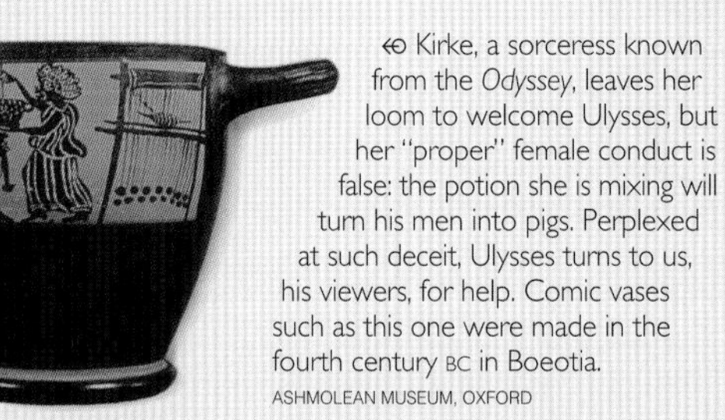

Kirke, a sorceress known from the *Odyssey*, leaves her loom to welcome Ulysses, but her "proper" female conduct is false: the potion she is mixing will turn his men into pigs. Perplexed at such deceit, Ulysses turns to us, his viewers, for help. Comic vases such as this one were made in the fourth century BC in Boeotia.
ASHMOLEAN MUSEUM, OXFORD

Attacked by Etruscan pirates, the god of wine, Dionysos, performs a miracle by making his mast sprout leaves like a vine and turning the terrorized pirates into dolphins. The cup, dating from about 540 BC, was painted by Exekias, the foremost of the Athenian painters working in the black-figure technique.
STAATLICHE ANTIKENSAMMLUNGEN UND GLYPTOTHEK, MUNICH

An oil flask in the shape of a charming little owl. Such exquisitely stylized works were already turned out by Corinthian vase painters by the middle of the seventh century BC.
ERICH LESSING/ MAGNUM

NATIONAL MUSEUM OF VILLA GIULIA, ROME/SCALA

Greek foot soldiers engaging in battle to flute music. This small-scale painting with its sharp, precise details has rightly made Corinthian vase painting of the seventh century BC famous.

Supervised by Hermes, Death and his brother Sleep, all with their names inscribed, are about to carry a Homeric hero to his last rest. Dating from about 515 BC, this large bowl was painted by the famous Athenian red-figure painter Euphronios.
METROPOLITAN MUSEUM OF ART

Satyrs cavorting and doing the things that Greek men normally could not do—this was a favorite motif and suitably so, considering that many of the vases were intended for the men's symposia (banquets). This vase is a wine-cooler, painted by the Athenian Douris, and dates from about 480 BC.
BRITISH MUSEUM

H. LEWANDOWSKI/THE LOUVRE/RMN

Ganymedes, still a beautiful young boy playing with his hoop, is pursued by Zeus, who appears on the other side of the vase. The cock is a gift of love from the enamored god. Dating from about 470 BC, it was painted by the Berlin painter, an Athenian, who was named after the location of his most famous vase.

Unlike the vases painted in the black and red-figure techniques, this Athenian oil flask with a muse playing her lyre was painted with many different colors on a white background after firing, giving us an idea of what the large-scale painting of the time was like. It dates from about 440 BC.
STAATLICHE ANTIKENSAMMLUNGEN UND GLYPTOTHEK, MUNICH

ROBERT HARDING PICTURE LIBRARY

THE HELLENISTIC AGE: 323 BC TO 31 BC

With Alexander's death in 323 BC, his vast empire was divided up between his generals and successors. After a period of utter confusion, three of these kingdoms proved to be of longer duration than just a generation or two. One was Egypt, where Ptolemy established himself and his family so securely at Alexandria that the dynasty continued to rule the country for 300 years, until the battle of Actium, in 31 BC, and the Age of Augustus. The dynasty's last ruler was Queen Cleopatra.

The second kingdom to endure was the Seleucid, which took over the old Persian Empire and Alexander's eastern conquests. This was a vast country, which lost most of its territory when the Romans conquered Greece and Asia Minor in the second century BC, and the Parthian kingdom rose in the east.

The third lasting kingdom was the old Macedonian kingdom, the capital of which was Pella. It was defeated by Rome in the battle at Pydna, in 168 BC.

Apart from Ptolemaic Egypt, none of the Hellenistic kingdoms survived more than 150 years. From the mid-second century BC, Rome was the undisputed ruler of the eastern Mediterranean. It confirmed this fact by its ruthless destruction of Corinth, in 146 BC, and the sale of all survivors into slavery. Greek cities throughout the Hellenistic world were, to a large extent, left to rule themselves. Most had democratic constitutions insofar as all male citizens made up the assembly to elect their magistrates. The rules for nomination, however, made it easy for those in power to manipulate the election procedure. Of course, no city under the rule of a Hellenistic kingdom, or under Rome, could make decisions concerning foreign policy.

Although not a political power, Greece continued to play an important role throughout this era. Hellenism's cultural basis was strictly Greek. Throughout the Hellenistic world, the language was Greek, literature and art were Greek, and political and cultural life were in accordance with Greek customs. Barbarians (non-Greeks) who wanted to take part in Hellenistic culture had to Hellenize by learning the Greek language and by adopting Greek customs. To an extent, even Rome conformed to this rule, once it had extended its influence into the Hellenistic world.

In one field of culture, Athens remained the focal point. In philosophy, two new schools rose to fame with philosophers who had moved to Athens. These were the school of Epicurus of Samos, who moved to Athens in 307 BC, and the Stoic school, founded in 310 BC by Zeno of Kition. The philosophical schools provided teaching of a high order, and Athens remained the most important university city until the Roman emperor Justinian ordered the schools to be closed in AD 529, a date that marks the end of antiquity, and the final victory of the Christian faith.

A coin portrait of Ptolemy I (305 BC to 283 BC), one of Alexander's companions and the founder of the Ptolemaic dynasty, which ruled Egypt for 300 years. At Alexandria, he built the largest library of the ancient world.
C.M. DIXON

The colossal temple of the Olympian Zeus at Athens, built in the Corinthian order by the Roman architect Cossutius from 174 BC, was not finished until AD 132.

⊖ Reliefs from the Pergamon altar (181 BC to 159 BC). The sea god Triton (left), son of Poseidon, the ruler of the sea, fights together with his mother Amphitrite (right) against three giants. Triton is a creature with a human chest, wings, a fishtail, and a horse's leg.

Scientific and Architectural Achievements

In the Hellenistic post-Aristotelian age, philosophy and science went separate ways. Science was not a field of interest for the philosophic schools of Hellenistic Athens. The major scientific institution of the period was the library of Alexandria. There, literary scholarship flourished, thanks to its collection of some 500,000 books. The library also became the world's foremost research institute in the fields of mathematics, astronomy, geography, and medicine.

Among scientists who worked at Alexandria was Euclid, the author of *Elements*, the systematic presentation of mathematical theorems that is still valid. Another scientist was Eratosthenes, who managed to calculate the circumference of the Earth with an error of only about 300 kilometers (180 miles). This calculation would, of course, not have been possible without the knowledge, later forgotten, that the Earth is a sphere. The ancient world believed, however, that the Earth was the center of the universe, although Aristarchos of Samos, a third-century BC astronomer, had suggested that the Earth revolved round the sun. His treatise is lost, so we do not know his arguments and evidence.

The Hellenistic age witnessed some imposing architectural achievements. Builders used retaining walls to construct rising sequences of terraces, surrounded by colonnades and connected by monumental processional stairs. Examples of this style can be seen in city planning, as at Pergamon, and in the layout of sanctuaries, such as that of Asclepius, on Cos, off the coast of Asia Minor. In Italy, the sanctuary of Fortuna, at Praeneste, is a striking example of this tendency. These achievements were inspired by the architecture of fourth-century BC Caria.

Classical sculptors had shown much restraint in movement and feeling; in the Hellenistic period, such restraint was discarded. The most outstanding piece of Hellenistic art clearly illustrates this point: it is the frieze of the great altar of the gods Zeus and Athena at Pergamon, probably built about 181 BC to 159 BC to commemorate the victory over the Galatians—three warlike Celtic tribes that had immigrated to Asia Minor (around present-day Ankara) in the third century BC. There, the Hellenistic baroque style finds its most eloquent expression in sculpture, depicting a battle between gods and giants, which is, of course, an allusion to the Pergamene royal victory over the Galatian barbarians. The many fighting bodies obscure the background, so that the colonnaded altar of Zeus and Athena seems to float above the uproar of the cosmic battle.

⊖ The open-air theater at Epidauros, built from about 360 BC by the architect Polykleitos. The acoustics of this theater, which could seat some 12,300 spectators, are remarkable.

C.M. DIXON/PHOTORESOURCES

The Greek Heritage

Classical Greece was the most important source of European culture, and continues to exert its influence on the rest of the world in many ways, good and bad. This is not only a question of quite naturally transferred, and sometimes superficial, traditions—for example, the tradition that coins should be flat and round with impressed texts and symbols on both sides. Nor is Classical inspiration for modern architecture more than an interesting feature of contemporary society: the influence of heritage is not very strong in this case. Columnar architecture is, however, definitely a Greek gift of importance to world architecture, although Egyptian columns are older. This is not just a question of borrowed forms: Greek columns were bearers of meaning, and so are columns of later epochs. Even if the meaning has changed, the columns remain symbols of power.

Much of the Greek heritage is abstract—for example, democracy. There is certainly no direct line of tradition from Classical Greece to the modern world, but Athenian democracy, however imperfect (and however different from today's imperfect democracies), gave the world a new idea to work on.

Another idea from Classical Greece is the appreciation of individuality and creativity. It is easy to forget that these qualities are products of culture, and are not inherited. Closely attached to the cult of individuality is admiration for the fighter, the invincible hero. This admiration appeared in early Greek fiction, in Homer's histories of Odysseus, the adventurer. Odysseus was the first European or, if one prefers, the first modern man in the European sense—inventive, creative, and selfish, for good and for bad. One wonders whether the ancient Greek obsession with war and violence is not also a bequest to the world, spread by European thinking.

In the field of science also, the modern world owes a great debt to Greece, and especially to that universal genius Aristotle. His analytic work in many fields was directed towards the creation of a coherent, encyclopedic conception of the world. Through the ages, he has had an enormous influence on scientific thinking, from the time of medieval Arabic scholars to that of later European scientists.

Aeschylus, Sophocles, and Euripides—the three major tragedians of fifth-century BC Athens—have exerted a lasting influence. By using ancient myths to illustrate contemporary human conflicts, they created drama that would remain up to date through the ages. The inflammability and never-ceasing topicality of some of the issues dramatized by these tragedians become only too apparent whenever a modern dictatorship bans Sophocles' *Antigone*. The classical dramas have been a constant source of inspiration to poets, novelists, painters, composers, dramatists, and film-makers.

Greece gave the Western world an alphabet containing both consonants and vowels, the first of its kind, in the late eighth century BC. Several local alphabets soon developed in Greece, with slightly different signs used from place to place. It is because Cumae (Kyme), one of the earliest Greek colonies in Italy, was founded by settlers from the island of Euboea, and because early Rome was in close contact with Cumae, that the Euboean set of letters came to form the Roman alphabet. The Greeks today use letters different from those in our Latin alphabet, because theirs are of Athenian origin, not Euboean.

A posthumous bronze portrait of Aristotle (384 BC to 322 BC), the most influential of the philosophers of ancient Greece.
NATIONAL MUSEUM, NAPLES/SCALA

This early representation of the famous Wooden Horse dates from about 675 BC. In Greek legend, the siege of Troy lasted for 10 years. Pretending to give up, the Greeks left by sea, leaving a wooden horse behind, filled with warriors. When the Trojans pulled the horse into the city, the soldiers came out at night and opened the city gates to the Greek army. In many languages, a wooden horse or Trojan horse has ever since been an expression used to describe the infiltration of enemy troops or agents.

MYKONOS MUSEUM, CRETE/C.M. DIXON/PHOTO RESOURCES

D. & J. HEATON/AUSTRALIAN PICTURE LIBRARY

THE RISE AND FALL OF ROME

900 BC – AD 500

From City-state to Worldwide Empire

ÖRJAN WIKANDER

THE PREHISTORY OF ITALY was very much a product of Italy's geographical position. The peoples of southern Italy and Sicily were influenced by cultures in the eastern Mediterranean area, particularly those of Greece; whereas the peoples of northern Italy had strong contacts, through the alpine passes, with the metal-producing cultures in central Europe. Towards the end of the Bronze Age, between the fourteenth and twelfth centuries BC, there is ample evidence of Mycenaean trade, and possibly settlements, along the Italian coasts as far north as southern Etruria. At the same time, traits typical of the central European Urnfield cultures spread deep into northern and central Italy, with some examples found further south and even in Sicily. New metalworking techniques appeared, and the discoveries of new funerary rituals—with cremation and inhumation of ashes in biconical urns (hence the term "Urnfield")—suggest immigration. From the north came the skill of beating bronze into sheet form, and warriors were able to be equipped with heavy armor: helmets, corselets, and circular shields, giving rise to a new, armored fighting technique.

The "Pont du Gard", a Roman aqueduct near Nîmes, in southern France, was built about 20 BC to carry water across the river valley. One of the most impressive of its kind, it is 49 meters (160 feet) high and 270 meters (885 feet) long.

This inscribed sheet of gold, dating from about 500 BC, was found at Pyrgi, the main port of Cerveteri. The dedication inscriptions—to the Etruscan goddess Uni (Juno) and her Phoenician equivalent, Astarte—are in both Punic (the language of ancient Carthage) and Etruscan, indicating close trading contacts between the Carthaginians and Etruscans.
NATIONAL MUSEUM OF VILLA GIULIA, ROME/SCALA

⚱ Dating from the early seventh century BC, this oriental-style bronze cauldron on a conical stand was recovered from the Barberini Tomb at Praeneste (Palestrina). It is decorated with four lion and griffin heads.
NATIONAL MUSEUM OF VILLA GIULIA, ROME/SCALA

The change from the Bronze Age to the Iron Age at the beginning of the last millennium BC was gradual. Contacts between the Italic peoples and the Greek peoples were interrupted, but central European influences, particularly from the Hallstatt culture (in modern Austria), remained important.

The Iron Age and the Italic Peoples

A number of Italic Iron Age cultures have been identified, and they are often presented in two main groups according to their burial customs: cremation in the northwest; inhumation (the burial of unburned bodies) in the southeast. In various parts of the peninsula, Iron Age cultures persisted for centuries with few changes—in some cases, up to the Roman conquest in the last centuries BC.

In southern Italy and in the western part of central Italy, the arrival of eastern merchants in the eighth century BC and the ensuing Greek colonization greatly affected the lives of the Italic peoples. Traditional forms of Italic art and crafts took completely new directions; local social and economic structures changed rapidly.

Perhaps the most interesting change is the adoption of the Greek alphabet. Ancient Italy had a number of languages and dialects—most of them were Indo-European, the major family of the languages of Europe. These Italic languages can now be defined, and a historical map of languages and peoples may be juxtaposed with an archaeologically based map of cultures. The two correspond only in parts; for instance, the people of the Este culture apparently spoke Venetic.

PALAZZO DEI PRIORI, GUBBIO/SCALA

⚱ One of the *Tabulae Iguvinae*, seven bronze tablets discovered in AD 1444 at Gubbio, in Umbria. In the third or second century BC, they were inscribed with religious regulations in Umbrian, an Italic language distantly related to Latin.

The Etruscans

Particular interest has been devoted to the relationship between the Iron Age Villanova culture and the highly advanced Etruscan culture. Today, when few scholars would see the Early Archaic (seventh century BC) culture of central Italy as a phenomenon caused by recent Etruscan immigration from Asia Minor, we are rather inclined to trace its gradual development from the Villanova culture under strong Greek influences.

The copper mines of Etruria were one of the few mining resources in Italy. In the eighth century BC, there was evidence of growing social classes among the Etruscans. In among common graves—in which such items as a bronze razor or a bracelet and a few fibulas (clasps or brooches) and pins were found—a

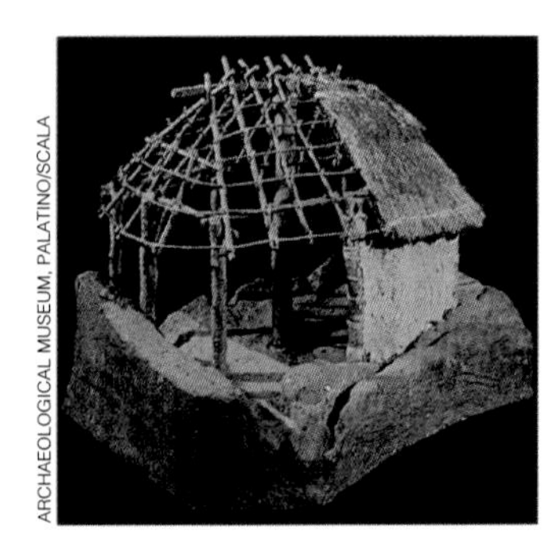

ARCHAEOLOGICAL MUSEUM, PALATINO/SCALA

⚱ A reconstruction of an Iron Age hut (*capanna*) from the Palatine hill in Rome. These huts have been dated to the eighth century BC.

ANCIENT ITALY

As the maps show, culture and language areas correspond only in part; for instance, the people of the Este culture apparently spoke Venetic.

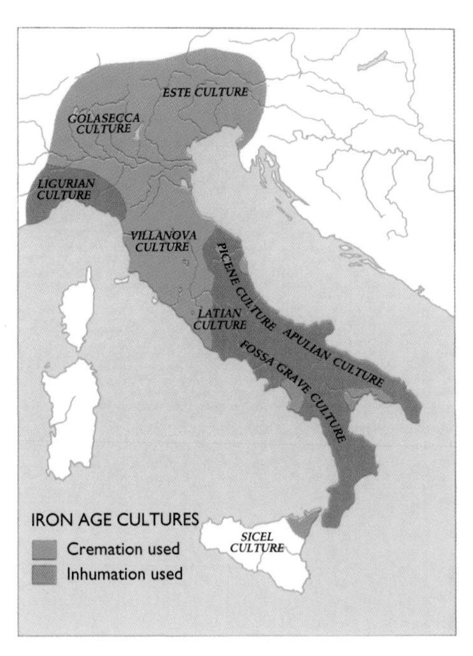

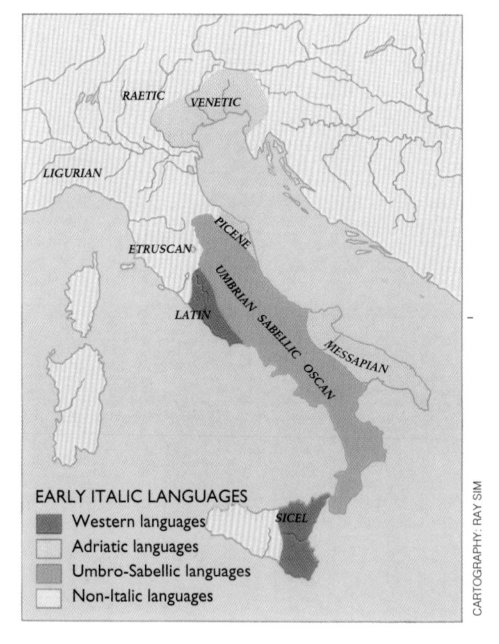

CARTOGRAPHY: RAY SIM

small number of richer graves have also been found. In these, there are items of pottery, bronze vessels, axes, swords, and horse bits. From these finds, it appears that an aristocratic, warrior class may have been emerging.

Between 725 BC and 650 BC, there is more evidence of wealth in a few extremely rich tombs at several major sites along the Tyrrhenian (Etruscan) coast: at Populonia, Vetulonia, Tarquinia, Cerveteri, and inland Praeneste. There, the grave goods include gold, ivory, and bronze show-pieces—imports from the east. These Early Archaic tombs could have been those of local chieftains, enriched by trading Etruscan metal to the Greeks, at Greek colonies at Pithekoussai and Cumae (Kyme), in southern Italy. The growth of local aristocracies was largely a result of the rapid accumulation of wealth through successful trade. It was also certainly promoted and influenced by contacts with Greek aristocratic ideology. Some Greek nobles visited and settled in Etruria; at Tarquinia, for instance. It is possible that the use of horses and two-wheeled carriages may have been introduced from the north, but the practices of drinking wine and holding symposia (banquets) among the aristocracy doubtless reflect Greek influences. After about 650 BC, noble families buried their dead in huge, circular mounds (tumuli). (See the feature *Death in Etruria*.) Towards the end of that century, Etruscan inscriptions provide us with the first examples of particular inherited family names. From then on, the material wealth of the aristocracy was coupled with class consciousness and pride.

Changes in Society

The emergence of a central Italic aristocracy is not isolated. It is closely linked with an extraordinary transformation of Italic society. There was the creation of a substantial class of craftsmen, including bronze smiths and potters, and increasing urbanization. Pottery became a specialized craft with the break-through of the fast-spinning potter's wheel, imported from the Greek world. In later Roman tradition, King Numa (of the early seventh century BC) instituted eight craftsmen's guilds—including the guilds for bronze smiths and potters—for goldsmiths, carpenters, dyers, tanners, leather-workers, and flute-players.

C.M. DIXON/PHOTO RESOURCES

Part of the Banditaccia necropolis outside Cerveteri. The circular tombs (known as tumuli) were built by aristocratic families in the sixth century BC.

The increasing specialization of labor led to greater population concentrations, such as in Tarquinia. From the middle of the seventh century BC, settlements that were virtual cities were established on the Tyrrhenian coast and even in the hinterland of Etruria—along the river valleys, connecting inland areas with the seaboard.

As Etruscan settlements became larger, there was a rapid change from huts with thatched roofs to sturdy, rectangular buildings with tiled roofs. Roof tiles were a recent innovation imported from Greece, but their general use on private buildings in the growing towns was a central Italic achievement. It was not until several centuries later that they were used this way in the Greek world. Terracotta tiling proved to be an efficient roof-cover. A simple module system, it also offered rich possibilities for architectural decoration. Painted and relief-molded roof terracottas remained an Etruscan specialty for more than 500 years. Technical progress has its drawbacks, however: Etruscan metalworking and the firing of tiles and pottery are largely to blame for the deforestation of central Italy.

An Etruscan ridge tile from Acquarossa, about 1 meter (3 feet) long, with an acroterion (gable decoration) in the shape of two mythical animals. It dates from about 600 BC.
ÖRJAN WIKANDER

This reconstructed Etruscan roof from a private house at Acquarossa, dating from about 550 BC, consists of flat pantiles, semicylindrical cover tiles, and ridge tiles covering the ridgepole.
ÖRJAN WIKANDER

SCALA

⇧ The Tomb of the Reliefs, in Cerveteri, dates from about 300 BC. On the walls are hung all the paraphernalia the dead would require in their new life. The beds are prepared with plumped-up cushions, and the slippers stand ready.

DEATH IN ETRURIA

CHARLOTTE SCHEFFER

THE TOMBS OF THE ETRUSCAN dead are more impressive than the dwellings of the living. Research and archaeological excavation have concentrated on the Etruscans' funeral culture, and our knowledge of that civilization is largely based on the cities of the dead, because the extensive writings of the Etruscans are lost.

Etruscan civilization has been approximately dated to the period from the end of the eighth century BC to the end of the first century BC. Even though the Etruscan language does not belong to any known language group, it is fairly easy to read, being written in the Greek alphabet. Before that time, a people who were probably their ancestors—members of the Iron Age Villanova culture—cremated their dead and buried the ashes in simple tombs with, at most, some fibulas (clasps and brooches), bronze weapons, and, occasionally, a lid in the shape of a helmet. The Villanovan necropolises give little or no indication of differences in social status.

Towards the end of the eighth century BC, there is evidence that this society was gradually transformed as a result of contact with Greek and Phoenician civilizations. In the seventh century BC, inhumation (the burial of unburned bodies) replaced cremation as the dominant funerary form. From that time, large separate tombs, expensively furnished with imported luxury goods, were built to house the remains of single families.

An Elegant Society

The great centuries in Etruscan history are the seventh and sixth BC. At this time, the Etruscans dominated most of central Italy, including Rome, and also spread into northern Italy and Campania. Having grown rich through trade with the Greeks, the Etruscan noble families who lived in the southern Etrurian cities spent lavishly on both their tombs and funerals.

The wall paintings in underground chamber tombs in Tarquinia depict an elegant society that appreciated good living. They are painted in bright colors with no shading, the central activity being the drinking of wine, a custom the Etruscans learned from the Greeks. However, the Greeks drank in male groups,

⇧ A terracotta figure from the Tomb of the Five Seats, in Cerveteri, dating from about 600 BC. Male and female figures were seated on chairs carved from the living rock. They probably represent ancestors of the tomb's occupants.

RONALD SHERIDAN/
ANCIENT ART & ARCHITECTURE COLLECTION

mainly for political reasons, whereas Etruscans drinkers are usually depicted as husband and wife—master and mistress of a great house.

Although the members of the drinking parties look very much alive, it may be that what we see is not of this life but rather the owners of the tomb in the company of their dead forebears. The shadow of death rarely falls over these painted scenes—an occasional empty couch, closed door, gesture of mourning providing the only hint. The essential meaning eludes us.

Belief in an Afterlife

The Etruscans filled their tombs not only with furniture and textiles, but also with food and drink, weapons, and cooking utensils, which seems to indicate that they believed in an afterlife, although they did not embalm their dead. Tombs were furnished as houses, with all that a living person needed. Ash urns could depict human features or be made in the shape of a house. In a tomb in Cerveteri, dating from about 600 BC, a row of seated terracotta figures represents ancestors awaiting the latest arrival. Although the scene is ambiguous, the existence of such figures, and the care extended to dead forebears, probably indicate ancestor worship.

A husband and wife on the lid of a sarcophagus from Cerveteri, dating from about 525 BC. The couple is shown taking part in a symposium (banquet), reclining on a couch in the oriental way made fashionable by the Greeks.

C.M. DIXON/PHOTO RESOURCES

Towards the end of the fifth century BC, the wall-painting motifs become more somber, the colors are darker, and shading occurs frequently. The borrowed Greek myths often involve fighting, bloodshed, and killing. From earliest times, the shedding of blood was probably connected with funerals and the continuing existence of a dead person. Not surprisingly, the Etruscans are believed to have originated gladiatorial games.

Motifs depicting scenes of traveling and the presence of monstrous figures have led some scholars to conclude that the Etruscan concept of a happy afterlife changed to a belief in an underworld, where the shades of the dead await punishment for their former sins. There is, however, no evidence for such an interpretation. The Greek motifs are superficial borrowings, and the monstrous figures and winged females are included to suggest the funerary content of the scenes rather than as active participants in them.

From the fourth century BC, Etruscans gradually became part of the Roman world. The symposium lost its significance as a status symbol; the banqueter is alone on his or her couch with an offering bowl. Status at that time was to be a magistrate from a family of magistrates. The facades of tombs became more important than their interiors. Visible from afar in cliff faces, they surrounded the cities of the living.

The Etruscan attitude to death—their belief in a continued, reasonably happy existence, and their view of the funeral and tomb as proper for the display of family unity and position in society—appears to be consistent throughout the changing forms of expression. Like many ancient peoples, the Etruscans probably believed that time was not linear but cyclic, so that after a cycle of time (*saeculum*), all returned to the beginning and the start of a new *saeculum*. In the same way, generation followed upon generation. Their world was preordained and regulated by the gods, who revealed their divine will in omens. The human world was intimately interwoven with that of the gods and of the dead: all were part of the great plan revolving through the *saecula*.

SCALA

A wall painting from the Tomb of the Augurs (interpreters of bird flight), in Tarquinia, dating from about 510 BC. Two mourners salute a large, painted door. The door may represent the dead person's house or may be a symbolic barrier separating the living and the dead.

The Founding of Rome

Urbanization in Etruria soon spread southwards along the Tiber Valley into Latium. Rome was one of the towns emerging in that area towards the end of the seventh century BC. It was situated in a fordable place at the Tiber island, where two important roads crossed: the "salt-road" (*Via Salaria*)—leading from the saltworks around the mouth of the Tiber up to the country of the Sabines—and the inland road through Latium. This was also the border between the Fossa Grave culture to the southeast, which practiced inhumation, and the Villanova culture to the northwest, which cremated its dead. Iron Age villages founded on the Palatine, Esquiline, and Quirinal hills, between 900 BC and 700 BC, have traits of both cultures.

With the royal dynasty of the Tarquins, who were of Etruscan descent and ruled from about 616 BC to 510 BC, Etruscan influence grew strong in Rome. The thatched huts were replaced by tiled buildings, and the marshy valley between the main hills was drained and became the site of a central marketplace, later known as the Forum Romanum. Temples and public buildings were erected in various parts of Rome. The great Temple of Jupiter, on the Capitoline Hill, was inaugurated in 509 BC, immediately after the last Etruscan king was overthrown.

The transition from monarchical to republican rule was occurring not only in Rome. In the late sixth and early fifth centuries BC, a number of Etruscan kings and southern Italian and Sicilian tyrants were toppled. Their places were taken by aristocratic cliques: in Rome, by the patrician *gentes* (nobles), families once represented in the council of the kings. This council, the Senate, remained the kernel of government.

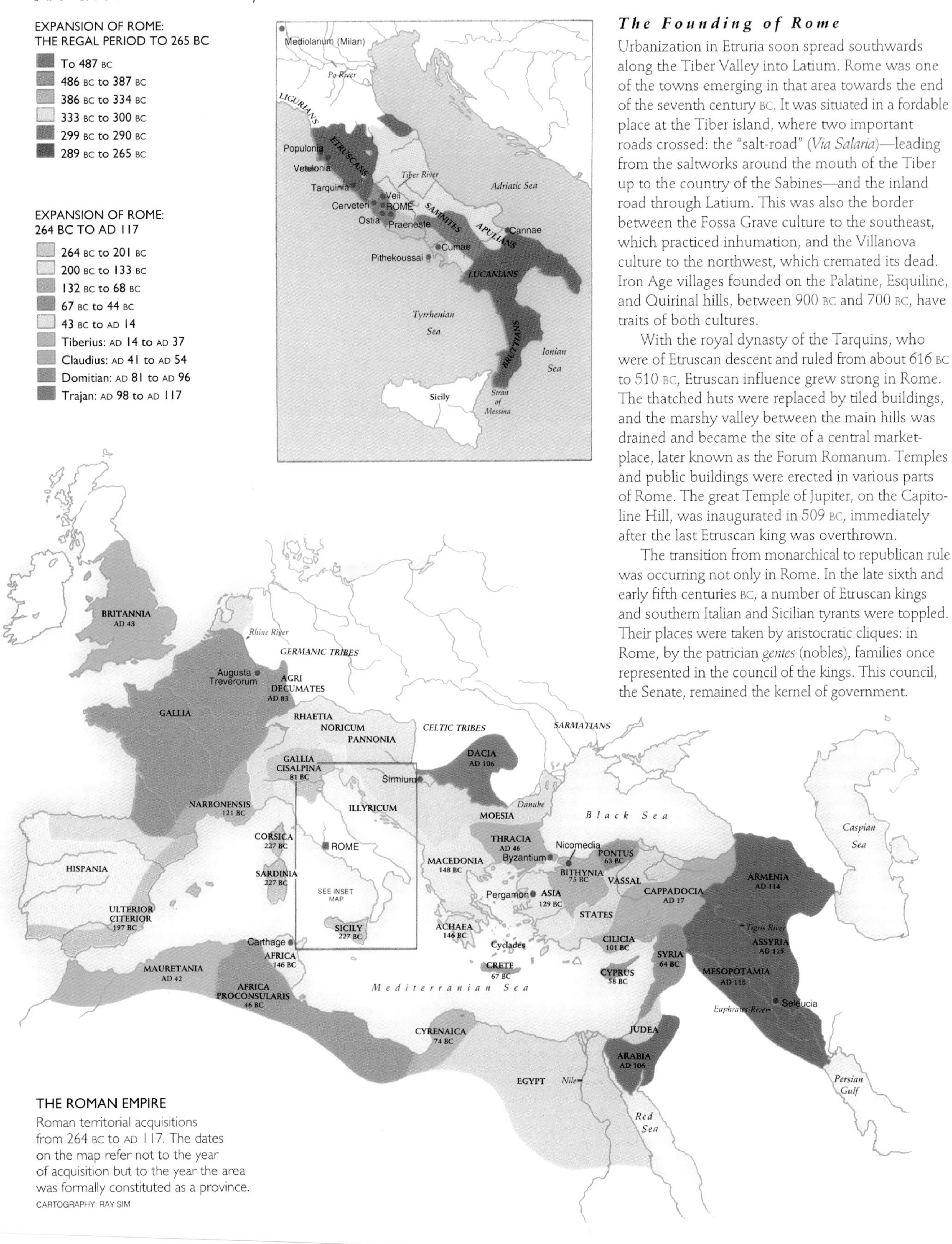

THE ROMAN EMPIRE

Roman territorial acquisitions from 264 BC to AD 117. The dates on the map refer not to the year of acquisition but to the year the area was formally constituted as a province.

CARTOGRAPHY: RAY SIM

The Social and Political Structure

The Senate delegated executive powers to annual magistrates, to two consuls (chief magistrates) in particular. The consuls retained supreme power in war and peace, but a series of new magistracies was created eventually to take over various functions of a growing administrative structure. The censors were responsible for the census registration; the praetors for the jurisdiction; the aediles for the maintenance of temples and public buildings; and the quaestors for revenue and public finance. In cases of emergency, particularly in wartime, the supreme command was entrusted to a dictator, governing alone, for a period of no more than six months.

Other than the patrician inhabitants of Rome, there were clients (followers of the nobles), free-born plebeians (commoners), and a growing number of slaves and freed people. In later records, the first centuries of the republic of Rome are seen as dominated by class struggles between patricians and plebeians. The accounts are confused, however, by the insertion of material about the history of the Late Republic, several centuries later. Led by the powerful and sacrosanct "tribunes of the people" (*tribuni plebis*), the plebeians eventually enforced equal rights with the patricians. In 445 BC, plebeians obtained *conubium*, the right of intermarriage with patricians; in the next century, accordingly, a growing number of plebeian leaders could claim patrician descent on their mother's side. In 366 BC, the consular lists mention the first plebeian consul, Lucius Sextius Lateranus. In 300 BC, the plebeians won access to the most important religious offices, and in 287 BC, the struggle was brought to an end when plebiscites passed by the assembly of the plebs (*concilium plebis*) were accepted as valid for the whole people—that is, as public laws.

Roman Expansion

Even during the period of the kings (about 700 BC to 510 BC), the people of Rome started to expand the city boundaries by subduing their closest Latin neighbors, including the city of Alba Longa, in the Alban hills, about 20 kilometers (12 miles) southeast of Rome, and the saltworks by the mouth of the Tiber. Involved in continuous fights with other neighboring tribes—Etruscans, Sabines, Aequi, Volsci, and Hernici—in the fifth century BC, Rome became the leader of the Latin League, a confederation of city-states in Latium.

The climax of this development was the conquest of Veii, the southernmost Etruscan metropolis, 17 kilometers (10 miles) north of Rome. The capture of Rome by Senonian Gauls (who had crossed the Alps from the north), in 390 BC, was a temporary setback, as Rome soon regained its position as leader. In 338 BC, the Latin League was dissolved after a war between Rome and other Latin cities, and shortly afterwards, Rome came into conflict with the powerful Samnites, in the

ORJAN WIKANDER

The so-called Servian Wall at the Aventine hill, in Rome, was originally built between 378 BC and 353 BC. The upper arch shown here, intended for catapults (*ballistae*), was a later addition, dating from 87 BC.

mountainous hinterland of central Italy. The Samnites were finally subdued in 295 BC, and within 25 years, Rome was in possession of the entire Italic peninsula. Etruscans, Gauls, and the Greeks of Magna Graecia (Greater Greece) yielded to the superior force of Roman armies.

The Hellenistic Period and the Roman Empire: 323 BC to AD 395

Rome's capture by the Gauls is the first event in Roman history mentioned in a contemporary Greek source, but 200 years later, Rome was a political power of importance all over the Greek world. The fourth and third centuries BC gave rise to states larger than city-states in both the western and the eastern Mediterranean area. In 334 BC, Alexander the Great started his campaign against the king of Persia, Darius; and Alexander's uncle, Alexander of Epirus, embarked upon an adventure in the West, allegedly to help Greek colonies in southern Italy against increasing attacks from native tribes. He had more far-reaching ambitions, but failed. So did his successor, Pyrrhos, in about 275 BC, even though he temporarily controlled considerable parts of southern Italy and Sicily.

The sarcophagus of a Roman patrician, Lucius Cornelius Scipio Barbatus, consul in 298 BC. It was cut about 280 BC and clearly shows the influence of contemporary Greek art in southern Italy and Sicily.
MUSEO PIO-CLEMENTINO, VATICANO/SCALA

HERCULANEUM: A BURIED TOWN

Örjan Wikander

THE MOST FAMOUS eruption of the volcano Vesuvius, which began on 24 August in AD 79, buried more than the city of Pompeii. It also buried a number of smaller towns and villages. Herculaneum was one of these. Situated 14 kilometers (9 miles) southeast of Pompeii, it was hit not only by the fine ash-rain that buried Pompeii, but also by a stream of mud-mixed lava, which hardened to form a layer of tufa more than 20 meters (65 feet) thick.

ÖRJAN WIKANDER

SCALA

These apartment blocks for poorer people, on the so-called Cardo IV, were built in a half-timbered style, a cheaper building method that was not unusual in Roman towns.

Private houses in the southern part of the town. To the right of center is the "atrium" of the Casa del Rilievo di Telefo. Most of these houses are more advanced architecturally than Pompeii houses.

ÖRJAN WIKANDER

⇧ The town possessed a theater, a large gymnasium (or palaestra), and at least two public baths. The gymnasium, shown here, took the form of a large courtyard, its northwestern portico almost 90 meters (300 feet) long. The end of the excavated area can be seen in the background, with the houses of the modern-day village of Resina above.

SCALA

DAVID LONGLEY/MICK SHARP

⇧ The mud-lava that buried the town has helped to preserve organic material, such as this charred wooden bed frame. Even a library with books of papyrus was preserved.

⇨ A grocery store on the *Decumanus inferior*, one of the main streets of the town. In and behind the marble-covered counter, there are eight large storage jars (*dolia*) for grain and vegetables. The presence of a cooking stove suggests that the shop may also have been a *thermopolium*, supplying hot meals to customers.

ÖRJAN WIKANDER

⇧ Regular excavations began only in 1927, and over the years since, substantial areas of the town have been revealed and restored. Apparently much smaller than Pompeii, Herculaneum had fewer than 5,000 inhabitants. The Forum has not been found, and only one temple has been uncovered. Most buildings, both public and private, were erected during the last century of the town's life. The most impressive, upper-class, houses have been discovered in the southwest. Shown here is the Casa del mosaico di Nettuno e Anfitrite.

LUIS CASTANEDA/THE IMAGE BANK

A Roman bridge over a deep gorge at Ronda, in Spain.

The final victory fell to Rome, which did not halt at the Strait of Messina. Long-standing, peaceful contacts with the other great power in the West, Carthage, came to an end in 264 BC, when a conflict about Carthage's influence in Sicily led to the three Punic Wars. These lasted a little more than a century, and the victory led to complete Roman dominance in the western Mediterranean.

The first Punic War (264 BC to 241 BC) gave the Romans their first provinces: Sicily, Sardinia, and Corsica. The second, known as the Hannibalic War (218 BC to 201 BC), gave Rome eastern and southern Spain. The third Punic War (149 BC to 146 BC) caused the total destruction of Carthage, and the division of its African territory between a native vassal king and a new Roman province. The Spanish hinterland remained a military problem for 200 years, but the main parts of the Iberian peninsula were subdued during devastating wars in 154 BC to 133 BC. A land link from there to Italy was gained by lengthy campaigns against the Ligurians along the Italian Riviera (the Gulf of Genoa) and Celtic tribes in southern Gaul (part of present-day France). In 118 BC, southern Gaul became a Roman province, Gallia Narbonensis, which was of interest for the increasingly important trade into central Gaul.

The first two Punic Wars involved enormous strains upon Rome's economic resources and military capacity. After these victories, however, there was no power left in the Mediterranean world that could match Rome's strength. To follow Rome's gradual move into the Greek East is like watching a cat toying with a mouse. In some parts, the conquest passed almost unnoticed; elsewhere, when necessary, it was conducted with unrestrained, brutal force. Both Macedonia and the Seleucid kingdom were rebuked on several occasions, punished with cession of land, and weakened militarily. For a long time, however, Rome preferred to rule through agents: only in 148 BC was Macedonia turned into a formal province, followed by Achaea, in 146 BC. The year 133 BC was notable in the East, because of the bequeathing of western Asia Minor (present-day Turkey) to Rome by the last king of Pergamon. At that time, both Seleucid Syria and Egypt were, in practice, under Roman control.

The establishment of larger states or empires is, of course, not the sole characteristic of the later Classical Antiquity—the Hellenistic period (323 BC to 31 BC) and the Roman Empire (31 BC to AD 395)—as compared to the preceding Archaic and Classical periods. Indeed, the differences are so great and crucial that it is a matter of doubt whether they should be considered as parts of one and the same historical epoch.

The conquests of Alexander the Great completely changed the foundations of Greek economy and culture. Greek settlements; Greek political organization; and Greek language, literature, and art spread to India, in the East, and Egypt, in the south.

ÖRJAN WIKANDER

These two well-preserved Republican temples in the Forum Boarium, in Rome, date from the late second century BC. The round temple on the left is one of the earliest surviving Roman buildings erected in marble.

NATIONAL MUSEUM, NAPLES/SCALA

The large harbor depicted in this wall painting from Stabiae, near Pompeii, dating from the first century AD, may be the one at Puteoli. Puteoli was Rome's most important port until Trajan's harbor was constructed at Ostia some time after AD 100.

⚲ An aerial view of Masada, located about 50 kilometers (30 miles) southeast of Jerusalem, in Israel. The cliff was transformed into a well-defended stronghold by King Herod the Great (37 BC to 4 BC). During the rebellion against the Romans from AD 66 to AD 70, Masada was occupied by 1,000 Zealots, who managed to hold out until AD 73.

ILLUSTRATION: KEN RINKEL

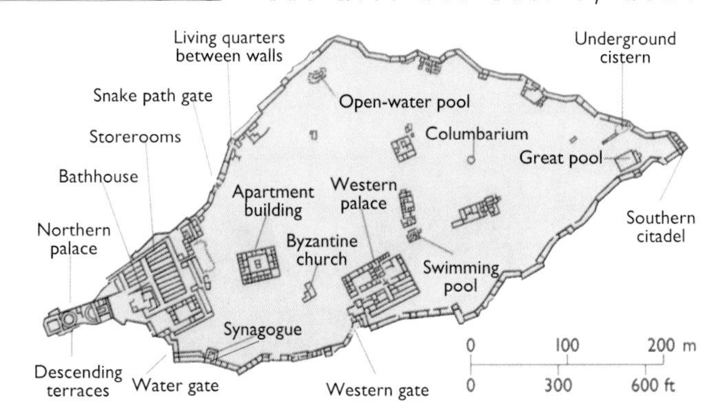

THE PHOTO LIBRARY, SYDNEY

⚱ Dating from about AD 100, this marble relief from the Tomb of the Haterii, in Rome, shows a crane powered by men in a treadwheel being used in the construction of a temple.
MUSEO GREGORIANO PROFANO, VATICANO/SCALA

With Greek colonization and far-reaching Hellenization already present in the western Mediterranean, Alexander's empire laid the foundations of a new and, at least superficially, uniform world around the Mediterranean. Trade and slave-based production grew rapidly, and so did the many new cities founded in that area.

Even in the fourth century BC, one Greek philosopher had called Rome "a Greek town", but it was only after the conquest of Magna Graecia (282 BC to 270 BC) that the true Hellenization of Rome began. Greek sculptures are mentioned occasionally in Rome, members of the Roman aristocracy started learning Greek, and Romans came into contact with Greek literature. In 216 BC, a Roman noble, Fabius Pictor, led a delegation to the Delphic Oracle following the disastrous defeat suffered against Hannibal at Cannae, and he later composed a Roman history in Greek in order to introduce his country to the Hellenized world.

The conquests of the second century BC had immense cultural implications. Greek works of art were stolen and taken to Rome, and the capital attracted Greek artists, philosophers, and writers. Less well known is the fact that, in the same period, Rome and Italy as a whole became strongly influenced by the most recent Greek technology, particularly in agricultural production. The invention of the screw, the crank, and various kinds of gear, at the beginning of the third century BC (or slightly earlier), opened up opportunities for a series of labor-saving devices and machines. The rotary hand mill dramatically increased the volume of grain processed as compared to earlier querns (mills). The principle of the rotary hand mill led to the development of the animal-powered "hourglass" mill (about 200 BC) and the water mill (in the first century BC). By means of other new devices, animals in a capstan could raise water in a geared bucket-chain (*saqyia*), crush olives or metal ore in an edge-runner mill (*trapetum*), or knead dough in the many bakeries that were necessary to supply the growing towns. (See the feature *Cato's Agricultural Machines*.) New modes of production transformed parts of the terracotta industry—for example, roof tiles, brick, and, in particular, fine tableware pottery—into mass production. A constantly growing market in the urban centers throughout the empire, and the emergence of a well-to-do middle class, increased the demand for such commodities to a level never before achieved in the ancient world.

People consumed, production increased, and trade prospered. Larger and better equipped harbors were constructed all over the empire. Archaeological finds, such as stamped storage amphoras (two-handled vessels), help historians to plot the major trade routes. The increase in trade is demonstrated by the discovery of a number of shipwrecks from the period 300 BC to AD 300. These, by far, surpass those from both earlier and later periods.

NATIONAL MUSEUM, RAVENNA/C.M. DIXON/PHOTO RESOURCES

⚱ A Roman tombstone from Ravenna, in Italy, depicting the shipbuilder Titus Longidienus at work.

CATO'S AGRICULTURAL MACHINES

ÖRJAN WIKANDER

The agriculture of Hellenistic Italy was transformed not only by the introduction of a large number of technical innovations, but also by a profound structural change. The last two centuries BC witnessed decisive steps towards the establishment of large-scale estates, *latifundia*, which were to play an important role in the course of the empire. Even though the cultivation units remained relatively small for a long period, there was a gradual transition to more extensive farming, largely based on slave labor.

C.M. DIXON/PHOTO RESOURCES

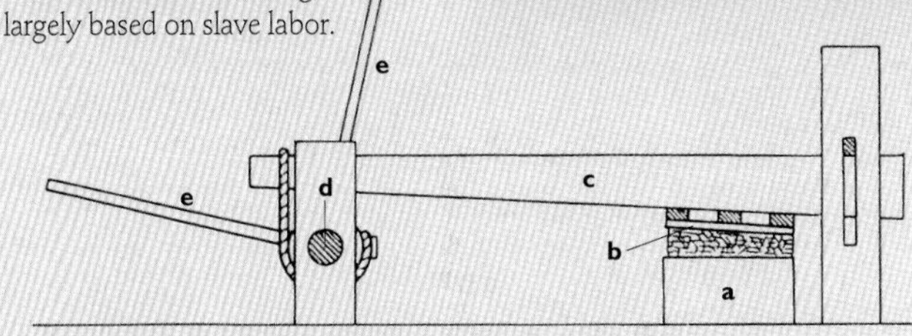

A reconstruction of a lever-and-drum press for crushing olives, or grapes for winemaking, in the Villa dei Misteri, at Pompeii, dating from the first century AD. The olive pulp or grapes were placed on the press bed (**a**) and covered with a lid (**b**). The pressing beam (**c**) was drawn down with levers (**e**) and a rope running around a drum (**d**), shown here in the foreground.

Fortunately, we are able to gain a detailed insight into the agricultural life of the time. About 160 BC, a Roman statesman, Cato the Censor (234 BC to 149 BC), wrote a book called *De agricultura* ("About agriculture"). It is not a well-arranged manual, but rather a collection of unconnected notes comprising, apart from general instructions and a mention of religious customs, a description of two of Cato's own estates near the border of Latium and Campania.

One farm—with an extent of 240 *iugera* (about 60 hectares, or 150 acres), managed by 13 people, mainly slaves—specialized in the cultivation of olives. The other specialized in viticulture, occupied 100 *iugera* (about 25 hectares, or 60 acres), and was managed by 16 people. Even though the descriptions refer to these two particular farms, they are doubtless fairly representative of normal cultivation units in Late Republican Italy.

Besides workers and animals, all kinds of tools and equipment are listed, including the precise number of spades, axes, tongs, working tables, and so on used at each farm. As well as this specialized agricultural equipment, Cato describes a series of machines, showing that—in spite of his well-known aversion to everything foreign—he was perfectly aware of the recent achievements of Greek technology.

The olives were crushed in five edge-runner mills (*trapeta*) of various sizes (a recent invention), and the pulp was then transferred to five presses of the most recent models, at least some of which were provided with block and tackle to hoist the weights. The wine was pressed in similar machines, and there was a series of mills to process grain cultivated for household use: on the olive farm, there was an Olynthian mill, an improved saddle quern, a rotary hand mill (invented about 300 BC), and a donkey mill (a recent invention); in the vineyard, there was one Olynthian mill and three donkey mills.

Cato describes his machines in detail, but they are best illustrated by slightly later archaeological finds—from the cities of Vesuvius, in particular. Variants of the same devices were used throughout the Roman Empire, from Britain and the Rhine frontier to Africa and Southeast Asia. Some of the machines survived in Mediterranean countries well into the twentieth century.

An edge-runner mill (*trapetum*) from the Athenian Agora (marketplace), dating from the fifth or sixth century AD. Two spherical segments hanging on a horizontal beam were rolled over the olives in order to separate the pulp from the stones.
RABAT MUSEUM, MALTA/C.M. DIXON/PHOTO RESOURCES

Animal mills are depicted in this relief from a Roman sarcophagus, probably dating from the second or third century AD. The hourglass-shaped upper stone is raised slightly above the conical lower one by means of a wooden construction resting upon a vertical beam inserted into the top of the cone. The grain was placed in the funnel-shaped upper part, passed between the millstones, and ground to flour, which was collected by the man seen on the right.
VATICAN MUSEUM

THE ROMAN EMPIRE: 900 BC – AD 500

Timeline scale: 500 · 400 · 300 · 200 · 100 · AD 1 · 500 · 1000 BC

SIGNIFICANT EVENTS

- The last Roman emperor of the West, Romulus Augustulus, is dethroned AD 476
- Rome sacked AD 455
- Rome sacked AD 410
- Christian Church officially acknowledged AD 311
- Diocletian creates a constitution, the "Tetrarchy" AD 285
- Period of "military anarchy" AD 235 – AD 284
- Eruption of Vesuvius buries Pompeii and Herculaneum AD 79
- Fire destroys major part of Rome AD 64
- Julius Caesar's reign ends the republic 48 BC – 44 BC
- Pompey's victories in the East 67 BC – 62 BC
- Caius Marius crushes barbarian invaders 101 BC
- 3rd Punic War 149 BC – 146 BC
- 2nd Punic War 218 BC – 201 BC
- 1st Punic War 264 BC – 241 BC
- Rome master of the Italic peninsula 270 BC
- Plebeian laws become valid for all people 287 BC
- Etruscans gradually become part of Roman world
- First plebeian consul 366 BC
- Plebeians gain right of intermarriage with patricians 445 BC
- Royal dynasty of Tarquins 616 BC – 510 BC
- Rise of Rome
- Adoption of Greek alphabet
- Etruscan language used
- Greek colonization of southern Italy and western part of central Italy
- Gradual change from use of bronze to iron

ART, ARCHITECTURE, AND TECHNOLOGY

- Aurelian builds a 19 kilometer (12 mile) wall to protect Rome
- Use of water-powered mill spreads over large parts of the empire
- Public baths, aqueducts, bridges, theaters, amphitheathers, circuses, and libraries are erected all over the empire
- Hadrian's Wall built in Britain
- Fired bricks in use for covering concrete walls
- *Terra sigillata*
- Bronze artifacts common in domestic use
- Invention of glass-blowing creates new category of household utensils
- Two large aqueducts constructed
- Greek works of art stolen and taken to Rome
- Inventions such as the screw, crank, and gear herald technological progress
- Great Temple of Jupiter inaugurated on the Capitoline Hill 509 BC
- King Numa institutes eight craft guilds

MAJOR ROMAN EMPERORS

- Valentinian III AD 425 – AD 455
- Theodosius II AD 408 – AD 450
- Theodosius I AD 379 – AD 395
- Valens (eastern empire) AD 364 – AD 378
- Valentinian I (western empire) AD 364 – AD 375
- Julian AD 361 – AD 363
- Constantine I AD 306 – AD 337
- Diocletian (eastern empire) AD 284 – AD 305
- Aurelian AD 270 – AD 275
- Gallienus AD 253 – AD 268
- Caracalla AD 211 – AD 217
- Septimius Severus AD 193 – AD 211
- Marcus Aurelius AD 161 – AD 180
- Antoninus Pius AD 138 – AD 161
- Hadrian AD 117 – AD 138
- Trajan AD 98 – AD 117
- Domitian AD 81 – AD 96
- Titus AD 79 – AD 81
- Vespasian AD 69 – AD 79
- Nero AD 54 – AD 68
- Claudius AD 41 – AD 54
- Caligula AD 37 – AD 41
- Tiberius AD 14 – AD 37
- Augustus 31 BC – AD 14

The Hellenization of Rome

Gradually, the attachment of Italy to the Hellenistic Greek economy grew tighter. Trading contacts between the western and eastern Mediterranean had long traditions, and for some time, there were no drastic changes. The Greek colonies in southern Italy, together with occasional representatives of the native Italic population, remained in control of the eastern trade. But the Greek cities were badly afflicted by the devastations of the Hannibalic War and Rome's ruthless postwar policy, from which they never completely recovered. Instead, Campanian and Roman traders took over, extracting great fortunes in a Greek world under increasing political pressure from Rome.

Settling in the East, Romans did business as slave-traders and bankers. We know the names of many such traders, particularly from inscriptions on Delos—a small island among the Cyclades, which became a free port in 166 BC and soon developed into the center of trade in the eastern Mediterranean. Most traders were of the semi-aristocratic class of Roman knights (*equites*). They grew rich from private enterprises or as partners in the powerful companies of *publicani*, who were contracted by the Roman state to collect public revenues and to oversee the work of mines in the newly established provinces. Together, in little more than a century, the aristocracy—as military commanders, plunderers, and robbers—and the *equites*—as profiteers and extortionists—managed to turn the East from prosperity to poverty and destitution.

The second century BC was a period of unbounded Roman success abroad—political, military, and economic—yet the situation in Italy grew continually worse. The Hannibalic War had meant disaster, not only to the Greek colonies, but to considerable parts of central and southern Italy in general. Arable land lay waste, and the Roman policy after the war did not encourage its recultivation by Italic peasantry. Instead, more and more land passed into the possession of members of the Roman aristocracy, while impoverished peasants flocked into the towns. Rome grew rapidly, and to meet the city's increase in population, two large aqueducts were built, in 144 BC and 125 BC. The two older aqueducts, constructed in 312 BC and 272 BC, had been sufficient for more than a hundred years.

Problems in Rome

The growing urban poor could be pacified with food and water, but the problems were not only social and economic. They had even more serious implications for Rome's existence as an imperialistic state: the supply of free men to enroll for the army. Rome's military strength depended on freeholders, and the proletarization of parts of the Italian peasantry made it very difficult to enlist sufficient freeholders for the wars in Spain.

Presumably, this was one of the main reasons why the two Gracchi brothers, who were of aristocratic birth, tried to use the office of tribune of the people—a position intended to defend popular rights—in 133 BC, and in 123 BC to 122 BC, respectively, to accomplish far-reaching changes in Roman society. Both brothers were killed, but as a result of their actions, considerable areas of land were distributed to unpropertied citizens. Although the Gracchi were unsuccessful in their efforts, they recognized the need for reform. In part, they used unconstitutional methods in trying to achieve their goals, and in due time, these methods were instrumental in putting an end to the republic.

Throughout Italic society and the growing empire were contradictions that could no longer be handled, or solved, within a political and social system that had been created for a city-state governed by the representatives of a small, landed aristocracy. The last century of the republic is characterized by the political struggles between the *optimates*—who were nobles basing their actions upon the authority of the Senate—and the *populares*—who followed the example of the Gracchi by appealing directly to the people over the head of the Senators.

The problem of finding men for the army was solved by Caius Marius, a parvenu from the class of knights who had won military successes in Africa. In a national crisis, when Rome was under threat from two barbarian tribes from the north—the Cimbri and Teutoni—which had defeated several consular armies, unpropertied citizens were taken on as paid soldiers. Caius Marius organized new legions that finally crushed the barbarian invaders in 101 BC.

Marius had created a professional army, no less loyal to its generals than to the state. In 83 BC, Sulla, the leading *optimate*, returned from victories in the East and defeated the followers of Marius. He conquered Rome and made himself dictator for life, proscribing and murdering thousands of his enemies, between 82 BC and 79 BC. Pompey won a similar position by impressive victories in the East (67 BC to 62 BC), but he hesitated to draw the formal, political consequences of his position. A coalition between the three most powerful men in Rome—Pompey, Julius Caesar, and Crassus ("the first triumvirate", in 60 BC)—postponed the decision. In the end, a civil war brought death to Pompey, in 48 BC, and dictatorship to Julius Caesar. Four years later, Caesar was murdered by aristocratic followers of the former oligarchic rule.

Augustus and the End of the Roman Republic

Caesar's short reign ended the republic. Through Caesar's highly developed military and organizational skills, and through his open-minded and imaginative analysis of the requirements of Rome and the Roman Empire, he had demonstrated that the republican Senate was incapable of handling the empire's affairs.

After Caesar's death, there was a long struggle for power: first, between his heirs and his murderers; then, among the heirs—his closest associate, Mark Antony, and Caesar's adoptive son, the future emperor, Octavian Augustus. After his naval victory at Actium, in 31 BC, Augustus remained sole ruler, and in 44 years, he reorganized the Roman Empire. Wisely, he avoided the dictatorship and every formal monarchical title, basing his rule, instead, upon existing republican offices and institutions, which he gradually transformed to suit his personal ambitions. On the whole, this pseudo-republican imperial constitution (the "Principate") was to last for 300 years.

A Roman coin with a portrait of Emperor Augustus, struck about 19 BC.
RONALD SHERIDAN/ANCIENT ART & ARCHITECTURE COLLECTION

Augustus's reforming zeal intervened at almost all levels and sections of Roman society, but there is little doubt that his most important achievement was the transformation of the haphazard, disorganized Roman Empire into a well-arranged and well-functioning realm, controlled firmly by the hand of the emperor. The conquests of Pompey in Southwest Asia and Caesar in Gaul had added vast territories to the empire. The boundaries of the Asian and African provinces were defined in Rome's favor, owing to the easily defendable Euphrates border, the African desert, and a number of client kingdoms. However, the situation in Europe was less favorable, with an unreasonably long border leaving considerable parts of the Alps and the northern Balkans outside the empire. For the first time in the history of Rome, Augustus made detailed plans for creating a more easily defendable border. During most of his reign, his generals fought fierce mountain tribes in the Alps and the Balkans and even Germanic tribes in the north; by the time of his death, Augustus left an empire neatly bordered by the two great northern rivers, the Rhine and the Danube.

This marble statue depicting a Roman aristocrat holding portrait busts of his ancestors dates from the late first century BC.
MUSEI CAPITOLINI, ROME/SCALA

The administration of the provinces changed: the former attitude, which treated them basically as conquered territories, gave way to a new policy in which provinces were rather to be seen as more or less fully integrated parts of a peaceful nation. The military forces were concentrated along the borders, and the former economic extortion was replaced by a new system of collecting revenues. The *Pax Augusta* brought peace to the empire; the provinces and their cities prospered.

ANCIENT ART & ARCHITECTURE COLLECTION

⇧ A Roman relief dating from the second or third century AD, showing peasants using the *vallus*, a type of harvesting machine driven by a donkey that was in common use in northern Gaul in this period.

Technology and Trade

In combination with rich archaeological finds, the agricultural writers Varro and Columella provide a clear and detailed picture of the forms and organization of agrarian production. The large estates (*latifundia*) offered opportunities for extensive farming, based upon slave labor and made more efficient by the adoption of new technical devices. The harrow was taken into general use, the heavy plow was introduced from the north to work the clay soil of the Po Valley, and in Gaul, the grain was reaped with special harvesting machines (*vallus* and *carpentum*). In the second century AD, the use of the water-powered mill had spread over large parts of the empire.

⇧ These two Roman glass bottles, dating from the second or third century AD, come from Nîmes, in southern France.
C.M. DIXON/PHOTO RESOURCES

The terracotta industry developed further. Fired bricks became the general covering for concrete walls from the first century AD. The relief-molded *terra sigillata* (clay vessels) offered a method to produce fine pottery cheaply without requiring highly skilled potters and painters. Bronze artifacts became common for domestic use, and the recent invention of glass-blowing, between 50 BC and 20 BC, created a new category of household utensils.

Long-distance trade increased in volume. Grain, wine, olive oil, pottery, marble, and other heavy goods were transported over the Mediterranean, but to the almost exclusive benefit of those living on the coast or navigable watercourses.

⇩ A reconstructed wall painting from a tomb outside Rome, dating from the third century AD. A riverboat (the *Isis Giminiana*) is being loaded at the port of Ostia before being towed up the Tiber to Rome.

C.M. DIXON/PHOTO RESOURCES

In spite of the impressive road system constructed over the empire, land transport remained extremely expensive—50 times as costly as sea transport, according to a convincing estimate. Sea transport was promoted, and lighthouses were built and protected harbors were developed. Rome's port, Ostia, was rebuilt by the emperors Claudius (AD 41 to AD 54) and Trajan (AD 98 to AD 117) to fulfill the needs of the capital.

The appearance of Rome changed considerably. Augustus and his successors erected or rebuilt public buildings. A more complete transformation followed upon the devastating fire in AD 64, which destroyed the major part of the city. Rome, as we know it from most archaeological excavations—with brick-covered house walls and temples shining with marble—was created mainly between the time of the fire and the early fourth century AD. Multistoried residential buildings, up to more than 20 meters (65 feet) high, housed a population of approximately one million people, whose provision with the necessities of life remained a constant challenge to the emperors. A sophisticated organization (*annona*) brought grain from Africa and had it transformed to bread in public bakeries; wine and oil came up the Tiber in barges, with the grain; and impressive amounts of fresh water flowed from the mountains in 11 major aqueducts.

The rest of the empire, comprising Italy and the provinces, was organized around both established and newly founded towns, built according to a more or less uniform plan. The central forum was surrounded with religious and civic public buildings—most important, the Temple of Jupiter ("Capitolium"), the center of official cult, and the meeting place of the local "senate". In the second century AD, building activity was intense: public baths, aqueducts, bridges, theaters, amphitheaters, circuses, and libraries were erected, even in small towns, all over the empire. Together, the investments reached such a level that they strained the economic resources of many communities.

The Efficiency of Roman Emperors

Roman history droops under the load of imperial evil and madness. The importance attached to the eccentricity of certain emperors, in both ancient and modern history-writing, has tended to conceal the fact that most Roman emperors were very competent administrators, who managed the realm far better than did their republican predecessors. For a very long time, the empire prospered. Never before in the history of civilization did such a large proportion of a huge population benefit from peace, material welfare, education, and other human privileges.

A standing army of more than 300,000 men ensured interior stability; it protected the borders from aggression from Germanic tribes in the north and the armies of the Parthian Empire in the east.

ÖRJAN WIKANDER

This house facade still standing in the Via Biberatica, a Roman Imperial street near the Forum of Trajan, dates from the second century AD. The ground floor was occupied by shops, while the upper floors contained apartments and lodgings for ordinary citizens.

ÖRJAN WIKANDER

A view of the Forum Romanum from the southeast. In the foreground are the podium and three standing columns of the Temple of Castor and Pollux; to the left is the Basilica Iulia; and in the background, the Arch of Septimius Severus and the Curia (the meeting hall of the Senate).

On the whole, Augustus's borders were maintained, and only in a few cases were new provinces established. Besides four former client kingdoms (Cappadocia, Mauretania, Thracia, and Arabia), three new areas were annexed, all along the northern border: Britannia (Britain), the Agri Decumates (in southern Germany), and Dacia (in modern Romania). (See the feature *The European Frontiers of the Roman Empire*.) Emperor Trajan's attempt to force the Parthians back beyond the Euphrates in AD 114 to AD 115 failed; the new provinces in Mesopotamia and Armenia were given up after a few years.

C.M. DIXON/PHOTO RESOURCES

The interior of a *thermopolium*, a shop selling hot meals, at the Roman port of Ostia. It dates from the third century AD.

Economic Instability and "Military Anarchy"

The organization of the empire and the comparatively high standard of living among its inhabitants, the impressive building activities, and the great size of the standing army all depended upon the prospering economy. But, apparently, the Romans exploited their resources to the utmost, leaving small margins for economic decline or increasing expenditure. The growing pressure on the northern and eastern borders from AD 160 onwards could only just be met with existing military forces. The situation grew manifestly worse after AD 226, when the faltering Parthian Empire was overthrown by the Persian, Sassanid dynasty. A series of severe wars with Persia followed, and the military crisis was further complicated by Germanic tribes crossing the Rhine and forcing their way through Gaul into Spain and Italy. Economic life collapsed, and the military situation grew critical; it soon became obvious that one supreme leader could no longer manage the defense of the entire empire. Usurpers appeared in numbers: to posterity, the period from AD 235 to AD 284 is known as one of "military anarchy".

It is a sign of Rome's fundamental vigor and strength that the empire survived. After a period of disruption and chaos, the legitimate emperors started recapturing and reorganizing the divided

NATIONAL MUSEUM, NAPLES/SCALA

A wall painting from Pompeii, dating from the first century AD, showing a baker selling bread in his shop.

ROBERT HARDING PICTURE LIBRARY

⇧ This Sassanid rock relief at Bishapur, in Iran, commemorates the capture in AD 260 of the Roman Emperor Valerian by King Shapur I.

realm. The most important contribution was made by Aurelian (AD 270 to AD 275), who took control of the entire empire and built a city wall, 19 kilometers (12 miles) long, to protect Rome from future barbarian attacks. He did not live to conclude his restoration of the government, and his achievements were unjustly overshadowed by those of two of his successors, Diocletian (AD 284 to AD 305) and Constantine (AD 306 to AD 337).

The Empire Is Divided

Diocletian created a constitution, the "Tetrarchy", which acknowledged that the empire was too large to be controlled effectively by one ruler. The provinces were split into more than 100 smaller units under 12 dioceses, subordinate in turn to 4 prefectures: 2 in the West and 2 in the East. Four emperors, two *augusti* and two *caesares* (their designated successors), were responsible for these basic parts of the empire, with their new capitals in Augusta Treverorum (Trier), Mediolanum (Milan), Sirmium (near Belgrade), and Nicomedia (at the Marmara Lake). From then on, the city of Rome lost all political importance, although it retained its symbolic value for a very long time. Many emperors favored Rome economically, but few bothered to visit it. The status of Italy no longer differed from that of other provinces: the empire's focus had moved towards its borders.

The immense differences between the Greek East and the Latin West became more pronounced in all respects: economy, politics, warfare, art, religion, and so on. Restoration of military and political authority was the first prerequisite of the renaissance of the empire, but it had no real future without settling the economic anarchy, too. During the Tetrarchy, economic life revived, but debased currency and uncontrolled inflation counteracted the efforts of reorganization. Several monetary reforms failed, and so did the Price Edict of AD 301, an attempt to stop inflation by freezing the prices of goods and services.

The Tetrarchy collapsed only a few years after Diocletian's abdication. In AD 324, one of his successors, Constantine, assembled the entire empire under his rule and established a parallel seat of government in Byzantium (Constantinople), in the East—the door to the trade between Europe and Asia. Only Constantine succeeded in bringing order to the monetary system by introducing a new gold coin, the solidus. At that time, however, the importance of money was rapidly diminishing. Trade receded, a barter economy prevailed, and the towns were depopulated, their functions being gradually replaced by self-supporting rural estates. The husbandmen, *coloni*, lost their freedom and were gradually transformed into villeins, taking the place of the former rural slaves. In reality, Classical Antiquity as an urban civilization had ceased to exist. After Constantine's death, the empire split again and was ruled by his three sons. It was seldom to be in the hands of a single ruler. The last time was in 394 BC to 395 BC.

For some time, the cities retained their importance as cultural centers, not least for the Christian Church. After centuries of work and struggle, and after grave persecutions (under Decius, AD 249 to AD 251, and Diocletian, AD 303 to AD 305, in particular), the church was officially acknowledged in AD 311. Its power and importance grew constantly until, at the very end of the fourth century AD, it became the sole legally admitted religion in the empire. Paganism survived in the countryside and its small villages (*pagi*), but the towns became centers in the hierarchic organization of the church. Bishops and archbishops built richly decorated cathedrals, and churches and monasteries gradually took over responsibility for the transmission of the cultural heritage of antiquity.

The Roman Empire Disintegrates

While the eastern, Byzantine, part of the empire prospered around its new capital, Constantinople, the western emperors finally lost the struggle against invading barbarians and a collapsing economy. Almost simultaneously, the western Roman Empire disintegrated. In AD 406, Germanic tribes crossed the Rhine and founded a series of new states upon the ruins of the empire—Vandals in Africa, Visigoths in southern Gaul and Spain, Salian Franks in northern Gaul, and so forth. Rome was sacked in AD 410 and in AD 455, and in AD 476, the last emperor of the West, Romulus Augustulus, was dethroned—a symbolic event, but one of little real consequence by this time.

In the East, Roman emperors were to rule for a thousand years more, until Constantinople fell to the Ottoman Turks in AD 1453. In the West, the Christian Church represented continuity, until a new emperor—Charlemagne, king of the Franks—was crowned by the Pope, Leo III, in Rome on Christmas Day, AD 800.

⇨ *Opposite page*: The magnificent apsis of the Basilica of St Apollinare in Classe, in Ravenna, Italy. The walls are covered with polychrome mosaics from the first half of the sixth century AD.

SCALA

⇨ A detail of the reliefs on the Column of Trajan, erected in the Emperor's forum to commemorate his victories over the Dacians (in present-day Romania) between AD 101 and AD 106. The reliefs depict a variety of scenes, including battles, Roman soldiers building fortifications, and Trajan addressing his troops.

+SANCTUS APOLENARIS

THE EUROPEAN FRONTIERS OF THE ROMAN EMPIRE

P.J. Casey

THE ROMAN EMPEROR AUGUSTUS abandoned ideas of world conquest when the Roman army, invading Germany north of the Elbe, was massacred in AD 9. He established a European empire ending at Germany's borders on the banks of the Rhine and the Danube rivers. Along this line, a system of forts and fortresses protected the provinces and served as bases from which he could conduct punitive campaigns against the barbarians. Flotillas of river-craft prevented incursions by raiders and smugglers.

MUSEI CAPITOLINI, ROME/SCALA

↑ The emperor Hadrian. A restless traveler within his empire, he ended imperial expansion and formalized the frontiers. Hadrian's Wall is an enduring monument to this policy of consolidation.

↓ A regularly paid army guarded the frontiers of the provinces, and each regiment occupied a fort built to a standard plan. At Chesters, on Hadrian's Wall, the underground strongroom, in which the unit's pay and savings were stored, survives to the present day.

There were minor changes to this grand design. Between the two rivers, various schemes of forts and fortifications—which represented attempts to gain strategic locations—have been identified. Early in the second century AD, Trajan crossed the Danube, adding the province of Dacia (modern Romania) to the empire. Dacia was abandoned in the late third century AD; the Danube was once again the frontier line. Claudius added Britannia (Britain) to the empire in AD 43, but once it was decided to conquer only part of the island, the task of establishing a viable frontier against the northern barbarians presented a major problem.

Frontier Defense Strategy

The strategy of frontier defense was based on the two main elements of the army: the citizen legionaries and the noncitizen auxiliaries. The legionary heavy infantry was usually deployed in units of about 5,500 men; their fortresses provided them with accommodation, workshops, and technical and medical facilities. Auxiliaries were recruited from defeated tribes or enrolled from unenfranchised peoples within the empire. They served for the reward of Roman citizenship, conferred at the end of 25 years' service with the colors. Auxiliary regiments varied in their make-up; most comprised 480 infantrymen or a similar number of cavalry troopers. A minority of regiments comprised 1,000 horse or foot soldiers; some others were a mixture of both. Sensibly, the Roman administration tended to post newly recruited auxiliary units to provinces, distant from their homelands. There, they settled for long periods in garrison, forming liaisons with the community and attracting traders, until a distinctive frontier culture evolved, and a population grew up that depended on the local fort for its livelihood and existence. Some of these civilian settlements grew into substantial towns. From these communities (*vici*), new members of the local regiment were recruited. In time, units with names derived originally from distant tribes were entirely served by locally born *vicani*.

PHILIP ABRAMSON/MICK SHARP

This strategy, and its modification and development, are best demonstrated by Hadrian's Wall in Britain, constructed during the reign of Emperor Hadrian (AD 117 to AD 138). Along its 130 kilometer (80 mile) line were 17 forts, manned by infantry units totalling some 8,400 men. At 1.6 kilometer (1 mile) intervals, fortified gates allowed passage through Hadrian's Wall under military supervision. Towers at 500 meter (1,750 foot) intervals allowed surveillance of the landscape. Approach to Hadrian's Wall from the south was prevented by a vast ditch (the *Vallum*), which followed the wall, up hill, down dale, through bog, and through scrubland, across the width of Britain. For a 130 kilometer (80 mile) deep zone south of the wall, further auxiliary forts protected the rugged uplands of the frontier zone. A full legion at Eburacum (York) reinforced the wall garrisons in case trouble erupted that could not be dealt with by local resources. The *vici* attached to auxiliary forts flourished, especially in the third century AD. After AD 350, most *vici* were abandoned, probably because unit size was reduced to about one-third of the strength in the first century AD. This created accommodation space for soldiers and their families within the forts.

PHILIP ABRAMSON/MICK SHARP

↑ Frontier forces were accommodated in barrack blocks designed to hold 80 soldiers. Eight men shared a two-room unit in cramped company with their equipment, personal effects, and bedding.

Community Response to Frontiers

The presence of these frontiers had profound effect on the communities living beyond them. Local people adopted different strategies at various times and in various places. The simplest response was attack, but the instances of successful penetration of Roman defenses, before the end of the fourth century AD, were very rare. Hadrian's Wall was crossed in AD 181, but the resulting punitive campaign certainly outweighed any advantages gained by the attackers.

On the Danube, a long campaign was fought by Marcus Aurelius (between AD 161 and AD 181) against the Marcomanni (literally, "people of the frontier"). In the third century AD, attacks launched across the Rhine resulted in devastation in Gaul and the creation of a separatist dynasty of Roman emperors, ruling Germany, Gaul, and Britain. They were devoted to protecting regional defense interests.

Trade across the frontiers was regulated, not discouraged, and access to Roman goods may have been used to create pro-Roman elites among the tribes beyond the frontier. Evidence from Germany suggests that chieftains and leaders with access to such goods used them to reward their followers. Through trade, Rome acquired amber, furs, wild animals, and slaves. Barbarian soldiers also crossed the frontiers to serve in the Roman army.

The Frontier Falls

The collapse of the frontier system was swift in northwestern Europe. In the winter of AD 406, the Rhine froze over, and a mass of refugees—driven west by the expansion of eastern tribes—crossed the river and quickly moved through Gaul and on to Spain. These peoples created their own kingdoms inside the empire, and these eventually superseded the Roman administration.

In Britain, the forts on Hadrian's Wall were probably occupied into the middle of the sixth century AD, perhaps under some sort of local dynastic control. On the Danube, the frontiers crumbled slowly, following the defeat of the East Roman army in AD 378 by the Visigoths at Adrianople. Frontiers had ceased to be effective barriers; depleted of a labor force and served by inferior troops, they were a minor deterrent. In the event of a major incursion, mobile armies, kept in reserve within the provinces, were rushed in to attack the invaders. This system worked well until the army was reduced in numbers, and as recruiting became more difficult, barbarian armies were hired to fight barbarian invaders.

Frequently, the hired "allies" set up self-ruling barbarian kingdoms in the heartland of the Roman Empire. Moreover, improvements in marine technology brought shiploads of invaders to the coastal regions, and this further stretched the logistic base of the Roman frontier defenses. It was then clear that the tide of history had undermined even the strongest frontier defenses.

B. GERARD/EXPLORER/AUSCAPE

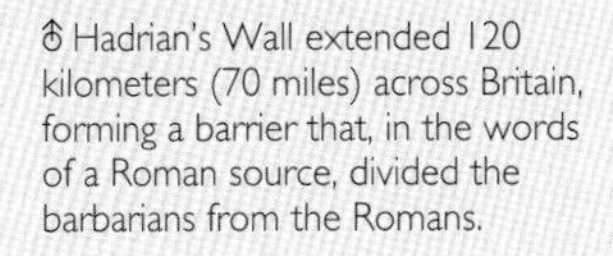

⇧ Hadrian's Wall extended 120 kilometers (70 miles) across Britain, forming a barrier that, in the words of a Roman source, divided the barbarians from the Romans.

PHILIP ABRAMSON/MICK SHARP

⇧ In the fort at Housesteads, on Hadrian's Wall, comforts provided for the troops included bathing facilities and elaborate sanitary arrangements. The lavatory block shown here seated up to 20 men and was flushed by running water.

BRUCE COLEMAN LTD

⇦ The fort at Hardknott (Cumbria) guards a high pass through the bleak spine of hills that passes through northern Britain. Forts such as this one ensured the safety of travelers and military convoys in the remote frontier area.

PAT ODEA/BORD FAILTE

THE IRON AGE IN EUROPE

8 0 0 B C – A D 1 0 5 0

Horsemen, Ironsmiths, and Vikings

GÖRAN BURENHULT

THE INTRODUCTION OF iron-working in Europe during the eighth century BC was to have truly revolutionary consequences, not the least of which was that it brought about the rapid collapse of the continent's ancient social systems, which had their roots far back in the Stone Age. For the first time, a raw material that could be used to make tools, weapons, and ornaments was accessible to everybody. Power could no longer be based on the control of the trade routes for precious materials, such as copper, tin, and zinc. From about 500 BC, more and more parts of Europe appeared in the limelight of history as a result of intensified contacts with the Mediterranean world. At the same time, the westward thrusts of the nomadic Scythian horsemen from Siberia and the Russian steppes significantly influenced art, clothing, and military strategies in the powerful chiefdoms of central Europe. The rich Hallstatt culture, centered in present-day Austria, became a melting pot of cultural influences from the Scythians, the Etruscans, and the Greeks—giving rise to the Celtic tradition that would soon spread across much of Europe.

⟲ Facing the roaring Atlantic, the Celtic Iron Age hill-fort of Dún Aenghus, on the island of Inishmore, off the western coast of Ireland, constantly braves the fury of the elements. This magnificent site once may have been a religious center, but its location and fortifications, in the form of so-called *chevaux de frise* (closely spaced, erect stones), indicate that its function was mainly defensive.

⊙ This miniature bronze cult wagon from a Hallstat burial at Strettweg, in eastern Austria, dates from the seventh century BC. Its frame bears figures of mounted warriors, flanking a large, naked woman, who is thought to be a goddess. It was probably used as a ritual object.
RONALD SHERIDAN/ANCIENT ART & ARCHITECTURE COLLECTION

C.M. DIXON/PHOTO RESOURCES

This bronze Tarquinia sword found in Bavaria, in southern Germany, is a typical weapon of the Urnfield period.

But while the Mediterranean world and increasingly large parts of central and western Europe now stepped into historic times, the people of the Germanic world in the north were to experience another 1,500 years or so of unwritten prehistory. Nevertheless, contacts with the "civilized" world to the south would leave a deep mark on society on both sides—politically and culturally.

A New Europe

To understand these far-reaching changes, and the subsequent rise of Celtic dominance, we need to look at both the relationship between and the events of the three main cultural phases that characterized the period between about 1200 BC and 400 BC—the Late Bronze Age and what are known as the Hallstatt and La Tène periods—as well as at the important role played by increasing contacts with the Mediterranean area.

The Late Bronze Age societies in central and northern Europe, and their ruling classes in particular, were marked by a high degree of uniformity. New burial practices prevailed in these societies. Bodies were cremated and the remains deposited in clay urns in grave-fields, giving the tradition its name: the Urnfield culture. The Urnfield tradition, which is equivalent to the first two phases of the Hallstatt period (A and B)—so named after an important site in western Austria—between 1200 BC and 800 BC, was notable for the gradual introduction of iron.

During these last phases of the Bronze Age, contacts with the Mediterranean area were intensive. Powerful chiefs lived in heavily fortified settlements strategically situated on high ground. Society was hierarchic, with power based on control over the surplus production of both staple and luxury goods in exchange for the security offered by a strong and successful leader. A desire for prestige and status is reflected in finds of rich hoards and sacrificial offerings.

During the Hallstatt C phase (about 800 BC to 600 BC), some notable changes took place. In many areas, from present-day France in the west to the Czech Republic and the Balkans in the east, inhumation (the burial of unburned bodies) once again became the dominant form of burial. At the same time, a number of remarkably rich, princely burials (burials of the leading elite, or so-called *Fürstengräber*) took place. These usually take the form of timbered chambers containing four-wheeled carts, horse trappings, and exceptionally rich grave goods. Similar burial practices are also found further east—for example, in the so-called Timber Grave culture of the South Russian steppes, where the custom may have originated. These magnificent burials reflect the development of a warrior aristocracy in Europe. An all-embracing political power probably never existed; rather, the many mutually warring tribes were led by their respective chiefs. During this period, contacts with the Mediterranean world appear to have all but ceased.

The Lake Hallstatt area, in the Austrian Alps, was the heartland of the emerging Iron Age. Its rich resources of salt—an important trade item—and copper and iron spurred the development of the first major metal cultures in central Europe.

ERICH LESSING/MAGNUM

Undoubtedly, the transition from bronze to iron, with the immense social upheavals this brought about, lay behind these changes.

One of the most significant local groups within the Urnfield tradition lived in the Lausitz region, located in present-day Poland, eastern Germany, and the Czech Republic. The Saale River region and the southern shores of the Baltic Sea were also important. The Urnfield period was a time of technological innovation. In particular, an advanced bronze-working technique was developed that allowed the thin metal plates used to make shields, helmets, bronze vessels, and other objects to be embossed with ornamental motifs, often in the form of animals. Alloy and casting techniques were also refined. Glass production, too, was introduced from Egypt, and ceramic technology reached a high level in many areas. Painted pottery appeared in the Hallstatt area, and the Lausitz ceramics influenced pottery-making all over northern Europe. About 1000 BC, iron swords came into use within the Urnfield area; a few centuries later, iron tools and weapons were commonplace throughout central Europe.

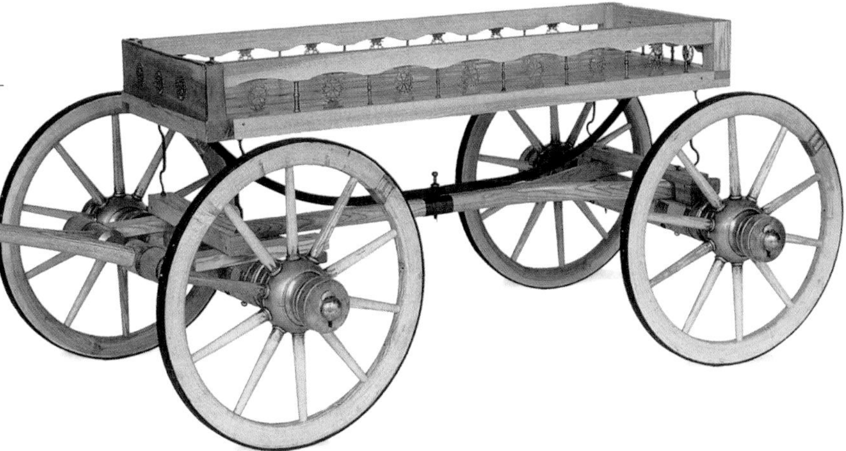

A reconstructed wagon from the Hallstatt wagon grave of Vix, in eastern France. The grave is that of a woman, and dates from the end of the sixth century BC. Among the imported luxury items it contained were a black-figure cup and a large bronze crater (wine bowl) from Greece, and bronze flagons from Etruria.

RÖMISCH GERMANISCHES ZENTRALMUSEUM

GÖRAN BURENHULT

Numerous settlements dating from the Late Bronze Age have been found in Europe. All were situated near water, in the form of rivers, springs, or lakes. In some regions, heavily fortified artificial islands—so-called lake dwellings—were built. Lake dwellings were particularly common in Ireland, where they are known as crannogs, and a large number have been found there. Shown here is a reconstructed crannog at the "Craggaunowen Project", at Quin, in County Clare, Ireland.

Wealth and Turmoil

After 600 BC, the political situation in central Europe changed radically, and the region once again came into direct contact with the Mediterranean world. It was during this period that Greek colonization reached its high point, beginning about 750 BC and culminating in the foundation of Massilia (present-day Marseilles), about 550 BC. In the process, Greek culture spread to large parts of southern France and also to Italy, where it strongly influenced the Etruscan culture. About 500 BC, the Classical Age began in Greece, and a few centuries later, Rome emerged on the scene—an event that was to have a considerable impact on subsequent developments in Europe.

The contacts between the peoples north and south of the Alps were reflected in the import of magnificent luxury items, which have been found in the princely burials of this period. The wagon grave at Vix, in eastern France, is a particularly important example. But the peoples of central Europe were also inspired to advance their own artistic and technical skills. The architect who designed the fortified settlement of Heuneburg, in Germany, with its walls of clay blocks, was surely influenced by Mediterranean prototypes. Other important fortified settlements of this period have been found at Hohenasperg and Breisach, in Germany; and at Mont Lassois, Château-sur-Salins, and Châtillon-sur-Glâne, in France. Feudal society had appeared in Europe.

Excavation sites such as Heuneburg have shown that this feudal society came to an abrupt end during the last phase of the Hallstatt period, in the sixth century BC. Currently, there is no evidence to suggest that these powerful chiefdoms survived into the La Tène phase of the Early Iron Age in Europe, and this is one of the great problems faced by prehistorians in trying to establish continuity in the history of settlement in the region. Ludwig Pauli of the Bavarian Academy of Science, in Munich, has pointed to a series of fundamental changes that occurred in central Europe during the fifth century BC. The destruction of the fortified settlements coincided with the end of the tradition of princely burials. At the same time, princely burials appeared in new areas that had previously been only sparsely populated—areas in which iron was apparently common. A new kind of princely burial, primarily containing adornments and ritual objects of the early Celtic La Tène type, appeared in many places. Cultural influences from the south and east were manifested in art, handicrafts, and symbols: Greek–Etruscan palmettes (fan-shaped ornaments), Oriental motifs, and Celtic circular motifs. At the same time, the characteristic symbols of the Late Bronze Age and the Hallstatt culture, including solar disks, waterfowl, and horses, disappeared. In fact, Europe was going through its own process of "orientalization": Celtic expansion had begun.

A gold vase from the burial mound (*kurgan*) of Kul-Oba, in the Crimea, depicting a Scythian legend recorded by the Greek author Herodotus.
STATENS HISTORISKA MUSEUM, SWEDEN

Horsemen from the East

It was not only contact with the developing states in Greece and Italy that transformed the feudal societies of central Europe into a uniform Celtic culture. For the first time in the history of Europe, the ancient nomadic horsemen of the South Russian and central Asian steppes made their presence known—the Scythians had begun to move west.

Most of our knowledge of these colorful peoples springs from the Greek author Herodotus, who devoted his fourth book about the Greek struggle against alien tribes to the Scythian wars against the Persian king Darius. As early as the seventh century BC, the Greeks had founded trading ports along the northern shores of the Black Sea, where they came into contact with these mounted nomads. This led to an extensive exchange of goods, and Scythian chiefs also commissioned items from Greek craftworkers and artists, especially goldsmiths, whose products have been found in richly adorned mound burials on the steppes. About 450 BC, Herodotus visited one of these Black Sea trading ports—Olbia, at the mouth of the Bug River—and came in contact with people who had dealings with the steppe nomads.

The nomadic horsemen had developed an advanced culture that stretched from the Great Wall of China, in the east, to the Danube River, in the west—a distance of more than 7,000 kilometers (4,350 miles). The Scythians, a western nomad group, roamed the area north of the Black and Caspian seas. Over thousands of years, their ancestors had developed a way of life centered on the horse: at Dereivka, in the Dnepr River area, for example, 74 percent of the animal bones excavated were those of horses. The Dereivka finds belong to the Sredny Stog culture, which was followed by the so-called Pit Grave culture, which, in turn, developed into the Catacomb Grave culture. Dating from about 2500 BC, the graves of this latter culture have yielded the world's oldest known examples of wheeled vehicles. The previously mentioned Timber Grave culture emerged about 1900 BC, and it is in the graves of this culture that light, horse-drawn carts are found for the first time. Not until about 1500 BC, when

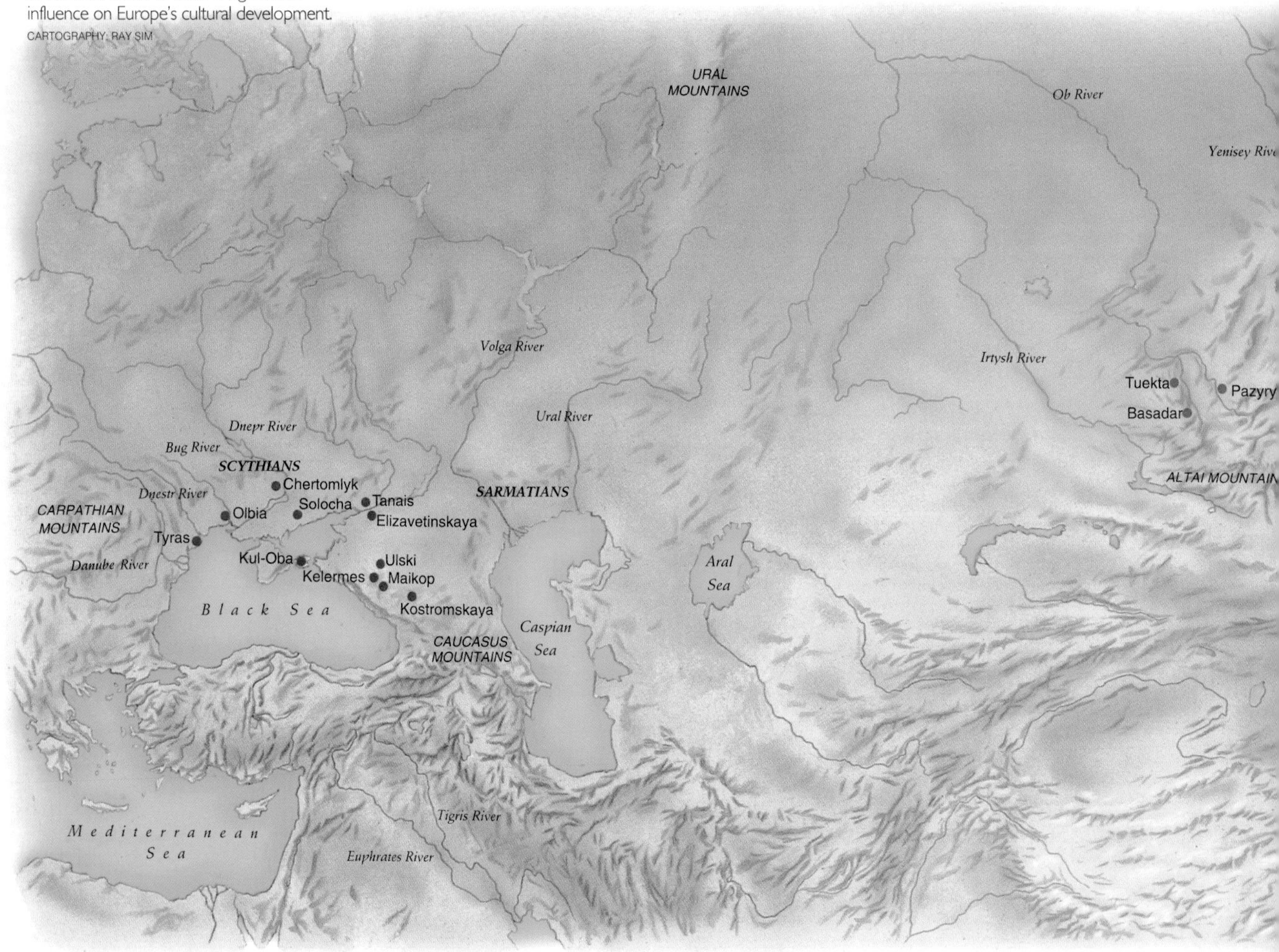

THE WIDE WORLD OF THE STEPPE NOMADS

During the Iron Age, tribes of nomadic horsemen roamed the Eurasian steppes, from the Carpathian Mountains, in the west, to the Altai Mountains, in the east. The Scythians, a western group of these horsemen, were to have a significant influence on Europe's cultural development.
CARTOGRAPHY: RAY SIM

the Andronovo culture first appeared in the same region, did true nomadic societies begin to develop from these hitherto relatively sedentary herding peoples. About 500 BC, the Scythians appeared.

During periods of drought, the nomads traveled beyond their regular migration areas, and their thrusts towards the east, the south, and the west can be distinguished more or less clearly at different times. The oldest parts of the Great Wall were built by the emperor Qin Shi Huang between 221 BC and 210 BC as a defense against attacks from eastern groups of these horsemen. Warlike nomadic horsemen of Scythian origin are also thought to have taken part in the destruction of the Assyrian capital, Nineveh, in 612 BC.

It has been said that the Scythians were the world's foremost light cavalry. What is certainly true is that these master horsemen were largely responsible for introducing horses to European warfare during the Late Bronze Age and Early Iron Age. Because it was easy to subdue crowds of people from horseback, the horse became an important adjunct to the exercise of power. Rich finds of sacrificial offerings of horse trappings from this period surely reflect this new development.

But it was not only in the ongoing social transformation and in military strategies that Scythian influence was significant. The manners and customs of the nomadic horsemen also left their mark on clothing and ornamental decoration in Celtic and Germanic Europe. Trousers were introduced in Europe, and naturalistic motifs featuring horses, deer, and birds were further elaborated in the Germanic world.

The superior fighting techniques of the Scythians, which included use of the bow and arrow, made them indomitable masters of the steppes for a long time. It was not until the fourth century BC that another tribe, the Sarmatians, managed to shatter their power. It has been suggested that the Sarmatians invented the iron stirrup, which allowed them to carry lances in their saddles, and thereby push their enemies off their horses. It was to be about another thousand years, however, before the iron stirrup came into widespread use in the Germanic world of northern Europe.

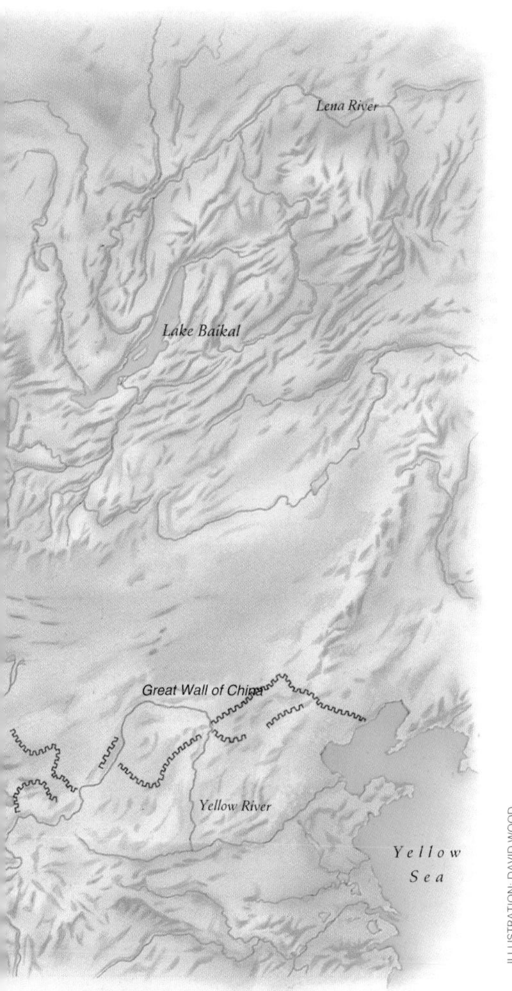

Magnificent burial mounds on the South Russian steppes, so-called *kurgans*, are impressive reminders of the Scythians' heyday. They contain the remains of the most powerful chiefs, along with those of their wives, servants, and horses, who accompanied their masters to the land of the dead.

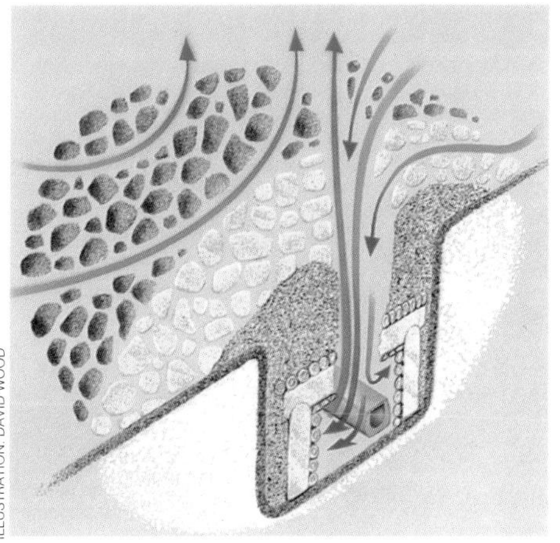

FROZEN TOMBS IN THE ALTAI

At Pazyryk, in the High Altai, Russian archaeologists have made some sensational discoveries. Stone burial cairns in this region were found to have prevented the soil underneath them from warming up in summer, and allowed frost to penetrate to the bottom of the grave during winter. The permafrost thus formed around the timbered burial chamber has preserved organic materials for posterity, including wood, body tissue, and magnificent textiles. (After L.L. Barkova)

ERICH LESSING/MAGNUM

The site of La Tène, on the shores of Lake Neuchâtel, in western Switzerland, has given its name to the Iron Age phase that succeeded the Hallstatt period, about 500 BC. Votive offerings of bronze, iron, and wooden objects were found here in the shallow waters at the lake's edge.

La Tène and the Celtic Expansion

While the nomadic Scythian culture flourished on the eastern steppes, Celtic tribes in central Europe were spreading out over vast areas from their homeland along the upper reaches of the Rhine River. The reasons behind this expansion are not fully known—overpopulation and internal conflicts have been put forward as probable causes—but the course of events is evident from both classical literary sources and the archaeological record. Herodotus described these "Keltoi" as "living further west than any other European people, except the Kynetians". The latter inhabited the southwestern corner of the Iberian peninsula, in present-day Portugal. Another Greek author, Eforos, classified them as one of the four great barbaric peoples: Celts, Scythians, Persians, and Libyans. Later, during Roman times, the Celts were known by the Romans as Gauls.

Celtic societies grew rapidly and markedly during the fifth and sixth centuries BC, with the rise of a number of warrior societies. These emerged in two main centers in central Europe: the Hunsrück-Eifel region of the central Rhineland, in Germany, and the Champagne district of northeastern France. Both were associated with powerful Hallstatt chiefdoms: Hunsrück-Eifel with the Hohenasperg complex, and Champagne with the Mont-Lassois complex.

Clearly, trade with Massilia played a decisive role in this process. Products from the north, such as foodstuffs, gold, iron, furs, and slaves, were exchanged for goods from the eastern Mediterranean area and Italy, and the main transport route into the Celtic heartland followed the Rhône River valley. It has been suggested that slaves were the main commodity in this interchange of goods. Celtic warrior societies "collected" slaves in the far north and northwest and sold them to more sedentary Celtic chiefdoms in the western Hallstatt region. These, in turn, had contacts with the Mediterranean area, where Phocaeans (from Phocaea, an ancient Greek city in present-day Turkey) and Etruscans in particular were reputed to be notorious pirates and slave-traders.

Towards the end of the seventh century BC, however, the Celtic warrior societies had forged their own, direct contacts with Massilia, becoming more or less independent of the merchants in the old Hallstatt region. This led to great political changes in central Europe. Beginning about 500 BC, a number of other events in the Mediterranean area also influenced the situation. Widespread Greek

colonization, including the foundation of Alalia, in Corsica, meant that Greek merchant fleets could reach Massilia without having to enter Etruscan ports. At the same time, the Greeks' interest in their western colonies waned, following political events in Asia Minor (present-day Turkey), such as the Persian Wars. As a result, these colonies eventually formed an independent, western Mediterranean region. The Greek cities in southern Italy and Sicily, strategically situated in the middle of the Mediterranean, were in a key position. Together, these events resulted in the beginning of the traditional Celtic societies' disintegration, and the consequent spread of their influence far afield. The Celtic peoples of Europe never formed a unified state or even an ethnic group. Many of their dialects were closely related, but they often spoke completely different languages. The different ruling families and chiefs, with their roots in the Hallstatt tradition of the Late Bronze Age, created a great number of independent regions, governed from strategically situated so-called *oppida.* These often consisted of heavily fortified cities built on high ground, but they were also important cultural centers, with skilled craftworkers and flourishing trade. It has been estimated that there were 700 *oppida* in Gaul alone (which covered the area of present-day France and parts of Belgium, western Germany, and northern Italy), including Alesia, Bibracte, and Avaricum, which became famous in connection with Caesar's campaigns. Manching, in southern Germany, is in a class by itself and is one of the best-studied examples of these city-like settlements.

The Celtic tribes became the first historically known peoples north of the Alps, and their role as intermediaries of eastern, Mediterranean, and Oriental culture was significant. The Celtic world became a melting pot, combining local traditions and the cultural influences of Scythians, Etruscans, and Greeks within its religious, artistic, and social life.

From the fifth century BC, Celtic tribes apparently spread throughout much of Europe, sometimes by means of peaceful colonization, sometimes by war campaigns. About 400 BC, Celts from present-day Switzerland reached Italy. In 386 BC, they defeated a Roman army at the Allia River, and with the exception of the Capitolium, burned the city of Rome to the ground. From there they pushed southwards to Apulia and Sicily. At the same time, Celtic tribes settled in large parts of southern England, including Cornwall, and Wales and Scotland, and soon after, also in Ireland. In the third century BC, other Celtic tribes penetrated into the Balkans, where they were defeated in 279 BC, after having burned down the temple of Delphi. Another group of Celts migrated into Asia Minor, where they founded the state of Galatia.

The Celtic world, however, was centered on an area that includes parts of present-day France and northern Italy. These regions, called "Gallia Narbonensis" and "Gallia Cisalpina" by the Romans,

The "Battersea Shield", a splendid example of Celtic craftmanship, was found in the River Thames, in London, in 1857. Dating from the early first century AD, it is made of bronze, has glass inlays, and is decorated with cast-bronze disks featuring bosses and tendril-shaped designs.
C.M. DIXON/PHOTO RESOURCES

NATIONAL MUSEUM, PRAGUE/ERICH LESSING/MAGNUM

This Celtic stone bust from Mšecké Zehrovice, in Bohemia, in the Czech Republic, was found near a ritual site. Possibly representing a god, it dates from between 150 BC and 50 BC.

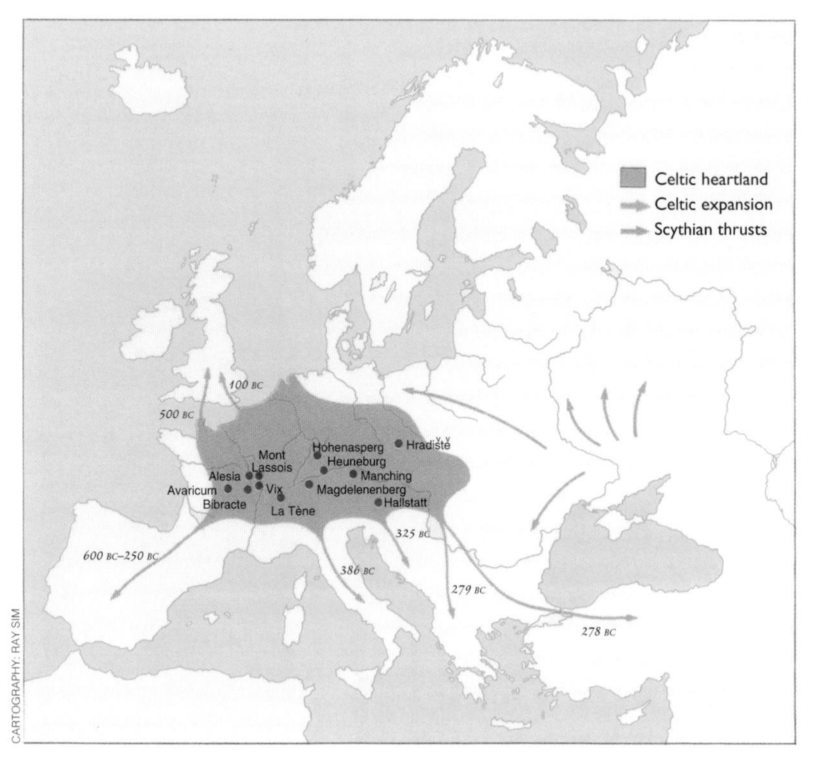

CARTOGRAPHY: RAY SIM

This large, silver cauldron was found in a bog at Gundestrup, in Vesthimmerland, Jutland, Denmark, in 1891. Manufactured by Celtic craftsmen about 100 BC, possibly in Thrace, in the Balkans, it eventually found its way deep into the Germanic regions of northern Europe.
NATIONAL MUSEUM OF DENMARK

Opposite page: This spectacular bronze face was mounted as decoration on the side of a four-wheeled wagon found at Dejbjerg, at Als, in Jutland, Denmark. It dates from the first century BC.

CELTIC EXPANSION
From the fifth century BC, Celtic culture began to spread from its central European homeland to the British Isles, Iberia, Italy, the Balkans, and Asia Minor. At the same time, the nomadic Scythians were thrusting westwards into Europe.

A Celtic bronze statue of a warrior-god from Saint-Maur-en-Chaussée, in Oise, northern France.
A. LE TOQUIN/EXPLORER/AUSCAPE

were intimately linked to subsequent events in Roman history. In 225 BC, Celtic tribes once again penetrated into the Apennine peninsula, but at Telamon, on the coast of Etruria, they were defeated by joint Roman and Etruscan forces. The Romans then conquered Gallia Cisalpina, and, soon after, turned it into a Roman province.

In 121 BC, Gallia Narbonensis also became a Roman province, although conflicts with rebellious tribes continued there for a long time. The Gauls rose under the leadership of the famous chief Vercingetorix, but the revolt was put down following the siege of Alesia, in 52 BC. Celtic power came to an end, and Caesar conquered the rest of Gaul.

Although the political power of the warlike Celts had been crushed by Caesar's campaigns and the subsequent expansion of the Roman Empire, Celtic culture, art, music, and beliefs were to survive into modern times. This was particularly evident in marginal areas such as Brittany, Wales, and Ireland, where Celtic tribes lived on relatively undisturbed.

It was the Celtic tribes of central Europe who introduced iron-working during Hallstatt times, and this surely accounts for much of their political and economic success. The Hallstatt soon transformed into the La Tène period, after an important site on the shores of Lake Neuchâtel, in Switzerland, and rich chiefly burials dating from this time bear witness to a considerable concentration of power. Skillful artists transformed Scythian, Greek, and Oriental motifs into vivid, naturalistic compositions with spirals, whirls, and stylized animals. Ornamentation on such items as jewelry, weapons, and drinking vessels included founded (molded) glass pearls and inlays of red enamel. Ceramics were characterized by beautifully painted, thrown pots of high quality. The Celts also struck their own coins on the model of Hellenistic and Greek prototypes. This bears witness to intensive and far-reaching trading contacts, in which metalwork goods served as the basic commodity of exchange.

Several splendid bog finds in northern Europe, notably in Denmark, include objects that originated in Celtic workshops in central Europe and reached the Germanic world through trade, such as a famous silver cauldron from Gundestrup, in Vesthimmerland, and two four-wheeled carts from Dejbjerg, at Als, in Jutland. While these finds most likely represent sacrificial offerings to the gods, the famous and remarkably well-preserved Danish and North German bog bodies dating from this period are probably those of executed criminals. The Roman author Tacitus described how thieves, homosexuals, and traitors were put to death by garrotting, and then were placed in swampy watercourses. Most of the bog bodies show signs of severe ill-treatment, and only a few are fully dressed. (See the feature *Lindow Man: A 2,000 year-old Human Sacrifice*.)

The political developments taking place in the south also involved the Germanic peoples of the north in an extensive interchange of goods—but this time with a totally different power: Rome.

LINDOW MAN: A 2,000-YEAR-OLD HUMAN SACRIFICE

I.M. STEAD

LINDOW MAN is the name given to an ancient body found in a bog at Lindow Moss, near Manchester, in England, in 1984. The previous year, workers digging up peat had found the remains of a human head, and so they were not very surprised when a human leg came to light at the same site. They contacted an archaeologist, who located the rest of the body, which was removed, still encased in a large block of peat, and sent to the British Museum for excavation.

The block of peat contained the upper half of a body that had been sliced by the peat-cutting machine; the rest had been ripped apart and scattered. The remaining pieces, including the leg the workers had found, were discovered in the loose peat. Much of the skin was well preserved, being dark brown and leathery, but the body was almost flat, having been compressed by the great weight of the peat. It had been lying face down in a bog pool. Thanks to the presence of a relatively high concentration of humic and fulvic acids in the peat, which acted as antibiotics and attacked any bacteria present, and the absence of oxygen, the body was preserved for posterity.

The dating of Lindow Man posed problems. He was unclothed and had nothing with him, so the body could not be dated by means of associated artifacts. The position of the body, more than 2 meters (6 feet) beneath the original surface, showed that it was ancient. An examination of associated pollen, together with radiocarbon dating of the peat, indicated that he had lived nearly 2,000 years ago. Initial radiocarbon dates from the body itself varied considerably, but the latest results from Oxford University, where 19 dates have now been processed, suggest that he died in the first century AD, or perhaps early in the second century.

Lindow Man was subjected to photogrammetry (taking measurements from photographs), xeroradiography (high definition X-rays), and body scanners (CAT scans and Magnetic Resonance Imaging) before being thoroughly examined by a surgeon. Specialists determined that he had been in his mid-twenties, some 168 centimeters (5 feet, 6 inches) tall, and perhaps 60 kilograms (130 pounds) or more in weight. He had been quite healthy, although some of his vertebrae had Schmorl's nodes (cavities in the end-plates of vertebrae, perhaps related to severe strain) and he had suffered from worms. No DNA had survived, but his blood group was O. His moustache and beard had been cut by shears, and his fingernails were neatly rounded. Nothing remained of his liver, lungs, or heart, but a length of gut was found, which contained digested food. His last meal consisted of griddle cakes made from flour containing a mixture of wheat (spelt and emmer) and barley and cooked over an open fire.

Lindow Man had not drowned in the pool but had been killed before he entered it. A pathology report revealed that a blow from a small axe had stunned him and fractured his skull. He had then been garrotted (the knotted ligature was well preserved) which broke his neck, and his throat had finally been cut. The position of the garrotte would have speeded up blood loss, and this deliberate bleeding suggests ritual slaughter rather than common murder. One slight clue may point to the identity of the murderers: some mistletoe pollen was found in the man's gut, which is a rare occurrence in an archaeological context. Mistletoe was used by the Druids, the philosopher-priests of the Celtic world, who appear to have taken part in human sacrifices. Little is known about them, but Druids were certainly active in Britain in the first century AD.

Once the body had been taken out of the bog, it was in danger of drying, shrinking, and falling to pieces. Decomposition was prevented in the short term by keeping the body cool and damp. Its long-term preservation was achieved by freeze-drying: the body was immersed in polyethylene glycol (water-soluble wax) for 10 weeks, and was then frozen for three days and freeze-dried for three weeks, the ice being converted directly to vapor and removed to a condensor, where the temperature was minus 60 degrees Celsius (minus 76 degrees Fahrenheit). The outcome was successful, with only slight shrinkage, no color change, and no variation in the texture of the skin. The body is now on permanent display at the British Museum.

The body of another adult male was found in the same bog in 1987, but it had been badly mauled by the peat-cutting machinery. It seems likely that the head found in 1983 belongs to this body. The cause of death has not yet been established, but it seems clear that this second body was more or less contemporary with Lindow Man.

BRITISH MUSEUM

The upper part of Lindow Man's body, with the detached leg on the left, on display at the British Museum.

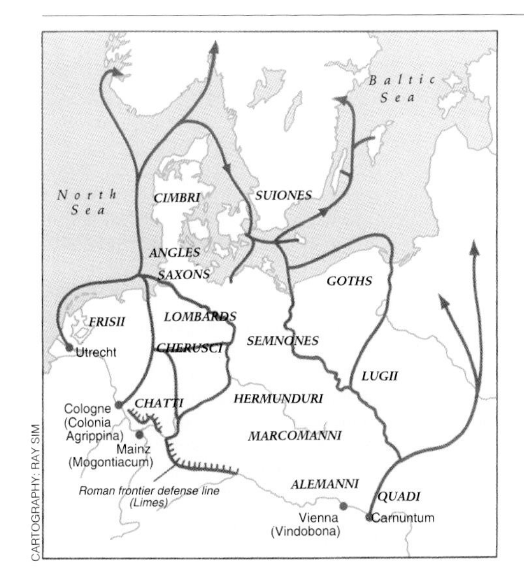

Germanic Peoples and Rome

Following Caesar's pacification of Gaul, the Germanic peoples in northern Europe came in contact with the Roman Empire. The different tribes were now described in detail by Roman historians, and for the first time in history, individual tribes were mentioned by name, giving us a fascinating, contemporary glimpse into prehistoric customs, beliefs, and political conditions. Germanic chiefs were described as skillful commanders, capable of challenging the Roman legions' supremacy. Our knowledge of these historic events comes largely from the brilliant accounts of Tacitus, in his *Annales* and *Germania*, but also from other Roman authors, such as Pliny and Virgil, and the Greek writer Strabo.

During the reign of Caesar Augustus (31 BC to AD 14), the borders of the Roman Empire were consolidated, and for several centuries, peaceful trading with the Germanic tribes in the north alternated with periods of conflict. In northern Europe, the period between the beginning of the first century AD and AD 400 is for this reason called the Roman Iron Age. The borders followed the Rhine and Danube rivers. When, in AD 9, Augustus decided to shift the borders northwards to the River Elbe by annexing large parts of present-day Germany, this attempt came to a sorry end in the Teutoburg Forest. Here, the Roman army, under the command of Publius Quinctilius Varus, was wiped out to the very last man by joint Germanic forces led by the Cherusci chief Arminius. Thereafter, the Roman border, or "Limes", as it was known, largely followed the Rhine River, whose strategically and commercially important mouth was under Roman control. The long border was heavily fortified, and ditches and palisades were constructed from present-day Holland, in the north, to the Balkans, in the south.

The social and economic changes that took place in the Early Iron Age society of northern Europe also resulted in a different system of goods exchange. The circulation of prestige items and "status symbols", which was characteristic of the Bronze Age, was closely linked to the control of the trade routes that carried bronze from central Europe to Scandinavia. Such items were often placed in lakes or marshlands as offerings to the gods, thereby acquiring prestige. During the Late Bronze Age and the Early pre-Roman Iron Age, this traffic ceased; the focus of Europe's interest had switched to the Mediterranean world.

Imported finds once again appear in the archaeological record in the last few centuries BC, but they now reflect a different kind of exchange system. More than ever before, the distribution of luxury items by chiefs and ruling families was probably aimed at securing friendship and loyalty both from other tribes and from within their own tribal group. Rich warrior graves show that men who were capable of bearing arms were more and more closely linked to the political system. At the same time, chiefs seem to have become richer and fewer in number: power was concentrated in a few hands, indicating the beginning of a process of centralization had begun. Luxury items from this period are usually found in rich graves and rarely as sacrificial offerings to the gods. Increasingly, offerings included weapons and other articles of war instead, bearing witness to military events and the emergence of a more solid machinery of power. Centralization was fully consolidated by about AD 100, and a network of trade routes was built up, linking northern Europe with the developing feudal societies and their handicraft centers in the Roman provinces. There are some splendid examples of luxury commodities that reached the Germanic world in this way, including various Roman utensils for wine-drinking, such as bronze situlas (bucket-shaped vessels), wine dippers, strainers, and drinking vessels.

GERMANIC TRADE ROUTES
As a consequence of their intense trading contacts with the Roman Empire, a number of Germanic tribes living along the northern banks of the Rhine and Danube rivers assimilated aspects of Mediterranean culture and passed them on to the tribes further north. In some cases, goods were transported from craft centers and bronze industries in the motherland, Italy, but more often, the objects that reached northern Europe originated in nearby Roman provinces, such as Gaul. There is also evidence to suggest that Roman fleets, sailing from the mouth of the Rhine, reached as far north as Scandinavia: Augustus's famous temple inscription, *Monumentum Ancyrarum*, at Ankara, in Turkey, tells of voyages to the land of the Cimbri, in present-day Jutland, Denmark.

The Rhine marked the boundary not only between the Roman Empire and the Germanic domains, but also between written history and unwritten prehistory.

CARL O. LÖFMAN/PROMEDIA

Following the collapse of the Roman Empire in the fifth century AD, huge amounts of gold circulated among the Germanic tribes of northern Europe, much of it finding its way to Scandinavia. This gold hoard from Timboholm, in Sweden, consisted of 2 ingots and 26 spiral rings, with a combined weight of more than 7 kilograms (15 pounds).

Clearly, the Germanic tribes in the north must have offered something attractive in return for these luxury goods. Hides and furs were presumably of great importance, the Roman armies requiring enormous amounts of hide for clothing, tents, shields, and harnesses. Rich finds of Roman imports on the Swedish island of Öland, together with evidence of skin-working and large-scale sacrificial offerings of horses, may indicate the large-scale production and export of hides and, possibly, of live horses as well. Iron, amber, beeswax, and wool, and surely also slaves, were other important commodities, while in many southern Germanic areas, salt and copper were the main items of merchandise. Foodstuffs, such as dried meat, fish, and cereals, may also have been exchanged.

During the last pre-Christian century, the sought-after Roman products arrived directly from Italy, including magnificent bronze objects from the major metal industries established at Capua, in Campania. Clay vessels (so-called *terra sigillata*), gold objects, Roman coins, and glass products also made their way via Aquileja, on the Adriatic coast, through the Alpine passes, to the Roman province of Noricum (present-day Austria), and onwards, via Carnuntum and through Bohemia and Moravia, to the Germanic peoples along the coasts of the Baltic Sea. Somewhat later, workshops and trading posts in Gaul supplied the north with industrial products, including *terra sigillata* and glass. The Danish island of Zealand appears to have been a center of economic and political power within this exchange system.

Roman silver, such as this magnificent cup found at Hoby, on Lolland, in Denmark, traveled far beyond the borders of the Roman Empire as gifts, trade items, and war booty.

NATIONAL MUSEUM OF DENMARK

Peoples on the Move

At the beginning of the second century AD, the Roman Empire had reached its zenith. During the reign of Emperor Hadrian (AD 117 to AD 138), a large, defensive wall was constructed in northern England. Patrolling the long borders of the empire entailed tremendous expense, and economic difficulties in combination with far-reaching internal disintegration had dramatically weakened the empire towards the end of the second century. At the same time, the Germanic peoples had begun to realize that unity meant strength.

Between AD 161 and AD 181, the so-called "Marcomanni Wars" took place when the joint forces of Marcomanni, Quadi, Hermunduri, and Lombards temporarily crossed the Limes for the first time. Then, in AD 260, Saxons, Franks, and Alemanni pushed the borderline south of the Rhine once and for all. This was the prelude to a series of Germanic migrations and military adventures, the reasons for which are not fully known. Gothic tribes left their homeland in northern Poland and conquered Dacia, in present-day Romania, in AD 275. At the same time, the Franks penetrated as far south as the Iberian peninsula. But the definitive starting point of the migration period can be pinpointed to AD 375, when the Huns, a tribe of horsemen from central Asia, pushed into the heart of Europe from the

RURAL SETTLEMENT IN ANGLO-SAXON ENGLAND

HELENA F. HAMEROW

AN INCREASING INTEREST in the history of the English landscape and the origins of the English village has fueled archaeological investigations into the earliest Anglo-Saxon communities of Britain. The buildings, size, layout, and distribution of Anglo-Saxon settlements of the fifth to eighth centuries AD, when the English landscape was overwhelmingly rural, are now the subjects of extensive research. Archaeology, place-name studies, topographic work, and historical documents have all contributed to our understanding of the early English village. Yet archaeological traces of these villages are difficult to detect, and it is only relatively recently, since the 1960s and 1970s, that such villages have been excavated in a systematic way.

The conventional picture of the Anglo-Saxon community is of "Ye Olde English Village": a small, stable community of several extended families, established soon after the migrations, in the fifth and sixth centuries AD, of the ethnically mixed group of Germanic peoples who came to be known as the Anglo-Saxons.

The first early Saxon settlement to be scientifically recorded was excavated in the 1930s. It was not until the 1960s and 1970s, however, that excavations were undertaken on a sufficiently large scale to reveal how these early Anglo-Saxon communities actually functioned. It is now known that the Anglo-Saxons lived in settlements consisting of two main types of buildings: rectangular, post-built timber dwellings with wattle-and-daub walls and thatched roofs, and so-called sunken huts, small constructions with sunken floors, used mostly for storage or as workshops for activities such as weaving. Fifth and sixth-century AD settlements were loosely structured, and had few enclosures or well-defined trackways. No obviously "high-status" settlements incorporating exceptionally large buildings are known from this period, despite the number of burials accompanied by rich grave goods. The size of these settlements varied widely, from just two or three families at West Stow, Suffolk, to a community of up to 100 at Mucking, Essex.

⟲ A reconstruction of the largest hall excavated at Cowdery's Down, in Hampshire. ROYAL ARCHAEOLOGICAL INSTITUTE

Economy and Trade

Just as our knowledge of the size and structure of early English communities has grown, so, too, has our understanding of their economic base. Exceptionally complete assemblages of animal bones, seed remains, and industrial debris found at West Stow, and current excavations at West Heslerton, in North Yorkshire, will add further detail to the picture we already have of mixed arable farming, dominated by barley, oats, rye, and wheat, and animal husbandry, with varying emphasis on rearing cattle, pigs, sheep, or, occasionally, horses.

Despite the traditional view of these communities as "self-sufficient" and rather isolated, long-distance trade continued throughout this period, as evidenced by regular finds of amber, precious metals, crystal, amethyst, coins, and imported ornaments, such as brooches from the continental European homelands of the Anglo-Saxons and from the Mediterranean world. Local and interregional trade in commodities such as iron, scrap bronze, and, perhaps, pottery also played a significant role in these economies.

The excavation of settlements, with their associated burial grounds, such as at Mucking and West Heslerton, should yield still more information about the demographic structure and economy of the earliest English villages. Inevitably, this will raise as many questions as it answers. At Mucking, for example, two cemeteries were excavated that contained a number of rich burials, suggesting social stratification. The settlement, however, consisted of a rather haphazard scattering of between 50 and 60 small timber "halls" and more than 200 sunken huts (not all contemporary), but no large, "high-status" buildings. Could this apparent paradox reflect stratification within, rather than between, families? The rich burials may be of heads of families, buried in a more ostentatious style, rather than of particularly rich members of the community. It certainly appears that until the seventh century AD, at least, power was relatively fluid, and was not monopolized by certain lineages.

A Social Elite Emerges

The archaeological record reveals that there were a number of interrelated socioeconomic developments in the seventh century AD. The majority of burials were accompanied by only a few grave goods, or none at all, yet a small number of graves were very rich indeed. The most striking example is the presumably royal ship burial at Sutton Hoo, in Suffolk. At the same time, a number of identifiably high-status settlements with large, central buildings and a carefully structured layout appear, such as at Yeavering and Milfield, in Northumberland, and, on a somewhat less grand scale, at Cowdery's Down, in Hampshire. These settlements and burials suggest the emergence of an aristocratic elite. Even in "ordinary" settlements dating from the beginning of the seventh century AD, such as West Stow, enclosures and what appear to be property boundaries were being built.

It is clear that many early Anglo-Saxon settlements were not fixed in one place. In continental Europe, the phenomenon of gradually "wandering" settlements is well known. Abrupt shifts of several hundred meters could occur, but more often, the shifts were gradual, occurring when houses fell into disrepair and were rebuilt on a new site, leaving the old farmyard to be brought under cultivation. Evidence from Anglo-Saxon settlements such as Mucking suggests that this was frequently also the case in England, where truly stable settlements may not have developed for several more centuries.

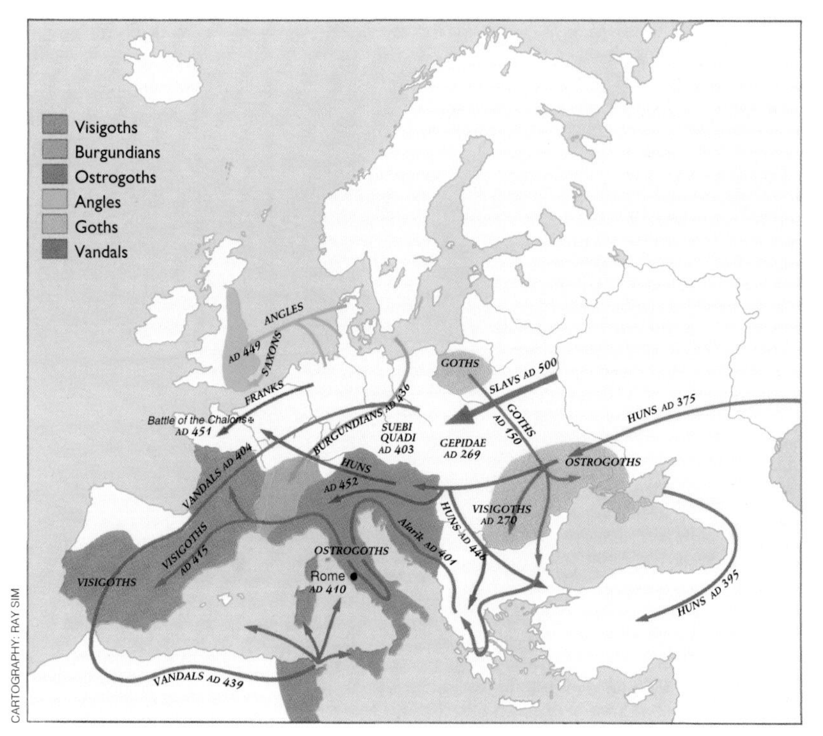

CARTOGRAPHY: RAY SIM

THE MIGRATION PERIOD
The collapse of the Roman Empire triggered a series of large-scale migrations by Germanic peoples. Several tribes left their northern European homelands and ventured to far-flung places, such as northern Africa, sometimes founding new kingdoms. The Angles and Saxons of southern Jutland and northern Germany crossed the North Sea and established themselves in Britain at this time. The Goths were located on the southern shores of the Baltic in the second century AD, and north of the Black Sea in the third century AD.

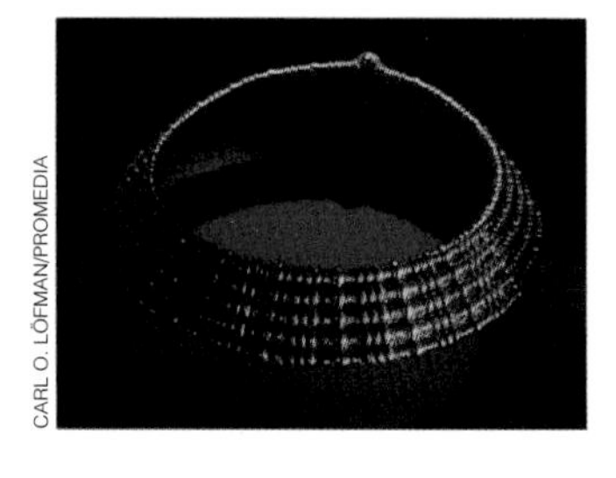

CARL O. LÖFMAN/PROMEDIA

↑ This gold collar was found at Färjestaden, on the island of Öland, in Sweden, and may have been a sacrificial offering. Dating from the migration period, it is one of a series of spectacular jewelry finds and has unparalleled decorations of filigree and granulation.

South Russian steppes. For a century, they ravaged large parts of central Europe, and the whole Germanic world was stirred into motion.

The Goths had split into two groups, the Ostrogoths and the Visigoths. The former were defeated by the Huns, while the latter penetrated into the Balkans in AD 378 and into Italy in AD 401. In AD 395, Emperor Theodosius split the Roman Empire into two parts, the Western and Eastern empires. In AD 410, the Goths, under the command of Alarik, captured the city of Rome. At about the same time, the Romans left Britain, which soon afterwards was occupied by Angles and Saxons from southern Jutland and northwestern Germany.

Gaul now lay open for the Germanic onrush: about AD 400, the Franks arrived from the north, and in AD 406, Vandals, Suebi, Lombards, Quadi, Gepidae, Heruli, Alemanni, and Burgundians poured in from the east. Their barbaric ravages have been vividly described by contemporary authors. In AD 446, Attila became ruler of the Huns in the east, and in AD 451, he pushed westwards with an enormous army made up of Huns and their allies, including Ostrogoths, Gepidae, and Heruli. Having devastated large parts of northern Gaul, he finally stood face to face with an army consisting of Visigoths, Franks, Burgundians, and Saxons, under the command of Aëtius. The battle took place in the Catalaunian Plains, near the River Seine. Attila and his band were defeated. Soon after, the Huns disappeared from the European stage. The Germanic peoples had now taken over Rome's role in western Europe, and about AD 500, King Clovis founded the Frankish kingdom, which became the dominating force and the cultural intermediary of western Europe for the next 500 years.

Rising Powers in the North

The Gothic historian Jordanes and the Greek author Procopius both give us a glimpse into the great number of tribes that inhabited Scandinavia around AD 500. Some of these tribes can be quite accurately located on a map, whereas the names of others are probably based on misunderstandings. These writers may well provide the first historical accounts of the Laps (referred to as the Screrefennae, or Skrithifinoi) and the Swedes, who lived further south (referred to as the Suehans, or Suetidi). The former were mobile hunter-gatherers, while the Swedes were said to be a sedentary people. A region referred to as Raumaricicae is probably identical to present-day Romerike, in Norway, and the Rygi people may have inhabited modern-day Rogaland, also in Norway. Obviously, the Dani lived in Denmark, and the Finni in Finland.

In this multitude of Germanic peoples, some areas seem to have been particularly important, and during the course of the Late Iron Age, these regions developed into significant centers. The basin of Lake Malar, in eastern Sweden, the Baltic islands of Öland and Gotland, southern Norway, and Denmark all played an important part in the subsequent formation of states.

A stream of luxury items from the continent continued to reach Scandinavia's central regions. They derived largely from the same countries as during the heyday of the Roman Empire, but now it was Frankish craftsmen who manufactured the glass and bronze products. Large amounts of goods destined for the Scandinavian markets were produced in the Namur and Picardy regions of Belgium and France. The Danish island of Zealand appears to have lost its commercial importance, which was so evident during late Roman times, and Sweden and Norway now traded directly with central Europe. As time went on, a number of trading centers developed, from where goods were distributed across the countryside. At Dankirke, in the Jutland peninsula, in Denmark; and on the island of Helgö, in Lake Malar, veritable business houses were established in the fifth and sixth centuries AD.

Most conspicuous, however, are the rich finds of gold that have caused this period to be called Scandinavia's Golden Age. Evidently, huge amounts of gold circulated among the tribes of northern Europe after the collapse of the Roman Empire. Attila the Hun, for instance, received 432,000 solidi (Roman gold coins) from

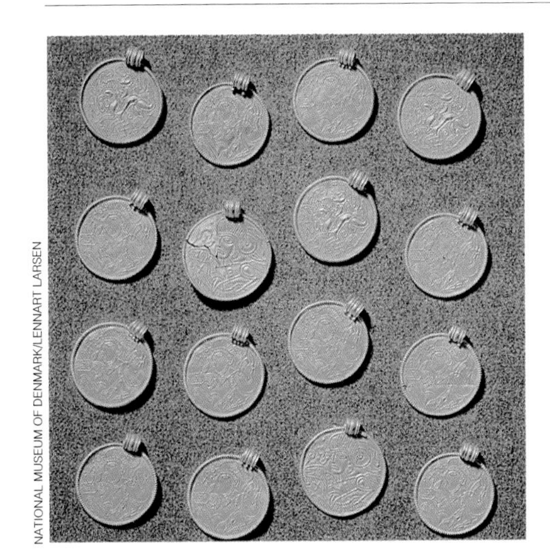
NATIONAL MUSEUM OF DENMARK/LENNART LARSEN

Theodosius II, emperor of the Eastern empire, in 443 AD, in exchange for not plundering the country. This is equivalent to about 2 tonnes (2 tons) of solid gold! Large numbers of solidi were imported into Scandinavia. Most were used as ornaments or melted down by local goldsmiths and reshaped into magnificent objects, including collars and necklets. Hidden hoards of these items, which may have been sacrificial offerings, have been found, among other places, at Ålleberg, Storegården, and Möne, in western Sweden, and at Färjestaden, on Öland.

Somewhat later, in the seventh century AD, rich so-called boat graves appeared, possibly representing warrior burials of people close to the king. Members of this warrior aristocracy also owned large farms, and almost certainly played an important part in the formation of the Swedish state. Particularly magnificent are the boat graves at Vendel and Valsgärde, in east central Sweden, where great men were buried with all their possessions: helmets, shields, weapons, household utensils, horses, cattle, dogs, and gyrfalcons. Iron probably played a major part in the development of the land of the Swedes. The abundant supply of this metal apparent from the contents of the boat graves can be explained by extensive trade with continental Europe and the British Isles.

This gold buckle from the boat grave at Sutton Hoo, in Britain, was found next to the purse lid (top right).
BRITISH MUSEUM/C.M. DIXON/PHOTO RESOURCES

One of the boat graves at Sutton Hoo, on the east coast of England, also bears witness to Sweden's long-distance contacts. Boat graves are not found in continental Europe, and the only true parallels of the Sutton Hoo grave are to be found in the grave-fields of Vendel and Valsgärde, in Sweden. The superb helmet from the Sutton Hoo grave was very likely made in Sweden, although it may have been manufactured locally under continental influence, since all the helmets of this period are derived from Roman prototypes. The shield also appears to have been made in Sweden, and it has even been suggested that it was manufactured by the same craftsperson as one of the Vendel shields. The motif, scale, and animal ornamentation are very similar in both cases.

The most obvious link between the two areas is the boat grave itself. With one or two exceptions, this type of grave is not found elsewhere. British archaeologist David Wilson has pointed out, however, that the eighth-century AD heroic

These Danish gold bracteates (thin, ornamental plates) are replicas of Roman emperor medallions (medallions bearing the emperor's face) and date from the migration period.

The lid of an elegant purse from the boat grave at Sutton Hoo, adorned with gold and cloisonné enamel. The purse contained 37 gold coins, 3 coin blanks, and 2 small gold ingots.
RONALD SHERIDAN/ANCIENT ART & ARCHITECTURE COLLECTION

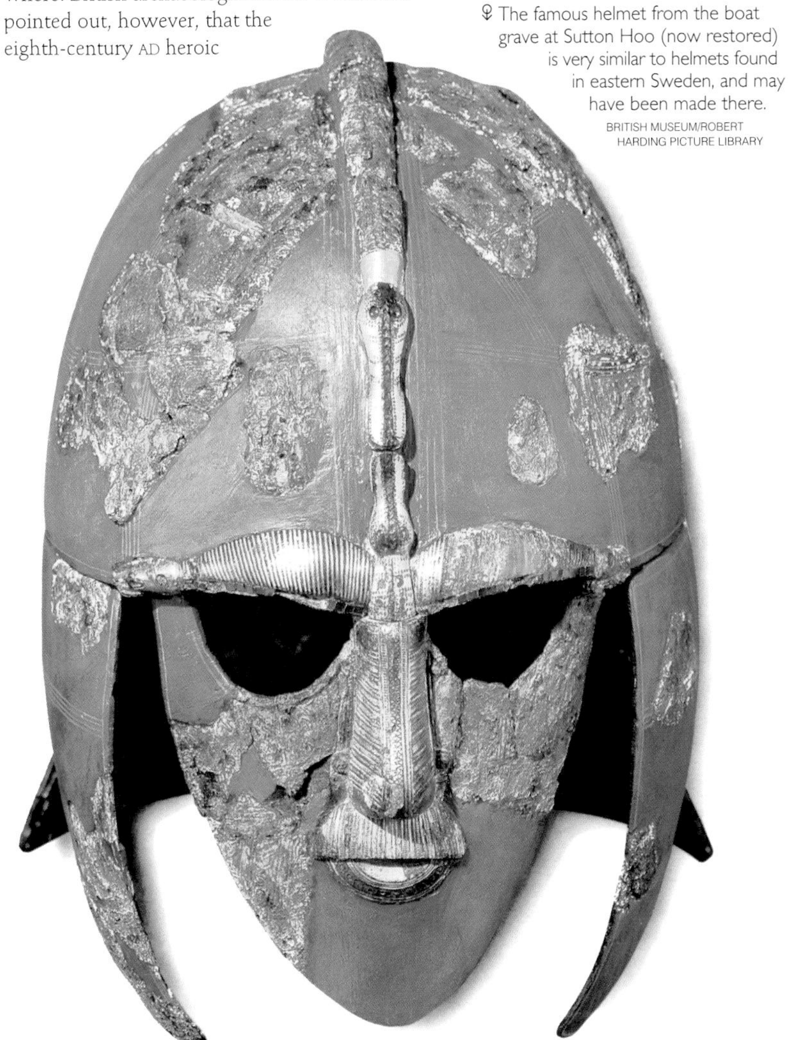

The famous helmet from the boat grave at Sutton Hoo (now restored) is very similar to helmets found in eastern Sweden, and may have been made there.
BRITISH MUSEUM/ROBERT HARDING PICTURE LIBRARY

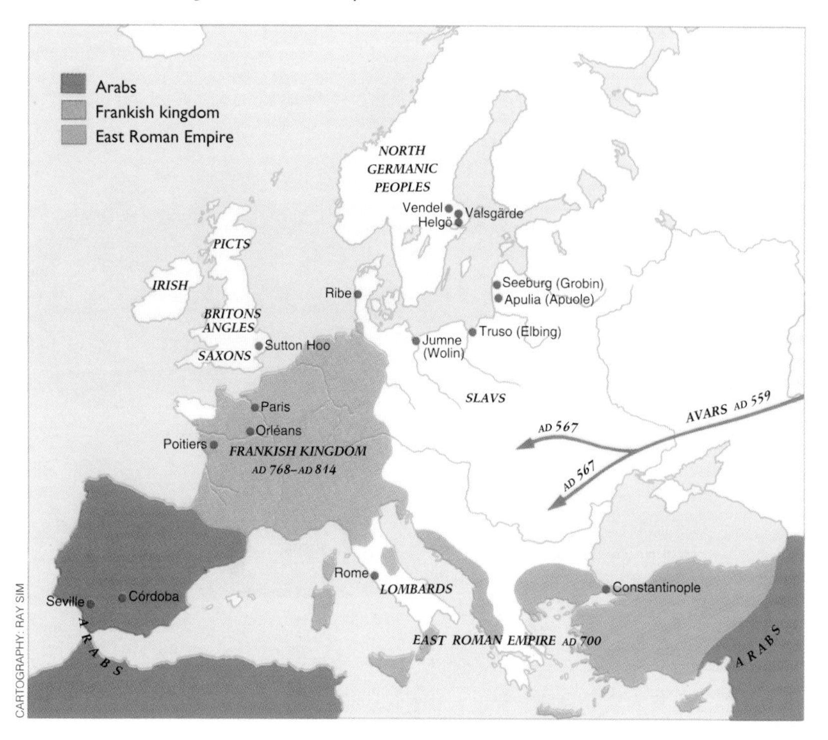

EUROPE: AD 500 TO AD 800
The political situation in Europe towards the end of the Germanic Late Iron Age was dominated by three major powers: the Frankish kingdom, in the west, the East Roman (or Byzantine) Empire, in the eastern Mediterranean area, and the Arabs, in North Africa and the Iberian peninsula.

poem *Beowulf* contains an account of the burial of Scyld, who was placed in his boat together with rich treasures. The boat was not buried, but was put out to sea. Such a practice could explain why boat graves are not found along the coasts of the North Sea. The custom of placing the dead in boats may have been much more widespread than is revealed by the archaeological record.

The Viking Age

The period of Scandinavian expansion between AD 800 and AD 1050, usually referred to as the Viking Age, did not follow a single pattern. In reality, different motives lay behind the Vikings' long journeys, which began towards the end of the eighth century. The differences are particularly evident between Denmark–Norway on one hand, and Sweden on the other. In the west, the expansion took the form of straightforward colonization or forays for plunder. In the east, a fine-meshed network of trade routes and colonies was developed, which supplied the Baltic area with large amounts of silver and exotic products, especially from the Abbasid caliphate, an Islamic empire encompassing much of southwestern Asia.

The new conquests in the west are largely reflected in increased levels of settlement, which are clearly visible in the archaeological record. In Denmark and Norway, as the demand for new land exceeded supply, population pressure was channeled to the islands north of Britain—Orkney, Shetland, and the Hebrides. At the same time, the Frankish kingdom in western Europe gained an increasingly powerful trade position, and important commercial towns developed on the English Channel: Quentowic, in France, and Dorestad, at the mouth of the Rhine. As the Scandinavian communities expanded, northern Europe attracted the interest of the Frankish kingdom.

It is often thought that the dramatic Viking voyages, with constant war expeditions to the east and west, were characteristic of Scandinavian society as a whole, but this was never the case. The people we call Vikings were only a minority of the population; most Scandinavian people of this time were farmers, who had little to do with these undertakings. They cultivated their land as they had done for generations, and it was only at the intersection of different trade routes, where harbor conditions were favorable, that more outward-looking communities developed.

There were two main reasons for the success of the Viking enterprises. First, the political situation in the Frankish kingdom and in Britain alike was characterized by disunion, with internal power struggles and fighting between the many small states. A unified resistance was therefore impossible. Indeed, there are many examples of local rulers allying themselves with the Vikings for their own political ends. Clearly, the Scandinavians made the most of these periods of division.

The second factor was the element of surprise. Thanks to their seaworthy, clinker-built ships (built of overlapping boards), the Vikings were able to carry out rapid surprise attacks on horseback along coasts and rivers. As the boats could be pulled out of the sea onto any beach under the cover of the morning fog, the Vikings' arrival could never be anticipated.

→ The style of ornamentation used in Late Iron Age Scandinavia resembles Celtic ornamentation found in England and Ireland during the same period, one example being the famous *Book of Kells*, an illustrated copy of the Bible dating from the early eighth century.

Towards the end of the eighth century, Norwegian Vikings had already occupied the Faeroe, Shetland, and Orkney islands. About AD 825, the Irish author Dicuil described how the Christian Picts living on some of these islands were driven off by the Scandinavians—events that are clearly visible in the archaeological record. The Viking Age settlements all postdate those left behind by the Celtic-speaking Picts. In the Hebrides, however, the Celtic population lived side by side with the Scandinavian settlers.

About AD 820, the Scandinavians began to attack the coasts of Ireland. Here, they came into contact with a culturally prosperous area: Celtic art was to exert a great influence on Germanic ornamentation in Scandinavia. Since Ireland was firmly divided between five rival kings and a number of tribes and clans under the leadership of local "chieftains", it fell an easy prey to the Vikings. In AD 840, Turgeis arrived with a large fleet and founded Dublin.

Recently, excavations at Wood Key, in central Dublin, have thrown new light on its early development and the earliest Viking Age houses. Both Irish and Scandinavian kings governed in Dublin till AD 1169, when English conquest of the island began. The Scandinavians in Ireland formed some sort of warrior aristocracy, and only a few of them supported themselves peacefully by farming. The Irish entered into alliances with Danish Vikings several times in order to drive off the Norwegians. Finally, however, the heroic Irish king Brian Boru managed to defeat the local Irish kings in AD 1004, and in AD 1014, the Scandinavians were crushed at the battle of Clontarf, outside Dublin. Both Brian Boru and his son, as well as a number of local Irish kings, were killed in the battle, but the victory was a turning point in rebuffing Scandinavian colonization of the island.

This magnificently carved wooden head was mounted as decoration on a wagon found on the well-preserved Viking ship excavated at Oseberg, in Norway.

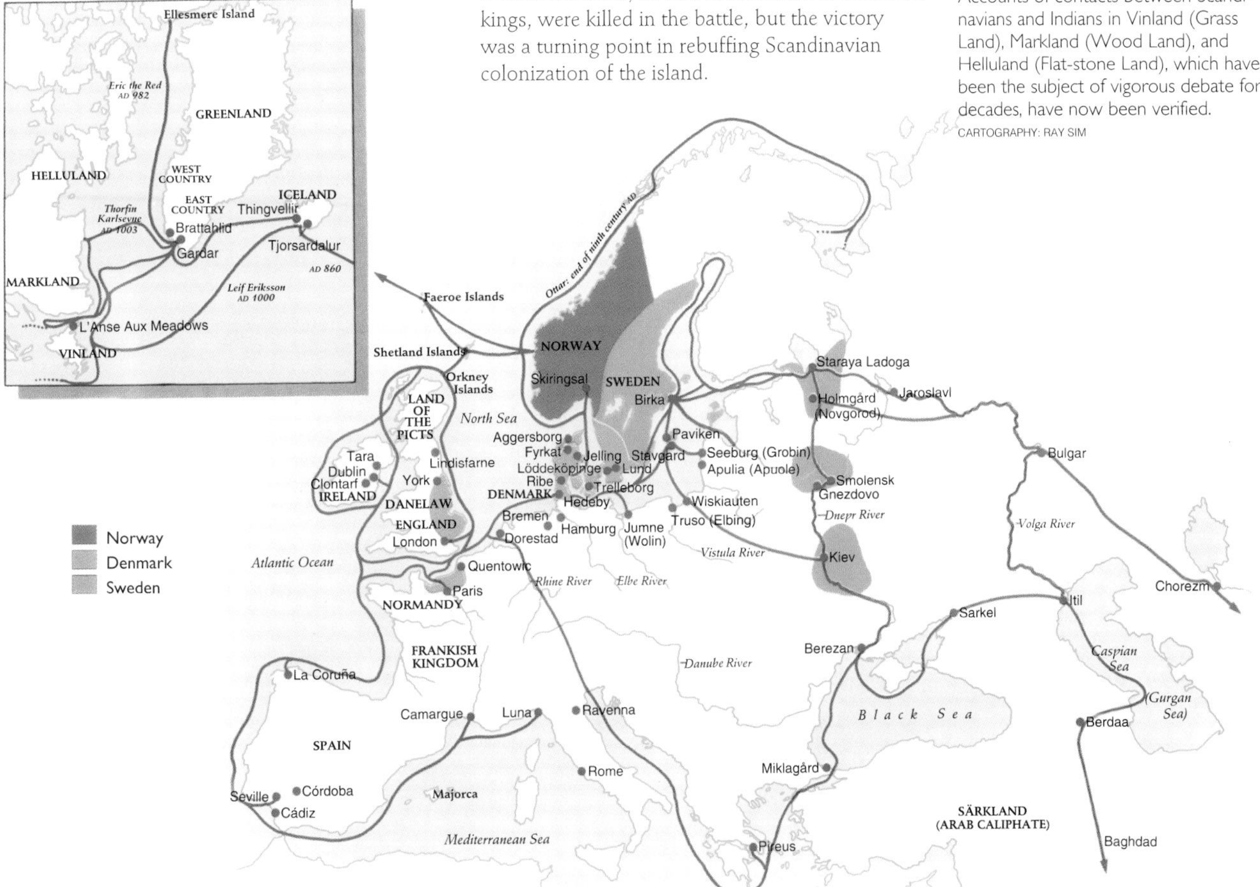

THE VIKING WORLD

The red lines indicate the routes of Viking journeys. The expansion in the west by predominantly Danish and Norwegian Vikings took the form of sheer colonization and forays for plunder. In the east, Swedish Vikings built up a network of trade routes and colonies. Leif Eriksson, son of Erik the Red, is usually credited with being the first European to discover America, in AD 1000. Accounts of contacts between Scandinavians and Indians in Vinland (Grass Land), Markland (Wood Land), and Helluland (Flat-stone Land), which have been the subject of vigorous debate for decades, have now been verified.

CARTOGRAPHY: RAY SIM

ROBERT HARDING PICTURE LIBRARY

⇧ Large farms dating from the earliest settlement of Iceland, in the tenth century AD, have been excavated in Tjórsárdalur, in the south of Iceland. The buildings shown here are a reconstruction of a farm, known as Stöng, which was destroyed by a volcanic eruption in AD 1104.

MARTYN F. CHILLMAID/ROBERT HARDING PICTURE LIBRARY

⇨ The entrance to the main farm building, made of timber and turf, at Stöng, in Iceland.

Iceland was colonized quite late. About AD 900, a period of intense settlement took place, and it is estimated that about 30,000 people had made their home on this northerly and previously uninhabited island by the middle of the tenth century AD. Our knowledge of these events comes not only from the archaeological record, but also from the *Book of the Icelanders* and the *Book of Settlements*, dating from the twelfth and thirteenth centuries AD. In many cases, farms and settlements named in these sources have been verified by excavations—for example, Stöng, in Tjórsárdalur, which was destroyed in a volcanic eruption in AD 1104. The political reasons behind the large-scale emigration to Iceland are also touched upon in these early scripts. The *Book of Settlements* tells of "outlawed and political emigrants from Norway", many of whom were probably opponents of King Harald Fairhair, who seized power in Norway towards the end of the ninth century AD. Perhaps it was due to distrust of royal power that Iceland never formed a kingdom, but rather a "republic of chiefs". It seems likely, however, that the settlement of Iceland is at least partly to be explained by the need for new land; a considerable number of people also arrived from Ireland.

In AD 930, the first Althing (legislative assembly), which consisted of 39 of the island's most prominent chiefs, was held at Thingvellir. The country was divided into 12 "thing areas", and the Althing was presided over by three so-called "godar", who were elected from among the most important chiefs.

DR ECKART POTT/BRUCE COLEMAN LTD

⇨ At its peak, the Scandinavian colony in Greenland is estimated to have had 3,000 inhabitants.The settlement was abandoned in the fifteenth century AD, possibly because the climate became much colder. In the 1960s, the remains of the site of Brattahlid, including a church built by Tjodhilde, Erik the Red's wife, were discovered at Kagssiarssuk.

The first indisputable Viking settlement in North America has been excavated at L'Anse Aux Meadows, in northern Newfoundland, Canada. Remains of house sites and of iron-working have been found, together with find material that has clearly Scandinavian characteristics. The houses shown here are reconstructions.

Danish Colonization

Whereas the journeys to northern Scotland, Ireland, Iceland, Greenland, and America were predominantly carried out by Norwegian Vikings, the interest of their Danish colleagues was primarily focused on England and the Frankish kingdom. The first major attacks were carried out as early as the 830s, when Danes successfully exploited periods of weakness in these two areas.

The extensive Danish settlement in east central England was subject to Danish law and administration. When William the Conqueror occupied England after the Battle of Hastings, in AD 1066, a register of lands, known as the *Domesday Book*, was established.

Notably, there are many surviving place-names with Scandinavian suffixes—villages and towns with names ending in "by", "thorp", and "toft". More than 700 East English place-names today end in "by". Moreover, the English language still has many Old Danish loan-words, such as "window" and "happy", all of which bear witness to the massive Scandinavian influence on the English community during the tenth century AD.

Swedes in the East

As early as the eighth century AD, growing Swedish interest in eastern trade contacts had led to the establishment of trading colonies on the east coast of the Baltic—for example, at Grobin and Apuole. During the early Viking Age, these contacts resulted in the development of an extensive communication network with the Orient via Russian rivers. Several Scandinavian colonies at posts along the trade routes developed into virtual nations. A number of Swedish rune stones describe voyages to "Gårdarike" (Russia), "Särkland" (the Arab caliphate), and "Miklagård" (Constantinople, capital of the Byzantine empire). Even more important sources of information include Nestor's *Chronicle* (from the twelfth century AD), Constantine VII Porphyrogenitus's *De Administrando Imperio* (a Byzantine work from the tenth century AD),

MAJOR VIKING EVENTS IN THE WEST

AD 793	Vikings destroy the Lindisfarne monastery on Holy Island, off the coast of eastern England.
AD 795	The monastery of Saint Columba on Iona, in the Hebrides, is ravaged.
AD 795	First attacks on the Irish west coast.
AD 812	120 Viking ships are thought to have rounded Ireland and reached the Kerry peninsula.
AD 820	First major Viking attacks on Ireland.
AD 825	The Christian Picts are driven off the islands north of Scotland.
AD 834	Dorestad, in the Frankish kingdom, plundered.
AD 835	First major Viking attacks on England.
AD 840	Turgeis arrives in Ireland and founds Dublin.
AD 841	First attacks along French rivers: Seine, Loire, Garonne.
AD 843	Nantes, in France, plundered.
AD 844	Vikings reach the Iberian peninsula; La Coruña and Lisbon plundered, Cádiz and Seville captured.
AD 845	Viking fleet sails up the River Elbe; Hamburg, in Germany, is burned to the ground.
AD 845	Paris plundered.
AD 850	Viking settlement in France, primarily in Normandy and at river mouths.
AD 859	Vikings reach the Mediterranean and plunder Majorca, off the coast of Spain, as well as Pisa and Luna, in Italy.
AD 865	A large Danish army, under the sons of Lodbrok, arrives in East Anglia, in England; 10 years of war begin.
AD 867	York (Jorvik), in England, attacked and captured.
AD 869	Mercia and Wessex, in England, attacked and occupied.
AD 878	The Danes are beaten by Alfred the Great, king of Wessex, but are awarded Northumberland, East Anglia, half of Mercia, and part of Essex.
AD 896	The Danelaw, one of three judicial ares in England, becomes the unified Danish possession, and Danish settlement is established.
AD 900	Iceland is colonized from Norway.
AD 911	Charles the Simple, king of the Frankish kingdom, gives Normandy to the Vikings under the chief Rollo.
AD 930	The first Althing in Iceland is held at Thingvellir.
AD 980	Greenland is colonized by the outlawed Icelander Erik the Red.
AD 986	Leif Eriksson sails from Greenland to America
AD 988	Sweyn Forkbeard inherits the Danish throne from Harald Bluetooth.
AD 994	Sweyn Forkbeard sails up the Thames with 93 ships and attacks London, together with Olaf Tryggvason, king of Norway.
AD 1002	Torfin Karlsevne from Greenland spends three years in Vinland, in America.
AD 1013	Sweyn Forkbeard occupies all of England and proclaims himself king of the whole country.
AD 1014	Brian Boru crushes a Viking army on 23 April at Clontarf, outside Dublin, in Ireland; Brian Boru and a number of Irish chieftains are killed, but the battle is a turning point in the process of rebuffing Scandinavian colonization.
AD 1016	Sweyn Forkbeard dies and is succeeded by his sons Edmund and Canute.
AD 1017	Edmund dies and Canute the Great, who spends most of his time in England, takes over the whole North Sea kingdom.
AD 1035	Canute the Great dies and the vast Danish kingdom is divided between his sons, Harald Harefoot (England), Hardecanute (Denmark), and Sweyn (Norway).
AD 1047	Harald the Ruthless becomes king of Norway and tries to conquer both Denmark and England.
AD 1066	Harald the Ruthless is killed in the battle at Stamford Bridge, in England.
AD 1066	The Battle of Hastings, on 14 October; the Normans, under William the Conqueror, defeat the English army and become the dominating power in western Europe. This event marked the end of Viking activity in western Europe. The establishment of effective naval forces, which could avert attacks on the open sea, and fortifications along exposed coasts put an end to Viking supremacy.

↑ During the Late Iron Age, Birka developed as an important trading port on the island of Björkö, in Lake Malar, in eastern Sweden. (Lake Malar was at that time part of the Baltic Sea.) The town was situated on the shore next to a fortified hill known as Borgberget. Recent excavations in the central part of the town, the so-called "Black Earth" (a residential area named after the black color of the soil, indicating human activity), have greatly added to our knowledge of city life, craftwork, subsistence, and trade in the Viking Age.

→ Thanks to historical accounts and recorded tales, we know a great deal about the pre-Christian religious beliefs of Scandinavians. Thor was the god of war and thunder, and the thunderbolt was represented by his hammer, called Mjollnir or Mjölner. Many protective amulets in the shape of Thor's hammer have been found throughout Scandinavia and other parts of Europe. This one comes from Erikstorp, in Östergötland, Sweden.

and the Arab authors and travelers Ibn Khordabeh and Ibn Fadlan of the ninth and early tenth centuries AD. Their vivid descriptions have given us a unique insight into the everyday life of Vikings in the East—knowledge that also provides a glimpse into the conditions and customs in Scandinavia in that period.

During the ninth century AD, the ar-Rus (the Arab name for the Swedish traders) found their way along two major routes: along the Dnepr River to the Black Sea, and along the Volga River to the Caspian Sea. Towards the end of the ninth century AD and during the tenth century AD, the former became increasingly important. Both routes started at Lake Ladoga, where an important Scandinavian settlement was established early on at Staraya Ladoga, by the Volchov River. Archaeological excavations have revealed a city-like community very similar to Hedeby, in Denmark, and Birka, in Sweden, with a conglomeration of houses and narrow alleys surrounded by a wall.

The Dnepr River was reached via the Dyna, and it was along this route that the Swedish settlements and colonies developed. Although the extent of these settlements is unknown, it is probable that the Scandinavians' primary aim was to control the trade routes. At Smolensk, there was intensive Swedish settlement over a long period, as evidenced by a grave-field outside the city containing more than 4,500 burial mounds. A number of Scandinavian burials have been

excavated here, the finds including sets of weights, "Thor's hammers" (a type of amulet), and women's ornaments of Scandinavian type, as well as a boat grave containing weapons, boat rivets, and ornaments. The find material provides a significant insight into Swedish trade in the East and into the colonies that developed in its wake. A well-organized system of transportation, involving transshipment and reloading, developed at an early stage at junctions such as Staraya

This eastern trade of the Swedish kingdom is reflected in the great amounts of Arabic silver found in Viking Age hoards in Sweden, particularly the island of Gotland. But this represents the final destination of only a very limited part of the interchange—the part that for some reason was taken out of circulation. Viking goods were much sought after by the caliphate: furs of sable, beaver, squirrel, and fox; axes; honey; wax; walrus tusks; and slaves. The Scandinavians received in return silver, bronze vessels, pearls, and Chinese silk. Many of the commodities traded by the Scandinavians originated in the region of Russia—particularly furs and Slavic slaves.

In the first half of the tenth century AD, the importance of the Volga route was greatly diminished, following uprisings among the Kazars and the Volga–Bulgarians. Similarly, the Dnepr route declined in importance as the Slavic kingdoms in Russia grew more powerful. About AD 970, the two routes were abandoned, and all trade with the Byzantine empire now traveled along the rivers of central Europe. This is reflected in the increasing number of western European coins found in Scandinavian silver hoards of this period.

By about AD 1050, the whole of Scandinavia had officially converted to Christianity: the entire continent of Europe had thereby entered historic times, and the Iron Age had come to an end.

A bronze figure from Rällinge, in Södermanland, Sweden, depicting the phallic pagan deity Freyr, also known as Frö. Worshiped mainly in eastern Sweden, Frö was the god of fertility, peace, sunshine, and rain; and phallic cults, fertility rites, and sexual symbolism, relating to such objects as this figure, were linked to him.

A silver hoard found at the Viking Age town of Birka, situated in the Lake Malar basin, in Sweden. Along with different kinds of silver objects, it contained Arab coins, the most recent of which were minted in AD 963 or AD 967. More than 1,100 Viking Age silver hoards have been found in Sweden, most of them on the two Baltic islands of Öland and Gotland. Seven hundred hoards have been found on Gotland alone, yielding more than 130,000 imported silver coins.

Ladoga, Novgorod, and Smolensk. Merchants settled here with their families, under the protection of garrisons stationed in the area. The Scandinavians soon intermixed with the Slavic population, and as a result, an increasingly large number of Slavic objects are found in graves.

Further south, the Dnepr route passed through Kiev, eventually ending up in Berezan, an important reloading station and trading post on the Black Sea coast. From Berezan, Miklagård (Constantinople) and the eastern Mediterranean were reached via the open sea. Regular trading contacts with the capital of the Byzantine empire are reflected in the strict regulations the Scandinavians had to observe when visiting the city: only unarmed men with permits were admitted; the amount of goods that could be exported was limited; and all goods had to be stamped upon departure. On the other hand, the Scandinavians were offered women, baths, food, and drink, indicating that they were coveted trading partners, if not to be trusted.

The major trading post on the other important route, the Volga River, was Bulgar, situated at the center of the Volga–Bulgarian kingdom. It was here that the Scandinavians came in contact with the Silk Road. The Volga route ended at Atil, on the Caspian coast, the capital of the Kazar people. From the Caspian Sea, the Scandinavian traders sailed on to Berdaa and Baghdad, in the Arab caliphate.

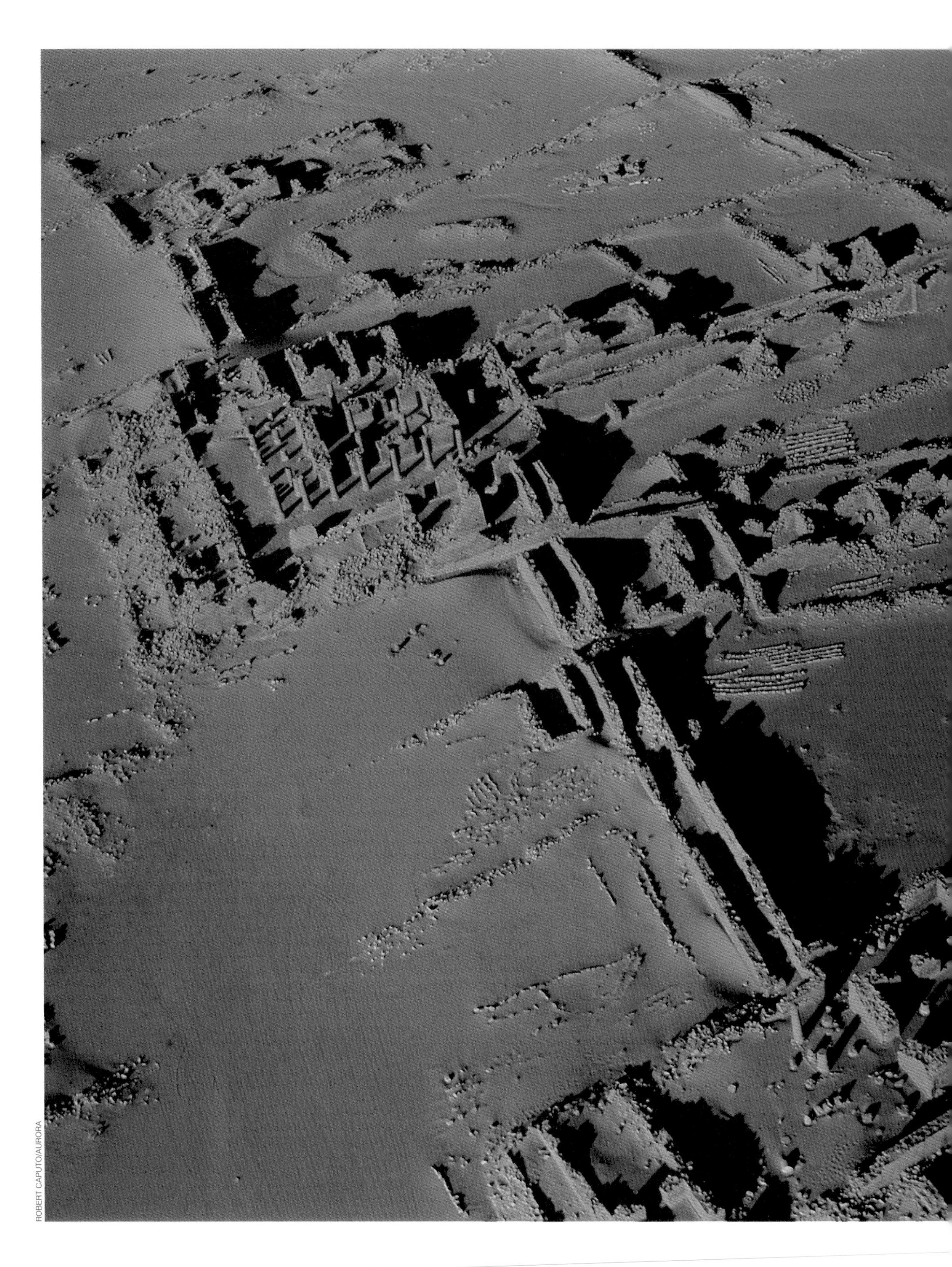

ROBERT CAPUTO/AURORA

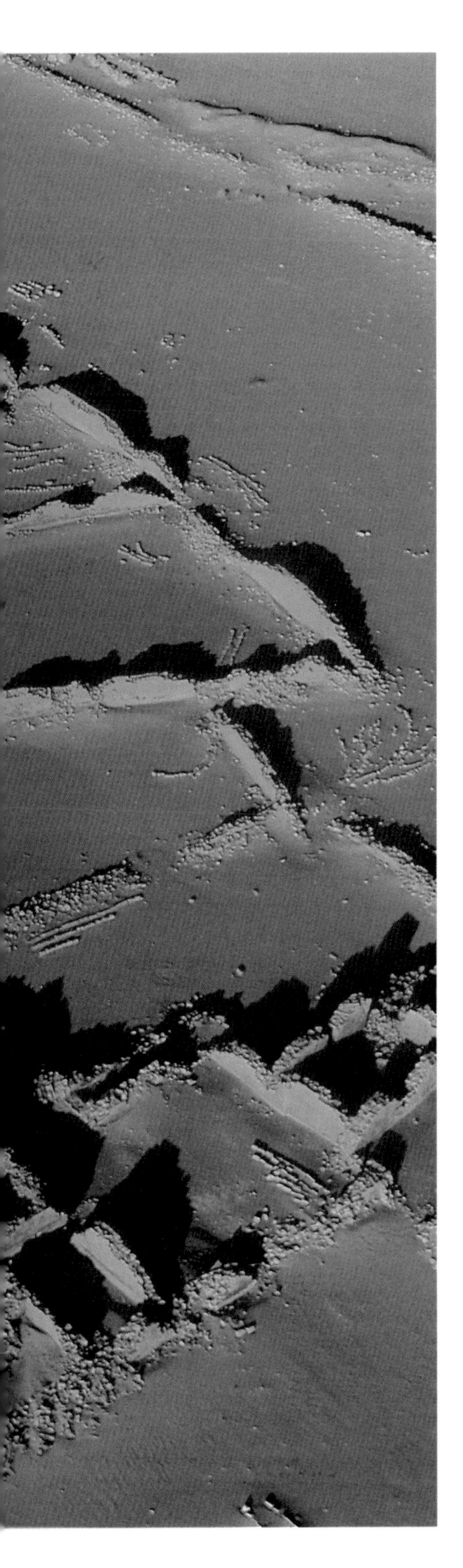

THE DEVELOPMENT OF AFRICAN STATES

3000 BC – AD 1500

Loosely Organized Political Communities

CHRISTOPHER FYFE

DURING MUCH OF the long period from 3000 BC to AD 1500, most Africans lived in small, loosely organized political communities, without monarchs, hereditary nobles, or permanent officials. Each community had its own distinctive form of government, which enforced rules its members accepted. These forms of government had to be devised and agreed to by individuals, and were based on rational decisions. They did not somehow "evolve" in a notionally organic way.

When and how they were devised and agreed to, we cannot now tell. Nor can we know how they operated. We have no records to enlighten us as to the remote African past. Inevitably, then, historians are tempted to try to infer the past from the present—to take, for instance, what social anthropologists have written about similar communities in our own era and apply it to earlier societies. This is not how historians should operate, however. African societies were not "timeless" (although some people have asserted that they were). Like everything else, they changed over time. When the Sahara began to dry up, in the third millennium BC, the inhabitants' ways of life changed, and so did their political structures. Similarly, the spread of iron-working through Africa, from the middle of the first millennium BC, altered political as well as social arrangements. Africans innovated in all spheres when it suited them—political, economic, and the arts.

A general view of Meroë, in modern-day Sudan. For more than a thousand years, it was one of the major centers of Meroë kingdom. There may have been a major center here, or in the vicinity, as early as the second century BC.

This terracotta head, from the Nok culture of modern-day northern Nigeria, was sculptured during the first millennium BC.
ANCIENT ART & ARCHITECTURE COLLECTION

⊕ The headpiece of a ceremonial society mask that covered the whole body, made in the Kuba country, in modern-day Zaire. Constructed of raffia and cloth, it was mounted on a wooden frame and sewn with leather beads and cowrie shells.
PRIVATE COLLECTION/WERNER FORMAN ARCHIVE

⊕ This face mask, made by a society among the Dan people of modern-day Liberia, would originally have been part of a body mask made of raffia or some other fabric that covered the wearer's whole body.
BONHAMS, LONDON/THE BRIDGEMAN ART LIBRARY

PICTUREPOINT LTD

⊕ The people who executed this rock painting found at Kondoa-Iringi, in modern-day Tanzania, would have been members of a loosely organized political community.

Historians are therefore in a dilemma. If we interpret political behavior in the remote past by reference to similar-looking behavior in the present, we are guilty of "presentism" (looking at the past in terms of the present) and of suggesting falsely that African societies were timeless. If we stick to our normal methods, however, and put down only what we can deduce from verifiable data, we shall be forced to erase from the historical record all reference to many millions of Africans; and that we must try not to do. We should not present the African past in the way historians have regularly presented the past of Europe and Asia—solely as the achievements of highly organized states. We must swallow our principles, however unwillingly, and infer how these loosely organized political communities are likely to have been organized in the past from our knowledge of similar communities in the present.

Such communities are sometimes described as "stateless societies". This is misleading. Though loosely structured, they were, like most structured states, self-governing sovereign entities, each with its own distinctive political constitution. The constitutions varied, but seem to have followed a basic pattern. The community was divided into small groups distinguished by descent, age, or some other feature. Each was separate from the others, but ready to combine with them to resist outside pressure or to solve problems of common concern. No one group was allowed by the others to become too strong, and the rivalry between groups held them together.

Normally, the members of each group carried on their own daily life without reference to the other groups, and groups combined only when common concerns arose. Hence, there was no need for a permanent administration; there were no career officials or judges. Administration was contingent on events, not continuous.

Similarly, no individual within a group was allowed to become too powerful. Those who gained wealth were under strong pressure to redistribute it to others. Among the Igbo (in modern Nigeria), a term for a rich man was "Give Me Something". Those who were too successful were liable to be accused of witchcraft. In this way, power remained dispersed and classes were prevented from forming.

A Patriarchal Political Structure

The political model tended to be the patriarchal family in which age confers authority. Women and young people had their recognized place in society, but it was below that of the old men. Marriage was used as a means of social control. The older men apportioned out the marriageable young women as wives for themselves or for appropriate young men. Such societies were not, therefore, egalitarian. Although there were no kings or aristocracies, and social differentiation by wealth was prevented, the men dominated the women, and the old dominated the young.

Over the generations, power was regularly transferred from older to younger. Where the basic unit was the age-group, children were initiated together into an age-grade. This determined their place in society for the rest of their lives. The young age-grades had no authority. Every few years, however, at a formal ceremony, the age-grade above them handed over new responsibilities, and they moved up to a higher status.

Those in the prime of life held the dominant grade, although older people were still given respect and high status.

In other communities, power was vested in "secret societies"—societies, that is, whose members claimed to have secret, supernatural knowledge. (See the feature *Holding Society Together*.) Boys were initiated at an early age, and decisions were made in secret conclaves. The decision-makers were concealed behind body masks that gave them a supernatural sanction, enforceable, if need be, as a death sentence. Women were excluded. Although women sometimes had their own powerful societies, with their own secret knowledge, the decisions of these societies were usually binding on women only.

All these political activities were validated by supernatural sanctions, which also guided people in their everyday lives—hunting, farming, child-rearing. These sanctions were reinforced by communal rituals, performed with special music, dances, and costumes. All members of the community were thus constantly made aware of the bonds that united them.

These loose, flexible political structures could hold large numbers of people together. An estimate made in the mid-twentieth century suggested that in West Africa alone at that time, there were something like 35 million people living in such communities, let alone those living elsewhere in Africa. One cannot, therefore, just write these communities off as "primitive" or "vestigial", or leave them out of African history altogether.

M. & A. KIRTLEY/ANA

Constructed out of plaited straw, this mask reveals the wearer's arms and legs but conceals his identity. It was made for use in a society in the Baule country, in modern-day Côte d'Ivoire.

PICTUREPOINT LTD

These rock paintings, too, in the Tassili N'Ajjer mountains, now in the middle of the Sahara, in modern-day Algeria, were painted by people living within a loosely organized political community.

A terracotta portrait head of a queen of Ife, from the Yoruba country, modern Nigeria.
ANCIENT ART & ARCHITECTURE COLLECTION

A Benin bronze plaque, showing a royal or noble figure with subordinate attendants. Hundreds of such plaques were formerly fixed to the walls of the royal palace in Benin, modern Nigeria.
BRITISH MUSEUM/WERNER FORMAN ARCHIVE

The Rise of African Kingdoms

The forces that united these loosely organized polities often broke down. One group, or one powerful individual, came to dominate the rest and established a centralized structure of government. This process of centralization is customarily presented as progress into a "higher stage" of social organization. Yet, when one recalls that many people today are perturbed by trends towards centralized authority and bureaucratization, one has to question whether the change is to be applauded unthinkingly. It is a question some Africans seem to have asked themselves. There is evidence that the Igbo people gave up centralized, monarchical rule and reverted to decentralization.

The oral traditions that record the histories of African kingdoms usually start with a male founder who persuaded or forced people to accept his rule. Often he is presented as a stranger endowed with a supernatural power, such as being able to make rain or to work iron. There are many traditions in which the founder-king was a blacksmith. Armed with a supernatural sanction, rulers could enforce their authority. Sometimes, it was enforced peaceably. Some traditions record that the new ruler was welcomed gladly by his people (although this may well be no more than royal propaganda). Or a ruler and his followers might simply have seized power and ruled by force, subjecting the people to the authority of an alien monarchy and aristocracy.

Sometimes, economic changes generated political change. As long-distance trade developed, markets were established along the trade routes. Organizing a market offered political opportunities to enterprising individuals. Controlling the market meant controlling the people who used it. In Africa, as in other parts of the world, large states thus grew up round market centers, notably the kingdoms of the western Sudan that exploited the wealth of the trans-Saharan trade, and the kingdoms of south central Africa that controlled trade down the Zambezi to the Indian Ocean.

Vestiges of the previously loosely organized structures often survived. The local economies were usually still organized on the familiar small-group pattern, though now under rulers who appropriated the surplus product as taxes. Royal power was still limited by practices surviving from the old community-based days. African kingdoms were constitutional monarchies, where kings were subjected to checks and balances. Their authority was restricted by their councilors, whose opinions they could not ignore. Sometimes, secret societies survived as a check on royal power.

Outwardly, and in view of their lesser subjects, kings may have seemed to be absolute monarchs. The trappings of majesty invested many of them with what appeared to be supernatural authority (like the "divine right of kings" claimed by many European sovereigns). People acted out allegiance to their rulers in gestures of abasement. In the kingdom of Ancient Ghana, they fell on their knees and sprinkled their heads with dust when they approached the king. Indeed, physical prostration of inferiors before superiors, wives before husbands, juniors before seniors—the visual, day-to-day enactment of the rules of a hierarchical society—was widespread. Every day, every hour, people were reminded of their political and social status.

Some kings lived invisibly, secluded in their palaces, seen only on state occasions with their faces veiled. Yet, although they might appear to have been absolute, in practice, African kings were controlled by their councils. The council members might have had to approach their sovereign groveling on the ground, but once they reached his ear, he had to listen to them. When policy was decided, their voices were decisive. In some kingdoms—for example, among the Yoruba (in modern-day Nigeria) and in some of the East African Great Lakes' kingdoms—a king's council could even make him commit suicide if they had had enough of him.

HOLDING SOCIETY TOGETHER

CHRISTOPHER FYFE

Many African political communities chose to retain a loosely organized political system rather than accept the constraints of centralized kingship. Each had its own constitution and laws. There were no monarchs, hereditary nobles, or permanent officials. Yet these loose forms of government held together large numbers of people. Historians and political scientists must, therefore, take them seriously.

JEAN M. BORGATTI

This spirit mask from the Dafing people of Burkina covers the whole body ("mask" including not only the face mask but the full costume), making the male wearer invisible and his appearance mysterious. The wooden headpiece gives him extra, domineering height. Altogether, the mask presents an alarming image of supernatural authority.

Performance as Social Control

Whatever form the constitutions took, they had to be made comprehensible and acceptable to their constituent members. In societies where people did not read and write, constitutions could not be written down. If the law was to be enforced and maintained, people had to be made aware of its authority, and of the sanctions that upheld it, by visual means, in performance. It had to be publicly enacted in ceremonies in which everyone participated, with songs and dances that gave them meaning for the participants, and these ceremonies thus acted as political controls.

The illustrations have been chosen to show some of the ways in which political control was enforced. They are all photographs taken recently, and do not, therefore, illustrate what was done in the remote past. Styles changed over time. But even if the styles have changed, the photographs indicate how such African political communities functioned. The visual record illustrates the constitutional mechanisms.

Law and custom were given supernatural sanction by reference to some outside force or spirit that, when presented visually, seemed to be overpowering and beyond human control or questioning.

Secret Societies

Many political communities were controlled by a secret society. The Ngbe society, open only to men, gave political solidarity to the Ejagham people of the Cross River, Nigeria. A figure wearing a mask represents the society in public, for the existence of the society is not secret, only its esoteric knowledge. The mask hides everything but the wearer's hands, and the face has no mouth (as befits a society with secrets).

Women, too, had their secret societies. Members of the women's Bondo society (in Sierra Leone and Liberia), where girl initiates received their education as women, were genitally mutilated as a mark of womanhood. It is believed to be the only African society in which a spirit mask is worn by a woman.

The Edo peoples (in Nigeria) had an age-grade political structure. Every five to seven years, a masquerade marked the admission of an age-grade into its new, higher status. The specially designed masks worn were destroyed before the next admission ceremony.

The Power of Dead Ancestors

Continuity in government could be maintained by appeal to dead ancestors, whose opinions had to be respected. The community was seen as a community of the living and the dead, still bound together politically. Hence, some proposed political innovation could be rejected on the grounds that the ancestors had never known it.

These few illustrations do no more than indicate the inventiveness and creativity that underlay the exercise of political power in Africa over thousands of years.

MARILYN HOULBERG

The Yoruba people (in Nigeria) had royal governments, but this Yoruba mask is a spectacular example of an ancestral presence. The dead ancestors were believed to parade in the annual Egungun masquerade—fully hidden under their elaborate masks—whereby they exerted their moral influence as guardians of the community.

FREDERICK LAMP/BALTIMORE MUSEUM OF ART

These boys are being prepared by a masked instructor for admission into the Rabai society, one of the secret societies of the Temne people, in Sierra Leone. They were instructed in the ways of manhood, taught the society's secrets, and circumcised.

AFRICAN STATES: 3000 BC – AD 1500

	SAHARA, NILE VALLEY, AND NORTHEAST AFRICA	WESTERN SUDAN AND WEST AFRICAN FOREST COUNTRY	CENTRAL AND SOUTHERN AFRICA	EAST AFRICA
1500			Luba and Lunda kingdoms	
1400	Muslim states	Songhai AD 1400 – AD 1591	Great Zimbabwe	Bunyoro and Buganda
		Mali AD 1300 – AD 1470		
1300		Benin AD 1300 – AD 1897		
1200		Ife AD 1200 – AD 1900		Kilwa, Malindi, and Mombasa
1100				
1000	Ethiopia	Igbo-Ukwu AD 700	Mapungubwe Migrations of Bantu speakers	Migrations of Luo people AD 1000
500	Christian Nubian kingdoms Gold trade from AD 300	Ghana AD 600 – AD 1300		
AD 1				
500				
1000	Napata/Meroë Aksum 1000 BC – AD 700			
1500				
2000	Sahara drying up 2200 BC – 200 BC			Migrations of Bantu speakers from about 2000 BC
2500	Kush 2500 BC – 1500 BC			
3000 BC	Indigenous societies	Indigenous grassland and forest societies	Indigenous societies (migrations of Bantu speakers from about 5000 BC)	Indigenous societies

When a king died, his successor was usually chosen by "kingmakers", often after armed conflict known as "The Choice of Spears". Anarchic though it may seem to regularly make a king's death an occasion for civil war, this acted as a constitutional mechanism. The balance of power that shifted to the king in his lifetime, shifted back to the king-making nobles on his death. Thus, kings were prevented from accumulating new powers to pass on to their eldest sons or other chosen successors.

Similarly, restrictions on accumulating private wealth remained. Although kings and private individuals could grow rich, they were still under strong pressure to redistribute their wealth. People demanded, and expected to receive, rewards. Kings who failed to give lost popular support. In the kingdoms, as in the loosely organized polities, capital formation was restricted, and class formation based on the accumulation of private wealth was kept firmly in check.

In some kingdoms, queen mothers were powerful. Women occasionally reigned as queens, but this was a rarity. In Africa, as in most parts of the world, male rule was the norm, and female rule, the exception.

A glazed stone animal from Meroë, in modern-day Sudan.
KHARTOUM MUSEUM/WERNER FORMAN ARCHIVE

The Kingdom of Kush–Meroë

The first African kingdoms, founded in the Nile Valley by the peoples of Upper Egypt and the Nile delta, coalesced into the kingdom of Ancient Egypt. The peoples living south of the Egyptian frontier, in what the Egyptians called Kush (the northern part of the modern Republic of the Sudan), organized regular trade down the Nile with Egypt. About 2500 BC, they united as one kingdom, with its capital at Kerma.

Kerma was plainly a large city: the cemetery contains tens of thousands of graves. Its kings were buried in vast, brick-built tombs surmounted by a domed mound of earth. The largest to have been excavated is more than 90 meters (295 feet) wide. At royal funerals, hundreds of victims were sacrificed. About 1500 BC, however, the Egyptians, in a period of imperial expansion, advanced up the Nile and conquered Kush. Kerma was then abandoned, until archaeologists found it in the twentieth century.

The Egyptians ruled Kush as a province of Egypt. By at least the ninth century BC, however, it had once again become an independent kingdom. During the period of Egyptian rule, Kushite culture had become Egyptianized. The kings adopted the royal Egyptian religious cults. Early in the eighth century BC, Pi-ankhi, King of Kush, invaded and conquered Egypt, and for the next 70 years he and his successors ruled the Nile Valley from Kush to the Mediterranean as pharaohs. Eventually, the Kushites were driven back up the Nile, although their kings still considered themselves to be the kings of Egypt. For about another thousand years, ruling first from Napata, near the Egyptian frontier, and then from Meroë, higher up the Nile, they maintained the ancient Egyptian traditions long after Egypt itself had been conquered, first by the Greeks and then by the Romans. (See the feature *Meroë: Capital of a Prosperous Kingdom.*) Temples and palaces were built in the Egyptian style, with inscriptions in the Egyptian hieroglyphic script and figures depicted according to the traditional Egyptian canon of proportion. When the kings died, they were buried in pyramid tombs.

As in Egypt, queen mothers had great power. Moreover, there were at least five ruling queens of Meroë. One of them is depicted on a stone monument wearing the double crown of Egypt, originally designed some 3,000 years earlier. As the years passed, however, the culture became more distinctively Meroitic, with locally devised styles of sculpture and handicrafts. Lion-headed Meroitic gods appeared. Queens were depicted with wide hips instead of in the slim Egyptian style. Eventually, Egyptian hieroglyphs were superseded by a Meroitic script, which reproduced the local language.

Meroë was situated within the rainfall belt, surrounded by fertile land that was suitable for growing grain and pasturing cattle to feed a large urban population. Here, as in other parts of Africa in this period, iron was mined and worked. Archaeologists have still not determined when or where iron was first mined in Africa. Nor are they sure whether the technique of iron-working was an imported skill or invented locally in a number of different places.

Meroë's prosperity was maintained by regular trade with Roman Egypt, with exports of gold, ivory, wine, and slaves and imports of luxury goods. As Roman power slackened, however, the neighboring peoples began raiding the Nile Valley, eventually cutting Meroë off from Egypt and thus undermining its prosperity. These invaders founded their own state, Ballana, between Meroë and Egypt, where royal burial sites full of imported luxury goods have been discovered. Eventually, during the fourth century AD, the kingdom of Meroë came to an end, presumably as a result of pressures from these peoples (but the evidence is uncertain).

PEOPLES AND STATES IN AFRICA: 3000 BC TO AD 1500

Most Africans lived in small, loosely organized political communities throughout the long period from 3000 BC to AD 1500. An estimate made in the mid-twentieth century suggested that in West Africa alone at that time, there were about 35 million people living in such communities.

CARTOGRAPHY: RAY SIM

ENRICO FERORELLI

A stone pillar at Meroë bearing an inscription in the Meroitic script. This script can be read (in the sense that individual characters can be identified) but has not yet been deciphered.

WERNER FORMAN ARCHIVE

⇧ Only a few of the pillars built at Aksum, in present-day Ethiopia, to commemorate kings survive today.

⇩ A worshiper emerges from one of the rock-face churches of Lalibela, in modern-day Ethiopia.

The Kingdom of Aksum-Ethiopia

During the last centuries BC, the peoples in the upland country along the Red Sea coast (in modern-day Ethiopia) created the kingdom of Aksum. Aksum was an inland city on the Red Sea, with its own seaport at Adulis. By the first century AD, it had become a major trade center, trading with the other Red Sea ports and India, its main export being African ivory.

Temples and royal palaces were built in Aksum. The kings were commemorated by tall, flat-sided pillars up to 30 meters (100 feet) high, a few of which survive today. In the mid-fourth century AD, at about the time Emperor Constantine made the Roman Empire Christian, a Greek from Alexandria converted King Ezana of Aksum to Christianity. His coinage is evidence of his conversion: the early coins bear non-Christian symbols; the later, Christian. Aksum became a Christian kingdom, owing religious allegiance

ROBERT CAPUTO/AURORA

to the Coptic Church of Egypt (as the Ethiopian Church still does today).

The kings of Aksum progressively conquered an empire in southwestern Arabia. In the seventh century AD, however, the tide turned. When Mohammed converted the Arab peoples to Islam, he inaugurated a great period of Arab conquest. Arabs crossed the Red Sea and took over the coastal regions, gaining control of the Red Sea trade. Aksum became an inland kingdom. Its kings gradually moved their power base southwards, through the high mountainous plateau around and beyond Lake Tana, the source of the Blue Nile, creating the kingdom of Ethiopia (sometimes referred to as Abyssinia).

As the Askum kings moved inland, the peoples they conquered were converted to Christianity. In the tenth century AD, their advance was stalled by protracted opposition led by a non-Christian queen (whose name has not been recorded). Distinctive styles of Christian worship and practice developed. Theological debates generated civil wars. The nominal head of the Ethiopian Church, the Abuna, was an Egyptian, sent from

ED MULLIS/ASPECT PICTURE LIBRARY

⊕ One of the Lalibela churches, showing how the building has been carved out of the surrounding rock.

⊖ Lalibela is famous for its churches hewn directly out of huge rock faces in the tenth century AD. The interiors are decorated with paintings.

ROBERT CAPUTO/AURORA

⊕ The church of St George at Lalibela. St George is an important saint in the Ethiopian Church. Here, in accordance with local custom, a worshiper places his forehead against the wall and kisses it, as a mark of reverence.

Alexandria, but in practice, the king controlled the church and used it as an instrument of government. Richly endowed churches and monasteries, their walls decorated with paintings and jeweled plaques, were built throughout the country as guardians of state authority. Some, like the famous churches of Lalibela, were hewn out of rock. The Aksum kings themselves claimed descent from the biblical King Solomon and the Queen of Sheba, giving the royal family a mystical status that was officially asserted until the fall of the Ethiopian monarchy in 1974.

The precipitous mountain countryside made it easy for dissident nobles to defy the king from their isolated fortresses. So royal discipline was harsh, and rebellion was punished ruthlessly. Moreover, to reinforce royal authority, the king, once he had been crowned at Aksum, moved around the country continuously instead of ruling from the capital. A Portuguese priest who visited Ethiopia in the early sixteenth century was amazed by the vast royal court of about 150,000 people, accommodated in tents and always on the move, and by the enormous number of richly

WERNER FORMAN ARCHIVE

BRITISH MUSEUM/WERNER FORMAN ARCHIVE

This ornament worked in gold was worn by a senior official at the court of Asante, in modern-day Ghana, in the eighteenth or nineteenth century.

decorated churches and monasteries. This was a high point for the Ethiopian monarchy, to be followed by two and a half centuries of invasion and civil war.

The Kingdoms of Nubia

After the fall of Meroë, the mid-Nile peoples regrouped into three new states. These were the kingdoms of Nubia: Nobatia, Makuria, and Alwa. In the sixth century AD, Christian missionaries converted the Nubian kings. Nubia, like Ethiopia, owed allegiance to the Coptic Church in Alexandria. As in Meroë, there was regular import–export trade with Egypt. When, in the seventh century, the Muslim Arabs conquered Egypt and then the whole North African coast, they tried without success to invade Nubia. Defeated, they made a trade treaty with the Nubian kings instead, and henceforth goods were regularly exchanged between the Christian and Muslim countries.

For another 600 or 700 years, the Christian kingdoms flourished, their densely built-up towns and villages ranged round cathedrals and churches (now being excavated by archaeologists). They coexisted peacefully with their Muslim neighbors, and tolerated any who chose to settle among them, particularly Arab pastoralists who came to pasture their cattle in the Nile Valley grasslands.

In the thirteenth century AD, a Nubian king unwisely sent an army to help the European Christian crusaders who were trying to conquer Palestine. The Muslim Egyptian army retaliated and invaded northern Nubia. Although the Egyptians were driven out, Muslim rulers took over the northern kingdom. The royal cathedral became a mosque. In the south, too, Muslims gained power, until by the end of the fifteenth century, all the kingdoms were ruled by Muslims.

The new Muslim governments made no attempts to forcibly convert the Christians to Islam. Christians were tolerated in Nubia as they were in Egypt (where, after 1,300 years of Muslim rule, there are still four million Coptic Christians). Deprived of their Christian governments, however, and remote from Alexandria, the center of their church, these peoples gradually became Muslims and the Christian Church faded away. Today, few Sudanese realize that their country was Christian for nearly a thousand years.

The Western Sudan

For about 6,000 years, the Sahara was well watered, and substantial communities lived alongside its rivers and lakes. From about the third millennium BC, it began to dry up. Increasingly, it became uninhabitable, although people continued to live around the surviving oases.

The art of domesticating camels—first practiced in Arabia—spread across the Red Sea to inland Africa, and by the early years of the Christian era, had reached the Sahara. The introduction of camel transport revolutionized the economy. Camels could carry heavy loads over long distances, covering 30 to 40 kilometers (20 to 25 miles) a day without food or water. They could cross the desert without needing artificially constructed roads. Although there is archaeological evidence to suggest that there may perhaps have been trade across the Sahara at earlier periods, camel transport introduced regular, efficient long-distance trading of a completely new kind.

In the forest country of West Africa, there were large mineral deposits, and people here had been mining and working copper and iron for at least 500 years. Now, with camel transport available, they began extracting gold to exchange with traders who carried it northwards across the

ANGEL MARTINEZ BERMEJO/SYGMA/AUSTRAL

PETER CARMICHAEL/ASPECT PICTURE LIBRARY

Blocks of salt, mined in the central Sahara, were a regular commodity in trans-Saharan trade. They were carried on camelback to the trading cities of the Niger to be exchanged for gold or slaves. These blocks are from Bilma, in modern-day Niger.

The main mosque at Jenne, in present-day Mali, has been rebuilt over the centuries, but it probably originally dates from the introduction of Islam, about the twelfth century AD.

Known as a *kuduo*, this brass container from the Asante kingdom, in modern-day Ghana, was used to hold valuables. *Kuduos* were sometimes buried with their owner after death.

MUSÉE ROYAL DE L'AFRIQUE CENTRALE/ WERNER FORMAN ARCHIVE

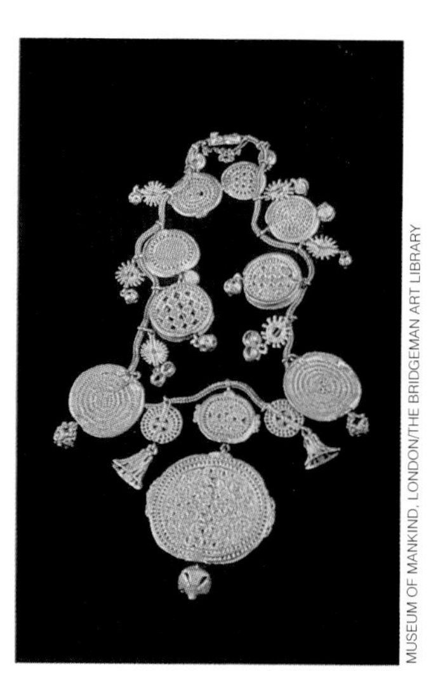

MUSEUM OF MANKIND, LONDON/THE BRIDGEMAN ART LIBRARY

This gold necklace, also from the Asante kingdom and now mounted on a European chain, was made using a method of casting known as the lost-wax technique.

Sahara. There is evidence of gold coins being minted in Roman North Africa in the third century AD, presumably from West African gold, and within three or four centuries, substantial quantities were being minted there.

When the Arabs conquered North Africa, there was a demand for an additional commodity: slaves, captured in the sub-Saharan countries and exported across the desert to supplement the traditional supply of slaves to the Mediterranean area from eastern Europe and central Asia. Much of the gold was re-exported from Muslim North Africa to Europe, which received most of its gold supply from West Africa until the sixteenth century. The slaves worked chiefly in North African households. Manufactured luxury goods were imported into West Africa in exchange for exports of mineral and slaves. Horses, too, were imported. Because disease makes them difficult to breed in West Africa, they were in great demand, revolutionizing warfare in the grassland countries. The volume of trans-Saharan trade increased steadily. Although often referred to as an "Arab trade", it was mostly conducted by Africans, particularly by Berber, Tuareg, and related Saharan peoples, and by the Mandinke peoples of the mid-Niger region.

The country south of the desert, stretching from the Nile to the Atlantic, was called in Arabic "Bilad-es-Sudan"—"The Land of the Blacks". Already, in the western Sudan, in the mid-region of the Niger Valley and westwards, people had

M. & A. KIRTLEY/ANA

One of several terracotta figures of great beauty and complexity that have been excavated at Jenne, in present-day Mali. They cannot be properly studied by scholars, most of them having been smuggled out of Mali into private collections in Europe, but plainly, they date from before the period when Islam became the dominant religion.

started living together in small, stone-built towns. With long-distance trade established, these towns could develop into market centers. Powerful individuals took control of the markets and turned the towns into kingdoms. Sometimes intruders from the desert took over, sometimes local people. In Ghana, the first kingdom to attract international attention, there was, according to tradition, at first a white (light-skinned, desert-based) ruling family, which was then superseded by a black ruling family.

Kumbi Saleh, identified as the capital of Ghana, was in what is now a desert region of modern-day Senegal (well north of modern-day Ghana). We have a description of this kingdom from an eighth-century AD Arab geographer. The king (by this period, black) presided in state in a palace within a walled city. He and his attendants, his horses, and even his dogs were decorated with gold ornaments. His revenue was drawn from customs duties on imports and exports, including salt, mined in the central Sahara and transported in blocks. He controlled the gold trade, deliberately restricting production to prevent inflation.

Ghana declined during the twelfth century AD, possibly as a result of warfare, but more likely because of the environmental deterioration of its heartland. The political and economic center shifted east to the market cities of the mid-Niger—Jenne, Timbuktu, and Gao—where the Mandinke people created the state of Mali. From this period, historians have narrative records they can turn to in the form of oral histories, both those translated into Arabic and written down by historians working in Timbuktu in the seventeenth century, and those still being recited in the twentieth century. Sunjata, the founder of Mali, was the hero of great epics. By the fourteenth century, Mali had become the dominant power, controlling territory southwards into the gold-producing forest country and westwards to the Atlantic, making it larger than any state in fourteenth-century Europe.

Through trade, Islam spread into the western Sudan. The long-distance traders were usually Muslims, finding in their religion a useful bond of commercial solidarity. The kings of Ghana kept their own religion. In Mali, however, they adopted Islam. Mansa Musa, the most famous king of Mali, made a spectacular pilgrimage to Mecca, traveling with a vast train of attendants and lavishing presents of gold on his way. But kings who became Muslims risked cutting themselves off from their subjects, whose daily way of life was closely tied to their religious observances. However unwillingly, kings had to go on performing the old rituals in order to retain their people's allegiance, and Islam remained the religion of a small minority.

Holding together an empire such as Mali (for so it may properly be called) depended very much on the personality of the rulers. If their power slackened, provinces would secede under new leaders, or the people would simply revert to their own community-based forms of government. By the fifteenth century, Mali was in decline, eclipsed by Songhai, a breakaway province, centered at Gao. Like Mali, Songhai had a great conquering hero, Sunni Ali. In his case, however, the historical record diverges. He alienated Muslim scholars and was remembered in their writings as a man of evil, but in popular epic he was a great warrior and a mighty magician.

The rulers of Songhai waged wars against the grassland peoples to the south, who grouped together into kingdoms of their own, including Mossi and Dagomba. Mossi horsemen raided the Niger cities and even sacked Timbuktu. The Songhai empire had also to be defended against attacks from the desert Tuareg. It remained the dominant power, however, until the end of the sixteenth century.

Southeast of the Niger bend, the walled cities built by the Hausa people (of modern-day Nigeria) attracted long-distance traders and grew into commercial centers. By the fifteenth century, they had developed into (by tradition) seven kingdoms. Eastwards, around Lake Chad, was the kingdom of Kanem (later enlarged as Borno), founded in the eleventh century by a member of the Sefuwa family. This family reigned until it was displaced by a usurping ruler in 1846—one of the longest-reigning royal dynasties in the world.

West African Forest Country

Much of what we know of the early history of the West African forest kingdoms comes from archaeological work concentrated on Nigeria, which began intensively only in the 1940s. The most spectacular find has been a royal burial dated to the ninth century AD at Igbo-Ukwu, west of the Niger, in Igbo country. The burial contained regalia worked with sculptural techniques of greater sophistication than anything found in ninth-century Europe. Locally mined metal alloys were used, showing that the people had their own way of processing metals as well as sculpting them. The burial also contained thousands of imported glass beads, indicating that the kingdom was linked to the trans-Sahara trade network. Nothing more is known of it. Today, the Igbo peoples have no tradition of centralized monarchy—although the Igbo language contains many words that describe its trappings. One might infer that, at some later period, they renounced their kings and returned to their former loosely organized political systems, which they retained until the twentieth century.

West of the Niger, in Yoruba country, kingdoms were established by about 1000 AD. Yoruba history has been confused by myths invented in the nineteenth century to confer prestige, alleging ancestral migration from Arabia or Egypt. The archaeological and linguistic

Shaped like a horse and rider, this brass weight from the Asante kingdom, in modern-day Ghana, was used to weigh gold dust. Millions of these gold weights survive in museums and private collections around the world.
BRITISH MUSEUM/WERNER FORMAN ARCHIVE

NATIONAL MUSEUM OF DENMARK

A decorated ivory cup from Sierra Leone, carved from an elephant's tusk in the fifteenth century AD.

evidence, however, points to long, continuous occupation by the same peoples. Tradition gives primacy among the Yoruba kings to the *oni* (king) of Ife. Archaeologists working at Ife have discovered a magnificent series of royal portrait busts, dating from the eleventh or twelfth century, which bear witness to an elaborate court life. In these Yoruba kingdoms, a powerful secret society (*ogboni*) survived, a relic of the pre-royal past.

In Benin, in the Niger delta, royal tradition dates the present royal family back to the fourteenth century, when it was said to have superseded an earlier family. Archaeologists date the first urban occupation of Benin to about a century earlier. A great period of building followed in the fifteenth century, when the city was rebuilt with a new street plan and a city wall enclosing about 1,400 square kilometers (540 square miles). Here, as at Ife, bronze-casters worked at the royal court, making portrait busts of the kings and queens. Sculptors also worked in ivory. During the British occupation of 1897, much of the vast royal treasure was looted and scattered over museums in Europe and America.

West of the Yoruba kingdoms, in the gold-producing forest country of present-day Ghana, the Akan peoples were linked to the Niger cities through regular trading routes. Here, too, small states arose. East of the Niger River, in the inland grassland country of modern Cameroon—an area of great linguistic diversity, which suggests long occupation by the same peoples—kingdoms developed among the Bamenda and Bamilike peoples.

Central and Southern Africa

Most of Africa south of the equator is inhabited by peoples who speak one of the many Bantu languages. Linguists and archaeologists have pieced together the story of their movements. From a homeland in the country between the Benue River and Lake Chad (in modern-day Nigeria and Cameroon), they began moving out in small groups about 3,000 years ago and gradually expanded over the continent, reaching the Indian Ocean coast of the present-day Republic of South Africa about the fourth century AD.

They used iron tools and lived by farming. They also kept cattle when the environment was suitable. They settled in small, scattered villages, and when a village grew too large, some inhabitants would move away to form a new village. There was a pattern of dispersed settlement, unlike the heavy urban conglomerations of West Africa, where the soil and vegetation allowed more intensive cultivation and high population densities. Even when kingdoms formed, the royal capitals were smaller and less permanent than the West African capital cities.

Individuals as well as communities moved about. Many royal traditions relate how a stranger arrived, alone or with followers, and persuaded or forced people to accept his rule. Or a cluster of adjacent villages might come together for protection and eventually be formed into one unit by a powerful leader. The traditions of the Kuba people of modern-day Zaire relate how two rival contestants and their followers strove for power, the victor founding the Kuba kingdom. Here, later on in the eighteenth century, sculptors carved a series of wooden portrait statues to commemorate their founder kings.

This bronze portrait head of an *oni* (king) of Ife, is one of a magnificent series from the eleventh or twelfth century discovered in Yoruba country, in modern-day Nigeria.
ANCIENT ART & ARCHITECTURE COLLECTION

Of intricate design, this velvet pile cloth was woven from raffia in Kuba country, in modern-day Zaire. Such cloths were worn by important people and were highly cherished. Traders carried them over long distances.

E. ANSPACH COLLECTION, NEW YORK/WERNER FORMAN ARCHIVE

TOM NEBBIA/ASPECT PICTURE LIBRARY

↔ "Great Zimbabwe" is the most famous and extensive of the stone palaces called "zimbabwes", which were built from about the tenth century AD.

As elsewhere, mineral resources provided an exploitable base for royal wealth. In the coastal forest kingdom of Loango (in modern-day Zaire), and in the Kongo kingdom southeast of it, copper was mined and exported over long distances with other commodities, including sea salt and a special kind of cloth woven from fiber. Long-distance trade brought wealth to rulers. The Luba and Lunda kingdoms of the central grassland country around the headwaters of the Zaire and Zambezi rivers grew powerful through controlling trade.

There were vast deposits of copper under the grasslands (later known as the Copperbelt), and also gold. Here, royal burials dating from the sixth to the tenth centuries AD have been found, containing fine copper ornaments. Copper, which can be burnished to a beautiful surface, tended to be used for personal body decoration. At Mapungubwe, in the Transvaal, just over the border of the present-day Republic of South Africa, small gold sculptures have been found in royal graves.

There was also an export market for gold. In central Africa, mined gold and alluvial gold washed from the riverbeds was transported down the Zambezi River for export to countries along the Indian Ocean coast. Sofala, on the seacoast (in modern-day Mozambique), became the main export emporium. Eastern commodities, including Chinese porcelain and Asian beads, were imported in exchange, and are found in royal burials. Thus, there were two unconnected gold trade routes from Africa: from the West African deposits northwards across the Sahara to Europe, and from the south central African deposits eastwards to the countries of the Indian Ocean.

Much of the central African gold lay far below the surface, inaccessible to miners working with iron picks. So the rulers here derived far less wealth from gold than those in West Africa. The real wealth of those who ruled the grassland plateau country around the Zambezi lay in cattle. Cattle were a political as well as an economic asset; those who had power distributed cattle to their dependants. But cattle-based states tend to be unstable, since herds can easily be rustled away by rivals, and a long series of successive kingdoms rose and fell in the Zambezi region.

From about the tenth century AD, people began building large stone buildings called "zimbabwes" for their kings, siting them away from land where the tsetse fly, which infects cattle fatally with trypanosomiasis, breeds. About 150 survive today as ruins (many having been demolished in the nineteenth and twentieth centuries by Europeans looking for gold). Over the centuries, the building styles became more sophisticated. The most famous and extensive of these palaces is "Great Zimbabwe", from which the Republic of Zimbabwe took its name. It was built over a period of 200 years and formed a vast elliptical enclosure, with high granite walls ornamented with soapstone sculptures. People no longer lived there after the middle of the fifteenth century, probably because the soil had become eroded by overintensive cultivation for the royal court, but it continued to be used as a religious shrine. Other "zimbabwes" continued to be built elsewhere over succeeding centuries, notably at Khami, although none on the scale of "Great Zimbabwe".

↓ The doorway of "Great Zimbabwe". The palace walls were built using a dry-stone technique, the granite blocks shaped and laid without the use of mortar.

ROBERT HARDING PICTURE LIBRARY

East African Kingdoms

Peoples who spoke Bantu languages settled around the Great Lakes. Here, the development of kingdoms has often been seen as part of a regular pattern, as warlike cattle-keeping peoples from the vast swampy region to the north (the Sudd) invaded and, as conquerors, lorded it over the sedentary lakeside farmers. This is a misleading oversimplification, however. While some of the first state-builders were invaders from the north, notably the Luo people, others were of local origin. Pastoralists did not necessarily wield power over those who cultivated crops. The Luo, originally a cattle people, eventually settled down and cultivated the soil. Historians have studied the oral genealogies of the Great Lakes kingdoms, which record the names of the successive kings. By assigning notional life-spans, they have constructed a rough chronology, which indicates that most of the states were founded in the thirteenth and fourteenth centuries AD. One date is more precise. The traditions of the Nyoro kingdom record that during the reign of the fifth *mukama* (king), the sun was darkened. This solar eclipse would have been visible in the region in 1520. Moving five reigns back gives a probable date for the first *mukama* in the fifteenth century.

As elsewhere, powerful individuals and their followers took power by persuasion or force. In some, notably the Nyoro and Nkore kingdoms (in modern-day Uganda), the kings and ruling families formed a hereditary elite, marrying only among themselves. They maintained a strict social distance from their subordinates, whose lower status was deliberately emphasized and acted out in daily living. In neighboring Buganda, social relations were rather more relaxed. There, the *kabaka* (king) took a wife from each clan, integrating the monarchy into the lineage system and making his subjects his relatives.

East of the Great Lakes, people retained their loosely organized political systems. Towards the coast, the land turns to arid semidesert, called the Nyika, which forms a wide barrier between the lakeside country and the sea. Although people ventured across it from the interior to the coast, there is evidence to show that no coastal traders traveled inland. No imported goods are found in the royal burials in the lakeside kingdoms before the eighteenth century.

The Bantu-speaking peoples who settled along the Indian Ocean coast had opportunities for overseas trade with seaborne traders from Arabia and the Persian Gulf. The trading towns that developed there are often described inaccurately as "Arab colonies". This is a misnomer, because there was no colonizing power in Arabia at this time. Arabs came in as individual traders, and although they were allowed to settle in the coastal towns and marry (since they did not usually bring their own wives), they lived there under the rule of the existing governments. In time, the two populations merged, helped by the diffusion of Islam, which had become the prevailing religion by at least the fourteenth century AD. A distinctive coastal language developed in the form of Swahili, a Bantu language strongly influenced by Arabic.

About 40 city-states grew up along the East African coast, including Malindi, Mombasa, Kilwa, and Zanzibar. They were filled with mosques of a distinctive local style, palaces, and merchants' houses, built of locally worked coral. Their wealth came from trade—exports of ivory, which was in great demand in India and China, and other local commodities, and also gold shipped north from Sofala. They stretched out along a thousand or so kilometers of coast, each politically independent and in commercial rivalry with the others. So when the Portuguese invaded in 1498, there was no concerted resistance, and one after another, they were looted and conquered.

GEOFF TOMPKINSON/ASPECT PICTURE LIBRARY

In common with other cities on the East African coast, the ancient port of Suakin has buildings constructed from blocks of coral.

African Kingdoms by AD 1500

By AD 1500, much of Africa was under the control of centralized, royal governments, although large numbers of people still chose to live under their own noncentralized form of government. The kingdoms had some common features—for instance, constitutional checks on royal power and social mechanisms to restrict the accumulation of individual wealth. Each kingdom had evolved in its own distinctive way, however, with its own particular political constitution and rituals, its own forms of economic and financial organization and policy, and its own characteristic styles of art and music.

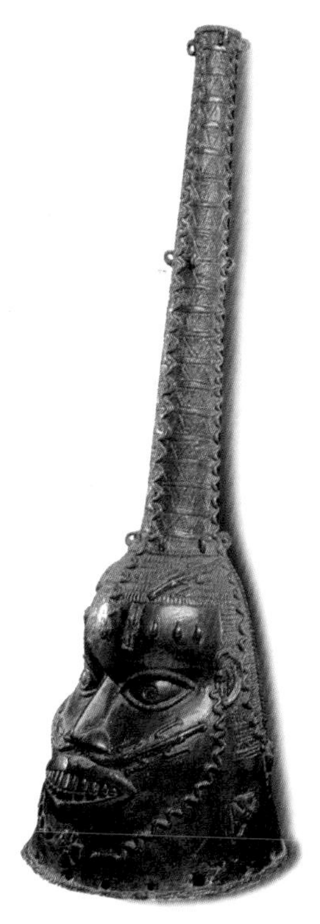

The bronze headpiece of a ceremonial mask from the Benin kingdom, in modern-day Nigeria.
BRITISH MUSEUM/THE BRIDGEMAN ART LIBRARY

ENRICO FERORELLI

⊕ The royal cemetery at Meroë was in use from about 300 BC until the fourth century AD. Some chapels and small pyramids have been restored in recent times.

MEROË: CAPITAL OF A PROSPEROUS KINGDOM

ROBERT G. MORKOT

MEROË FLOURISHED for more than a thousand years as one of the two major centers of a state that at its greatest extent (between 710 BC and 664 BC) stretched from the Mediterranean to the south of modern-day Khartoum, in the Sudan. It was well placed to control the fertile savanna land of the central Sudan, and the routes by which its precious commodities—notably ivory, ebony, and incense—traveled north to Egypt.

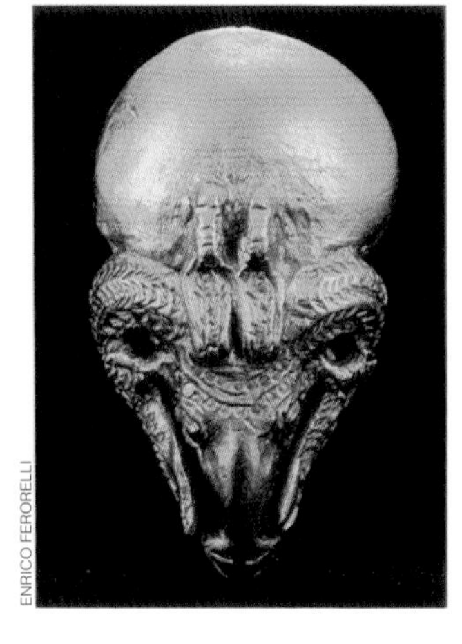

ENRICO FERORELLI

⊕ An earring from Meroë depicting a ram's head with a solar disk.

The name Meroë first occurs in the second half of the fifth century BC, in both indigenous Kushite texts and the writings of the Greek historian Herodotus. Archaeological remains, however, have been dated to as early as the seventh century BC, and there may have been a major center here, or in the vicinity, as early as the second millennium BC. The town and cemeteries were in continuous use until the fourth century AD, the town flourishing particularly in the third century BC and first century AD, when economic contacts with Egypt were strong.

The Town Site

The town site of Meroë covers an area of approximately 1,000 meters by 1,000 meters (3,300 feet by 3,300 feet). It remains largely unexcavated, with the exception of the royal compound, a large, stone-walled enclosure. This "Royal City", with the adjacent religious center, may have been separated from northern and southern "suburbs" by branches of the river. The stone wall encloses an area of about 200 meters by 400 meters (650 feet by 1,300 feet) and was probably built in the third century BC, since the excavators noted Greek masons' marks.

Some of the buildings may be considerably older. Two-story buildings lined a broad street on the north-south axis, and there were signs of rebuilding over a long period. An extraordinary structure in the southwest of the enclosure

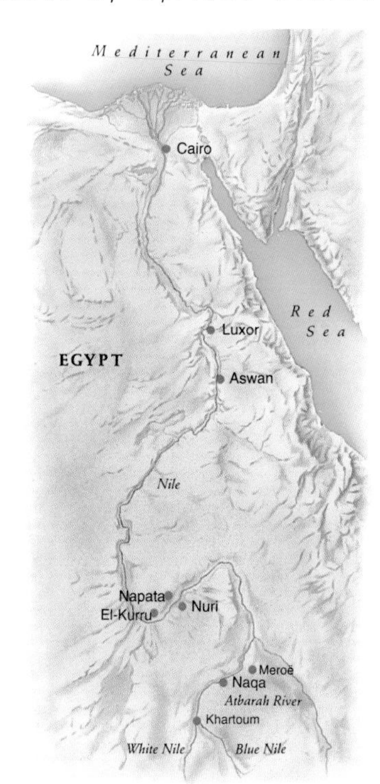

THE KINGDOM OF MEROË
At its greatest extent, between 710 BC and 664 BC, the kingdom of Meroë stretched from the Mediterranean to the south of modern-day Khartoum, in the Sudan.
CARTOGRAPHY: RAY SIM

This gold sheath, with its delicate engravings of winged goddesses and relief decoration of sacred cobras, ram's heads, and papyrus plants, probably held a rolled papyrus bearing protective spells.
ENRICO FERORELLI

The so-called "Roman kiosk" at Naqa, an important royal and religious city south of Meroë, was a resting place for statues carried in procession. The style of the kiosk shows the influence in Egypt of Alexandria's Hellenistic architecture. It was probably built in the late first century AD, but the date is uncertain.
ENRICO FERORELLI

ENRICO FERORELLI

A painted decoration in the tomb of a king's mother in the earliest of the royal cemeteries, el-Kurru, dating from about 660 BC. The scene is from Egyptian funerary literature.

BRITISH MUSEUM/WERNER FORMAN ARCHIVE

This bronze head of the Roman emperor Augustus was taken from a statue in the Egyptian frontier town of Aswan, which was attacked by the Meroitic armies about 24 BC, during a war with Rome. It was discovered buried beneath a victory temple in the city of Meroë.

ROBERT CAPUTO/AURORA

The lion-headed god Apedemak was the most important indigenous god of the Meroitic pantheon, standing alongside the Egyptian god Amun. Apedemak was a solar and warrior god—here depicted carrying a military standard. He was also a god of vegetation.

This pair of gold tweezers is one of three from the grave of King Aspelta, who was buried about 580 BC.
ENRICO FERORELLI

was almost certainly a water sanctuary. Called "The Roman Bath" by the excavators, it featured a deep, open water tank, fed by a complex of pipes. Painted scenes and glazed tiles decorated the walls of the room, and stuccoed and painted sculptures lined the edges of the tank. The architecture and decoration were derived from Egyptian, Hellenistic, and Roman models, as well as typically Meroitic styles, pointing to influences on the court culture of the first century BC and first century AD. There was also a small chapel with painted walls within the "Royal City". Beneath its floor was a magnificent, larger than life-size head of the Roman emperor Augustus, probably buried ceremonially after being brought from the Aswan region during the conflict between Meroë and the Romans about 20 BC.

The main temple at Meroë, dedicated to the Egyptian god Amun, adjoined the palace enclosure. Built on an east-west axis, it was a massive building of brick and stone, 120 meters (400 feet) long. Little survives of the scenes depicted in the relief sculpture, painted columns, and tiled floors that originally decorated the temple. A ceremonial way extended to the east from the main entrance. This was lined with granite rams as far as a small, pillared resting place for the processional statues, and continued eastwards, flanked by other temples. There is some reason to think that the Amun temple originally (in the seventh to sixth centuries BC) faced a branch of the Nile, and was enlarged—the processional way extended, and new temples built—at a time when the river channel had dried up (perhaps in the first century AD).

Although the main religious district was in the center of the town, other temples have been located, the most important being the "Sun Temple", so named by the excavators after Herodotus's description of a "Table of the Sun" outside the city walls. Probably built by King Aspelta in the early sixth century BC, it was rebuilt in the late first century BC. The temple itself consists of a chapel with a towered gateway standing on a platform in the center of a colonnaded court. Some fragmentary remains of relief sculpture show that the original decoration was largely military, possibly connected with the royal cult. Blue-glazed tiles cover the floor and walls of the sanctuary itself.

PICTUREPOINT LTD

↑ The colonnade of the temple of Musawwarat es-Sufra, an important Meroitic temple in the savanna of the central Sudan. Musawwarat seems to have been a place where the king was crowned and also, perhaps, hunted elephants. Although elaborately decorated, the columns carry no royal names. The temple was probably built about 300 BC.

ROBERT CAPUTO/AURORA

↑ The flat-topped sacred mountain of Gebel Barkal rises 90 meters (300 feet) high, near the fourth Nile cataract. An enormous temple to the ram-god Amun was built here about 700 BC.

→ This gold ewer was found in the tomb of King Aspelta, who ruled in the early sixth century BC at Nuri, on the opposite bank of the Nile to Gebel Barkal. Nuri was the main royal cemetery from the mid-seventh century BC until about 300 BC, when it was superseded by Meroë.

ENRICO FERORELLI

Cemeteries for the Elite

Three elite cemeteries lie to the east of the town: the northern and southern cemeteries are situated on sandstone ridges; the western one, on the plain.

The southern cemetery contains more than 200 graves. The earliest, from the twenty-fifth dynasty (seventh to sixth centuries BC), are mainly pit burials, but there are also mastaba tombs (with sloping sides and a flat roof) and pyramid tombs. Some members of the royal family were buried here, although at this early date, the kings and major royal women were buried near Napata, at el-Kurru, and Nuri.

The west cemetery, consisting of about 500 graves, contains some pyramid tombs, but none of these appears to belong to a ruler.

The north cemetery was the main burial place of rulers from the mid-third century BC. These pyramid tombs have small funerary chapels attached and are mostly built of local sandstone, although some of the latest are of mudbrick. The body was buried in a rock-cut chamber beneath the pyramid.

The pyramids have rather steep angles, resembling the pyramids of private tombs in Egypt rather than the royal pyramids of the Old and Middle Kingdoms. Styles changed at different periods, some being smooth-faced and others slightly stepped. Although badly plundered, the cemeteries have yielded large quantities of objects, including many fine pieces imported from the Mediterranean world.

CARL FRANK/PHOTO RESEARCHERS, INC.

THE EMERGENCE OF CIVILIZATION IN MESOAMERICA

1500 BC – AD 1521

The Development of Complex Societies in a New World Region

RICHARD E. BLANTON

A CIVILIZATION IS A PARTICULAR TYPE of social system that is made up not of a single society but, rather, of many interacting societies found within a large region on the scale of China, South Asia, or Europe. Despite local cultural differences, common cultural features can be identified within such regions, usually relating to such matters as religious belief, artistic style, and systems of weights and measures. Within civilizations, there are different kinds of societies, some more complex than others. Groups in the "core" are more complex than the more "peripheral" groups, their institutions including cities, temple hierarchies, and complex systems of government. In some cases, a single core government maintains hegemony over the whole interactive system (as has been the case in China during many periods), while in others, local governments remain politically independent. Long before Europeans arrived in the New World, a civilization emerged in what is now Mexico and parts of Central America. This civilization is known as Mesoamerica.

The main plaza of Monte Albán, the political center of the prehispanic Zapotec state, in the Valley of Oaxaca, Mexico. The buildings seen here date to the latest construction phases (AD 500 to AD 750).

A mask in the Mixtec mosaic style, decorated with jade and turquoise. The Mixtecs were one of many groups that made up the ethnically and linguistically diverse civilization of Mesoamerica.

MUSEO PREISTORICO ED ETNOGRAFICO L. PIGORINI, ROME/SCALA

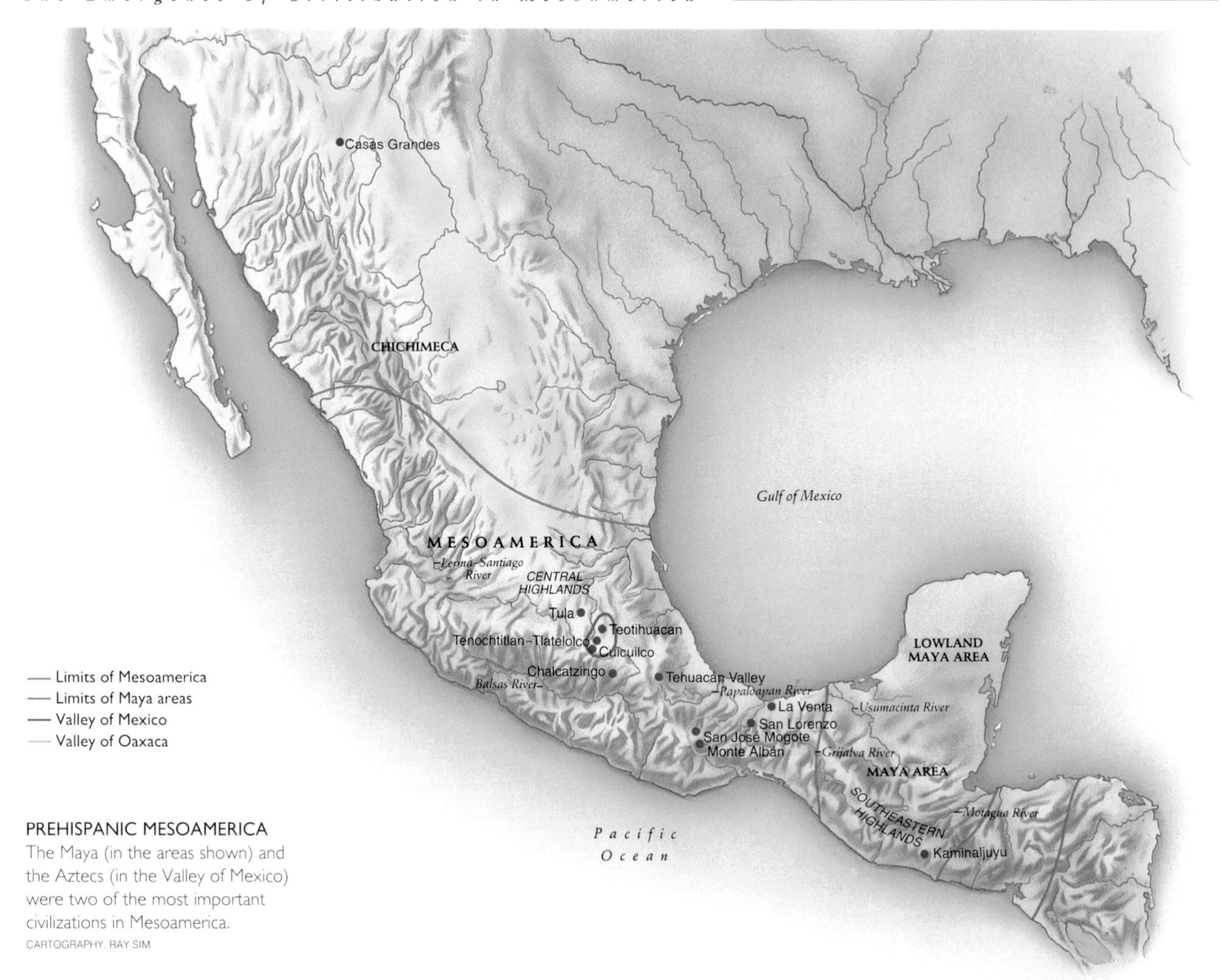

PREHISPANIC MESOAMERICA
The Maya (in the areas shown) and the Aztecs (in the Valley of Mexico) were two of the most important civilizations in Mesoamerica.
CARTOGRAPHY: RAY SIM

CAROLYN BROWN/PHOTO RESEARCHERS, INC.

⮉ The Pyramid of the Niches in Tajín, Veracruz, Mexico, is named for its horizontal panels decorated with 365 niches, one for each day of the solar year. While this pyramid reflects the general style of Mesoamerican monumental architecture, some elements of its design are particular to the Totonac culture, which emerged in Veracruz during the Classic period.

The Mesoamerican (or Middle American) civilization lasted from about 1500 BC to AD 1521 (the date of the Spanish conquest). With its northern boundary in what is now central and western Mexico, it extended over a large region to the south and east, through the present-day Central American nations of Guatemala, El Salvador, and Honduras. The southeastern boundary is inevitably somewhat arbitrary, as settled agriculturalists living in much the same way as their Mesoamerican neighbors were also to be found further east in Central America in that period. The northern boundary is more clear-cut, corresponding to the division between the farmers and city dwellers of Mesoamerica and the foragers of the arid Chichimeca region of northern Mexico. Mesoamerican influence, however, sometimes extended quite far north into the arid zone, to sites such as Casas Grandes, close to the present Mexico–United States border. The shifting northern limit of Mesoamerican civilization probably reflected varying degrees of interaction between Mesoamerican

traders and the populations of the American Southwest (a cultural area that today includes the states of Arizona and New Mexico, together with parts of Colorado and Utah, and extends into the Mexican states of Sonora and Chihuahua).

Just as the physical boundaries of Mesoamerican civilization cannot always be sharply drawn, neither can its temporal boundaries. The date of 1500 BC is a somewhat arbitrary starting point, since it was the social and technological changes that began thousands of years earlier in this region—particularly the domestication of maize (corn) and other plants in the semi-arid highland areas—that set the stage for what was to come in later centuries. It is generally accepted, however, because it was by about this time that settled agricultural village life, one of the hallmarks of Mesoamerican civilization, had become widespread throughout the region.

Geography and Climate

Mesoamerica is a difficult area to characterize in terms of its natural environment. Unlike most other early civilizations—in Egypt, the Indus Valley (Pakistan), North China, and Mesopotamia, for example—Mesoamerican civilization was not centered on a major river drainage or drainages. There are several major river systems in the Mesoamerican region, notably the Lerma–Santiago, Balsas, Papaloapan, Grijalva, Usumacinta, and Motagua, and these were important as transport routes. Typically, however, the regions at the center of the political, social, and cultural changes that gave rise to Mesoamerican civilization were located some distance from the major rivers.

M PATTERSON/PHOTO RESEARCHERS, INC

The ruins of Yagul, a Zapotec settlement in the Valley of Oaxaca, in Mexico. The mountainous terrain and arid-lands vegetation seen here are characteristic of the semi-arid highland regions of Mesoamerica.

Probably the most characteristic feature of the Mesoamerican environment as a whole is its extreme diversity. The terrain ranges from wet lowland tropics (for example, in the lowland Maya area and coastal Veracruz) to high, often semi-arid, mountainous regions (most notably, the central highlands), where the highest mountain peaks, under permanent cover of snow, reach up 5,500 meters (18,000 feet). In this central highlands area, several large valleys, more than 2,100 meters (7,000 feet) in elevation, were the birthplace of significant early societies, in particular the Valley of Mexico, the site of Mexico City. Two other highland regions are also found in Mesoamerica—the southern highlands and the southeastern highlands, both of somewhat lower elevation.

In the mountainous highland valleys grew various kinds of cactuses and other plants adapted to arid conditions, some of which were important sources of food and fiber for early peoples. Crops, including corn, the basic element of the Meso-

The diversity of climate and topography found within the Mesoamerican region extends to zones of lowland tropics, as here on the east coast of the Yucatán peninsula. This platform-mound is at the Maya site of Tulum, in Quintana Roo, Mexico.

JEAN-GERARD SIDANER/PHOTO RESEARCHERS, INC

A detail of a mural dating from the Classic period, discovered in a Teotihuacan residential compound called Tepantitla. The scene portrays the paradise known as Tlalocan, the realm of the rain-god Tlaloc. In this scene, figures dance animatedly beside flowing water, butterflies, and flowering trees.

WERNER FORMAN ARCHIVE

Merchants known as *pochteca*, who specialized in long-distance trade, honored a patron deity called Yacatecuhtli, shown here carrying the merchants' symbol of a crossroads marked with footprints. The merchant portrayed in the panel at right carries a cargo of valuable tropical bird feathers.
LIVERPOOL MUSEUM, LIVERPOOL/ WERNER FORMAN ARCHIVE

Pods of the cacao tree, one of the many tropical crops grown in lowland regions. A beverage made from cacao (chocolate beans) was popular with the Mesoamerican nobility.
DOUG BRYANT/D. DONNE BRYANT STOCK

american diet, were at the mercy of seasonal frosts and inadequate rainfall. In parts of the tropical lowlands as well, there was sometimes insufficient water for agriculture or even for drinking purposes.

The riskiness of agriculture was an important factor in the growth of complex societies in Mesoamerica. Farmers often faced shortfalls, and could survive only by giving their allegiance to large-scale political and economic institutions, which, in turn, supported them during difficult years. Such institutions included the emerging central governments and their religious cults, and also the market systems that became one of the most important structures within Mesoamerican civilization. The fact that the most common Mesoamerican deity was a god of rain and fertility ("He Who Makes the Plants Spring Up", or Tlaloc, in the Aztec language) is evidence that the hazards of agriculture were a matter of overriding concern to these early communities.

The diversity of environmental conditions in Mesoamerica gave rise to one of the most important features of the emergent civilization in this region—namely, the interaction between widespread populations, who exchanged products across different environmental zones (although there were also other kinds of specialized production not directly related to the environment). Highland groups imported tropical products, such as colorful bird feathers, cacao (chocolate beans), and rubber. In return, they exported local materials, such as obsidian and magnetite, and manufactured goods, including pottery. These long-distance contacts were important, because they fostered the commonality of cultural and social practices that identifies Mesoamerica as a distinct civilization.

Cultural Diversity and Unity

For all its similarities, Mesoamerica encompassed (and still encompasses) a considerable degree of linguistic, social, and cultural variation. According to one scheme of linguistic classification, more than 200 languages were spoken in this region (many of which are still spoken today), representing at least three distinct major language families. Because of these linguistic differences, which go hand in hand with some degree of cultural difference from region to region, parts of the larger Mesoamerican whole are often identified as separate civilizations in their own right, including the Maya and the Aztec peoples. Other groups that are sometimes separately identified include the Zapotecs of the southern highlands region and the Tarascans of West Mexico. These distinctions notwithstanding, Mesoamerica can usefully be seen as a relatively homogeneous civilization, which, overall, functioned as a distinct social and cultural entity with meaningful boundaries to the north and southeast.

What were the factors that gave rise to a single civilization within this large and diverse area? First, despite the existence of local social systems with their own peculiarities of organization, culture, and language, there was extensive interaction between different groups. Goods were exchanged, people migrated, elites married distant elites.

Second, there were a number of cultural and social practices common to all groups in the region. An example is the so-called calendar round, which meshed the days of two calendars: a 365-day solar year and a 260-day ritual cycle. The two calendars ran in parallel, beginning on the same day only once every 52 years. The 52-year cycle had great significance for Mesoamerican peoples, the rituals carried out at its beginning ensuring the continuation of life (as they knew it) for the coming round.

Third, social stratification was central to the Mesoamerican way of life, the basic distinction in all communities being between a ruling elite (the nobility) and various categories of commoners.

This Aztec calendar stone (or sun stone) was originally located in the main ceremonial plaza of the Aztec capital of Tenochtitlan–Tlatelolco (now Mexico City). It measures 4 meters (13 feet) in diameter and weighs 24.5 tonnes (24 tons). The inner panels depict the history of the world as four previous cycles of creation and destruction, with the current era, the Fifth Sun, represented by the center figure. In the ring just outside these panels, 20 segments represent the 20 days that make up each of the 18 "months" of the Mesoamerican year. (The year was composed of 360 days plus 5 extra days, which were considered to be unlucky.)

NATIONAL MUSEUM OF ARCHAEOLOGY, MEXICO/ GEORGE HOLTON/PHOTO RESEARCHERS, INC.

MESOAMERICAN WRITING

JOYCE MARCUS

WHILE THE OLD WORLD is famous for its ancient scripts—Sumerian cuneiform, Egyptian hieroglyphs, proto-Elamite, proto-Indic, Cretan, Hittite, and Chinese, among others—the New World also produced its share of writing systems. At least four different civilizations in Mesoamerica possessed a system of hieroglyphic writing—the Zapotec, Maya, Mixtec, and Aztec. The Zapotecs produced the earliest known hieroglyphs (existing by 600 BC); the Maya had the most complex system, with the greatest correspondence with the spoken language (AD 200 to AD 1500); and the Mixtecs and Aztecs used simpler, more recently evolved systems, in which pictures conveyed much of the information (AD 1000 to AD 1521).

This Zapotec slab is divided into two registers, showing a marriage in the upper zone and ancestors in the lower. The bride (called 3 Serpent/Water) is shown at left; the groom (6 Earthquake), at right. The female ancestor (11 Monkey) is at lower left; the male ancestor (6 or 8 Glyph D), at lower right. The text begins at the bottom and wraps around the exterior of the stone, and includes the names of 13 of the couple's relatives.
ILLUSTRATION: MARK ORSEN

A Zapotec genealogical register focusing on the early life of a noble named 2 Water/Vessel. The lowest register shows his grandparents; the middle register shows him shortly after birth; and the upper register shows him having his headband adjusted. Slabs such as this were placed in the antechamber of tombs, to be read by nobles at the funeral or when the tomb was reopened for the burial of deceased relatives.
ILLUSTRATION: MARK ORSEN

All four of the major Mesoamerican writing systems combined pictographic, logographic, and syllabic elements. The only kind of writing not present in the New World was the alphabetic system, a development that occurred solely in the Old World.

In Mesoamerican states, writing skills were restricted to members of the elite, who were educated in special schools that excluded commoners. The ruling class not only restricted access to writing, but also controlled what was written, presenting only the version of events that served its current political needs. Scribes are known to have read public inscriptions to commoners, often relying on accompanying pictorial scenes to reinforce the message.

Writing Mediums

The earliest known Zapotec and Maya writing was carved into stone, but writing is also found on polychrome murals, fired pottery, and portable objects of stone, bone, and clay, and also in screenfolds, or "books", consisting of bark paper covered with layers of lime sizing and then painted. Since few books have been preserved, most early writing has survived in the form of stone monuments, which number in the hundreds in the case of the Zapotec, and in the thousands in the case of the Maya. In contrast to these earlier systems, most Mixtec and Aztec writings occur in the form of colorfully painted books, maps, and other types of manuscripts.

Content

Although the four writing systems were not in use at the same time, and each group used different mediums, there were strong similarities in the content of most Mesoamerican texts. All four communities recorded genealogical information about their hereditary nobles, emphasizing their links to former rulers and other nobles. Texts featured important events, such as rites of passage, in the lives of rulers and close family members. We learn the rulers' names, and the dates on which they were born, were inaugurated, married, and died; we read their claims of having won major victories in battle. Commoners were ignored in the inscriptions, and even information about the nobles was carefully selected. Clearly, such texts do not represent objective or complete historical records that can be taken at face value.

Events in the lives of Mesoamerican rulers were placed within a chronological framework. All four groups used two calendars: a ritual calendar consisting of 20 day names, each prefixed by a number from 1 to 13, giving a total of 260 days (with names like 8 Deer and 5 Crocodile), and a secular calendar of 365 days (18 "months" of 20 days each, plus 5 extra days). In addition to specifying the dates of important activities, the calendars allowed people to schedule future events so that they would coincide with the anniversaries of past events. The inauguration of a new ruler, for example, might be timed to coincide with that of a prominent ruler who had lived centuries earlier.

Function

Much of the information given in hieroglyphic monuments or painted books seems to have been propaganda used in the endless competition between nobles for important positions of leadership. Political and genealogical data were frequently manipulated. For example, an ambitious noble who seized power without the proper genealogical credentials might destroy his or her predecessor's books or monuments and commission new ones that provided the desirable details.

Even before the rise of true states in Mesoamerica, chiefs made use of writing to record the names of enemies taken in raids, some of whom were destined for sacrifice. After major states had emerged, writing was also used to set down the territorial limits of a ruler's domain, and to list the names of the places a ruler claimed to have conquered or from which he or she received tribute.

Maya Hieroglyphs

Of all the hieroglyphic writing systems in Mesoamerica, that of the Maya has been the most intensively studied. There are perhaps 800 known hieroglyphs in Maya writing (about the same number as used in Egyptian writing during some periods). Among these glyphs, nouns, verbs, adjectives, prefixes, suffixes, numbers, and proper names have been identified. Currently, the meaning and pronunciation of perhaps 30 to 40 percent of the noncalendrical Maya hieroglyphs are known.

Ancient texts constitute an important source of information, complementing data from such areas of research as ethnohistory, regional settlement patterns, architecture, and subsistence patterns. The challenge remains for us to integrate all these lines of evidence, and thus to explain the similarities and differences between New World and Old World states.

A captive in puma or jaguar military garb, his arms bound behind his back, is depicted on the front of this Zapotec monument from Monte Albán, in Oaxaca.
ILLUSTRATION: MARK ORSEN

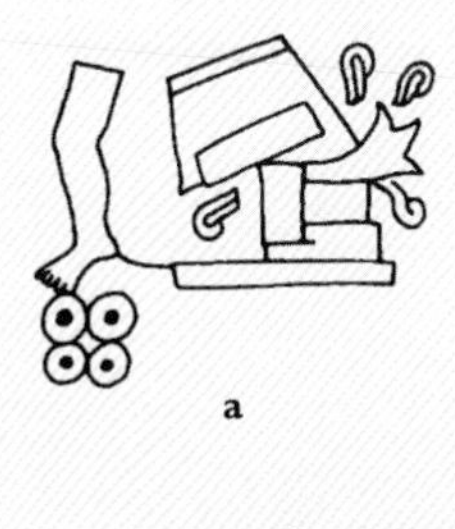

a

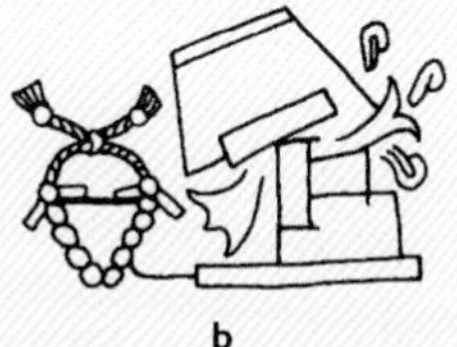

b

c

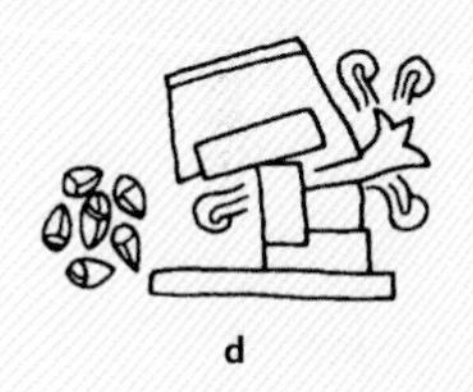

d

e

f

g

The Aztec ruler Tizoc (shown at bottom) reigned from AD 1481 to AD 1486. Listed here are the places he claimed to have conquered, conquest being signified by the flames emanating from beneath the toppled roofs of the vanquished temples.
ILLUSTRATION: JOHN KLAUSMEYER

- **a** Tonaliymoquеçayan ("Where the Sun Rises")
- **b** Toxico
- **c** Ecatepec
- **d** Çilan
- **e** Tecaxic
- **f** Tulucan
- **g** The ruler Tizoc

THE EMERGENCE OF CIVILIZATION IN MESOAMERICA: 1500 BC – AD 1521

	MESOAMERICAN PERIODS	MAJOR PHASES AND EVENTS
1521		Spanish conquest
1400	Late Postclassic (AD 1200 – AD 1521)	Aztec empire (AD 1400 – AD 1521)
1200		Toltec empire (AD 1000 – AD 1200)
900	Early Postclassic (AD 750 – AD 1200)	Decline of Maya centers of the Classic period
750		Decline of Teotihuacan, Monte Albán
	Classic (AD 200 – AD 750)	Classic period of Teotihuacan influence (AD 200 – AD 750)
200		
AD 1	Terminal Formative (100 BC – AD 200)	Pyramids of the Sun and Moon; Street of the Dead; grid layout of Teotihuacan
100		Cuicuilco destroyed by lava flow
	Late Formative (500 BC – 100 BC)	Formation of states in central highlands and Valley of Oaxaca
		First city at Monte Albán
500		Earliest Mesoamerican writing, including calendar glyphs
	Middle Formative (900 BC – 500 BC)	
900		Widespread Olmec symbolism (1200 BC – 500 BC)
	Early Formative (1500 BC – 900 BC)	Early emergence of social strata and chiefdoms
1500 BC		First settled agricultural villages; pottery

This social cleavage could be somewhat blurred, for social mobility was possible. In addition, some non-noble merchants and craftspeople were able to accumulate considerable wealth and prestige, and constituted a kind of middle class. In general, however, Mesoamerican societies were strongly stratified, and the nobility exerted considerable control over the major activities and institutions, including religion and the temples (prominent priests were members of the nobility), city governance, warfare, and even, to some extent, the production and distribution of many kinds of goods. The elite also sponsored most art and public architecture, which commonly incorporated characteristic elements of the major Mesoamerican styles found in a range of areas. The primary purpose for which writing was used, whether in books or on carved stone monuments, was to record significant events in the life of the nobility. (See the feature *Mesoamerican Writing.*) Nobles also had almost exclusive access to such precious goods as cotton garments, jade, and tropical bird feathers.

SOTHEBY'S, NEW YORK/WERNER FORMAN ARCHIVE

Dating from the Classic period, this hollow ceramic figurine of a seated Maya noble is characteristic of the portraiture that accompanied burials on the island of Jaina, off the coast of Campeche, in Mexico.

The common set of beliefs that upheld the social dichotomy of nobility and commoner was largely what distinguished Mesoamerica from other regions of North America. In addition, frequent contact between members of the elite from widespread regions created a common social system that transcended regional economies and cultures. Members of any particular elite had more in common with members of other elites from distant regions than they had with the commoners of their own region, and these wide-ranging contacts were one of the most important sources of their legitimacy, power, and wealth. For example, royal marriages between distant groups conferred prestige, at the same time as they affirmed political alliances between regional polities. The elite obtained goods from their distant social contacts, traded with them, and even joined with them in the causes of warfare and empire-building. The exotic products thus acquired, heavily laden with symbolic significance, could be displayed, consumed during public rituals, or presented to followers in order to create and maintain political obligations. Some were also used as royal insignia to reinforce political status.

At the other end of the social spectrum were the commoners. Their social world was much more localized than that of their noble overlords, except in the case of the few traders who carried goods between distant markets. The growth of complex societies over the whole of Mesoamerica, however, tended to produce a pattern of everyday life in which some central themes can be identified. These common themes make it possible for us to distinguish Mesoamerican households from, for example, Plains Indian, Northwest Coast, or Great Basin forager households, despite the regional differences that existed between Mesoamerican cultures and languages.

Most Mesoamerican commoners lived in nuclear family households consisting of a married couple and their unmarried offspring, although in some cases, related families lived together as extended families—for example, when married children remained in their parents' house. Houses were substantial, often constructed of wattle-and-daub (sticks and mud), mudbrick, or stone, and were occupied year round. Households grouped together to form permanent communities, which ranged in size from small hamlets and villages to larger towns and cities. The degree of urbanism (the percentage of the population living in cities) varied from region to region, but cities grew up in most regions. Most commoners were farmers, although some, especially those living in cities, specialized to varying degrees in craft production, trade, various kinds of construction, or even warfare. Most of what was produced or earned was used to provide for the household's own requirements, but a proportion was given (along with labor) as tribute to noble overlords or

NATIONAL MUSEUM OF ANTHROPOLOGY, MEXICO/WERNER FORMAN ARCHIVE

A stone lintel carving portraying Maya nobility of the Classic period, from Structure 23 at the site of Yaxchilan (AD 726). Noble status is signified by such characteristic features as the deformed heads; the feathered headdresses; the elaborate items of personal adornment, including earplugs, necklaces, and bracelets (probably of jade); and the costly clothing, such as the padded jacket worn by the figure on the left.

The style of this ceramic piece, probably from Nayarit or Jalisco, is characteristic of the tomb art of West Mexico. It appears to depict a birth scene.

WERNER FORMAN ARCHIVE

A cylinder vase from Tikal, the ancient center of Classic Maya culture, in present-day Guatemala, depicting a noble in a characteristic pose, seated on a decorated stone bench.
TIKAL MUSEUM, GUATEMALA/D. DONNE BRYANT STOCK

landowners, who were exempt from production. The remainder could be exchanged in the marketplaces for goods households did not produce themselves; for example, corn farmers might acquire at least some of their cloth, pottery, stone tools, and ritual items through market exchange.

There were some regional differences in the crops grown by commoner households, but maize was the dominant crop wherever the environment was suited to its cultivation. A field of maize was a common sight in the ancient Mesoamerican landscape, as it still is today, and maize symbolism was prominent in Mesoamerican beliefs and ritual. The lowland Maya area was somewhat different, since parts of it are not favorable to the cultivation of maize. Research into ancient Maya subsistence practices is ongoing, but it is likely that the lowlanders grew a complex mix of crops suited to local conditions, with less emphasis on maize than was the case in the highlands.

Many techniques were used to intensify agricultural production, including the terracing of slopes, the construction of raised fields to reclaim swampland (such as the *chinampas* of the Valley of Mexico), fertilizers, and irrigation. The latter helped to overcome the problem of uncertain rainfall and often made it possible to cultivate a second or third crop well into the dry period. These agricultural regimes were very labor-intensive, leaving most commoner households with little time to produce other goods.

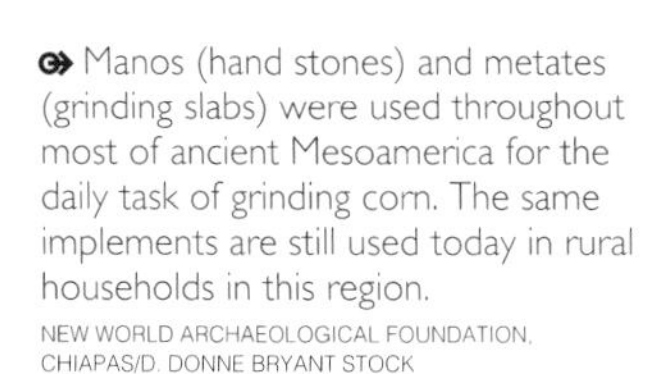

Manos (hand stones) and metates (grinding slabs) were used throughout most of ancient Mesoamerica for the daily task of grinding corn. The same implements are still used today in rural households in this region.
NEW WORLD ARCHAEOLOGICAL FOUNDATION, CHIAPAS/D. DONNE BRYANT STOCK

Mesoamerican commoners used many kinds of tools and implements, variously made from stone, bone, wood, or fired clay, among which were stone implements called manos and metates for grinding corn. Maize was most often shaped into tortillas and cooked on a clay griddle, and tortillas are a central feature of Mesoamerican cuisine to this day. Households possessed numerous well-fired pottery vessels, and an obsidian blade served as an all-purpose knife. This basic household tool kit, along with a diet based on maize, was common to nearly all societies in the Mesoamerican region.

Opposite page: This mural by modern-day Mexican artist Diego Rivera portrays nobles of the Totonac culture, which emerged during the Classic period in what is now the state of Veracruz. The elaborate clothing, headdresses, jewelry, and other paraphernalia, such as the staffs, are typically Totonac styles, but such items would have signified noble status throughout Mesoamerica.

Settled Villages: The Early and Middle Formative Periods

The 3,000-year duration of prehispanic Mesoamerican civilization can be divided into three broad periods: the Formative (about 1500 BC to AD 200); the Classic, sometimes called the Middle Horizon (AD 200 to AD 750, but lasting until AD 900 in the Maya lowlands); and the Postclassic (about AD 750 to the Spanish conquest in AD 1521). During the Formative period (which, in turn, can be divided into Early, Middle, Late, and Terminal phases), most of the characteristic features of Mesoamerican civilization developed. These include a settled village way of life, the growth of an elite class, the emergence of the first cities, intensive methods of agricultural production, the development of writing systems and the calendar round, the beginnings of monumental public architecture, and the spread of common cosmological themes and artistic styles throughout the Mesoamerican region.

By about 1500 BC (the starting date varies from place to place), a settled form of village life based on the cultivation of domesticated crops had become the preferred way of life for most Mesoamerican households. Previously, households had moved seasonally between different kinds of camps. Archaeologists distinguish between sites dating to the preceding Archaic (or Preceramic) period and the earliest village sites (from the Early Formative period) largely on the basis of the pottery found in the latter sites, although other changes can be noted as well, including a more substantial style of house construction. Once people adopted a sedentary, agricultural way of life, they needed more vessels for storage and food preparation, and probably more eating utensils, and did not have to worry about transporting heavy and fragile ceramic objects. In the Early Formative period, the new ceramic technology impinged on many aspects of life, from everyday household activities to the more rarified realms of artistic and symbolic expression.

During the first few centuries of the Early Formative period, there was considerable diversity among Mesoamerican societies. For example, although most households were beginning to make and use pottery vessels, the other elements of the later household tool kit, including obsidian blades, manos, and metates, were not in use everywhere, probably indicating substantial differences between regional farming communities and household economies. In addition, although there may have been fledgling elites in some areas, societies were generally highly egalitarian.

From about 1200 BC to 500 BC, however, household tool kits everywhere began to look more alike, and for the first time, there is evidence of frequent long-distance contact between members of emergent social elites. Anthropologists use the term "chiefdom" to refer to societies in which inherited social position determines access to power

This jade figurine embodies several aspects of Olmec symbolism that are seen especially in ceramics and objects carved out of stone (usually jade). The cleft baby-face has jaguar-like features, and the skirt design incorporates jaguar motifs, probably representing the belief that the nobility originated from the mating of a jaguar with a human female. The figure holds a torch, a symbol of elite status.
DALLAS MUSEUM OF FINE ARTS/ WERNER FORMAN ARCHIVE

A hollow figurine of a crying baby in the Olmec style.
DR KURT STAVENHAGEN COLLECTION/ WERNER FORMAN ARCHIVE

Valley of Mexico sites dating from the Early Formative period, such as Tlatilco, have yielded artifacts with Olmec characteristics along with objects that reflect a more localized cultural complex. Many Tlatilco burial offerings included terracotta figurines in the local style. Most depict unclothed or partially clad females with elaborate headdresses: many different forms were produced, including grotesque figurines such as this.
J.P. COURAU/D. DONNE BRYANT STOCK

and resources. The term is a useful one to describe many local social systems that existed in Mesoamerica during the Early and Middle Formative periods. Among the first themes expressed in the art and iconography of these periods were divine descent, hereditary rulership, and lineage (descent group) affiliation. At the same time, interaction between members of widespread elites became much more frequent, indicating that Mesoamerica was beginning to develop a multisocietal social system.

The Growth of Chiefdoms and the Rise of Olmec Style and Iconography

Olmec is the name given to an artistic style, and its associated symbols, that appeared at the time the first chiefdoms evolved. Emphasizing jaguar images and symbols, including human babies with jaguar-like features, it seems to reflect a belief that the nobility stemmed from the mating of a jaguar with a human female. It is seen in local ceramic phases dating from the Early Formative period (about 1200 BC to 900 BC) in such centers as Ajalpan, in the Tehuacán Valley, San Lorenzo, in the Gulf Coast lowlands, San José Mogote, in the Valley of Oaxaca, and Ixtapaluca, in the Valley of Mexico. Olmec art and iconography persisted, with modifications, throughout the Middle Formative period (900 BC to 500 BC).

The rapid spread of the Olmec style and its associated cosmological themes reflected a deepening division between the elite and commoners in Mesoamerica. Evidently, participation in rituals that gave expression to a cosmological belief system was an important part of the emergent elite's developing power base. The exotic elements of these rituals were common to elites over a wide region, leading to the exchange of such prestigious items as magnetite mirrors, jade, and even pottery vessels and figurines invested with potent symbols. These goods confirmed the elite's social status, and sanctified its power by linking its members with the religious themes expressed in Olmec iconography.

The nature and origins of the Olmec style and religion remain one of the central issues in Mesoamerican archaeology. Since there is so much local variation in its expression, Olmec culture probably did not develop as a single entity in one place and then spread to other areas. Some researchers do take this view, however, proposing the site of San Lorenzo, in the Gulf Coast lowlands, as the probable point of origin. It is true that this site has the best-established ceramic sequence leading up to the pottery types identifiable as Olmec. It also has the most elaborate monumental construction found anywhere in Mesoamerica in the Early Formative period—an architecturally modified ridge surmounted by a cluster of pyramid-mounds—as well as someof the earliest carved stone monuments in Mesoamerica, including colossal stone heads, which are thought to portray individual rulers. A more plausible theory takes as its starting point the fact that societies throughout Mesoamerica were becoming more socially stratified during the Early and Middle Formative periods. Households of the ruling class in such places as La Venta, in Veracruz, San José Mogote, in the Valley of Oaxaca, Tlatilco, in the Valley of Mexico, and Chalcatzingo, in Morelos, were part of a widespread elite network that helped to legitimize the growing social gulf between nobles and commoners. Olmec culture, accordingly, was probably not the creation of a single group but may have emerged from a process of social differentiation that was taking place in many regions simultaneously.

Colossal stone heads, such as this one, possibly depicting rulers, are typical finds in Gulf Coast Olmec sites dating from the Early and Middle Formative periods.
D. DONNE BRYANT STOCK

TONY MORRISON/SOUTH AMERICAN PICTURES

Cities and States: The Late and Terminal Formative Periods

Anthropologists distinguish between the state, as a form of government, and a chiefdom on the basis of the complexity of the governing apparatus —including the number of bureaucrats and the number of hierarchical levels of decision-makers that separate the general population from the highest level of decision-making—and the scale of the governing institution (its size and territorial extent). Ethnographic studies show that chiefdoms usually consist of fewer than 10,000 people living within a prescribed region, and have only one or two hierarchical levels of administration. State governments control much larger populations and regions—in effect, they incorporate numerous chiefdoms into a single structure, with three or more levels of hierarchy.

The first Mesoamerican states evolved during the Late and Terminal Formative periods (about 500 BC to AD 200), notably in the emerging core zones of the central and southern highlands regions. A number of related social and cultural changes were taking place during this time, including greater specialization in the goods produced by households, an increase in market participation, intensification of agricultural activity (including canal irrigation), and the growth of large communities to house the increasing population of government personnel, craft specialists, and priests. These communities formed the basis of the first Mesoamerican cities.

Two archaeological sequences in particular, in the Valley of Oaxaca (in the southern highlands) and the Valley of Mexico (in the central highlands), have much to tell us about the nature of the changes that evolved over these periods in the emergent core regions.

The Rise of Complex Societies in the Valley of Oaxaca

During the Early and Middle Formative periods, the most important chiefdom center in the Valley of Oaxaca was San José Mogote. By about 600 BC, this center was becoming more militaristic, as we know from the evidence of a stone monument carved with figures known as Danzantes (meaning dancers)—a misleading name, since the figures clearly portray dead bodies, often with their hearts torn out and limbs cut off.

Massive platform-mounds are ranged along the eastern boundary of the main plaza of Monte Albán, the ancient Zapotec capital, in the Valley of Oaxaca, Mexico. This plaza complex was the center of government for the Zapotec state from 500 BC to AD 700. The city is located on top of a mountain; the valley floor can be seen in the distance.

THE ANCIENT ZAPOTEC CAPITAL OF MONTE ALBÁN

RICHARD E. BLANTON

ANDREW RAKOCZY/PHOTO RESEARCHERS, INC.

For approximately 1,250 years, from 500 BC to AD 750, the archaeological site known as Monte Albán was the foremost political and cultural capital of the Zapotecs, the inhabitants of the Valley of Oaxaca and adjacent areas of Mexico's southern highlands region. Monte Albán is the colonial Spanish name for the mountain on which the ancient city was built. We do not know what the capital was called during prehispanic times, although carved stone glyphs in several of the excavated buildings suggest that it may originally have been named "Hill of the Jaguar". Most of the information we have about Monte Albán comes from studies of the remains of its elaborate architecture and artifacts.

With its elegant main plaza and its majestic setting high on a mountaintop, Monte Albán is one of the most beautiful of the major archaeological sites to be found in Mesoamerica. It is also one of the most important sites for anthropologists investigating the evolution of complex society in prehispanic Mesoamerica. Not only did it serve as an important regional political capital for a long period—possibly for longer than any of the other major Mesoamerican capitals—but it was also one of the first Native American settlements to attain the population size and the degree of urban density that qualify it as a city.

From its very beginning, Monte Albán was unique, being set apart by its isolated mountaintop setting and its expansive plaza surrounded by public buildings. One of these early buildings, unlike any other in the region, housed a gallery of hundreds of stone monuments carved with figures of slain warriors, which publicly proclaimed the new capital's military might. Inappropriately, these figures were originally named the Danzantes, meaning "dancers", and the name has endured, referring both to the figures and the monuments

⬆ This complex of buildings, known as System IV, is located along the western boundary of Monte Albán's main plaza. It consists of a large pyramid platform, fronted by a courtyard and a lower platform.

themselves. Early Monte Albán was also unique for its rapid increase in population, from 5,000 during its initial stage to more than 15,000 during the Late Formative period (locally, 350 BC to 200 BC)—a higher growth rate than occurred in any other settlement in the region. By the Late Classic period (AD 500 to AD 750), the city had reached its peak population of more than 30,000.

The Growth of a City

Over many hundreds of years, the capital acquired a complex cityscape of palaces, temples, and other public buildings; plazas (some of which served ritual and government purposes, while others were used as markets); minor and major roads; defensive walls; and water control systems for channeling and storing domestic water supplies and for irrigating agricultural fields on the slopes below the city. Owing to the steepness of the terrain, houses were built on stone-faced terraces, more than 2,000 of which have been located and mapped by archaeological teams. Houses had a central courtyard, under the floor of which a tomb for the interment of household members is typically found.

CHARLES LENARS/EXPLORER/AUSCAPE

ROBERT F. KAY/D. DONNE BRYANT STOCK

A fragment of a Danzante figure from Monte Albán's main plaza, dating from the Late Formative period (500 BC to 200 BC).

Ceramic funerary urns, often adorned with a figure (probably a venerated ancestor), are a distinctive feature of Zapotec culture.

A reconstruction of Monte Albán's main plaza by the artist Antonio Trejo, showing how it would have looked at the ancient city's height in AD 700.

NATIONAL MUSEUM OF ANTHROPOLOGY, MEXICO/ BARBARA CERVA/D. DONNE BRYANT STOCK

After about AD 750, the main plaza was abandoned, and its buildings eventually fell into ruin. At the same time, the population of the city declined substantially, although some areas of the settlement continued to be occupied over the eight centuries between AD 750 and the arrival of the Spaniards in the sixteenth century. But the city never again regained its position of regional dominance. After the main plaza was abandoned, Monte Albán became just one of several competing towns in the Valley of Oaxaca in the Postclassic period.

The Main Plaza

The massive main plaza served as the center of government activity for the city and the region. The form of the plaza evolved over more than a thousand years of almost continuous construction projects, in the course of which the plaza space was enlarged and made more elaborate, and surrounded with various building complexes. These architectural changes gradually closed off the space and its buildings, increasingly isolating the plaza and its inhabitants from the city's general population.

The final construction phase of the main plaza, dating to the Late Classic period (AD 500 to AD 750), the last major period of occupation, has been partly reconstructed by Mexican archaeologists. By this time, the plaza measured 150 meters by 300 meters (160 yards by 325 yards). It was bounded north and south by massive platforms 12 meters (37 feet) high, each with a broad staircase providing access from the plaza to buildings at the top of the platform. Other platform-mounds and a ballcourt (for the ritual ball games so important to Mesoamerican societies) defined the plaza's east and west boundaries, and a central spine of buildings extended between the north and south monumental platforms. Additional plazas and platform-mounds on top of the north platform formed a complex of buildings that housed the ruling families and also provided formal spaces for rulers to meet with high-ranking government officials and ambassadors from other polities. Judging from carved stone commemorative monuments placed at the base of the south platform, some of these official visitors represented Monte Albán's counterpart in the Valley of Mexico—Teotihuacan.

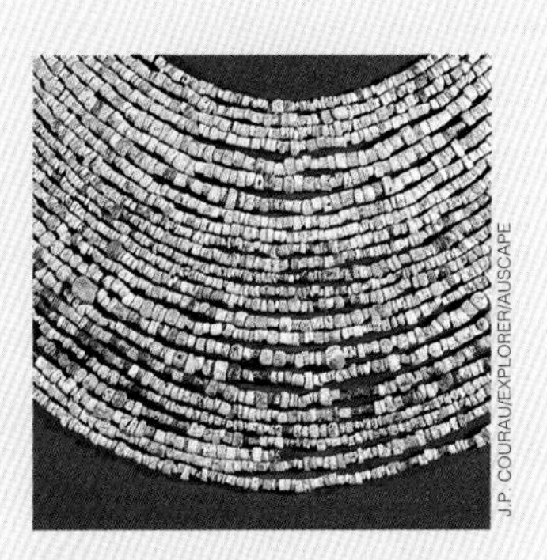

J.P. COURAU/EXPLORER/AUSCAPE

This necklace was part of the fabulous burial offerings found in Monte Albán's Tomb 7, dating to the Postclassic period, some time after AD 1000.

The Pyramid of the Sun is the major temple at Teotihuacan. The buildings in the foreground, with their rectangular panels resting on a sloping base, are characteristic of the city's architecture, known as the Talud-Tablero style.

D. DONNE BRYANT STOCK

D. DONNE BRYANT STOCK

The Quetzalpapalotl Palace, at Teotihuacan, dates from the Classic period. Located near the Street of the Dead, this excavated and reconstructed building, although comparatively elaborate, illustrates the characteristic form of Teotihuacan domestic architecture. Rooms with entrances framed by columns face onto a roofless central courtyard with a plaster floor.

Soon after this monument was carved, a most extraordinary political change took place in the Valley of Oaxaca. The archaeological evidence indicates that before 500 BC, there were three discrete (although probably interacting) chiefdoms in the Valley of Oaxaca, located in the three arms of the valley. Suddenly, about 500 BC, a new regional political capital was established on a previously unoccupied mountaintop in an area located between these three chiefdoms. Now known as Monte Albán, this mountaintop was to remain the site of the region's major city until AD 750—a period of 1,250 years!

Located in a neutral position, away from the existing chiefdom centers, the new capital was evidently established in order to integrate the entire valley into one political system. The change was most likely made to reduce the level of fighting between the three chiefdoms, and to allow them to combine their fighting forces to counter external military threats. Unfortunately, we have little written information from the period that would throw light on these striking political changes, but it is clear that early Monte Albán had a strongly military orientation: hundreds of Danzante monuments—far more than at any other site—were erected there during its earliest period of occupation (300 having been discovered to date).

The establishment of Monte Albán, during what is locally referred to as Period I, signifies the origin of the state and the beginnings of urban life in the Valley of Oaxaca. In later periods, the capital exerted an influence on regions outside the valley, and its elite maintained contacts with other elites as far away as the Valley of Mexico and the Maya area. The founding of the city marked a turning point. Local society was transformed in many ways, as can be seen even in the changing pattern of everyday life within its commoner households. The population grew rapidly, both in the city itself and throughout the region, probably as the result of higher fertility rates, reduced mortality, and immigration, although our archaeological and human biological (skeletal) data are too limited to allow us to assess these factors accurately. Commoners began to build houses of more durable and costly mudbrick, rather than wattle-and-daub. There is evidence of an increase in the specialized production of goods; for example, pottery-making villages are found for the first time, and it is likely that specialist products were exchanged through a system of marketplaces. Remnants of the region's first canal irrigation systems date from the same period. Some of these features—and even the regular eating of tortillas—have endured to the present day in the Valley of Oaxaca.

Monte Albán continued as the region's major city and political center until the end of the Classic period, at which time it was largely abandoned and other centers began to dominate the region. Because the city was deserted, its main public buildings have been preserved, and thanks to

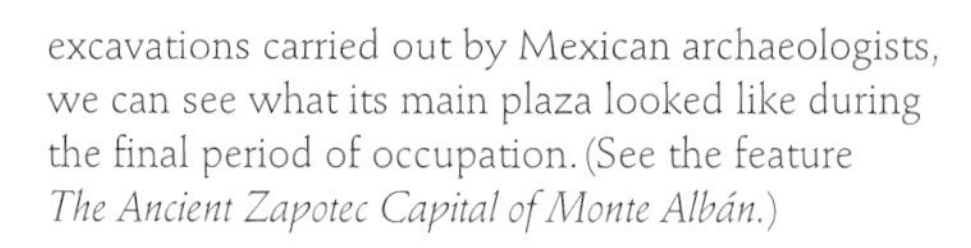

excavations carried out by Mexican archaeologists, we can see what its main plaza looked like during the final period of occupation. (See the feature *The Ancient Zapotec Capital of Monte Albán.*)

Cultural Evolution in the Valley of Mexico

By the end of the Middle Formative period (which occurred locally as early as 600 BC), a series of chiefdom centers dotted the landscape of the Valley of Mexico. Two of these—Cuicuilco, in the west, and Teotihuacan, in the east—gradually emerged as the region's most important centers. The archaeological survey data from the valley indicate that by about 100 BC, the two centers were vying for regional prominence. At this time, however, a singular event radically altered the

course of the valley's history. A major volcanic eruption buried Cuicuilco under meters of lava, destroying it completely, so that until about AD 750, Teotihuacan had unchallenged supremacy over the Valley of Mexico and other parts of the central highlands region.

During what is known as the Tzacualli ceramic phase (AD 1 to AD 100), Teotihuacan grew rapidly, while many other sites in the Valley of Mexico were abandoned. It seems that many people either voluntarily migrated to the city or were forced to move there, perhaps because of a state policy of resettlement. The population of the city grew rapidly during and after this period, reaching an estimated 80,000 by the end of the Tzacualli phase and a maximum of probably 150,000 or more during the Classic period (AD 200 to AD 750), which made Teotihuacan one of the largest cities in the world at that time.

The scale of public building works undertaken in Teotihuacan during the Tzacualli phase was greater than that at any other time or in any other place in Mesoamerican history. During this phase, most of the work was completed on the Pyramid of the Sun, one of the ancient world's greatest temple buildings (with a volume of a million cubic meters, or 1,300,000 cubic yards). The great north–south avenue, now called the Street of the Dead, was intersected by a major east–west avenue. Later, two massive structures were built at the intersection: a market plaza, known as the Great Compound, and a government building, the Ciudadela. During the subsequent ceramic phase, the Miccaotli (AD 100 to AD 200), the

A panoramic view of central Teotihuacan, in the Valley of Mexico. The northern end of the main avenue, the Street of the Dead (at the top of the photograph), terminates at a plaza fronting the Pyramid of the Moon (top right). The avenue is lined with important government buildings, temples, and residential areas.

COMSTOCK

A detail from the western facade of the Temple of Quetzalcoatl. The temple faces the massive plaza of the Ciudadela, a government center in Teotihuacan. Elaborately sculptured panels depict feathered serpents (representing the god Quetzalcoatl), snails, seashells, and grotesque heads of the rain-god Tlaloc.

TONY MORRISON/SOUTH AMERICAN PICTURES

Decorated with mosaic, this mask from Teotihuacan dates from the Classic period. Masks were important in Teotihuacan culture, although their functions are not yet fully understood. They were sometimes placed on the faces of the deceased, and may have been worn on ritual occasions and placed on statues.

MUSEO PREISTORICO ED ETNOGRAFICA L. PIGORINI, ROME/SCALA

The wooden drums used in major rituals were often elaborately carved. Here, members of the nobility are seen wearing masks representing the rain-god Tlaloc. The drum was held horizontally, and a skin was stretched over each end to provide two tones.

BRITISH MUSEUM/WERNER FORMAN ARCHIVE

Ciudadela eventually attained a volume of 750,000 cubic meters (about 980,000 cubic yards): its main plaza area was large enough to hold 100,000 people on ritual occasions. During the Tzacualli phase, the whole city had begun to develop a strongly planned aspect. By the Tlamimilolpa phase (AD 200 to AD 400), walled residential compounds were added, in careful conformity with the grid established by the two major avenues.

During the Classic period, Teotihuacan's influence spread far beyond the territory in the central highlands over which it had direct control. Elements of Teotihuacan style—in ceramics and architecture, for example—are found nearly everywhere, revealing this as a period during which Mesoamerican societies were highly interconnected. There was never a Mesoamerica-wide empire, but Teotihuacan did control outposts as far away as Veracruz and Guatemala (at Kaminaljuyu), and was engaged in commercial activities involving the production and exchange of obsidian and other goods over a very broad area.

Understanding the nature of government in Teotihuacan and its role in the society is still a major challenge for archaeological researchers. The state was clearly involved in influential religious cults, many of which emphasized agricultural fertility and worshiped a fertility goddess. It was a massive institution, which appears to have affected many aspects of people's daily lives. At the same time, it was impersonal, which makes it a difficult entity for archaeologists to study. No rulers are named in written texts or portrayed by statues. In fact, although the Ciudadela was clearly an important center of government, we are still not certain about the location of the rulers' quarters or the state's central offices. It seems that there was no tradition of building royal funerary monuments, although future research may uncover such structures.

A ceramic incense burner dating from Teotihuacan's Classic period. The masked figure peering through the opening, framed by a feathered headdress containing birds, probably represents the important Great Goddess of Teotihuacan religion.

NATIONAL MUSEUM OF ANTHROPOLOGY, MEXICO/WERNER FORMAN ARCHIVE

The Final Period of Indigenous Civilization: The Postclassic

Monte Albán and Teotihuacan endured as pre-eminent Mesoamerican metropolises for many centuries, but about AD 750, conditions changed, making the old centers obsolete. (In the lowland Maya area, the predominant centers of the Classic period, including Tikal, declined somewhat later, about AD 900.) We do not know what caused the decline of the old order, but data from Teotihuacan indicate that the city met a violent end. The whole Street of the Dead was systematically burned—possibly the work of dissidents who rose up against their noble overlords.

The pattern of long-term dominance by a few major centers that had characterized the Classic period in Mesoamerica did not recur during the ensuing period. The Postclassic was a much more dynamic time, with many centers emerging and jockeying for power and economic dominance, although few endured for long. There were two more major cycles of empire formation during this period, both emanating from the central highlands. The Toltecs of Tula, north of the Valley of Mexico, attempted to re-establish a Teotihuacan-like domain, but failed after only a century or so. By the end of the prehispanic period, the Culhua Mexica (Aztec) city of Tenochtitlan–Tlatelolco, in the Valley of Mexico, had emerged as a major core center, and was beginning to exert an influence over large parts of Mesoamerica. We will never know whether its rulers' imperial ambitions would have been any less ephemeral than those of the Toltecs, as the Spaniards under Hernán Cortéz defeated the Aztecs in AD 1521. This conquest brought an end to indigenous civilization in the region, initiating the process that eventually led to the blending of Mesoamerican and European cultures in Mesoamerica.

MUSEUM OF MANKIND, LONDON/THE BRIDGEMAN ART LIBRARY

Decorated vessels like this cylindrical, flat-bottomed ceramic vessel with tripod supports are one of the hallmarks of the Teotihuacan style, which was widespread during the Classic period.

HANS NAMUTH/PHOTO RESEARCHERS, INC

THE MAYA

2000 BC — THE PRESENT

Lords of the Forest

WILLIAM L. FASH

WHEN THE AMERICAN EXPLORER and diplomat John Lloyd Stephens arrived at the Maya ruins of Copán in 1839, he described the scene as follows: "Architecture, sculpture, and painting, all the arts which embellish life, had flourished in this overgrown forest; orators, warriors, and statesmen, beauty, ambition, and glory, had lived and passed away, and none knew that such things had been, or could tell of their past existence ... It lay before us like a shattered bark in the midst of the ocean, her masts gone, her name effaced, her crew perished, and none to tell whence she came, to whom she belonged, how long on her voyage, or what caused her destruction ... All was mystery, dark, impenetrable mystery."

Scattered mentions of the Copán ruins and other imposing monuments of the Classic period of Maya civilization, which spanned the period from about AD 250 to AD 900, had made their way into the Spanish colonial archives, only to be forgotten. Stephens' book, with its compelling illustrations by the English artist Frederick Catherwood, gave the world at large the opportunity to admire the achievements of this creative and energetic people, and to speculate on the reasons for the demise of their once imposing centers of the arts and sciences. Abandoned when the original inhabitants migrated from much of the region, shrouded in jungle, and obscured by the passage of centuries, the Classic Maya ruins presented a formidable mystery.

Temple I in Tikal, northern Guatemala, is the majestic final resting place of one of the greatest kings of the Classic Maya period, known to us only as Ruler I. His stucco portrait adorned the roof crest above the temple doorway, while his tomb lies deep inside the pyramid.

One of a famous series of Maya illustrations by the nineteenth-century artist Frederick Catherwood, showing the corbeled arch leading into the Palace of the Governor, in Uxmal, Yucatán, Mexico.
COLLECTION E.S./EXPLORER/AUSCAPE

➜ The tops of Temples I, II, and III in Tikal, as seen (from left to right) from Temple IV, pierce the upper canopy of El Petén rainforest, in northern Guatemala.

TONY MORRISON/SOUTH AMERICAN PICTURES

Besides the issue of what caused the collapse of the Classic Maya city-states, these ancient ruins posed a whole series of questions for the Western scholars who took up the challenge of reconstructing the history of this lost civilization. Where did it come from? How long did it flourish? What was the nature of the society that gave birth to such remakable monumental art and architecture? And what did its ancient hieroglyphic writings record: what matters of state and religion were documented there? The answers to these and many other questions have been pursued by a wide range of scholars over the past 150 years, with dramatic and often surprising results. They have shown that, far from being a monolithic culture, the people we refer to as the Maya (on the basis of a sixteenth-century reference to the Yucatán peninsula as "Maya" or "Maia") were, in fact, a number of widely diverse peoples, who occupied distinct environments and arrived at different solutions to the common challenges they faced.

Geography and Culture

At the time of the Spanish conquest in the early sixteenth century, Maya speakers inhabited about one-third of the land surface of Mesoamerica, extending from the Isthmus of Tehuantepec in the west to the western sections of the present-day republics of Honduras and El Salvador in the east. Within this area of about 125,000 square kilometers (48,000 square miles), there was tremendous geographical and cultural diversity.

The lands these peoples occupied range from humid tropical mangroves in the south to a lush foothills zone further north, which, in turn, gives way to the cool, steep slopes of the highlands of Chiapas, in what is today Mexico, Guatemala, Belize, and the far western parts of Honduras and El Salvador. The highlands slope down to the immense, flat region referred to as the Maya lowlands, the heart of the dramatic cultural flowering that took place in the so-called Classic period. The lowlands are themselves divided into the southern lowlands —consisting of northern Guatemala, Belize, and adjacent parts of Chiapas, a region characterized by fully fledged tropical rainforests and an average annual rainfall of 2,000 to 3,000 millimeters (80 to 120 inches)—and the northern lowlands—comprising the modern-day Mexican states of Campeche, Yucatán, and Quintana Roo, which are characterized for the most part by scrub vegetation, thin soils, little surface water, and a mean annual rainfall of less than 2,000 millimeters (80 inches).

Of the 31 Mayan languages recorded at the time of the Spanish conquest, only two are now extinct. Speakers of the other languages still occupy different parts of the Maya area. The languages recorded in the hieroglyphic texts of the Classic period include Cholan, in the southern lowlands, and Yucatecan, in the northern lowlands, and speakers of these two languages still outnumber speakers of the other Mayan tongues.

The archaeological remains attest to considerable cultural diversity in pre-Columbian times. This probably reflected regional differences, but it is evident that there was also a great wealth of beliefs and customs that the people of this region held in common.

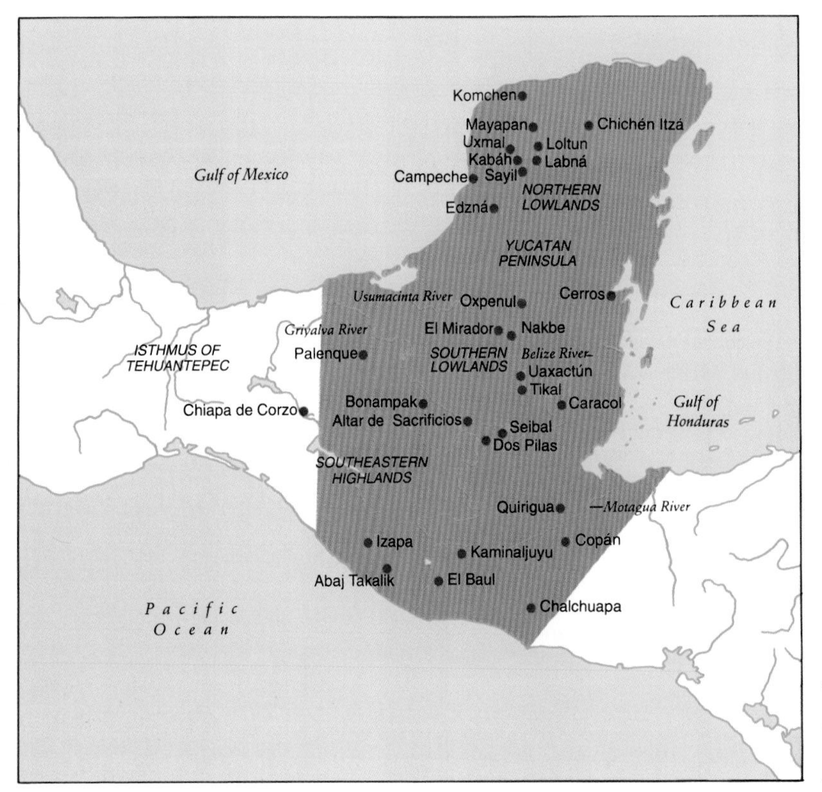

THE MAYA IN MESOAMERICA
The locations of major archaeological sites of the Maya civilization.
CARTOGRAPHY: RAY SIM

ALAIN THOMAS/EXPLORER/AUSCAPE

A view of the heart of Uxmal, a major Classic Maya center in Yucatán. On the left is the so-called Nunnery Quadrangle, and on the right, the Temple of the Magician.

The Origins of Maya Culture

It is truly extraordinary that a Stone Age people such as the pre-Columbian Maya should have made such great advances in urban development, art, and architecture in the tropical rainforests of Mesoamerica, one of the most challenging environments on Earth in which to establish such a civilization. Indeed, many anthropologists have concluded that the rainforest of the southern lowlands area (considered to be the geographical and cultural core of Maya civilization) was such an inhospitable setting for urban, civilized life that the seeds of Classic Maya culture must have been imported from outside. For many years, it was thought that the large metropolis of Teotihuacan, in the arid highlands of central Mexico—an environment more similar to those in which the Mesopotamian and Egyptian civilizations flourished—must have been the "donor culture". Classic Maya culture reached its peak, so the thinking went, several centuries after the founding of Teotihuacan, then the world's sixth-largest city. Recent investigations have shattered this view, however, showing that the Maya were among the most innovative and energetic indigenous peoples of the New World.

The Early Preclassic Period

Evidence for the earliest settled villages in the Maya region dates to about 1600 BC, during what archaeologists call the Early Preclassic period (2000 BC to 1000 BC), and takes the form of ceramic remains found in the Pacific coastal areas of Chiapas and adjacent Guatemala. Referred to by the names given to the ceramic styles characteristic of different phases of this period, the Barra and the Ocos, these early coastal dwellers apparently subsisted largely on seafood and freshwater fish, supplemented by plant foods from the estuaries and adjacent upland zones. Eventually, people moved into the slightly higher areas to the north, where maize agriculture gradually became the predominant means of livelihood. The decorative techniques used in Ocos ceramics are strikingly similar to those of contemporary pottery from coastal Ecuador and Pacific coastal Costa Rica, indicating that there was some form of seafaring trade between South America and Mesoamerica even at this early date.

D. DONNE BRYANT STOCK

This remarkably sophisticated pottery was produced during the Barra phase (1600 BC to 1400 BC) of the Early Preclassic period in the Soconusco region, on the Pacific coast of Chiapas, in Mexico.

COPÁN: THE CLASSIC MAYA CENTER

WILLIAM L. FASH

THE DISTINGUISHED MAYA SCHOLAR Sylvanus Morley believed that "Copán may be aptly called 'the Athens of the New World', a title the writer has been wont to bestow upon her in drawing analogies from the ancient cities of the Old World ... it may be claimed with perfect assurance that no other city of aboriginal America ever attained so high a level of cultural achievement."

Morley's enthusiasm comes as no surprise given the grace and beauty of Copán's art and architecture, and the fact that Copán, in present-day Honduras, contains more hieroglyphic inscriptions and sculptured monuments than any other Maya ruin—or any other site in the New World, for that matter. The sculptors who shaped Copán's soft, green, volcanic stone succeeded where most of their contemporaries failed, creating reliefs of great depth and sometimes carving fully in the round. Theirs is a style of sculpture that appeals to Western aesthetics, with its appreciation of naturalism and movement. Given the abundance of dateable inscriptions, the clearly defined styles of art and architecture, and the sheer number of sculptures at Copán—including tens of thousands of surface fragments of the mosaic sculpture that once adorned the facades of the Acropolis temples and other important buildings—it is little wonder that Copán is seen to be of such central importance in Maya archaeology.

WILLIAM L. FASH

A mosaic sculpture of the Maya maize god, from an elite residential complex about a kilometer (two-thirds of a mile) east of the civic-ceremonial center at Copán, in Honduras.

Settlement Patterns

Excavations in Copán in recent years have gone a long way towards giving us an insight into the ancient city's ecological setting and into the lives of the people who created such a wealth of monuments to their illustrious god-kings. In the mid-1970s, Gordon Willey pioneered a study of settlement patterns and human ecology that set the course for a subsequent series of projects sponsored by the Honduran government and directed by Claude Baudez, William Sanders, and David Webster. This research has shown that, about AD 800, a peak population of about 20,000 people lived within the 24 square kilometer (9 square mile) area of the Copán Valley immediately adjacent to the site-core, whose ruins are known as the Principal Group.

The remnants of the Copán Valley settlements consist of so-called house-mounds, the ruins of stone platforms that once supported buildings of stone or perishable materials, generally arranged in groups around patios. Willey divided them into four types, which have proved to be accurate reflections of their occupants' relative social status. Type 1 sites consist of small groups of low stone platforms that supported perishable dwellings where commoners, and perhaps slaves, lived. Type 2 sites are slightly larger, with structures grouped around one or more patios and stone platforms up to 2.5 meters (8 feet) high. These were the abodes of what could be called the lower middle class. Type 3 sites are both larger and more complex, with platforms up to 4.5 meters (15 feet) high, some of which support vaulted masonry structures that are sometimes decorated with elaborate sculptures. These are thought to have been the residences of the lower nobility. Type 4 sites are very large, multipatio compounds, whose architecture varies greatly in terms of size and elaborateness. The largest buildings contain vaulted, sumptuously decorated masonry palaces, with hieroglyphic inscriptions detailing the genealogy of the noble families that once resided there.

The investigations directed by Baudez and Sanders within the site-core have recently been followed up by a larger project known as the Copán Mosaics Project (now incorporated in the Copán Acropolis Archaeological Project), directed by the author and similarly sponsored by the government of Honduras, as well as by research institutions in the United States. This research has enabled us to describe and explain the ideological changes brought about by the last four Copán rulers (18 Rabbit, Smoke-Monkey, Smoke-Shell, and Yax Pac) in response to the political and ecological pressures under which they reigned. One of the project's objectives was to locate, document, analyze, and reconstruct what proved to be more than 30,000 fragments of the tenoned mosaic facade sculpture scattered about the surface of the Principal Group. This work has involved the coordinated efforts of archaeologists, epigraphers, artists and art historians, architectural restorers, and conservation specialists, and has produced a wealth of new information about the religion, political symbolism, dynastic history, and government strategies of Copán's rulers. Recently, by tunneling into the temple-pyramids of the Acropolis, we have uncovered early monuments and hieroglyphic texts relating to the earlier rulers, and these have added much to our understanding of historiography and statecraft within this ancient centre.

WILLIAM L. FASH

This head of a royal scepter, of elaborately carved flint, formed part of a temple offering in the Rosalila Structure. It had been wrapped in cloth.

Looking down on the ballcourt from the upper steps of the Hieroglyphic Stairway of the Temple of Structure 26. This ballcourt was situated in the very center of the city, reflecting the ritual importance of ball games for kings and commoners alike.

The Hieroglyphic Stairway bears the longest inscribed text of the pre-Columbian Americas. It records the glorious deeds of 15 of the 16 Copán kings, who are portrayed on the stairs and the temple at its head.

A Succession of Kings

A dynasty of 16 kings was founded in AD 426 by the ruler K'inich Yax K'uk Mo' (Sun-eyed New Quetzal Macaw), who claimed to have obtained the symbols of office from outside Copán and wore the goggles and bird imagery characteristic of Teotihuacan warrior-merchants. His successors expanded Copán's domain—which at its height, in the sixth and seventh centuries AD, may have been as large as 500 square kilometers (190 square miles)—only to see it contract during times of competition and crisis in the eighth century. A particularly dramatic event was the capture and decapitation of the thirteenth Copán king, 18 Rabbit (who reigned from AD 695 to AD 738), by a vassal from the formerly subservient center of Quirigua, some 70 kilometers (40 miles) away. The fourteenth Copán ruler, Smoke-Monkey (who ruled from AD 738 to AD 746), built a Council House known as *popol nah*, or the mat house, whose facade bore sculptured images of the mat that symbolized political authority, the hieroglyphic names of the eight most important communities in the kingdom, and portraits of his councilors seated above the names of their respective communities—as if to publicly acknowledge the importance of his subordinates, while at the same time making them responsible for the kingdom's future. The fifteenth ruler, Smoke-Shell (who reigned from AD 746 to AD 763), built the Hieroglyphic Stairway and Temple, which is inscribed with more than 1,200 glyphs recording the days of glory of all previous Copán kings and adorned with portraits of the rulers attired as warriors.

The sixteenth and final ruler, Yax Pac (New Dawn), reigned from AD 763 to AD 820 and built two large temple-pyramids that mirrored the imagery and themes of his predecessors. He made regular visits to the nobles in their palaces in the valley, and dedicated several hieroglyphic monuments in their honor during elaborate ceremonies. Ultimately, his long and distinguished reign was overshadowed by the fact that the Copánecs could not agree on his successor. After an interregnum of nearly two years, a pretender to royal power started to build, but never completed, a stone altar hailing his "accession" in AD 822.

After that time, no new monuments were added to the Principal Group, although periodic burials and other ceremonies took place there, and the two ballcourts continued in use. Evidence gathered by William Sanders, David Webster, and their students has shown that while the houses of the noble families in the Copán Valley were continually occupied in this period, and some new buildings were constructed, the commoners gradually migrated from the crowded, unsanitary city center, in search of more fertile land and to escape both from communicable diseases and from the increasing demands made by the elite.

WILLIAM L. FASH

This jade statuette of an early Copán king was part of a ritual offering buried under the Hieroglyphic Stairway on the day the stairway was dedicated.

WILLIAM L. FASH

Slightly larger than the statuette shown above, this Maya god formed part of the same ritual offering. The markings on the face and body identify this deity as the patron of a month in the solar calendar.

Temple I in Tikal was the funerary temple of Ruler A (or "Ah Cacao"), a distinguished Late Classic king who reigned from AD 682 to AD 734 and oversaw the refurbishment of the entire area of the North Acropolis and Great Plaza (including the soaring Temples I and II). The temple is seen here from the Central Acropolis, which was the residence of the royal family and the members of the royal court.

Olmec Culture and the Middle Preclassic Period

Referred to as the Mother Culture of Mesoamerica, the Olmec culture flourished from 1200 BC to 300 BC in the Gulf Coast states of Veracruz and Tabasco, in Mexico. It set the pattern of civilized life in this region, encompassing such developments as monumental art and architecture, an elaborate cosmology, and the divine right of kings. Elites in all parts of Mesoamerica emulated the Olmec chiefs, and sought to acquire goods from them and to exchange ideas with them through emissaries and visits.

In the Maya area, by the beginning of the Middle Preclassic period (1000 BC to 300 BC), the cultural impetus had shifted northwards. Evidence from a number of sites in the upland zones of the Maya area shows that the culture in this region was becoming more complex. At Abaj Takalik, in the piedmont zone of southern Guatemala, an impressive range of monumental stone art and architecture has been found. Excavations by John Graham and Miguel Orrego have uncovered a number of monumental sculptures, among which are represented all the styles of stone monuments found in the Olmec heartland except for tabletop altars. Indeed, Graham believes that the origins of the colossal stone heads characteristic of the Olmec culture, an example of which he found at Abaj Takalik, are to be found in this region rather than in the Olmec area itself.

Other scholars doubt that Olmec culture started in the Maya area, but do note the presence and significance of Olmec cultural elements at a number of Maya sites. These include Olmec-style sculptures and monumental architecture at Chalchuapa, in El Salvador; Olmec-style design motifs and numerous jade offerings in burials at Copán, in Honduras; an Olmec-style votive cache, complete with a jade bloodletter (a ritualistic instrument used in sacrifices), at Seibal, in Guatemala; and numerous jade, celt (stone axe), and ceramic offerings in upland Chiapas that are clearly similar to Olmec ritual offerings. All these finds indicate that there was a lively system of exchange between the southern Maya area and the Olmec heartland during the early part of the first millennium BC. Recently, E. Wyllys Andrews has documented an impressive cache of Olmec artifacts at Oxpenul, in Yucatán, arguing that there was active trading between that region also and the Olmec heartland during the Middle Preclassic period.

The Late Preclassic Period

Excavations in the 1930s by the Carnegie Institution of Washington at the site of Uaxactún, in the heart of the northern Guatemalan rainforest of El Petén, brought to light a fascinating Late Preclassic (300 BC to AD 250) structure in the form of a small pyramid, known prosaically as "E-VII-sub". Its most intriguing feature was the stucco anthropomorphic masks flanking the stairway, which had mouths strikingly similar to the drooping mouths found on Olmec monumental and portable art. This find opened archaeologists' eyes to the possibility that the Preclassic period in the Maya area had been much more than just a prelude to the compelling art and architecture of the Classic period.

That promise has recently been fulfilled by the excavation of impressive Preclassic remains at a number of sites in the core area of the southern Maya lowlands. From 1958 to 1971, the University of Pennsylvania, in collaboration with the government of Guatemala, conducted a massive research and restoration project at the ruins of Tikal. Under the direction of William Coe, a great deal of decorated Late Preclassic and Early Classic architecture from the massive North Acropolis, in the heart of that ancient Maya metropolis, was uncovered. At the site of Cerros, in northern Belize, David Freidel has excavated Late Preclassic architecture whose imagery has helped scholars to unlock the meaning behind the stucco masks and has given us an insight into the nature of early Maya kingship. The massive site of El Mirador, north of Tikal, is now known to have been occupied in Preclassic times by an extremely large, dense, and tightly nucleated population, who built some of the largest man-made structures in the Americas in the last centuries of the pre-Christian era. Indeed, the monumental architecture of El Mirador is larger in scale than that of the central zone of Classic Tikal, and compares favorably with that of Teotihuacan, which also flourished after the heyday of El Mirador.

Near the city of El Mirador, and connected to it by a broad elevated causeway known in Yucatec Maya as a *sacbe*, or white road, is the

SASSOON/ROBERT HARDING PICTURE LIBRARY

This Late Preclassic stela from Kaminaljuyú, in Guatemala, depicts a highland Maya ruler dressed as a god and wearing a headdress representing the head of the patron deity of Maya rulers. Impersonating gods in this way was a central feature of a Maya ruler's ritual repertoire.
FILMTEAM/D. DONNE BRYANT STOCK

large site of Nakbe (which means "by the side of the road"). Rediscovered in the 1960s by Ian Graham, along with El Mirador and other important sites in this area, Nakbe has yielded even earlier remains of complex forms of art and architecture than its neighbors: recent excavations by Richard Hansen have shown it to have some of the earliest examples of monumental art, pictorial stone sculpture featuring human figures, and hieroglyphic inscriptions in the Maya area. Hansen's evidence supports the growing body of data indicating that the people of Nakbe and other Late Preclassic centers of the southern lowlands were among the earliest Maya peoples to use the hieroglyphic script that was to become widespread during the Classic period.

The highlands and Pacific piedmont areas also experienced rapid development during the Late Preclassic period. Sites such as Abaj Takalik, El Baul, Chiapa de Corzo, and Kaminaljuyú all boasted elaborate stone sculptures with hieroglyphic writing, and the people of Izapa developed a highly figurative and narrative style of art that many scholars believe represents a transition between Olmec and Maya art. The center of Kaminaljuyú, which stood on the site of present-day Guatemala City, was ruled by chiefs who had access to goods that came from

THE MAYA: 2000 BC – AD 1524

	GENERAL CULTURAL PERIODS	PACIFIC PLAIN AND HIGHLANDS	SOUTHERN LOWLANDS	NORTHERN LOWLANDS
1524	Colonial AD 1524 +	Spanish conquest Conquest and formation of states by Quiche and Cakchiquel	Cortéz expedition visits Tayasal and Nito	Spanish conquest Political fragmentation Fall of Mayapán
	Postclassic AD 900 – AD 1524	Penetration of Quiche warrior elites into highlands from Gulf Coast	Itzá occupation of Lago Petén Itzá region	Mayapán domination Chichén Itzá abandoned Domination by Chichén Itzá
1000	Terminal Classic AD 800 – AD 900	Occupation of hilltop and fortified sites	Population loss; many centers eventually abandoned Putun Maya expansion	Reoccupation of Chichén Itzá by Itzá Putun Maya expansion
	Late Classic AD 550 – AD 800	Corzumalhuapa sculptural style	Most lowland centers reach peak population and size	Growth in size and population of many centers
500	Classic AD 250 – AD 900			First sculptured stone monuments with hieroglyphic texts and dates; development of dynastic rule (beginnings of state systems)
	Early Classic AD 250 – AD 550	Kaminaljuyú mimics Teotihuacan architecture; possibly port-of-trade for lowlands	Expansion of Maya elite culture into peripheries of lowlands	
	Protoclassic AD 100 – AD 250	Eruption of Ilopango Many southern sites reach peak population and size	Initial sculptured stone monuments; development of dynastic rule	
AD 1	Late Preclassic 300 BC – AD 250	Sculptured stone monuments, often with hieroglyphic texts and dates; probable development of dynastic rule (beginnings of state systems)	Initial monumental architecture, including tombs and stucco-decorated facades	Early monumental architecture (beginnings of complex social, political, and economic systems)
500			Expansion of settlement into nonriverine areas	
	Middle Preclassic 1000 BC – 300 BC	Olmec influences in Maya area, with probable Olmec "colonies" along Pacific coastal plain; early monumental sculpture and architecture (beginnings of complex social, political, and economic systems)		
1000			Expansion of settlement along rivers into lowlands Beginnings of village life at Cuello and coastal Belize	
1500	Early Preclassic 2000 BC – 1000 BC			
2000 BC		Early sedentism along the Pacific coast (beginnings of village life?)		Early sedentism at Loltun and Mani (?)

A detail from the stucco facade of a building in Toniná, Chiapas, showing a supernatural animal participating in an important ritual in the Maya underworld.

far and wide and were buried in elaborate tombs along with hundreds of ceramic vessels and other finely crafted offerings.

In the northern lowlands, too, sites such as Komchen and Edzná had large populations in the Late Preclassic period. A very early bas-relief sculpture in the cave of Loltun is similar to the stone art of its more southerly contemporaries in terms of its artistic style and the religious rituals it depicts. At Edzná, raised fields have been discovered that converted swamplands into highly productive, intensively cultivated agricultural lands. The same practice is believed to lie behind the large growth in population at El Mirador that made possible the construction of such enormous public works.

Three major developments: the growth of El Mirador into the largest urban center of its day in Mesoamerica, the widespread use of monumental art and architecture (sometimes embellished with hieroglyphic writing) throughout the Maya world, and the archaeological evidence indicating that nearly all parts of the Maya area were occupied both extensively and intensively during the Preclassic period, together show that far from being merely a stepping stone to, or precursor of, the later developments of the Classic period,

The five-storied Temple of Edzná, in Campeche. The rooms of the first four "stories" of this pyramid were built onto the exterior walls of four rubble-filled terraces. The surmounting temple is of a more conventional form.

the Preclassic period witnessed the emergence of civilization and urbanism in this part of Mesoamerica. The cultural patterns laid down during the Preclassic period (and elaborated during the ensuing Protoclassic period) set the stage for the flowering of Maya culture during the succeeding Classic epoch.

The Classic Period

During the Classic period (AD 250 to AD 900), Maya culture everywhere reached a peak, although developments were particularly dramatic in the core area of the southern lowlands. Western scholars named this period the "Classic", because it was the time when the Maya peoples dedicated themselves to those cultural endeavors that were most appealing to researchers familiar with the Classical civilizations of the Mediterranean world. Their legacy includes elaborate hieroglyphic inscriptions bearing dates in the linear system of time-reckoning known as the "Long Count"; beautiful bas-relief sculptures in stone, and modeled and incised works in stucco, bone, wood, and other media; massive yet graceful architectural monuments featuring corbeled (or "false arch") roofs; and spectacular polychrome pottery decorated with mythological scenes and hieroglyphic texts.

Although the southern Maya area, including the Pacific coast, piedmont, and highland zones, was at the forefront of cultural innovation for most of the Preclassic period, it was the dense tropical rainforest of the southern lowlands that saw the greatest achievements in urban development, art, and architecture during the Late Preclassic and Classic periods. But the abandoned cities of the core area have yet to yield up all their answers to the questions that continue to intrigue scholars: how were the Maya able to rise to such cultural heights in this challenging environment, and why were they eventually forced to abandon these centers?

The Rise of Tikal

Tikal, in northern Guatemala, assumed the mantle of the largest Maya city after El Mirador declined in population and importance in the early centuries of the Christian era. Excavations at the North Acropolis of Tikal by William Coe and his University of Pennsylvania Tikal Project colleagues,

D. DONNE BRYANT STOCK

The North Acropolis of Tikal, in northern Guatemala, as seen from Temple I. This complex of temples served as the burial ground for most of the Tikal kings throughout the Classic period. Buried below the complex are constructions dating back to the origins of the city, about 500 BC.

PRIVATE COLLECTION, NEW YORK/WERNER FORMAN ARCHIVE

This terracotta incense burner from Palenque, in Chiapas, Mexico, depicts the face of the jaguar sun-god, complete with jaguar ears.

and subsequently at other parts of the site by Juan Pedro Laporte, have shown that the city's population and the number of public works projects carried out increased dramatically during what can be seen as two major bursts of activity. The first took place between the beginning of the first century AD and AD 75 (which Coe refers to as "Time Span 11"), when roughly 23 percent of the buildings comprising the North Acropolis and the Great Plaza (the heart of ancient Tikal) were constructed. The second occurred between AD 170 and AD 325 (Coe's "Time Spans 8 and 9"), when a further 25 percent of the buildings at these two sites were added.

This latter burst of building activity at the center of Tikal corresponds roughly to a period of time some scholars refer to as the Protoclassic (about AD 100 to AD 250). The transition to the cultural patterns refined during the Classic period is thought to have taken place during this time, fueled in part by population pressure and intense competition between emerging centers. But what were these centers like? How were they organized, who ruled them, and what was the purpose of their monuments?

Civic-Ceremonial Centers in the Jungle

During the early stages of the decipherment of the Maya hieroglyphic script, scholars concluded that Maya stone monuments and the few surviving bark-paper books reflected an obsessive preoccupation with the movements of the sun, moon, and stars, and their endless, cyclical repetition over the millennia. Early decipherments of some of the Long Count (also known as the Initial Series) dates showed that they recorded events stretching millions of years back in the past and forward into the future. These readings fueled speculation that the purpose of the stone monuments was to appease the gods and to record the astrological predictions of astronomer-priests whose task it was to weigh up the influence of the various gods associated with the heavenly bodies, the months, the days, and even the numbers themselves. When the calendar resulted in the pairing of a "lucky" day number with an "unlucky" day name, month, or year, it was for them to decide which influence was the stronger one for a particular purpose. These priests, it was reasoned, lived exclusively in the temple-pyramids found at the core of each Maya center, ruling as a benevolent theocracy over peasant farmers scattered throughout the countryside. The common people were thought to have visited the temples solely for important ceremonies and for the purpose of raising ever higher monuments to the gods, giving rise to the notion that the site-cores of such ruins as Tikal, Palenque, and Copán were "vacant ceremonial centers".

This view of ancient Maya society, along with the "vacant ceremonial center" model, were demolished by two significant advances in Maya studies made during the late 1950s and early

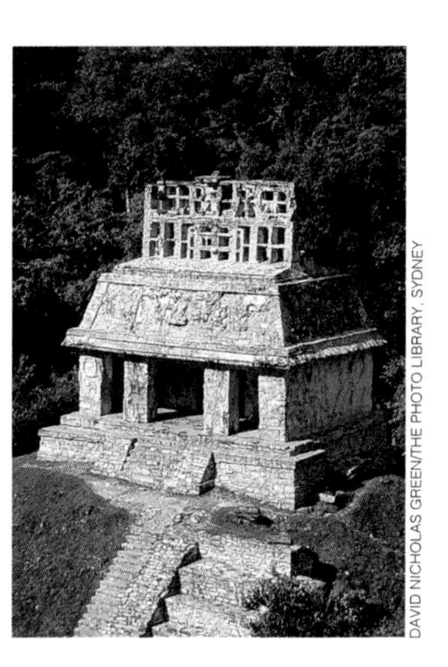

DAVID NICHOLAS GREEN/THE PHOTO LIBRARY, SYDNEY

The Temple of the Sun, in Palenque, is named for the jaguar sun-shield, a shield bearing the visage of the jaguar sun-god, which is the central image on the beautiful bas-relief panel in the inner sanctuary. The Maya believed that when the sun set in the west, it had to fight off the jaguars in the underworld in order to rise, triumphant, in the east the next morning.

A detail from Altar Q at Copán, showing 2 of the 16 kings carved into its four sides. Each king sits on a hieroglyphic throne that bears his name.

Stela H at Copán shows the king known as 18 Rabbit bedecked in a feminine costume for an important ritual. The creator god of many present-day Maya groups has both male and female attributes.

1960s. In a new series of readings that has come to be called the "epigraphic revolution", the historical parts of the Maya hieroglyphic texts were deciphered, and this led to the realization that the Maya political leaders were just as vainglorious and materially oriented as leaders in other parts of the globe. At the same time, the scientific revolution in archaeology resulted in more accurate dating methods and a better understanding of the ecological and economic underpinnings of Maya culture, and also allowed the archaeological remains of the house-mounds (the decayed remnants of stone platforms that once supported stone or perishable buildings) of entire regions to be precisely mapped, revealing that the site-cores were, in fact, administrative centers for vast, densely packed residential areas.

The epigraphic revolution began with Heinrich Berlin's decipherment of the names of the different Maya city-states (or "emblem glyphs") and the recognition by Tatiana Proskouriakoff that the dates in the Classic Maya stone inscriptions did not refer only to mythological time but also recorded the birth, the accession to power, the important conquests and anniversaries, and the death of named Maya rulers, who were the individuals portrayed on the numerous slab-like statues (or stelae) and altars. Yurii Knorosov's subsequent discovery that the Maya writing system was, in fact, a mixed script with a fundamental phonetic component has since led to a burst of new decipherments. Writings on subjects not previously encountered by glyphic experts are now being deciphered at a blistering pace. Records of royal visits; marriage alliances between royal houses; place names; the names of monuments and buildings, subsidiary lords, and political offices; and many other records are once more being read. The phonetic approach enables scholars to translate the dates, names, places, and events that were central to ancient Maya history directly into ancient Mayan languages. (See the feature *Maya Hieroglyphic Writing*.)

In terms of archaeological methods, a more scientifically rigorous approach to designing research projects, as well as to excavation methods, surveying and mapping techniques, and materials analysis, has produced a treasure trove of new information about the nature of ancient Maya societies and how they adapted to their physical environments. In particular, the study of Maya settlement and land utilization patterns has given us dramatic new insights into the size and complexity of the Maya city-states.

The pioneer of settlement pattern studies, Gordon Willey, of Harvard University, whose distinguished career of field work extended from the 1950s through to the late 1970s, showed that there were densely packed residential zones in close proximity to the centers of Seibal, Altar de Sacrificios, and Copán, and, somewhat more surprisingly, also in an area previously thought to have been relatively rural, the Belize River Valley. Not only were there thousands of house-mounds, but their arrangement and size indicated that there were different levels of status within Classic

Maya society. Excavations at these sites revealed that segments of the general population shared the trappings of elite culture to a greater degree than the old theocracy model had postulated. Ongoing studies of both archaeological remains and hieroglyphic inscriptions are revealing that there was a great deal of variation in the kinds and degrees of economic and political ranking in Maya society, both within and between the different centers.

Agricultural Practices

Studies of the ecological setting of the ancient Maya world have also shown, not unexpectedly, that agricultural practices were very diverse and often adapted to particular localities. The old view of Maya agriculture was that it was based on a simple slash-and-burn, or swidden, system. From observations of modern-day practices in some areas, scholars concluded that in ancient times, plots were cleared in the forest by felling and burning off trees and vegetation, and then planted with maize, beans, and squash (the Mesoamerican "trinity"), which were cultivated there for a few years. Thereafter, the plot was allowed to revert to forest to enable the soil to regain precious nutrients, only to be cleared once more after a fallow period of between 5 and 10 years. It was believed that this type of subsistence system could not possibly have sustained large numbers of people—in the order of 5 to 10 million for the entire Maya area—lending support to the then entrenched notion of small populations of peasant farmers scattered through the countryside. The large, dense populations revealed by the surveys of settlement patterns contradicted these views, and forced botanists, palynologists, and cultural geographers to come up with new models for Maya agricultural practices that would explain how so many people could thrive for so long, particularly in the southern lowlands rainforest.

New studies of fossil pollen recovered from lake beds and swamps, of botanical remains found in archaeological contexts, and of the remnants of such structures as raised fields in swampy areas and stone-lined terraces on hillsides—indicating that land was intensively cultivated—have shown that many innovations in agricultural practices took place during the Preclassic and Classic periods. In the highlands and upland areas, terracing reduced soil loss from erosion and maintained higher humidity levels in the topsoil thus retained. In the tropical lowland areas, the work of botanists and pollen experts, including Fred Wiseman and Nicholas Dunning, has shown that the Maya increased agricultural productivity by planting their tree crops and garden plots so as to mimic the biodiversity of life in the rainforest, maintaining the different canopy levels and dispersing different species over wide areas. In their subsistence strategies as well as in their level of social and political development, the Maya were considerably more sophisticated than Western scholars had earlier believed. Indeed, the modern world has a great deal to learn from the ancient Maya about how to maintain large human populations for hundreds of years within a stable rainforest environment.

Nobility and Commoners

The picture of Classic Maya life that is emerging after a century of scholarly investigation is that of a complex society very much like other preindustrial state societies. The Classic Maya centers ranged in size from small towns, such as Bonampak, to big cities controlling large territories. At its peak, Tikal is estimated to have accommodated 70,000 people within the 12 square kilometers (about 5 square miles) that constituted the heart of the city, with several thousand more people scattered in its rural hinterland. These centers were ruled by hereditary elites, with the office of god-king (*ch'ul ahau*, meaning holy lord) passed on from father to son, or to another eligible noble if the sons of the previous king were considered unworthy. In Yucatán, at the time of the Spanish conquest in the sixteenth century, the ruler's second sons were inducted into the priesthood, whose ranks were made up entirely of the sons of nobles.

Excavations at the residential compounds of noble families have shown that nobles were able to commission impressive works of art and architecture, with their own name, title, and genealogy literally carved into the stone. Adjoining buildings are thought to have been the living quarters of their offspring and some of their servants. During the Classic period, the nobility probably controlled the best agricultural land close to the centers, along with the labor of the peasants who worked the soil.

L. GIRARD/EXPLORER/AUSCAPE

Like their ancient forebears, the present-day Maya near Lake Atitlán, in Guatemala, use terracing to allow them to grow crops on the steep hillsides. Maize, prepared in various ways, is not only the Maya's main staple but also their favorite food. In the *Popol Vuh* (or "Book of Counsel") of the Quiche Maya, and in other less well-known accounts, the ancient Maya referred to themselves as the Maize People, believing that their creator fashioned them from corn.

The tower that rises above the royal residences and shrines at the Palace of Palenque, in Mexico, provides a commanding view of the lowland plain to the north. Many of the palace buildings contain important inscriptions, paintings and stucco reliefs.

ALAIN THOMAS/EXPLORER/AUSCAPE

MAYA HIEROGLYPHIC WRITING

DAVID STUART

ONE OF THE HALLMARKS of Maya civilization is its complex system of hieroglyphic writing. But the Maya were not unique among ancient Mesoamericans in possessing a writing system. To the west, in what is now Oaxaca and Veracruz, earlier cultures had developed and refined writing systems that, although still largely undeciphered, have many principles and visual elements in common with the Maya script, including oval or rectangular signs and the use of a columnar format in texts. While the origins of these systems remain obscure, it appears that several early Mesoamerican cultures developed scripts with similar characteristics at about the same time. The Maya script was by far the longest-lived, coming into use about AD 100 and surviving until the Spanish conquest of the last of the Maya people in the late seventeenth century.

Hieroglyphic inscriptions are found mainly in the lowlands of the Maya area, at sites associated with the Classic period of Maya civilization, including Tikal, Palenque, Copán, Calakmul, and many other smaller city-states. At the time of the Spanish conquest, this broad area was occupied by speakers of two branches of the Mayan language family, called Cholan and Yucatecan. The vast majority of extant hieroglyphic texts are thought to belong to these two languages. Modern linguists have identified more than 30 different Mayan languages, most of which are spoken in the highland areas, which did not possess Maya hieroglyphic writing.

D. DONNE BRYANT STOCK

A large *ahau* (a hieroglyph representing one of the 20 days of the Maya calendar) painted on a ceramic vessel of the Late Classic period. Pottery texts often take the form of dedications specifying the ritual uses, and the owner, of the pot.

This elegantly incised stone panel, known as the "Tablet of the 96 Glyphs", was excavated at Palenque, in Mexico.

D. DONNE BRYANT STOCK

An Intricate Script

At first glance, Maya inscriptions, most commonly carved in stone or painted on pottery, might seem absurdly intricate. Like Egyptian hieroglyphs, Maya writing was always highly pictorial, its thousand or so signs representing animals, supernatural beings, parts of the body, and objects from nature and daily life. This visual complexity hindered decipherment for many years, and it was assumed that each sign must have a subtle range of meanings associated with the actual image. Today, we know that the system was not quite so complicated.

Almost all Maya signs can be grouped into one of two categories: logographs, or word-signs, and syllables. Logographs include, for example, the sign for "hill", which is pronounced *wits* (like the English "wheats") in Mayan. We probably would not recognize this sign as a representation of a hill or mountain,

LOGOGRAPHS AND SYLLABLES

wits or hill

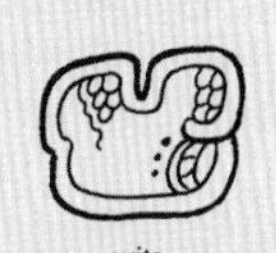

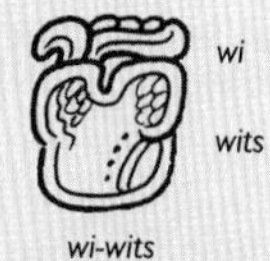

pakal or shield

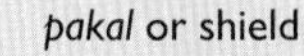

ILLUSTRATION: DAVID STUART

J.P. COURAUD/D. DONNE BRYANT STOCK

Part of Copán's great Hieroglyphic Stairway, which was dedicated in the mid-eighth century AD and recounts the city's dynastic history from the early fifth century AD.

D. DONNE BRYANT STOCK

but the image resembles supernatural mountain spirits that are portrayed throughout Maya art. Sometimes, the sign for the syllable *wi* is attached to the hill sign. This syllable functions simply as a phonetic prefix. In fact, scribes could drop the hill logograph altogether and spell the word with the combination *wi-tsi*. Another illustration of the way Maya signs work is provided by the glyph for "shield", pronounced *pakal*. The *pakal* logograph is a simple representation of a round war shield. Often, however, it is also written with *pakal* and a final *la* complement, or simply by the syllabic combination *pa-ka-la*.

Apart from straightforward choices between logographs, syllables, and combinations thereof, one feature of the script that makes Maya writing very complicated is the principle of substitution. Both logographs and syllables have many variant forms, and may be replaced by completely different signs that are functional equivalents. Note, for instance, the different signs that stand for the syllables *pa*, *ka*, and *la* in *pakal*. These are called allographs. The syllable *na*, to take another example, can be written with six distinct signs, with apparently no real difference in meaning. The vast assortment of signs, therefore, can be classified into sign sets that have logographic or syllabic readings in common. Decipherment largely involves working out such equivalences and discovering their phonetic values.

A Key to the Past

Since we are closer to reading entire inscriptions than we were even 10 years ago, what new insights do we have into Maya civilization itself? The hieroglyphic texts on stone monuments record the dynastic histories and ritual activities associated with the many city-states that dotted the southern Maya lowlands during the Classic period. Sites such as Copán and Palenque have fairly complete lists of kings extending over several centuries. More recently, texts identifying different political and ritual offices have been deciphered, revealing previously unknown details of the internal structure of Maya city-states. Moreover, detailed records of the relationships between some of these polities reveal wars and alliances that shaped the history of the Classic Maya civilization until its rapid collapse in the ninth century. Aside from historical events, the window on Maya religion has been very revealing, providing the names of deities and supernatural beings, and describing aspects of the Maya world view that can be clearly linked with aspects of modern Maya culture.

A collection of the plaster hieroglyphs that fell from the facade of Temple 18 at Palenque, in Mexico. The temple itself still stands. These hieroglyphs formed part of an important historical inscription that is now too jumbled to be deciphered.

The Great Ballcourt at Chichén Itzá, in Yucatán, is the largest of all the ballcourts in Mesoamerica. It was the scene of spirited competition and also of occasional human sacrifice.

A rubber ball had to pass through this carved ring in the Great Ballcourt at Chichén Itzá—no mean feat, given its considerable height above the playing field.

These rural landholdings are what allowed them to maintain their lavish way of life, and from the combined evidence of Maya settlement patterns and the practices recorded by sixteenth-century Spanish priests, it seems likely that the nobility would also have maintained elaborate country estates within their confines.

Other commoners lived in independent so-called patio groups—the smallest unit of Maya settlement, comprising two or more structures fronting a shared patio—on the lands belonging to noble families, or, in more rural settings, on plots of land they had cleared for themselves. The commoners were probably dazzled by the brilliantly painted and sculptured monuments erected in the site-cores by the god-kings in honor of their ancestors and the gods themselves, and by the elaborate ceremonies and ritual ball games that took place there. Ball games were considered to perpetuate natural cycles, such as the movement of the sun and other celestial bodies, the transition of the seasons, and, above all, the timely rains on which agricultural fertility depended. The wide roads found within and between the centers indicate that thousands of people made pilgrimage to and were witness to, if not participants in, the public pageants staged by the god-kings. It was by means of such ceremonies, as well as by intervening with the gods and royal ancestors and expressing their concern for their people, that the god-kings maintained the loyalty of (and tribute from) commoners and nobles alike.

Yet one cannot escape the feeling that the common people were ultimately more concerned with their own agricultural pursuits, and with the spirits of the forest and the skies that made it possible for their maize fields (*milpa*) to produce a good harvest each year. Kings who were successful in producing good rains and abundant harvests had the people's support; those who were less successful probably did not. For commoners, life during the Classic period was probably not so different from what it had been before or was after. Slavery existed during the Postclassic period, however, and probably also during the Classic period, if not earlier. There was thus a great deal of social inequality in the ancient Maya world, just as there has been in virtually every other civilized society.

War and Politics

The mastery of such agricultural techniques as raised fields dates back to the Late Preclassic period, and helps to explain why so many centers were able to draw large numbers of people into their service. Less easily understood is why a city-state of the size and complexity of El Mirador eventually declined and was eclipsed by Tikal and other centers. Why, also, did Tikal have its ups and downs, with periods of great growth, during which many public works were constructed (Coe's "Time Spans 11, 8, and 4"), interspersed with times of little activity? Indeed, the end of the sixth century AD is often referred to as the hiatus, because of the paucity of inscribed and dated public monuments from that period at Tikal and several neighboring centers. Two reasons for this have been put forward.

As the Classic period wore on, the inscriptions blazoned on the public monuments of art and architecture that were the centerpieces of the Classic Maya cities recorded the events of war, the taking of captives, and conquests with increasing frequency. From the warrior figures adorning temples, stelae, and mural paintings, such as those that survive at the ruins of Bonampak, and from references in hieroglyphic texts, it is obvious that success in war was an important means by which the Maya god-kings built and maintained their political prestige. (See the feature *The Wall Paintings of Bonampak*.) Inscriptions at a particular site often refer to an episode in which that site prevailed over another site in a so-called "war event". Caracol claimed to have prevailed over Tikal in two such "war events", and the center of Dos Pilas claimed to have captured a Tikal king and to have sacrificed him in an elaborate ceremony in the royal court at Dos Pilas. Of great interest is that the hiatus at Tikal corresponds to the years that followed the first such encounter with Caracol, in AD 556. Furthermore, Arlen and Diane Chase have found that the population of Caracol increased some 325 percent in the 130 years after the "war event" against Tikal, and believe that this was due to the Caracol rulers' success in attracting the population of the vanquished Tikal to their center.

Another reason that has been put forward for the waxing and waning of most Classic Maya centers is the structure of their political system. Arthur Demarest has suggested that the Classic Maya city-states were similar to the competing segmentary state systems of Southeast Asia, which Stanley Tambiah has referred to as "pulsating galactic polities" or "theater states". Such political entities are characterized by weak control over the land and its products, with political authority based more on the ruler's charismatic leadership, and on the frequency and effectiveness of his ritual displays of concern for his subjects, than on real, institutionalized power. This combination results in a highly volatile

GEORGE HOLTON/PHOTO RESEARCHERS, INC

political landscape, with competing towns and cities constantly expanding or contracting according to the political fortunes and prestige of their individual rulers—hence the so-called "pulsating" effect, with one polity growing as another one recedes in size and importance. Such a political system has so many inherent structural weaknesses that political unification under a single royal house is extremely difficult.

As the landscape filled with ever greater numbers of people, and more centers were competing for land, subjects, and access to such elite trade goods as jade, quetzal feathers, prized ceramics, and other prestigious products, the stakes of warfare rose and war probably came to have a greater effect on the common people. Add to the long-term problem of political instability a number of short-term crises—communicable diseases, shortfalls of staples during years of bad harvests, disruption of trade routes by outsiders, ethnic conflicts with neighboring Maya and non-Maya peoples—and it is clear that the Classic Maya civilization was doomed to decline.

The Collapse of Classic Maya

Perhaps no other question in the field of New World archaeology has attracted as much scholarly and popular attention as the causes of this collapse. The process is hardly unique to the Maya, but perhaps because of the encroachment of tropical

Stela 1 at Bonampak, in Chiapas, Mexico, portrays a ruler of the Late Classic period. This small, short-lived center yielded one of the world's great artistic treasures in the form of a series of beautifully painted murals. The few stone carvings discovered at this site are also exceptionally well executed.

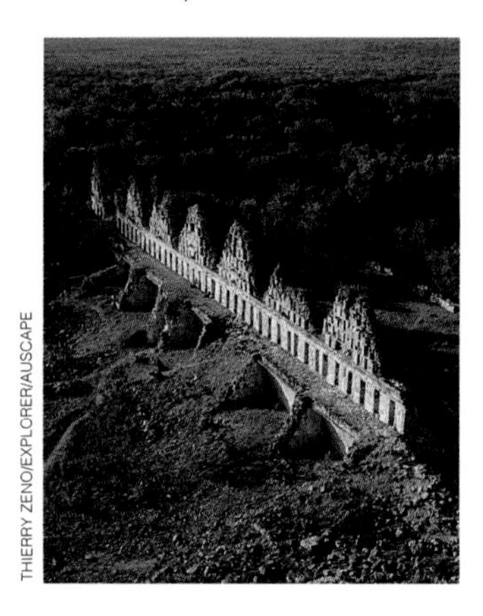

THIERRY ZENO/EXPLORER/AUSCAPE

The elaborate roof crest of the Temple of the Doves, at Uxmal, in Yucatán, is a masterwork of Puuc-style architecture.

D. DONNE BRYANT/STOCK

The Castillo at Chichén Itzá is the largest and most imposing building of its kind in the northern lowlands. Built during the Terminal Classic period, it incorporates numerous Maya architectural and design features, and includes elements made popular by the Toltec culture of central Mexico. The north side faces the natural sinkhole or cenote that gives the site its name ("Chichén Itzá" meaning "at the mouth of the well of the Itzá").

Opposite page: At the Temple of the Warriors, in Chichén Itzá, the semireclining figure of the Chacmool (a deity of the Early Postclassic period) holds a stone bowl—a receptacle for human hearts offered in sacrifice in front of this imposing monument. The Chacmool and the feathered serpent column in the background are icons within the Toltec style of art, which was incorporated into the architecture and sculpture of this center at the end of the Classic period.

rainforest on the centers of the Classic period, and the physical disappearance of these now "lost cities", their case has been emphasized, and to a degree mystified, by numerous writers. The consensus of several important scientific symposia on the subject is that internal problems, particularly those related to what T. Patrick Culbert has referred to as "ecological overshoot", and the increasingly parasitic role of the elite, were the primary causes of the social, political, and demographic collapse of the southern lowland Maya city-states in the ninth and tenth centuries AD. Demitri Shimkin has pointed out that communicable diseases pose a particular threat to urban centers in tropical forest settings. Others have emphasized the disruption of long-established trade routes by rival Maya kings, and possibly by outsiders, as a contributing factor to the internal failures of the system.

Recently, Arthur Demarest has concluded that the end of Maya civilization in the Petexbatun region of east-central Guatemala was due to war. Research on defensive fortifications by Demarest, and on hieroglyphic texts by epigraphers Stephen Houston, Peter Mathews, and David Stuart, has shown that the territorial ambitions of the kings of Dos Pilas, combined with a political backlash by the local elites that controlled the other centers and subsequent changes in the rules of engagement in battle, resulted in endemic warfare throughout the Petexbatun region. This forced the common people to huddle their settlements—and, more importantly, their fields—close to the centers, for protection from the onslaughts of warriors from rival kingdoms. The concentration of populations in too small an area forced people to abandon their dispersed and diverse food production strategies in favor of the short-term solution of slash-and-burn cultivation close to their stone-wall-enclosed settlements. After only a few decades, these practices resulted in the deterioration of the habitat and systemic collapse.

While Demarest's scenario for the Petexbatun region is amply borne out by the impressive findings of his multidisciplinary research project (which successfully models the diverse ideas of the academic community), scholars continue to debate the degree to which his explanation can be applied to the many other regions and political contexts that made up the Maya world during the final century of the Classic period. The diversity of environments, economic strategies, and political histories within the different regions gave rise to a cultural patchwork of such complexity that it is doubtful whether a single cause (or prime mover, as it is sometimes called) can account for the collapse of each and every Classic Maya kingdom. Ultimately, competing hypotheses for explaining the collapse need to be objectively tested at each center in the way that Demarest has done at Dos Pilas, and David Webster, William Sanders, and the author have done at Copán.

In analyzing Copán's collapse, there are three facets to consider: the decentralization of power during the eighth and early ninth centuries AD; the political collapse of Copán kingship in AD 822; and the demographic decline of the surrounding population and ecological deterioration of the Copán Valley, which was occupied by ever-decreasing numbers of people during the following two or three centuries. The author has long held the view that the proliferation of noble families, and the relatively few political offices they could fill, resulted in a sort of nobles' revolt when the successor to the last Copán king, Yax Pac (New Dawn), could not be agreed upon. Demarest also suggests that the expansion of the nobility's power and privilege accelerated political instability to the point of collapse. In Copán, the demographic decline that followed the dissolution of a central authority was clearly a protracted process, tied to a long-term process of environmental degradation. This helps us to answer the question Gordon Willey and Demitri Shimkin posed long ago: why was there no recovery? First, the environment itself was depleted to the point that urban concentrations were not feasible. Second, the conflicts and stresses that prevailed during the last century of dynastic rule at Copán mitigated against any one faction attempting to re-establish a centralized system, at least within the confines of the Copán Valley. There, the site-core and its falling monuments stood as witnesses to the failures, as well as the successes, of the Classic Maya way of life.

The Postclassic, Colonial, and Modern Periods

As the centers of the southern lowlands succumbed to the numerous ills that plagued them in the ninth century AD, those in the northern lowlands experienced a cultural flowering. The centers of the Puuc and Chenes regions saw increases in construction and population growth that scholars have long claimed were fueled by immigrants from the collapsing kingdoms to the south. Such centers as Uxmal, Sayil, Labná, and Kabáh all became larger and more elaborate at this time, but the site of Chichén Itzá assumed the mantle of the largest and most powerful Maya city.

Archaeologists used to believe that Chichén Itzá was invaded and taken over by the Toltecs of central Mexico. More recent studies of hieroglyphic texts, pictorial sculptures, mural paintings, and ceramics, however, indicate that the Itzá—who gave their name to the famous well, or *cenote*, at that site—were not Toltecs but Chontal (Putun) Maya from the western fringes of the Maya area. *Cenotes* are sinkholes that tap into underground water. As there is no surface water on the Yucatán

DAVID NICHOLAS GREEN/THE PHOTO LIBRARY, SYDNEY

peninsula, they are vital to life, and for this reason the Maya considered them to be sacred.

The use of central Mexican symbolism was nothing new in the Maya world. In both the fourth and eighth centuries AD, the symbols of war and warriors used at Teotihuacan became very popular among the Maya of the Classic period, and connections to the legendary Toltecs were much ballyhooed not only by the Itzá and other lowland elites but by most of the reigning dynasties in the highlands of Guatemala. The legitimacy provided by a connection with a more powerful political force from outside the Maya world was a political strategy that apparently proved useful to many powerful Maya kings over the centuries.

The Itzá forged a series of alliances with other centers, forming a system of joint rule (*mul tepal*) that held the political rivalries of the Yucatán peninsula in check for some 200 years. This alliance eventually collapsed, however, and the Cocom lineage of Mayapán subsequently formed a new alliance with both the Xiu lineage of Uxmal and the Itzá lineage during the Late Postclassic period, although this, too, gave way after some 200 years of relative peace and prosperity. By the time of the Spanish conquest in AD 1524, the Yucatán peninsula was divided into a series of 16 provinces, which were constantly at odds over land rights.

The diseases introduced by Europeans decimated the Maya populations of the highlands and lowlands alike, and the forced conversion to Catholicism resulted in a syncretism of pre-Columbian and Christian beliefs that today varies markedly in content and practice from region to region. Many Maya rituals, religious concepts, and other cultural constructs have somehow survived the onslaught, if sometimes in modified form, and continue to be a source of fascination to anthropologists. In perhaps the most heartening development in Maya studies to date, the living Maya are beginning to exert their right to self-determination and to take steps to preserve their natural and cultural heritage. As the Maya themselves become deeply aware of, and involved in, the study of their culture and their heritage, new opportunities are opened to them and to the world at large for understanding this fascinating people and their ancient civilization.

Market day in Chichicastenango, Guatemala, where Maya from many different highland communities gather to trade. The diverse range of goods, traditional clothing, customs, and languages that comes together at this market reflects the wide cultural variation that has existed in Maya lands for 4,000 years.

THE WALL PAINTINGS OF BONAMPAK

MARY ELLEN MILLER

At Bonampak, in Chiapas, Mexico, Maya artists left a unique record of the courtly and warlike world of the Maya nobility in a series of paintings covering the stuccoed interior walls and vaulted ceilings of a small, three-chambered palace. Commissioned at the end of the eighth century AD by the last known king of Bonampak, Chaan-muan (who reigned from AD 775 to AD ?792), the famous paintings and dated texts in the main building, Structure 1, reveal the pageantry and bloodshed of noble Maya life at the end of the Classic period.

In Room 1, Chaan-muan presides over the presentation of a child heir to the throne, an event witnessed by other nobles. We then see the king and his entourage being ceremoniously attired in preparation for the next scene, where, after a period of 336 days has passed, the regional governors (*sahals*) confirm the heir's installation on the throne. A musical band and masked performers join in the celebration.

In Room 2, the king leads his warriors in battle and then directs the sacrifice of prisoners at dawn on the day the planet Venus rises as Morning Star, in August of AD 792, a time deemed appropriate in Mesoamerica for sacrifices. A captive on the steps in Room 2 has had his heart cut out; a severed head lies on the step below him, and victorious warriors pull out the fingernails of other unfortunates. Although monumental Maya art rarely portrays emotional states, the pathos of the victims reaches out to modern-day viewers.

In Room 3, the sacrifice of prisoners continues, now on stepped pyramids. While royal women and the little heir retreat to their private chambers to draw blood from their tongues, the king and his entourage, with so-called "dancers' wings" inserted through their penises, whirl and spin across the pyramid, blood streaming from their groins. This final act of human sacrifice seals the ritual begun in Room 1. But the paintings were not completed, the little heir probably never saw the throne, and Bonampak was apparently abandoned as widespread warfare engulfed the region.

Brought to modern attention in 1946 by Giles Healey, these Maya murals are the most complete indigenous paintings in the New World, and in color, craft, and complexity, are among the finest wall paintings in the world. Several fine sculptures have also been found at Bonampak.

MARY ELLEN MILLER

In a scene from Room 2, warriors with feather shields rolled up on their backs stand guard during the public display and bloodletting of captives seized in war.

MARY ELLEN MILLER

The Bonampak paintings capture surprisingly informal moments. Here, in Room 1, a regional governor turns as if to chat with the parasol bearers following in procession.

A painted pyramid wraps around three walls of the small chamber known as Room 3. At left, captives are decapitated as they enter, while nobles in feathered costumes whirl and dance among them. Meanwhile, royal women (upper left) draw blood from their tongues with spines.

HILLEL BURGER/PEABODY MUSEUM, HARVARD UNIVERSITY

The royal family draws blood in their private chamber.
During the sacrifice, the dancers, with blood streaming from their groins, whirl across the pyramid.

DAVID HISER/PHOTOGRAPHERS ASPEN

THE RISE OF THE AZTECS

A D 1 2 0 0 – A D 1 5 2 1

The Evolution of a Postclassic Mesoamerican Civilization

RICHARD E. BLANTON

ARCHAEOLOGISTS IDENTIFY a final period in the development of indigenous Mesoamerican civilization, which they call the Postclassic. In western Mesoamerica—the region west of the Maya area—the Postclassic spans the years from the decline of Teotihuacan and other centers of the Classic period, about AD 750, to the Spanish conquest in AD 1521. It was a time of complex changes, during which numerous cities rose to prominence and then fell into decline, and some ethnic groups, including the Mixtecs of the southern highlands region, exerted considerable influence beyond their own territories.

During the final phases of the Postclassic period (AD 1200 to AD 1521), a group known as the Aztecs came to dominate a large part of the Mesoamerican world. They achieved great renown, even in the most remote corners of Mesoamerica. To this day, the Aztecs are the most famous of all the native Mesoamerican societies.

From a combination of several sources of information, including archaeological data, painted manuscripts in the aboriginal style, and Spanish accounts written during and after the conquest, we have been able to develop a uniquely detailed picture of the prehispanic imperial society of the Aztecs.

A traditional Mexican farmer from Xochímilco navigates his boat along a canal, between raised agricultural fields (*chinampas*) of a type first developed by the Aztecs in the Valley of Mexico.

An Aztec pectoral ornament of turquoise mosaic, depicting a double-headed serpent.

BRITISH MUSEUM/WERNER FORMAN ARCHIVE

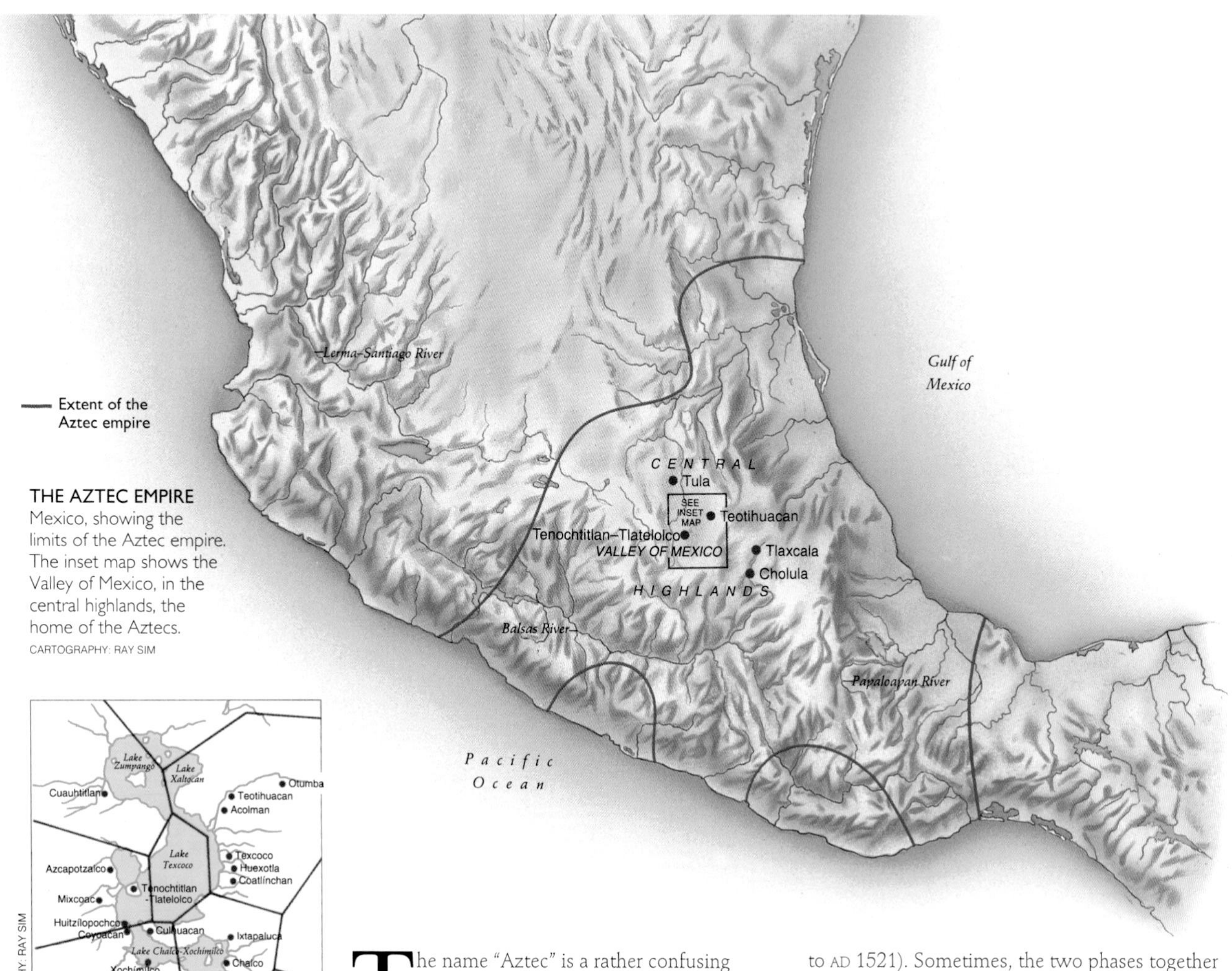

Extent of the Aztec empire

THE AZTEC EMPIRE
Mexico, showing the limits of the Aztec empire. The inset map shows the Valley of Mexico, in the central highlands, the home of the Aztecs.
CARTOGRAPHY: RAY SIM

CARTOGRAPHY: RAY SIM

Boundaries of city-states

The name "Aztec" is a rather confusing one, having been used in various ways over the years. In this chapter, it refers to the people who lived in the Valley of Mexico during the later phases of the Postclassic period. It is unlikely, however, that these people would often have referred to themselves by this name. Although most of the residents of the Valley of Mexico spoke one language, Nahuatl, some local subgroups, wishing to assert their separate identity, referred to themselves by such ethnic names as "Chalca", "Culhua", "Tepaneca", and "Mexica". No native society of Mesoamerica referred to itself as Aztec.

The term came into common usage following the Spanish conquest, probably because one of the ethnic groups, the Mexica (pronounced "Mesheeka"), who had risen to prominence in the Valley of Mexico, claimed to have migrated into the valley from a mythical place to the north and west called Aztlan. (For this reason, "Aztec" is sometimes used to refer to the Mexica alone.) The term is also used to identify the last two prehispanic archaeological phases in the Valley of Mexico—the Early Aztec (AD 1200 to AD 1400) and the Late Aztec (AD 1400 to AD 1521). Sometimes, the two phases together are referred to as the Late Postclassic period. During this period, the Valley of Mexico retained its multi-ethnic character, but local tribal domains came under the political control of the Mexica and their allies. The valley was integrated economically by a growing system of marketplaces, and cultural integration was enhanced by the construction of a civic-ceremonial complex in the Mexica capital, where the region's most important rituals were conducted on a grand scale.

The base of a carved stone box depicting the rain-god Tlaloc overturning a vessel filled with corn, amaranth, and water. In this way, he was believed to bring rain for crops.
BRITISH MUSEUM/WERNER FORMAN ARCHIVE

R. CUNDY/ROBERT HARDING PICTURE LIBRARY

Agriculture in the Valley of Mexico

The home of the Aztecs was the Valley of Mexico, one of a group of valleys in the central highlands of Mexico. The high and rugged volcanic mountain ranges that are characteristic of this area rise up to 5,500 meters (18,000 feet) above sea level, encircling several high, large, broad valleys. The Valley of Mexico is one of these, lying 2,100 meters (7,000 feet) above sea level and covering an area of 7,000 square kilometers (2,500 square miles). These highland valleys are semi-arid, with an average annual rainfall of less than 750 millimeters (30 inches). There is considerable fluctuation in the amount of rainfall during the rainy season, which occurs from May to October.

Agriculture is a risky venture in this environment, where the high elevation also results in low temperatures, so that early or late frosts can damage crops. Yet high yields were required every year to support the dense population of the valley, which numbered well over a million by AD 1521.

Since earlier prehispanic periods, people had continually devised strategies for coping with agricultural risk. These included extensive use of domesticated xerophytic (dry-adapted) plant species, including the ubiquitous maguey cactus, which was a source of food, fiber for cloth, and the alcoholic beverage *pulque*.

The techniques of terracing, to catch water and retain soil on slopes, and irrigation canals, to bring water to agricultural fields, go back to as early as 600 BC in the Valley of Mexico, and large irrigation and terracing systems, involving thousands of hectares, were built or extended during the Late Aztec phase. The largest agricultural scheme devised by the Aztecs, however, involved the modification of the valley's system of shallow, swampy lakes, using a technique of constructing raised fields known as *chinampa* agriculture. Reclaiming these lakes for agricultural purposes was not an easy task. Lake levels varied seasonally, and this could result in the flooding of agricultural fields and lacustrine (lake-dwelling) communities. Moreover, because the valley is an internal drainage basin, much of the lake system was saline.

The reclamation process probably began at least several hundred years before the Postclassic period, but it was during the Early and Late Aztec

Popocatepetl (a Nahuatl name) is one of the towering volcanoes of the central highlands region surrounding the Valley of Mexico.

A traditional farmer of the Valley of Mexico collects juice from the maguey cactus, still one of the most important crops in the region.

DAVID HISER/PHOTOGRAPHERS ASPEN

THE RISE OF THE AZTECS: AD 200 – AD 1521

	MESOAMERICAN PERIODS	VALLEY OF MEXICO ARCHAEOLOGICAL PHASES	EVENTS	MEXICA RULERS
1521			Spanish defeat of Tenochtitlan –Tlatelolco	Cuauhtemoc (1520–1521) Cuitláhuac (1520) Moctezuma II (1502–1520)
		Late Aztec (1400–1521)		Ahuitzotl (1486–1502) Tizoc (1481–1486) Axayacatl (1468–1481) Moctezuma I (1440–1468)
1428	Late Postclassic (1200–1521)		Defeat of Tepanecs; establishment of Triple Alliance	Itzcoatl (1426–1440) Chimalpopoca (1415–1426) Huitzilihuitl (1391–1415) Acamapichtli (1372–1391)
		Early Aztec (1200–1400)	Independent dynasties	
1325			Foundation of Tenochtitlan	
1200			Decline of Tula	
		Mazapan		
1000	Early Postclassic (750–1200)		Growth of Toltec empire from Tula	
		Coyotlatelco		
750			Decline of Teotihuacan	
	Classic (200–750)			
200				

JEAN-GERARD SIDANER/PHOTO RESEARCHERS, INC.

phases that the *chinampa* system was perfected and implemented on a massive scale. The soil was dredged up from the lake bottom to create fields, and trees were then planted along the edges to shore them up and prevent erosion. Fields were separated by canals. Plants had water even in dry years and during the dry season, because their roots extended into the water-soaked lower levels of the *chinampa* plot, and this allowed two or even three crops to be cultivated each year. Local canals were used as transport routes, connecting the fields to larger canals, which served as the interstate highway system of the day. Farmers could thus transport produce directly to urban markets.

The Aztec *chinampas* of the Valley of Mexico have to be counted among the most productive large-scale agricultural systems of the ancient world. By the end of the Late Aztec phase (AD 1521), *chinampas* extended over some 13,000 hectares (32,000 acres). A complex system of dikes and gates permitted lake levels to be regulated, to prevent flooding and to maintain a steady water level throughout the year. This agronomic system, highly productive but requiring extensive government planning and management, has barely survived to the present day. Since the Spanish conquest, the system has gradually been allowed to decline, until now there is only a remnant in a small part of western Lake Chalco–Xochímilco (commonly, but mistakenly, referred to as the "floating gardens").

The *chinampas* near Xochímilco, south of Mexico City, are among the last remnants of a highly productive agricultural system developed by the Aztecs, by means of which swampland was reclaimed for the purposes of cultivation. At its height, about AD 1521, the system extended over some 13,000 hectares (32,000 acres).

Mexica Migrations and the Foundation of Tenochtitlan

During an earlier phase of the Postclassic period, from about AD 1000 to AD 1200, the empire forged by the Toltecs of Tula (located in the present-day state of Hidalgo, north of the Valley of Mexico) extended over much of the central highlands and beyond. The collapse of the Toltec empire, in AD 1200, resulted in a fluid and fragmented political situation. During the Early Aztec phase, numerous small, autonomous city-states, each with its own ruling dynasty (or *tlatoani*, in Nahuatl), interacted with one another in the course of shifting alliances, wars, and trade. Several ethnic groups claimed to have migrated into the sparsely populated Valley of Mexico during that time of conflict, after AD 1200. According to later historical accounts, these newcomers referred to themselves as Chichimecs, meaning they were comparatively uncultured wanderers from the arid northern fringes of Mesoamerican civilization. Among the immigrants was a tribe called the Mexica, after whom the modern nation of Mexico is named.

Over many decades, the Mexica and other Chichimecs came to adopt the languages, arts, and productive skills of the resident Nahuatl speakers, whom they regarded as being more civilized than themselves. Eventually, they settled into their own communities and territories in the Valley of Mexico. As newcomers, the Mexica faced a treacherous situation, because they lacked access to the land and other resources they needed to support themselves. However, they thrived for a time by serving as mercenary soldiers for the then prominent city-state of Culhuacan. About AD 1325, the Mexica were ejected from this haven for sacrificing the daughter of a ruling Culhua family to the glory of their bloodthirsty patron deity, Huitzilopochtli, and were forced once more into marginal swampland along the western limits of Lake Texcoco. While crossing an island there, the Mexica saw an eagle perched on a spiny cactus, and took this as a sign that they had finally reached their destination. There, they established the community they named Tenochtitlan (now Mexico City), in the year AD 1325.

MARIE UEDA/THE PHOTO LIBRARY, SYDNEY

A stone sculpture depicting the eagle perched on a cactus that the wandering Mexica tribe took as a sign that they had reached their destined home. They founded the city of Tenochtitlan on the island where the sighting took place.

MUSEUM FÜR VÖLKERKUNDE, BASEL/ WERNER FORMAN ARCHIVE

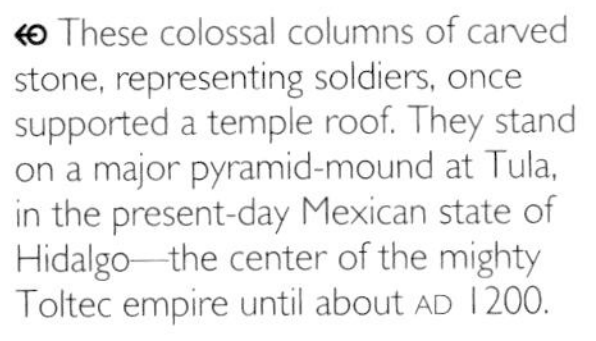

These colossal columns of carved stone, representing soldiers, once supported a temple roof. They stand on a major pyramid-mound at Tula, in the present-day Mexican state of Hidalgo—the center of the mighty Toltec empire until about AD 1200.

This Aztec warrior's shield is decorated with a geometrical design in feather mosaic.
WÜRTTEMBERGISCHES LANDESMUSEUM/RAINBIRD/ ROBERT HARDING PICTURE LIBRARY

The Triple Alliance: AD 1428 to AD 1521

By the end of the Early Aztec phase (about AD 1400), following the long period of fragmentation that ensued after the decline of the Toltec empire, a process of political consolidation was once more apparent in the Valley of Mexico. The Tepanec city of Azcapotzalco was at the center of these early attempts to re-establish an empire, but by the early 1400s, the Mexica, allied with the Acolhua of Texcoco, managed to defeat Azcapotzalco, thus bringing an end to the Tepanecs' hegemonic designs.

At the beginning of the Late Aztec phase, nearly 50 independent *tlatoani* centers dotted the Valley of Mexico, the Mexica, in their fledgling center of Tenochtitlan, among them. In spite of an inauspicious beginning, the Mexica prospered in their new location, establishing a marketplace in the sister community of Tlatelolco. (The two communities really made up one city, referred to as Tenochtitlan–Tlatelolco.) The succession of Mexica rulers forged alliances that advanced them politically, notable among which was Acamapichtli's marriage to a woman from the royal lineage of Culhuacan. This provided the Mexica with a legitimate genealogical link with the much-venerated Toltecs of Tula. The city grew in population and area, eventually outgrowing its island space. So Mexica commoners made use of the *chinampa* technique, learned from the older communities of Lake Chalco–Xochímilco, and with great effort reclaimed swampland for agricultural plots, house sites, and public spaces.

Following the defeat of the Tepanecs, the regional social system of the Valley of Mexico did not devolve into a system of independent city-states, as it had at the beginning of the Early Aztec phase. The processes of political consolidation and regional economic interaction—the latter mediated through a growing series of minor and major marketplaces—had gone too far for that. Henceforth, two major powers had the potential to achieve regional control and economic dominance—the Mexica of Tenochtitlan–Tlatelolco and the Acolhua of Texcoco—and they faced each other nervously across Lake Texcoco. The two cities, under the Mexica's Itzcoatl and the famous Acolhua poet-ruler Nezahualcoyotl of Texcoco, initiated a cycle of imperial expansion, both within and outside the Valley of Mexico. Following the defeat of Azcapotzalco, an alliance, known as the Triple Alliance, was struck between the two dominant powers, the Mexica and the Acolhua, and a remnant group of Tepanecs. Although some tensions remained throughout the life of the alliance, which endured until the Spanish conquest, no other polity or group of polities in the central highlands was successful in challenging the combined military might of these three powers. The empire quickly expanded to encompass a large part of western Mesoamerica, and by AD 1521, it ruled over some six million people.

A stone vessel bearing an image of the rain-god Tlaloc. Vessels of this type were buried as offerings beside the major Tlaloc temple in the great *teocalli*, the central ritual complex of Tenochtitlan.
JEAN-PIERRE COURAU/EXPLORER/AUSCAPE

A detail from a codex, showing four Aztec soldiers of high military rank, in full battle dress, armed with obsidian-tipped lances.
OXFORD, BODLEIAN LIBRARY, MS. ARCH. SELDEN. A. 1, 67R

Tenochtitlan–Tlatelolco in the Late Aztec Period

A combination of archaeological survey data and accounts and maps from the early period of Spanish conquest has allowed us to reconstruct the settlement pattern in the Valley of Mexico during the Late Aztec phase. Such sources are particularly important for studies of the regional capital of Tenochtitlan–Tlatelolco and its surrounds, as Mexico City lies over the ancient site and has largely destroyed it. Tenochtitlan–Tlatelolco was massive compared with contemporary settlements. It was probably the largest city in the New World at the time, with an estimated population of about 250,000 people (out of a total regional population exceeding one million). An island city set in a swampy lake, it was connected to the mainland by broad causeways, as well as by aqueducts that conveyed spring water to the city for domestic consumption.

Scattered among the various residential neighborhoods within the city were about 40 public building complexes. These civic-ceremonial complexes included temples, administrative buildings, *calmecac* (schools for boys of the noble class), the palaces of the nobility, and local market plazas. The central ritual complex, the great *teocalli*, was built at the intersection of the major north–south and east–west avenues. This consisted of a vast walled complex, each of its sides measuring some 400 meters (1,300 feet). Within the walls were 18 major pyramid-mounds and a number of other structures, all dominated by the massive Templo Mayor, a twin temple dedicated jointly to the patron deity of the Mexica, Huitzilopochtli, and the rain-god Tlaloc. Mexican archaeologists have been excavating this fascinating complex since 1978. Around the great *teocalli*, a succession of rulers built their vast palaces.

While the major civic-ceremonial buildings of the capital were in Tenochtitlan, its sister community, Tlatelolco, contained the city's major market plaza. This large and bustling commercial zone was the most important of the dozens of market plazas then operating in the Valley of Mexico. According to early Spanish accounts, the Tlatelolco market served some 25,000 people on normal market days, and 50,000 on special market days. A listing of some of the goods and services it offered included gold; silver; copper; seashells; bright tropical bird feathers (a major medium of artistic expression for the Aztecs); building materials; medicinal herbs and other medicines; yarn, cloth, and clothing of many colors; pottery; stone tools; many varieties of domesticated and wild food (raw, or processed and cooked); restaurants; and hairdressers. Similar categories of goods and services were grouped, so that customers could easily find what they wanted. Cacao (chocolate) beans, brought from the tropical lowlands in the east, were the most common form of currency for market transactions, although copper items and gold were sometimes used. Many kinds of craft specialists produced their wares within Tenochtitlan–Tlatelolco, including lapidary workers, feather workers, and potters, to name just a few. Some of their products were destined for the market, but others were produced as a form of tribute for the ruler.

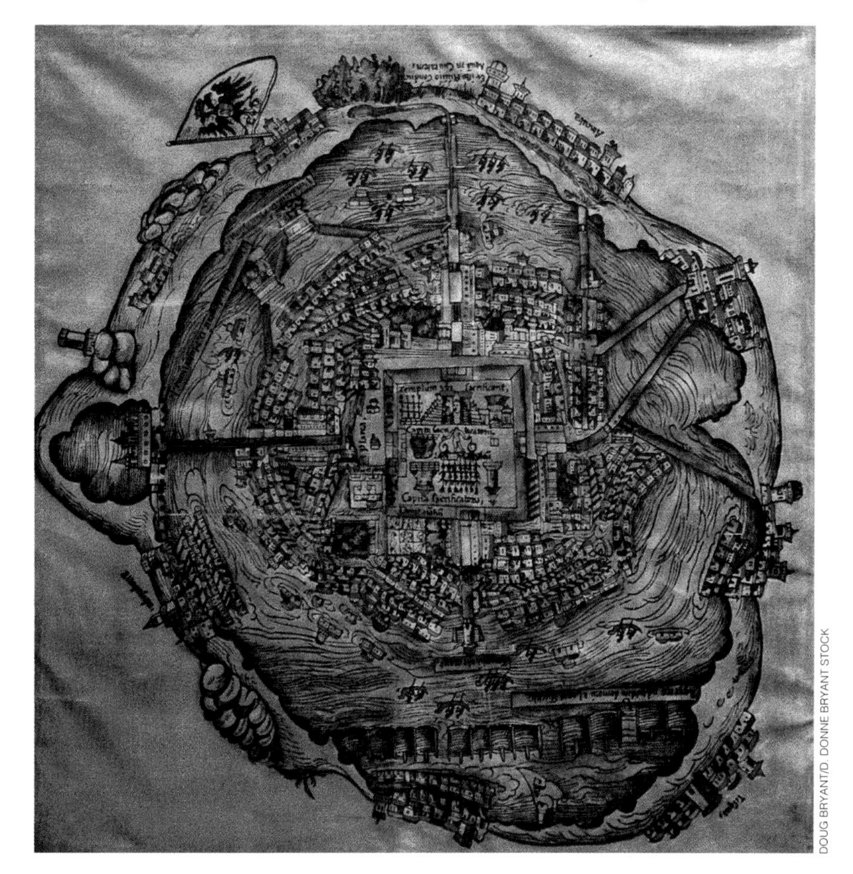

DOUG BRYANT/D. DONNE BRYANT STOCK

This early Spanish map of Tenochtitlan was based on information provided by the Spanish explorer Hernán Cortéz in his first letter to Charles V, in 1519. Although inaccurate in many respects, it shows the island city linked to the mainland by numerous causeways.

Moctezuma II's feather headdress was sent to Charles V by Hernán Cortéz, and is now held in the Vienna Museum. An elite guild of Aztec craftworkers specialized in making items decorated with exotic bird feathers, which were a major medium of Aztec artistic expression.

VOLK MUSEUM/RAINBIRD/ ROBERT HARDING PICTURE

AZTEC TRADE: A MARKETPLACE TRADITION

MARY G. HODGE

DIEGO DURÁN, A DOMINICAN FRIAR, wrote an account of prehispanic Aztec life in the late 1500s, based on the recollections of Aztecs who had lived through the Spanish conquest of AD 1521. In this, he described the central role marketplaces played in the social, political, and religious life of most Aztec communities, over and above their practical function as places for the exchange of goods. Market days were held to coincide with a calendar of rituals that took place at intervals of 5, 9, 13, or 20 days. Only in the largest and most important Aztec cities were markets held daily.

"Thus they came from all parts, from two, from three, from four and more leagues away, to the marketplaces ... The markets were so inviting, pleasurable, appealing, and gratifying to these people that great crowds attended ... The markets in this land were all enclosed by walls and stood either in front of the temples of the gods or to one side. Market day in each town was considered a main feast in that town or city. And thus in that small shrine where the idol of the market stood were offered ears of corn, chili, tomatoes, fruit, and other vegetables, seeds, and breads—in sum everything sold in the *tianguiz* [market]."

DOUG BRYANT/D. DONNE BRYANT STOCK

An artist's impression of merchants and customers in the Tlatelolco market. Shoppers bartered for a wide range of goods and services here, from ordinary household items to prestigious goods of great value.

From the eyewitness accounts of Durán and other Spaniards, we know that Aztec markets were not independent economic entities but were under the control of political leaders. According to Durán, laws prohibited exchange outside marketplaces, and determined the types of goods that could be sold. Vendors paid a fee to the city's ruler for the privilege of offering goods in the market, and were then allotted a space in an area devoted to their product.

Each market specialized in local goods—wooden products were a specialty of the forest area of Coyoacan, while the market of lakeside Cuauhtitlan offered reed mats and ceramics, for example—but some cities also had specialized markets. At Azcapotzalco, slaves were sold, while Acolman specialized in dogs (for food) and Texcoco was known for fine cloth, painted gourds, and finely crafted ceramics. At most markets, traders offered everyday goods such as food, pottery, cloth, and tools, and larger, more frequent markets offered a greater variety of goods.

In all markets, products were bartered for other goods or for any of a range of relatively nonperishable goods that were valued in themselves as a form of wealth. These included cotton cloth, cacao beans, quills filled with gold dust, copper bells and axes, and beads of shell and various green stones.

Traders of Privilege

Aztec merchants specialized in distributing particular products and trading in certain areas. Local marketplace traders in utilitarian goods were very different from the elite group of traders called *pochteca*. *Pochteca* were authorized to trade at markets outside the immediate region of Tenochtitlan–Tlatelolco, the capital. Only 12 cities had resident *pochteca* guilds, and even these were ranked: only those from Tenochtitlan, Tlatelolco (its sister city), Azcapotzalco, Cuauhtitlan, and Mixcoac were permitted to trade outside the empire's formal borders and had direct access to such exotic goods as cacao and tropical feathers. Significantly, these cities were near Tenochtitlan, while the other cities with *pochteca* guilds (Texcoco, Huexotla, Coatlínchan, Chalco, Xochímilco, Huitzílopochco, and Otompan) were more distant.

In Tenochtitlan, an important part of the *pochteca*'s function was to bring to the capital the kinds of luxury goods the ruler gave as gifts to foster loyalty and create obligations. *Pochteca* are also reputed to have served as imperial spies for the city's ruler, returning with information as well as goods. The *pochteca* were clearly an important aspect of the Aztec economy. Socially, they ranked somewhere below the nobility but above commoners, along with members of some other high-status specialist guilds.

Another chronicler of Aztec culture, Bernardino de Sahagún, notes that, like such craftworkers as the lapidaries, the *pochteca* had their own deity and their own ceremonies. The *pochteca* of Tlatelolco had a system of internally selected leaders, and served as magistrates to settle disputes in the great market of Tenochtitlan –Tlatelolco.

Sources of Evidence

The reports of Aztec trade written by Spanish explorers, friars, and administrators tell us that nearly 40 cities and towns (that is, communities of 5,000 or more people) were located within the Aztec empire's core zone, the Valley of Mexico (now the urban zone of Mexico City). Of these 40 cities, only 15 were major market towns. We can infer from the reports that some markets were larger and held more frequently than others, the largest and most important being those at Tlatelolco and Texcoco. Although they give general descriptions of the markets and list some of the products offered at them, these reports are of limited scope and deal mainly with the major centers. The archaeological record is indispensable for what it tells us about small communities and everyday trading practices.

Painted ceramics, for example, were widely traded in Aztec society. Decorated bowls, plates, cups, and dishes were used at feasts as well as for everyday meals. In the Valley of Mexico, a distinctive kind of pottery was made, having a bright orange surface color painted with black designs. Known as Black-on-Orange Ware, it has been found in communities far from the Valley of Mexico. Archaeologists therefore believe it was a popular trade ware, and use its presence in ancient cities as an indication of trade with the Valley of Mexico and the Aztec empire. It is also found at almost every archaeological site of Aztec times in the Valley of Mexico, as emerged during regional surveys undertaken in the 1970s to map the locations of Aztec communities. Because of the popularity of Black-on-Orange Ware, and because the surveys collected ceramics from all sites, large and small, it has been possible to use this distinctive ceramic to learn more about patterns of trade among Aztec cities and smaller communities, and about how the Aztec empire changed them.

Patterns of Trade

Before the Aztec empire (AD 1150 to AD 1350), Black-on-Orange ceramics were made in several different areas of the valley. It is clear that this ware was a specialty product made by particular workshops in only a few cities, because distinctive groups of designs are concentrated in particular sections of the valley. After AD 1430, when all cities in the Valley of Mexico had been consolidated into the Aztec empire and were ruled from Tenochtitlan, ceramics became much more uniform. It is thought that craftworkers in the provinces emulated the capital's style, perhaps seeing it as prestigious. Nonetheless, they continued to produce their characteristic designs, although in smaller quantities (representing about 15 percent of total production), and to offer them in regional markets.

The distribution of these distinctive ceramics in Aztec sites not only tells us which of the large markets the people of different small communities visited, but also gives us an insight into trade in the imperial period that we could not gain from the historical record alone. Concentrations of particular designs were found (in sites of all sizes) within five areas of the valley: near Texcoco, known to have had the second-largest market in the valley; near Chalco, a provincial capital; in the southern central part of the valley, near the Ixtapalapa peninsula; on the west side of the valley, near Tenochtitlan–Tlatelolco; and in the northwestern sector of the valley.

The boundaries of these trade zones correspond directly with the boundaries of the pre-imperial city-state confederations in the Valley of Mexico, and this confirms the documentary evidence that trade was under the control of regional rulers. The different designs may thus have been of special significance to people within these different political zones. It also shows that, despite the emphasis in the historical records of the size, grandeur, and importance of Tenochtitlan's market, the imperial capital did not monopolize production and trade, but rather influenced and utilized a pre-existing network of artisans and markets.

The type of pottery known as Black-on-Orange Ware was the most widely traded Aztec ceramic product.
BRITISH MUSEUM/WERNER FORMAN ARCHIVE

An Early Aztec plate from Texcoco, painted with the most popular combination of decorative motifs, feathers, and scrolls.
TEXCOCO FIELD MUSEUM/MARY HODGE

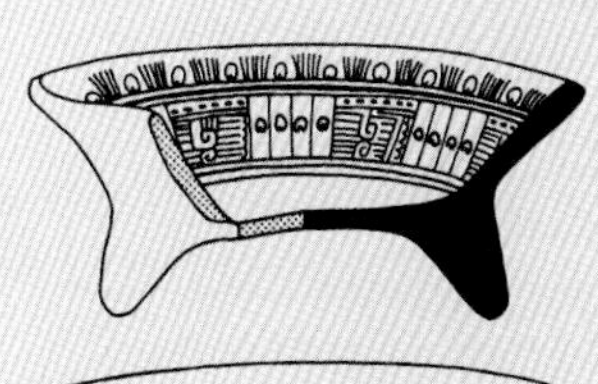

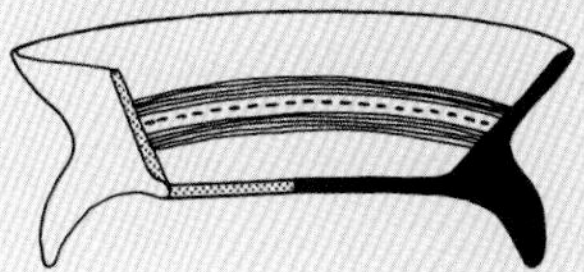

An elaborately decorated Black-on-Orange tripod dish from the Early Aztec period (above) contrasts with a plain, sparsely decorated Black-on-Orange dish of the Late Aztec period (below).
MARY HODGE

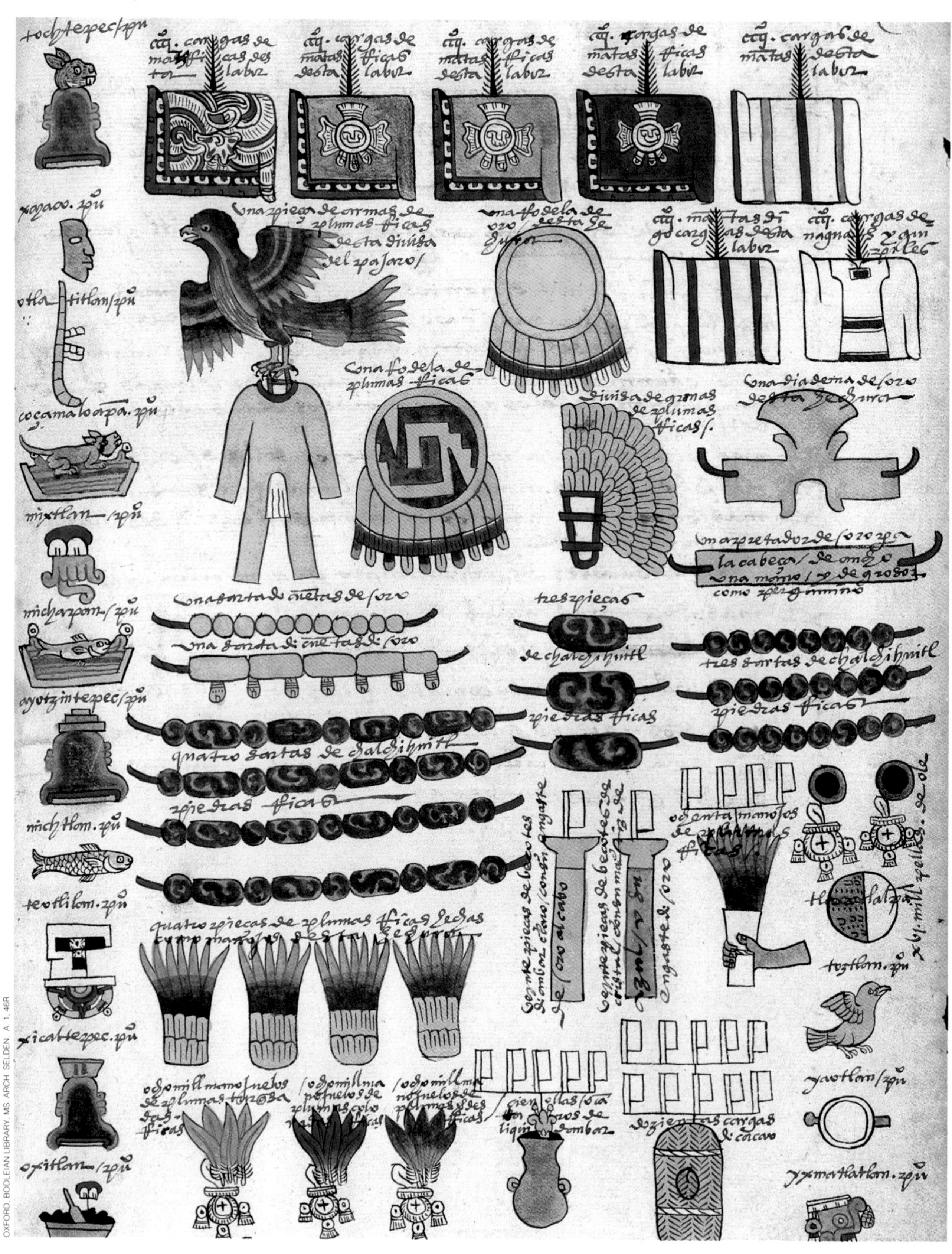

OXFORD, BODLEIAN LIBRARY, MS. ARCH. SELDEN. A 1, 46R

Market and Command Economies

Groups of people who specialized in particular crafts or other forms of production were found in cities other than Tenochtitlan–Tlatelolco, and also in rural areas—for example, the communities of the Lake Chalco–Xochímilco district were known for their agricultural products. Market transactions accounted for much of the economic activity in the Valley of Mexico: probably two-thirds of Tenochtitlan–Tlatelolco's food supply came through the market system, which included the main market at Tlatelolco and neighborhood markets scattered throughout the city.

In addition to commercial transactions, there was a form of "command economy" engendered by the rulers. This involved two main types of transactions. The first flowed from the fact that some members of the nobility (and others, such as high-ranking military officers) owned or in other ways controlled agricultural land. (The royal families had vast landholdings.) Some of this land was worked by serf-like farmers called *mayeque*, whose surplus produce went directly to the person who controlled the land. Many noble households had slaves, but slave labor was used mostly for household chores, not production. By the Late Postclassic period, there were apparently more *mayeque* commoners than there were of the other main class of commoners, known as *macehualli*. These were people who lived in communities that retained control over their land (although they, too, were required to hand over a portion of their production as tribute to noble overlords). The payment of tribute, which could take the form of the labor of *macehualli* and other commoners, was the second main type of transaction. These tribute payments funded the activities of the state, including its bureaucracy, military activities, and building projects, and also supported the noble households that controlled the state apparatus. The *Codex Mendoza*, a book written in the aboriginal style, probably shortly after the Spanish conquest, gives us a glimpse of the dazzling array of tribute goods that flowed into the Mexica state storehouses. (See the feature *The* Codex Mendoza*: A Window into the Past*.)

OXFORD, BODLEIAN LIBRARY, MS. ARCH. SELDEN. A.1, 65R

The burning of incense in decorated ladles was an important part of the offerings made to the gods during Aztec ritual events. The decoration on this handle (showing the "smoking mirror"), and the turkey-claw shape at its end, symbolize Tezcatlipoca, the god of duality.

BRITISH MUSEUM/WERNER FORMAN ARCHIVE

In theory, the members of the Triple Alliance were obliged to share imperial tribute, but the Mexica clearly benefited the most. The command economy controlled a smaller quantity of goods and services than did the market economy, but consumed a substantial portion of the region's economic output. Ethnohistorian Frances Berdan has estimated that the following quantities of food (to take just a few examples) were consumed daily within the palace of the Texcocan ruler Nezahualcoyotl (AD 1427 to AD 1472): 1,200 kilograms (2,650 pounds) of maize (enough to make 20,000 tortillas), 140 kilograms (310 pounds) of beans, 32,000 cacao beans, and 100 turkeys. The corresponding figures for Mexica palaces would have been substantially higher, although we lack the information on which such estimates might be based.

The rulers needed substantial amounts of goods and labor to finance such government initiatives as warfare and construction, and also to achieve their political goals. Rulers gave gifts of prestigious goods to the members of their cadre (for example, successful warriors) to reward them for service and to create obligations that could cement allegiances. Similarly, they sometimes distributed agricultural land captured from enemies. Prestigious goods, including cotton garments, jade and obsidian jewelry, and fine feathers, were recognized as the most precious and symbolically significant possessions in the Aztec world. The early colonial writer Friar Diego Durán relates how Moctezuma II (also known as Montezuma) distributed rewards on one occasion: "… he instructed that they be dressed in fine mantles, loinclothes, and sandals … he ordered they be given maize, chian seed, and cacao in large quantities … the next day … the king gifted his noblemen with fine mantles, rich loinclothes, sandals, lip-plugs, ear-plugs, shields, beautiful weapons, insignia, and gold armbands. These were rewards for men who had proven their bravery."

Pottery stamps are often found at Aztec sites, and may have been used to imprint designs on cloth or to apply facial paint to those taking part in ceremonies.

BRITISH MUSEUM/WERNER FORMAN ARCHIVE

Opposite page: A page from the *Codex Mendoza* recording an Aztec imperial tribute list. The painted figures indicate the types and quantities of goods scheduled for periodic delivery to the empire's tribute collectors—in this case, the tribute obligations of the conquered province of Tochtepec. Among the items (top center) are feather-mosaic shields and warrior costumes.

High-ranking warriors renowned for their success in battle and the taking of prisoners (as depicted here) were awarded elaborate insignia of honor. Aztec armies were dressed in a variety of colorful regalia, which was invested with symbolic significance.

BIBLIOTECA NAZIONALE, FLORENCE/SCALA

The Aztec ritual of human sacrifice is graphically depicted in this illustration from the *Codex Magliabechiano*, a painted manuscript in the aboriginal style. A priest cuts out the victim's heart with a large knife made of chipped stone.

DAVID HISER/PHOTOGRAPHERS ASPEN/AUSCAPE

This Teotihuacan-style mask was included in an offering cache from the Templo Mayor (Great Temple) at Tenochtitlan.

Political and Religious Rituals

Prestigious goods were consumed during Aztec rituals as a public symbol of the rulers' power. Among the most important events of this kind were coronations. Diego Durán had this to say about the coronation of the ruler Ahuitzotl: "... this feast was prepared by the Aztec people with the intention of showing the enemy—Tlazcala, Huexotzinco, Cholula, and other cities in that direction, together with those of Michoacan, and Metztitlan—the greatness of Mexico. It was designed to bewilder them, fill them with fear, and make them see the grandeur and abundance of jewels and gifts that were exchanged on such an occasion. All this was based on ostentation, vaingloriousness, in order to show that the Aztecs were the masters of the riches of the earth."

Rituals commemorating the completion of construction projects, such as a temple, required the placement of elaborate dedicatory caches of valuables, including pottery and jade. Mexican archaeologists have unearthed many such caches in recent excavations.

CHARLES LENARS/EXPLORER/AUSCAPE

An artist's impression of the Aztec capital city of Tenochtitlan, on the shores of Lake Texcoco, in the Valley of Mexico. The volcanoes lining the lake's opposite shore and, behind them, the even more massive volcanoes defining the valley's southeastern boundary, typify the generally rugged topography of the central highlands region.

ANDREW RAKOCZY/PHOTO RESEARCHERS, INC.

The Coyolxauhqui Stone, in the Templo Mayor at Tenochtitlan, still lies where it was placed to commemorate an Aztec victory. The goddess Coyolxauhqui was the sister of the god Huitzilopochtli, the patron deity of the Mexica.

DAVID HISER/PHOTOGRAPHERS ASPEN

These objects from a dedicatory cache were exposed during excavation of the Templo Mayor at Tenochtitlan. At left is a mask made from a human skull.

A carved stone figure of Xipe Totec ("The Flayed One"), a god associated with spring. The distinctive priest's costume for this god's ceremony was a human skin, representing the annual renewal of the Earth's vegetation.

MUSEUM FÜR VÖLKERKUNDE, BASEL/ WERNER FORMAN ARCHIVE

Coronations, temple dedications, and religious rituals in the great *teocalli*, particularly those dedicated to Huitzilopochtli, often included the ritual sacrifice of humans, usually war captives. Many kinds of human sacrifices took place in Aztec society, for many different reasons, the most important of which was to provide the blood required by Huitzilopochtli. The major sacrificial events, however, such as the one described by Durán, were performed in a manner calculated to instill awe and fear in those who observed the bloodshed, including the enemy rulers who had been summoned to witness the events. Although exact figures are hard to come by, sometimes as many as 20,000 people were sacrificed in one ritual event. The skulls of thousands of sacrificial victims were displayed in the great *teocalli* of Tenochtitlan, a gory reminder of the military prowess of the Aztec ruler and his armies.

DOUG BRYANT/D. DONNE BRYANT STOCK

The Great Tzompantli, or stone skull rack, is located near the Templo Mayor at Tenochtitlan. The skull effigies reflect the countless ritual human sacrifices that took place in the temple.

Why the Mexica?

The later prehispanic periods in the Valley of Mexico were characterized by the cyclical rise and decline of powerful centers of empire. Major cycles of regional centralization had emanated from Teotihuacan (AD 200 to AD 700), Tula (AD 1000 to AD 1200), and, finally, Tenochtitlan–Tlatelolco (AD 1400 to AD 1521). These expansionist periods were punctuated by periods of decentralization, in which numerous local centers retained autonomy, as was the case during the Early Aztec phase. Given that nearly 50 *tlatoani* centers (communities with ruling elites) existed during this phase, why did only one come to dominate the valley in the final cycle of empire-building?

The handle of this Aztec sacrificial knife is decorated in the Mixtec style, with a mosaic of turquoise, jade, shells, and coral.

BRITISH MUSEUM/VICTOR R. BOSWELL JNR/ NATIONAL GEOGRAPHIC SOCIETY

DOUG BRYANT/D. DONNE BRYANT STOCK

The results of past and continuing research by archaeologists and ethnohistorians are as yet insufficient to give us a satisfactory answer to this difficult question, but asking it can help to give us an insight into some important aspects of the social changes that took place in Central Mexico during the Late Postclassic period. Many factors need to be considered to understand the Mexica's comparative success, but here we will focus on three: location, alliances, and religion.

Although Tenochtitlan–Tlatelolco was founded in the middle of a marginal swampland, this was a site that eventually proved an ideal location for a major market of regional importance. (Moreover, with great effort, the Mexica were able to convert the swamps into highly productive *chinampas*.) Settlements in the middle latitudes of the Valley of Mexico have always had potential for commercial growth, because they have relatively easy access to other regions in the valley, and merchants therefore based themselves there. It was vital for a ruling family to have an important marketplace within its domain, for the tax on market transactions was a major source of state revenues. An important marketplace also attracted prominent traders and craftworkers, from whom rulers could obtain the kinds of exclusive goods they distributed to followers and allies as part of their political strategies.

The Mexica were usually very astute in the political alliances they made. For example, Acamapichtli married a woman from Culhuacan who was descended from Toltec rulers. This was crucial for a group of newcomers with imperialist designs. Boasting of their early history, the Mexica characterized themselves as a rugged and aggressive band of Chichimec immigrants, and this, no doubt, gave them a certain prestige. In Postclassic Mesoamerica, however, their successes in battle and their growing wealth were still not sufficient to allow them to attain leadership. Political legitimacy, however tenuous in the Mexica's case, demanded an hereditary connection to the great imperial families of the past.

Huitzilopochtli ("Hummingbird-on-the Left"), the patron deity of the Mexica, was a relatively obscure figure compared to the more famous Mesoamerican gods, such as Tlaloc, the major rain-god, or Quetzalcoatl, the feathered serpent. He was one of a class of deities now referred to as warfare–sacrifice gods. Huitzilopochtli was one of a group of sun deities whose nourishment, in human blood, was necessary to ensure that the sun would rise and cross the sky each day. At death, successful warriors were thought to dwell with Huitzilopochtli for a time, and then to return to Earth as hummingbirds, sipping wild honey for eternity. For this reason, Huitzilopochtli is often portrayed with a hummingbird headdress. This craving for blood was to prove advantageous to the Mexica rulers.

A portrayal of life in the capital of Tenochtitlan–Tlatelolco by modern-day Mexican muralist Diego Rivera. Seated on a throne, Moctezuma II observes the activities of the Tlatelolco market. The structures behind him are part of Tenochtitlan's central complex of pyramid-mounds *(teocalli)*.

This stone statue of the god Quetzalcoatl ("Feathered Serpent") shows him in one of his guises as a fertility god, bearing a load of maize cobs.

ST LOUIS ART MUSEUM, MO / WERNER FORMAN ARCHIVE

THE *CODEX MENDOZA*: A WINDOW INTO THE PAST

FRANCES BERDAN

The people of the ancient Mesoamerican civilizations, including the Aztecs and their neighbors, produced painted manuscripts in enormous quantities. These books, painted on paper made from the bark of the native fig-tree, recorded many aspects of their lives, ranging from genealogies, religious events and calendars, through maps and migration histories, to accounts of conquests and lists of tributes paid into imperial coffers. Unfortunately, only a handful of these prehispanic manuscripts have survived to the present day, and none of the known Aztec manuscripts can be indisputably dated to preconquest times, even though large and magnificent libraries once graced the powerful imperial cities of the Aztecs. We do not know why so many books were destroyed during the Spanish conquest, but some were certainly victims of the destruction that inevitably accompanies warfare.

A great many manuscripts, however, were painted shortly after the Spanish conquest of the Aztecs. The native scribes who produced these documents continued to use local conventions in their painting, sometimes even copying directly from then-existing preconquest manuscripts. In this way, they preserved indigenous styles of painting and writing, and even duplicated the content of some books. One famous example is the *Codex Mendoza*.

The historical section of the *Codex Mendoza* records the founding of the Aztec imperial capital, Tenochtitlan, and its division into four quarters. The city's foundation is symbolized by the eagle perched on a cactus above a rock. Two conquests are commemorated below, and glyphs representing years border the page. OXFORD, BODLEIAN LIBRARY, MS. ARCH. SELDEN. A. 1, 2R

A Unique Record

The *Codex Mendoza* was produced in the early 1540s, just 20 years after the fall of the Mexica imperial capital of Tenochtitlan–Tlatelolco to Spanish conquistadors under Hernán Cortéz. Compiled in Mexico City (the new capital, built on top of the ruins of Tenochtitlan–Tlatelolco) by order of King Charles V of Spain, this remarkable manuscript came to carry the name of the viceroy of central Mexico (called New Spain at that time), Antonio de Mendoza. The *Codex* was hurriedly finished to meet a scheduled sailing of Spanish treasure ships to Spain. En route, however, French privateers (or pirates) attacked the flotilla. Miraculously, the document survived, later reappearing at the French royal court. It changed hands only a few more times before finally coming to rest in the Bodleian Library at Oxford, in England.

The *Codex Mendoza*'s content is no less amazing than its history. Although painted on European paper and composed under Spanish supervision, it records preconquest events and activities of the Aztec world. The *Codex* includes 72 pictorial pages, briefly annotated in Spanish at the time the work was composed. In addition, there are 63 pages of extended Spanish commentary describing the events and information illustrated.

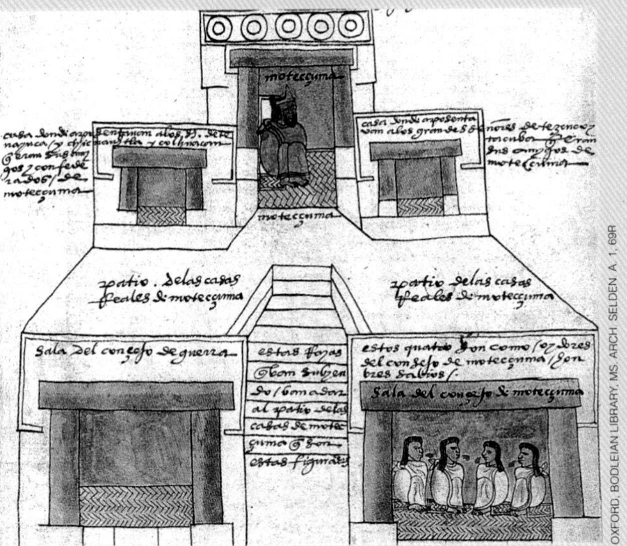

The palace and courtyard of the Aztec ruler Moctezuma II. As well as the royal residence, the palace was a center for political and legal activities, as the courtroom at lower right indicates. OXFORD, BODLEIAN LIBRARY, MS. ARCH. SELDEN. A. 1, 69R

Three Distinct Parts

The *Codex* is divided into three distinct parts: a history of imperial Aztec conquests, a listing of tributes paid to the empire by 38 conquered provinces, and a description of Aztec daily life from the cradle to the grave.

The historical section begins with the founding of the island city of Tenochtitlan (with its symbol of the eagle perched on a prickly pear cactus) in the Aztec year 2 House, AD 1325. The remaining pages in this

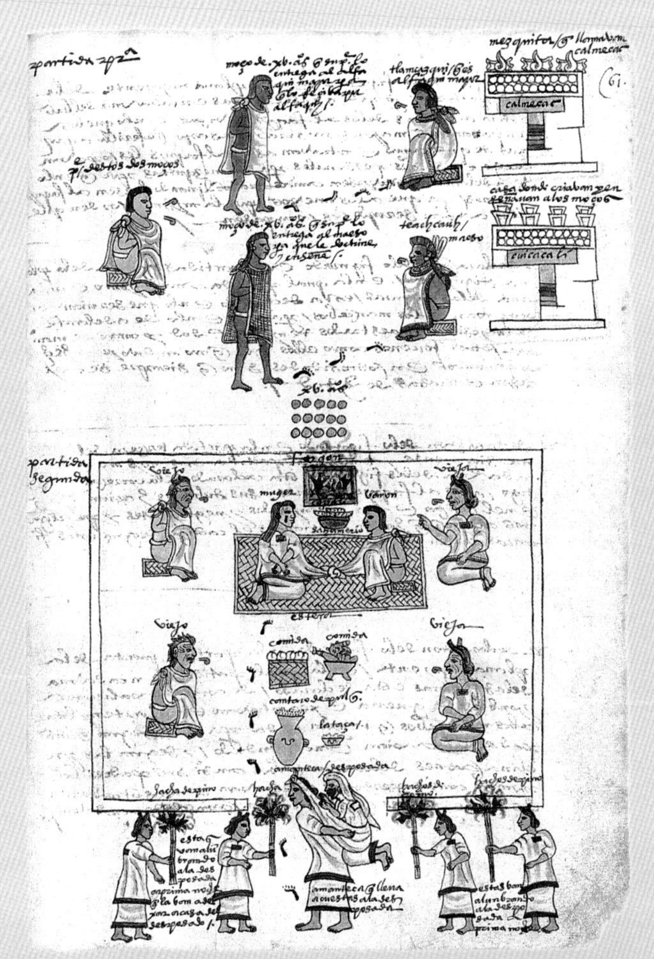

This page from the *Codex Mendoza* shows a variety of scenes from Aztec daily life. At the top, 15-year-old boys are sent to school. Below, a wedding ceremony takes place, complete with a form of bride-capture, exhortations by elders, and the symbolic "tying of the knot".

OXFORD, BODLEIAN LIBRARY, MS. ARCH. SELDEN. A.1, 61R

section commemorate the military conquests of the city's 9 successive rulers. The record of each ruler's achievements includes a drawing of the ruler with his personal name glyph, a shield with arrows (a symbol of warfare), and glyphs representing the names of defeated towns. Accompanying each town's name glyph is a drawing of a toppling, burning temple—the symbol of conquest, the conquest of a community being complete when a town's temple was captured. This conquest history relates the development and growth of the Aztec empire, from the small island domain of the first three Mexica rulers to the unprecedented imperial expansion of the later kings throughout most of central and southern Mexico.

The second part of the *Codex* builds logically on the first, being a tally of tributes received from the conquered provinces. The towns in these provinces were conquered over the 90-year history of the empire, and their residents paid heavy tributes in the form of goods ranging from maize and beans to feathered warrior costumes and jadeite beads. Almost all the provinces were obliged to deliver huge quantities of clothing to their imperial overlords, amounting to hundreds of thousands of items each year. The tributes that poured into Tenochtitlan–Tlatelolco reflected the enormous environmental diversity of the imperial domain: exquisite feathers from tropical jungles, wooden beams and planks from highland forests, seashells from the coast, and live eagles from the dry northern regions.

These first two sections of the *Codex Mendoza* were almost certainly copied directly from preconquest manuscripts. The third part, however, dealing with Aztec daily life, appears to be an innovation. It shows the lives of Aztec men and women from birth, through childhood, schooling, marriage, entry into the priesthood, and passage through the warrior grades, to old age and its privileges. It also illustrates a distant war, the activities of judges, the Aztec ruler's palace, and a wide variety of occupations (for example, featherworking) and vices (such as gossiping and thieving).

More than any other early Aztec painted manuscript, the *Codex Mendoza* is a true window into the past. In vivid pictures and clever glyphs, it eloquently depicts a people's history, the wealth of an empire, and everyday patterns of life among the Aztec people in prehispanic times.

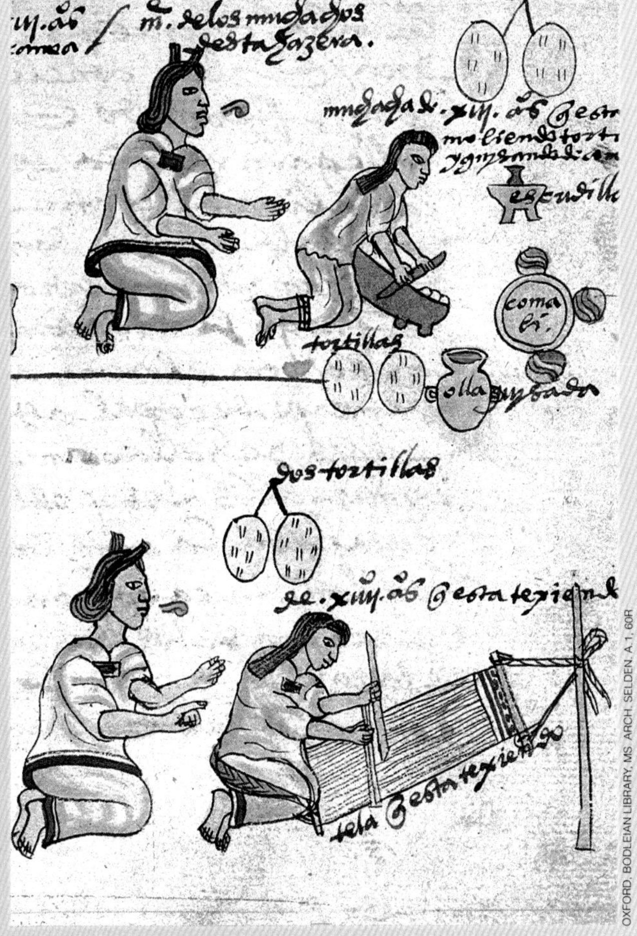

Another page illustrates the education of Aztec girls. By the age of 13, a girl was expected to have mastered the necessary culinary skills, under her mother's instruction. By the age of 14, she was expected to be proficient at weaving.

OXFORD, BODLEIAN LIBRARY, MS. ARCH. SELDEN. A.1, 60R

The priests and rulers used this demand for blood—preferably that of captured enemy warriors sacrificed at the summit of the temple dedicated to Huitzilopochtli—to persuade the people to support war and to motivate warriors to take great risks in battle. (There were other reasons why men went to war, however, including the promise of rewards—both in this life, for success in battle, and in the afterlife, for those who perished.) While the desire for tributes that would demonstrate that the Mexica were "the masters of the riches of the earth" may have underlain the Mexica's drive towards imperial expansion, we should not overlook the role played in this process by a religious belief requiring human sacrifice.

The Spanish Conquest and the End of Aztec Domination

By the final decades of the prehispanic period, Mexica human sacrifice had become such a gory spectacle that enemies and allies alike were unnerved and disgusted, making them less likely to challenge or oppose the Mexica's demands and expansionist aims. Word of the immense scale of their sacrificial rituals—most notably, the sacrifice of 20,000 victims at the dedication of the temple of Huitzilopochtli, in AD 1487—spread throughout Mesoamerica. These rituals enhanced the prestige of Huitzilopochtli and the Mexica, but it was a prestige tinged with dread. The human sacrifices, and the heavy tribute obligations and brutal military reprisals suffered by conquered groups, caused widespread fear and hatred of the Mexica. This proved to be their undoing when a new element exploded on the Mesoamerican scene in the year AD 1519, during the reign of Moctezuma II.

When Hernán Cortéz and his band of 350 soldiers landed on the coast of what is now the Mexican state of Veracruz, news of his arrival quickly reached the court of Moctezuma, and Mexica envoys were sent to greet the strange newcomers. Given the small number of the Spaniards, why didn't Moctezuma, with his vast armies, respond to what was clearly a threat and take military action against the invaders? The Mexica ruler was unwilling to act decisively, because he thought that Cortéz might be a god. On the other side, Cortéz quickly sensed the possibility of carving out alliances with those who despised the Mexica. He began this process with the Spaniards' Cempoallan hosts in Veracruz, and then moved on to the powerful Tlaxcallans, a central highlands group even the powerful Mexica had not been able to subdue. Moctezuma's reticence and the widespread hatred of the Aztecs, particularly the Mexica, go a long way towards explaining the course of ensuing events.

The Spaniards and their Tlaxcallan allies first arrived in Tenochtitlan–Tlatelolco in November of 1519, where they were greeted by Moctezuma. At first, relations were peaceful, but Cortéz soon outraged his hosts by displaying his dislike of the Mexican gods and idols. As tensions mounted, Cortéz took Moctezuma captive, whereupon the whole fabric of Mexica society began to unravel. The Spaniards, who were under siege, barely escaped from the city, but managed to return to Tlaxcalla during the summer of 1520.

The Aztecs' first encounter with the Spaniards, in AD 1519, was peaceful. A representative of Moctezuma II is shown here presenting Cortéz with a necklace of gold and precious stones. This illustration is from an account of the conquest of Mexico by the Spanish chronicler Friar Díego Durán.

Following these events, Cortéz began to organize an invasionary force. He enlisted recruits from the Spanish ships that had followed him to Veracruz, and his men carried ships' cannons from the coast to Tlaxcalla, where the elements of a fleet were being assembled for later transport overland. He also forged new alliances, the most important of which was with the Texcocans, who had been powerful members of the Aztec Triple Alliance. Later, other groups followed suit. Cortéz and his army of Spaniards and native allies then marched back to the Valley of Mexico, to Texcoco, where the fleet brought from Tlaxcalla was put together and launched on Lake Texcoco. Fierce battles took place, but the Spaniards finally prevailed, largely because they were able to blockade the island city of the Mexica, bringing this once powerful people to the brink of starvation. The Spaniards finally captured the Mexica ruler, Cuauhtemoc, on 13 August 1521. They had toppled the imperial apparatus of the Mexica, but soon replaced it with another—this one of their own design.

This Aztec warrior's shield, with its decorative feather mosaic, features a design symbolizing the rain goddess Chalchiuhtlicue ("Jade Glowing"), the consort of the rain-god Tlaloc.
NATIONAL MUSEUM OF ANTHROPOLOGY, MEXICO/ WERNER FORMAN ARCHIVE

AZTEC ART

EMILY UMBERGER

The Aztecs' development of a monumental style of art and architecture, which found expression particularly in stone sculptures, paralleled their rise to political power and economic wealth in the middle of the fifteenth century AD. Between military campaigns, the Aztec ruler (or *tlatoani*) Moctezuma I redesigned the capital of Tenochtitlan to serve as a dramatic setting for the great ceremonies held to celebrate his victories. Within a period of 20 or 30 years, sculptors and other artisans, under his direction, had developed a distinctive style by making a study of imported works, objects in nature, and antiquities at deserted ancient cities in central Mexico. The result was an eclectic body of work inspired by diverse sources and emanating from foreign as well as local artists.

It was probably also in the time of Moctezuma I that the myth of the birth of the patron god Huitzilopochtli ("Hummingbird-on-the-Left") attained its official form, and that the Templo Mayor (Great Temple) and its surrounding structures—notably, the skull rack and ballcourt—were decorated to recreate the mythic Mexica landscape. Colossal sculptures of serpents designated the pyramid itself as representing the hill Coatepec ("Serpent Hill"), on which Huitzilopochtli was born, and a sculpture of his defeated enemy-sister Coyolxauhqui ("Golden Bells") lay at the foot of the pyramid, where her body landed at her death.

Monuments and Idols

The majority of Aztec sculptures took the form of anthropomorphic figures of deities representing the forces of nature and the communal patrons of particular towns and their neighborhoods (*calpultin*). Unfortunately, only one of the great idols of Tenochtitlan has survived intact, a 2.5 meter (8 foot) tall image of Coatlicue ("Serpents Her Skirt"), the earth goddess who was Huitzilopochtli's mother.

The majority of Aztec figurative sculptures depict deities, but few of those in the imperial capital survived the Spanish conquest. This figure, from the nearby city of Tlamanalco, is typical of the Aztec imperial style. The god of spring, Xochipilli, wears a mask, and a suit of animal skin decorated with flowers.
NATIONAL MUSEUM OF ANTHROPOLOGY, MEXICO CITY/SCALA

Otherwise, the most important surviving monuments are various images of Coyolxauhqui and three large, round sacrificial stones depicting the sun on their upper surface. All rulers had such "stones of the sun" carved, sacrifice being considered necessary to ensure the sun's continued movement across the sky. Other stone carvings included animals and plants; boxes and vessels of all shapes; models of musical instruments, weapons, batons, and such; relief-covered blocks, seats, and platforms; and reliefs on boulders and rock faces at natural sacred sites, such as hills, caves, and springs.

Despite their predominantly religious and cosmic imagery, Aztec sculptural monuments were firmly linked to imperial politics, playing a central role in the ritual life of this aggressive and warlike people. Important events were always marked by the erection of a monument, and whether the event were an accession to the throne or the completion of a civic project, warfare was a necessary adjunct, providing the means of acquiring the victims required to be sacrificed at the initiation ceremony. Often, the first act of aggression towards an enemy was a demand for the materials and workers needed to construct a monument or other building. When a town was defeated, sculptures of deities identified with the conquered group were taken to Tenochtitlan and kept in a prison temple, and images of such deities were sometimes included in humiliating contexts in Aztec monumental art. Although the main motifs on major relief-covered monuments, such as the sacrificial stones, are cosmic images and deities, there are also hieroglyphs of dates and rulers' names, linking the monuments to particular events and personalities.

A Range of Crafts

The Aztecs worked in materials other than the basalt used for major monuments. They made images of deities, masks, weapons, and furniture of wood; ceramic figures

Large ceramic urns with images of fertility gods were found at Tlatelolco, the island city adjacent to Tenochtitlan. Tlatelolco was defeated in a civil war in 1473 and incorporated into the capital city.
JEAN PIERRE COURAU/EXPLORER/AUSCAPE

This colossal stone head from the Templo Mayor at Tenochtitlan represents one of the fire serpents that carried the sun.
EMILY UMBERGER

and vessels; mosaic masks and shields of turquoise and shell; jewelry, containers, and small deity images of jade and other precious stones; obsidian ear and lip ornaments; gold and silver jewelry and reliefs; and textiles of featherwork, cotton, and maguey fibers for all types of clothing and costumes.

The artifacts that have survived in the greatest numbers are ceramics. The most prestigious local form, known as Aztec Black-on-Orange, was a distinctive orange ware with complex calligraphic patterns formed by fine black lines. Aztec nobles also used polychrome vessels decorated with figures, animals, and isolated motifs such as flint knives and skulls, in the traditional style of the ancient city of Cholula. Recent excavations, especially at the Templo Mayor, have revealed life-size ceramic figures of warriors and deities; vessels decorated with effigies of deities; and other containers in a variety of styles, including copies of ancient and foreign types.

The gold objects stored in the great treasuries were melted down by the Spanish, so examples of Aztec metalwork are scarce—to the point that we do not know how such works differed from those of the Mixtecs, which they emulated. Most other Aztec works were made of perishable materials—wood, fibers, feathers, paper, and even dough—and are known only from colonial illustrations.

The Archaeological Legacy

Because Aztec cities were so completely destroyed by the Spanish, and so many ancient monuments have been buried under modern-day cities, the development and context of Aztec art are as difficult to reconstruct as are the forms of Aztec architecture. Sculptures that escaped the initial phase of destruction, when buildings were razed and sculptures smashed, were cut up and reused as building stones in the colonial period. Only after 1790, as Mexico moved towards independence, did colonial elites find it politically useful to preserve the relics of Aztec culture, in order to re-create an ancient past distinct from that of Europe.

Among the monuments preserved were the great Coatlicue sculpture and the Calendar Stone, a "stone of the sun" from the reign of the last prehispanic *tlatoani*, Moctezuma II. Hundreds of sculptures have since been excavated from construction sites in Mexico City and elsewhere in the Valley of Mexico, culminating in the uncovering of a great, circular relief sculpture of the goddess Coyolxauhqui (measuring 3 meters, or about 10 feet, in diameter), still in the place where it was laid to commemorate a victory, probably in the 1470s.

After the Conquest

With the fall of the empire, Aztec stone carvers and other artisans were re-employed to decorate the great sixteenth-century Spanish monasteries with Christian imagery. A few traditional types of objects were still made. A range of ceramic vessels was produced throughout the colonial period, and feather costumes and wooden drums were made for use in the native dances (*tecontin*) featuring impersonations of preconquest nobles and warriors that were performed before Spanish audiences. The costumes have perished, but some drums in the original Aztec style have survived and are now in museum collections. Small "idols" of stone, ceramic, and paper are covertly made in rural areas to this day.

Unlike the other major goddesses of deathly aspect, this less than life-size sculpture depicts the water goddess Chalchiuhtlicue ("Jades Her Skirt") dressed as a noblewoman.
JEAN PIERRE COURAU/EXPLORER/AUSCAPE

JOHN DOWNER/PLANET EARTH PICTURES

CIVILIZATIONS IN THE ANDES

3500 BC – AD 1470

The Rise of Andean Civilization before the Inka

TERENCE N. D'ALTROY

IN 1532, A CONTINGENT of 150 Spanish conquistadors, led by Francisco Pizarro, ascended from coastal Tumbez into the Peruvian Andes and the heart of the Inka empire. At the royal settlement of Cajamarca, they brazenly captured and garroted the emperor Atawalpa, recent victor over his brother Wascar in a five-year civil war. Pizarro's advance triggered the collapse of Tawantinsuyu, the largest prehistoric polity in the Americas. The century-long Inka empire, however, was only the last of a series of indigenous civilizations in the Andes, which began to emerge by 3500 BC.

This chapter explores the development of those societies, from simple villages to imperial empires. It traces the roles of politics, warfare, ideology, and economics in the rise and fall of ancient chiefdoms and states, in a region notable as much for its extraordinary cultures as for its spectacular landscapes.

Among the objects found in Tomb I of the third-century AD Royal Tombs of Sipán were a necklace of gold and silver peanut shapes, gold and turquoise earspools, and shell pectorals. This tomb belonged to a man who was 35 to 45 years old.

A gold and turquoise *tumi* (ceremonial knife) from the Sicán culture (AD 900 to AD 1100), on the north coast of Peru. This region was the center of metallurgical innovation in the New World. Most metal objects were symbolic and status-related rather than utilitarian.

ORO DEL PERU/LOREN MCINTYRE

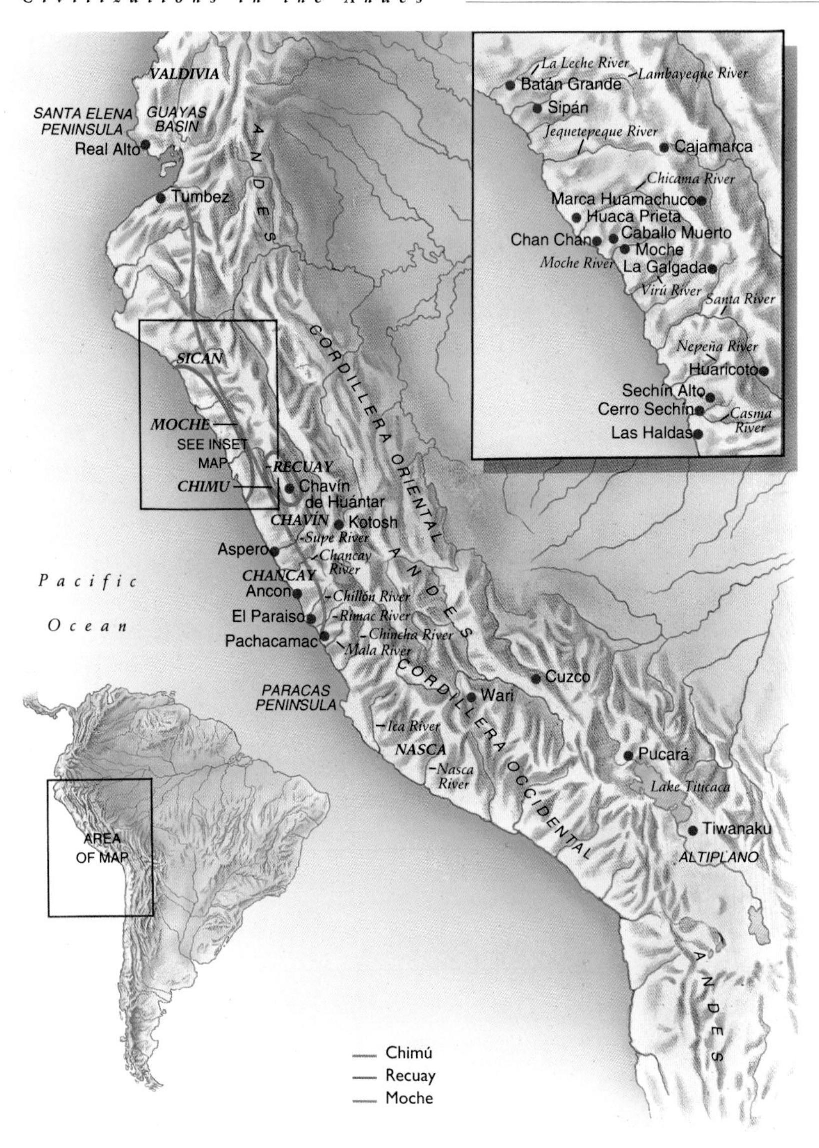

NORTHERN PERU
Sites and cultures of central importance arose within this region of dense residential occupation and monumental construction.

THE ANDEAN REGION
The major cultures and key sites in the development of prehistoric Andean civilization (3500 BC to AD 1470) arose between northern Peru and Lake Titicaca.
CARTOGRAPHY: RAY SIM

Western South America is a region of striking environmental contrast, dominated by the rugged Andes mountains. Along most of the Andes, there are two parallel ranges, the Cordillera Oriental (east) and the Cordillera Occidental (west). From Peru north, transverse ranges (*nudos*) divide the landscape into many valleys. Further south, the ranges are separated by the Altiplano, a windswept plain that encloses Lake Titicaca, which, at 3,800 meters (12,500 feet) above sea level, is the world's highest navigable lake.

The coastal area from central Chile to central Ecuador is a desert that is transected by river valleys, whose croplands cut swaths of green through a spectacular landscape. From Bolivia north, the Amazonian jungle borders the eastern side of the mountains, above which is the *montaña*, an area productive in coca and fruits. The sharply cut highland Peruvian valleys support the grains maize and quinoa; beans; the legume *tarwi*; and the tubers potato, *mashwa*, *ulluco*, and *oca*. Above 4,000 meters (13,000 feet) is the *puna*, a cold grassland that is the habitat of the Andean camelids—the llama, alpaca, *guanaco*, and vicuña.

Agricultural and pastoral strategies were complementary adaptations to the varied, vertically compact, Andean environment. By 3000 BC, all the major crops and animals were domesticated, most from natural progenitors in South America. Potatoes were grown by 8000 BC in Bolivia, maize in the northern Andes by 6000 BC to 5000 BC, and beans and peppers in highland Peru by 8500 BC. Lowland cultivars (plant varieties developed from naturally occurring species), including cotton, squash, and *lúcuma*, appeared in Peruvian sierra sites between 4200 BC and 2500 BC. Remains of the earliest known domesticated camelids come from caves in central Peru, dating to 4500 BC. Guinea pigs were important in the highland diet by 7000 BC, but may not have become fully domesticated until after 4200 BC.

Early Sedentary Societies in the North Andes: 3500 BC to 1800 BC

The beginnings of complex Andean society are best known from Valdivia culture sites from the Santa Elena peninsula and the Guayas Basin of western Ecuador. Architectural and mortuary evidence from permanent villages at these sites suggests that differences in social status may have been present by 3500 BC, or shortly thereafter. The site of Real Alto is notable for its size (12 hectares, or 30 acres), planning, and ceremonial architecture. Most construction occurred after 2300 BC, although the site plan was present for some centuries before. Long, low habitation mounds bounded an open plaza, into which projected two mounds containing ritual deposits. One mound contains a ritual burial of a woman in a stone-lined pit, with the dismembered bones of a male to one side, and those of seven other males in a nearby pit.

The Valdivia people gathered most of their food, but cultivated bottle gourds for containers and beans for food by the early fourth millennium. Maize, which appeared in the middle of the third millennium, was not an important food until after 1000 BC. The ceramics recovered from Valdivia deposits are among the earliest in the Americas. They are roughly contemporary with pottery from Puerto Hormiga, Colombia, radiocarbon-dated to 3090 BC (±250) and 2252 BC (±250). A similarity between Valdivia pottery and Japanese Jomon ceramics has been noted in the past; however, this resemblance is most reasonably attributed to stylistic convergences rather than trans-Pacific contact.

⬆ Llamas grazing in their natural habitat, the high *puna* grasslands found below permanent snow caps. Llamas and alpacas were the main sources of wool and meat for highland peoples throughout prehistory.

The Late Preceramic Period: 3000 BC to 1800 BC

Although foreshadowed by the Valdivia culture, Peruvian societies rapidly surpassed their northern neighbors in scale and complexity. From about 3000 BC to 1800 BC, simple foraging groups were transformed into complex agricultural polities that built grand monuments and encompassed thousands of people. On the Peruvian coast, where the major changes occurred, this era is often called the Cotton Preceramic.

The major coastal settlements lie between the Rimac and Chicama valleys, where sites such as Ancon and Huaca Prieta are preserved mainly as vast accumulations of mollusk shells and decayed organic matter. Their middens contain numerous well-preserved objects made from non-food plants, including gourd containers, cotton textiles, fishing nets, and reed mats. The few food crops were jack beans, squash, capsicum peppers, legumes, and the root crop *achira*. The known tools were primarily used in fishing, and architectural features are simple house foundations or terraces. Painstaking study by Junius Bird, however, has revealed fine artistic imagery in cotton textiles, carved gourds, and basketry that is belied by the middens' drab outward appearance. Animal figures woven as part of the cloth fabric are especially arresting.

A few sites display multilayered mound architecture. El Paraiso, in the Chillón Valley, is the largest preceramic site in the Andes. It covers more than 50 hectares (125 acres) and contains 13 or 14 rock mounds up to 6 meters (20 feet) high. The site's brief occupation at the end of the Preceramic, and its scant residential debris, may indicate rapid social change, pressure on food resources, or both. Excavations at Aspero, in the Supe Valley, show that some rooms were filled in to form foundations for later buildings. Dedicatory caches, including human burials; spondylus shell from coastal Ecuador; brilliant feathers; shell, bone, plant, and stone beads; and unfired clay figurines, were placed in these structures when new buildings were erected.

The food sources for Preceramic populations are a matter of contention, as scientists debate whether humans needed to control their food production to sustain a complex society. Some archaeologists argue that the abundant maritime species, especially mollusks and small fish, sufficed to nourish the builders of the early mound architecture. They observe that the immense shell middens—some over 3 meters (10 feet) deep and covering several hectares—mostly lack cultivated, staple crops. Another view holds that marine foods were too unreliable and low in calories for an

⬆ The modeled ceramic head and hand of a woman from the Valdivia culture of coastal Ecuador (3500 BC to 1500 BC). The incised ceramics from this region were among the earliest pottery in the Americas.

TONY MORRISON/SOUTH AMERICAN PICTURES

CIVILIZATIONS IN THE ANDES: 3500 BC – AD 1532

	ECUADORIAN HIGHLANDS (h)/ COAST (c)	CENTRAL ANDEAN PERIODS	CENTRAL ANDEAN KEY *SITES* AND CULTURES	BOLIVIAN HIGHLAND PERIODS
1532	Spanish contact	Spanish contact	Spanish contact	Spanish contact
	Inka	Late Horizon AD 1440 - AD 1532	Inka (h)	Inka
1500				
			Killke (h)	
	Cãnari (h) Mantẽno (c) Milagro (c)	Late Intermediate period AD 750 - AD 1440	Chimú (c) Ica (c) Sicán (c)	Qolla, Lupaqa Pacajos
1000				
				Tiwanaku V
		Middle Horizon AD 600 - AD 750	*Wari* (h) Sipán (c)	
500				Tiwanaku IV
		Early Intermediate period 200 BC - AD 600	Moche (c) Nasca (c)	Tiwanaku III, Pucara
AD 1				Tiwanaku II
	Guangala (c) Jama-Coaque (h)		Salinar/Gallinazo (c) Paracas (c)	Tiwanaku I
500	Chorrera (c)	Early Horizon 800 BC - 200 BC	Chavín (h)	
			Cupisnique (c)	Late Chiripa
				Late Qaluyu
1000			*Las Haldas* (c) *Caballo Muerto* (c)	Early Chiripa
	Machalilla (c)	Initial period 1800 BC - 800 BC	*Kotosh* (h)	Early Qaluyu
1500				
			Cerro Sechín (c) *El Paraiso* (c)	
2000				
	Cerro Narrio (h)		*Huaca Prieta* (c) Ventanilla (c)	
2500	Valdivia (c)	Late Preceramic 3000 BC - 1800 BC		
3000		Preceramic		Preceramic
3500 BC	Preceramic			

TERENCE GRIEDER

The multilayered north mound at La Galgada, in Peru's Tablachaca Valley, spans the Preceramic and Initial periods, having been repeatedly modified between about 2500 BC and 1200 BC.

adequate diet. As intensified foraging failed to keep pace with population growth, people would have been forced to adopt agriculture. The limitations of the marine diet would have been accentuated during the unpredictable El Niño climatic episodes, when southward-flowing tropical waters kill off fauna and cause torrential rains to fall on the coast. There are still insufficient data to sustain either position with certainty. At present, it appears that most groups lived on a mixed marine–terrestrial diet that increasingly included cultigens throughout the third millennium BC. The explosion of monumental construction in the succeeding Initial period, in contrast, was unequivocally based on farming.

Parallel cultural developments occurred in the Peruvian highlands from about 2500 BC to 1200 BC. Among the most prominent highland sites are Kotosh, on the eastern slopes, and Huaricoto and La Galgada, in western valleys. Each site covers only a few hectares, but contains multiple strata of elaborate, well-maintained architecture. The Temple of the Crossed Hands, at Kotosh, is a fine example of early ceremonial architecture. At Kotosh and Huaricoto, central enclosures contained sunken hearths used for ritual offerings. La Galgada had extensive residential occupation, but it is distinguished by two large mounds containing layers of fancy masonry, burials, and unusual artifacts made from parrot feathers and deer antlers.

Late Preceramic societies ranged from simple local polities to incipient chiefdoms. The emergence of social ranking, marked by the early mound architecture and a few elaborate burials, was a localized phenomenon. Some investigators infer, from the scarcity of residential remains at Kotosh and Huaricoto, which date from the Mito phase, that people gathered at some ceremonial locations only periodically. The dense residential occupation near La Galgada suggests, alternatively, that an agricultural society lived among its ceremonial buildings. Together, this evidence implies that the broad trend towards complexity was marked by significant variation among regions.

The Initial Period: 1800 BC to 800 BC

The Initial period, also called the Early Formative period, derives its name from the appearance of simple ceramic vessels, which came into use for cooking and for storing staple agricultural foods. The importance of the transition from the Preceramic, however, lies more in social and agricultural innovation than in craft technology. During this era, people began to occupy the inland parts of the coastal valleys, where they erected spectacular ceremonial complexes. Similarities in design suggest that the builders shared cosmological notions, although the nature of their ideas is still unknown.

The monumental architecture in many sites was laid out in a U-shape, with the open end facing eastwards or upstream. Pyramids formed the base of the U, and mounded arms enclosed plazas that often contained sunken circular pits. There are 45 sites with this layout between the Mala and Moche valleys, 27 of which also contain pits. The visual imagery of the pyramids, some with pillared entrances, stairwells, and friezes, was truly imposing. Although El Paraiso's layout anticipated these sites, the complexes of the Initial period dwarfed their antecedents. The scale of construction is exemplified by San Jacinto, in the Chancay Valley, where more than 2 million cubic meters (2,600,000 cubic yards) of earth was moved for leveling.

The Casma Valley contains the greatest architecture of the era, including major sites at Pampa de la Llamas-Moxeke, Cerro Sechín, Sechín Alto, and, nearby, at Las Haldas. None of these massive complexes seems to have been built at a single blow. Sechín Alto, for example, exhibits at least five distinct construction phases. It covers 56 hectares (140 acres), including an immense pyramid and five plazas with associated architecture, all arranged along a central axis. The main pyramid is the largest construction of its kind in Peru, and two plazas contain spacious pits, about 50 meters (165 feet) and 80 meters (260 feet) across.

The major coastal sites contained organized residential areas, but most people probably lived in smaller villages or among nearby farmlands. Population estimates, although conjectural, suggest that the largest settlements may have housed several thousand people. The social elites probably drew their elevated status from a combination of kin ties, politics, and religious sanction. Highland societies, in contrast, do not seem to have kept pace with the coastal developments. The main Late Preceramic centers, such as Kotosh and La Galgada, were enlarged and elaborated, but no constructions on the scale of major coastal settlements were undertaken.

Many settlements of the Initial period lay where the topography was suited to the construction of irrigation intake canals. People still inhabited some coastal sites, but the move inland signaled a

THOMAS POZORSKI

This anthropomorphic feline adobe frieze, about 2 meters (6 feet, 6 inches) high, adorns the facade of the Huaca de Los Reyes architectural complex at the site of Caballo Muerto, in Peru's Moche Valley. Huaca de Los Reyes is a large, important complex of the Initial period, with well-preserved friezes.

TERENCE N. D'ALTROY

A reconstruction of the two-story building that formed the base of the U-shaped monumental architecture at the preceramic site of El Paraiso, in the Chillón Valley, in Peru.

THOMAS AND SHELIA POZORSKI

Las Haldas, in the desert south of Peru's Casma Valley, was a major center during the Initial period. The main pyramid was built in stages, using a natural hill as the base. The plaza fronting the pyramid is bordered by two mounds about 400 meters (440 yards) long.

JOHN PHELAN/AL PAMAYO/D. DONNE BRYANT STOCK

The Tello Obelisk, at Chavín de Huántar, in Peru, dates from between about 900 BC and 600 BC. This ornately carved granite monolith, 2.5 meters (8 feet) tall, may depict an origin myth concerning the role played by caymans (alligators) in introducing tropical food crops.

The fortress of Chauvillo, erected on a bluff above the Casma Valley, provides evidence of the conflict endemic to the Early Intermediate period on the northern Peruvian coast.

commitment to agriculture. Middens show an increased range and proportion of cultivars, including cotton, gourds, squash, beans, maize, *achira*, peppers, peanuts, *pacai*, *lúcuma*, avocados, and guavas. These crops were adopted gradually at varying rates in different areas. Although farming supported larger populations, the gains were partly offset by a lowered return on labor investment, shortened life spans, and increasing malnutrition and communicable diseases. Hints of these problems had appeared centuries earlier in settled foraging villages, but became more noticeable with the shift to growing staple crops. People were probably unaware of the drawbacks until the population was too dense to revert to foraging.

The coastal societies of the Initial period were undeniably more complex than those of the Late Preceramic, but archaeologists disagree as to the organization needed to build the architecture and irrigation systems. Some researchers contend that the construction of canals or pyramids with dedicatory human burials implies that a coercive authority was present, whereas others suggest that the earliest canals were probably built communally. Paradoxically, the erection of ceremonial architecture may signify that the social elites lacked coercive power, and relied on religious sanction for status. Other scholars note that many early monuments arose from the addition of multiple layers, each requiring only a modest labor investment. Because some valleys contained several contemporary mounds built over centuries, fairly simple societies may have erected some mounds through intermittent collaborative efforts. Together, the variations in diet, settlement, and ceremonial construction show that the societies of the Initial period were increasingly complex and diverse, but this was not without cost.

The Early Horizon Period: 800 BC to 200 BC

The era following the Initial period is most frequently associated with the crystallization of the distinctive Chavín art style, which is usually considered to be the religious iconography of an expansive cult. Rather than being a time of social integration, as has traditionally been thought, however, the zenith of Chavín "integration" was concurrent with the demise of the social formations that built the great coastal ceremonial complexes. The spread of Chavín imagery was preceded, or paralleled, by important independent social and artistic developments along the coast of Peru. South of Lake Titicaca, the site of Chiripa was the center of a developing regional culture. Its rectangular array of buildings around a sunken plaza, built between about 600 BC and 100 BC, foreshadowed ceremonial architecture of later eras in the basin.

Chavín art is identified by a range of fantastical and representational figures that coalesced into their classic form by about 500 BC. Some scholars maintain that Chavín art represents the pinnacle of Andean artistry, and that this style found its most elegant expression at the site of Chavín de Huántar (after which the culture was named), in Peru's highland Mosna Valley. Occupation of the 40 hectare (100 acre) site is divided into the Urabarriu, Chakinani, and Janabarriu phases, radiocarbon-dated to within the period 1092 BC to 241 BC. The classic style of Chavín art is most widespread in the second phase, Chakinani. The temple at Chavín de Huántar, modified several times, contains elements of the earlier coastal complexes, including a U-shape and a circular pit in its plaza. Its finest stonework is found on the

LOREN MCINTYRE

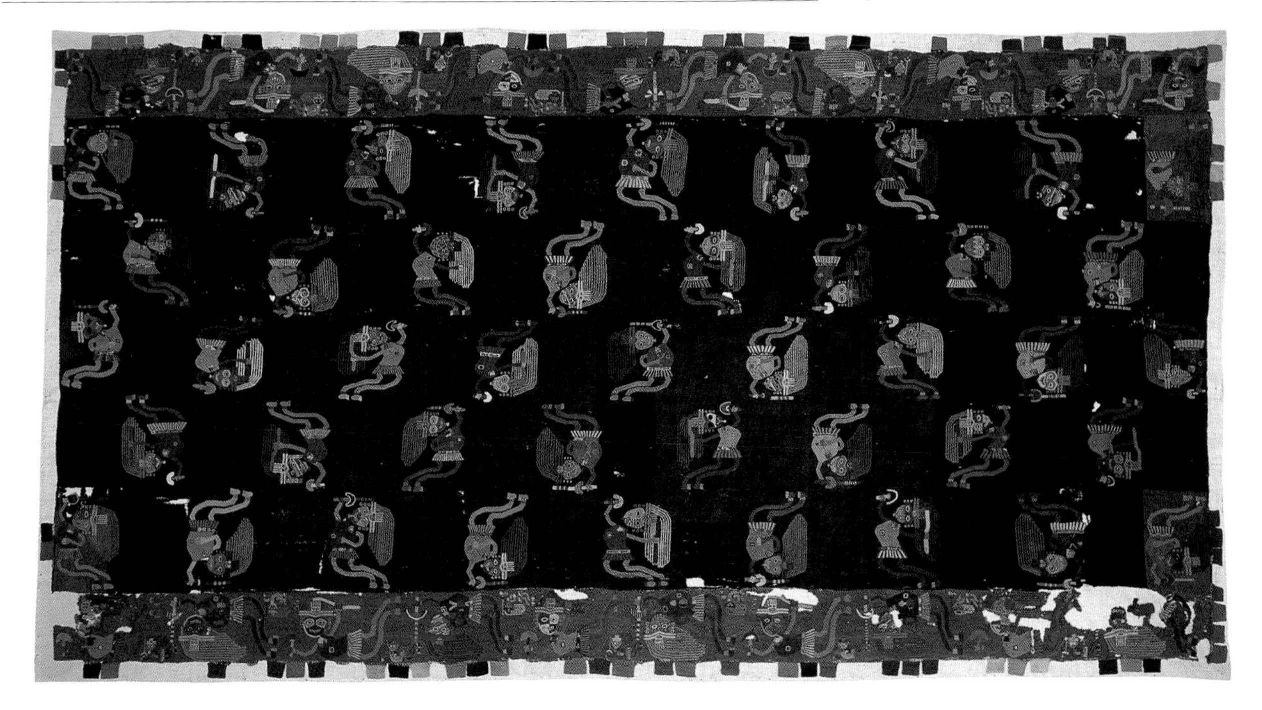

Tello Obelisk, the Raimondi Stela, and the Lanzón (a monolith). Two of the most spectacular images are anthropomorphic beings, known today as the Smiling God and the Staff God. The images also combine elements from diverse environmental zones, such as the cayman from the tropical forest, spondylus shell from coastal Ecuador, and the hawk from the Peruvian sierra.

The Chavín era also saw important advances in craft technology. Potters made ornately modeled and incised pieces; metallurgy included soldering, sweat welding, repoussé, and silver–gold alloying; and the heddle loom, a major innovation in weaving, was first used during this period. The most spectacular textiles from prehistoric South America date to the end of this era, from the Cavernas and Necropolis cemeteries, on the arid Paracas peninsula. Excavated in the 1920s by the father of Peruvian archaeology, Julio C. Tello, the mummy wrappings from bodies found in these cemeteries contain dazzling textiles decorated with myriad small figures and geometric forms. Despite their artistic mastery, the people who produced the textiles lived in a much simpler society and devoted less effort to public monuments than did their neighbors further up the coast.

The preoccupation of researchers with Chavín artwork has limited the study of daily life, population size, and social organization. Recent research has shown that Chavín de Huántar itself was the center of a local settlement hierarchy, although it was a town housing only 3,000 to 4,000 people. In comparison, the entire coastal Santa Valley, downriver from Chavín, housed about 6,000 people, with most settled in the upper valley, where canal irrigation was easiest. There, and in adjacent valleys, the temple complexes were associated with the residences of social elites. The fortified citadels in the Virú and Santa valleys also testify to an increase in local conflicts.

Despite the artistic similarities, coastal social developments could not have been stimulated by a cultural climax in the Peruvian sierra, as has often been proposed. The principal construction phases of the Initial period on the coast ended more than a century before the major spread of classic Chavín-style iconography began, and some coastal Chavínoid artistry preceded the highland center's cultural climax by 500 years. Constructions at coastal sites were also far larger than those at Chavín de Huántar and contained extensive areas of dwellings. For example, Caballo Muerto, in the Moche Valley, contained eight pyramid complexes, the earliest of which dates to about 1500 BC.

Recovered from the Cavernas or Necropolis cemeteries on the Paracas peninsula, this cotton funerary textile dates from about 300 BC. Mummies were sometimes wrapped in as many as eight of these colorful textiles.
MUSEO NACIONAL DE ANTROPOLOGÍA Y ARQUEOLOGÍA, LIMA/LOREN MCINTYRE

An embroidered anthropomorphic figure from a Paracas textile. Some of these beautiful cloths contained as many as 100 threads per centimeter.
MUSEO NACIONAL DE ANTROPOLOGÍA Y ARQUEOLOGÍA, LIMA/LOREN MCINTYRE

A late Chavín stirrup-spout bottle, with lustrous black surface.
ORO DEL PERU/LOREN MCINTYRE

Chavín religion undoubtedly contributed to the structure of society in many places during the Late Early Horizon period, and stylistic parallels and long-distance exchange of obsidian and spondylus shell also show that interaction among societies increased during this time. We do not yet know, however, how much the proponents of this ideology triggered change or helped fill a leadership vacuum left by local strife. Past notions of conquest, migration, or evangelism are not widely accepted today. Many scholars think that some societies adopted and tailored an evolving ideology to local circumstances without creating much social upheaval. Others suggest that a Chavín cult gained influence because local authorities elsewhere collapsed, perhaps as a result of environmental disaster or the general populace's resistance to elite demands. Similarly, the end of the Chavín phenomenon is an enigma. It may be surmised, however, that Chavín, as a religious movement that complemented regionally organized societies, did not have the independent political or economic bases to sustain itself over time.

J. DONOSO/SYGMA/AUSTRAL INTERNATIONAL

Monumental adobe architecture in the city of Pachacamac, in the Lurin Valley, Peru. The facades of some buildings retain traces of bright clay murals. A revered oracle in this city was destroyed by the Spaniards in AD 1532.

The Rise of the Coastal States: 200 BC to AD 600

During the following millennium, usually called the Early Intermediate period, societies in Peru and in the Altiplano experienced a surge of development. On the north coast, the Salinar and then the Gallinazo cultures held sway for about 300 years. The largest polities of these two cultures united only single valleys, but the population grew rapidly and settled nascent urban communities. For example, the site called the Gallinazo Group, in the Virú Valley, contained 30,000 rooms in an area of 500 hectares (1,200 acres).

These cultures were succeeded by the Moche culture (AD 100 to AD 700), the first Andean state, centered in the Moche Valley. State organization is inferred from the scale of the polity, and the evidence for settlement and social hierarchies and economic complexity. Between AD 200 and AD 600, the Moche polity expanded to rule the coast from Nepeña to Lambayeque, and built its greatest monuments. Information about settlement patterns is sketchy for the core region, but most people probably lived in villages among agricultural lands, as they did in Virú and Santa. They relied on maize-based agriculture, fed by canal systems that encompassed entire valleys.

Warfare may have played a prominent role in Moche expansion. In the Virú and Santa valleys, the people built scores of citadels before being incorporated into the Moche polity, after which the population dropped. Painted and modeled images of warriors and prisoners also imply that conflict was an element of state rule.

The Huaca del Sol (Pyramid of the Sun) at the site of Moche was the largest adobe structure in prehispanic America. Built from some 143 million adobe bricks laid in columns, the pyramid measured at least 340 meters by 160 meters by 40 meters high (1,100 feet by 525 feet by 130 feet high). In the late sixteenth century, Spanish treasure-seekers diverted a watercourse to erode the pyramid, recovering 2,788 kilograms (6,134 pounds) of precious metal. Many bricks have marks that some scholars interpret as signifying either payment of labor taxes or voluntary contributions by patrons. Across a plain from the Huaca del Sol stands the smaller Pyramid of the Moon, on which courts and rooms with multihued murals were built. Smaller pyramids, some still retaining fragments of bright murals, were constructed all along the north coast.

Like their predecessors, the Moche rulers apparently did not distinguish between political and religious authority. States typically develop administrative offices, but we cannot yet determine if these were present among the Moche. Nonetheless, the rich tombs found between the two main pyramids at Moche, and in other monumental architecture, provide strong evidence of an upper tier of a class-based society. Ceramic and mural iconography also depict either mythical or high-status individuals conducting lavish ceremonies. (See the feature *Moche Crafts*.)

Moche crafts reflect both superior artisanry and large-scale manufacturing by specialists producing for elite patrons and a large consumer populace. Moche ceramics were mass-produced, often by using molds. Scholars have also inferred textile production in workshops from an illustration on a flared-rim bowl. Metallurgist Heather Lechtman has said, "New World metallurgy means Andean metallurgy", and the Moche artisans and their successors were the experts of the Andes.

Using sheet metals, they created copper–gold and copper–silver alloys, and developed gilding and surface-enrichment techniques. Their products were primarily symbolic, status-related, and decorative, rather than utilitarian, although many copper tools were produced.

One of the most spectacular recent finds of American prehistory is the multilayered grave of the Lords of Sipán—members of the elite interpreted as being royalty by archaeologists Walter Alva and Christopher B. Donnan—who were buried in a deep chamber tomb in an adobe pyramid. If the array of gold, silver, copper, turquoise, and ceramic figurines, masks, and other artifacts accompanying these adult males is any indication, the wealth accumulated by the region's nobility was simply astonishing.

As is the case with many cultures, the demise of core Moche society is puzzling. Some archaeologists suggest that tectonic uplift, drifting sands, or a long drought (from AD 562 to AD 594) caused agricultural failure. The populace resettled, some going inland to fortified settlements, but most went about 150 kilometers (90 miles) north into the Lambayeque region. Evidence of external conquest is scant, although fortifications such as those at the site of Galindo do imply conflict with societies of the western Andes.

ERIC PASQUIER/SYGMA/AUSTRAL INTERNATIONAL

Excavations at the deep shaft tomb of the adobe pyramid at the Royal Tombs of Sipán. The principal coffin lay in the center of the shaft, and ceramic vessels lay in niches along the sides of the burial chamber.

During Moche's heyday, the urban settlement of Pachacamac was the hub of a major polity on the central coast. Renowned in late prehistory as an ancient oracle, the site boasted an immense pyramid and extensive residential areas. Pachacamac maintained an unusual place among Andean cultures, as it housed foreign enclaves and enjoyed almost 2,000 years of continuous occupation until the arrival of the Spanish.

On the south coast, the Nasca (or Nazca) culture flourished from about 200 BC to AD 600.. The two principal sites of the Nasca Valley, Cahuachi and Tambo Viejo, differ radically. Cahuachi consists largely of 150 hectares (370 acres) of monumental archi-tecture and open plazas, built on and among natural hills. The scarcity of residential remains suggests to some archaeologists that Cahuachi was more a focus of periodic rituals than an urban center. In contrast, one sector of Tambo Viejo alone contains 8,800 densely packed rooms. To many scholars, this nucleated settlement was the first really urban Andean community. Like the Moche, the Nasca people made exquisite pottery, but pieces were manufactured individually, not mass-produced. Nasca culture may be best known for its extraordinary geoglyphs, or ground drawings. (See the feature *The Nasca Lines*.) As striking as they are, the Nasca lines were only the most elaborate of a series of figures executed from northern Chile to northern Peru.

Bright, multihued Nasca ceramics were decorated with human, anthropomorphic, and naturalistic images. Unlike the modeled, mass-produced ceramics of the north coast, each Nasca vessel was handcrafted.

NATIONAL ARCHAEOLOGICAL MUSEUM, LIMA/GIRAUDON/ART RESOURCE

ERIC PASQUIER/SYGMA/AUSTRAL INTERNATIONAL

The appearance of looted objects, such as this gilded copper bell, on the illegal antiquities market led to the discovery of the Sipán tombs in 1987. Standing 12 centimeters (5 inches) high, the bell is topped by a magnificent gilded copper bead (16 centimeters, or 6 inches, high) in the form of a feline head with shell teeth.

MOCHE CRAFTS

CHRISTOPHER B. DONNAN

THE MOCHE CIVILIZATION flourished on the north coast of Peru between the first and eighth centuries AD. Although they had no writing system, the Moche left a vivid artistic record of their activities, environment, and supernatural realm. Their extraordinary ceramics depict animals, plants, and anthropomorphic deities, and individuals engaged in hunting, fishing, combat, and elaborate ceremonies.

Moche metalworkers made remarkable jewelry and ornaments of gold, silver, and copper. Weavers created sumptuous decorated textiles of cotton and wool, and artisans carved and inlaid bone, wood, and stone, and painted colorful murals.

This tapestry panel shows warriors in procession, each carrying a large war club over his shoulder and holding a goblet in front of his body.
DENIS NERVIG/FOWLER MUSEUM OF CULTURAL HISTORY, UCLA

A ceramic bottle representing a fanged deity paddling a tule (bulrush) boat in the form of a large fish. In front of the deity is a human captive.
MUSEUM RAFAEL LARCO HERRERA, LIMA/LOREN MCINTYRE

CHRISTOPHER B. DONNAN

CHRISTOPHER B. DONNAN

Two examples of ceramic bottles showing human figures. The seated man at left is holding a piece of fruit. His headdress has two large feathered ornaments, and his shirt has an elaborate tapestry-weave pattern. The drummer at far left wears an elaborate spangled costume, the circles representing decorative metal disks.

Opposite page, top: This gold ear ornament with a decorative inlay depicts a bird warrior holding a club and shield in one hand, and a sling in the other.
MUSEUM RAFAEL LARCO HERRERA, LIMA/LOREN MCINTYRE

Bottom: A gilded copper headdress ornament showing a large headless human in silhouette, with a smaller human on its torso.
SUSAN EINSTEIN/FOWLER MUSEUM OF CULTURAL HISTORY, UCLA

THE NASCA LINES

TERENCE N. D'ALTROY

ROBERT FRANCIS/SOUTH AMERICAN PICTURES

On the south Peruvian coast, in the elevated desert zone of the Nasca *pampa*, is found an extraordinary series of geoglyphs—figures and lines etched into the Earth's face by removing rocks and topsoil. These geoglyphs were first recognized archaeologically by Alfred Kroeber in 1926, and hundreds of them have subsequently been studied and described by María Reiche and others. The animal figures are mostly birds and fish, and include a hummingbird, a spider, a killer whale or shark, a fox, a monkey, a lizard, a condor, and a frigate bird. Of the plant forms, flowers are the most easily recognized. Geometric figures, which are more numerous and larger, include trapezoids, triangles, rectangles, spirals, and zigzags. There are almost 1,000 straight lines, some of them extending for several kilometers, and hundreds of them radiate out from scores of central points.

The plant and animal figures were probably made by members of the Nasca culture during the Early Intermediate period, about 200 BC to AD 600. Most linear motifs were probably created a little later.

Interpretations of the lines are varied and hard to confirm. The full meaning of the markings may remain a mystery forever. Fanciful tales that they were inspired by extraterrestrial visitations have been popularized by Erik Von Daniken, but have no scientific credibility. It is thought that some groups of lines mark the passage of the sun across the zenith, but the popular idea that the entire array formed an enormous calendar has not been supported by the meticulous investigations of astronomers. The figures could also be representations of images envisioned in constellations. It is likely that the images delineated sacred spaces where ceremonies were conducted, perhaps to reinforce bonds of kinship or mutual responsibility. In part because the line centers lie near watercourses, astronomer Anthony Aveni has also suggested that the lines marked natural cycles, especially water flow.

The spider figure, about 46 meters (150 feet) across, is one of the most representational of the Nasca images. María Reiche's premise that its layout reflects a precise understanding of geometry or numerology has been challenged by astronomer Anthony Aveni.

One of the most elegant geoglyphs on the Nasca *pampa* is the hummingbird, with its elongated beak. This image is about 91 meters (300 feet) long. Elongated beaks are a feature of a number of the Nasca bird images.

TONY MORRISON/SOUTH AMERICAN PICTURES

The Rise of the Highland States: AD 100 to AD 900

While Moche culture ruled the northern coast of Peru, the two urban centers of Tiwanaku and Wari rose to power in the south-central Andes, reaching their peak during an era often called the Middle Horizon. The residents of Tiwanaku, just south of Lake Titicaca, began major architectural and agrarian projects about AD 100. Between AD 375 and AD 725, Tiwanaku became fully urban, and the polity's hegemony expanded into the Bolivian jungles, the south Peruvian and north Chilean coasts, and northwestern Argentina. The capital covered more than 400 hectares (1,000 acres), and housed between 30,000 and 50,000 people. Its core included the temples of Pumapunku and Kalasasaya and the pyramid of Akapana, all notable for their carved megalithic sculptures, especially the Gateway of the Sun. Other stonework depicts humans, stylized animals, and composite figures. Ongoing research has shown that Tiwanaku contained rather poorer dwellings, some of which housed craftsmen, such as potters. Elaborate tapestries and ceramics, especially drinking cups and jars, provide striking examples of the skill of Tiwanaku's artisans.

Tiwanaku lay at the apex of a settlement hierarchy that included Altiplano and lakeside settlements, such as Luqurmata and Pajchiri. Of all the civilizations of the Andes, Tiwanaku relied most heavily on camelid herding, but its people also reclaimed lacustrine wetlands for farming in a system that covered 75 square kilometers (30 square miles). Modern reconstructed fields in this area are highly frost-resistant and productive for tuber crops.

Wari, a great Andean city in the Ayacucho Basin, gained dominion over the south Peruvian highlands from AD 500 to AD 750. This settlement had an urban core of 250 hectares (625 acres) and a periphery of similar size. Like Tiwanaku, it was a demographic magnet, concentrating much of the region's population into a single locale. Although Wari developed a strong central administration, the capital itself grew irregularly by accretion. Some temple construction is present, especially in the early Moraduchayuq sector, but most of Wari's architecture consists of large compounds in rectilinear patterns. Craft production has survived best in the form of fine ceramics, which closely resemble the pottery of Tiwanaku. Concentrations of obsidian tools found in some areas also suggest textile or meat production.

CAROLYN KERSON/D. DONNE BRYANT STOCK

DALLAS MUSEUM OF FINE ARTS/WERNER FORMAN ARCHIVE

This woolen poncho from the coastal Nasca Valley (about AD 600 to AD 700) is an example of the highland Wari style. Woolen textiles provide evidence of exchange between adjacent mountain and coastal societies.

The Kalasasaya temple, in Tiwanaku, in highland Bolivia, dates to between about AD 300 and AD 900. Built of finely hewn stone, the temple was aligned with the four points of the compass. The carved stelae, such as the Ponce Monolith framed in the doorway, were key symbols of power.

Andean ceremonial items often combined metal and lapidary work in turquoise and lapis lazuli. Exotic materials, such as marine shell and feathers, were also highly prized. This Tiwanaku-style pendant, dating from about AD 500 to AD 600, is made of shell, stone, silver, and copper.
ROBERT FRERCK/ODYSSEY, CHICAGO/ROBERT HARDING PICTURE LIBRARY

Researchers differ as to the nature of the Wari expansion, which lasted only from AD 600 to AD 700. Some envision an empire based on military conquest, whereas others see relations built on religious or mutual economic interests. With the exception of the south sierra, material evidence of the Wari presence is highly localized, suggesting that direct Wari control was geographically limited. The strongest evidence for Wari dominion lies in planned settlements, which intruded into other regions where transport and communications could be controlled. Pikillacta, near Cuzco, contains a large complex of cellular architecture, and is associated with subsidiary settlements. Pikillacta has recently been found to contain residential debris, rather than being essentially uninhabited, as was long thought. Viracochapampa, in northern Peru, is the northernmost Wari-related site, but it was abandoned during construction. Wari presence elsewhere is most evident in ceramic vessels at probable oracles, such as Wariwillka, in the Mantaro Valley, and Pachacamac; and in ritual caches, such as Pacheco, in the Nasca Valley. The collapse of Wari is likely attributable to the dynamics of its growth. The city and polity may have overreached their subsistence and administrative capacities, and collapsed during political or environmental stress.

The relationship between Wari and Tiwanaku is one of the mysteries of Andean prehistory. The two cultures shared symbolic motifs and styles of megalithic architecture, but their ceramic styles are distinguishable, and there is little firm evidence for trade, warfare, or political interaction. Many scholars view the two urban centers as nonbelligerent rivals, each focused away from the other in its expansion. Others suggest that Wari was a subsidiary of Tiwanaku that gained independence, or that the two cities were dual capitals of one polity, as were Cuzco and Tumipampa in the Inka empire. The last two views are challenged by scholars who see Wari rising autonomously from local antecedents.

Several other highland cultures emerged at this time. During Tiwanaku's early phases, Pucará was an important center north of Lake Titicaca, notable for its stone sculpture. Pucará culture's brightly colored ceramics and textiles were widely distributed, the cloth as far as coastal Peru and Chile. The Recuay culture, in north-central Peru, is renowned for its modeled whiteware ceramics. Further north, the site of Marca Huamachuco was the center of a powerful polity from AD 400 to AD 1000. Covering 240 hectares (590 acres), this site contains multistory, stone architectural complexes with galleries that are several hundred meters long.

Parallel Developments in the Northern and Southern Andes

Indigenous societies in the northern and southern Andes were generally less elaborate than those of the central Andes throughout prehistory. By the end of the first millennium BC, societies in Ecuador, Colombia, northwestern Argentina, and Chile had formed agricultural communities. Each region exhibited local settlement hierarchies, social differences, reflected in mortuary treatments, and extensive use of status goods by AD 400 to AD 600. However, the most complex northern societies probably held only 10,000 to 20,000 members.

In coastal Ecuador, the principal cultures were the Milagro, Manteño, and Atacames, whereas the highland groups are better known by names of the contact period, such as Cañari, Puruha, and Cara. In Colombia, the groups formed social hierarchies, constructed irrigation and terracing systems, and expended group labor in building mounds. Among the most notable Colombian cultures are the Tairona, Quimbaya, Chibcha, Tolima, and Colima. They are best known for their artistry in gold–copper alloy (*tumbaga*) objects, but prestige items were also made of platinum, emeralds, and shell. At Buriticá, in Colombia, the gold-mining operations of the contact period were enormous. Smiths appear to have been attached to particular chiefs, who could lend them out to other chiefs.

This seated gold figure, 16.5 centimeters (6 inches) high, comes from Colombia's Quimbaya culture (about AD 1000 to AD 1500). Colombian metalsmiths created exquisite objects of gold and gold–copper alloy (*tumbaga*), including masks, crowns, earrings, pendants, and figurines.
BRITISH MUSEUM/THE BRIDGEMAN ART LIBRARY

LOREN MCINTYRE

In the Argentine Andes, the principal culture of the first millennium AD, called the Aguada, was succeeded by the Santamariana and other localized cultures. Regional cultures also dominated in Chile. Each society was a relatively small-scale local development, but the most northerly groups exhibited close ties to Tiwanaku from AD 400 to AD 700. Both long-distance trade and direct colonization have been suggested to explain this relationship.

The Late Intermediate Period: AD 750 to AD 1440

The final pre-Inka era is often called the Late Intermediate period. As Wari and Tiwanaku collapsed—about AD 750 and AD 900, respectively—highland power became fragmented, and the Peruvian coast resurged as home to the dominant Andean polities. About AD 600, the Moche polity shifted north to the Lambayeque region, while Wari and Tiwanaku were still at their peak. The relocated Moche polity occupied the area from the Jequetepeque Valley to the La Leche Valley, and built centers at Pampa Grande and Batán Grande, in the Lambayeque Valley. By AD 700, Sicán societies were supplanting the Moche. Sicán reached its peak between AD 900 and AD 1100, when vast pyramid complexes were erected, including Huacas Chotuna and Chornancap. About AD 1050 to AD 1100, there was extensive flooding, the core Sicán precinct was burned, perhaps deliberately, and the power center shifted west to the area around El Purgatorio. Between about AD 1375 and AD 1400, Sicán fell to the expanding Chimú state.

The Sicán region contained the most extensive irrigation systems in South America. As at Moche, adobes exhibit makers' marks, probably associated with recording labor contributions. Sicán metallurgy, the culture's most distinctive craft, was technically, aesthetically, and organizationally advanced. A workshop at Batán Grande contains smelting furnaces, ore, slag, and processing tools used in the mass production of arsenical copper. The most pervasive image in metals and ceramics is the "Sicán Lord", thought by some to be Ñaymlap, the legendary founder of the dynasties of the northern Peruvian coast.

By AD 900, a new group, called the Chimú, had emerged in the old Moche Valley heartland. Their empire, called Chimor, expanded from AD 1100 to AD 1400, through three to five waves of growth, until it engulfed Sicán and the entire north coast. Early expansion was marked by the construction of fortifications, but Chimú imperialism probably combined diplomacy and conquest. Recent analyses suggest that the expansion was tied to efforts to compensate for agricultural failures in the Moche Valley. Unquestionably, the Chimú invested enormous energy and engineering expertise in canals and drained fields, but more limited efforts on the ceremonial architecture so prominent earlier. An unfinished canal, intended to join the Chicama and Moche valleys, is emblematic of Chimú labor projects.

Túcume, or El Purgatorio, is a pyramid complex in the Lambayeque Valley, on Peru's northern coast, dating from the Late Intermediate–Late Horizon period (about AD 1100 to AD 1532). In late prehistory, it was the most important site in the region, but it fell to ruins soon after the Spanish conquest.

This plumed headdress is from the Chimú culture (about AD 1100 to AD 1470), on the northern coast of Peru. Many of the feathers used for such elite garb probably came from birds of the tropical forest beyond the Andes.

L. PIGORINI/ROME MUSEUM/SCALA

THE ROLE OF METALS IN MIDDLE SICÁN SOCIETY

Izumi Shimada

Large gold masks with slanted eyes have been displayed in museums and galleries throughout the world as stunning examples of the expertise of goldsmiths in pre-Columbian Peru. These familiar objects were looted from ancient tombs in the Batán Grande region of Peru's northern coast from the mid-1930s to the early 1970s—at times with the aid of bulldozers. Often, and understandably, misidentified as pertaining to the Chimú or Inka empires, they are now known to belong to the Middle Sicán culture (also known as the Classic Lambayeque), which was dominant on the Peruvian coast from about AD 900 to AD 1100. The name Sicán—derived from the indigenous Muchik name for the Batán Grande region, signifying the house or temple of the moon—designates the prominent cultural tradition that emerged following the demise of Moche culture between about AD 700 and AD 750 and persisted until the Chimú conquest, about AD 1375 to AD 1400. Sicán also refers to the capital, a ceremonial city with some 12 monumental adobe pyramids and associated tombs of elite members of society.

The Huaca Loro Tomb

To clarify the nature of Middle Sicán social organization and political leadership, the Sicán Archaeological Project, under the author's direction, has excavated more than 20 tombs of various sizes and in different locations in Sicán, including two major shaft tombs of the elite—the first ever to be scientifically excavated.

The six months' long excavation (1991 to 1992) of a tomb at the north base of the Huaca Loro pyramid far exceeded the excavators' expectations in its complexity and material wealth. The tomb consisted of a 3 meter (10 foot) square burial chamber, about a meter (3 feet) in depth, at the bottom of a 10 meter (33 foot) vertical shaft that had been cut into consolidated clay–sand flood deposits. The diverse contents of the chamber, weighing about a tonne (just over a ton), were arranged around the centrally placed but inverted body of a man about 40 to 50 years old. He was surrounded by his full ceremonial regalia, including a *manta* (a large shawl), to which nearly 2,000 small gold foils had been sewn (the textile has long since perished); a pair of ceremonial gloves 90 centimeters (3 feet) long, made of *tumbaga* (an alloy of gold, silver, and copper), one of which holds a gold and silver cup, and the other, a wooden staff with gold and *tumbaga* ornamentation; a pair of gold shinguards; a heavy silver *tumi* (ceremonial knife), with a semicircular blade; a number of gold headdresses; a standard with various gold trimmings; and six pairs of large gold earspools. The noble's face was covered by a large gold mask and three pairs of gold ear ornaments. His chest was adorned with at least four layers of beads, including amethyst, blue sodalite, and crystal.

Excavation of the burial chamber at the bottom of the shaft tomb at the north base of Huaca Loro.

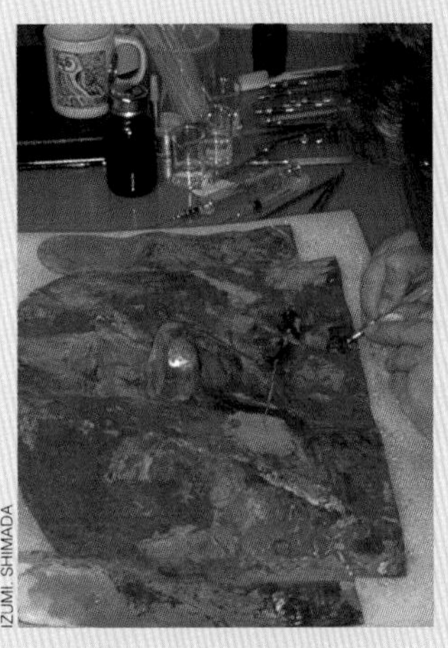

The large gold mask covering the face of the centrally placed body in the tomb required extensive conservation, as shown here.

The burial chamber also included the remains of two young women and two juveniles (all sacrificed); a disassembled litter, which had presumably borne the noble to his tomb; some 400 shells imported from coastal Ecuador; four large clusters of diverse beads, weighing some 50 kilograms (110 pounds); 15 bundles of cast arsenical copper implements, weighing some 200 kilograms (440 pounds); five piles of *tumbaga* scrap, weighing some 500 kilograms (1100 pounds); and thousands of arsenical copper sheet objects, thought to have been used as a primitive form of currency. At the northwest corner of the chamber was a mat-lined "box" containing at least 60 objects of a ritual and personal nature, including rattles, crowns, headbands, head ornaments in the form of gold feathers, and *tumis*.

Most of the metal objects listed above were fashioned from sheets of 14 to 18 karat gold, mostly 0.1 to 0.2 millimeters thick, skillfully hammered from ingots using stone hammers and anvils. The earspools and the gold mask covering the noble's face represent some of the finest examples of pre-Columbian goldwork thus far documented. These goldsmiths were masters of techniques rarely seen in combination, including a sophisticated technique of joining without the use of solder and innovative designs that show an intimate knowledge of the potential and limitations of the materials and techniques available. Decorative motifs take the form of cut-outs and repoussé, the most common being mythical feline heads and the Sicán Lord: the most noble lord, the earthly personification of the Sicán deity, who is shown wearing a mask and holding staffs. The power symbolism is evident.

A Metalworking Industry

The scale of production of *tumbaga* sheets indicated by the quantity of the scraps that are an inevitable part of any metalworking is equally impressive. The Huaca Loro finds suggest that a sizable group of sheet-makers, goldsmiths, and finishers were engaged in this task. *Tumbaga* approximating 10 to 12 karat gold in composition was treated with acid(s) to deplete the baser metals from the surface, leaving it high in gold concentration. This technique, called depletion gilding, was a practical and economic way to produce gilt sheets and was used extensively

Y. YOSHII

⮉The gold face mask after undergoing conservation measures. The mask is largely covered with cinnabar, and each eye is formed of tree resin and an emerald bead.

Y. YOSHII

⮊ Some of the gold earspools recovered from the Huaca Loro tomb. Their technical features suggest that they were crafted in the same workshop.

within the Middle Sicán culture—for example, to wrap wooden objects and ceramic vessels. The scrap thus constituted an important resource to be melted down to make new ingots. In this respect, the presence of the scraps in this tomb may well reflect the control exercised by members of the elite not only over the services of many metalworkers and lapidarists and over finished luxury goods, but also over raw materials. If political power can be gauged by control over human and material resources, then the nobleman buried at Huaca Loro was powerful indeed.

The use of diverse metals and the scale of metal production in Middle Sicán society, as revealed by the Huaca Loro tomb finds, were unprecedented in the pre-Columbian New World. Metals permeated all facets of culture and society, serving as the prestigious medium of political, social, and religious expression. From a comparison of the excavated tombs, it is clear that the different metals to which people had access (gold, silver, *tumbaga*, and arsenical copper) were a ready marker of their social status. For the people of the Middle Sicán culture, who brought the "bronze age" to northern Peru, metallurgical production was one of the prime movers of cultural development.

Y. YOSHII

⮈ Made from thin, hammered gold sheet, these cut-out figurines representing the Sicán Lord, each mounted on a plaque, may have been clothes ornaments.

The Chimú often incorporated feathers and shells in their textiles. This featherwork pectoral is decorated with the figure of a deity.
DALLAS MUSEUM OF FINE ARTS/ WERNER FORMAN ARCHIVE

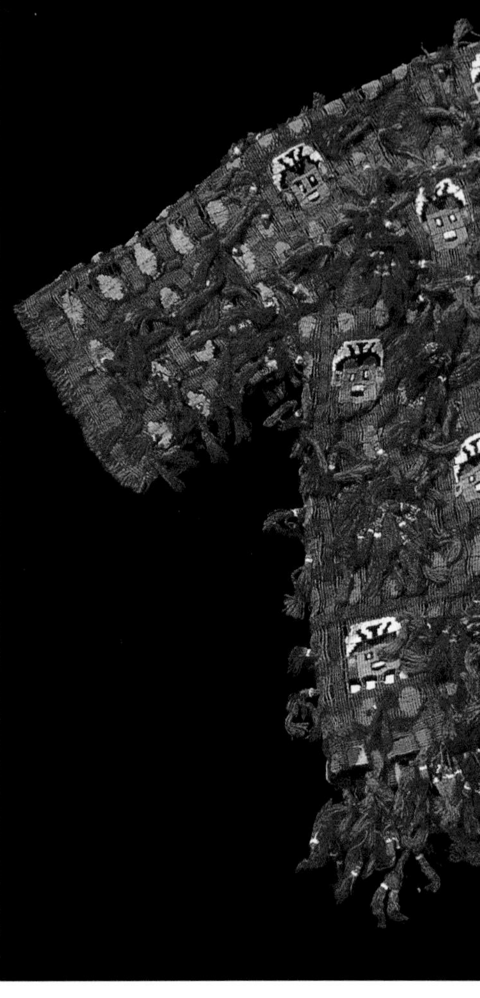

Chan Chan, in the Moche Valley, formed the apex of the Chimú settlement hierarchy. (See the feature *Chan Chan*.) Below it were the centers of Pacatnamú, Farfan, and Manchan, in subject valleys, and a populace of a million or more in lesser communities. Architectural and early documentary evidence suggests that Chimú social structure became highly stratified over time. The sociopolitical hierarchy was based on divisions by two, four, and ten, each division controlling a territory and perhaps a canal system. Origin myths recorded in Spanish documents say that the royalty descended from the king Tacaynamo through 10 successors. The documents also narrate that the moon was worshiped as the greatest god; the stars known as the Pleiades were the patron of agriculture; and the sea was a powerful deity. Many communities specialized in agriculture and fishing, while others focused on crafts such as pottery, metallurgy, and sandal-making.

A gold and turquoise *tumi* (ceremonial knife) from the northern coast of Peru. The *tumi* was a pervasive image in state-sponsored religion from Moche times onwards. Moche art shows it being used for ceremonial decapitations.
ORO DEL PERU/LOREN MCINTYRE

Even with political unification, coastal societies exhibited substantial cultural variation. In the southern Chimú domain, people of the Chancay culture produced distinctive ceramic whiteware figurines and delicate gauze textiles. Further south were diverse regional societies, the strongest centered in the Chincha and Ica valleys. About AD 1470, Chimor fell to the Inka armies attacking south from coastal Ecuador. Minchançaman, the last emperor, was taken to Cuzco along with many metalsmiths, renowned as the most skilled in the Andes, and the empire was dismantled.

The highland cultural origins from which the Inka empire arose were volatile and fragmented, and both oral histories and archaeological evidence suggest that warfare was rife in the sierra by AD 1200. Many communities were situated on high peaks, well above farmlands, and were encircled by massive stone walls. Sierra sites usually consisted of *barrios* (neighborhoods) of densely packed, circular buildings crosscut by serpentine pathways. Major settlements in northwestern Argentina, such as Quilmes and Fuerte Quemado, housed populations approaching 10,000, but unified polities encompassed no more than 20,000, as in the central Andes.

Alongside Lake Titicaca, the Lupaqa and Qolla polities boasted populations of tens of thousands, based on tuber farming and the herding of great flocks of llamas and alpacas. These groups had well-developed social hierarchies, but most highland polities were only moderately socially differentiated. The *ayllu*, a kin group including up to several hundred households, was the dominant social unit. Often divided into two or three ranked parts, the *ayllu* owned resources communally,

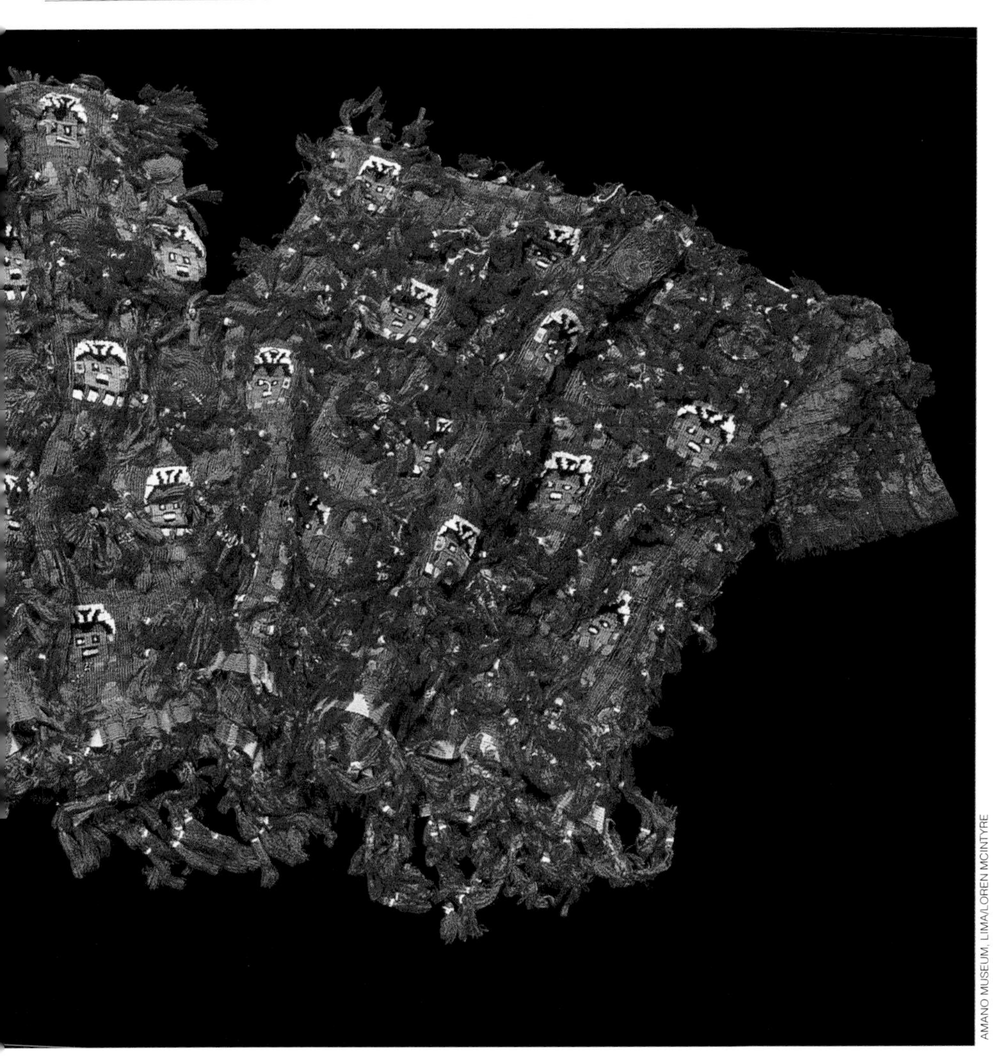
AMANO MUSEUM, LIMA/LOREN MCINTYRE

A funerary wool tunic (*uncu*) of the Chancay culture (about AD 1300), from the north-central Peruvian coast. It is 92 centimeters (36 inches) long by 130 centimeters (51 inches) wide. Such textiles were probably reserved for ceremonial occasions and for burials, in contrast to the more common cloth made from coastal cotton.

AMANO MUSEUM, LIMA/LOREN MCINTYRE

A Chimú-Chancay funerary textile from the northern coast of Peru, dating to the thirteenth to fourteenth centuries AD. Such textiles sometimes combined cotton and wool and incorporated different weaves, including gauze and more tightly woven fringes.

usually in several adjoining environmental zones. Religious systems appear to have been locally organized throughout the highlands. Although the populace exhibited little of the skilled artisanry of their predecessors or coastal neighbors, there was some elegant craftwork in the far northern and southern Andes, where metalsmiths manufactured fine pieces. The northernmost societies also used monetary goods and held markets, neither of which is thought to have existed further south.

By AD 1200, the Cuzco area may have been an oasis of relative tranquillity. The region shared a ceramic style called Killke, the antecedent to the imperial Inka style. The distribution of this style, and a lack of fortified settlements, suggest to some archaeologists that a wide region was already consolidated under prestate Inka dominion. This development set the stage for the meteoric rise of Tawantinsuyu, the empire of the Inka.

DAVID BERNSTEIN COLLECTION, NEW YORK/WERNER FORMAN ARCHIVE

This painted cotton textile from the Chimú culture, in the Chancay Valley (about AD 1100 to AD 1470), depicts a standing warrior wearing a loincloth and helmet and holding a long club in each hand. Serpents issue from his waist and head, and the figure is encircled by a double-headed serpent.

CHAN CHAN

JOHN R. TOPIC

Chan Chan was the capital of the empire of Chimor, which, at its height, controlled the whole north coast of Peru, from modern-day Lima to the Ecuadorian border. Over 600 years, Chan Chan grew from a town oriented toward farming and fishing into a truly urban center, characterized by occupational specialization and administrative activities.

The site was founded about AD 850 by the Chimú, and was continuously occupied, growing and changing, until at least AD 1470. The sequence of growth can be ascertained partly from changes in ceramic styles, but changes in social organization are best reflected in the architecture. As much of the early monumental architecture is still preserved on the surface of the site, it is a more useful indicator of social change than the domestic architecture, which was repeatedly remodeled and rebuilt. Archaeologists who have worked at the site since the 1970s have proposed a number of sequences for the monumental architecture. While they differ in detail, there is general agreement as to the broad outline of change.

Elite Housing

Before AD 1100, the site appears to have been a sizable town, with a population of perhaps 7,000 to 8,000 people, who may have been largely involved in farming and fishing. There were elites present, nobles and administrators of varying rank, who lived in monumental enclosures, or *ciudadelas*, such as those now called Tello and Uhle. The elites were buried within artificially constructed platforms located either in those same enclosures, or in the mounds and enclosures now called Huaca Tacaynamo, Chaihuac, and Huaca El Higo. The elite *ciudadelas*, or "palaces", have courtyards, storage areas, *audiencias*, and wells. The *audiencias* are rooms with only three walls, each containing several niches. *Audiencias* often have floors raised about 10 centimeters (4 inches)

LOREN MCINTYRE

The central core of Chan Chan is dominated by the ruins of palace enclosures (*ciudadelas*). Between the *ciudadelas* are smaller compounds that served as residences of the lesser elites, workshops, and administrative facilities. Most of the population lived in *barrios* (neighborhoods) around the core. Sunken gardens are situated near the ocean.

LOREN MCINTYRE

The entrance to the Ciudadela Laberinto is at lower right and leads into the large courtyard. A ramp led from the entry courtyard up to an area with rows of storerooms. In the smaller courtyards, surrounded by storerooms, there are *audiencias*, where administrators kept the kingdom's accounts. The same pattern of courtyards, storerooms, and *audiencias* occurs in the central sector. A *barrio* is in the top right-hand corner.

above the surrounding area and dedicatory burials located beneath the floor. Both of these features are associated with elite status, and the occupants of the *audiencias* were probably nobles or high-ranking officials who acted as courtiers and administrators to the elites.

Chimú Expansion

Between about AD 1100 and AD 1400, the Chimú expanded north and south along the coast to control more than 400 kilometers (240 miles). During the twelfth and thirteenth centuries, an unsuccessful attempt was made to construct a canal to bring water from the Chicama Valley to the Moche Valley. Perhaps as a partial alternative to the lost potential of the canal, the Chimú then built large sunken gardens at the southern end of Chan Chan. These gardens of 5 to 25 hectares (12 to 62 acres) were excavated to a depth of almost 10 meters (33 feet), so that the roots of the crops could tap the ground water.

The *ciudadelas* built during this phase, of which Laberinto and Gran Chimú are the best examples, have exceptionally large storage areas. Both of these have a repetitive layout, consisting of three sectors: a northern sector, containing the entrance to the enclosure, which leads into a large formal courtyard; *audiencias* and storerooms; a central sector, with the same components; and a southern sector, consisting of an open space, sometimes containing cane-walled huts. The repetitive layout and the increased storage capacity suggest that these enclosures were used for administrative purposes to a greater extent than the earlier palaces, although it is assumed that they still functioned

ROBERT HARDING PICTURE LIBRARY

An adobe frieze decorates the wall of Ciudadela Tschudi's courtyard. This section of the wall is at the entrance to the storage area at the top of the ramp. The animals shown are probably *viscachas,* which resemble squirrels.

as palaces. It is thought that the goods stored in the enclosures were obtained from conquests and agricultural reclamation projects, and were used to support the workers and soldiers involved in those activities.

The Rise of Artisans

About AD 1350, some major changes began to be made at Chan Chan. There is much more evidence of craft production, especially weaving and metalworking, but also of wooden, shell, and stone artifacts. These changes in the economy had a profound effect on the city, and may have resulted from the importation of artisans from conquered territories, such as the Lambayeque region.

Some artisans were housed on top of specially built platforms adjacent to the *ciudadelas;* these may have been the king's retainers. Others lived in the four *barrios* (neighborhoods), each of which had houses, workshops, wells, and cemeteries. There is evidence of both weaving and metalworking in individual houses, suggesting that both men and women were full-time artisans. These artisans were supplied with raw materials and food from the storerooms in the *ciudadelas,* and this is reflected in subtle changes in the enclosures dating from this period: the northern sectors began to have many more *audiencias* and fewer storerooms, and the central sector had fewer *audiencias* and more storerooms. This change indicates a higher turnover of goods in the northern sector, and a lower turnover in the central sector. Commodities were moved in and out of the city by llama caravan, and the caravan drivers were accommodated near the city center. Craftworks were given as gifts by the Chimú elite to show their generosity to their subjects and to create mutual obligations.

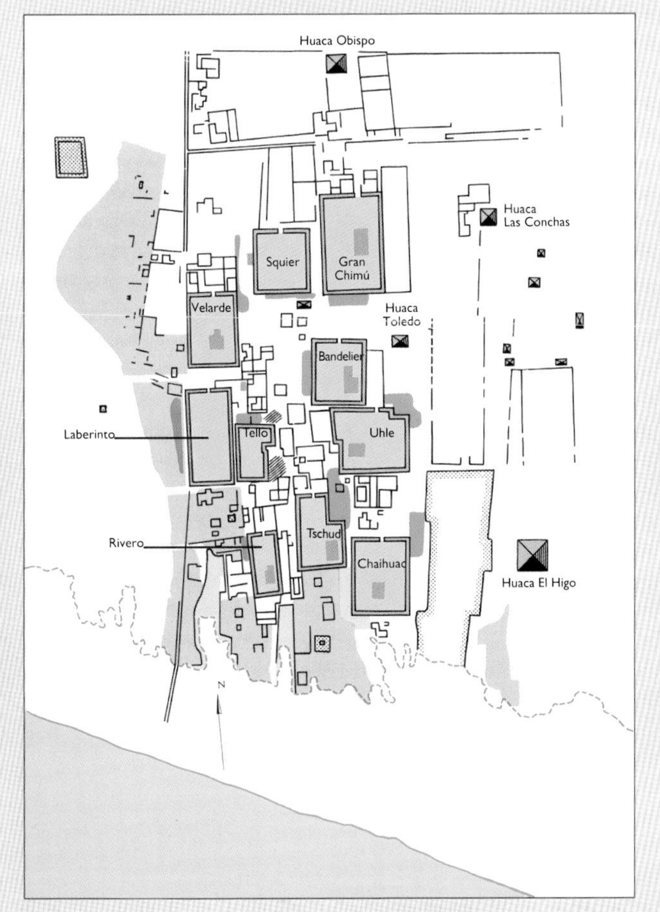

CHAN CHAN

The major features of Chan Chan as it appeared about AD 1460. The *ciudadelas* (palace enclosures) occupy the central area, and are interspersed with retainer areas and smaller enclosures. The *barrios,* the neighborhoods where most of the population lived, were located mainly to the west and south. Pyramidal mounds were located to the north and east. The ancient coastline is a cliff 10 meters (33 feet) above sea level.

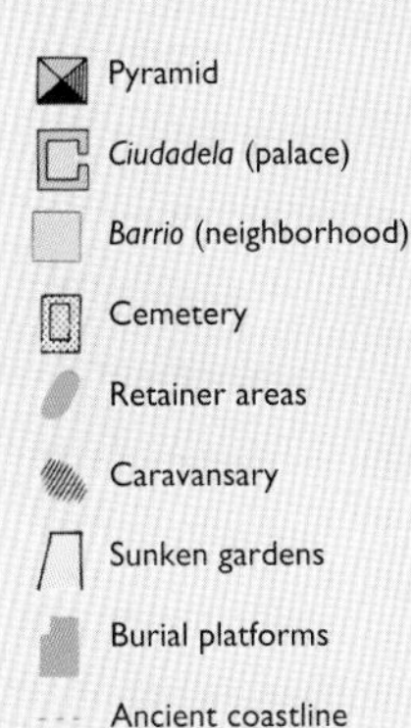

LOREN MCINTYRE

THE INKA STATE

A D 1 4 0 0 – A D 1 5 3 2

An Andean Empire of Great Diversity

CRAIG MORRIS

AT THE TIME THE INKA were conquered by the Spaniard Francisco Pizarro, in AD 1532, they ruled the largest empire in the Americas. It ran for more than 4,000 kilometers (2,500 miles) down the western course of South America, and included the western coastal deserts of Peru and Chile as well as the highland areas of Peru, Ecuador, Bolivia, northern Chile, and northwestern Argentina. It brought together hundreds of different ethnic groups, many of them speaking different languages, as well as greatly varied environments—high grassy plains, steep mountainsides, warm irrigated valleys, deserts where it rained about one year in twenty, and the lushly forested eastern Andean slopes. ("Inka" is the modern spelling used in Quechua, the language spoken by the Inka.)

The successful management of this enormous environmental and cultural diversity was the Inka's most important achievement. Economically, they were able to combine rich, but scattered, resources; politically, peoples of differing cultural and linguistic backgrounds were brought together into a very diverse but coordinated empire. Evidence is beginning to suggest that this strategy of expansion was accomplished not by great military force, as was once thought, but largely by means of traditional Andean political alliances, fostered by elaborate feasts and reciprocal gift-giving.

Inka storehouses on a steep hill above the site of Ollantaytambo, in the Urubamba Valley, near Cuzco, in Peru. Since the warm Urubamba Valley was devoted mainly to maize farming, these buildings were probably used for storing the crop.

This Inka ceramic plate, decorated with painted catfish and modeled snails, was found on the south coast of Peru.

JOHN BIGELOW TAYLOR/AMERICAN MUSEUM OF NATURAL HISTORY, NO. 5061(2)

The Inka are as noted for their great wealth as they are for the vast size and diversity of their empire. In a vain attempt to ransom their captured ruler, Atawalpa, they were easily able to fill a large room with exquisite gold objects. Pedro Sancho, one of Pizarro's scribes, gives a glimpse of the great Inka treasure as it was destroyed: "It was a thing worthy of witnessing, this house where the melting was done, full of so much gold in plates of eight and ten pounds [four and five kilograms] each, and in table service; jars and pieces of various forms with which these lords were served, among other singular things to be seen were ... ten or twelve figures of women, of the size of women of this land, all of fine gold and as beautiful and well made as if they were living."

While it was gold that most impressed the Europeans, in Andean terms the real wealth was held in thousands of warehouses throughout the realm, filled with foodstuffs, fine textiles, and other goods. It was also held in rich and varied lands improved with thousands of kilometers of irrigation canals and terraces, and in great herds of llama and alpaca, animals that served as beasts of burden and sources of wool. These investments, combined with their experience in managing lands, herds, and natural resources inherited from pre-Inka peoples, made possible a society that was famous for minimizing hunger among the common people at the same time as providing a rich court life for the elite.

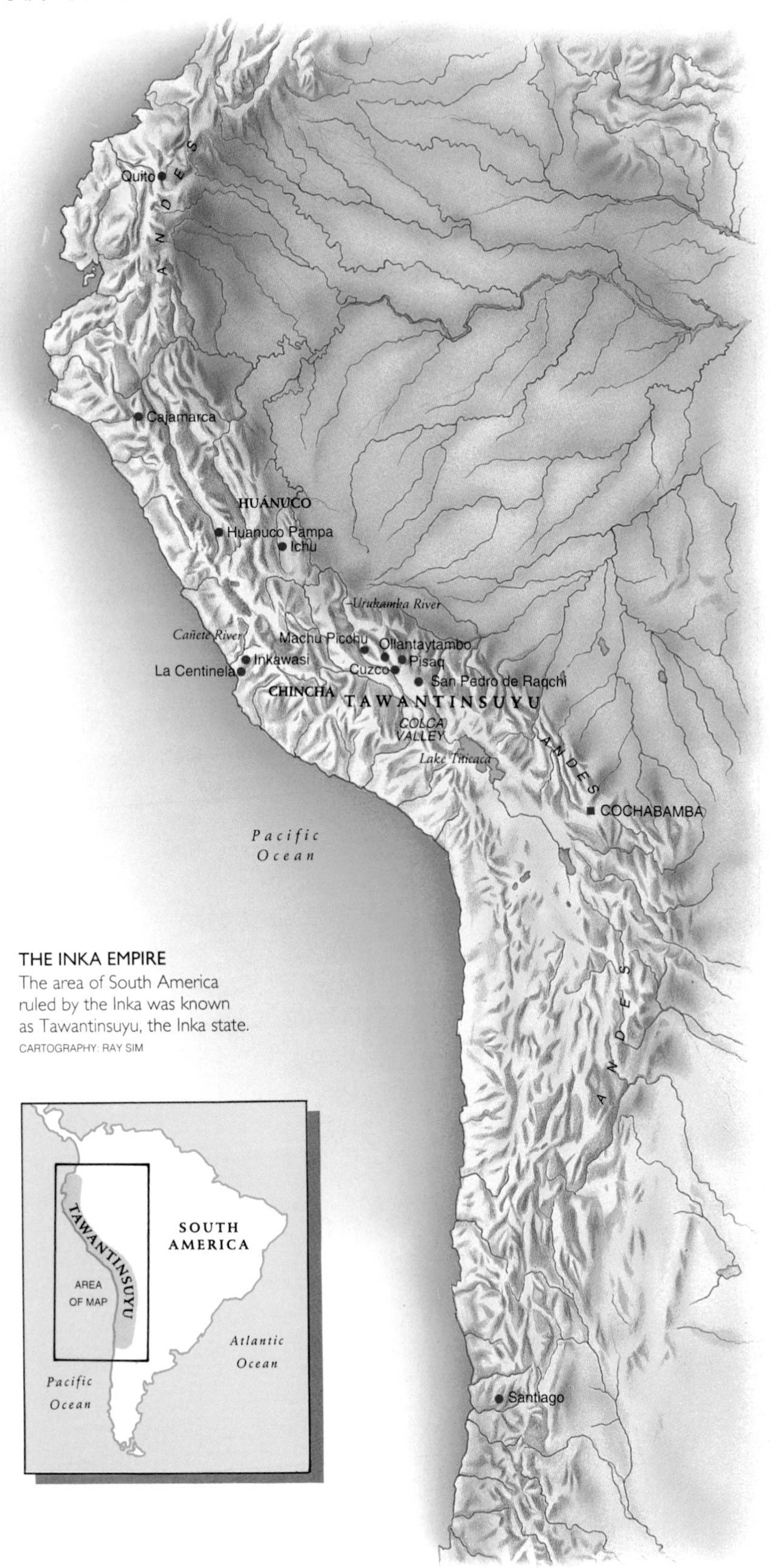

THE INKA EMPIRE
The area of South America ruled by the Inka was known as Tawantinsuyu, the Inka state.
CARTOGRAPHY: RAY SIM

Agricultural terraces in the Colca Valley of Peru. The Inka practice of building terraces to expand agricultural production, especially of areas suitable for growing maize, extended to many areas of the Andes. Many of the terraces in the Colca Valley were built before the Inka.

TONY MORRISON/SOUTH AMERICAN PICTURES

INSTITUTO DE ARQUEOLOGIA, UNIVERSIDAD NACIONAL DE SAN ANTONIO ABAD DEL CUZCO/LOREN MCINTYRE

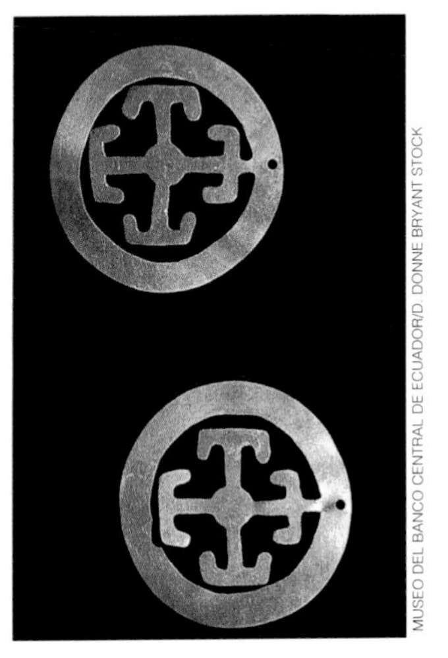

MUSEO DEL BANCO CENTRAL DE ECUADOR/D. DONNE BRYANT STOCK

These Inka gold artifacts are held in the Central Bank Museum, in Quito, Ecuador.

A gold figurine of a woman. Figurines of humans and animals were often buried as religious offerings. This figurine is unusual as human figurines were usually clothed.

INKA TEXTILES

VUKA ROUSSAKIS

The Inka inherited one of the world's greatest textile traditions from their Andean predecessors. By the time of the rise of the Inka empire early in the fifteenth century AD, Andean textile artists had developed a vast range of techniques for making cloth. Textile or fiber technology was so pervasive that it extended into areas not normally associated with cloth—such as the building of bridges, the construction of roofs, and the use of knotted cords (*khipu*) for record keeping.

The earliest textiles were made by twining. They appeared at archaeological sites such as Huaca Prieta more than four thousand years ago. Completely faded, they were little more than rags when excavated. However, a microscope reveals thread designs of condors (vultures), snakes, and other themes that became part of the Andean artistic tradition. Later the heddle loom came into use followed by a technological and artistic fluorescence that encompassed a vast array of designs and fabric structures.

Andean fabric structures ranged from plain weaves of simple warp and weft relationship through to weaves of great complexity. Tapestry techniques included slit tapestry (different colors of weft are separated between the warps); interlocked tapestry (wefts are interlocked at color change points); compound weaves with supplementary and complementary sets of warps and wefts; and gauze weaves, that create a lace-like pattern. Twining and other non-loom structures, such as looping, braiding, and knotting, were also used.

The principal fibers used in Andean textiles were cotton and wool. Cotton was cultivated in at least five natural shades ranging from white to dark brown. Wool came from the hair of Andean camelids: the domesticated llama and alpaca and the wild vicuña. Little is known of dyeing procedures but mordants were used to fix the colours. Most of the dyes were derived from plants, with the exception of cochineal red and a marine snail purple.

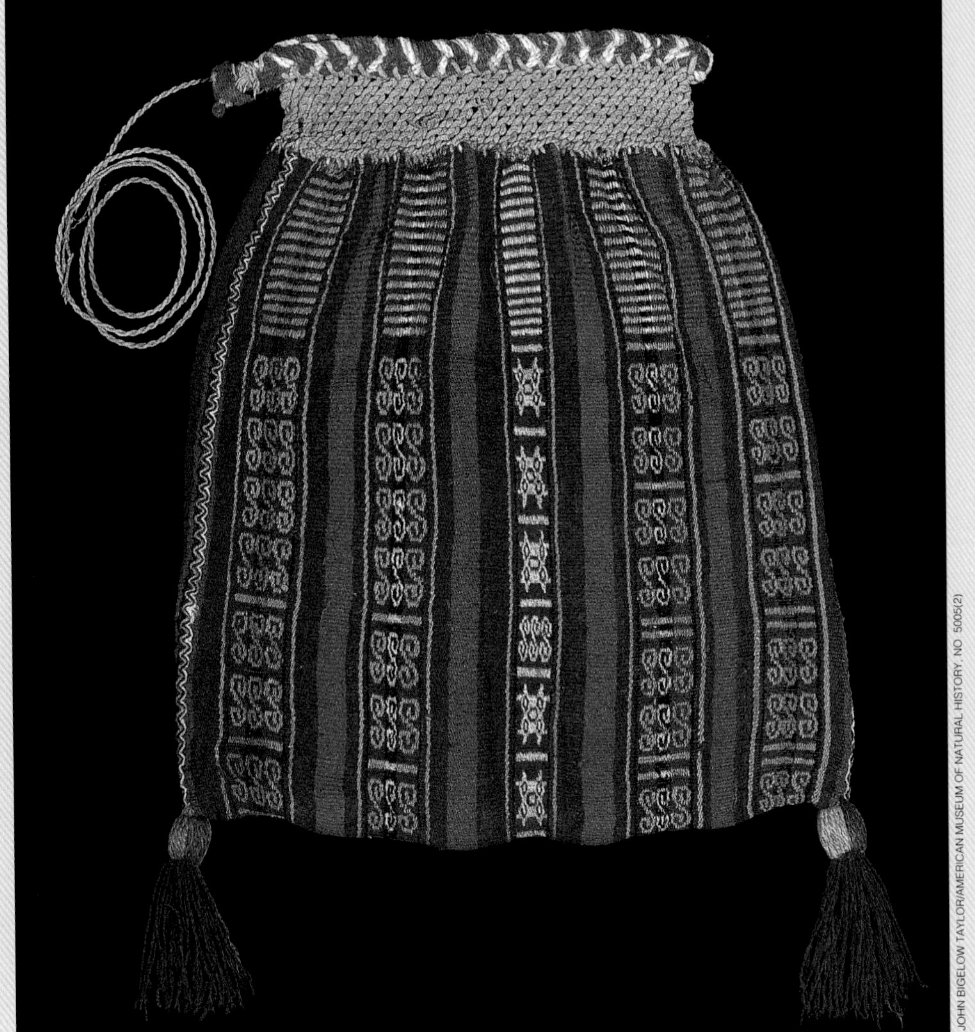

JOHN BIGELOW TAYLOR/AMERICAN MUSEUM OF NATURAL HISTORY, NO. 5005(2)

A warp-patterned bag made of camelid fiber. To create warp-patterned designs, more than one set of warps can be used on the loom, and interlaced in various ways. Bags such as this were used by the Inka primarily for carrying coca leaf.

The most important garment in Inka times was the man's tunic: this was made from a rectangular piece of cloth woven to size, folded over and sewn up the sides with openings left at the top for the arms, and a slit woven in the center to allow for the passage of the head. The tunics made for the elite were woven of extremely fine interlocked tapestry, which is completely reversible. In this labor-intensive tapestry technique, discontinuous wefts were linked, or interlocked at points of color change, revealing a strong, clean color separation between the designs. The lower edges, arm holes, and slit for the head were finished with embroidery. The bold, abstract designs on these tunics were symbolic and standardized under state control.

Accessories, such as bags and belts, were often decorated with warp-patterned designs. In warp-patterned weaves, more than one set of warps can be used on the loom and the warps inter-worked in various ways to produce the designs.

After the Inka conquest of the coastal regions of Peru, a number of provincial Inka styles developed, combining Inka features of size, design, and color with local weaving traditions. There are examples in the archaeological record of tunics of typically Inka shape and layout, but woven in slit tapestry, a traditional technique of coastal cultures.

The Rise of the Inka Empire

It is frequently assumed that the growth and strength of Inka control had its base in military conquests and the maintenance of invincible military power. Recent research has suggested, however, that military strength was only one factor among many in the rapid emergence of this Inka state. Most scholars now feel that the army was not the primary instrument of expansion and that military activities frequently had a ritual basis—rather different from our European image of war.

The lack of complete and reliable historical information makes any reconstruction of Inka political organization and the growth of the empire somewhat speculative. There are some clues, however, that allow us to begin to piece together a picture of a state that was very different from modern nation-states or sixteenth-century European states.

The first of these clues is the traditional name of the state, Tawantinsuyu, meaning "the four divisions together", immediately suggesting a combination of parts rather than a nation-state built on a single identity and set of traditions. Tawantinsuyu was closer to our idea of a loose empire, in which each unit maintained considerable independence, the threat of rebellion being a constant concern for the rulers.

A second clue is the rapidity with which the empire had been assembled. Evidence suggests that most of the expansion took place in a few decades. Traditionally, this rapid spread of Inka rule has been attributed mainly to military successes. While military force was certainly a factor, especially later in the expansion, it is difficult to see how in the early years such a powerful military force, along with its necessary economic base, could have been constructed so quickly when the Inka was only one group among many others.

Inka myths and legends were carefully manipulated to create an image of power. This mythic history had an effect on the people they ruled or sought to rule. It has also affected interpretation of the nature of Tawantinsuyu. Power and the use of force was magnified and embellished, and, at the same time, the myths underlined the association of power with gods and supernatural forces, giving the rulers an element of divine right and their expansion a suggestion of inevitability. Whatever the ultimate explanation of the rapid Inka expansion, it was not the first time in the Andes that a powerful and well-organized state had spread rapidly, to rule and prosper for just over a century and then decline, also quite rapidly.

A miniature tunic made of camelid fiber and decorated with a typical Inka checkerboard design. Tunics were often used to clothe the metal figurines used in ritual offerings.
JOHN BIGELOW TAYLOR/AMERICAN MUSEUM OF NATURAL HISTORY, NO. 5091(2)

A group of buildings at Machu Picchu, a site of ceremonial and religious significance in the Urubamba Valley. The site was covered with heavy vegetation when it was discovered. Most of the ruins have now been cleared, and many of the walls reconstructed.
SASSOON/ROBERT HARDING PICTURE LIBRARY

GEORGE HOLTON/PHOTO RESEARCHERS, INC.

The "stone of the twelve angles" in the wall of an Inka palace in Cuzco shows the care and precision of Inka stonework.

Saqsawaman, located on a hill above Cuzco, included three levels of terraces made of megalithic polygonal masonry. Early European visitors thought the site was a fortress, but it was probably an area devoted mainly to rituals and included a sun temple and areas of storage.

Cuzco: The Capital City

Further clues to understanding the process of the rapid rise and fall of the Inka empire, and perhaps of other Andean states, can be found by taking a closer look at how Tawantinsuyu functioned. Cuzco, the Inka capital, was composed of a central sector of palaces, temples, and public buildings. This monumental zone consisted of buildings made of stone blocks, so finely cut that they needed no mortar. Some sources suggest that it was laid out in the form of a puma. According to this version of animal representation in city planning, the temple and fortress of Saqsawaman formed the puma's head, and the area between the two rivers formed its tail. The area of the tail was known as *puma chupan*, "tail of the puma".

Around this administrative and ceremonial sector of Cuzco, lay a much larger area of less dense construction. Most of the population of the city lived in this area. Their dwellings were interspersed with cultivated fields, storehouses, terraces, and irrigation canals. Most of the inhabitants of Cuzco belonged to the Inka ruling elite, or to groups of state functionaries, or to groups of craftspeople, who made luxury goods for the state and its elite. Others were members of groups that apparently had been native to the region before the Inka moved there. Still others were members of noble families from the provinces. These people had been brought to the capital to learn Inka customs or to assist with administration. One of the most powerful reasons for bringing them to Cuzco, however, may have been to assure that they did not encourage rebellion in their home provinces. The elite population was augmented at certain times of the year by people paying their labor tax by cultivating fields and working on construction and other projects for the Inka state. The city's population was also swelled during certain periods of the ritual calendar by people participating in the important ceremonies hosted by the Inka rulers in the capital.

Rituals and the Land

Some of the most important towns in Tawantinsuyu line the sides of the Urubamba Valley, north of Cuzco. This deep valley, known as the "Sacred Valley", runs from the high altitude of Cuzco itself, 3,395 meters (11,135 feet), to low, almost impenetrable jungle. Because of the lower altitude of most of its course, the Urubamba enjoys a warm climate, well suited to the production of maize. Maize was important because of its nutritive value and its storability, but its most crucial use was in the making of *chicha*, the maize beer drunk in vast quantities on ceremonial occasions. Sponsorship of rituals and

LOREN MCINTYRE

ROBERT HASHIMOTO/BUCKINGHAM FUND 1955.2587/THE ART INSTITUTE OF CHICAGO

A sixteenth-century head-shaped Inka beaker made of hammered gold.

The Urubamba Valley, north of Cuzco, is a deep valley well suited to growing maize. Maize was an important food source and component of the ceremonial life of the Inka.

TONY MORRISON/SOUTH AMERICAN PICTURES

ceremonies by the ruling elite was an essential ingredient of the achievement and maintenance of power in the Andes. Ceremonies could not be sponsored unless the availability of substantial amounts of maize could be assured. The Urubamba Valley was the nearby source of maize to support the rich ceremonial life of Cuzco. To increase maize production in the Urubamba Valley, the Inka completed some of the most remarkable public works projects of the ancient Americas. Systems of irrigation made water supplies more reliable and shortened the growing season. The irrigation canals frequently flowed through newly-built terraces, bringing steep slopes under cultivation and greatly increasing tillable land in this warm climatic zone.

Changing the Landscape

The Inka matched the transformation of the landscape of the Urubamba with social and political transformations that were no less remarkable. In many parts of the Andes today, communities exploit the great variety of ecological zones by sending their own people to cultivate, pasture, or otherwise utilize the resources of zones some distance from their nuclear settlement. This direct exploitation of a varied ecology, by distributing the various communities to manage the natural resources, is essentially an alternative to trading. It was already an old tradition in the

MIKE ANDREWS/COMSTOCK

Inka terraces at the site of Pisaq, in the Urubamba Valley. Pisaq, constructed as an estate for Inka royalty, is one of the most spectacular examples of Inka agricultural engineering.

Machu Picchu, on the eastern slopes of the Andes, shows the extraordinary ability of the Inka to shape their settlements as an organic part of the environment in which they were built.

Andes by Inka times. The state modeled one of its labor institutions, known as *mitmaq*, on this tradition of moving populations from one region to another. Some people were moved as *mitmaq* for security reasons. Friendly peoples could be moved to watch over untrustworthy ones, and rebellious groups could be divided and settled in various places. Other *mitmaq* groups fulfilled state economic goals. For example, experienced maize growers were brought to newly terraced and irrigated maize lands, such as those in the Urubamba Valley and others near what is now Cochabamba, in Bolivia. Pastoralists could similarly be sent to grassland regions where state herds were being developed to increase cloth production.

The results of the Inka capacity to effect transformations are evident in the changed landscape of the Urubamba Valley. There are few details of the peoples who occupied and cultivated the valley, but the fine architecture in the archaeological sites gives modern visitors a vivid impression of the area's beauty and importance. Pisaq, with its spacious terraces and spectacular views, the great megalithic wall and hillside storehouses of Ollantaytambo, and the high terraces of the Inka ruler's fields at Yucay, all demonstrate the intricate planning and massive effort that went into this breadbasket of the capital.

The most famous site of the Urubamba Valley, Machu Picchu, lies at its end. Beyond Machu Picchu, the combination of rough terrain and thick vegetation makes the lower valley almost impenetrable. Machu Picchu remains almost as mysterious as it was when Hiram Bingham brought it to the world's attention in 1912. What is not in question is its spectacular beauty; few towns in the world so successfully integrate architecture with landscape. Its narrow terraces were probably not capable of producing a significant surplus so that agricultural products could be shipped to Cuzco or elsewhere in Tawantinsuyu. Hints of its meaning may lie in its location at the eastern edge of the empire, and the way its planning fits with its natural setting. Temples perched on precipices, water flowing downwards through stone channels and fine cisterns, sculpture carved in living rock: all of these underscore the integration of land with people and culture. One carved stone even seems to echo the hills behind it. Whatever else Machu Picchu may have been, it was permeated with symbolism and is not easy to explain in strictly utilitarian terms. Its main significance must have been religious and ceremonial.

GEORGE HOLTON/PHOTO RESEARCHERS, INC.

Economics and Politics in Chincha

Research in two regions far away from Cuzco gives an idea of the economic and political workings of Tawantinsuyu. The information it provides leads us to ask political and economic questions related to the expansion and prosperity of the empire. On the one hand, what were the bases of the authority of the rulers, and, on the other, what were the sources of revenue that allowed the growth of the governmental apparatus and the support of the elite?

One of the regions of Tawantinsuyu, from which we have considerable information, is that of Chincha, on the south coast of Peru. Before its incorporation into the Inka empire, Chincha was a rich desert kingdom. According to an anonymous sixteenth-century source, the Chincha kingdom had three specialized groups: farmers, fishermen, and merchants. The basis of Chincha's wealth and power apparently was primarily commercial. The traders controlled important maritime connections to the north and south. Trade with the north, now Ecuador, involved large fleets of boats. The document does not specify exactly what was traded, but the waters of that part of the Pacific Ocean are much warmer than those to the south where there is an upwelling of cold water called the Peruvian Current. The warm Ecuadorian waters are rich in the spiny oyster, spondylus, whose red shell had long been sacred further south in the Peruvian Andes, and, in some areas, was regarded as food for the gods. It was also believed to bring rain. Perhaps that belief came from the association of the spiny oyster with the rare, rainy years on the Peruvian coast, referred to as Niños.

Political ties between Cuzco and Chincha were evidently close. The lord of Chincha was traveling with the Inka Atawalpa at the time of the fateful encounter with Pizarro, in Cajamarca. Two of the factors that determined relationships between the Inka and the peoples they brought into Tawantinsuyu, were the size of the conquered group and the degree to which authority was centralized within it. The incorporation of Chincha into the empire appears to have been basically peaceful. The archaeological record also suggests that in the Chincha area there was a long tradition of social and political complexity and centralized authority. The Inka were able to take advantage of this and established themselves at the top of the pyramid of power, probably exerting some control over the process by which local people were selected for positions of authority. Rule was largely indirect, however, using the existing structure of power and administration.

The Chincha capital, now the archaeological site of La Centinela, is a group of impressive, locally built compounds that continued to function during the period of Inka domination. In their midst, the Inka built an adobe brick compound of their own. In contrast, the earlier Chincha construction was of the coursed adobe known as *tapia*. The Inka compound also contained a rectangular plaza and used the trapezoidal niches and doorways characteristic of Inka architecture. Alongside the buildings that appear to have served as an Inka palace, however, was a pyramidal platform more reminiscent of Chincha architecture than Inka, in spite of the fact that it was constructed of uncoursed adobe bricks. Several of the Chincha compounds of *tapia* construction have been modified with adobe bricks, indicating Inka involvement in the alterations—in one case, the alterations are extensive. These local compounds were probably related to Chincha social units and were the settings for important ceremonies and rituals, such as initiation, marriage, and other rites of passage. From within the city, the Inka indirectly supported and controlled various local Chincha groups. While using existing administrative structures, they were obviously not content to leave the mechanisms of power entirely in local hands. Elements of Inka identity, as can be seen in both architecture and artifacts, were evident at many points in the social and political ceremonies that held the upper levels of local society together.

SHIPPEE JOHNSON/AMERICAN MUSEUM OF NATURAL HISTORY, NO 334671

An aerial view of La Centinela in the Chincha Valley, photographed in 1931. The kingdom of Chincha was incorporated into the Inka empire and the Inka palace compound may be seen in the lower right.

The Inka palace compound at La Centinela was part of the substantial modification made by the Inka to the massive capital of the Chincha kingdom.

CRAIG MORRIS/AMERICAN MUSEUM OF NATURAL HISTORY, NO. K16781

The Region of Huánuco Pampa

Huánuco Pampa, in the Peruvian central highlands, more than 600 kilometers (375 miles) north of Cuzco, was among the largest of the administrative, religious, and warehousing centers built along the vast Inka road network. Huánuco Pampa served as a provincial capital from which several small local groups were administered from about AD 1460 to AD 1532. It was built on a high *pampa*, or plain, about 3,800 meters (12,450 feet) above sea level. Although it probably housed only a small permanent population, it had nearly 4,000 structures, providing for thousands of people who came for ceremonial festivals of state, at intervals filling the city with color and life.

These public ceremonies were held in the great central plaza and the surrounding buildings. Royal dwellings and temples formed a compound on the city's eastern edge. The thousands of jars for corn beer and plates, found in buildings around the smaller plazas between the royal compound and the central plaza, suggest that public feasts took place in these areas. More than 500 warehouses held food and other supplies to support the elaborate feasts. A compound including 44 houses provided work and living space for women weavers and brewers, who produced cloth and maize beer. These goods conferred prestige on the people who received them, and gave respect and power to the Inka who provided them.

Archaeological sites of local, non-Inka peoples in the region near Huánuco Pampa contrast markedly with the city the Inka built. In most of these sites, there is no material evidence of the existence of the Inka state. Local sites continued to be occupied as they had been for decades, and the ceramic vessels they used were essentially unchanged. Early in the Colonial period (AD 1532 to AD 1821), an inspection of part of the Huánuco

Compound for women weavers and brewers

Royal compound

Ushnu platform

Central plaza

Road from Cuzco enters here

Storehouses

HUÁNUCO PAMPA

A plan of the Inka administrative center of Huánuco Pampa, in the Peruvian central highlands. Huánuco Pampa lies at an altitude of about 3,800 meters (12,500 feet) and has nearly 4,000 buildings, planned around a large, central plaza. The *ushnu* platform (the center of Inka ceremonial activity) stood in the center of the plaza. The main Inka road from Cuzco to Quito entered at the southeast corner of the plaza and exited at the northwest corner.

DELFÍN ZÚÑIGA/AMERICAN MUSEUM OF NATURAL HISTORY

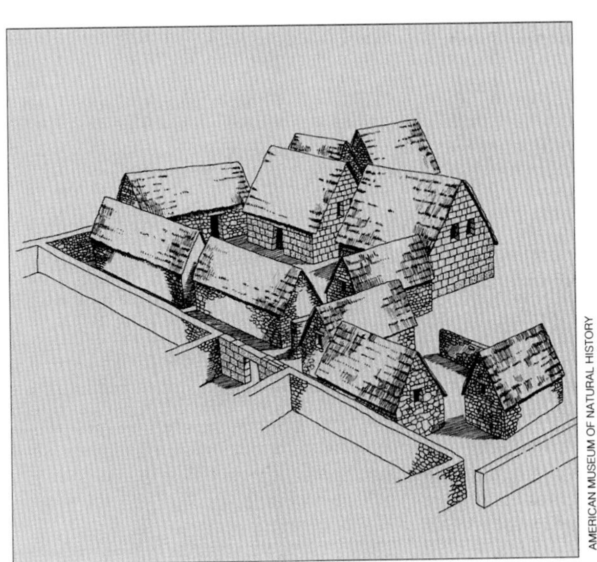

AMERICAN MUSEUM OF NATURAL HISTORY

An artist's reconstruction of the palace complex at the Inka administrative center of Huánuco Pampa. Inka palaces were more elaborate versions of Inka domestic architecture, which usually consisted of a group of rectangular buildings located around a courtyard.

region, mandated by the Spanish government, supplied important information on the organization of the local people. From this information, we can identify—for example—the towns where local leaders lived. An archaeological survey based on the inspection discovered substantial quantities of state-style pottery in the ruins of the town of Ichu, home of the leader of the Chupaychu, one of the numerous small groups the Inka ruled through Huánuco Pampa. Ceramic vessels made in the Cuzco style, but produced for use in Huánuco Pampa, followed Inka designs, emphasizing their power and authority. They were found in what is thought to have been the household of the leader of the Chupaychu. Apparently, the brightly painted pots, plates, and jars allowed the local leader to symbolize the Inka in the hospitality he offered to his own followers.

A Flexible System of Government

The contrasts between the Huánuco and Chincha regions exemplify Inka flexibility in adapting their policies and strategies of rule to the great variety of situations they encountered as the empire expanded. If a region was viewed as essential but its people recalcitrant, the Inka were capable of violent warfare. This appears to have been the case in the Cañete Valley, just north of Chincha, where a garrison town, now the archaeological site of Inkawasi, was built specifically for the subjugation of the area. If a region was wealthy and important, as well as amenable to collaboration, they would form a closely integrated alliance, as in Chincha. In a region fragmented into numerous small polities, the Inka were able to implement a strategy of sociopolitical combination in which they attempted to bring groups together and organize them hierarchically to form larger units. These units would have their own internal administrative levels that the Inka could more easily govern.

The *ushnu* platform in the central plaza of Huánuco Pampa. The *ushnu* were centers of ceremonial activity and a symbol of the Inka state.

An Inka bowl and two small Inka plates. Vessels with imperial Inka designs were used to serve meals provided by the Inka and their representatives throughout the empire.
BRITISH MUSEUM/ROBERT HARDING PICTURE LIBRARY

THE INKA ROAD SYSTEM

JOHN HYSLOP

WHEN THE SPANISH CONQUERED the Inka empire, in AD 1532, they found a massive and elegant road system covering much of the Andes. Some of the first European eyewitnesses wrote in praise of these routes, commenting on their superiority to those of Europe. The Inka road system is the most extensive ancient construction in the Americas. It is now possible to chart approximately 23,000 kilometers (nearly 13,000 miles) of this vast network, which may once have been almost twice as large.

RICHARD BERGMANN/PHOTO RESEARCHERS, INC.

⇑ This section of a road near Machu Picchu is part of a massive Inka-built road system that wound its way through the Andes.

The network of roads ran the full extent of the Inka empire, which was the largest native state in the Americas. It stretched from the modern-day Colombian–Ecuadorian border to an area just south of Santiago, in Chile.

The Inka empire was short-lived, enduring for little more than a hundred years before it collapsed during the Spanish invasion. How was such a massive road system constructed in such a short time? First, some roads built by pre-Inka Andean civilizations were incorporated into the Inka system. Complex civilizations had held sway in the Andes for several thousand years, and had left roads in some places. Secondly, the Inka genius for organization ensured the labor necessary for building new roads. All able-bodied Inka subjects were required to contribute a labor tax to the state. This labor service (often for several weeks annually) made millions of people available for work on state projects, such as building bridges and administrative centers, and tending state herds. The builders of the Inka roads thus came from many subject groups. Although the Inka supervised the work, the road system was, in fact, built by Andean peoples, many of whom were not ethnically Inka.

The road system was crucial to the growth and maintenance of the Inka state, providing a means of communication as well as transport. On all the roads that have been surveyed so far, roadside lodgings called *tampu* have been found, built at intervals of approximately a day's walk. Here, travelers, usually on state business, could eat and rest. It seems that at least a thousand *tampu* were maintained on the roads, and possibly many more. The roads also allowed armies to be mobilized and moved rapidly. The Inka state maintained very few garrisons within its territory, relying on its ability to move troops to any zone where trouble had broken out. A whole series of administrative centers was located along the road system, serving as a link between the hinterlands and the Inka capital, Cuzco, in the south-central Andes.

One of the more unusual aspects of the road network was a system of messenger-runners, known as *chaski*. The messengers waited in posts set at frequent intervals along major roads, and, by relay, could carry messages from Cuzco to the most distant parts of the empire—for example, to Quito or Santiago—within about a week. The roads made much mundane but also significant state business easier. Sons of the local non-Inka nobility wishing to further their education had to travel the roads to Cuzco. Inka officials and bureaucrats traveled the roads on state tasks and inspections, as did the Inka emperors, who constantly moved about their domains to ensure local loyalty was maintained and to direct military ventures.

Inka roads were not built by any one method. Several dozen construction techniques have been recorded. They range from simple paths to broad, paved thoroughfares with retaining walls. Many factors affected the construction and appearance of an Inka road: the labor supply available, the topography, a route's symbolic importance, and the nature of the land surface where the road was to be laid. For example, routes became narrower when passing through valuable agricultural terrain or over steep slopes. When the same roads continued over flat grasslands or deserts, they were often built 15 meters (50 feet) or more wide, which must usually have exceeded the requirements of the traffic using them.

Roads in Inka culture assumed a symbolic importance well beyond that attributed to roads in our modern-day culture. They were a symbol of the state, a type of "flag" of the empire, a physical presence known to every Inka subject. Inka roads were used to define the state's geography, and the relationship of different peoples to each other, a group's location being indicated by its position within the sequence of place names on a road. Roads were also used to define territories. Each of the four main routes leading out of the capital of Cuzco was named after one of the empire's four main divisions, and provided access to that division.

The overwhelming size of the Inka road system has meant that only small sections of it have been surveyed by specialists. Much still remains to be learned about this engineering wonder of the ancient world.

Imperial Symbols of Communication

The relationships between members of a society are based in communication that depends on a series of shared symbols; language is the primary example of the symbolic systems that allow a society to function and to reproduce itself. In complex societies, such as that of the Inka, the population was large with a great number of groups based on ethnicity, social class, and economic specialization. To attain a degree of participation and cooperation that would assure the functioning and growth of the polity and the economy, it was necessary to communicate with, and mediate between, all of these groups. There had to be a set of shared ideas relating to group identities and appropriate behavior. Identities, structures, and relationships not only had to be specified, the symbolic system also had to have mechanisms of negotiation, adapting and allowing for change and the creation of new structures as new situations were encountered. In an expanding state, constantly having to incorporate new groups, the system of communication had to be flexible and creative to realign positions and create new policies.

Most complex societies eventually develop systems of writing. They write down laws, and send messages and orders from one area or one group to another. They keep records of tributes, population, and economic transactions. They record their calendar, the events it regulates, and they set down their history, at least the version they want passed down to succeeding generations.

It is rather surprising that writing, in the sense of a set of symbols that can record spoken language, was never developed in the Andes, given the achievements in management and technology. The Inka did use, however, elaborate codes woven into garments that stated identities and guided social relationships. They also had a system of recording numbers and perhaps other kinds of information on knotted strings. The *khipu* used specific types of knots and clusters of knots to indicate numbers; the positions of the knot clusters signified the number's position in a decimal system of notation. Secondary and summary cords made it possible to record complicated numeric information, and the order in which groups of number cords were recorded probably related to a tradition of hierarchies and categories of information. A *khipu* could be rolled up and stored and carried from one place to another. It was a substitute for writing in the critical area of bureaucratic records.

The Inka road system utilized way stations and messengers to communicate between one part of the realm and another. This infrastructure for transportation and communication was remarkable for its day (see the feature *The Inka Road System*). Regional administrative centers that allowed many decisions to be made and carried out

JOHN BIGELOW TAYLOR/AMERICAN MUSEUM OF NATURAL HISTORY, NO 5001(2)

A *khipu* (system of recording numbers) of several colors of cotton cords. The knots indicated numbers, and the positions of the cords are thought to be related to various categories of information.

Opposite page: An Inka-style tunic of interlocked tapestry. The embroidery near the bottom edge probably suggests that the tunic was made during the Colonial period (AD 1532 to AD 1821). The checkerboard motif near the neck and the design band at the waist contain important symbolic elements.
JOHN BIGELOW TAYLOR/AMERICAN MUSEUM OF NATURAL HISTORY, NO. 4960(2)

locally by various levels of provincial authorities were part of the infrastructural system. The Inka maintained a balance in decision-making between the efficiency of local control and the security of frequent checks by central authorities. With notable flexibility, they adapted to local circumstances, while at the same time directing large scale and long-term state planning and building.

The royal headband worn by the Inka ruler supposedly had a red fringe that hung in front of the eyes and a golden plume mounted on the top. This headband is similar to eyewitness descriptions, except that it lacks the plume.
JOHN BIGELOW TAYLOR/AMERICAN MUSEUM OF NATURAL HISTORY, NO. 4959(2)

Identification through Design

One of the most important elements in establishing identities and relationships between peoples was the incorporation of symbols into clothing, ornaments, buildings, and items of daily use to identify the group of origin or status of Inka officials and others. The utility of clothing was not limited to warmth, of buildings to shelter, nor ceramic or metal vessels to holding food or drink. The designs we regard as decoration, even art, were filled with meaning. The world of manufactured goods was richly embedded with insignia that identified the people and groups who used them.

A gold Inka figurine wrapped in a tapestry weaving which suggests a high rank, possibly that of emperor.
MUSEUM FÜR VÖLKERKUNDE, BERLIN/WERNER FORMAN ARCHIVE

Clothing signified social identity; people were what they wore. As historian Bernabe Cobo wrote, "The men and women of each nation and province had their insignias and emblems by which they could be identified, and they could not go around without this identification or exchange their insignias for those of another nation, or they would be severely punished. They had this insignia on their clothes with different stripes and colors, and the men wore their most distinguishing insignia on their heads … "

Tunics showed the status of their wearers, while headdress was a main indicator of ethnicity. Belts and slings were also associated with group identities. Gifts of cloth and clothing were frequently made by the Inka rulers to the non-Inka peoples they brought into their empire. We have little specific information on the designs of these gifts, but it seems likely that they were of state design and state manufacture. Such gifts honored the recipients, and, at the same time, furnished new insignia that would redefine their social and political identity in ways the state desired.

The Inka had the custom of moving and resettling populations within areas already occupied by other peoples. Given the pattern of discontinuity produced by the custom, it was important to identify settlements with the groups who built and used them. The stamp of identity was often given through architecture (see the feature *Inka Architecture and Carved Stone*). Imperial Inka architecture, with its simple, but elegant rectangular buildings and frequent use of fine-dressed stone masonry, is frequently cited among the world's great architectural accomplishments. The use of trapezoidal windows and doorways is also a hallmark of Inka builders.

JOHN BIGELOW TAYLOR/AMERICAN MUSEUM OF NATURAL HISTORY, NO. 4996(2)

A solid silver figurine of a man holding ears of maize in his hands and with maize on his shoulders. The figurine is cast in a mold of 19 interlocking parts.

Throughout the empire, therefore, the installations built by the state were easy to distinguish from the towns of the local people who lived in the region. Even when Inka buildings were placed in an existing local town, as was the case in Chincha, the identity is evident. Architecture was a clear signal that the Inka had arrived to stay.

The design of the ceramic vessels in which state feasts were served frequently adhered to state-prescribed patterns of shape and painted decoration so that the source of the hospitality was clearly indicated. The architecture of the setting, and the dishes in which food and drink were provided, constantly reminded the beneficiary of the "generous Inka" who had bestowed them. The Spanish chronicles imply that even the music and the ritual performances were programmed to reflect the state's image and aims. They were all part of the government's communication with the people, the way it conveyed their obligation to tribute work and continued loyalty.

An Inka jar painted in the style of the Lake Titicaca region. Inka ceramics produced for state use were very standardized, but minor differences in style indicated the region where they were made.

JOHN BIGELOW TAYLOR/AMERICAN MUSEUM OF NATURAL HISTORY, NO. 4958(2)

Organization by Season

The *khipu*, the elaborate road system with its administrative cities, and the symbols borne on objects manufactured by the state, give us clues to the ways the Inka orchestrated people, space, and goods. Another important organizational element was the way time was structured to take advantage of the seasons. The Inka achieved this through a complex calendar—the details are still being worked out. It appears that the Inka actually used two 12-month calendars: a daytime calendar based on the yearly cycle of the sun; and a night-time calendar, linked to the cycles of the moon and certain stars.

The daytime calendar was marked by periodic sacrifices of llamas. It scheduled feasts, pilgrimages, and exchanges of goods related to important economic activities. These events helped coordinate various kinds of work, including agriculture, herding, travel and transportation, mining, construction, and warfare. The night-time calendar concerned natural forces: wind, water, and sacred places. Ceremonies seeking help from these forces occurred in an orderly sequence at sacred sites, called *waka*, creating a calendar of religious events. Because the night-time calendar used 12 periods, based on observations of the moon and stars, it did not account for 37 days in the solar year. The Inka related this 37-day period to the disappearance of the stars known as the Pleiades. The details of how the two calendar systems were coordinated are not as yet well understood.

Land Distribution, Labor, and Wealth

Most archaic states did not try to maintain the appearance of a separation between the political and economic aspects of their relationships with the people they ruled. In the Inka case, gifts and state hospitality involving large quantities of goods were a basic element of power. As at Huánuco Pampa, the dispersal of food and maize beer was a part of activities held in the city's architecturally most impressive public areas. Early Spanish observers describe massive issues and gifts of cloth and other goods to state officials, the army, and to recently conquered or incorporated peoples.

The major economic problem facing the state was how to provide for these enormous hospitality expenses and cover the living costs of increasingly large numbers of leaders, bureaucrats, and others providing services to the state. In theory, the state functioned without tribute of goods. Its revenues were based on labor given by the subjects to till the state's fields, care for its herds, make its cloth and other manufactured goods, build its roads, bridges, and cities.

Lands throughout the empire were divided into several classes: the lands of local communities provided for the subsistence of the great majority of the people; lands for religion provided goods related to various cults; state lands supported the Inka rulers, the armies, and the massive labor force working for the state. We do not know the proportions of land in the various categories; nor do we know many details about how the state and religious lands were acquired. Some of the land that passed into state use must have been taken from land dedicated to local purposes before the Inka expansion. The Inka created or greatly improved additional land through terracing and irrigation projects, investing some of the state's labor revenues in projects to increase production —for example, in the Urubamba Valley.

The "labor tax", or *mita*, was an extension of Andean principles, whereby leaders received labor from the people of their communities. The leader, in return, was expected to provide food and drink for the workers. Work was couched in a festival context with food, drink, and music. Economics, politics, and religion were part of events that combined work, ritual, and festival. The evidence of feasting and drinking found at Huánuco Pampa was an extension of the state's community principles, as played out against the backdrop of an imperial city.

Most of the labor the state received was provided by the *mita*, able-bodied male heads of households working for the state in turn. They cultivated the state's fields and carried out construction projects. The army was staffed mainly by soldiers serving in rotation. Other people worked full-time for the Inka, the most famous being a group of women known as *mamakuna*. These women, chosen for state service, were sometimes referred to as "virgins of the sun", suggesting two of the women's characteristics— they were unmarried, and many of their duties were related to sun worship and other religious functions. These qualities led the Spanish to draw a parallel between the *mamakuna* and nuns.

Written sources note that these women were also spinners, weavers, and makers of maize beer. At Huánuco Pampa, excavation of one of the places where they lived and worked uncovered hundreds of spinning and weaving tools, and sherds from large numbers of the jars used in brewing. It is clear that the economic importance of *mamakuna* equalled that of their religious duties.

The frequent mention of the *mamakuna* in census and other administrative documents shows that their numbers were large and their importance to the Inka state economy was pervasive. Evidently, they lived mainly in state cities, where they could be carefully controlled by the state. The Inka apparently sometimes gave *mamakuna* in marriage to local leaders as a means of forming or re-enforcing alliances, but we do not know how common this practice was. Since both real and fictive kinship were important factors in Andean political relations, however, it seems logical that the Inka would have found a way to manipulate alliances through such marriages. The large numbers of single women serving the state would have provided them with a substantial reserve of female workers and functionaries, and, at the same time, have provided the rulers with the opportunity to create social ties for their political benefit. As with most other state workers, the Inka provided the *mamakuna* with food, clothing, and housing. While these women had little in the way of personal liberty, they enjoyed a relatively high material standard of living.

The *yanakuna* were men in permanent service to the state. There was a tendency in early literature on the Inka to equate these men with slaves. Like the *mamakuna*, the *yanakuna* were dependent on the wishes of the rulers in a wide range of their activities. The Inka, however, lacked the concept of property to be bought and sold, much less of

A Chimu–Inka style ceramic ceremonial vessel (*paccha*) modeled in the form of a pointed digging tool, topped with a human head. *Pacchas* were used during fertility ceremonies to pour maize beer from the top which would flow out through the pointed tip.
JOHN BIGELOW TAYLOR/AMERICAN MUSEUM OF NATURAL HISTORY, NO. 4998(2)

JOHN BIGELOW TAYLOR/AMERICAN MUSEUM OF NATURAL HISTORY, NO. 4999(2)

Ceramic bowls from the Lake Titicaca region with handles of modeled pumas, and stylized maize or spondylus shell molded on the interior. Pumas, symbols of power and authority, were often associated with the ruling Inka.

An Inka storehouse with bricked-up trapezoidal windows at Ollantaytambo, in the Urubamba Valley.

NICK SAUNDERS/WERNER FORMAN ARCHIVE

A copper–tin *tumi* (ceremonial knife), with a blade in the form of a fish, and a human figure perched on the handle. Copper–tin, the hardest metal of the Andes, was a hallmark of fifteenth-century Inka expansion.

JOHN BIGELOW TAYLOR/AMERICAN MUSEUM OF NATURAL HISTORY, NO. 5006(2)

people as property. Interestingly, local leaders sometimes had *yanakuna* in their service, and their marital status was less rigid than that of the *mamakuna*; *yanakuna* were often married. One of the major services performed by *yanakuna* for the Inka state was caring for the royal herds.

A final category of labor service involved communities, rather than individuals or families. These were the *mitmaq* groups, discussed earlier in relation to the resettling of the Urubamba Valley. The state frequently moved them hundreds of kilometers, and they played major roles in both the political and economic development of newly incorporated areas.

Most state goods were produced by these labor categories, with the state supplying land and raw materials. Some artisans had specific titles, such as *kumpikaymoq*, the weavers of fine cloth. These skilled people supplemented and cross-cut the main labor classes in ways that are not always evident. The resulting wealth, however, was very clear. It could be seen in the rich cities with their palaces, temples, and more gold than the world had seen assembled under a single authority. It could also be seen at the feasts the Inka provided and the system of warehouses that guaranteed their ability to provide them. Storehouses were found throughout much of Tawantinsuyu, especially in areas where climatic or social and economic circumstances made the reliability of deliveries questionable, as described by the historian Pedro Cieza de Leon: "... in the more than 1,200 leagues [6,000 kilometers] of coast they ruled they had their representatives and governors, and many lodgings and great storehouses filled with all necessary supplies ... When the lord was lodged in his dwellings and his soldiers garrisoned there, nothing, from the most important to the most trifling, but could be provided."

Thousands of the storehouses can still be seen in orderly rows above the ruins of many Inka provincial centers. Excavations have uncovered primarily maize and other foodstuffs. The administrative center at Huánuco Pampa had warehouses with a volume capacity of almost 40,000 cubic meters (52,320 cubic yards). The realm must have had overall millions of bushels of goods in storage. Stored goods assured state workers that feast obligations would be fulfilled regardless of the time of year or climatic circumstances. The state preferred to leave responsibility for day-to-day local subsistence in the hands of local communities. That would not prevent it from increasing its hospitality, however, and perhaps also its use of labor, in times of crisis.

Overall wealth is one measure of the success of an economy. Another is the distribution of sufficient wealth so that the people are well provided for and content. We do not have information to really describe the standard of living of the common people of Tawantinsuyu. European inspectors, however, recorded enough complaints contrasting Inka and Colonial times to leave little doubt that the situation for most had been better under the Inka.

Yet another measure of economic success is how extractive economic practices were balanced to make maximum use of available resources but not depleting them for future generations. Disruptions after the fall of the Inka make it difficult to assess the long-term impact of Inka economic practice, but comparisons between the native and European management of the Andes is easier.

An early seventeenth-century drawing by Andean native Guaman Poma showing the Inka ruler and an "accountant" with his *khipu*. The structures are apparently storehouses. The drawing was part of a 1,200-page letter written by Guaman Poma to the king of Spain, Felipe III.

MARION AND TONY MORRISON/SOUTH AMERICAN PICTURES

The productivity of the Inka economy depended on careful management of the Andean ecological mosaic and an almost equal diversity of human labor resources. Many of the Inka practices for combining and utilizing these factors had been handed down from previous Andean cultures. They had assured thousands of years of long-term growth in environments that often seem hostile. The European invaders brought many useful practices along with new plants and animals, but their success in assuring the continued well-being of the people and their environment has not so far matched that of the Inka and their Andean predecessors.

A Natural Order

The ways the Inka combined diverse landscapes and peoples to create a large and wealthy empire were intricate and ingenious. All successful societies have a set of beliefs and visions that help justify their ruling structures and guide their activities. In the case of the Inka, these were embodied in religion and expressed in the myths that justified their right to rule and envisioned the political and social order of the empire as part of the natural order. Sociopolitical growth and agricultural growth were analogous processes. The sun, the moon, thunder, rain, earth, water, stone, and other elements of nature were all systematically considered, and an attempt was made to rationalize human activities so that they became a harmonious part of nature's scheme.

A rich oral tradition of religious myths, and myths of the origins of the Inka as rulers, served to inform the people of this order and justify the power of the Inka as a legitimate mediator between human groups and the forces that created growth in the world of nature. Not enough research has been done in Andean religion to allow us to write a short synthesis that can do justice to the way a wealth of details were brought together to form a system of beliefs that was both coherent and sufficiently flexible to adapt to different regional religions as the empire expanded. In its most fundamental sense, religion seems almost to have been both a metaphor and a guide for the Inka skills in the management and coordination of the great diversity of people and natural resources that constituted Tawantinsuyu. It provided a vision and a pattern for the rational treatment of social groups and the resources of nature, by combining them in the same way as nature combines earth, water, sunlight, and the other forces of earth and sky for the growth and prosperity of plants and animals. There was ample room in Inka religion for the conflict and calamity that characterized nature as well as human experience, but these negative aspects of the world were also seen as ultimately part of the creative process.

Some of the best symbols of the Inka interest in combining peoples and nature and in mediating may be seen in perhaps their most original art: the carving of sculpture from living stone. Visitors to the Cuzco region and other parts of the Inka realm have long admired these stones. Many of them are strikingly simple; some are complex; almost all are enhanced by the landscapes in which they are set. They share a sensitive cultural transformation of living stone, one of the most sacred of materials for the Inka. Perhaps the most spectacular example of the careful balance between culture and nature is Machu Picchu. Inka builders literally carved a mountain, turning it into a city. The sensitivity of detail in the city, such as creating a platform to call attention to a stone that echoes the shape of the mountains behind it, is as remarkable as its overall drama.

Some features of Inka civilization are still alive. Quechua, the Inka language, is spoken by several million people. The Andean textile tradition survives in remote villages in the highlands of Peru, Bolivia, and Ecuador. After AD 1532, however, the top levels of Inka society were quickly replaced by foreign domination. Native management of a complex set of landscapes, with their natural and human resources, had produced thousands of years of growth in economy, polity, and technology. For nearly 500 years, that management has been primarily in hands that have yet to learn how to manage the Andes effectively.

Note: Some material in this chapter is similar to text prepared by the author for the book *The Inka Empire and Its Andean Origins*, Craig Morris and Adriana von Hagen, American Museum of Natural History and Abbeville Press, 1993.

MARION MORRISON/SOUTH AMERICAN PICTURES

This famous Inka sculpture at Machu Picchu, now known as the "hitching post of the sun", is carved into bedrock.

An Inka stone offering container (*conopa*), carved in the form of an alpaca. *Conopa* were filled with a mixture of llama fat and blood and placed in pastures to insure the herd's fertility. Simple versions are still used in the Andes today.

JOHN BIGELOW TAYLOR/AMERICAN MUSEUM OF NATURAL HISTORY, NO. 5000(2)

INKA ARCHITECTURE AND CARVED STONE

CRAIG MORRIS

INKA ARCHITECTURE is world famous for its starkly elegant buildings with their finely dressed blocks of stone so precisely fitted together that the blade of a knife could not pass between them. The most famous Inka buildings are the palaces and temples of Cuzco, the imperial capital, but elaborate structures were built in the same style along the imperial road system that ran the length and breadth of the empire. These buildings served as the seats of Inka government in the provinces. The characteristically fine masonry, trapezoidal doors and windows, and spacious open plazas set Inka state architecture apart from the settlements of the local peoples who had lived in these outlying regions of the empire since before the time of Inka expansion.

JOHN CURTIS/D. DONNE BRYANT STOCK

DANIELE PELLEGRINI/PHOTO RESEARCHERS, INC.

Inka stone-working is so impressive that it has inspired many fanciful theories of secret Inka techniques. The careful research of Jean Pierre Protzen and others has revealed that the imposing granite structures were, in fact, built by relatively prosaic, but nonetheless effective, methods. The Inka used techniques similar to those the ancient Egyptians employed to construct their obelisks. The stones were dressed by flaking, using hammerstones of a material of similar hardness to, but tougher and less friable than, the stone being dressed.

⇐ The temple to Wiraqocha, the Inka creator deity, at San Pedro de Raqchi. This temple is one of the largest Inka buildings; the lower part of its walls are dressed stone, the upper sections are adobe.

Hammerstones of various sizes have been found. The larger and heavier ones were used for squaring and shaping the stones; the small, light ones, for fine dressing. Pumice was sometimes used to polish the stone and remove the pit marks left by the hammerstones.

The stones were typically laid in courses. The tops of the stones in a course were sightly concave, so that the stones of the course above it could project into the lower course, forming a stable "bedding joint". Inka buildings were as sturdy as they were beautiful. When an earthquake toppled the church of Santo Domingo in Cuzco in the 1950s, the beautiful Inka walls of dressed stone that were below it, and had earlier been part of the Temple of the Sun, were largely undamaged.

⇐ A trapezoidal window in a dressed stone building at Machu Picchu. The trapezoidal shape of doorways and windows was a characteristic feature of the buildings the Inka erected throughout the empire.

⇓ Some of the Inka's most striking works of art were produced by carving them into living bedrock. This example is in a small grotto beneath a structure in Machu Picchu known as the "*torreón*" (tower).

GEORGE HOLTON/PHOTO RESEARCHERS, INC.

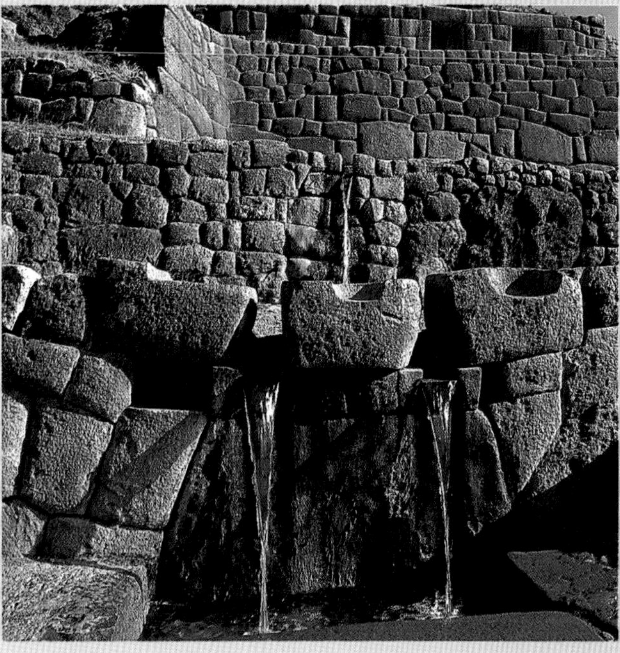

TONY MORRISON/SOUTH AMERICAN PICTURES

⇐ At the Inka site of Tambo Machay, near Cuzco, water flows through stone channels to produce two water fountains. The reason for this is unknown, but flowing water and duality were both important elements in Inka religion.

ENGLEBERT/PHOTO RESEARCHERS, INC.

⇑ This circular construction in the upper part of Saqsawaman incorporates a complex system of ducts. Early Spanish visitors to Cuzco referred to a large, circular tower with many rooms at Saqsawaman. The present structure may have been the base of that tower.

CONSTRUCTING JAPAN

400 BC – AD 1600

Diversity and Unification

Mark J. Hudson

UNTIL RECENTLY, most accounts of Japanese history portrayed Japan as a homogeneous and largely isolated civilization. The past few years, in contrast, have seen a growing awareness among scholars of the widespread contacts that existed between Japan and its neighboring regions in the premodern period, and of its cultural diversity at this time. This chapter provides an overview of the history of the Japanese islands during the 2,000 years from the beginning of wet-rice cultivation, about 400 BC. The period around AD 1600 is an important cut-off point for a number of reasons: the central islands (Honshu, Shikoku, and Kyushu) were unified politically under the Tokugawa shogunate, marking the end of more than a century of civil war; Catholicism, which had reached Japan in AD 1549, came under persecution; and with the establishment of trading posts in Hokkaido and the conquest of Okinawa in AD 1609, direct Japanese political influence was extended to the north and south.

At no stage during these 2,000 years did the islands as a whole form a unified political or social entity. Rather than thinking of a single Japan, it is more appropriate to think in terms of a complex mosaic of cultures. Although Japanese written history extends back to very early times, archaeology is invaluable in giving us an insight into the "other" Japanese cultures, because most historical records are biased towards the activities of the central state, and largely ignore the ethnic and social diversity of the peripheral regions.

The Daisen keyhole-shaped tomb mound in Osaka dates from the fifth century AD. At 486 meters (530 yards) long, it is the largest tomb in Japan. Daisen is controlled by the Imperial Household Agency, which believes it to be the grave of the Emperor Nintoku, and excavation is prohibited.

A female *haniwa*, or tomb sculpture, dating from the early sixth century.

TOKYO NATIONAL MUSEUM/TETTONI,CASSIO & ASSOCIATES/PHOTOBANK

AUSTRALIAN PICTURE LIBRARY

Despite modern urban sprawl, about two-thirds of Japan is still forested. A similar proportion is mountainous, and the narrow coastal plains are consequently intensively cultivated and crowded with human settlement.

The period in Japan from the end of the last Ice Age, about 12,500 years ago, to 400 BC is known as the Jomon. The people who lived on the Japanese islands at this time were primarily hunter-gatherers, but during the latter half of this period, they also cultivated a few plants, including bottle gourds, burdock, and the beefsteak plant *Perilla*. None of these would have formed a major part of their diet, but about 1500 BC, rice appeared in the islands.

Rice had been cultivated in southern China since at least 7000 BC. Many aspects of its spread into northeastern Asia remain unclear, but it appears to have arrived in Korea and Japan at more or less the same time. While direct evidence is lacking, it is likely that people grew rice on a limited scale late in the Jomon period, perhaps only in upland fields. A much clearer transition to agriculture occurred about 400 BC, when wet-rice farming based on the technique of irrigated paddy fields was introduced from the Korean peninsula.

THE ISLANDS OF JAPAN

The Japanese islands extend some 3,000 kilometers (1,900 miles) from north to south, although their total surface area is only slightly larger than that of Italy. There are four main islands, Hokkaido, Honshu, Shikoku, and Kyushu, and thousands of smaller ones. The archipelago is extremely mountainous and also environmentally diverse, ranging from the subarctic climate of northern Hokkaido to the subtropical Ryuku Islands.

CARTOGRAPHY: RAY SIM

Rice Farmers of the Yayoi Period

This marked the beginning of the Yayoi period, which lasted until about AD 300. For the first time, a large proportion of the population of the central islands became dependent on food production.

The evidence of biological anthropology suggests that the Yayoi period was marked by large-scale immigration from the Asian continent, a process that continued at intervals until about AD 700. The Japanese people can be said to have developed as a distinct racial group during this

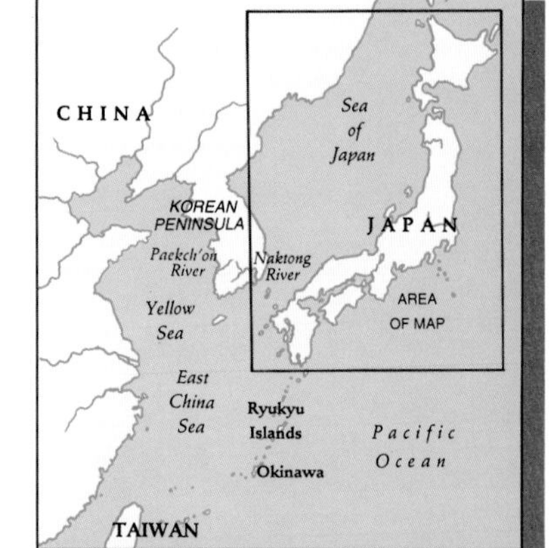

period, as immigrant rice farmers intermixed with the indigenous Jomon population. The genetic contribution of the immigrants was much greater in the central part of the islands. In Hokkaido, by contrast, the Jomon people evolved into the Ainu, with little genetic influence from the rest of Japan. Although its wider affinities are still hotly debated, the Japanese language may also have spread through the islands in the process of agricultural colonization during the Yayoi period, replacing the previous Jomon languages, except for Ainu.

The people who arrived in Kyushu in the Yayoi period brought with them a tradition of more complex social structures than had existed among the Jomon. Here, moated villages are found from the very beginning of the Yayoi period. This type of settlement is almost unknown from the Jomon period, and was probably derived from northeastern Asian prototypes. The largest moated Yayoi site is Yoshinogari, in Saga. At the height of this settlement, about the second century AD, the outer moat enclosed an area of at least 40 hectares (100 acres), while a smaller inner ditch marked out a residential precinct of about 1.5 hectares (3.7 acres). It is thought that a wooden palisade was erected along the moats to afford the village further protection.

The prevalence of moated settlements implies that warfare was widespread, and this is confirmed by other evidence: weapons for killing other humans appear for the first time, and arrowheads and sword tips have been found embedded in many Yayoi skeletons. Chinese records also mention periods of unrest in Japan in the second and third centuries AD. The causes of this warfare are not known for certain, but disputes over land and irrigation water no doubt figured prominently.

The official history of the Wei dynasty (AD 220 to AD 264) provides a brief description of third-century Japan seen through Chinese eyes. This document, completed in AD 297 and known as the *Wei zhi*, mentions some 30 "countries" in Japan, most of which are said to be under the overall control of a Queen Pimiko, who resided in Yamatai. Distances and directions from Korea to Yamatai are given, but taken literally, they lead into the ocean, and it has proved impossible to determine the location of Pimiko's capital from this text alone.

The location of Yamatai has been the subject of historical controversy for centuries. The two main contenders are northern Kyushu and the Kinai (Kyoto–Nara) region. The Kinai theory is based on the obvious similarity of the name Yamatai to Yamato, the ancient name for the Nara area, the center of the early Japanese state. On the other hand, several of the polities named in the *Wei zhi* as being controlled by Yamatai are known from other place-name evidence to have been on the island of Kyushu, and this could mean that all of Pimiko's dominions were located there. Certainly, there is no archaeological evidence that a polity centered in the Kinai region had any real power over Kyushu in the third century. Despite these puzzling inconsistencies, the testimony of the *Wei zhi* is important for two reasons. First, it confirms the archaeological picture of small chiefdoms centered on large moated settlements, where elaborate burials took place, and second, it suggests that informal interregional alliances of some kind were important as early as the late Yayoi period.

Kofun Tombs and the Yamato State

As time went on, these interregional alliances became more pronounced. Large keyhole-shaped tomb mounds first appeared in the Kinai some time between AD 250 and AD 300, marking the start of the Kofun, or Tumulus, period, which lasted until about AD 700. Although quite large burial mounds are found in the Yayoi period, Kofun tombs are remarkable for the standardization of their shape,

This bronze spearhead from the Middle Yayoi period was probably attached to a wooden shaft. During the Yayoi period, many bronze objects of types originally imported from the Asian continent became ritualistic rather than functional in form. Yayoi spearheads and daggers often have wide, impractical blades, and bells are large and ornate.

MUSEE GUIMET, PARIS/ LAUROS-GIRAUDON

YOKOHAMA HISTORICAL FOUNDATION ARCHAEOLOGICAL CENTER

The site of Ostuka, in Yokohama, which dates from the first century AD, is a typical moated settlement of the Yayoi period. Although only about a fifth of the houses would have been in use at any one time, the remains of almost 100 buildings have been excavated from the area within the moat, which covers about 2 hectares (almost 5 acres). Twenty-five contemporary moated burial precincts have been discovered 100 meters (110 yards) southeast of the village.

THE JAPANESE ISLANDS: 400 BC – AD 1600

Date	CENTRAL ISLANDS	HOKKAIDO AND OKINAWA	RELIGION AND PHILOSOPHY	CULTURE AND TECHNOLOGY
1600	Unification under Tokugawa shogunate	Satsuma conquest of Ryukyu Islands		Developments in mining technology
	Arrival of Portuguese		Christianity	
1500	Civil war			
				Castle towns
	Muromachi shogunate (AD 1378 – AD 1573)		Noh drama	
		Ainu/*gusuku* periods		Medieval economic development
	Kamakura shogunate (AD 1185 – AD 1333)		Zen Buddhism	
			The Tale of Genji	
1000				
				Rise of samurai
	Heian period (AD 794 – AD 1185)			
				Todaiji temple
700	Establishment of capital at Nara	Satsumon/Okhotsk periods	First Japanese chronicles	Grid-plan capitals
	Ritsuryo state (c. AD 650 – AD 900 or 1200)			
			Confucianism	
			Buddhism	
500				
				Be system
	Kofun period (c. AD 300 – AD 700)		End of Yayoi bronze rituals	Keyhole tombs
	Death of Pimiko			
AD 1				First tributary mission to China
		Epi-Jomon/Late Shellmound periods	Bronze bells	
	Yayoi period (c. 400 BC – AD 300)		End of Jomon stone and figurine rituals	Moated villages
				Wet-rice farming
500 BC				

SHOICHI UMEHARA, OSAKA

↑ The Hashihaka tomb mound, in Nara prefecture, is one of the earliest of the standardized keyhole-shaped mounds that give their name to the Kofun period. It is thought to date from about AD 275.

construction, and burial furnishings. Keyhole-shaped tombs spread very quickly to northern Kyushu, and then east to the Tohoku, in northern Honshu, in the fourth century. (See the feature *The Nakamichi Tomb Cluster*.) Some Japanese archaeologists see the tombs as evidence that these regions were brought under the control of a paramount ruler based in the Kinai. A more likely explanation is that provincial chieftains received status objects such as bronze mirrors, and perhaps the technology to build elaborate tombs, from Yamato in exchange for their nominal political allegiance. A third possibility is that the tomb mounds simply show that the elite of different regions shared a common subculture. This last idea cannot be ruled out, particularly since the tombs' significance may have changed over time, as the technology became more accessible.

The formation of states followed close on the heels of the spread of agriculture both on the Korean peninsula and in the Japanese islands. Chiefdoms based on moated settlements such as Yoshinogari had developed in the islands in the Yayoi period. By the third or fourth century AD, large regional chiefdoms probably existed in a number of areas, including Kyushu, Izumo, Okayama, and the Kinai. The processes by which they became subordinate to the Yamato state are still not fully known, but the fifth century AD marked an important watershed in the incorporation of local elites into the administrative structure of the Yamato court. A system developed whereby groups of people known as *be* (pronounced "bay") came to specialize in the production of particular crafts and foods, and this brought Yamato a step further towards the economic centralization essential to state formation. Archaeologically, the changing position of provincial chieftains in the fifth century AD is reflected in inscriptions on swords found in tombs in Kumamoto and

THE NAKAMICHI TOMB CLUSTER

MARK J. HUDSON

ONE OF THE MOST CONTROVERSIAL aspects of the transition from the Yayoi to the Kofun period, between AD 250 and AD 300, is the nature of the relationship that existed between provincial elites and the increasingly powerful Yamato state in the Kinai region. Burial remains found in the Nakamichi district of Yamanashi prefecture, in eastern Japan, have provided a remarkable insight into this transition, and have a unique potential for increasing our understanding of the eastward expansion of the Yamato state.

The Late Yayoi period is represented in Nakamichi by the square, moated burial precincts found at Uenodaira. These range in size from about 25 to 720 square meters (30 to 860 square yards). While no burials have been preserved, finds at other sites suggest that they would have been simple. There are 124 precincts divided into 8 groups, which the excavators see as evidence for kin-based social units.

Immediately after Uenodaira, a keyhole tomb 45 meters (50 yards) long, with a square rear section, was built on the next ridge. This was followed by the Choshizuka tomb, which, at 169 meters (185 yards) long, is one of the largest keyhole mounds in eastern Japan. In the style of its construction and its burial facilities, Choshizuka is typical of the standardized tombs of the fourth century. A stone-lined burial chamber 6.6 meters (7 yards) long was located on top of the rear section of the mound. The grave goods included 2 Chinese and 3 Japanese bronze mirrors, 7 iron swords, 3 iron axes and 2 sickles, 150 tubular jasper beads, and 11 bracelets, one made of shell and 10 of jasper. Facing stones are presumed to have covered the whole mound. The three elements of keyhole tomb construction thought to reflect Chinese influence were also present: the rear mound was built in three steps; vermilion was used inside the burial chamber; and the head of the coffin would have pointed north.

Despite their proximity, the contrast between Choshizuka and the communal cemetery at Uenodaira is staggering. Unlike many parts of western Japan, Yamanashi has no burial mounds dating to the Yayoi period. Society here seems to have undergone a sudden and drastic transformation, from minimal stratification in the third century AD to rule by powerful chiefs in the fourth century. There is no evidence, however, that Yamanashi was conquered by Yamato. The only links with the Kinai region are the tombs themselves. At present, the best explanation seems to be that the chief buried in Choshizuka had entered into an alliance with Yamato, and that the ensuing political contacts between the elites stimulated the development of more complex social structures in eastern Japan.

A reconstruction of a bronze mirror found in the burial chamber of Choshizuka.
SEIJI NAKAYAMA/ARCHAEOLOGICAL CENTER OF YAMANASHI PREFECTURE

SEIJI NAKAYAMA/ARCHAEOLOGICAL CENTER OF YAMANASHI PREFECTURE

This jar-shaped earthenware sculpture (*haniwa*) was found on the outer surface of the Choshizuka mound.
SEIJI NAKAYAMA/ARCHAEOLOGICAL CENTER OF YAMANASHI PREFECTURE

The Choshizuka tomb in the Nakamichi district of Yamanashi is one of the largest keyhole-shaped mounds in eastern Japan.

This bronze Buddhist statue dates from the Kamakura period (AD 1185 to AD 1333). The arrival of Buddhism in the sixth century AD had a far-reaching influence on all the Japanese arts.
MUSEUM OF ORIENTAL ART, ROME/SCALA

Saitama. These show that at least some local chiefs in both Kyushu and the Kanto recognized the suzerainty of the Yamato king Yuryaku, who is reputed to have reigned from AD 456 to AD 479.

Korean Connections

The rise of the Yamato state cannot be understood solely in terms of its expansion within the islands. Its development within the wider context of northeastern Asia is equally important. During the Han dynasty (206 BC to AD 220), the Chinese extended their influence to the area of Bohai Bay and the Korean peninsula. Four commanderies (administrative outposts) were established on the peninsula in 108 BC, and this region was brought into the Han tributary system, whereby "barbarian" states received gifts, such as seals and bronze mirrors, in return for acknowledging Han authority. The presence of Chinese commanderies on the peninsula opened the way for diplomatic relations between the Han court and the Japanese islands, stimulating the development of more complex societies throughout the so-called Yellow Sea Interaction Sphere.

In the islands, the pervasive influence of this interaction sphere is shown archaeologically by finds of Chinese mirrors and other prestigious items, and historically through written Chinese records of island envoys. The *Wei zhi* implies that the whole Yamatai phenomenon was intimately linked with the commandery tributary system, as Yamatai's main access to the mainland was through the country of Ito (the modern-day Itoshima area of western Fukuoka), which both Pimiko's own senior officials and the representative of the peninsular commandery of Daifang visited on official duties.

Relations with the Han commanderies proved an important means for the chiefdoms of the islands and the peninsula to increase their prestige and power. The more or less simultaneous transition from chiefdoms to states in both regions, however, took place in the political vacuum that followed the decline of Chinese influence after about AD 300. On the peninsula, the Three Kingdoms period (AD 300 to AD 668) saw the establishment of the states of Koguryo, Silla, and Paekche, with a smaller confederation of polities in the Kaya region, along the Naktong River. In the islands, the predominance of the Yamato state seems to have stemmed partly from its close contacts with the peninsula. Yamato's main interest was probably the iron that could be obtained from the Kaya region, but it is not yet clear how Yamato managed to seize control over access to the peninsula from the Kyushu region.

Yamato chronicles such as the *Nihon Shoki* (AD 720) make much of Japanese military intervention on the peninsula in the Kofun era, and contain accounts of a Japanese "headquarters" in Mimana, in the Kaya region. Although Mimana was traditionally assumed to have been a Japanese colony, its real status is unknown. It may have been a facility for traders or, perhaps, for the Japanese soldiers who are known to have fought in allegiance with the state of Paekche. The presence of such soldiers has been independently confirmed by an inscription on a stone stele erected in the north of the peninsula in AD 414, which recounts the exploits of the Koguryo king Kwanggaet'o, who reigned from AD 391 to AD 412. While it naturally glorifies his deeds, it also makes several references to Japanese armies fighting against Koguryo. The identity of these soldiers is not clear. Were they opportunistic mercenaries, or were they dispatched by rulers in Kyushu or Yamato? The non-Yamato texts are of little help, as they use the name "Wa" to refer to the Japanese islands in general. Recent excavations of Kaya royal tombs dating from the fourth and fifth centuries AD may help to provide an answer, as they contained bronze burial goods thought to show Yamato rather than Kyushu influence.

The Japanese military presence on the peninsula ended dramatically in AD 663, when Japan and Paekche were defeated by the forces of an alliance between the Tang dynasty and the kingdom of Silla, in the naval battle of Paekch'on River. The very real threat that the Japanese islands would be invaded next provided a strong impetus for increased centralization of power within the Yamato court. Power within the states of Silla and Yamato was similarly consolidated through the adoption of Tang Chinese political models.

The Ritsuryo State

In the formative stage of its civilization, Japan's debt to China was enormous. From the fifth century AD, Chinese characters were used to write Japanese, even though the two languages differ greatly in grammar and phonology. At first, records were kept in Chinese, but by the time the *Manyoshu* collection of poetry was completed, in AD 759, Chinese characters were regularly used phonetically to write Japanese sounds. By the early tenth century, the Japanese had compiled their own lists of syllables, known as *kana*, from Chinese characters. Since that time, these syllabaries have been used in combination with characters to write Japanese. Many Chinese words were also borrowed, so that today, more than half the Japanese lexicon is of Chinese origin.

Writing came to Japan by way of the Korean peninsula, and Buddhism arrived by the same route in the mid-sixth century AD. Buddhist teachings originated in India in the sixth century BC, but had become strongly sinicized after reaching China in the first century AD. The initial spread of Buddhism within Japan must therefore be seen as part of the Japanese nobility's admiration for things Chinese. The ambitious Soga clan, based in Yamato, used Buddhism, together with other aspects of continental Asian culture, to strengthen its position

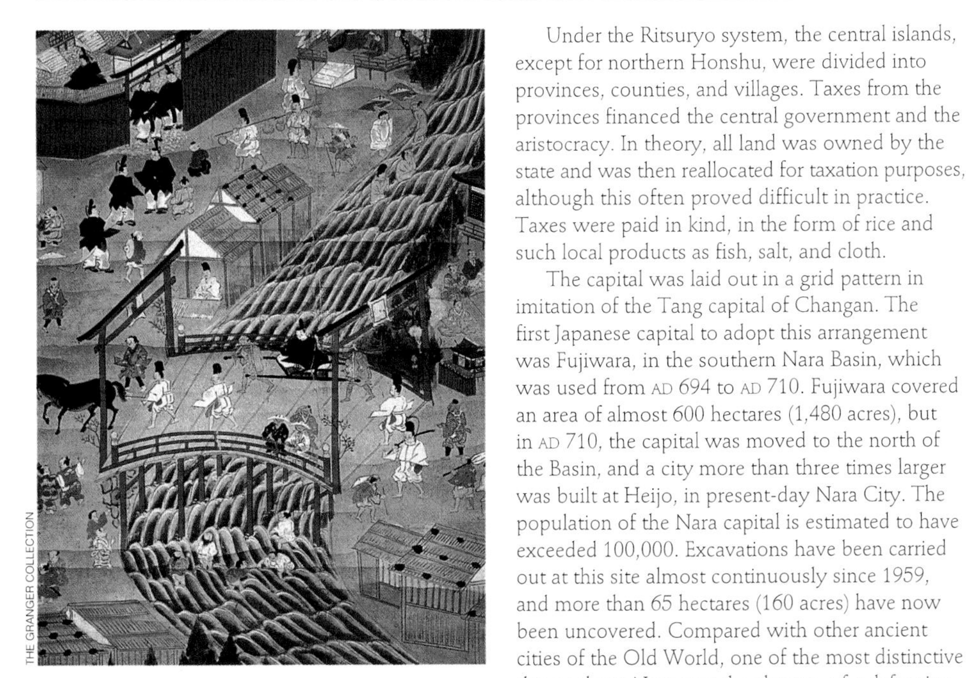

THE GRANGER COLLECTION

Purification was an important part of indigenous religious practices in Japan. This scroll shows worshipers taking ritual baths in the stream at the Shinto shrine at Ise, in Mie prefecture.

at court. In AD 592, the reigning king, Sushun, was assassinated on the orders of a Soga noble, who installed his niece Suiko on the throne.

Buddhism flourished under the Soga. Prince Shotoku (AD 574 to AD 622), who served as Suiko's regent, is regarded as the patron saint of Japanese Buddhism. As well as studying and lecturing on Buddhist teachings, he was influential in building a number of major temples in the Nara region. Shotoku also promoted the ideals of Confucianism, the Chinese system of ethics and social relations, which has had an enormous influence on Japanese life over the centuries. The arrival of foreign belief systems had a profound effect on native ritual practices in Japan, which were given a name for the first time: Shinto, or "The Way of the Gods". Shinto can properly be called the indigenous religion of Japan, but it is a mistake to think that pre-Buddhist rituals in Japan had remained unchanged for thousands of years. Change seems to have been particularly vigorous during the Yayoi period.

In AD 645, the Soga lost power in a coup as bloody as the one in which they had gained ascendancy. Support for Buddhism and political centralization through Chinese systems of government continued, however, and the latter was given added urgency by the threat of invasion from the peninsula after the battle of Paekch'on River. Building on the Taika Reforms of the latter half of the seventh century AD, the Taiho Code of AD 702 gave effect to a fully fledged bureaucratic state based on Chinese legal codes, known in Japanese as *ritsuryo*. This state was the prelude to the development of the first unified Japanese civilization, which saw a flowering of the arts and literature and the rise of the first urban centers.

Under the Ritsuryo system, the central islands, except for northern Honshu, were divided into provinces, counties, and villages. Taxes from the provinces financed the central government and the aristocracy. In theory, all land was owned by the state and was then reallocated for taxation purposes, although this often proved difficult in practice. Taxes were paid in kind, in the form of rice and such local products as fish, salt, and cloth.

The capital was laid out in a grid pattern in imitation of the Tang capital of Changan. The first Japanese capital to adopt this arrangement was Fujiwara, in the southern Nara Basin, which was used from AD 694 to AD 710. Fujiwara covered an area of almost 600 hectares (1,480 acres), but in AD 710, the capital was moved to the north of the Basin, and a city more than three times larger was built at Heijo, in present-day Nara City. The population of the Nara capital is estimated to have exceeded 100,000. Excavations have been carried out at this site almost continuously since 1959, and more than 65 hectares (160 acres) have now been uncovered. Compared with other ancient cities of the Old World, one of the most distinctive things about Nara was the absence of a defensive surrounding wall. The center of the capital was the Nara palace, located in the north of the city. Large, aristocratic mansions were concentrated around the palace, whereas the smaller houses of the ordinary citizens were found in the southern area. Excavations in the palace area have confirmed that the capital was the bureaucratic center, with

PICTUREPOINT LTD

Construction of the Todaiji temple, in Nara, began in AD 745.

WERNER FORMAN ARCHIVE

The Great Buddha Hall of the Todaiji temple is said to be the largest wooden building in the world. The original eighth-century hall and statue were both destroyed, and the present structures date to about AD 1700. The bronze Great Buddha is nearly 15 meters (160 feet) high, about a meter smaller than the original statue.

THE GRANGER COLLECTION

An armor-clad warrior of the Heian period (AD 794 to AD 1185).

finds of inkstands, brushes, and more than 135,000 inscribed wooden tablets.

In the eighth century, Buddhism was a potent force as a state religion in East Asia. The idea that Buddhist deities would protect kingdoms that supported temples and monasteries was far removed from the beliefs of the early followers of the historical Buddha, but a close relationship between church and state was central to the spread of Buddhism in China, Korea, and Japan. In Japan, Buddhism reached its apogee as a state religion with the construction of the Todaiji temple, in Nara. The temple's huge bronze Great Buddha, begun in AD 745, was dedicated in AD 752, even though the hall that housed it was not then finished. The Todaiji was a massive undertaking, employing some 1.6 million laborers. Although rebuilt several times, it remains one of the world's greatest Buddhist monuments.

The Todaiji possessed hundreds of treasures, many of which were donated by the court. These objects were kept in wooden storehouses, such as the Shosoin Repository, which still stands in the temple grounds. In the eighth century, Nara was the eastern terminus of the Tang Silk Road trading route, and some of the Shosoin treasures came from as far away as Vietnam and Persia. The furniture, textiles, musical instruments, clothing, and accessories owned by the Shosoin help to give us a picture of life at the Nara court.

Excavations at the residence of Prince Nagaya, grandson of King Temmu, who reigned from AD 672 to AD 687, have provided further details of aristocratic life in Nara. Nagaya held the important government post of Minister of the Left, and his extensive residence adjoined the Nara palace. He died in AD 729. Some 50,000 inscribed wooden tablets were found at the site, providing a fascinating insight into his home life. We know, for instance, that he kept cranes as pets, had a private ice house, and received food and other items from all over Japan.

Life in the provinces would not have been as luxurious, yet the extent of the Ritsuryo state's authority beyond the capital is controversial. In many ways, the court's influence was considerable. Administrative centers were located in each province and county, and provincial monasteries and nunneries were built in imitation of a similar system in Tang China. In general, however, regional economic production remained underdeveloped. Apart from the imperial capitals, Japan produced no urban centers until the early medieval era. In the provinces, settlement was largely in small, dispersed villages.

The Ritsuryo system was at its height in the eighth century, but declined during the Heian period (AD 794 to AD 1185). The reasons for this decline are still debated. A traditional explanation is that economic growth led to increased private ownership of land, undermining the state's authority. Although decentralization of landholding remains both a cause and a symptom of the decline, historian Wayne Farris has recently argued that economic backwardness rather than growth was more characteristic of the Ritsuryo system. Farris proposes that between the eighth and tenth centuries, epidemic diseases such as smallpox kept population levels more or less constant, and imprisoned peasants in a vicious circle of underdevelopment.

Archaeology is proving crucial as a means of testing theories about the Ritsuryo economy. Archaeological remains can tell us about many relevant factors, such as technological diffusion, settlement patterns, and land clearance. Furthermore, while much of the debate has so far revolved around rice production, recent archaeological research suggests that other forms of regional economic activity were quite well developed under the Ritsuryo system, and need to be studied in more detail. (See the feature *The Ritsuryo State and Bonito from Izu*.)

Another important factor was the growing power of the military in the provinces, a development that contrasted strongly with the flowering of a sophisticated Heian court culture in the new capital of Kyoto. After the cosmopolitan atmosphere of the eighth century, there was a move away from Chinese influence towards indigenous expressions of art and literature. The literary world of the Heian court is particularly well known through works such as *The Tale of Genji*, written by Lady Murasaki Shikibu (AD 978 to AD ?1016) and often described as the world's first novel. The court nobles who appear in *Genji* and similar works are contemptuous of commoners and the rough life of the provinces, admiring instead the graceful, the elegant, and the refined. The Heian aristocracy lived in an extremely warlike age, but their ideals and aspirations were often remarkably distant from those of their subjects.

THE GRANGER COLLECTION

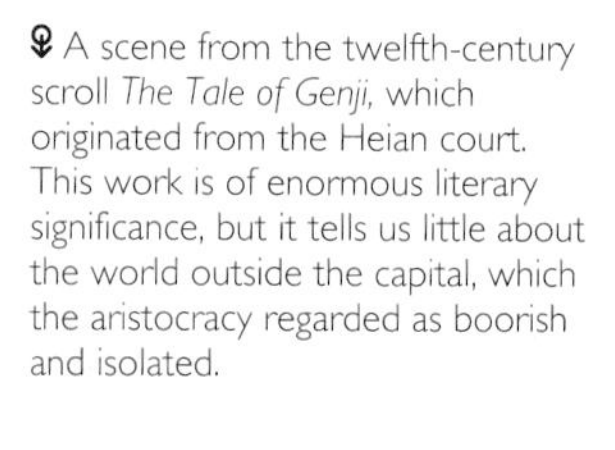

A scene from the twelfth-century scroll *The Tale of Genji*, which originated from the Heian court. This work is of enormous literary significance, but it tells us little about the world outside the capital, which the aristocracy regarded as boorish and isolated.

THE RITSURYO STATE AND BONITO FROM IZU

MARK J. HUDSON

Our understanding of the economy of the eighth-century Ritsuryo state has been revolutionized in recent years by the discovery of thousands of inscribed wooden tablets, most of which come from from the capital at Nara. These tablets were used as baggage labels for goods brought to Nara from the provinces as tax payments. More than 130 tablets mention offerings of bonito. While the name of the province can be read on only 112 of these tablets, two-thirds of them come from Izu province. Other archaeological evidence confirms that Izu was a major source of bonito in the eighth century, and these two lines of evidence clearly point to the fact that the power of the Ritsuryo state extended as far east as the Kanto at that time.

Bonito is a large, migratory fish that arrives off the Pacific coast of Japan in the spring and returns south in the autumn. It has been caught since the Jomon period and is still eaten in Japan today, both raw as sashimi and cooked in a variety of ways. Bonito flakes are also dried (when they are known as *katsuo-bushi*) and used as a condiment.

In the eighth century, the journey from the provincial capital of Izu to Nara was officially set at 22 or 23 days. Before such a long journey, the fish must have been processed in some way. Many bonito tablets, including that shown here, bear the words *ara katsuo*. Although their exact meaning is not known, they are thought to refer to some sort of dried bonito. This interpretation is strengthened by finds of distinctive ceramic pots at a number of sites in Izu and surrounding areas. Two thousand such vessels have been discovered at Fujiihara alone. They may have been used to boil the fish before flaking and drying it, much as is done in Japan today.

From the wooden tablets, we know that Izu province supplied at least 250 kilograms (550 pounds) of bonito to Nara in AD 735. This tells us not only that bonito fishing was an important economic activity in the eighth century, but that the Ritsuryo state was a real presence even in this region of eastern Japan. The study of the bonito industry in eighth-century Izu also provides an excellent example of how our knowledge of the past is deepened when we are able to combine historical and archaeological data.

Bonito has long been a favorite fish of the Japanese. Historical records are useful in helping us to interpret the archaeological evidence of bonito fishing. The illustration here, based on an illustration in the book *Nihon Sanka Meisan Zue*, published in 1799, shows bonito being processed in Shikoku in the late eighteenth century
KOWA SHUPPAN (HAND COLORED BY RAY SIM)

Pots such as this were probably used to boil bonito, possibly in preparation for flaking and drying it.
ILLUSTRATION: RAY SIM

The two sides of a wooden tablet from the Nara site recording a tax payment of bonito from Izu province. This tablet is 32 centimeters (13 inches) long and dates from AD 746.
NARA NATIONAL CULTURAL PROPERTIES RESEARCH INSTITUTE

The Warrior Age

Medieval Japan is currently the focus of some particularly exciting historical research. While a great deal of earlier work emphasized rice cultivation and its associated institutions of landownership, there has recently been a shift towards social history. Novels, picture scrolls, folklore, and archaeology have given us an insight into the many different ways of life that existed in this period, including that of fishers, hunters, tradespeople, and farmers who grew crops other than rice. Archaeology has provided concrete evidence of this diversity.

The political system established in the medieval period would be predominant in Japan until 1868. The rise of a warrior elite, known as *bushi* or *samurai*, led to full-scale military governments in Kamakura (AD 1185 to AD 1333), in the Muromachi area of Kyoto (AD 1378 to AD 1573), and, finally, in Edo (AD 1603 to AD 1868). These warrior governments were headed by a shogun, a commander-in-chief who was the emperor's military agent. The emperor himself was reduced to a nominal figurehead who gave legitimacy to the shogun. The major break in shogunal rule began in the middle of the fifteenth century, when Japan disintegrated into a civil war between competing warlords that lasted until the late sixteenth century.

Medieval Japan saw the spread of private (or, more accurately, semipublic) estates known as *shoen*. The first *shoen* appeared as early as the eighth century, when the government allowed land newly brought under cultivation to become private property. Exemption from taxation was a major stimulus to the establishment of *shoen*, and by the tenth century, they had grown in both size and number. Early *shoen* served as centers of production, rather like the manors of medieval Europe, although this role became less important after the rise of regional market economies in the late medieval era. The first *shoen* were owned by aristocrats and rich temples in the capital, but in the thirteenth century, a great many came under the control of provincial nobles. This trend continued until the sixteenth century, when the remaining *shoen* were absorbed into the territories of the warlords.

The medieval period witnessed major changes in the economic life of the archipelago. Agricultural production increased, markets sprang up, and occupational specialization became much more common. Commercial activities were stimulated by the use of coins imported from China. Urbanization was a natural consequence of these trends. Whereas the ancient cities of Nara and Kyoto had served as royal residences and centers of tax collection, new market and port towns came into being in the thirteenth century. (See the feature *Kusado Sengen: A Medieval Town on the Inland Sea.*)

STEVE VIDLER/AUSTRALIAN PICTURE LIBRARY

The principal tower of Matsumoto castle, in central Honshu. Built in the 1590s, the castle was designed to dominate the surrounding plain. The town that grew up around it was typical of the urban development that took place in Japan early in the modern period.

KITA-IN, SAITUMI/WERNER FORMAN ARCHIVE

An early seventeenth-century armorer's workshop in Kyoto. The man at right applies lacquer to parts for a helmet, while the master of the workshop ties the cords of a piece of body armor.

BOSTON MUSEUM OF FINE ARTS/WERNER FORMAN ARCHIVE

The Heiji insurrection was one of a series of civil wars that culminated in the establishment of military rule in Kamakura in AD 1185.

A contemporary portrait on silk of Tokugawa Ieyasu (AD 1542 to AD 1616), the warlord who unified central Japan in 1600, after more than a century of civil war.

THE GRANGER COLLECTION

The medieval pattern of urbanization changed in the fifteenth and sixteenth centuries, when the local warlords were at their height. In this period, the dominant urban type was the castle town, where settlement was huddled around a warlord's stronghold. These towns formed the basis for the phenomenal urban growth of the seventeenth century, during which Japan became one of the most urbanized societies in the world.

Distinctive religious and cultural trends mirrored the political and social changes taking place in medieval Japan. In the early medieval era, there was a widespread belief that the period of *mappo*, meaning the end of Buddhist law, had already begun, and that Japan was in its final, violent stage of decline as a result. The feelings of impermanence and nostalgia inherent in this pessimistic belief had a profound influence on the medieval Japanese world view and its expression in literary and artistic works.

Another important influence on medieval Japanese culture was that of Zen Buddhism,

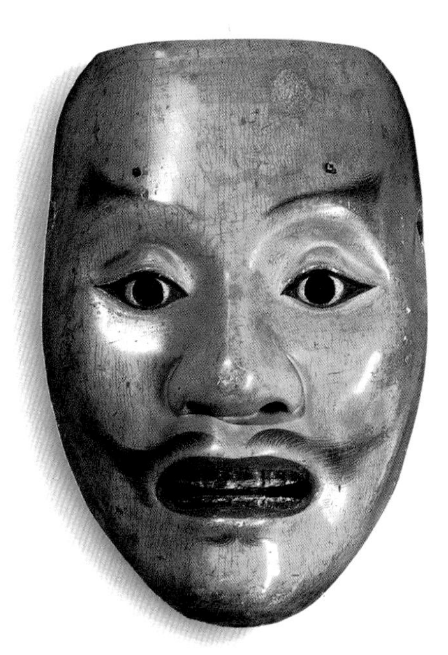

This mask, representing a *samurai*, was part of Noh theater, a formalized type of dance-drama that originated in the fourteenth century AD. Many traditional Japanese arts have their roots in the medieval era.

NOH THEATER COLLECTION, KONGO SCHOOL, KYOTO/ WERNER FORMAN ARCHIVE

KUSADO SENGEN: A MEDIEVAL TOWN ON THE INLAND SEA

AKIRA MATSUI

KUSADO SENGEN was a medieval town situated in the delta of the Ashida River in Fukuyama City, in Hiroshima prefecture. The town was first inhabited in the twelfth century, flourished from the fourteenth to the sixteenth century, and then vanished in a flood in 1673. Being waterlogged and largely undisturbed, the site has been exceptionally well preserved. Although some written documents relating to the town have survived, archaeological excavations have provided an invaluable insight into daily life in Japan's Middle Ages.

Excavation began in 1973, when the local government planned to build a dam at the river mouth. Over the following 20 years, most of the site, a total of 6.7 hectares (16.5 acres), was excavated. Abundant organic remains were found in good condition, including more than 4,000 inscribed wooden tablets. Most are trading documents and personal memoranda, and they confirm Kusado Sengen's status as a medieval trading town on the Seto Inland Sea. Finds of Chinese porcelains and thousands of coins also support this interpretation.

During the excavations, remains of many workshops and dwellings were recovered, together with ditches, fences, and wells. The workshops, identified from the artifacts found within them, include grocers, blacksmiths, lacquer shops, shoe shops, and fishmongers. Scenes of medieval towns are depicted on picture scrolls such as the *Ippen Shonin Eden* ("The Scroll of the Life of Saint Ippen"), but Kusado Sengen is one of the few archaeological remains of such a town.

Most buildings are small and simple. Because of floods and the superimposition of later constructions, many details of these buildings are unclear, but two main types can be distinguished. One was built on top of foundation stones; the other had wooden pillars sunk directly into the ground. The most abundant features are wells, many of which were reused as rubbish pits. Rubbish was also found in other pits and ditches, and has given us an insight into the town's economic life.

Plant and animal remains tell us what medieval people ate. Written records were left by monks and nobles rather than commoners, and are, therefore, not representative of common people's lives. The records suggest that Buddhist prohibitions against the eating of meat were in force in the Middle Ages, yet the animal remains at Kusado Sengen show that meat was eaten in quite large quantities.

The most common animals at the site were dogs, which account for two-thirds of the mammal bone fragments. Many of the dog bones show signs of butchering and cooking. Cattle and horses were also eaten, but fewer remains survive. One cow seems to have been sacrificed, probably in a rain-making ceremony. Other animal foods at Kusado Sengen include rabbits, martens, raccoon dogs (badgers), pheasants, ducks, and chickens, although all of these were found only in small quantities. Sika deer were also eaten, and their skin, sinew, and bone were used to make tools.

But the most common food was fish caught locally in the Seto Inland Sea. Here, as elsewhere in western Japan, red sea bream is the most abundant species. The bones of this fish are too tough to be eaten by humans or dogs, and have therefore been preserved. Black sea bream and sea bass were also popular, as they still are in this region today. The recovery of salmon and cod bones from Kusado Sengen is of particular interest, since these fish are found only in northern Japan. They were probably caught along the Sea of Japan/Hokuriku coast and then transported to Osaka, from where they were distributed along the Inland Sea. Remains of shellfish, fruit, nuts, rice, wheat, beans, and sesame seeds were also found. Kusado Sengen is truly remarkable for the unusually complete picture it has preserved of the diet of townspeople in medieval Japan.

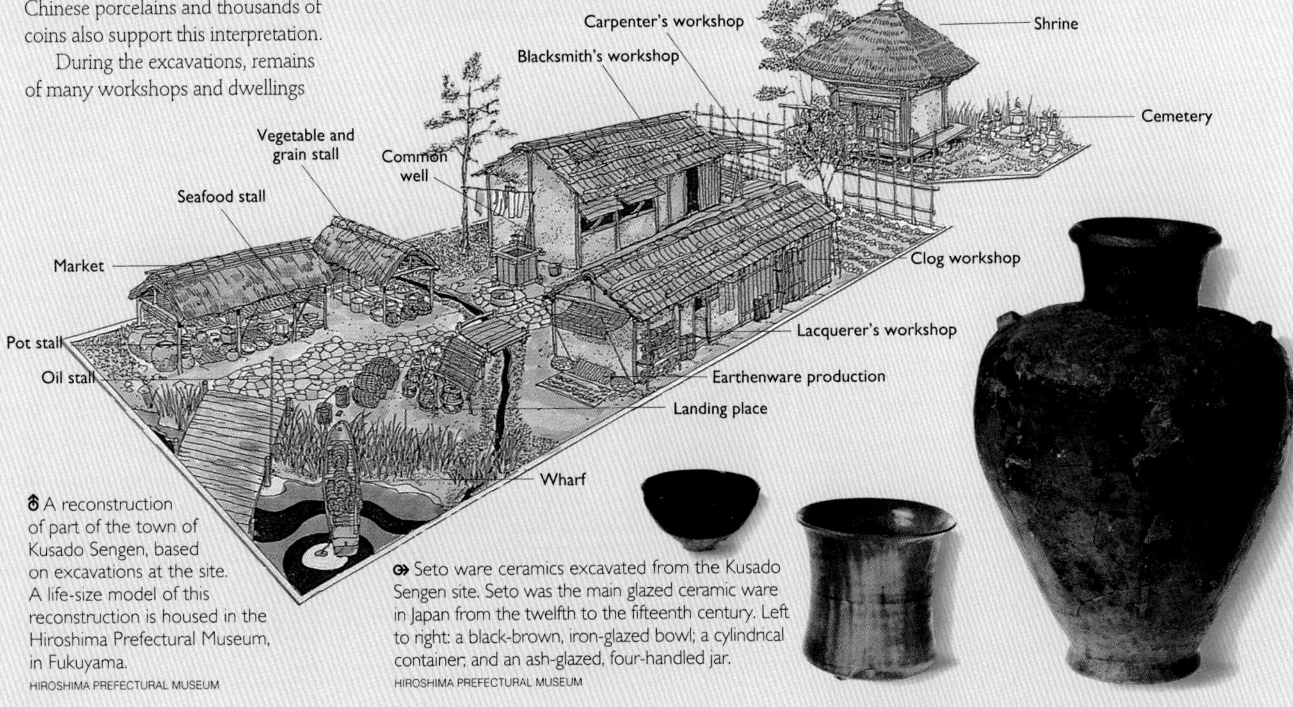

⇑ A reconstruction of part of the town of Kusado Sengen, based on excavations at the site. A life-size model of this reconstruction is housed in the Hiroshima Prefectural Museum, in Fukuyama.
HIROSHIMA PREFECTURAL MUSEUM

⇒ Seto ware ceramics excavated from the Kusado Sengen site. Seto was the main glazed ceramic ware in Japan from the twelfth to the fifteenth century. Left to right: a black-brown, iron-glazed bowl; a cylindrical container; and an ash-glazed, four-handled jar.
HIROSHIMA PREFECTURAL MUSEUM

which originated in China. Zen combined Indian meditative practices with Chinese Taoist elements. Practitioners followed a difficult path to enlightenment through meditation. Although it reached Japan in the Nara era, Zen did not gain a wide following there until late in the twelfth century. Zen aesthetics played a role in a number of medieval cultural developments, including Noh drama and the tea ceremony. Noh, which began in the fourteenth century, had its origins in earlier ritual practices and was a formalized type of dance-drama. Although tea was drunk in Japan as early as the ninth century, it became popular only after it was reintroduced by Zen monks late in the twelfth century. The aesthetic of tea drinking that developed over the medieval period actively incorporated Zen ideals of simplicity and restraint.

Contacts with the mainland continued through the Middle Ages. Since Han times, the Chinese had conceptualized the world in terms of tributary barbarian states surrounding the Middle Kingdom. In return for items of tribute, the barbarians received gifts from the Chinese court as tokens of investiture. The tributary system thus constituted a form of trade that was very important in East Asian history.

The first tributary mission from Japan took place as early as AD 57, when an embassy was sent to China from the kingdom of Na. Over the following centuries, official relations with China were interrupted and resumed at regular intervals. The Mongol Yuan dynasty (AD 1271 to AD 1368) attempted to enforce tributary relations by invading Japan in 1274 and 1281, but their fleets were repulsed on both occasions by storms, which the Japanese saw as *kamikaze*, or divine winds. Aside from the exchange of goods, the tributary system provided a model for diplomatic relations, which the Japanese adopted in their own contacts with Korea and the Ryukyu Islands.

Despite the importance of official trade, non-official contacts also played a crucial role. These contacts took many forms, from straightforward trading, with the authorities' silent agreement, to piracy. So-called *wako* (meaning Japanese pirates, although many were in fact Chinese and Korean) terrorized large areas of coastal East Asia until the sixteenth century and also engaged in illicit trade. It comes as no surprise that the first Europeans to reach Japan arrived on a Chinese *wako* ship. As one historian has noted, war, trade, and piracy were an inseparable trinity in the medieval period.

A pair of tea ceremony bowls. Apart from tea's aesthetic role, the spread of tea drinking through the Japanese islands from the early medieval era may have stimulated population growth by preventing intestinal diseases resulting from drinking unboiled water.
PRIVATE COLLECTION/WERNER FORMAN ARCHIVE

In this detail from a Chinese scroll painting, a Japanese fort is attacked by Korean and Chinese troops during the warlord Hideyoshi's second invasion of Korea, from AD 1597 to AD 1598.
THE GRANGER COLLECTION

The North and the South: Two Other Japanese Cultures

So far, the discussion has centered on "mainland" Japan—that is, the central islands of Honshu, Kyushu, and Shikoku. In Hokkaido, in the north, and the Ryukyus, in the south, very different cultures developed during the period considered in this chapter. Because of both ecological and cultural factors, agriculture took longer to spread to these regions. In Hokkaido, the people of the Epi-Jomon culture (150 BC to AD 700) continued to live as hunter-gatherers. Farming seems to have been well developed during the ensuing Satsumon period (AD 700 to AD 1300), however, at least in the southwest of the island. A variety of cultigens was excavated from the Sakushu–Kotoni River site in Sapporo, which dates from the ninth century AD, barley and millet being the most common. A contemporary culture to that of the Satsumon, known as the Okhotsk, existed along the northeastern coast of Hokkaido. This culture seems to have originated in southern Sakhalin about the fifth century AD, and from there, it spread to eastern Hokkaido and the Kuril Islands. Its subsistence basis was very different from that of the Satsumon, with a heavy emphasis on the hunting of sea mammals.

Okinawa was linked to networks of Kyushu Yayoi trade in tropical shells (some of which even reached Hokkaido), and contact between the Ryukyus and the mainland was greatly reduced when this trade ended about AD 150. Controversy surrounds the date of the introduction of agriculture into the Ryukyu Islands. The Late Shellmound period (300 BC to AD 1200) saw a trend towards specialization in lagoon marine resources, but records of Korean castaways show that millet, barley, and rice were being cultivated in the islands by the fifteenth century AD. The Okinawan economy was transformed at the end of the period considered in this chapter with the introduction of the sweet potato from China in 1605.

The early Japanese chronicles mention ethnic groups who resisted the expansion of Yamato power in the Tohoku, in northern Honshu, and in southern Kyushu. Those in the Tohoku were known as Emishi by the Japanese in the south. Yamato armies fought against the Emishi on the wild northern frontier until the ninth century AD.

Who were these Emishi? Many scholars have equated them with the Ainu, but the real picture is more complex. Biologically, the Ainu are clearly derived from Jomon ancestors, and place-name evidence also suggests that the Ainu language was once spoken in northern Tohoku. As used in the texts, however, the term "Emishi" may have referred to people who were beyond the borders

The Ainu were once seen as remnant hunter-gatherers occupying the northern islands of the Japanese archipelago. We now know, however, that economic and political interaction with the Japanese state to the south had a strong influence on Ainu culture. This is clearly reflected in this late nineteenth-century engraving.
TETTONI, CASSIO & ASSOCIATES/PHOTOBANK

An artist's reconstruction of the medieval fortress (*gusuku*) known as Gushikawa Castle, on Okinawa Island. The development of *gusuku* in the Ryukyu Islands was mirrored in Hokkaido by medieval Ainu fortresses known as *chashi*.

Swidden cultivation of buckwheat in southern Kyushu. Economic ways of life other than rice cultivation have always played an important role in Japanese history.

About AD 1200, stone-walled enclosures, such as the medieval fortress of Nakajin pictured here, began to appear on Okinawa Island. These *gusuku* appear to have been the fortresses of local chiefs who were already trading with the Chinese coast.

of the Ritsuryo state, rather than to a specific ethnic group. On this view, the Emishi would include mainland Japanese who had fled north to escape taxation. Ethnic differences between the mainland and the north were probably not as developed in this period as they would be later.

When considering the history of Hokkaido, it is crucial to remember that the Ainu culture described ethnographically in the nineteenth century was a relatively late development, formed largely through contact with mainland Japanese after the end of the Satsumon period. Following the decline of the Ritsuryo state, northern Tohoku was ruled by local warlords, who traded with the people to the north. Japanese settlement in southern Hokkaido increased in the fifteenth century, and by about 1600, the Matsumae domain had a monopoly over trade, which was conducted through trading posts known as *basho*. The main products in demand by the traders were furs and marine foods such as salmon and herring. In return for these items, the Ainu received rice, sake, tobacco, iron pans, and lacquerware.

In a pattern familiar from other parts of the world, the Ainu became more and more dependent on this trade. By prohibiting the introduction of seed, and by other measures, the Japanese did their best to prevent the Ainu from growing crops, so that they would be forced to concentrate on hunting and fishing to satisfy the merchants of Edo and Osaka. Despite major Ainu uprisings in 1669 and 1789, there was no change in this situation until 1799, when the Tokugawa shogunate took direct control of Hokkaido from the Matsumae and actively began to encourage the Ainu to farm. This change was not the result of a new-found benevolence towards the exploited Ainu, but rather a reaction to the growing threat of Russian expansion.

Trade was also important in the early history of the Ryukyu Islands, but here, unlike in Hokkaido, this trade led to the formation of an Okinawan state. About AD 1200, stone-walled enclosures, known as *gusuku*, began to appear on Okinawa Island. These seem to have been the fortresses of local chiefs who were already engaged in trade with the Chinese coast. In the early fifteenth century, the island was unified under the Chuzan kingdom. Its capital was the Shuri *gusuku*, which at its height covered an area of about 4 hectares (11 acres).

The Chuzan kingdom is a classic example of the role of trade in the formation of a state. The wealth that supported the king and the aristocracy came not from an agricultural surplus, but from the buying and selling of goods. The Okinawans acted as intermediaries between Southeast Asia, China, Korea, and Japan. Spices and pepper from Southeast Asia could be exchanged for Chinese pottery, iron, textiles, and coins. These Chinese goods were then sold to the Koreans and the Japanese. Archaeology provides ample evidence

for the extent of this trading activity, with finds of Chinese ceramics and coins at Okinawan sites.

In 1609, the Ryukyu Islands were conquered by the Satsuma domain of Kyushu. The Chuzan kingdom was allowed a facade of independence and continued diplomatic relations with China. The kingdom lasted until 1879, when the islands were forcibly turned into a prefecture of Japan. The Chinese lost all claim to the islands after they were defeated in the Sino-Japanese war of 1894 to 1895, but Okinawa remains a culturally distinctive part of modern Japan.

In contrasting the histories of Hokkaido and Okinawa with that of mainland Japan, there is the danger of seeing the latter as a uniform, unchanging entity. In reality, there were major local differences across the islands of Honshu, Kyushu, and Shikoku, which cannot be discussed in any detail here. There was considerable ecological diversity, leading to quite different ways of life in mountain and coastal regions. Social customs, dialects, and dietary preferences also varied a great deal. The Japanese islands as a whole did not become politically unified until the late nineteenth century, and modern notions of Japanese ethnic and cultural homogeneity date primarily to that time.

This sixteenth-century Japanese painted screen depicts a Portuguese merchant ship en route to Japan. Ships like this brought European muskets, along with American tobacco and sweet potatoes.

An early eighteenth-century Japanese portrayal of a Dutch ship's boy blowing a trumpet. The Dutch were the only Europeans allowed to trade with Tokugawa Japan.

BRITISH MUSEUM/WERNER FORMAN ARCHIVE

Zipangu and the Europeans

Largely through the writings of the Venetian explorer Marco Polo, Japan loomed large in the medieval European imagination. When Christopher Columbus left the Andalusian port of Palos in 1492, it was in the hope of finding not a new continent but Polo's fabled gold and spice island of Zipangu. Similar expectations figured strongly in the voyages of John Cabot, who reached North America from England in 1497. Long before Marco Polo, in the ninth century AD, Persian writer Ibn Khurdadhbih had described Japan as a land where even dog-chains were made of gold. But it was *The Travels* of Marco Polo that really seem to have inspired fifteenth-century Europeans, and Columbus took a copy with him on his voyages.

Some years before Columbus's first voyage, the Portuguese had rounded the southern tip of Africa, and in 1498, Vasco da Gama reached Calicut (now Kozhikode), in India, by this route. In 1510, the Portuguese seized Goa, and then Malacca in the following year: the European colonization of Asia had begun. The first direct European contact occurred in 1543, when a few Portuguese traders arrived at a small island off southern Kyushu. Relations with Europe continued for almost a century, but in the 1630s, shogunal edicts were issued banning Japanese from leaving the country and Europeans from entering. The only exception was the Dutch,

A sixteenth-century Japanese screen showing Portuguese merchants welcoming Japanese officials aboard their ship, and then spreading their wares along the beach.
THE GRANGER COLLECTION

ART INSTITUTE CHICAGO/WERNER FORMAN ARCHIVE

This seventeenth-century screen depicts Jesuit missionaries in Japan. The Jesuits arrived shortly after the European merchants. Some scholars estimate that there were as many as half a million Christian converts by 1615.

Opposite page: The Japanese fascination with the physique and dress of the *Namban* (southern barbarians) is reflected in this detail from an early seventeenth-century painting of a leading Portuguese merchant.

who, having first reached Japan in 1600, were allowed to retain a small trading post in Nagasaki. For many peoples throughout the world, the arrival of Europeans set in train a disastrous clash of cultures that forever altered the course of world history. Why was this not so for Japan? How did the Japanese manage to resist European expansion?

To begin with, Japan was not a new, unknown continent like the Americas. It was, in effect, the eastern extremity of the same Eurasian landmass Portugal occupied in the far west. Some degree of contact across the continent had always been maintained, however indirectly, and for this reason, the Japanese people were not ravaged by infectious diseases to which they had no resistance. This is perhaps the most important difference between the European encounter with East Asia and that with the New World.

Sixteenth-century Japan was a nation divided, where powerful warlords fought each other for overall control. The militarization of the country meant the Europeans had no hope of outright colonization. After about 1570, the fight between the warlords was largely over, and the Japanese state was stronger than it had ever been. The Europeans were content to derive whatever trading advantages they could, and in many ways, they could not have chosen a better time. Vigorous trade between Southeast Asia, China, and Japan afforded ready opportunities for European middlemen. East Asia became part of a global trading network: silver from Mexico was brought via Manila to China, where it was exchanged for silk; Chinese silk was resold in Japan, Europe, and the Americas; precious metals from Japan were sold in China to finance the purchase of goods for the European market.

Gold, silver, and copper were central to East Asian trade in the sixteenth and seventeenth centuries. Despite Marco Polo's tales of Zipangu's golden floors and windows, it took technological innovations from abroad to stimulate the mass production of these metals in Japan. Warlords took advantage of these advances to mine gold and silver to support their territorial expansion. Archaeology has given an insight into the spread of mining and smelting technology, with recent excavations of Takeda domain gold mines in Yamanashi, and of the eighteenth-century Sumitomo copper-smelting facility in Osaka.

Many historians speak of a "world system" of economic interdependence following the expansion of the Europeans from the late fifteenth century. Japan also became a part of that trade network, and yet the closure of most Japanese ports to international shipping in the 1630s set the country on a quite different historical course during the Tokugawa era (AD 1603 to AD 1868). The "closure" of Japan must be seen as a typically East Asian method of internal political control rather than as conscious isolationism. It was, moreover, during this period that the seeds were sown for Japan's rapid and phenomenally successful modernization, after the country was reopened to the world in the middle of the nineteenth century.

HANS-JÜRGEN BURKARD/BILDERBERG

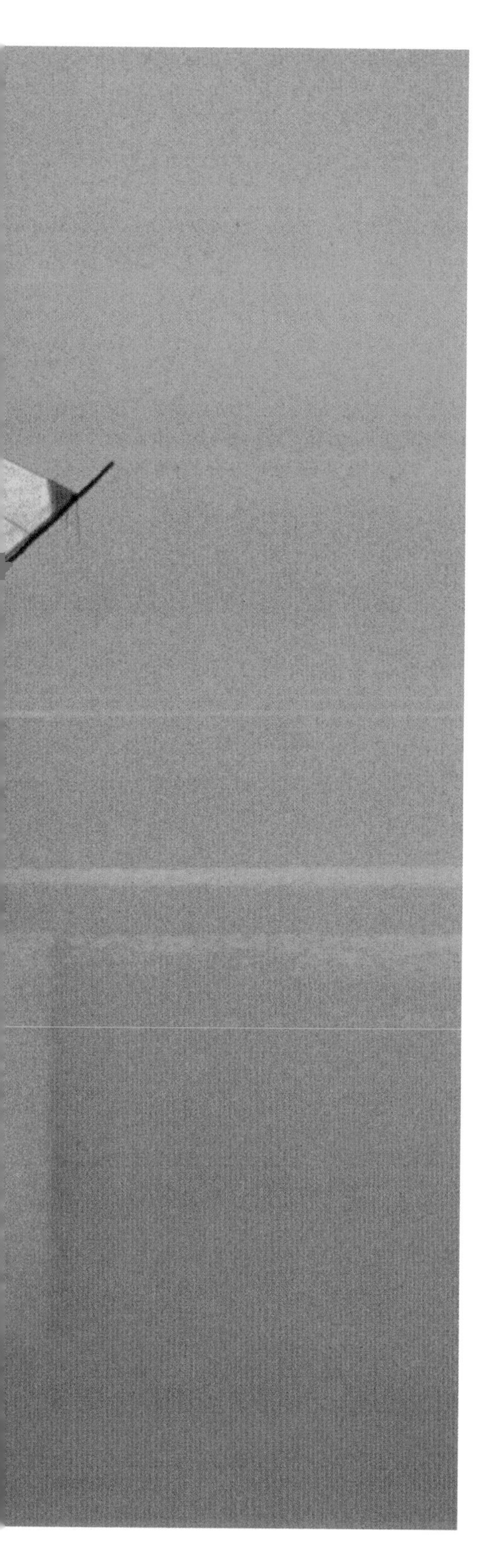

THE OCCUPATION OF THE PACIFIC ISLANDS

5 0 , 0 0 0 B C – A D 1 5 0 0

Voyagers and Fisherfolk

ATHOLL ANDERSON

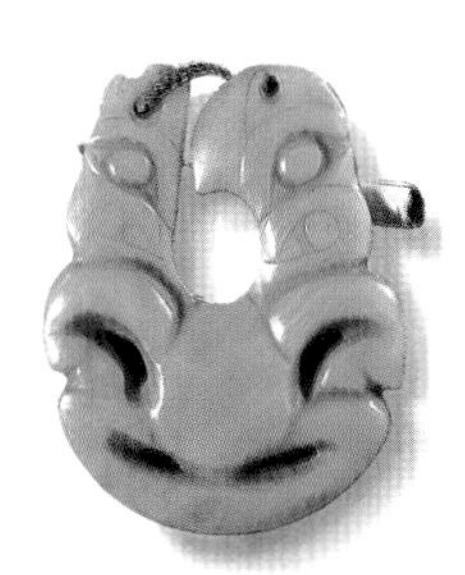

EAST OF ISLAND SOUTHEAST ASIA, the tropical Pacific Ocean stretches nearly halfway around the Earth to the coast of South America. Uninterrupted voyages across this vast and largely empty expanse of ocean were not accomplished until the arrival of European ships in the sixteenth century. Yet, prehistoric people, whose boat-building skills seldom escaped the limitations of the dugout canoe, had begun to venture along island chains more than 30,000 years ago, had reached the heart of the ocean 3,500 years ago, and by AD 500, were sailing up to 4,000 kilometers (2,500 miles) out of sight of land. At about that time, Pacific islanders ventured eastwards and probably reached South America, as there must have been some such contact to account for the introduction of the sweet potato into the Pacific Basin. Oceanic settlement then expanded to Hawaii in the north and, soon after, to New Zealand in the south, and this fixed the latitudinal boundaries of Pacific habitation until the eighteenth century.

Settlement of the remote Pacific islands depended on the development of vessels capable of long voyages out of sight of land. Multihulled craft proved to be the answer, including outrigger canoes, such as these from the Isle de Pins, in New Caledonia.

This nephrite (jade) ornament of a *hei matau* (fishhook) was given to a British captain in 1834 by a northern Maori chief. By the eighteenth century, nephrite was the principal Maori standard of wealth.

MUSEUM OF MANKIND, LONDON/ WERNER FORMAN ARCHIVE

The dugong, or sea-cow, is a marine mammal of the western Pacific Ocean. Melanesians prized it for its fat-rich flesh, spearing or harpooning it from canoes, as here in New Caledonia, about AD 1885.

What declared ambitions or unconscious motives propeled such persistent exploration we shall never know, but perhaps there was initial enticement in the geography of the Pacific environment. From just north of New Guinea, a broad band of nearly 800 habitable islands stretches 12,000 kilometers (7,500 miles)—about 110 degrees of longitude—eastwards between the Tropics of Cancer and Capricorn. For prospective settlers of the area to the north and east of New Guinea, colonizing was at first not difficult, because the islands through the Bismarck Archipelago and down the entire Solomons chain (the region often called "Near Oceania") were large and within sight of one another. Further east, and north into Micronesia (the area known as "Remote Oceania"), however, most of the islands are smaller and further apart.

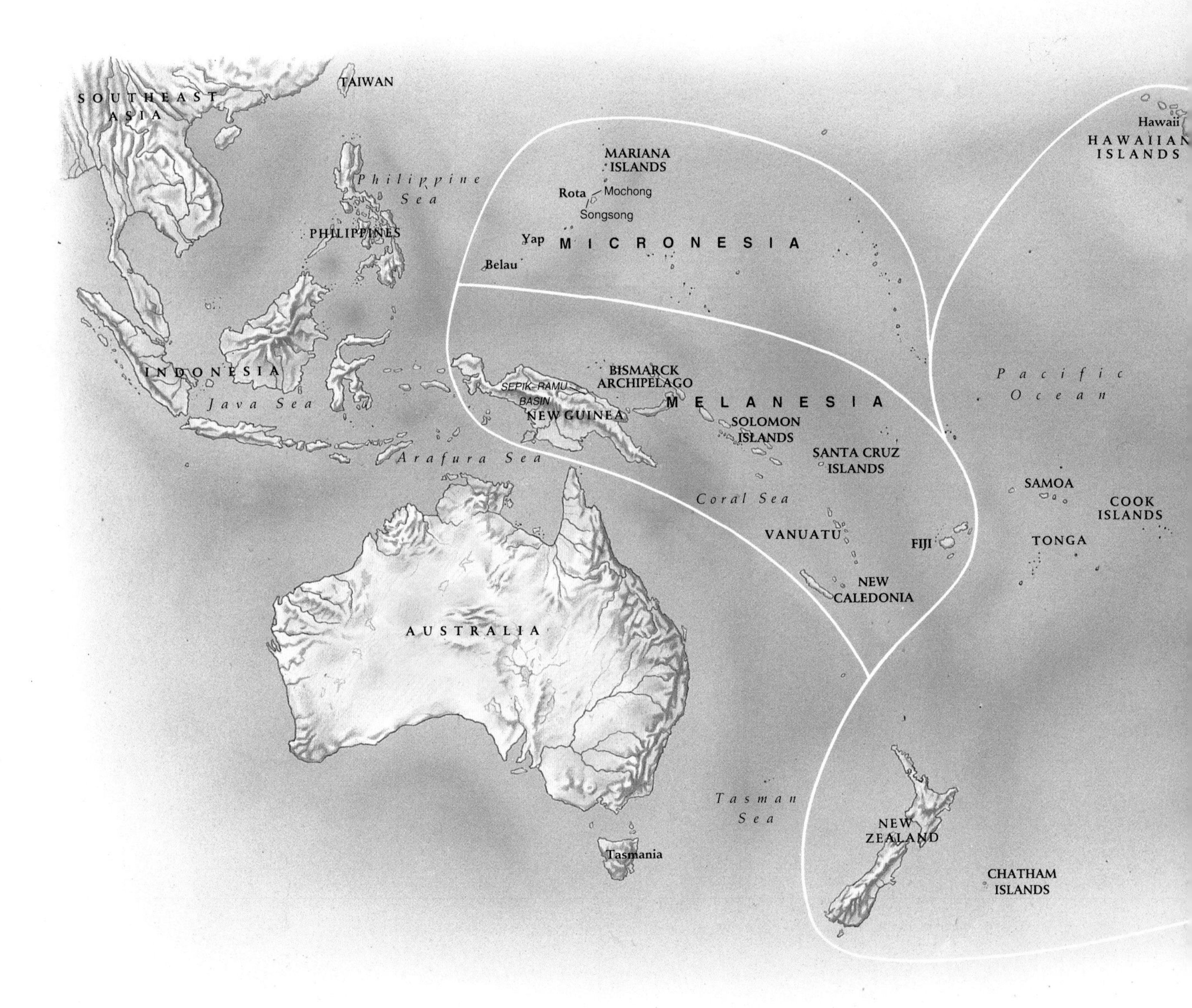

In general, island environments become less favorable for human habitation the further east one travels in the Pacific. The high islands of western Micronesia, Melanesia, and New Zealand are rich in continental rock types; those to the east are composed solely of oceanic basalts. All the islands were heavily forested, but useful plant varieties—notably, plants bearing large, fleshy, edible fruits or roots—were scarcer to the east, as were most kinds of edible animals. Dugongs and crocodiles are seldom seen beyond the Solomons group. Reef fish and shellfish, especially bivalves, become significantly less diverse east of Fiji. There are few terrestrial mammals, and of those that are found in western Melanesia, the pademelon wallaby, the common cuscus, and at least one species of large rat were deliberately introduced by prehistoric people. Only small rats, mice, and domesticated mammals are found beyond the Solomon Islands. The variety of land birds declines dramatically as a function of island size and distance: 520 species in New Guinea, 127 in the Solomon Islands, 54 in Fiji, 17 in the Society Islands, and only 4 on remote Henderson Island. It was only with the late discovery of New Zealand that settlers again encountered environmental diversity of continental richness. Therefore, nearly all human colonization beyond New Guinea had to cope with increasingly distant and less diverse environments.

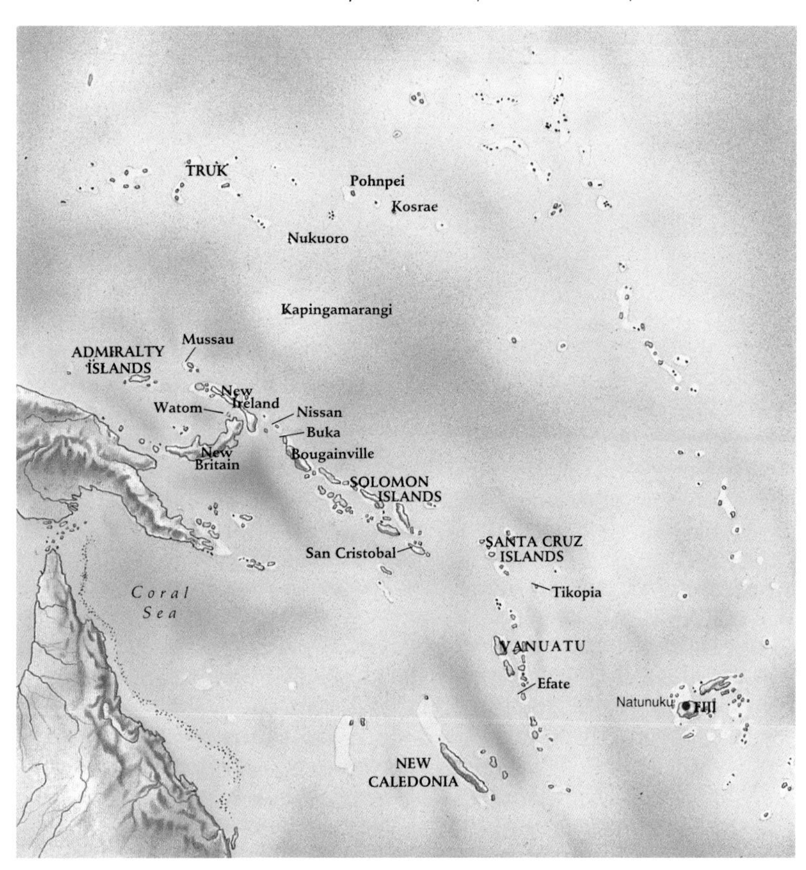

THE LARGE ISLANDS OF MELANESIA
Settlement began in the Pleistocene era and probably reached as far east as San Cristobal during that period, but Santa Cruz and the islands further east were settled much later, during the Lapita phase (about 1500 BC).
CARTOGRAPHY: RAY SIM

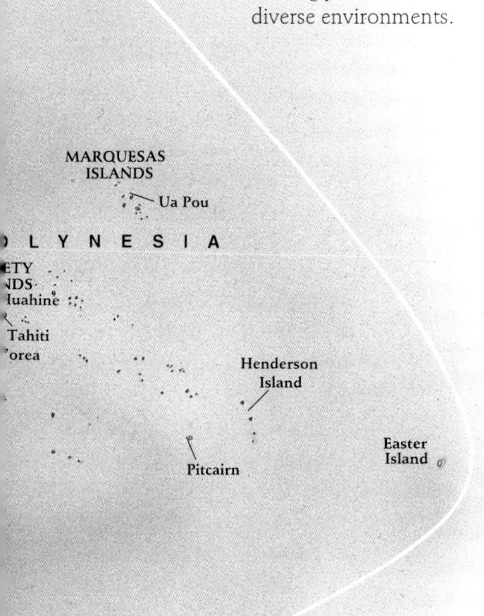

MELANESIA, POLYNESIA, AND MICRONESIA
The Pacific islands are conventionally divided into three groups: Melanesia ("black islands"), Polynesia ("many islands"), and Micronesia ("small islands"). Archaeologists today group the islands as Near Oceania and Remote Oceania (the latter starting at the eastern end of the Solomon Islands).
CARTOGRAPHY: RAY SIM

The settlement of the Pacific islands east of Southeast Asia occurred in two broad phases. During the first, Australia and New Guinea were occupied. Later, the large islands of Near Oceania were settled: New Britain and New Ireland at least 33,000 years ago, and—by a sea crossing of at least 50 kilometers (30 miles), presumably by raft—Buka Island (geographically in the Solomons group) about 28,000 years ago. Since much of the Solomons chain was dry land at that time, it is probable that people stood on the shores of San Cristobal before the peak of the last Ice Age. There was then a gap of nearly 25,000 years before people moved any further eastwards. The arrival of the Lapita culture, about 1500 BC, marks the successful negotiation of the 350 kilometer (220 mile) crossing to the Santa Cruz Islands, and beginning of settlement in Remote Oceania.

The Origins of Lapita Culture

There is broad agreement that Lapita culture first appeared in the Bismarck Archipelago, where its characteristic pottery was first uncovered in 1909 on Watom Island, just north of New Britain. (The name "Lapita" came from a site on New Caledonia.) Lapita ware, which includes jars, bowls, and dishes, is tempered with sand or crushed shell, fashioned by either the slab or paddle-and-anvil

OCCUPATION OF THE PACIFIC ISLANDS: 50,000 BC – AD 1500

Time scale: 1500 · AD 1 · 4000 · 50,000 BC

MELANESIA	POLYNESIA	MICRONESIA
Adoption of Polynesian forms of material culture in central Vanuatu and adjacent islands AD 1200	Moas become extinct (in New Zealand) AD 1500	Settlement of Micronesian islands by Polynesians AD 1100
Disappearance of dentate-stamped pottery AD 1000	Settlement of Chatham Islands AD 1400	Earliest inhabitation of eastern Micronesian atolls AD 1
Manufacture of late Lapita plainware in eastern Melanesia AD 1	Construction of *pa* (hill-forts) begins in New Zealand AD 1400	Settlement of volcanic islands in central and eastern Micronesia 500 BC – AD 1
Appearance of bronze on Lou Island 300 BC – 100 BC	Settlement of New Zealand AD 1200	Settlement of southern Mariana Islands 1000 BC
Manufacture of Mangaasi pottery in Vanuatu 600 BC – AD 500	Lapita culture displaced by local descendant cultures in western Polynesia AD 1000	Peak of post-Pleistocene sea levels 3000 BC
Development of new styles of incised pottery in New Caledonia and Fiji 1000 BC – AD 1	Settlement of eastern Polynesia AD 500 – AD 1000	
First successful crossing to Santa Cruz Islands 1500 BC	Settlement of the Marquesas Islands AD 500	
Settlement of Fiji by Polynesian ancestors 1500 BC	Cessation of pottery manufacture in western Polynesia AD 300	
Appearance of Lapita culture in the Bismarcks 1500 BC	Development of distinctive Polynesian culture in western Polynesia 500 BC	
First successful crossing to Admiralty Islands 3000 BC	Exclusive production of Lapita plainware in western Polynesia 500 BC	
Manufacture of giant clam shell adzes, shell ornaments, and pottery in the Sepik–Ramu Basin of Papua New Guinea 4000 BC – 3000 BC	Development of distinct proto-Polynesian language 1000 BC – 500 BC	
Establishment of pig husbandry and plant cultivation in mainland New Guinea 4000 BC	Appearance of Lapita culture in Tonga 1200 BC	
Intermittent forest clearance for agriculture in the Bismarcks 4,000 BC	Settlement of Samoa 1500 BC	
Establishment of agriculture and manufacture of ground stone adzes in highland Papua New Guinea 8,000 BC		
Development of obsidian trading in the Bismarcks 18,000 BC		
Settlement of Buka 26,000 BC		
Inhabitants of New Britain, New Ireland, and Bougainville become one of world's earliest fisherpeople 30,000 BC		
Settlement of New Britain, New Ireland, and Bougainville 31,000 BC		
Occupation of New Guinea 50,000 BC – 40,000 BC		

A fragment of decorated Lapita pottery from a Fijian site, probably Natunuku, on Viti Levu's northern coast. This piece was broken from a shouldered jar.
ROGER C. GREEN

technique, and fired at low temperatures. The classic form of Lapita decoration consists of complex geometric designs, including stylized faces, impressed into the clay by small dentate (toothed) stamps. Dentate-stamped ware is particularly common in early Lapita sites; incised ware and, especially, undecorated or plainware are more abundant later. In addition to pottery, Lapita material culture includes adzes made of giant clam shell (*Tridacna*), and beads, pendants, bracelets, armbands, vegetable peelers, and one-piece bait hooks also of shell; bone implements; stone adzes of quadrangular, oval, planilateral (planed to the side: mainly western Lapita), and plano-convex (one side planed and one side convex: mainly eastern Lapita) cross-section; stone pounders; hammerstones; and stone grinders, files, and cutting tools—the latter often of chert or obsidian.

Lapita sites are typically found in open localities on small islands or on the coast. Excavations have revealed the impressions of pole and thatch houses, and cooking shelters. There are stone hearths, earth ovens, separate activity areas marked by accumulations of pottery or food refuse, and, occasionally, storage pits. The evidence suggests that hamlets and villages were clustered and that villages in the western Lapita region were often large.

The people who lived here relied partly on coastal resources, gathering shellfish and netting, trapping, or spearing reef fish, but fish remains are not abundant, and relatively few sites show any evidence of turtles, crocodiles, or dugongs. Seabirds, rails, doves, and pigeons were taken infrequently, and there are rare remains of bandicoots or other forest mammals in the western sites. Although scarcely evident in the archaeological record, agriculture was probably important to subsistence here. Bones of domestic pigs, dogs, and chickens, and remains of various tree crops, have been found, but, so far, no evidence of the root crops taro and yam, which are presumed to have been the staples.

The origins of Lapita culture remain an enigma in Pacific prehistory. Who were the Lapita people? Where did Lapita culture come from, or how did it develop? One hypothesis is that it derives from Southeast Asia, suggesting, in its extreme form, that Lapita culture represents a rapid expansion of Neolithic Southeast Asian seafarers through Melanesia and into Polynesia after about 2000 BC. That view is not widely held today, but Southeast Asian connections of some kind are indisputable.

Few remains of Lapita people have been recovered, but studies of those from Watom and Mussau islands, and from Natunuku, in Fiji, reveal a tall, rather slender people who bear some similarities to modern Polynesian, to some eastern Melanesian, and, perhaps, to Indonesian populations: peoples who can be shown to have retained DNA characteristics of East Asian (although not necessarily Southeast Asian), rather than Papuan or Australian Aboriginal, ancestry. Analyses of historical linguistics tell a similar story. Outside New Guinea, most Melanesian and central and eastern Micronesian languages, and all Polynesian languages, belong to the Oceanic group of Austronesian languages. The latter originated in Southeast Asia, and Lapita culture is commonly regarded as the agent of their dispersal to Remote Oceania. At some level, therefore, the arrival of Lapita culture in the Pacific can be regarded as an eastward extension of later, or Neolithic, Southeast Asian prehistory.

The earliest known Neolithic sites in island Southeast Asia are in the Philippines, reliably dated to about 3000 BC, and people were present throughout the region by 2000 BC. The pottery associated with these early sites is often plainware or red-slipped ware, but after 1000 BC, elaborately decorated impressed or incised ware was made. By the beginning of the first millennium AD, pottery here is usually found in association with metal. There are some general indications of a Lapita connection—for instance, pottery with Lapita-like designs has been found at Bukit Tengkorak, in Sabah, a site dated to 800 BC, which also has obsidian from Talasea, in New Britain. Another, rather different, example is the discovery of bronze in a site dated to about 300 BC to 100 BC on Lou Island, in the Bismarcks, which is about the same time that bronze first appears in island Southeast Asia. There are further obvious similarities between the South-east Asian Neolithic and Lapita cultures in the forms of shell adzes and ornaments and some stone adzes, and in the incidence of domestic animals.

The outstanding difference is the absence of rice cultivation in the Lapita Neolithic, and that is possibly because a strong horticultural tradition of another kind was already established in Melanesia. Pig husbandry and gardening, particularly of taro, had begun by 4000 BC (possibly by 7000 BC) in mainland Papua New Guinea, although pig remains occur in only one of the Bismarck sites with pre-Lapita levels, the Balof 2 rock shelter, and then at a level dated to 1000 BC or later. Nevertheless, plant remains and pollen evidence from these sites suggest intermittent forest clearance in the Bismarcks from about 4000 BC, so Lapita culture may have been superimposed on an existing agricultural base.

COO-EE HISTORICAL PICTURE LIBRARY

Many islanders relied on coastal resources. These western Samoan fishermen have been successful in their hunt for turtles.

GEORGE W. BROWN COLLECTION/ AUSTRALIAN MUSEUM, NO. V.6537

The greater yam (*Dioscorea alata*) was grown in New Britain in hillside gardens carved from the bush. Huge tubers such as those shown here were used for competitive display and presentation, and were seldom eaten.

PREHISTORIC FISHING IN OCEANIA

FOSS LEACH

THE PACIFIC OCEAN presents an extraordinary range of marine environments surrounding many different kinds of islands. A coral atoll, for example, has a lagoon and surrounding reef flats, which support diverse species of edible fish. Although this type of island corresponds to the archetypal South Sea paradise, other forms of islands also present magnificent fishing opportunities, with outlying coral reefs or deep-water trenches harboring many Oceanic species. Given this diversity and wealth of fishing prospects, it is hardly surprising that the human communities that spread into the Pacific world were among the world's greatest prehistoric fishers.

In the Pacific islands, fishing was primarily an inshore pursuit, much of it concentrated on the shallow waters of reefs and the reef edges bordering the open sea. There, basket traps could be used to catch marine eels and other types of fish. The traps were commonly made from vines and coconut-fiber sennit, and were designed to prevent fish from escaping once inside. This New Zealand specimen has a tapering funnel, and was used to catch freshwater eels.

JAN NAUTA/MUSEUM OF NEW ZEALAND TE PAPA TONGAREWA, NO. B20092

An Ancient Fishing Tradition

The first people to enter the Oceanic world did so at least 33,000 years ago, crossing the narrow but deep oceanic trench between the Papua New Guinea mainland and the islands to the northeast, including New Britain, New Ireland, and Bougainville. Although the main thrust of Oceanic voyaging and settlement took place some 30,000 years later, the earliest inhabitants of these large islands were no strangers to the sea's resources, and are among the earliest fishers anywhere in the world. Remains of fish and shellfish have now been found in several archaeological sites in deposits of Pleistocene age. These include the sites known as Matenkupkum, Balof 2, Panakiwuk, and Matembek, on New Ireland; and Kilu, on Bougainville. A surprising range of marine species was being exploited, including reef shellfish, crab, lobster, sea urchin, turtle, saltwater crocodile, shallow-water reef fish (such as triggerfish and parrotfish), and at least three species of sharks. No evidence has been found of fishhooks, and it is currently thought that fish were caught by some other technique, such as netting, spearing, poisoning, or the use of fish traps on the reef platform.

A Varied Catch

Once prehistoric people moved beyond the large islands of Melanesia, about 3,500 years ago, they entered a region that offered fewer opportunities for land-based activities such as hunting, and they became more reliant on the sea. The nature of this dependence, however, varied greatly from one part of the Pacific to another. The Moriori people of the temperate waters of the Chatham Islands harvested at least 80 percent of their food from the sea. The main species they caught were seals, but rocky shore fish such as cod were also important. In the more tropical waters, by far the most common fish caught were various species of parrotfish. But the quarry of different fishing communities varied a great deal, and had less to do with environmental abundance than with cultural factors. Today, for example, the Polynesian people on Kapingamarangi Atoll spend a great deal of their time and energy trying to catch a fish known as the rainbow runner, and the men tell many fabulous stories about their adventures in search of these fish. The most common fish found in the ancient middens on this island, however, are various types of grouper, showing that in the distant past as in the present, what fishermen seek and what they catch are not always the same thing.

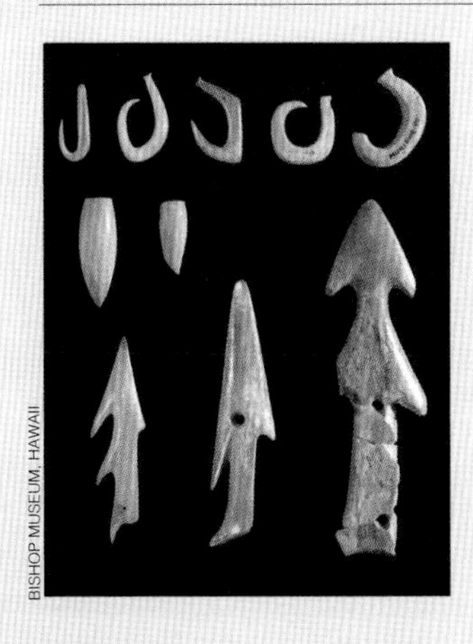

A small selection of the fishing equipment and amulets that have been recovered from archaeological sites on the Marquesas Islands.

Fishing Tackle

Prehistoric fishermen in the Pacific used a quite bewildering variety of techniques, including basket fish traps, kite fishing, poisoning techniques, frightening lines, lures, fishhooks, nets, spears, and bows and arrows. In each category, there are specialized forms to catch particular species. For example, there is a special lure made from the cobweb of the banana spider to entangle the numerous small teeth of the long tom. Some of the fishhooks of the Pacific qualify as works of art, especially those made from lustrous pearl shell. Fishhooks were even fashioned from stone on Easter Island, Pitcairn, and the Chatham Islands.

Toxicity of Fish

An important consideration for the prehistoric fishermen in the Pacific was the possibility that the daily catch contained fish with lethal poison in their flesh. Many species of Pacific fish are implicated in ciguatera poisoning, but whether an individual fish is toxic or not is not easy to tell in advance of eating, because toxicity varies with season and locality, and also with the diet of the individual fish. For example, moray eels are frequently poisonous, and modern ethnographic records testify to totemic and other forms of avoidance behavior towards eels on some islands. It is interesting that the archaeological record of individual islands shows eels to have been abundant in some periods and not in others.

It is clear that fishing in the prehistoric Pacific was not without hazards. An unusual case of this type of problem concerns the people who lived at Dongan, on the north coast of Papua New Guinea. The bones of pufferfish are quite conspicuous at this site, accounting for about 14 percent of the fish caught here, although the flesh and viscera of pufferfish are always highly toxic, and poison can be absorbed even by simple skin contact.

Despite the violently poisonous nature of pufferfish, it is a national pastime in Japan to eat Fugu, as they are known there. Fugu cooks must be licenced, and training and certification are exacting processes. The amount eaten must be tailored precisely to the customer's body weight if it is not to be lethal. One authority on Fugu makes the disconcerting comment that even the finest puffer cooks occasionally succumb to their own cooking, and that people who engage in this epicurean pastime must consider themselves, at best, to be "living dangerously". It seems that the ancient people at Dongan had mastered the art of preparing pufferfish for consumption some 6,000 years ago!

Big-game Fishing

Tuna fishing captured the imagination of early European observers in the Pacific, but it appears that few prehistoric fishermen caught tuna in abundance. There are some exceptions, such as early fishermen on Huahine, in the Society Islands, and Ua Pou, in the Marquesas Islands. These fast-swimming fish are at the bottom end of the big-game species, and provided great adventure for people fishing from canoes. In the northwestern Pacific, however, really spectacular big-game fishing was in vogue up to 2,000 years ago on the island of Rota, in the Mariana Islands. Archaeological sites near the present-day airport, and also at Mochong and Songsong, show that ancient fishermen were catching marlin, dolphinfish, and tuna. To catch and land a marlin, weighing at least several hundred and possibly as much as 1,000 kilograms (about 400 to more than 2,000 pounds), from a dugout canoe is a considerable achievement, and must have been a spectacular sight.

A late style of southern Maori bait hook. This finely decorated composite hook is of a type that was used to catch sharks and other large species, although this example may be decorative rather than functional.

COO-EE HISTORICAL PICTURE LIBRARY

Marine turtles, cultivated taro, and yangona root, or kava—three of the major resources of the Oceanic region—are gathered for display in a Melanesian village, possibly in Vanuatu.

A second theory is that Lapita culture developed locally, particularly in the Bismarck Archipelago. In addition to agriculture, ground stone adzes of oval and lenticular (curved on both sides) cross-section can be traced to the Early Holocene period in highland Papua New Guinea, and *Tridacna* shell adzes, shell ornaments, and pottery found in the Sepik–Ramu Basin may date back as far as 3000 BC to 4000 BC. Dentate-stamped Lapita ware is significantly older than equally elaborately decorated pottery from the Neolithic period found in Southeast Asia. It is possible, therefore, that while the art of potting and a range of Neolithic vessel forms came to western Melanesia from Southeast Asia, the decorative motifs were indigenous, and may have been transferred from other media, such as barkcloth (*tapa*) or tattooing.

With trade in obsidian established in the Bismarcks up to 20,000 years ago, and people there making ocean crossings of up to 200 kilometers (125 miles) wide (to the Admiralty Islands) as early as 3000 BC, it is apparent that many of the characteristic features of the Lapita cultural complex in this region are as old as or older than the same features in Neolithic Southeast Asia. According to this theory, the Lapita cultural complex developed in the Bismarcks on a foundation of local horticulture and a comparatively advanced maritime technology, the latter underpinning a particular interest in interisland trade in obsidian and other commodities. Pottery was then acquired once the exchange network took in the western margins of island Southeast Asia.

FRANK HURLEY COLLECTION/AUSTRALIAN MUSEUM, NO. V 4553

Neither of these theories accounts satisfactorily for all of the important evidence. East Asian affinities are undoubted, notably in the Lapita people and languages, and in some items of material culture, such as the quadrangular cross-sectioned adze and the manufacture of pottery, but there is more to Lapita than an expansion of the Southeast Asian Neolithic. Some of the material culture, including the plano-convex cross-sectioned adze and the distinctive decoration of Lapita pottery, probably has a Melanesian origin. It is assumed, as well, that taro, banana, coconut, breadfruit, and sugar cane were adopted by Lapita people from older Melanesian economies. At present, therefore, the precise mix of local and exotic elements that made up the Lapita cultural complex cannot be specified.

This man from Milne Bay province, in Papua New Guinea, is carrying a stone axe hafted in a wooden handle. Ground stone blades, some dating to as early as 9000 BC, could be mounted as axeheads (parallel to the handle) or transversely as adze-heads.

Stone axe-adzes such as this were manufactured at quarries throughout the highlands of Papua New Guinea and traded widely in the region, often for coastal products, including marine shells.

SYGMA/AUSTRAL INTERNATIONAL

A. LESSON/E.T. ARCHIVE/AUSTRALIAN PICTURE LIBRARY

The tropical islands of eastern Polynesia impressed early European visitors as visions of rural innocence: the lands of noble savages, whose customs and governance reflected a state of natural development assumed once to have existed in prehistoric Europe. This drawing of Matavai village, in Tahiti, by A. Lesson, with its ordered landscape of woodland, houses, and a quiet river, is clearly informed by a European sensibility.

Expansion into Remote Oceania

From Aitape, on the north coast of Papua New Guinea, to Mulifanua, in Samoa, 79 Lapita sites have been located. The fact that none have been found in the Solomons, except on Buka and Nissan, at the northern tip, is very odd, and is currently ascribed to insufficient searching for them. Similarly, when archaeological field work begins between the Sepik district and Sulawesi, a westward extension of Lapita can be anticipated. The same may not be true of the eastern boundary. It is possible that the expansion of Lapita culture stopped in western Polynesia, but there could be another explanation. East of Tonga, the tropical Polynesian islands are situated on a subsiding geological plate, and since Lapita sites are typically found on low, beach-front terraces, nearly all may have disappeared beneath the waves. The fact that the only Lapita site on the Pacific plate, Mulifanua, lies several meters (about 10 feet) underwater lends support to this hypothesis.

About 30 Lapita sites have been radiocarbon-dated, and the most important finding is that the Lapita culture first appeared at much the same time throughout the entire geographical range. The most reliable dates for Bismarck sites are 1500 BC; and for Tonga, 1200 BC. Most sites date to the period from 1200 BC to 400 BC, and sites containing dentate-stamped pottery probably do not date reliably beyond the beginning of the first millennium AD. The chronology suggests that Lapita culture developed or arrived very rapidly, was disseminated almost immediately, and was then modified according to local conditions.

The eastward spread beyond the continental islands to the high volcanic islands, raised coral islands, and true atolls of western Polynesia, with their increasingly restricted range of resources, seems to have influenced various aspects of Lapita culture. For instance, the change apparent in the forms of adzes—especially the rise of triangular and quadrangular cross-sectioned forms, and the loss of oval and planilateral cross-sectioned forms—seems largely to reflect the flaking properties of Oceanic basalts, the raw material available to the eastern adze-makers.

A similar explanation may be valid, at least in part, for the loss of pottery. The later history of Oceanic ceramics is complex. In Melanesia, local styles, which diverged early from the Lapita tradition, seem to have developed rapidly, and there is also evidence of intrusive traditions. In Vanuatu, for example, a distinctive style of incised and relief-decorated ware known as Mangaasi appeared about 600 BC and continued to about AD 500. Other styles of incised ware appeared in New Caledonia and Fiji during the first millennium BC, and pottery of many styles continued to be made throughout Melanesia until the nineteenth century.

There was also a broad west-to-east decline in the diversity of Lapita vessel forms and ceramic decoration. In the eastern regions, there tended to be a smaller variety of motifs, and design patterns were simplified to rectilinear forms. This trend was carried a step further in western Polynesia, where plainware was the only form being produced by about 500 BC and pottery manufacture ceased altogether by about AD 300. A few sherds of Polynesian plainware—probably imported, although some of those found at Atuona may have been made locally—have been found in the Marquesas Islands, but other than these, there is no evidence of pottery manufacture anywhere in eastern Polynesia.

The distribution of suitable raw materials certainly had something to do with this eastward decline in ceramics production. In general, potters preferred clays of the kaolin type, which were common as far east as Fiji. These were formed by the weathering of continental rocks, especially andesite. Further east, clays and tempering materials suitable for pottery were scarce, and were largely absent in eastern Polynesia, except for New Zealand. By the time New Zealand was discovered, however, eastern Polynesians were a thousand years removed from any ceramics tradition.

But there is more to it than this. Pottery manufacture declined quite slowly over a millennium in western Polynesia, and it is unlikely that only the relative scarcity of raw materials was involved. Increasing emphasis on large wooden vessels, such as kava bowls, for prestigious occasions may have gradually reduced the status of pottery to a utilitarian level, at which point the Polynesian emphasis on pit storage of root crops, and cooking in earth ovens, may have made pottery manufacture redundant.

By about the first millennium AD, then, the original form of Lapita culture had been transformed into various local cultures. All of these were based on much the same gardening and fishing economy, and had many similar tools and other artifacts in common, but while pottery flourished in island Melanesia, it was slowly dying in the east. The 700 kilometer (440 mile) crossing from Vanuatu to Fiji effectively removed the eastern Lapita people from all but occasional participation in the cultural changes that were taking place in Melanesia, and its widespread exchange networks, and in that relative isolation, these peoples developed the distinctive prehistoric cultures of Polynesia and eastern Micronesia. Both these cultures were then spread to numerous widely scattered islands by skillful voyagers.

COO-EE HISTORICAL PICTURE LIBRARY

Kava is a narcotic drink prepared by crushing the roots of the shrub *Piper methysticum* in water, or sometimes by chewing them. Kava was drunk on ceremonial occasions in Fiji and elsewhere in the central Pacific.

In Fiji, but no further east, the manufacture of pottery, begun in the Lapita era, persisted into modern times. Pottery shaped by the common paddle-and-anvil method, shown here, was fired in the open.

COO-EE HISTORICAL PICTURE LIBRARY

DAVID HISER/PHOTOGRAPHERS ASPEN

The *Hokule'a*, a modern Hawaiian voyaging canoe of traditional form, displays the characteristic features of two matched hulls and the Oceanic spritsail rig. This vessel completed unaided passages between Hawaii, Tahiti, and New Zealand.

Oceanic Voyaging

Since obsidian from New Britain and other rock types from the Bismarcks were exchanged fairly regularly as far east as Santa Cruz (even reaching Fiji), long passages out of sight of land must have been negotiated. It is apparent, therefore, that some advance in maritime technology was a significant, if unseen, factor in the Lapita expansion and the subsequent Polynesian and Micronesian dispersal. Voyaging technology in the prehistoric Pacific region is a complex subject, and one that has provoked passionate debate during the last 40 years. The main elements of this debate have been the nature of the water-craft and their sailing and sea-keeping qualities, the nature and effectiveness of navigation techniques, and the causes of, or motives for, long-distance voyaging.

The famous *Kon Tiki* voyage, in 1947, demonstrated that a large raft, if it cleared the coastal wind and current (across which the *Kon Tiki* was towed), could sail from the vicinity of South America to eastern Polynesia. It does not, however, add much to our understanding of Polynesian colonization. Rafts may occasionally have been used in Pacific voyaging, and were almost certainly the means by which voyagers reached the large islands of western Melanesia at least 30,000 years ago. It is much more probable, however, that sailing canoes were the principal form of water-craft in the Pacific region by the mid-Holocene period (about 4000 BC). This cannot be shown archaeologically, but there is some indirect linguistic evidence. If the meanings of words have remained more or less unchanged, then the widespread similarity of various words for the components of sailing canoes in Austronesian languages suggests an antiquity of that order.

Similarly, it is assumed that the main vessel used to colonize the Pacific was the double-hulled canoe joined by a platform on which a mast was stepped and a shelter constructed. The outrigger canoe was also used and, as it occurred in New Zealand, must have spread virtually throughout the Pacific, but it is not clear that it was always a sailing craft. The outrigger sailing canoe keeps its smaller hull to windward and shunts back and

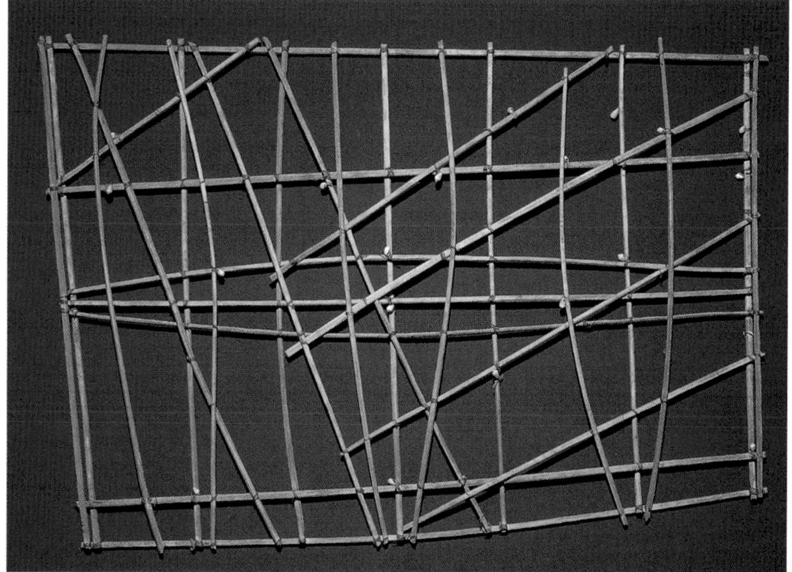

DEREK BAYES/ASPECT PICTURE LIBRARY

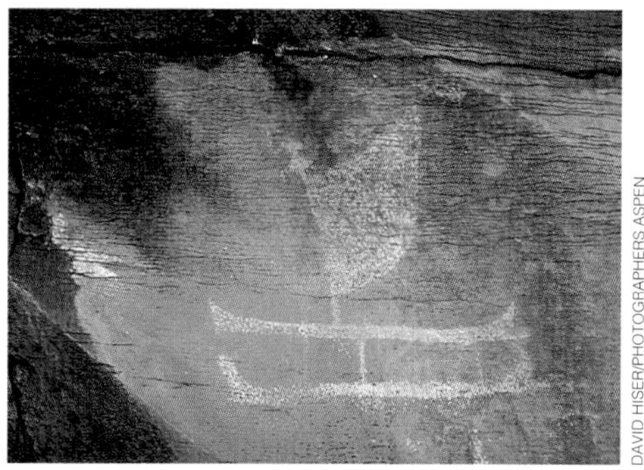

DAVID HISER/PHOTOGRAPHERS ASPEN

This bamboo lattice with small shells attached in some places was a navigational aid. Such devices, which represented currents, courses, and the disposition of islands, were used in Micronesia until recently.

Carvings chipped into rock surfaces (petroglyphs) are found throughout Oceania, as here in Maui, Hawaii. Canoes, people, and animals are common motifs and often occur in groups along traditional pathways.

forth across the wind by switching the apex of a lateen (triangular) sail to either end of the main hull—that is, bow and stern are interchangeable. The Oceanic lateen sail, however, was still spreading into eastern Polynesia at the time of European discovery, while the more primitive Oceanic spritsail—a narrow triangular sail, rigged apex-down between a mast and an upstanding yard—was already widespread. Double-hulled sailing canoes in eastern Polynesia used the spritsail, had a bow and stern of a different shape, and tacked by swinging the bow through the wind in the same manner as a modern yacht.

The qualities of such water-craft have been tested by building and cruising replicas, notably the Hawaiian double-hulled canoe *Hokule'a*. This 19 meter (62 foot) vessel, built to a traditional design, proved capable of sailing an upwind course to about 70 degrees off the wind. It has completed three Hawaii–Tahiti passages and made one voyage to New Zealand, sailing a total of 24,000 nautical miles. Such experiments suggest that the double-hulled canoe, although limited in capacity and sailing ability in comparison with contemporary plank-built craft, such as the dhow, the junk, and the longship, was capable of reaching, and returning from, any part of Oceania—although with some difficulty to the far east and south—provided there was an effective means of navigation.

Here, again, we have to rely on ethnographic accounts of traditional navigation, together with experimental voyages. These accounts and voyages indicate that fairly accurate courses could be set by observing the succession of stars that rise and set at the same points on the eastern and western horizons, and their relationship to other star patterns. In sailing star courses, there were undoubtedly some difficulties that Oceanic navigators could only partly overcome, such as allowing for the set of currents out of sight of land, and others for which they had no solution, such as estimating changes in longitude. Experimental voyaging suggests, however, that errors in dead reckoning tend to cancel each other out rather than accumulate. Thus, ancient navigators, by

THE POLYNESIAN VOYAGING CANOE

Ben Finney

The Polynesian voyaging canoe, one of the great ocean-going craft of the ancient world, was the means by which generations of adventurous voyagers were able to extend the human frontier far out into the Pacific, discovering and colonizing a vast realm of Oceanic islands. By 1000 BC, when Mediterranean sailors were sailing in their land-locked sea, the immediate ancestors of the Polynesians had reached the previously uninhabited archipelagos of Fiji, Tonga, and Samoa, in the middle of the Pacific Ocean. Their descendants went on from there to settle all the habitable islands in a huge triangular section of the ocean bounded by the Hawaiian archipelago, tiny Easter Island, and the massive islands of New Zealand—an area equivalent to most of Europe and Asia combined.

Ocean-going Canoes

The canoes in which people spread into the Pacific were not only humankind's first truly ocean-going craft, but also embodied a unique way of gaining the stability needed to carry sail in rough, open ocean waters. Trying to raise a sail of any size on a slim canoe hull leads to disaster. As soon as the wind fills the sail, the canoe will capsize. The builders of later ocean-going craft, such as European keelships, transcended this limitation by making broad-planked and ballasted hulls, but those who developed the Oceanic canoe gained the needed stability by adding outrigger floats to one or both sides of a single canoe hull, or by joining two hulls together by means of crossbeams and coconut-fiber lashings to make the so-called double canoe. The first Pacific voyages may have been made in outrigger canoes, but as interisland distances increased and people sailed further into the Pacific, the double canoe came to be the favored craft. The double canoe had greater stability and the capacity to carry migrating men, women, and children; their food and water; and all the tools, seeds, plants, and domesticated animals they needed to survive.

People Movers

Since unballasted canoes do not sink, and Polynesians, unlike Vikings, do not seem to have buried voyaging canoes with their chiefs, archaeologists have not found any ancient examples of these craft. Judging from the voyaging canoes seen by Captain Cook and other European explorers, however, they were large, swift-sailing vessels capable of carrying many scores of people over great distances. Indeed, they would have to have been in order for these seafarers to have crossed thousands of kilometers of open ocean to colonize such isolated islands as the Hawaiian Islands and Easter Island.

Fast Sails

The triangular sails that powered voyaging canoes were made of matting, typically woven from the saltwater-resistant leaves of the pandanus tree. Ethnographic reports from the contact period, and modern experiments, indicate that these sails drove the slim hulls of voyaging canoes easily through the sea, enabling voyagers to travel upwards of 240 kilometers (150 miles) a day in brisk winds. Although these canoes sailed best when reaching across the wind, they could tack to windward. Polynesians did not, however, try to make long crossings directly to windward. Instead, they waited for periodic wind shifts. To sail eastwards against the direction of the prevailing trade winds, for example, they waited for the seasonal changes that brought periods of favorable westerly winds.

The Tongiaki

By the time Europeans had entered the Pacific (AD 1520), Polynesian expansion had largely run its course. On most of the islands, the people had given up long-distance voyaging and were concentrating on internal matters. Not so the Tongans, however. At the time of European contact (AD 1616), they were ranging widely over western Polynesia and deep into Melanesian waters on voyages of trade, adventure, and plunder. Their chief vehicle was the *tongiaki,* a handsome double canoe with a single lateen sail. The Dutch navigator Willem Cornelis Schouten, the first European to see and describe a *tongiaki,* wrote in AD 1616: "The rig of these vessels is so excellent and they go so well under sail that there are few ships in Holland that could overhaul them." When, more than 150 years later, Captain James Cook saw these voyaging canoes, he was equally impressed. He describes one fine example as having two hulls, "each about 60 or 70 feet [18 to 20 meters] long", and being built from a dug-out log base to which planks were lashed to raise the freeboard. The two hulls were connected 1.5 to 2 meters (6 to 7 feet) asunder, by stout crossbeams lashed securely to the gunnels of each hull. On top of the crossbeams was a central platform, on which the mast was stepped, a low, arched shelter for the crew was erected, and a sand-insulated fire box for cooking was placed. The lateen sail was raised on a short, stubby mast, and the canoe was steered by two long steering oars, one for each hull.

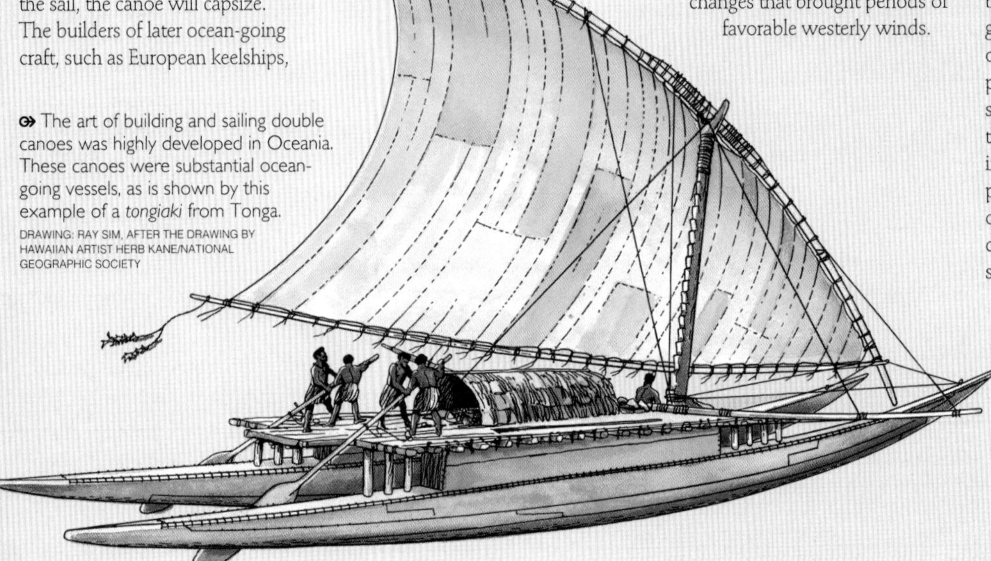

The art of building and sailing double canoes was highly developed in Oceania. These canoes were substantial ocean-going vessels, as is shown by this example of a *tongiaki* from Tonga.
DRAWING: RAY SIM, AFTER THE DRAWING BY HAWAIIAN ARTIST HERB KANE/NATIONAL GEOGRAPHIC SOCIETY

employing a variety of techniques, ranging from star bearings to keen observation of swell patterns and the angle of the wake, could steer relatively accurately over thousands of kilometers. Their success was partly due to the fact that, in most cases, their target was huge. Nearly all Polynesian islands lie within archipelagos, which presented targets that were 20 to 40 degrees wide to voyagers setting off from the nearest inhabited island.

Perhaps most important, it now appears that voyagers in Remote Oceania employed a rational and comparatively safe voyaging strategy. Navigation was easiest on east–west courses, and within the tropics, seasonal shifts in wind patterns were fairly predictable. So, whether voyagers sailed to windward, or waited for windows of reversed wind direction in an otherwise headwind pattern, their chances of return from an exploratory voyage were reasonably good in the event of finding no new land or if their vessel were disabled. Windward is more or less eastward for most of the year, and analysis of the pattern of colonization in Polynesia indicates that the earlier discoveries were made from west to east—that is, into prevailing winds. Later voyages, probably building on experience and developing maritime technology, searched for and found land at points, such as Hawaii, that lie across the wind, a somewhat more risky direction. The last discoveries were generally made downwind or to the far southwest, where New Zealand and its outlying archipelagos lie beyond the predictable tropical weather systems.

The hypothesis of systematic voyaging bears, to some extent, upon the question of what motivated regular long-distance voyaging. That is, rather than discovery by accidental voyages, such as by fishermen who were lost at sea, or by drift voyages, such as rafting from South America, the Polynesians seem to have been following a systematic process of exploration and colonization. With a confidence in their methods justified by success, the Polynesians had a continuing incentive to search for yet more islands that were suitable for settlement. In such a strategy, it could be expected that voyaging canoes would be equipped with all the basic requirements of a new colony, including fertile people and domestic plants and animals.

Expectation of success is, though, only a partial explanation. There was still a large element of risk, and what people found was, in most cases, not much different from what they had left. So why keep voyaging? Various ideas have been canvassed. The discovery of most islands, in eastern Polynesia especially, occurred so quickly that population pressure on resources was probably not a compelling motive in general. Perhaps the rapid depletion of pristine food reserves, especially of large, flightless, or colonial birds, encouraged some voyagers to keep seeking regions offering high-quality resources, instead of investing in the long-term development of agriculture and fishing. Cultural pressures, including the flight of exiles and also of losers in the interclan skirmishing endemic to Polynesian society—a common traditional explanation of prehistoric voyaging—and simple satisfaction of human curiosity are other likely motives.

The Settlement of Micronesia

The earliest voyages out of the eastern Lapita homeland may have been northwards into Micronesia, but to understand the colonization of this region, we need first to resolve the issue of whether many of the islands had emerged from beneath the high post-Pleistocene sea levels, which peaked about 1000 BC before falling to modern levels. Most of eastern Micronesia, in particular, consists of atolls rising only a few meters above the waves, and there are no archaeological sites on these that date to earlier than about the beginning of the first millennium AD. When Lapita settlers expanded throughout Melanesia to Fiji and into western Polynesia more than a millennium earlier, much of present-day Micronesia may simply not have existed. It is difficult to tell if that was a factor in colonization patterns, however, because the high volcanic islands in central and eastern Micronesia, such as the Truk Islands, Pohnpei (formerly Ponape), and Kosrae, were apparently also not settled until between about 500 BC and the beginning of the first millennium AD. Similarly, the Micronesian islands settled by Polynesians, Nukuoro and Kapingamarangi, have archaeological sequences dating back to only AD 1100, compared to about 1000 BC in other so-called Polynesian

ROSEMARY CHASTNEY/OCEAN IMAGES, INC/THE IMAGE BANK

Many Micronesian islands are low-lying coral atolls, like this one in Truk lagoon. Small, often short of cultivable soil and drinking water, and prone to devastation by storms, they are precarious habitats for people.

DAVID HISER/PHOTOGRAPHERS ASPEN

High islands, especially those with fringing coral reefs and lagoons, as here at Mo'orea, in Tahiti, offered Oceanic settlers a secure environment. Root crops could be grown in their fertile volcanic soils, and their sheltered waters offered excellent fishing.

outliers to the south in Melanesia (although a Polynesian culture was a late arrival here as well, about AD 1200). It is equally possible that eastern Micronesia was simply settled comparatively late.

The western Micronesian archipelagos, in which high islands are far more common, have a longer archaeological record. There are well-established dates of about 1000 BC for settlement in the southern Mariana Islands. Current dates of about the beginning of the first millennium AD in Yap and Belau (formerly Palau) probably do not reflect the period of colonization if settlers came from island Southeast Asia and through the closest archipelago, the Marianas.

The conventional account of Micronesian settlement certainly incorporates that view. It is argued, primarily on linguistic grounds, that the western Micronesians originated in island Southeast Asia, whereas most of the other Micronesian languages are closest to those spoken in eastern Melanesia. This division finds support in archaeological evidence. Early remains from western Micronesia, notably pottery from the Marianas and Belau, show unmistakable affinities with contemporary styles in Indonesia and the Philippines, although the similarities are not sufficiently marked to pinpoint the district of origin. The pottery of eastern Micronesia, however, resembles that of the late Lapita plainware found in eastern Melanesia at about the beginning of the first millennium AD. Artifacts similar to other early eastern Micronesian forms, including shell adzes, fishhooks, vegetable peelers, and ornaments, are also found in eastern Melanesian assemblages. A two-pronged colonization is thus envisaged: settlement of the western margins directly from island Southeast Asia, which took place about 1000 BC or earlier, and settlement of the remainder, somewhat later, from eastern Melanesia (or possibly western Polynesia).

Other explanations are possible, although there is as yet little, if any, archaeological evidence to support them. One is that Micronesia was settled entirely from eastern Melanesia by people who continued on to, and returned from, island Southeast Asia. Obtaining early dates from the high central Micronesian islands might swing some support in that direction. Another is that people migrated down the Marianas from the offshore archipelagos of East Asia, including Taiwan and Japan. The ancient and highly distinctive ceramic traditions of these areas should leave no room for confusion if potential evidence ever comes to light.

THE ROY MATA BURIAL, VANUATU

José Garanger

Oral traditions are often thought of as short-term history, wide open to distortion and even complete invention in the promotion of personal interests. In Vanuatu, as in most parts of the Pacific, they usually justify the present social structure—the hierarchical rules of chieftainship, the transmission of titles, and the tenure of land. But these traditions often have their origin in actual events, as the excavation of the burial of Roy Mata, from 1966 to 1967, demonstrated.

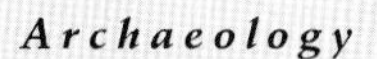

Skeletons surrounded by marine shells, megapod eggshell, and other debris at the Roy Mata excavations on Retoka, in Vanuatu. The archaeology of this site has revealed many features consistent with the account of this chiefly burial that has survived in the local oral tradition.

JOSÉ GARANGER

Traditions

Roy Mata was one of several "chiefs" who came in a fleet of canoes "from the south" to the island of Efate more than 500 years ago. They came first to the most easterly point of the 1,000 square kilometer (390 square mile) island, and from there Roy Mata directed the dispersal of various "chiefs" to different areas. He himself went to the northern part of the island, from where he organized the first of the five-yearly feasts of general "peace" known as *natamwate*. At this feast, new links between individuals of different clans on the island were forged by the distribution of objects with personal significance. He is also said to have introduced matrilineal descent into central Vanuatu.

When Roy Mata died, his body was carried around to the various clans who owed him allegiance before being buried on the small coral island of Retoka (Hat Island), 4 kilometers (just over 2 miles) west of Efate. Some men were sacrificed at his burial, but history also records that representatives from every clan, and some of his close associates, were willingly buried alive with him. The men, but not their wives, were drugged by chewing large amounts of kava root. After the burial ceremony, Retoka was declared forbidden land (*fanua tabu*): no one could live or stay on the island again. The burial location was marked by two large, upright stone slabs at the foot of a big tree.

Archaeology

Excavations over more than 100 square meters (1,000 square feet) around the stone slabs, still visible on the island, revealed three levels of burials. Two of these can be directly associated with Roy Mata.

Within the top 30 centimeters (12 inches) were three children's burials, the graves dug into coral and shell that may have been deposited by a tidal wave. So not everyone has stayed away from the island since Roy Mata's burial.

Not far beneath these burials was 30 to 50 centimeters (12 to 20 inches) of soil, clearly dumped and spread over an extensive area. On the surface of this soil were coral and basalt slabs, some now broken, forming a semicircle in front of the raised stones. Among them were large shells, perforated in the body for use as trumpets.

Below the burial soil were about 33 skeletons, all lying on a layer of very compressed earth, apparently trampled. The skeletons included individual bodies and the bodies of nine couples clasped in each other's arms. Secondary burials (bodies reburied from another site) were associated with three of the individual bodies. A bundle of limbs from six other bodies was found in the center of the graveyard, and the remaining parts of these bodies were found in the northern area, along with many other skeletons lying in different positions. These seem to be the people who were sacrificed at the burial.

The couples, buried to keep Roy Mata company in the next world, wore their finest jewelry and clothes—beads of bone and shell; pendants of whale teeth, crocodile teeth, bone and stone; bracelets of pig's tusks and trochus shell. They were lying in an arc around the two standing stones, where the soil was not trampled. On the soil were pieces of ornaments, sea shells, megapod eggshells (a bird related by tradition to the Country of the Dead), chips of pork bone, and small hearths left from the burial ceremonies.

Further excavation in the softer area in front of the two standing stones revealed a pit some 40 centimeters (16 inches) deeper. In the center was the body of a very old man, lying on his back. A bundled-up skeleton lay between his legs. In accordance with tradition, the body of a man rested at his right-hand side—Roy Mata's *Atavi,* the one in charge of his security. A couple lay to his left, and at his feet was the body of a young woman.

The old man is undoubtedly Roy Mata, as every aspect of his burial confirms the oral traditions. Even the radiocarbon date of 685 ± 140 is in conformity with them.

The Wider Context

About 700 years ago, significant changes occurred both in central Vanuatu and on some adjacent islands, such as Tikopia, where Polynesian languages are now spoken. Recognizably Polynesian forms of material culture became prominent, such as buildings constructed of coral conglomerate mined from beach rock, bone needles, pig-tooth beads, and shell tools. Production of pottery ceased (as in Polynesia), and some basalt adzes were imported from western Polynesia. The burial of Roy Mata was also similar to some chiefly burials found in western Polynesia.

What is not clear is whether the oral tradition surrounding Roy Mata, confirmed and expanded by the archaeology of his burial, is the remembrance of a major change in the social and political structure of central Vanuatu.

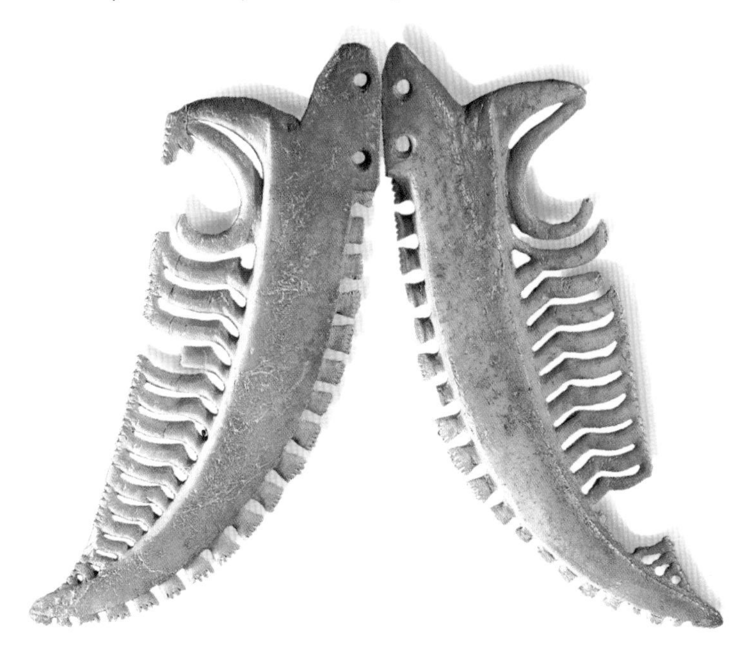

♁ Chevroned amulets made of whale ivory are a rare form of personal ornament from the later era of Maori prehistory, after about AD 1500. They were sometimes made as a matching pair, as in this example from Kaikoura, in the South Island of New Zealand.
NATIONAL MUSEUM OF NEW ZEALAND/ WERNER FORMAN ARCHIVE

OLIVER STREWE/WAVE PRODUCTIONS

♁ Pacific islanders devised many kinds of traps for catching fish and marine invertebrates on reef edges. This woven vine trap, with its funnel entrance, was used to catch crayfish (*Jasus edwardsii*) in New Zealand.

The Settlement of Western Polynesia

About 2,500 years ago, a distinctive Polynesian culture began to emerge in western Polynesia, which, until that time, had been part of the eastern Lapita world, along with Fiji. The evolution of Polynesian material culture is marked by the development of a distinctive adze kit, notably the manufacture of triangular cross-sectioned adzes and the loss of oval cross-sectioned and massive shell adzes; the replacement of arm rings and various types of ornaments made from long beads with other ornamental forms; and, above all, the gradual disappearance of pottery.

According to linguistic reconstruction, an inexact science at best, the proto-Polynesian language also became distinct from proto-Fijian between 1000 BC and 500 BC, and soon after began to split into its two main forms, Tongic and nuclear Polynesian. By perhaps the beginning of the first millennium AD, the latter was splitting into Samoic-Outlier and eastern Polynesian languages. Linguistic division resulted from the continuing dispersal by colonization, and it was also at that time, or after pottery production had ceased (unless older Lapita sites are found, underwater perhaps), that the colonization of eastern Polynesia began.

The chronology of this process is a matter of lively debate, in which there are essentially two schools of thought. One argues that the same colonizing impetus that brought people into western Polynesia continued eastwards, with settlement of the central eastern archipelagos, such as the Society Islands, the Cook Islands, and the Marquesas Islands, probably occurring more than 2,000 years ago. In the case of the Marquesas, this view is supported by the existence of plainware

BISHOP MUSEUM, HAWAII

♁ Stone-walled fishponds are a prominent feature of Hawaiian archaeological sites, especially here on Molokai Island. They functioned as tidal traps and as breeding ponds for favored species, such as mullet and milkfish.

pottery fragments and some other evidence that early material culture there was rather different from the so-called "Archaic East Polynesian" cluster of artifacts, which included various forms of tanged adzes, imitation whale-tooth pendants, and reel-shaped necklace units. Easter Island and Hawaii provide additional instances of what might be an early "pre-Archaic" assemblage of material culture. Research along other lines, such as looking for evidence of a human impact on island environments, notably in deforestation, erosion, and extinction of vulnerable indigenous birds, has also been used to support the hypothesis of early settlement in eastern Polynesia.

A great deal depends on the accuracy of radiocarbon dating, however, and there it is apparent that all is not well. In the Marquesas, the dates for early levels at sites such as Hane and Ha'atuatua are highly variable, and can be used to support both long (beginning about 2,200 years ago) and short (beginning about 1,500 years ago) chronologies. When radiocarbon dates on dubious samples, such as charcoal from old wood (wood that might have been hundreds of years old at the time it was burned in a Polynesian fire), are excluded from consideration, a different picture emerges. In this second hypothesis, no convincing evidence of human colonization is seen from either archaeological or natural sites that can be acceptably dated before about 1,500 years ago in the Marquesas, perhaps 1,000 to 1,200 years ago in most other groups, and 800 years ago in New Zealand.

Leaving aside timing, there is general agreement on the sequence of colonization and that the dispersal of Polynesians across 20 million square kilometers (7,700,000 square miles) of sea—in which there was only 0.3 million square kilometers (129,000 square miles) of land, and nearly all of that in New Zealand—had a profound impact on Polynesians as a people, and on their culture and way of life. As a people, Polynesians are distinguished by a noticeably robust body form, the origin of which is another matter for debate. One hypothesis argues that a large, robust body can more easily withstand the rigors of long-distance voyaging, notably the danger of hypothermia caused by exposure to wind and sea, and, therefore, that long-distance voyaging acted as a selective device in favor of the Polynesian body form. Another hypothesis argues that if the body form is an adaptation to long-distance voyaging, then it should have been developed in Lapita people, who were not of solid build, and probably in other Pacific populations as well. Instead, cultural factors may have been more important, such as the historical Polynesian preference for large people and the association of heavy build with status, or perhaps the advantage of large, strong men in the hand-to-hand skirmishing that was endemic to Polynesian society. Whatever the reasons, Polynesians were, and are, a tall, robust people.

Polynesian social and economic systems changed as people dispersed to a diverse range of island environments. In Hawaii, for example, there was substantial development of both irrigated gardening, to grow taro, particularly on the older soils of the western islands, and extensive dry-land cropping, mainly of sweet potato, and notably on the younger hill soils of the eastern islands. Coconut, sugar cane, banana, breadfruit, yam, and various other crops were also grown, pigs and dogs were husbanded, and mullet and milkfish were reared in specially constructed specialized forms of coastal ponds. Coupled with this intensive agriculture were specialized coastal and deep-sea fishing and forest fowling. On such a favorable economic base, the Hawaiian population flourished, eventually numbering more than 200,000 people. With increased population density, the older, kin-group patterns of authority and land-holding were transformed into highly stratified, landowning chiefdoms, and a huge class of landless commoners was created. By the time Europeans arrived in the eighteenth century, Hawaii had evolved from a tribal society into an incipient state, with the ranks and trappings of an aristocracy and a would-be "king", Kamehameha.

At the other extreme was New Zealand. Nearly the size of a continent, it contained the greatest variety of environments and resources in the

A taro garden on Viti Levu, in Fiji. Taro *(Colocasia esculenta)* was the most important cultigen in Oceania. It was grown in well-watered soils, often in specially prepared swamp gardens, and the root was eaten.

JEAN-PAUL FERRERO/AUSCAPE

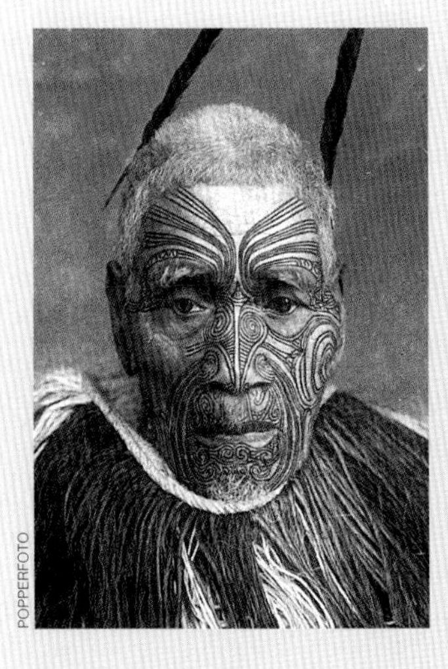

POPPERFOTO

⇧ In New Zealand, as throughout Polynesia, tattooing was a common custom. Patterns were pricked into the skin, using small-toothed chisels and a mallet, and a dye of soot and other materials was rubbed in.

THE ESTATE OF BRIAN BRAKE/JOHN HILLELSON AGENCY

⇨ Turuturumokai *pa* (fortress), in Taranaki province, New Zealand, is one of approximately 6,000 large, defensive earthworks built by Maori. It was last used in the 1860s, in fighting imperial British troops.

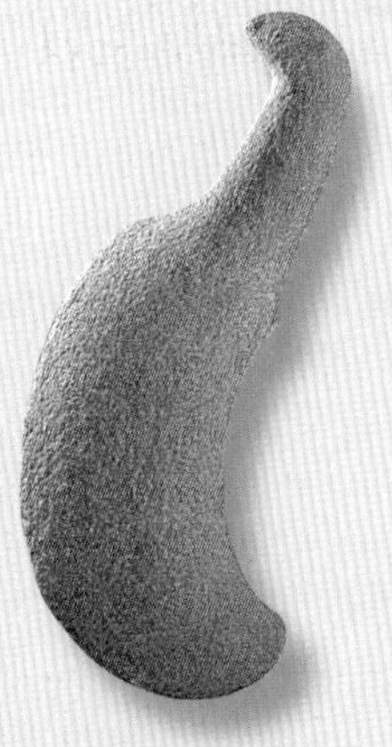

⇧ Polynesians used hand clubs of wood, bone, or stone as weapons and as badges of rank. This club, in a stylized bird form, is of Moriori origin, and comes from the Chatham Islands, off New Zealand.
NATIONAL MUSEUM OF NEW ZEALAND/WERNER FORMAN ARCHIVE

Pacific, but because it was a temperate land, only one of the Polynesian food crops—the kumara, or sweet potato—could be grown with much success. A few others, including taro and yam, straggled along, and the dog survived, but Polynesian agriculture was marginal nearly everywhere in New Zealand, and impossible in most of the South Island. Only in a few northern districts, particularly where there were "islands" of rich volcanic soils and almost no frost, did people rely substantially on cultivation. Instead, most food came from fishing, fowling, and foraging, notably for bracken-fern root.

In the early years in New Zealand, the hunting was particularly good, with huge moas (large, flightless birds) available and seal-breeding colonies dotted about the entire coast, but as the one became extinct and the other retreated to the far south, subsistence came to rely increasingly on fish and fern root. Population growth, to about 100,000 or less at contact, was slower than in Hawaii, and population densities were lower than anywhere else in the Pacific. Nevertheless, it was probably competition for resources that induced the later, prehistoric construction of *pa*, or hill-forts, beginning about AD 1400. Remains of about 6,000 have been found, and their elaborate ditch-and-bank defenses, once topped with stout palisades, testify to considerable military ingenuity and energy. They are located mainly in northern districts, where they are often situated close to patches of that scarce commodity, good agricultural land. The labor and organization required for building elaborate defensive structures, and for conducting large-scale military operations and alliances, may have led to the development of more complex chiefdoms in a few northern localities by the end of the prehistoric era (about AD 1800), but Maori, as a whole, remained in flexible, kin-based chiefdoms of a common ancestral Polynesian form.

With the settlement of New Zealand about AD 1200 and the outlying Chatham Islands about AD 1400, the expansion of prehistoric habitation in the Pacific came to an end. There were more islands available, especially to the south, in the sub-Antarctic region, but Pacific peoples of tropical origin and culture carried the wrong baggage to settle there.

MOA HUNTING IN NEW ZEALAND

ATHOLL ANDERSON

When people arrived in the southwestern Pacific region, large, flightless, ostrich-like birds inhabited each of the old continental landmasses. There were emus and cassowaries in Australia, cassowaries in New Guinea, and moas in New Zealand. All may have been descended from ratites (flightless birds with a flat breast bone) carried by each of the southern landmasses that split from the supercontinent of Gondwana—more that 80 million years ago, in New Zealand's case. There is some evidence to suggest, however, that the ancestors of moas and kiwis flew to New Zealand and later became flightless.

In every way, moas (Dinornithiformes) were the most diverse group. There were two families. Dinornithids comprised three species of relatively tall, slender birds, which reached 2 meters (6 feet, 6 inches) in back height and could stretch to 2.5 meters (8 feet). The largest, *Dinornis giganteus*, weighed more than 200 kilograms (440 pounds). The eight species in the second family, emeids, were generally of solid build, ranging from the size of a very large turkey, in the case of *Euryapteryx curtus*, to the massive *Pachyornis elephantopus*, which stood only 1.2 meters (4 feet) in back height but weighed about 150 kilograms (330 pounds).

Habitat

Moas occupied most terrestrial habitats of New Zealand. Some species were found mainly in beech forests and subalpine areas; others preferred dense lowland forest or the forest fringes, second-growth forest, scrub, and grassland. Where these habitats were prolific, notably in the eastern part of the South Island, population densities reached perhaps one to two moas per square kilometer (two to five moas per square mile), but moas were otherwise relatively scarce.

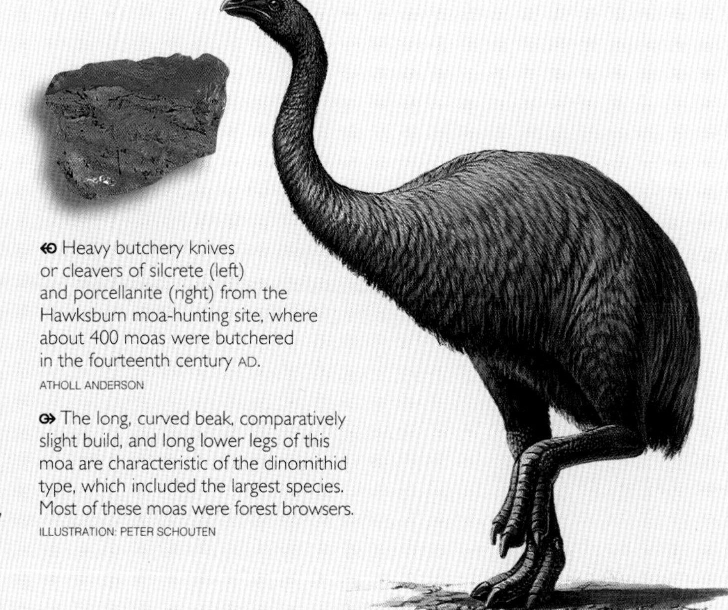

⇐ Heavy butchery knives or cleavers of silcrete (left) and porcellanite (right) from the Hawksburn moa-hunting site, where about 400 moas were butchered in the fourteenth century AD.
ATHOLL ANDERSON

⇒ The long, curved beak, comparatively slight build, and long lower legs of this moa are characteristic of the dinornithid type, which included the largest species. Most of these moas were forest browsers.
ILLUSTRATION: PETER SCHOUTEN

Predators

Although New Zealand had no dangerous reptiles or mammals, moas had one major predator. This was the largest eagle known, *Harpagornis moorei*—a "sit-and-wait" hunter, which plummeted from its perch with a weight of up to 13 kilograms (29 pounds) behind talons that opened to 30 centimeters (12 inches). Yet, fearsome as it was, it had evolved with moas and lived in balance with them. People were far more threatening. The huge moas were slow-breeding, highly conspicuous in a land where the next largest animals were rails, geese, and swans, and utterly unused to human predators. They quickly became the primary prey of the early Maori settlers on the eastern side of the South Island, and were sought after elsewhere.

Hunting Sites

About 300 archaeological sites containing moa bones have been recorded, and 50 of them have been investigated. Most are located in the South Island, nearly all of them east of the Southern Alps, where the annual rainfall is less than 800 millimeters (31 inches) and the original vegetation varied from light forest to tussock grassland. *Euryapteryx geranoides*, a medium-sized moa weighing about 80 kilograms (170 pounds), was the main species hunted.

Some sites are immense. At Waitaki Mouth, moa ovens are scattered over about 60 hectares (150 acres), and at Rakaia, there are two sites, one extending over perhaps 40 hectares (100 acres). Many thousands of moas were probably butchered and consumed at each of these sites and at others along the east coast of the South Island. These localities seem to have been used repeatedly, the moa carcasses having been brought downriver on reed boats from inland hunting grounds. Smaller moa-hunting sites are scattered through the interior basins and valleys.

Hunting Methods and Weapons

Exactly how moas were hunted is not known. There are no obvious hunting weapons at the sites, nor are there any authentic traditions of moa hunting. Dogs and spears were probably used, but snares were commonly used by Maori to catch other flightless birds and would have had the additional advantage of safety. With their powerful feet, moas were doubtless extremely dangerous at close quarters.

Moa-hunting sites contain distinctive butchering tools, including long blades of silcrete, fragments from sandstone boulders, and shaped slate knives. Moa bones were fashioned into many kinds of artifacts, including harpoon heads and spear-points, fishhooks, awls, needles, and necklace pieces. These sites seldom reveal remains of substantial houses, and it is assumed that hunting was generally a periodic activity, probably taking place mainly during spring (moa eggshells being common at the sites) and in the summer.

Hunted to Extinction

The age of moa hunting was shortlived. Peaking about AD 1300, moa hunting had declined to a rare catch by AD 1500, and moas were extinct soon afterwards. The lethal factors seem to have been overhunting of an easy prey by a growing population of efficient hunters, and a substantial reduction in moa habitats caused by forest firing. Many other species of flightless birds, along with their predators, including the great eagle, also became extinct at that time.

JOHN DOWNER/PLANET EARTH PICTURES

STONE-BUILT MONUMENTS OF THE SOUTH PACIFIC

A D 1 – T H E P R E S E N T

Sanctuaries for Gods and Ancestors

GÖRAN BURENHULT

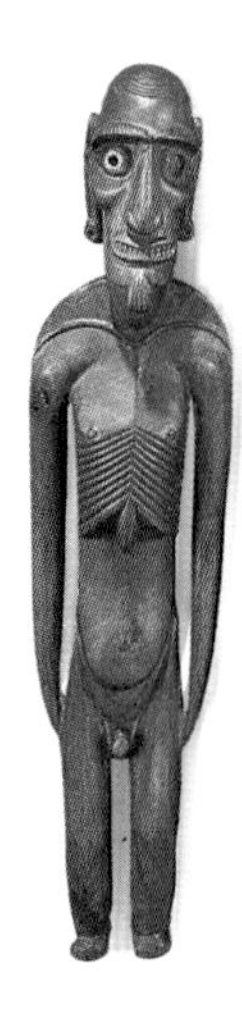

THE PACIFIC OCEAN covers 180 million square kilometers (about 110 million square miles)—more than a third of Earth's surface. It is easy to see why the scattered islands of this endless expanse of ocean were the last part of the world to be occupied by human beings, and also why they kept their secrets from European explorers for such a long time.

In many parts of this vast region, religious ceremonies have been linked to stone-built monuments. Stone structures—mainly in the form of menhirs, dolmens, statues, stone circles, mounds, and huge enclosures—have been recorded from eastern New Guinea, in the west, to the remotest outposts of Polynesia, in the east. Some, such as the gigantic statues of Easter Island, have fascinated humankind for centuries, while others are overrun with dense jungle on remote tropical islands and still remain secret and unknown. In some areas, the traditions linked to these monuments died out long before Europeans arrived. In others, the traditions were flourishing when the first explorers anchored, and in these cases we often have a wealth of ethnohistoric information as to why the monuments were erected and how they were used. In a few areas, ritual activities of various kinds are still performed at some monuments.

Nan Madol is a huge complex of artificial, stone-built islands off the coast of Temwen, near Pohnpei, in Micronesia. The central structure shown here is called Nan Douwas.

This *moai kavakaua*, a carved wooden figure of a thin man with ribs showing, is from isolated Easter Island, in easternmost Polynesia.
HILLEL BURGER/PEABODY MUSEUM, HARVARD UNIVERSITY

→ *Opposite page*: The gigantic, two-stepped megalithic platform called Manunu and Anini, on Huahine, in the Society Islands, is one of the largest stone-built structures in this part of Polynesia.

Little is known about the history of the monuments, as few modern excavations have been carried out on stone-built structures in the Pacific area. Did megalithic traditions spread with supposed waves of migrating Austronesian peoples from southern China? Or did they develop independently in many areas following the settlement of the island regions? In any case, the different traditions often seem to be widely separated in time. The similarities between the open-air temples in the Society Islands, Hawaii, Easter Island, and other parts of Polynesia point to a common Polynesian origin for that particular type of monumental tradition, perhaps in a supposed Polynesian homeland—presumably, somewhere in Melanesia—and linked to the highly hierarchic chiefdoms and the beliefs in deities that were characteristic of Polynesian societies.

The various megalithic structures in Melanesia are of a different character, however. Here, dolmens, menhirs, and stone circles predominate, and the monuments are always linked to an ancestor cult and less hierarchic societies. The pattern is the same from the Bismarck Archipelago, in the northwest, to Vanuatu (former New Hebrides) and New Caledonia, in the southeast. The grandiose temple cities of Pohnpei, in Micronesia, are unique to that particular area and are without parallels in the Pacific. Only future excavations can answer our questions as to the origin of the stone-built structures of the South Pacific. This chapter provides a brief overview of what is known about these monuments in Micronesia, Polynesia, and Melanesia.

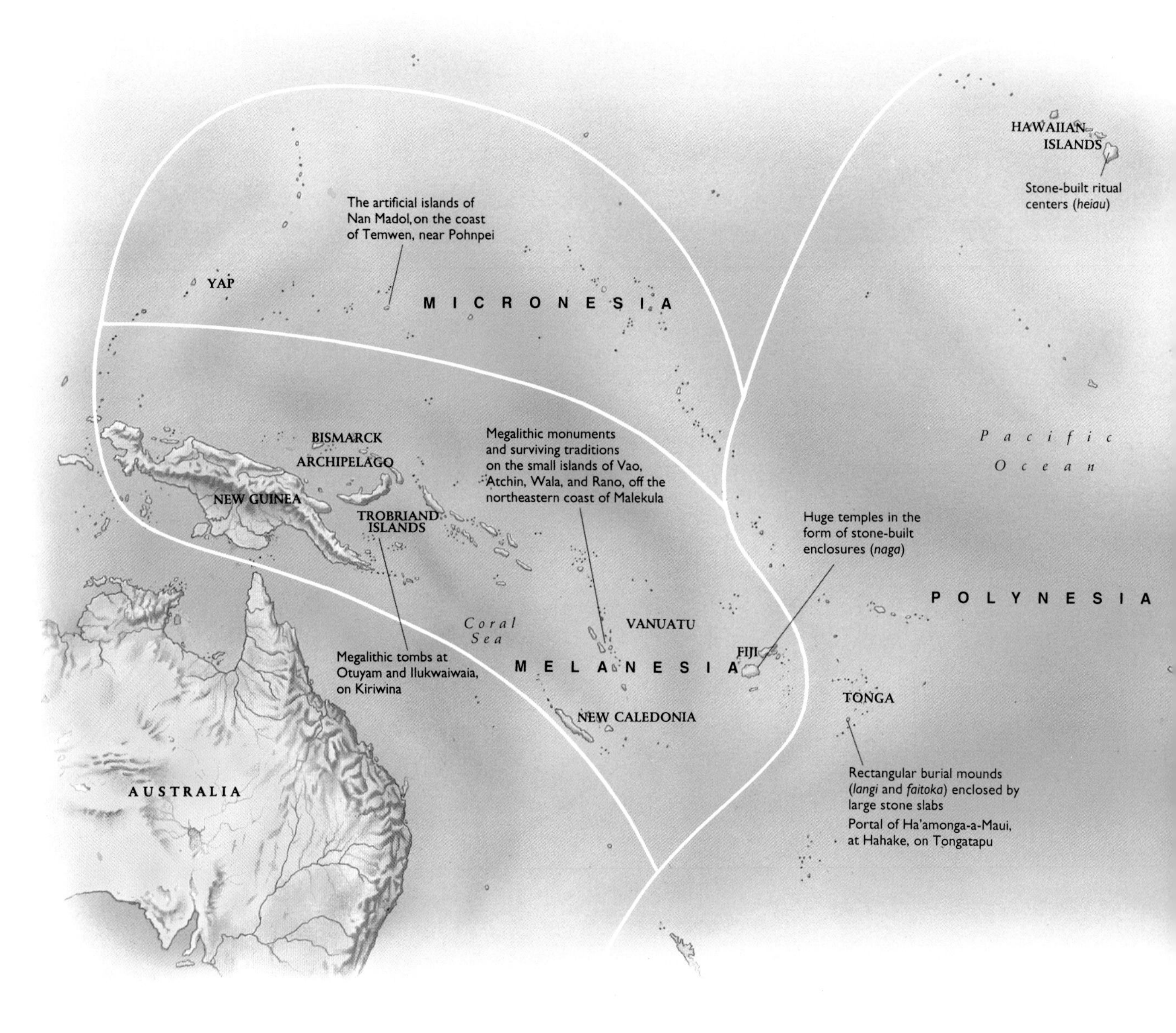

STONE-BUILT MONUMENTS
Stone-built monuments are found throughout the vast Pacific region. Although they vary greatly in size and shape, several major types can be identified. Local variants of these types are found in many other areas.
CARTOGRAPHY: RAY SIM

GÖRAN BURENHULT

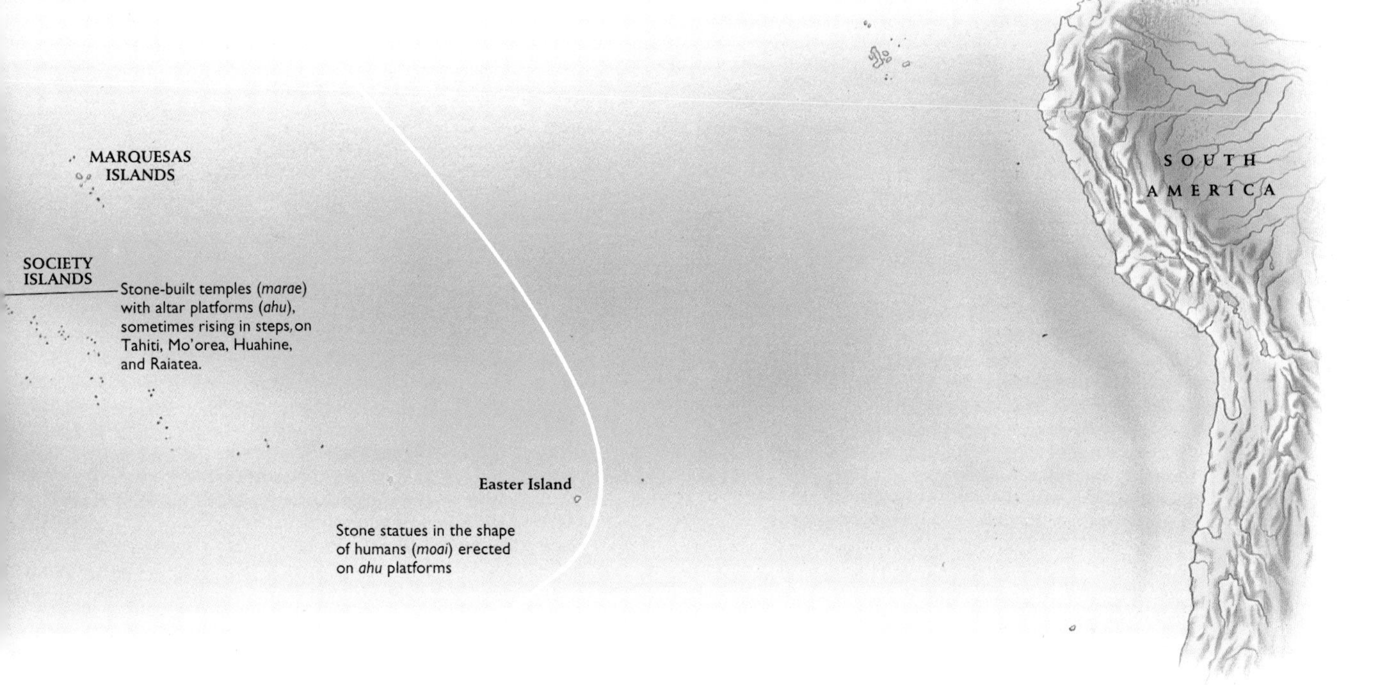
MARQUESAS ISLANDS
SOCIETY ISLANDS
Stone-built temples (*marae*) with altar platforms (*ahu*), sometimes rising in steps, on Tahiti, Mo'orea, Huahine, and Raiatea.
Easter Island
Stone statues in the shape of humans (*moai*) erected on *ahu* platforms
SOUTH AMERICA

JOHN DOWNER/PLANET EARTH PICTURES

Nan Madol: Venice of the South Seas

On the coast of the small island of Temwen, off the eastern shore of Pohnpei, in the heart of Micronesia, lies the most remarkable and enigmatic stone-built construction in the Pacific—Nan Madol. Here, on nearly a hundred artificial little islands, an unparalleled, possibly ceremonial, center was once erected. A network of canals was constructed around the presumed temples, which could only be reached by boat. Unlike most other stone-built monuments in the South Pacific, however, Nan Madol had long been abandoned and overgrown by the time Europeans discovered the site in the 1800s. The powerful chiefs and high priests who are thought to have once officiated here, and who probably also resided on the artificial platforms, had been altogether forgotten by the sparse population of fishers on Pohnpei. It is estimated that between 200 and 1,000 individuals once lived in this floating city.

Nan Madol is the largest individual stone-built complex in the Pacific, but a very similar temple city has been discovered on the small island of Lelu, in Kosrae, slightly east of Pohnpei. Nan Madol covers an area of more than 70 hectares (173 acres), its canals and surrounding stone walls included. A limited archaeological excavation in one of the constructions has provided a radiocarbon dating of between AD 1285 and AD 1485. It therefore seems probable that the floating city was in use for a few hundred years from the end of the thirteenth century. According to tradition, the grandiose construction was the work of the Sau Deleur family, rulers of Pohnpei.

All of the 100 platforms are built of interlocking natural basalt prisms. The stones were brought in from the opposite side of the island, and must have been transported along the coast on rafts. The largest and most important construction is called Nan Douwas by the locals. The 9 meter (30 foot) high walls of this central structure tower as a timeless monument to one of the most remarkable societies of the Pacific. Nan Madol still gloats over most of its secrets, however. Only future excavations can shed further light on its meaning.

The artificial platforms of Nan Madol are built of interlocking natural basalt prisms, which were brought in from the opposite side of the island. The section shown here is from the central structure, Nan Douwas.

One of the huge artificial platforms of Nan Madol, on the coast of Temwen, east of Pohnpei, in Micronesia. These mysterious structures, now overgrown, can only be reached by boat.

Chiefs and Deities in Polynesia

In spite of the cultural similarities between the various Polynesian societies, their adaptation to the different natural environments and climatic conditions has led to the development of regional peculiarities, both in terms of economy and social organization. This is also true of the megalithic traditions. The different types of stone-built monuments are easy to identify geographically, and are usually very characteristic of the different island groups.

In Tonga, rectangular burial mounds (so-called *langi*), 50 meters (164 feet) long and enclosed by kerbstones in the form of large, square-shaped slabs of coral stone, were built. These were used only by the sacred royal line Tui Tonga, whereas other important individuals in the society were buried in somewhat smaller but similar monuments, *faitoka*. Many of these monumental graves were used by members of the royal family well into the twentieth century. A portal or trilithon at Hahake, on the main island of Tongatapu—called Ha'amonga-a-Maui and often referred to as the "Stonehenge of the South Seas"—is the only structure of its kind in the Pacific. The large slabs of coral stone in all of these monuments were painstakingly cut loose from coral reefs during low tide. Long rows of half-finished slabs still dot the shallow waters around many of the Tonga islands, notably around Tongatapu, where most *langi* were built.

The stone-built monuments in Hawaii, the *heiau*, were generally never used as burial places, but instead served as large ceremonial (or ritual) centers. The same also applies to the *marae* of the Society Islands (in present-day French Polynesia), which is the most common type of stone-built temple in Polynesia. The megalithic tradition reached its peak with the builders of such *marae* at the time of Captain James Cook's three voyages in the South Pacific in the 1770s, and his logbook and the notes and books of his scientific passengers

GÖRAN BURENHULT

In Tonga, burial mounds were built of stone slabs cut loose from the coral rock at low tide. Unfinished slabs, such as this one on Pangaimotu, north of Tongatapu, still dot the shallow waters.

GÖRAN BURENHULT

The megalithic portal, or trilithon, of Ha'amonga-a-Maui, at Hahake, on Tongatapu, in Tonga, is without parallel in the Pacific. Its function is unknown.

probably form the most complete ethnohistorical description of any society's megalithic cult.

The island of Raiatea, northwest of Tahiti, appears to have been something of a religious center to most of the surrounding islands, but significant stone-built ritual centers are known also on Tahiti, Huahine, and Mo'orea. Many of them are still preserved, but several of the Tahitian ones have been destroyed during the past 150 years, as a result of the exploitation of the island, such as the use of stones for the construction of roads and buildings.

A *marae* is characterized by an altar, or *ahu*, which is situated on the short side of a stone-built rectangle with an inner pavement. Erected stones inside the stone enclosure mark the seats of different ancestors, deities, or important individuals taking part in the ceremonies. On many islands, and on Tahiti and Mo'orea in particular, the *ahu* rises in steps, usually less than five. A conspicuous exception is gigantic Marae Mahaiatea, on the southern coast of Tahiti, which was built in 1769 and boasted no less than 10 steps at that time. Alongside some *marae*, there are also a number of other stone-built monuments with different functions, among them a kind of crescent-shaped structure which was used as a "launching platform" during ceremonial archery competitions, the sacred sport of the aristocracy.

The Polynesians made a sharp distinction between different types of *marae*. The private ones, *marae tupuna,* were used during ceremonies for deceased relatives. Each family had its own temple, which was named after an ancestor, and here, pigs, fish, or vegetables were offered to the spirits. To protect the family ties, the name of the spirit or deity that had given its name to the *marae* should never be revealed. Often wooden or stone statues of different deities, so-called *tiki,* were erected within the tabooed area. The *marae* was the place where the Tahitian commoner fufilled religious obligations with respect and fear. Many

Marae Arahurahu, a stone-built temple on the west coast of Tahiti, in the Society Islands, has been partly restored. The stone enclosure and step-like altar are clearly visible. Inside the enclosure are *tiki* statues (of deities), and erected stones marking the seats of ancestors.

occupational groups had their own types of *marae*—for example, boat builders, fishers, and carpenters.

The large official *marae* were usually erected by tribal chiefs for ceremonies linked to the hierarchic social organization. The royal ceremonial centers were always built outside the settled areas and often by the sea, to make use of the purging powers obtained from the presence of the water, and also to facilitate the arrival of fleets of visitors from other islands during big, joint ceremonies. Human sacrifices were necessary during the construction of the royal *marae*. An individual chosen by the chief was attacked and clubbed to death, after which the remains were carried to the cult center in a basket. During the night, the rhythmic sounds of the *to'ere*, the drum of human sacrifice, were heard. Unlike many peoples in Melanesia, the Polynesians were not cannibals.

The construction of sacred, oval huts for the war god Oro also required a human sacrifice. In this case, the body served as a foundation for the centrally placed wooden post. During his last visit to Tahiti, Captain James Cook was present at a human sacrifice, which was also depicted by the artist John Webber. On Tuesday 2 September 1777, Cook wrote in his log: "The unhappy sufferer seemed to be a Middle aged man, and as we were told a Tou tou but I never understood he had done any crime so as to merit death; it is however certain that they make choise of such for these sacrifices, or else common low fellows who strol about from place to place and island to island without any vesible way of geting an honist livelyhood, of such sort here are enough at these islands. This man was bloody about the head and face, which we attributed to the manner he was killed having been privatly knocked on the head with a Stone, for those who fall a sacrifice to this barbarous custom are never apprised of their fate till the Moment that puts an end to their existence. Whenever any of the Great cheifs thinks a human Sacrifice necessary on any particular occasion, he pitches upon the Victim, sends some of his trusty Sevants who fall upon him and kill him; the King is then acquainted with it, whose presence at the Ceremony, as I was told is absolutely necessary, indeed except the Priests he was the only man that had any thing to do in it."

All ceremonies had one main purpose: to secure the support of the supernatural powers for the human society. Most official ceremonies were linked to events that were directly related to the royal family, such as birth, death, illness, or official installation. The seasonal cycle also played a

Based on a drawing by John Webber, this copperplate etching shows Captain James Cook present at a human sacrifice at a *marae* in Atehuru, in September 1777.

GÖRAN BURENHULT

significant role in the rituals. By making offerings, the people secured the coming and going of the seasons. Other rites were related to the first harvest of fruit, when fruits and flowers were offered on the *ahu*. During war campaigns, the gods were always consulted, and during these ceremonies, offerings of both pigs and humans—the favorite dishes of the war god Oro—were required. The heads and cut-up bodies of captured enemies were placed on the *ahu* after victorious battles. The skulls were left on display after the feasts and were a grim sight on the monuments. It was not until the first half of the nineteenth century, when missionaries started to subvert the traditional society on Tahiti, that the skulls were removed and hidden in caves in the mountains. Several of the original liturgies and prayers that once were recited in the *marae* have been rescued from oblivion. These include the sacrificial hymn "Parima Nui".

In many respects, the religion and values crushed by the missionaries were confusingly similar to the ones that were forced on the natives; the only difference being the fact that the original beliefs were adapted to the reality of the islands, while the new ones only resulted in the destruction of the original social system.

"Parima Nui"

The evil of the marae is repaired,
it has been weeded, accompanied
with the chant.

The evil of the ruler and the tribe is repaired,
our liturgy has weeded the sin,
the last prayer has been recited
and everything is pure.

Here are the 'ura feathers,
here is the peace token of
coconut flowers,
here is thy man long banana,
from his head down to his feet,
from his feet to his head,
to arrest thine anger of great growth,
o God.

For great crimes, for family discord,
for hasty words, for irreverence to
the gods, for imperfectly scraping off
the moss of the marae.

For rankling rage concealed, for mutual
estrangement of friends, for cursing,
for destruction by sorcery, for sending
evil spirits into fellowman.

These are the sins which displease thee,
o God.

Undo them, place them upon long banana stems
here present, cast them into the trackless ocean,
that thy devotees may be saved.

O God, dismiss these thy worshippers,
for they are now blessed.

GÖRAN BURENHULT

Easter Island: A Demystified Enigma

For the archaeologist, it is not an exaggeration to say that isolated Easter Island, the southeasternmost outpost of the Polynesian triangle, is one of the most fascinating spots on Earth. It is also easy to see why the curious culture of this extremely remote island has been the subject of a number of more or less imaginative interpretations, which at times have resulted in bitter academic dispute. The megalithic tradition on Easter Island is beyond all comparison.

Even the first European visitors wondered at the gigantic stone statues, erected on platforms, that turned their backs towards the sea and gazed into the island's interior. Following the arrival of Europeans, inadvertent disease and Chilean slavery resulted in an all but complete loss of knowledge of the original

Marae Mahaiatea, on the south coast of Tahiti—the largest stone-built temple in the Society Islands—was newly built at the time Europeans arrived, during the second half of the eighteenth century. The illustration is from a book by J. Wilson: *A Missionary Voyage to the South Pacific Ocean, Performed in the Years 1796, 1797, 1798, on the Ship Duff, Commanded by Captain James Wilson, Under the Direction of the Missionary Society*, London, 1799.

JOHN DOWNER/PLANET EARTH PICTURES

traditional society, and contributed to the creation of the so-called "enigmas" or "mysteries" that have characterized the discussion about the cultural and ethnic origin of the Easter islanders ever since.

The human-shaped statues, or *moai*, the largest of which are 10 meters (nearly 33 feet) high, and weigh more than 80 tons (81 tonnes), are unique in the whole Pacific area. The closest equivalents are to be found in the highlands of Peru, which has led some to believe that Easter Island was originally populated from South America, and that the Polynesian characteristics within culture and language resulted from later arrivals of people from the west. The classic picture of two conflicting populations on Easter Island thereby gained a foothold in the discussion.

In reality, the opposite seems to have been the case. All archaeological and linguistic data indicate that Easter Island was populated from the west by Polynesian sailors about AD 400. The Polynesian language spoken by the Easter islanders is of a very old type and has been preserved thanks to the remote location of the island, while Polynesian languages in other parts of the Pacific developed in other directions. Also, the tools found in the earliest settlement layers, such as stone adzes, are of a very early East Polynesian type. Tool forms that were developed later in other parts of Polynesia are not found on Easter Island.

The origin of the platforms and their statues is, however, less clear. One theory suggests that the Polynesian immigrants brought the *ahu/marae* concept with them from the west. Stone statues similar to the earliest ones on Easter Island have been found in the Marquesas Islands, from where the Easter islanders are thought to have arrived. Other experts have suggested that the *ahu* tradition developed on Easter Island and spread from there to Central Polynesia. This assumption is based on the fact that the earliest *ahu/marae* structures in Polynesia, dated to about AD 700, are found on Easter Island. The earliest known structures in Central Polynesia date to about AD 1400.

A third theory points out the close similarities between some of the early Easter Island *moai* and the statues of the contemporary Tiahuanaco culture in the Peruvian highlands. Also, the Easter Island platforms are very similar to ritual platforms in Peru. Contacts with South America would thus have spurred the development of the *ahu* tradition, which perhaps eventually would have spread westwards to Central Polynesia.The introduction of the sweet potato to the Pacific leaves it beyond all doubt that Polynesians were in contact with South Americans at some stage, although there is as yet no further support for such contacts in the archaeological record. The origin of the unique stone-building tradition on Easter Island is, therefore, still an open question. (See the feature *Easter Island Prehistory*.)

B. ANNEBICQUE/SYGMA/AUSTRAL INTERNATIONAL

Scattered pieces of white stone found beneath *moai* statues have been identified as the remains of stone eyes once placed in the statues' eye sockets. Perhaps this explains the Easter Islanders' way of describing their *moai: aina ora o te tu'puna*—the living face of our ancestors.

These *moai* statues (stone statues shaped like humans) stand on Ahu Nau Nau at Anakena, on the north coast of Easter Island. The site was reconstructed after excavation, and the "topknots" of red volcanic rock once again placed atop the statues.

EASTER ISLAND: A WORLD APART

PATRICK C. MCCOY

EASTER ISLAND, OR RAPANUI (a name applied in recent times to the island, its people, and their language), has fascinated and perplexed Westerners since the island was rediscovered by the Dutch on Easter Sunday in 1722. The human colonization of Easter Island, a tiny speck of land in the southeast Pacific, so isolated that it might have been settled only once, is one of the marvels of the ancient world. Who first settled the island and when has been the subject of much debate. Extensive research has failed to produce support for Thor Heyerdahl's theory that the island was settled by two culturally distinct populations: first by a group of maritime people from the coast of South America, and later by Polynesians. The orthodox view of Easter Island cultural origins, based on the combined evidence of oral traditions, linguistic characteristics, and archaeological evidence, is that the island was colonized by people from East Polynesia. Radiocarbon dates and dates based on linguistic analyses suggest that the island might have been settled as early as AD 400, although some archaeologists are now convinced that this event occurred several hundred years later.

LUIS CASTANEDA/THE IMAGE BANK

A small number of late prehistoric statues on *ahu* platforms were adorned with red scoria topknots called *pukao*, which have been variously interpreted as representing a hairstyle or some kind of headdress.

JEAN-PAUL FERRERO/AUSCAPE

Petroglyphs of *tangata manu* (birdmen) are common at Orongo, the site of the annual birdman festivities. Motu Nui, the largest of the seabird nesting grounds, can be seen in the distance.

One of the best indications that the island was settled by Polynesians is the *ahu*, a religious structure that in its earliest form may have consisted of nothing more than a row of upright stone slabs set into the ground or placed on top of a small stone platform, thus resembling many of the simpler *marae* of central and eastern Polynesia from which the Easter Island *ahu* is clearly derived. The best-known and most common of the several types of *ahu*, which number roughly 300, is the "image *ahu*" (those on which stone statues, or *moai*, were erected), which seems to have appeared about AD 900. Image *ahu* appear to have been frequently rebuilt, mostly to accommodate new statues. There is evidence for the gradual appearance of distinctive styles and the carving of increasingly larger images over time. Between a third and a half of the estimated 900 to 1,000 statues, including many of the largest ones, are located at one quarry, where all but a handful of the statues on the island were carved out of tuff. The quarry statues, many of which were abandoned in various stages of completion, probably for technical and aesthetic reasons, all lack eye sockets. The addition of eyes in the final stages of the production process might have been dictated by religious beliefs related to the power (*mana*) of the images, which are commonly interpreted as memorials to chiefs and other important persons, but might, in fact, have been regarded as both human ancestors and gods. The eye sockets, long thought to have been empty, are now known to have been inset with shaped coral and red scoria disks.

For reasons that are not yet entirely clear, the people stopped carving statues about AD 1700. Roughly coinciding in time with the demise of the ancestor worship cult was either the appearance—or, more likely, the elaboration—of what was probably a much older first fruits rite (the offering of the first seabird eggs to the gods) celebrated in the latter part of its history as the annual feast of the birdman (*tangata manu*) at a place called Orongo. The cult, which consisted of a competition to find the first egg of the migratory sooty tern, on a small offshore islet named Motu Nui, was controlled by the chiefs of the plebeian tribes, who through victory in the annual competition assumed a temporary sanctity of office for a year. Part of the ceremonies at Orongo involved the recitation of chants and prayers by priests from wooden tablets of inscribed hieroglyphic figures called *rongorongo*. None of the 23 surviving tablets has ever been completely translated, but it appears that they were mnemonic devices rather than texts. The origin and antiquity of the *rongorongo* is unknown. Some scholars have argued that it might have been inspired by the ceremony that made the island the property of Spain in 1770, during which the chiefs of the island affixed their "signatures" to the document of annexation.

The last few hundred years of local history, before the arrival of missionaries in the 1860s, was a period of instability characterized by internecine warfare, which was probably both a cause and a consequence of famines, the emergence of cannibalism, and the widespread destruction and concealment of image *ahu*, many of which were subsequently converted into communal grave sites. The deliberate destruction of many statues appears to be related to the desire to destroy the *mana* of the image. One explanation for this sequence of events, commonly interpreted as a classic instance of cultural decline or "devolution", is environmental change resulting from the long-term cumulative effects of population growth on the island environment. A peak population of perhaps 7,000 to 10,000 was attained about AD 1500. Even if the figure was lower, it is easy to envision near-total deforestation in a relatively short time on an island of this size, given the varied uses made of wood products, the long-established practice of clearing agricultural land by the slash-and-burn method, and the habit of burning the property of enemies defeated in war. The consequences of deforestation were far-reaching, but perhaps the most devastating was the eventual impossibility of emigration, because of the lack of sufficient wood to build canoes capable of long-distance voyaging. The people of Easter Island had become captives in a world of their own making.

Rongorongo tablets, which consist of directionally alternating lines of characters, were read across in one direction, and then turned 180 degrees and read back in the opposite direction.
ADRIENNE L. KAEPPLER/SMITHSONIAN INSTITUTION

Most Easter Island statues faced inland toward the community, but there are exceptions, such as these statues at the restored site of Ahu a Kivi, which look out to sea.
DAVID NICHOLAS GREEN/THE PHOTO LIBRARY, SYDNEY

JOHN LAYARD/GÖRAN BURENHULT

⬆ Taken by the British ethnographer and anthropologist John Layard around 1915, this photograph shows a villager, Ma-taru, beside a huge menhir (erect stone) on an abandoned dancing ground at Tolamp, on northeastern Malekula, in Vanuatu.

⬇ These grotesque carved stone faces are on top of an altar at the dancing ground of Norohure, on the island of Vao, off the northeastern coast of Malekula. They are linked to ancestor rituals and used in weather magic: the stone faces are the dwelling places of spirits that control the weather.

Megaliths of Melanesia

Megalithic structures are known in several parts of Melanesia, notably in the Milne Bay region of Papua New Guinea, Fiji, and Vanuatu. Little is known about the age of the monuments, as few excavations have beeen carried out in these generally remote areas. A date of about the end of the first century BC has, however, been claimed for a huge stone-built tomb at Otuyam, on Kiriwina, in the Trobriand Islands, east of New Guinea. This is one of the few indications we have that the megalithic traditions have their roots far back in Melanesian prehistory. The monument is 30 meters (100 feet) long and contained huge amounts of human bones and pottery, indicating that the human remains had been deposited in clay pots. Other monuments, such as Ilukwaiwaia, also on Kiriwina, and stone-built tombs on the neighboring island of Kitava, might be equally old.

In Fiji, offerings and other ceremonies were carried out at magnificent stone temples, so-called *naga*, that consisted of rectangular enclosures, nearly 60 meters (about 200 feet) long, with altars. These megalithic temples had many different functions. Some were linked to the Fijian New Year celebrations in October and November, while others were used during rites of passage and in the fertility rituals. They were also the scenes of human sacrifice and cannibalism. The earliest dates of human habitation in Fiji center around 1300 BC, but the tradition of constructing stone-built monuments is probably much younger, perhaps only a few hundred years. It has been suggested that the *naga* is related to the Polynesian *marae*.

In parts of Vanuatu, megalithic traditions have survived until recently, and in some areas, megalithic ceremonies are still performed, although—with a few exceptions—no new monuments are erected. A chain of small islands off the northeastern coast of Malekula—Vao, Atchin, Wala, and Rano—is famous for its distinct megalithic culture, which is very different from the cultures of inland Malekula, where megalithic traditions are nonexistent. Abandoned monuments on the mainland, however, indicate that the tradition was more widespread in earlier times. The interior of Vao is still a religious center with absolute sacredness. A number of megalithic ritual places form a chain of ceremonial units, connected by pathways lined with erect monoliths of different sizes. There are no less than six distinctly separated megalithic complexes with dancing grounds (open areas for ritual dancing) belonging to them—Pete-hul, Tolamp–Togh-vanu, Peter-ihi, Venu, Norohure, and Singon, one for each village on the island. A narrow opening in the curtain of green jungle behind the central part of Kowu Beach, on the western side of the island, forms the entrance to the path that runs between the different complexes. This path is believed to be holy and to have a special connection with the supernatural.

On the long sides of the dancing grounds, there are a number of stone-built tombs and altars of different sizes, overrun with the entwined aerial roots of age-old banyan trees. All of them are covered with moist green moss. None of them has been excavated, and it is not known if they have been in use for 500 years, or perhaps 1,000 years,

GÖRAN BURENHULT

GORAN BURENHULT

The stone-built tombs at Togh-vanu, on the island of Vao, are still in use, and the history of some of them is known in detail. The largest belongs to a chiefly clan originating in Tolamp, on mainland Malekula, and several generations of use can be traced. Many of the smaller megaliths at Togh-vanu may be even older.

A stone altar at Norohure, on the island of Vao, to which pigs are tied during so-called grade-taking ceremonies (*maki*). By conducting such ceremonies, which sometimes involve the killing of hundreds of pigs, individuals can climb in the complex social hierarchical system and ensure life after death.

or maybe even longer. What is known is that they still form the central part of an ancient religious and ceremonial system.

Huge hollowed wooden drums, whose upper parts are decorated in the form of carved and painted human faces, have been erected in front of the central altar. These represent ancestor spirits and also form the dwelling places of these spirits during the ceremonies.

No one knows today how old the megalithic tradition on Malekula and its satellite islands really is. On Vao, oral tradition can trace it back 18 named generations—that is, more than half a millennium—but it is probably considerably older than that. Archaeological excavations would provide a great deal of information, but the islanders would never allow such an encroachment on their cult centers. Possible excavations would have to be confined to other megalithic areas of Malekula, where the original religious and ceremonial systems have ceased to exist, but where oral tradition can still provide information about the generations that once used the megaliths and the dancing grounds for their offerings and ceremonies.

A Prehistoric Enigma

The fact that so little excavating has been done makes the stone-built monuments of the South Pacific one of the great enigmas of world prehistory. From ethnohistoric and ethnographic data, we know that there was a great variety of megalithic traditions throughout this vast area, with considerable regional differences, and often in completely different social and religious contexts. We also know that stone-building societies often existed side by side with populations that never used any stone structures for ceremonial purposes; indeed, the question why some communities did *not* build stone monuments is as important as why others did. It is also clear that many of the stone-

GORAN BURENHULT

Opposite: the carved, human-like face on one of the huge slit drums on the Togh-vanu dancing ground, on the island of Vao.

building societies of the Pacific are widely separated in time. It seems—again from ethnohistoric and ethnographic data—that a fairly high population density was one of the main factors behind the social need to erect monumental structures of different kinds, and that the access and privilege to use them was strongly connected with individual rank and social status, either inherited or acquired. As in most Pacific societies, human sacrifice and, occasionally, exocannibalism (the eating of people outside one's own tribe) were a crucial part of ritual activities within the stone-building communities. We also know that aggression and warfare were an integral part of these societies, and that they were male-dominated.

The rituals were, and in some cases still are, almost always associated with the worship of ancestors. In some heavily stratified societies, however, such as the Polynesian chiefdoms, stone-built monuments were associated with the worship of gods. More commonly, the stone structures represent ancestors whose spirits are considered to be always present and to take part in the ceremonies. Sacrificial offerings are made to appease ancestors and to secure admission to the kingdom of the dead, where the final reunion takes place.

What we do not know, in most parts of the Pacific, is when the first slabs were erected or how the traditions developed—whether they evolved locally in many places after a longer or shorter period of initial settlement; whether the concept was brought by the first settlers from their original homeland; or whether ideas diffused, in some way or other, from one or more heartlands to other parts of the Pacific. We cannot even exclude the possibility that all three of these explanations may be right, in different areas. Future excavations will not only provide information about the stone-built monuments themselves, their detailed function and chronology, but perhaps also some further answers to the intriguing question of how the Pacific was once settled.

GÖRAN BURENHULT

Chief Karasea in front of the main drum, known as "Albert-Marie", at Togh-vanu, on the island of Vao.

GÖRAN BURENHULT

At Norohure, on the island of Vao, wooden slit drums stand in front of a stone-built shrine that was traditionally the site of cannibalistic meals. The drums are decorated with human-like faces, and their sounds represent the voices of ancestors.

THE STONE MONEY OF YAP

Göran Burenhult

On the island of Yap, in the western Caroline Islands, in Micronesia, a unique and peculiar form of stone-working tradition has developed. Chiefs on the island own large perforated disks of calcite dripstone, so-called *vai*, which are used to exchange for various commodities, such as copra. These slabs are popularly referred to as "stone money", but since they are obviously quite impractical for market transactions, they are better described as prestige tokens.

The disks were quarried in the Belau islands, some 500 kilometers (300 miles) southwest of Yap, and transported to Yap by canoe. The origin of the tradition is obscure, but it is thought that it developed during a period when Yap was the center of a pre-European trade and tribute network (the so-called Yapese empire) stretching from Belau, in the west, to near Truk, in the east. This huge network, which involved a flow of tribute centered on politically dominant Yap, is without parallels elsewhere in the Pacific area.

BRYAN AND CHERRY ALEXANDER

DAVID HISER/PHOTOGRAPHERS ASPEN

Most stone money slabs can be carried on a log of wood by two men, but the largest known examples are about 4 meters (13 feet) in diameter, and have to be carried by at least 12 people.

A stone disk in front of a traditional Yapese men's house, or *falu*. In 1929, there were 13,281 disks in Yap. Today, only half this number remain.

Opposite page: A Yap chief in front of his *vai*. The stone money has an official exchange rate at the Bank of Hawaii of 72 American dollars per inch (22 millimeters).

GALE KOSCHMANN-BELINKY/PHOTO RESEARCHERS, INC.

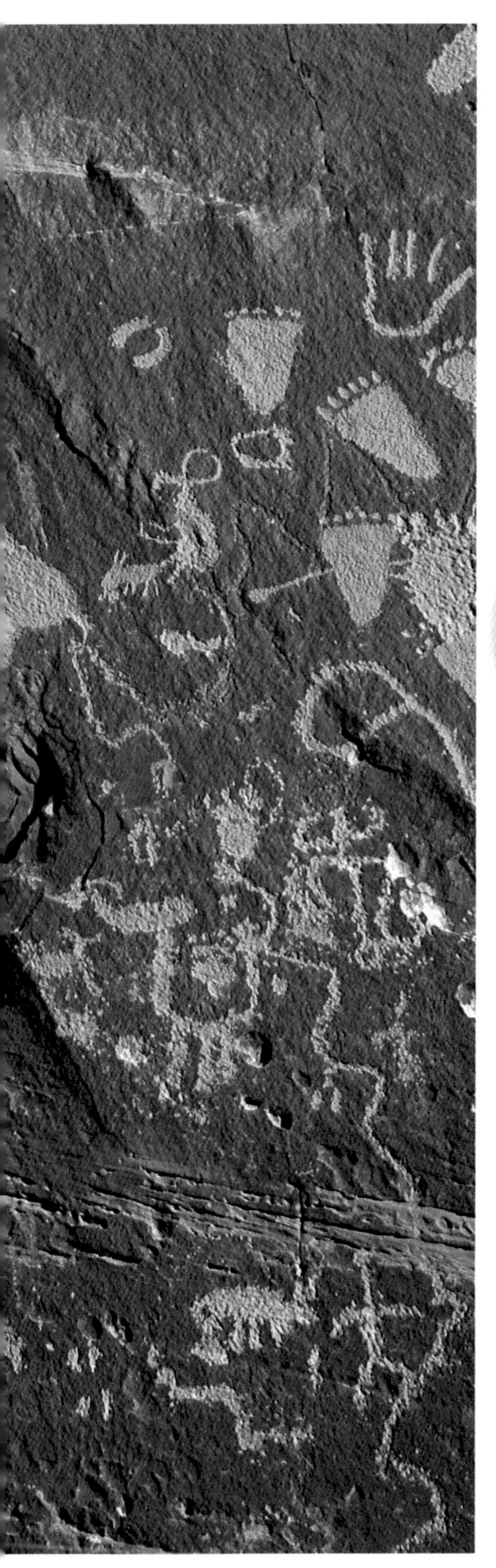

PREHISTORIC WAYS OF LIFE OF NATIVE AMERICANS

10,000 BC – AD 1850

Foragers and Farmers, Hunters and Herders

David Hurst Thomas

From the Arctic to Cape Horn, the continents of the New World stretch for a distance of 15,000 kilometers (9,300 miles), extending across 5,000 kilometers (3,000 miles) at their widest points. People have lived within this immense territory, covering a quarter of the Earth's habitable surface, for at least 12,000 years, and perhaps for much longer. Over thousands of years, native Americans developed many ways to win a living from this land: some hunted, some fished; others collected wild plants, herded domestic animals, or cultivated crops—their strategies as diverse as the environment itself.

← Petroglyphs at Newspaper Rock, in southeastern Utah. The symbols on this huge cave wall probably accumulated over about a thousand years, the earliest pecked into the rockface during Anasazi times (AD 900 to AD 1300) and the most recent probably made by the Ute people of the nineteenth century.

↑ This bowl from New Mexico, painted in the characteristic style of the Mimbres culture (AD 1000 to AD 1200) depicts two figures, which may symbolize male–female or life–death contrasts. The "kill" hole in the bottom, made when the bowl was included as part of a mortuary offering, helped release the vessel's spirit into the next world.

MAXWELL MUSEUM OF ANTHROPOLOGY, ALBUQUERQUE/WERNER FORMAN ARCHIVE

So-called effigy vessels of humans and animals, made of ceramics, are typical artifacts of the Mississippian period. This example, with sealed eyelids, stitched mouth, and facial decorations, may be the death portrait of a warrior chief. It dates from about AD 1000.

MUSEUM OF THE AMERICAN INDIAN, HEYE FOUNDATION, NEW YORK/WERNER FORMAN ARCHIVE

THE EVOLUTION OF MISSISSIPPIAN SOCIETY

The evolution of Mississippian society (AD 750 to AD 1540) represents a truly remarkable transformation within the cultural life of the American Southeast. The emergence of this new culture is marked in the archaeological record by the appearance of distinctive pottery (commonly tempered with crushed mussel shell); evidence of intensive, village-based horticulture; the rise of chiefdoms; and the construction of huge, regional ceremonial centers, characterized by a central plaza and large, earthern platform mounds that served as substructures for temples, elite residences, and council buildings. The available evidence suggests that Mississippian society arose independently, uninfluenced by contemporary state-level societies in Mesoamerica.

Although there is no firm evidence, people may have inherited the American Southeast before 10,000 BC. As elsewhere in North America, however, the earliest documented occupation was that of the Paleoindians (10,000 BC to 6000 BC)—a people who, very early, developed highly efficient techniques to harvest their river valley resources. Although they fashioned stone tools similar to those of contemporary big-game hunters in the Great Plains, their way of life was probably very different.

The people of the subsequent tradition, known as the Archaic (6000 BC to 700 BC), displayed an astounding ability to adapt to a variety of different conditions. Yet, despite local differences, Archaic peoples shared the same basic way of life, moving seasonally from one part of their home range to another to take advantage of the varying availability of grasses, fruits, nuts, fish, and game.

D. DONNE BRYANT STOCK

These fist-sized clay balls, called "Poverty Point" objects, were shaped by hand and baked. They were probably used to boil water, as this part of the Mississippi floodplain did not have the rounded cobbles from streambeds that were used as "boiling stones" elsewhere in native North America.

During Archaic times, the population was dispersed across the Southeast in small groups that were able to react rapidly to local variations in food supplies. This pattern of life minimized risk, providing a buffer against the failure of any particular plant or animal species.

In this period, there is evidence of people storing surplus foodstuffs as a hedge against seasonal fluctuations, and also of increased long-distance trade. Greater differences in social status begin to be reflected in the grave goods found in Late Archaic cemeteries. Valuable "exotic" items were restricted to a very few important people, suggesting that an earlier, egalitarian social structure was

D. DONNE BRYANT STOCK

An infrared aerial photograph showing the massive concentric earthworks at Poverty Point, in Louisiana. Built between 1000 BC and 700 BC, the six semicircular earthen ridges average about 25 meters (80 feet) in width, and were probably used as dwelling sites.

NATIVE NORTH AMERICA
The earliest archaeological site in native North America is the well-known Paleoindian mammoth-kill site at Clovis, in New Mexico. Pecos, Gran Quivira, Jemez, and Taos are traditional native American pueblos where Spanish missions were established during the seventeenth century.
CARTOGRAPHY: RAY SIM

breaking down as society became increasingly more "organized", probably in response to growing competition for scarce resources.

About 1300 BC, the Southeastern people began constructing earthworks in the lower Mississippi valley. A notable example is the Poverty Point complex, in Louisiana, a large, bird-shaped earthen mound nearly 23 meters (75 feet) high. Not far away is a series of extensive geometrical earthworks consisting of six concentric ridges, with an outer diameter of 1,200 meters (3,900 feet). The ridges were probably used as dwelling sites. At least a million cubic meters (1,300,000 cubic feet) of earth were used in the construction of these earthworks.

Sites such as Poverty Point are usually found in alluvial areas, which lack the stones commonly used by Archaic people for boiling and baking. Instead, they made "artificial stones" from baked clay balls, known as "Poverty Point" objects. The Poverty Point people also participated in far-flung exchange networks, trading for native copper and a wide range of stone goods.

The Poverty Point complex is an enigma. Despite the presence of massive earthworks, which suggests that this was an area of major ceremonial significance, the local culture does not appear to have differed greatly from that found in other Late Archaic sites. Some evidence suggests that Poverty Point groups were cultivating small garden plots of bottle gourd and squash, both for use as containers and for their edible seeds. Whatever the reason for its construction, the Poverty Point center was eventually abandoned, and nearly a thousand years passed before the Southeast once again saw evidence of such elaborate ceremonial activity.

PREHISTORIC WAYS OF LIFE OF NATIVE AMERICANS: 10,000 BC – AD 1850

	EASTERN NORTH AMERICA	WESTERN NORTH AMERICA	NORTHWEST COAST	SUBARCTIC	GREAT PLAINS
1850					
1600					European contact AD 1600
1500	Mississippian tradition AD 750 – AD 1540				Plains Village tradition AD 900 – AD 1850
1000	Late Prehistoric period AD 700 – AD 1540				
750					Plains Woodland tradition 250 BC – AD 950
250		Californian Archaic tradition 6000 BC – AD 1850	Classic Northwest Coast Culture 3500 BC – AD 1850		
AD 1	Sedentary period 700 BC – AD 700				
700					
1000		The Desert Archaic tradition 8000 BC – AD 1850			
2000					Plains Archaic tradition 5000 BC – AD 1
3000	Archaic tradition 6000 BC – 700 BC				
4000				Boreal and Maritime traditions 6000 BC – 1000 BC	
5000					
6000					
7000			Paleo-Plateau tradition 8000 BC – 6000 BC		
8000	Paleoindian tradition 10,000 BC – 6000 BC	Paleoindian tradition 10,000 BC – 6000 BC			Paleoindian tradition 10,000 BC – 6000 BC
9000			Paleoindian tradition 10,000 BC – 6000 BC		End of Pleistocene era 8000 BC
10,000 BC					

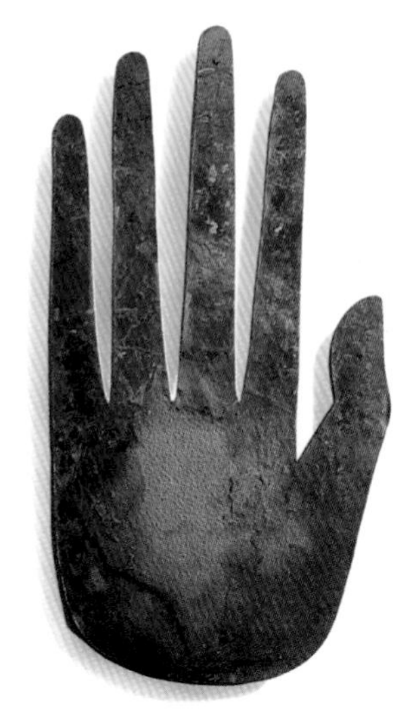

This oversized mica hand still glistens after centuries of burial in a Hopewell mound (about 100 BC to AD 400). The hand was a common shamanistic symbol throughout the eastern Woodlands during the Sedentary and Mississippian periods.
FIELD MUSEUM OF NATURAL HISTORY, CHICAGO/WERNER FORMAN ARCHIVE

The earliest pottery in North America appeared elsewhere in the Southeast about 2500 BC, and was not associated with any kind of agriculture. This simple pottery featured the use of organic fibers as temper to prevent the vessels cracking when fired. Some of the round bowls were adorned with what is known as "drag-and-jab" decoration.

Ceramics came into widespread use throughout eastern North America during the Sedentary period (700 BC to AD 700). While this probably does not signal great changes in Southeastern life, it does suggest that settlements were becoming more permanent.

Maize had arrived in the Southeast by about AD 100, but did not become a major staple until somewhere between about AD 800 and AD 1100. Previously, the cultivation of key native crops, such as sunflower, goosefoot (*Chenopodium*), sumpweed (*Iva*), and other river-bottom plants, had provided the basis for increased settlement and social development.

The most significant change to occur between the Archaic and Sedentary periods was in social organization and settlement patterns. Although society did not become complex overnight, the archaeological data reveal that mound-building on a monumental scale was becoming increasingly important. In addition, raw materials and finished goods were exchanged over great distances during the Sedentary period, effectively tying most of eastern North America into complex trade networks. This was an important factor in stimulating the development of hierarchical societies in this area.

Because burial mounds were built and plants domesticated earlier in Mexico than in the Southeast, it was once believed that mound-building and agriculture arrived as a "package" from Mesoamerica. There is no evidence, however, of any group movements from Mexico into the Southeast. Hunter-gatherers in southern Texas did interact with similar groups in neighboring northern Mexico, which ultimately led to the introduction of gourds and squash into the Southeast. Maize and beans, however, arrived in the Southeast at different times from the American Southwest, and it is unlikely that either was introduced directly from Mexico. Similarly, the known religious practices and beliefs of Southeastern Indians essentially reflect regional developments over thousands of years.

Throughout much of the eastern United States, the Late Prehistoric period (AD 700 to AD 1540) is characterized by an increased dependence on agricultural products. The term "Mississippian" is used to describe the highly complex Late Prehistoric societies that thrived along major river valleys of the eastern United States. People living along the Tennessee, Cumberland, and Mississippi rivers built huge earthen mounds and made pottery with crushed shell added to temper the clay.

The agriculture of the Mississippian peoples was vastly different from that practiced by European farmers. Because native Americans lacked domesticated draft animals, they were restricted to hoe cultivation. This, in turn, restricted agricultural activity to fertile river valleys or abandoned levee meanders in the Mississippi River valley. Major population centers and associated cultural developments arose in the interior rather than along the coast. These occurred not only in areas of high agricultural potential, but also where water and land routes provided ready communication with neighboring and distant settlements. As societies became more agricultural and centralized, so the authorities controlling the distribution of goods and services became more important. Conversely, the more centralized economic controls and population became, the more these new societies depended on agriculture for their survival.

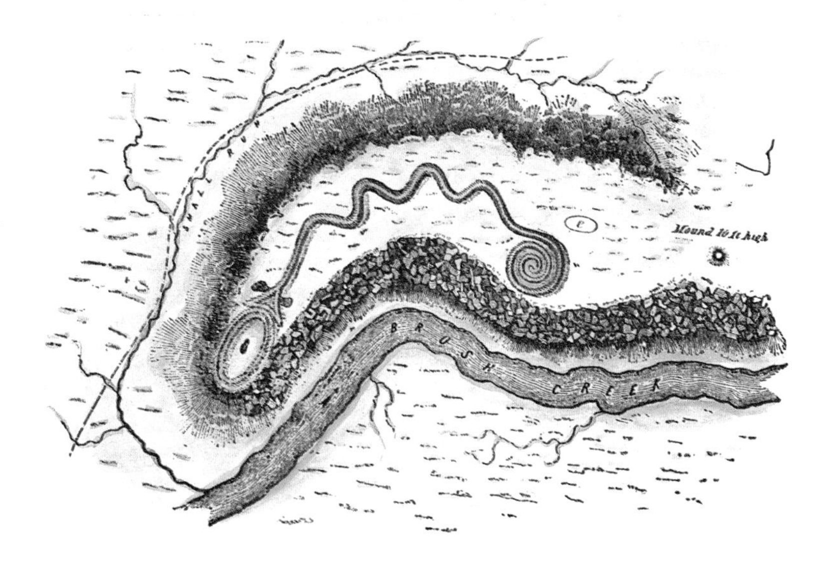

Made in 1846, this engraving of Ohio's celebrated Great Serpent Mound originally appeared in *Ancient Monuments of the Mississippi Valley*, by E.G. Squier and E.H. Davis. The snake is 210 meters (690 feet) long, and may be trying to swallow an egg, judging from the oval earthwork near its mouth. Although it has traditionally been assigned to the Sedentary period, new radiocarbon dates suggest that this earthwork may have been crafted during the Mississippian period.
THE GRANGER COLLECTION

Three examples of decorated bottles from the Mississippian period. At far left is an engraved bottle decorated with red and white bilobed arrows. The ceramic vessel at top left is encircled with alternating human hands and forearms, while that at bottom left is painted on both sides with a stylized human face. The forked-eye motif on this example is typical of Southern Cult ornamentation.
JACK C. ROBERTS/DAVID H. DYE

The organization of Mississippian settlements reflected the social hierarchy within these communities. Large central areas, with a number of platform-type mounds, served as administrative centers. A hierarchy of bureaucrats and priests (perhaps the same people), including community chiefs, military leaders, clan heads, and mortuary priests, supervised the production, collection, and distribution of food and materials. They also directed the construction of towns and mounds, and religious and political affairs. Mississippian towns were typically planned settlements, with rectangular, single-family houses arranged around an open central square and town meeting house. Adjacent to these stood towering earthworks, on which the chief's house and a charnel house (for the dead) were often built.

Many of the great Mississippian centers were thriving when the Spanish explorer Hernando De Soto first came to the American Southeast in AD 1539. The decline of these Late Prehistoric societies was directly related to European incursions into their territory. Early accounts indicate that some groups, such as the eighteenth-century Natchez Indians of the lower Mississippi Valley, continued to maintain chiefdoms during the early stages of European contact. The radical decline in population caused by European-introduced disease, however, led to the collapse of many Mississippian societies. Subsequently, several larger chiefdoms—some equivalent to states—arose in response to pressures from European settlers and conflicts that had broken out between various native American groups. Because of the rapid changes that occurred between the sixteenth and eighteenth centuries, it is difficult to trace historic tribes to specific prehistoric societies of the American Southeast, although the general lines of continuity are unquestioned.

FRANKE KEATING/PHOTO RESEARCHERS, INC.

The Emerald Mound, a ceremonial site near the Natchez Trace Parkway, in Mississippi (AD 1250 to AD 1600), is the second largest temple mound in the United States, its base covering an area of 3 hectares (8 acres).

A fragment of a copper repoussé plate from the Mississippian period, showing a human face, possibly a portrait. The motifs representing either painted ornamentation or tattoos are typical of the Southern Cult style.

MUSEUM OF THE AMERICAN INDIAN, HEYE FOUNDATION, NEW YORK/ WERNER FORMAN ARCHIVE

Caution: Agriculture Can Be Hazardous to Your Health

Thus arose and fell the most complex native American culture north of Mexico. Beyond the archaeological evidence, however, the development of Mississippian society highlights a problem that pervades our conventional view of the past. Too often, we view cultural evolution as a succession of great technological revolutions, which somehow made the world a better place to live in. We convince ourselves that through inventiveness and progress, prehistoric people gradually whittled down the list of problems and dangers once faced by all humankind.

The so-called Neolithic Revolution—when people began to cultivate domesticated plants—is one such transformation that has often been seen as solving the age-old problem of our reliance on nature and the seasons. Implicit in this view is a celebration of progress, as measured by rising population numbers, with people having more power over their lives. We are led to assume that with the agricultural way of life, people's workload became lighter, their nutrition improved, and they suffered from fewer diseases—in short, that the quality of human life has improved, representing a steady, if irregular, upward trend.

These assumptions about the progressive nature of the human past are today challenged by the results of new research suggesting that the changing health profile associated with the development of agriculture is more complex than was previously realized. For example, we now know that domestication—the genetic manipulation of crops—does not necessarily improve the nutrient value of plants; indeed, quite the reverse may be true. Moreover, since storage can result in a further loss of nutrients, settled communities living off stored staple foods end up with a poorer diet.

Several recent studies of human skeletal remains demonstrate the ill effects of an increasing reliance on domesticated plants and of the sedentary way of life that goes with this. For instance, at the Dickson Mounds, in Illinois, which span the Woodland period (AD 800 to AD 1250) and the following Mississippian period (AD 1250 to AD 1400), the health, nutrition, and longevity of Mississippian people can be seen to have declined significantly by the later period. There were higher rates of disease and malnourishment (probably as a result of overcrowding), singularly high rates of injuries (suggesting increased levels of violence), high rates of porotic hyperostosis (bone lesions probably caused by anemia), and a greater incidence of dental disease. In general, these people suffered greater biological stress and had a lower life expectancy than their predecessors. Some studies suggest that, with the transition from hunting and gathering to intensive maize agriculture, the incidence of infectious diseases within Mississippian societies may have doubled. In fact, "progress" exacted a higher cost than many might like to admit.

Conditions were apparently better in some areas than in others. At Moundville, in Alabama, and Etowah, in Georgia (AD 1250 to AD 1500), people were relatively healthy and long-lived, but there was a substantial difference between social classes. Although male adults accorded higher-status mound burial had a relatively high age at death (about 40 years, on average), those in surrounding village cemeteries (presumably a lower-status area) lived an average of only 23 years. But a contemporary group of hunter-gatherers living in an outlying settlement not far from Etowah were taller and more robust than their agricultural neighbors, and had lower rates of infection and arthritis.

Such recent studies not only highlight the downside of agricultural life but also point to the importance of setting aside widespread ideas about "progress". Surprisingly, nonagricultural people throughout the Americas and elsewhere may have lived healthier and longer lives than their agricultural contemporaries.

This colored engraving made in 1590 by Theodor de Bry, after a painting of 1587 by John White, depicts cornfields, domestic dwellings, and native people dancing around a circle of columnar idols. The scene is considered to provide a highly accurate ethnographic record, and probably took place in an Algonquin village somewhere in North Carolina.

THE SOUTHERN CULT

DAVID HURST THOMAS

AS COMMUNITIES DEVELOPED political and social hierarchies in the Late Mississippian period, about AD 1200, thereby becoming more complex, systematic ceremonial observances came to play a much more prominent role in people's lives. These rites were a means of paying homage to ancestors; of celebrating successful harvests, hunts, and warfare; and of expressing respect for the dead, through burial observances for community leaders.

The archaeological record bears eloquent testimony to these events, showing that a vast distribution network developed in the Southeast in this period, by means of which iconographic objects especially—but also, possibly, such basic commodities of life as food and salt—were exchanged between widespread communities throughout much of the east of North America. This traffic is known as the Southern Cult, but the term is also, and more often, applied to the characteristic artistic designs and motifs expressed in ceremonial objects found in this region between about AD 1150 and AD 1350. Emanating from three major regional centers—Moundville, in Alabama, Etowah, in Georgia, and Spiro, in Oklahoma—this phenomenon is also known as the Southeastern Ceremonial Complex. But it extended far beyond the limits of any single Mississippian cultural complex, involving communities from Mississippi to Minnesota, from the Plains to the Atlantic coast.

Southern Cult objects usually take the form of ceramic vessels (often representing animals and humans), ornaments of copper and shell, and shell cups. Their striking similarities in theme, motif, and medium transcend the sorts of influences commonly apparent in traded goods, suggesting, rather, a high degree of social interaction. Characteristic motifs include crosses, sun symbols, serpents, woodpeckers, falcons, and raccoons. Many of these objects and motifs can be linked to the belief systems of nineteenth-century native Americans of the Southeast, as expressed in their folk tales, myths, and religious observances.

A Mississippian effigy vessel (AD 1350 to AD 1550) from Arkansas, showing a kneeling hunchback with interlocking scrolls across the chest.

This painted effigy bottle (about AD 1500 to AD 1600), from Arkansas, depicts a stylized bear head.
JACK C. ROBERTS/DAVID H. DYE

JACK C. ROBERTS/DAVID H. DYE

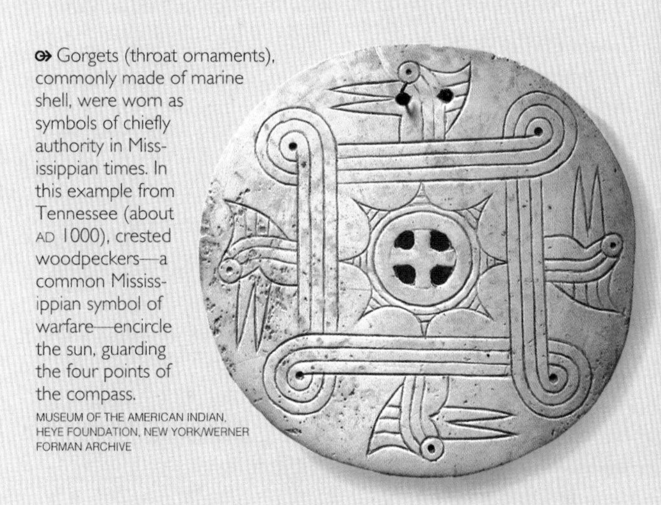

Gorgets (throat ornaments), commonly made of marine shell, were worn as symbols of chiefly authority in Mississippian times. In this example from Tennessee (about AD 1000), crested woodpeckers—a common Mississippian symbol of warfare—encircle the sun, guarding the four points of the compass.
MUSEUM OF THE AMERICAN INDIAN, HEYE FOUNDATION, NEW YORK/WERNER FORMAN ARCHIVE

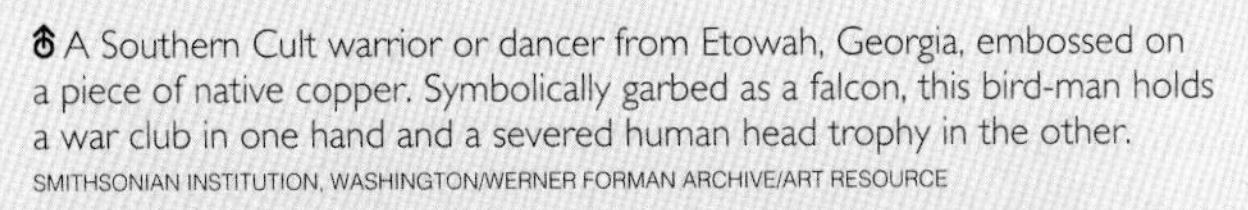

A Southern Cult warrior or dancer from Etowah, Georgia, embossed on a piece of native copper. Symbolically garbed as a falcon, this bird-man holds a war club in one hand and a severed human head trophy in the other.
SMITHSONIAN INSTITUTION, WASHINGTON/WERNER FORMAN ARCHIVE/ART RESOURCE

This remarkably well-preserved mask made of cedar wood, from the Spiro Mound (dating from about AD 1200), combines human features with deer antlers. Shell inlays indicate the mouth and eyes. It was probably worn by a Mississippian shaman during the Deer Ceremony, a ritual hunting dance.
MUSEUM OF THE AMERICAN INDIAN, HEYE FOUNDATION, NEW YORK/ WERNER FORMAN ARCHIVE

JACK C. ROBERTS/DAVID H. DYE

Cut from a marine conch shell, this pear-shaped Mississippian gorget (AD 1350 to AD 1550) from Arkansas takes the form of a face mask. The eye perforations are surrounded by engraved "forked eye" motifs typical of the Southern Cult, with zigzag extensions. The nose is represented in bas relief.

A fragment of a marine shell drinking cup from Spiro, Oklahoma (AD 1250 to AD 1350), incised with the image of a human head. The personal ornamentation includes facial tattooing (or painting); a beaded forelock and a hair bun, with the band of hair in between cut short in roach style; and earplugs. The lines issuing from the mouth may represent bands of woven cloth used to tie together human heads captured as war trophies, a common Southern Cult motif.
MEMPHIS PINK PALACE MUSEUM/ DAVID H. DYE

NATIONAL MUSEUM OF THE AMERICAN INDIAN

These ancient duck decoys were recovered from Lovelock Cave, in Nevada, in 1924. Made from bulrushes, a very buoyant material, they were often covered with feathered birdskins and were probably tied to a float to attract waterbirds. One of these decoys has recently been radiocarbon-dated to about AD 1.

ARCHAIC HUNTER-GATHERERS IN WESTERN NORTH AMERICA

Paleoindians rapidly made their way into far western North America, populating the vast areas between the Rockies and the Sierra Nevada mountains, and the Pacific slope to the west. They depended on a few key foods for survival. The two major staples of later periods—acorns and salmon—were not available to California Paleoindians, because they lacked the necessary knowledge and tools. Instead, they probably hunted mammoths and other animals that are now extinct, like their big-game-hunting cousins on the Great Plains. Since, moreover, pinyon pine nuts would not become available in the Great Basin area for another 5,000 years, the Paleoindians lived off the resources available along the shores and marshes of the great desert lakes left behind at the end of the Pleistocene era.

TOM WILLOCK/PHOTO RESEARCHERS, INC.

At the end of the Pleistocene era, pinyon pine woodland was restricted to the American Southwest. When the global climate became warmer during the ensuing Holocene era, the pinyon woodland moved northwards into the Great Basin.

PAT AND TOM LEESON/PHOTO RESEARCHERS, INC.

The hard-shelled nuts (seeds) contained within pinyon pine cones were an extremely nutritious food for the foragers of the American West, but yields vary radically from year to year. Pine nuts can be readily stored, and were a vital winter resource for Desert Archaic people.

The Desert Archaic: 8000 BC – AD 1850

Two important ecological shifts mark the boundary between the Paleoindian and Archaic periods throughout the western North American deserts. The gigantic desert lakes began to dry up at the end of the Pleistocene era (about 8000 BC), forcing some groups to cluster along the vastly diminished shorelines, where they collected bulrushes, cattail (*Typha*, a tall, reedy marsh plant), and insect larvae, fashioned clever decoys to hunt waterfowl, and fished during the rich spawning runs.

Others decided to shift territory altogether, abandoning the contracting lakes to live in upland mountain valleys. Here, they hunted the then plentiful bighorn sheep and collected plants in the ever-changing post-Pleistocene landscape. Before about 10,000 BC, pinyon pines had been restricted to the southern margin of the Great Basin, a massive area of internal drainage between the Sierra Nevada and Wasatch mountains. By about 4500 BC, they rapidly migrated northwards. The highly nutritious pinyon nut is a high-bulk food, which can be stored for two or three years. The upland Desert Archaic people followed a seasonal round, often moving several times throughout the year, relying on pinyon nuts as their staple food whenever, and wherever, they were available.

CHARLIE OTT/PHOTO RESEARCHERS, INC.

Desert Archaic people left thousands of petroglyphs throughout the West, but this rock art can rarely be dated precisely. The motifs. were made by pecking through the dark "desert varnish" to expose the light-colored, unpainted stone beneath.

Summer camps were commonly located in the interior hills and valleys, while winter camps were established close to where storable resources (such as pinyon) ripened—often on ridgetops, towards the base of major mountain ranges. The winter camp was often home to several families, who had come together in the autumn, when food was more abundant. In the spring, food was usually in short supply, and families would disperse.

The California Archaic: 6000 BC – AD 1850

The 8,000-year-long Archaic period in California was characterized by an economy without agriculture. No single food item became the single most important staple. Whereas the Paleoindians tended to focus their efforts on specialized activities, the Archaic peoples in California took advantage of the wider range of opportunities offered by the diversity of their environment. When big game became extinct, they continued to hunt smaller animals, but they also relied on literally hundreds of different plants for food, medicine, and craft materials.

In the oak chaparral forest, they collected the plentiful supplies of small, hard, protein-rich seeds, and hunted deer and smaller mammals. Along the coast, they found a great profusion of shellfish and seals, and the occasional beached whale. The mountains were home to deer, bear, and elk, plus a variety of plant foods that ripened by midsummer. The large rivers yielded huge quantities of spawning salmon, trout, and eel. As the Archaic period progressed, people continually expanded their range of food supplies, trying foods previously available but not previously used, and moved into areas that had never before been permanently settled.

About 2000 BC, the survival base of native Californians contracted once again, each group relying heavily on one or just a few species. The desert peoples focused on the pods of the screwbean mesquite (*Prosopis pubescens*), while valley groups depended on acorns, which increasingly became the most important natural resource in California. Once the tannic acid had been leached away, this edible nut could be ground into meal and flour, and stored for long periods. Groups living in the mountains had access to pinyon nuts and venison, while those living beside rivers relied on acorns and salmon.

Most of these resources had been available earlier, but by later Archaic times, population densities and group sizes had considerably increased, and societies had become more complex. This required a different strategy, and more people could be supported by collecting certain key foods in quantity and storing most of them for seasons when food was less abundant. By the time of Spanish colonization, in the late eighteenth century, California was home to more than 300,000 Indians, perhaps the highest native American population density north of Mexico. Native California may represent the upper limits of social development possible without agriculture.

TOM AND PAT LEESON/PHOTO RESEARCHERS, INC.

Today, mountain sheep are found mostly on the highest alpine crags and summits, where they can use their remarkable climbing and leaping ability to escape modern hunters. Before European contact, however, mountain sheep commonly ventured onto the flatlands, where they have been hunted for millennia by Desert Archaic people.

Desert Archaic people consumed the beanlike mesquite pods when green, and they also gathered the dry pods, which they sometimes ground in mortars or boiled.

KEN BRATE/PHOTO RESEARCHERS, INC.

HUNTERS AND HERDERS OF SOUTH AMERICA

JOHN W. RICK

IN SOUTH AMERICA, as in other parts of the world, many of the first hunter-gatherer societies transformed themselves into agricultural societies and complex state organizations, such as the Inka empire. We must be careful, however, not to think that these transitions were inevitable, or that the original hunting-gathering communities were simple societies that were all the same. The archaeology of South America has given us important examples of how these societies were structured, and how they changed and interacted.

The environmental diversity of South America fostered different hunter-gatherer ways of life. The Andes region of modern Peru is a prime example, including desert coasts, mountain valleys, high grassland plains, and tropical forests, all within a relatively small area. The proximity of abundant food from the sea along the Pacific shore, and the plant life of coastal valleys and the nearby seasonal hilltop meadows created by the moisture from coastal fog, encouraged some pre-agricultural communities to settle in one place. Other groups continued to be mobile, moving with the seasons between these different areas. In the sierra, the seasonal cycles of thorn forests kept foragers on the move, while annual droughts periodically forced them to break up into smaller groups.

Hunters of the Puna

With few animal species and a scarce supply of edible plants, the cold *puna* grasslands of central Peru, lying at an altitude of 4,200 meters (14,000 feet), seem an unlikely place for hunter-gatherers to congregate. Yet, a deer-sized relative of the llama, the vicuña, provided a good source of food for a very organized, largely settled, hunting society—as shown by cave sites virtually stuffed with vicuña bones and stone tools. About 10,000 BC, people started to live in the *puna*, and not long after, they began to develop conservative hunting techniques to preserve the vicuña population.

The great abundance of bones and tools tells us much about the *puna* way of life. In the earlier periods of occupation, from about 9000 BC to 6000 BC, the vicuña remains and rare plant foods suggest that people lived here seasonally. Gradually, they began to kill vicuñas all year round, judging from the dental age of the animal remains. These, along with carbonized plant remains from all seasons, suggests that people also lived here all year round in the three or four millennia leading up to 1500 BC.

Ever greater quantities of vicuña bones, from animals killed in the prime of life, testify to their hunting success. The many tens of thousands of stone tools excavated in the caves were used for hunting or processing animals. Hide-scrapers and knives are abundant, and there are even greater quantities of spearheads. A number of *puna* caves contain around half a million stone tools—easily enough to account for constant human occupation for thousands of years. At sites where people mostly stayed in one place, spearheads unique to that particular location are found. This suggests that small hunting groups may have lived for decades in a single cave, maintaining a distinct social identity.

Herding in the Andes

Perhaps as early as 4000 BC, some Andean peoples began to domesticate the ancestors of the present-day llama and alpaca. We know surprisingly little about this process, because the bones of wild camelids, the vicuña and the guanaco, are quite similar to those of the herded camelids, the llama and alpaca. Some archaeologists are trying to use bone characteristics to identify specific animals, but no one has yet identified a clear intermediate form between wild and domestic herded animals. Archaeologists

JOHN RICK

The limestone cave site of Panaulauca lies at an altitude of 4,200 meters (14,000 feet) in the grassland *puna* zone of Junin, in Peru. The cave mouth is partially choked with 4 meters (13 feet) of occupation deposits spanning hunting and herding periods.

A prehistoric herding village in the *puna* grasslands, near Junin, in Peru, as seen from the hillside above. The numerous small circles, which appear to be dwellings, are themselves in circular, corral arrangements.

JOHN RICK

search for patterns in the ages of the animals in prehistoric sites that might indicate the involvement of humans. Since modern alpaca herders lose many very young animals to disease, the presence of many newborn animals in a site suggests that herding was occurring.

For many reasons, herding sites have only rarely been found in the Andes. In the first place, herders needed to keep on the move in search of fresh pastures as their herds exhausted local food supplies. These short-term sites are difficult to find, since few permanent structures were built, and only a small amount of rubbish was accumulated. Second, the herders probably lived in small groups, within small areas. Third, herding was not an easy way of life, as it was quite difficult to increase herd size, whereas agriculture often produced vastly greater quantities of food than did the collection of wild plants. Unlike domesticated plants such as maize, with their greatly increased seed count and seed size, herded animals yielded about the same amount of meat as their wild ancestors. Some important conclusions can be drawn from this. For example, domestication did result in two new uses for Andean herd animals that were valuable in a rugged, cold land: transport and wool production.

Early Andean herders were undoubtedly used to hardship, and usually lived in independent groups. Their nomadic way of life may have led them to resist control by the large state organizations of the Late Prehistoric Andes, such as the Inka empire. On the other hand, herders may have had to rely heavily on trade or exchange with agricultural societies. As more complex societies developed, some herders were eventually absorbed into more diversified groups.

DANIELE PELLEGRINI/PHOTO RESEARCHERS, INC.

The vicuña, a member of the camel family and a relative of the llama, thrives in the *puna* grasslands of the Andes, being well adapted to this almost permanently cold environment. A favored prey of early hunters, it has fine fur and lives in highly territorial groups.

Andean herding should be seen neither as a great advance over hunting and gathering, nor as a way of life isolated from agricultural societies. The value of having herded animals at hand varied according to local conditions. Hunters in the heart of vicuña country would not have seen any advantage in switching to herding, whereas people living in areas with fewer game animals did. Unless game was quite scarce, the great amount of care and tending that herds required meant that herding compared poorly with hunting, in which nature took care of the nurture and reproduction of the animals, and humans merely harvested them. Thus, rather than herding being a great improvement over hunting, it seems likely that it was first adopted only when necessary, and primarily in areas poor in game. A particularly telling situation prevailed in Peru between 4000 BC and 2000 BC. In the *puna* region of Junin, some sites show clear evidence of sophisticated hunting societies, while nearby sites on the edge of the *puna* were evidently occupied by herders. These hunters and herders apparently lived in close proximity for thousands of years.

THE GRANGER COLLECTION

A nineteenth-century depiction of Pacific Northwest Coast fishermen employing a dip-net to catch whitefish in the rapids of the Columbia River. Weirs and fishtraps were also used here.

Spawning Kokanee salmon could be taken by the thousands, dried, and stored for winter use. Northwest Coast people considered salmon to be a race of eternal beings who lived in underwater houses during the winter, returning to their fish form in the spring.

THE NORTHWEST COAST

America's northwest coast extends along the Pacific Ocean from Yakutat Bay, in southern Alaska, to Humboldt Bay, in northern California. At the end of the Pleistocene era, the land subsided and valleys were flooded by the sea, creating a coastline intersected by a network of channels and fiords, with thousands of islands, both large and small. The upwelling of colder offshore water nourishes plankton communities, the start of the food chain that leads to the abundant fish, sea birds, and sea mammals in this region.

No significant differences are found in the earliest cultural remains of coastal and inland sites in southeastern Alaska, British Columbia, Washington, and Oregon. Distinctions did develop over time, however. Whereas hunters and river fishers came to dominate the inland region, the classic Northwest Coast culture (3500 BC to AD 1850) developed along the Pacific slope. Although agriculture was never practiced here, and ceramics were unknown, these are well known for their dense populations and lavish ceremonies, which emphasized property, rank, and personal pride.

An early hunting tradition, sometimes called the paleo-Plateau tradition, had developed by at least 8000 BC, in which elks, deers, antelopes, beavers, rabbits, and rodents were all favored prey. Two thousand years later, the list broadened to include salmon and river mussels. Most sites are clustered near major rivers in lowland areas. There is little evidence of upland occupation.

The population on the northwest coast increased significantly between 2000 BC and 1000 BC. At some point after that time, the northern and southern traditions merged along the Strait of Georgia, creating a coastal way of life directly linked to that of Northwest Coast Indians during the period following European contact in the sixteenth century. Prehistoric people had adapted their way of life to plentiful marine and intertidal food supplies, and a mountainous hinterland rich in fish and game. They achieved the spectacular "culture of abundance" that so impressed the earliest European and Russian explorers.

Large villages were invariably located at the water's edge, on a beach convenient for landing canoes. Smaller, special-purpose sites also existed, which suggests that local differences in ways of life had begun to spring up. In the north, houses were nearly square, 10 to 20 meters (33 to 66 feet) across, with vertical side planks and a gabled roof. A fireplace at ground level warmed sleeping compartments on the upper levels. The southern houses were long and narrow—one such house being 150 meters (490 feet) long and 20 meters (65 feet) wide. Each house was occupied by several families, each with its own hearth. Large wooden houses have been constructed on the northwest coast for more than 3,000 years, probably indicating that people lived in extended family groups.

Artifacts on the northwest coast became increasingly diverse, particularly after 1500 BC. Stone artifacts fashioned by grinding and pecking—including hammers, adzes, bowls, and lip-plugs—became commonplace, and bone, shell, and wooden tools are found in profusion. Woodworking was highly developed in this region; houses, canoes, bowls, spoons, boxes, drums, and masks were all carved with symbolic and artistic motifs.

The people of the interior lived in deep, semi-subterranean pit houses, often grouped into sizeable villages. Some of their houses exceeded 20 meters (65 feet) in diameter, and after European contact, up to 25 people wintered in such structures. Houses were covered with matting and bark and had a central fireplace. Early nineteenth-century explorers Meriwether Lewis and William Clark observed one such house at Kamiah, in Idaho, with more than 40 hearths.

WILLIAM H. MULLINS/PHOTO RESEARCHERS, INC.

PROVINCIAL MUSEUM OF BRITISH COLUMBIA NO. 14308/WERNER FORMAN ARCHIVE

PAT AND TOM LEESON/PHOTO RESEARCHERS, INC

⊕ This petroglyph in the Columbia River Gorge depicts Tsagiglalal ("She Who Watches"). This mythical being served as a guardian spirit, providing people with such desirable abilities as speed, bravery, hunting prowess, or invulnerability to wounds in battle. Tsagiglalal was a particularly powerful spirit, who formed part of a death cult ritual on the Columbia Plateau during the nineteenth century.

⊕ Made from the horn of a mountain goat, this Northwest Coast spoon is the work of either Haida or Tlingit craftsmen. The delicate carving depicts a raven and a doubled-up human figure. Items such as these were given to important guests at the conclusion of potlatch feasts: specialized ceremonies held to validate key cultural events, ranging from relatively minor events in a child's life through to more significant festivals.

FIELD MUSEUM OF NATURAL HISTORY, CHICAGO/WERNER FORMAN ARCHIVE

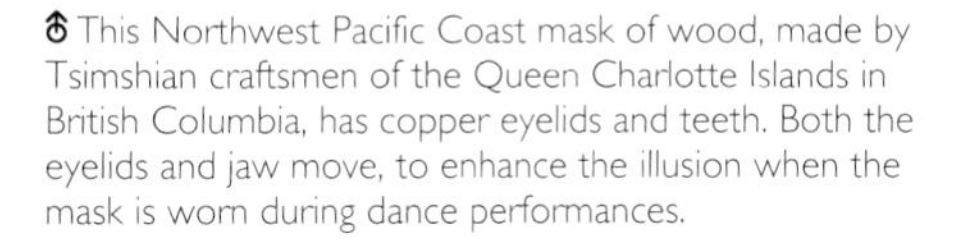

⊕ This Northwest Pacific Coast mask of wood, made by Tsimshian craftsmen of the Queen Charlotte Islands in British Columbia, has copper eyelids and teeth. Both the eyelids and jaw move, to enhance the illusion when the mask is worn during dance performances.

The concentrated network of waterways in the interior plateau greatly restricted human movement and reduced the availability of fish, such as salmon. Although the communities living there were not as socially stratified as contemporary coastal people, there is some evidence in British Columbia of hereditary leadership and exclusive ownership of salmon-fishing locations.

The people of British Columbia created thousands of petroglyphs, which even today adorn many cliff faces and boulders in the region. There are carvings of men (some with huge, square shoulders, short legs, and wearing horned headdresses), mountain sheep, deer, elks, salmon, and beavers. Others depict grotesque imaginary animals (such as water devils). A number of carved panels appear to tell a story, while others may be connected with death rites or clan symbols.

THE GRANGER COLLECTION

⊕ The massive red-cedar corner-post and other remains of a plank house constructed by Haida Indians of British Columbia, in Canada. Haida houses were usually named, and were commonly embellished with the owner's crest.

THE PLAINS INDIANS

DAVID HURST THOMAS

THE GREAT PLAINS comprise the very heartland of North America, and the Plains Indians who lived here developed one of the most distinctive ways of life in all of native America. By the late eighteenth century, the 120,000 surviving Plains Indian people lived within about 20 tribes. Some of these tribes, such as the Mandan of the upper Missouri River, continued to live in their palisaded semisedentary communities. These farming villages served as powerful trading centers, usually along major rivers and their tributaries. Other formerly sedentary tribes, such as the Omaha, were displaced by eastern tribes, themselves fleeing from the well-armed Iroquois. During the eighteenth century, most Plains Indian groups secured horses. For many tribes, such as the Sioux, Crow, Blackfeet, and Cheyenne, settled village life became too tame. As these Plains horsemen became fully mobile, they followed the massive bison herds on which they came to depend for survival.

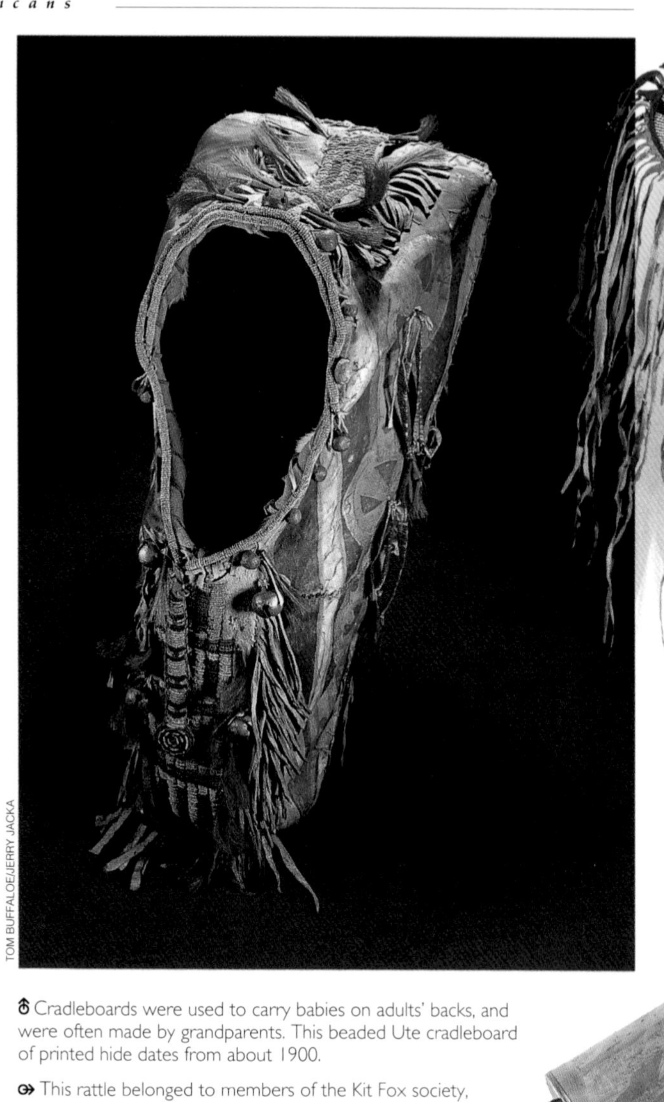

TOM BUFFALOE/JERRY JACKA

Cradleboards were used to carry babies on adults' backs, and were often made by grandparents. This beaded Ute cradleboard of printed hide dates from about 1900.

DIETRICH GRAF/STAATLICHE MUSEEN/MUSEUM FÜR VÖLKERKUNDE, BERLIN

Elegant shirts like this beaded, hair-fringed Blackfeet Indian man's shirt were usually worn only on special occasions. This example dates from about 1820.

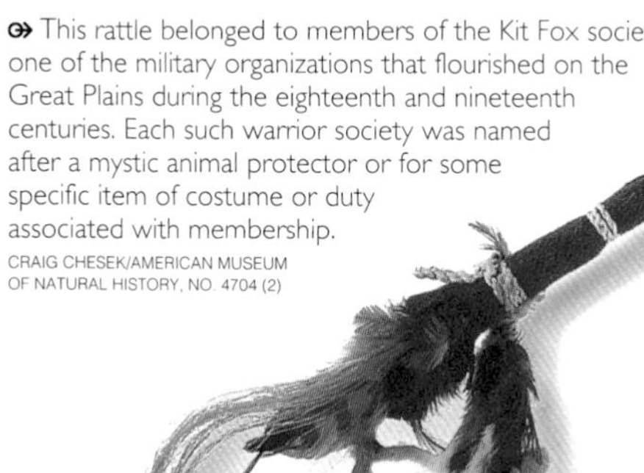

This rattle belonged to members of the Kit Fox society, one of the military organizations that flourished on the Great Plains during the eighteenth and nineteenth centuries. Each such warrior society was named after a mystic animal protector or for some specific item of costume or duty associated with membership.

CRAIG CHESEK/AMERICAN MUSEUM OF NATURAL HISTORY, NO. 4704 (2)

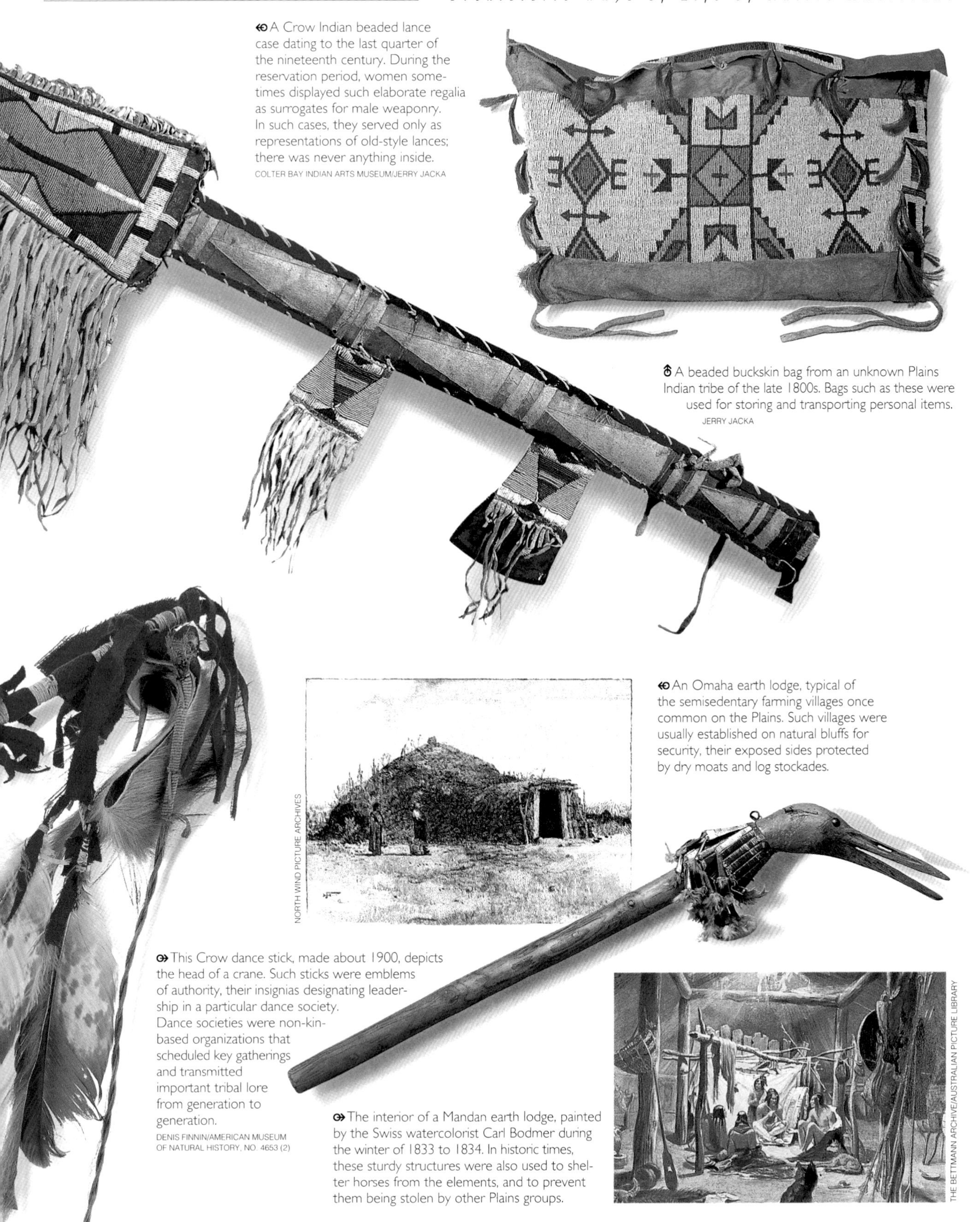

A Crow Indian beaded lance case dating to the last quarter of the nineteenth century. During the reservation period, women sometimes displayed such elaborate regalia as surrogates for male weaponry. In such cases, they served only as representations of old-style lances; there was never anything inside.
COLTER BAY INDIAN ARTS MUSEUM/JERRY JACKA

A beaded buckskin bag from an unknown Plains Indian tribe of the late 1800s. Bags such as these were used for storing and transporting personal items.
JERRY JACKA

An Omaha earth lodge, typical of the semisedentary farming villages once common on the Plains. Such villages were usually established on natural bluffs for security, their exposed sides protected by dry moats and log stockades.
NORTH WIND PICTURE ARCHIVES

This Crow dance stick, made about 1900, depicts the head of a crane. Such sticks were emblems of authority, their insignias designating leadership in a particular dance society. Dance societies were non-kin-based organizations that scheduled key gatherings and transmitted important tribal lore from generation to generation.
DENIS FINNIN/AMERICAN MUSEUM OF NATURAL HISTORY, NO. 4653 (2)

The interior of a Mandan earth lodge, painted by the Swiss watercolorist Carl Bodmer during the winter of 1833 to 1834. In historic times, these sturdy structures were also used to shelter horses from the elements, and to prevent them being stolen by other Plains groups.
THE BETTMANN ARCHIVE/AUSTRALIAN PICTURE LIBRARY

CHARLIE OTT/PHOTO RESEARCHERS, INC.

The subarctic environment consists of a belt of coniferous forest broken here and there by treeless tundra. Caribou and moose were the major source of food for the people of this region, and the many streams, lakes, and swamps made birch-bark canoes the most effective means of travel, although both snowshoes and toboggans proved useful during the winter.

LIFE IN THE SUBARCTIC

The subarctic of North America spans the formidable territory from Alaska to Labrador. The so-called "tree line" that separates the Arctic from the subarctic is not a line at all, but a broad transitional area of tundra and forest. The forested part is almost impenetrable, and travelers usually follow the waterways. Although the winter climate in these northern forests is as severe as on the tundra, the summers are warmer and longer, with up to 100 frost-free days.

The northeastern region of North America consists of the "newest" land surfaces to be found anywhere in the New World, as it was the last area to emerge from beneath the Pleistocene glaciers. People therefore spread into this region in a series of migrations towards the center, following the paths of the shrinking glaciers. As newly liberated landscapes surfaced around the edge of the icecap, tundra plants rapidly filled the resulting biological vacuum, followed by a variety of animals. Humans were last on the scene. In some areas, their arrival was delayed for centuries by obstacles left by the glaciers, such as ice-dammed lakes, which formed a physical barrier to human migration.

The first recognizable human activity in the subarctic dates to the Paleoindian period. As the climate improved and forests moved further north, however, an ever-thickening barrier of trees formed between the tundra country and the temperate grasslands. These barriers led to different cultural developments in isolated areas. The Boreal and Maritime Archaic traditions (6000 BC to 1000 BC), which represents early adaptations to forest conditions, emerged during this period of flux. As the regional population density increased, the land began to fill up with seasonal camps and more permanent settlements. People could not migrate, and became increasingly settled. As a result, they developed more sophisticated technologies.

Although it is not known precisely what became of the Boreal and Maritime traditions in the subarctic zone, most scholars assume that they evolved into the various Indian that occupied the region at the time of European contact. There is solid documentary evidence to show that the Beothucks of Newfoundland, the Montagnais-Naskapi of Quebec-Labrador, the Cree and Ojibwa of the Hudson Bay lowlands, and other Athapaskan-speaking tribes living further northwest, formerly lived as hunter-gatherers in this forested environment, and many elements of their culture can be traced back in the archaeological record to the Boreal and Maritime traditions.

BISON HUNTING ON THE GREAT PLAINS

The Great Plains of North America occupy roughly two million square kilometers (770,000 square miles). They comprise a flat land of cold winters and hot summers, and sparse and unpredictable rainfall, with a cover of perennial grasses. Trees grow only in stream valleys, on scarp lands, and in hilly areas. Early European explorers were impressed by the prodigious numbers of "wild cows" (bison) that roamed across an endless "sea of grass". It was these bison herds that gave the people of the Great Plains their distinctive culture.

The Clovis Complex site in New Mexico has provided the oldest reliably dated cultural materials in the Americas, clearly pointing to an association of humans and animals on the Great Plains. At the end of the Pleistocene era, between 8000 BC and 6000 BC, the northern forests were gradually replaced by deciduous forests. These, in turn, were replaced by grassland. Thus, about 10,000 years ago, large, grass-eating bison moved down into the Great Plains from the cooler, moister uplands, and were hunted in small numbers by the Paleoindians.

The people of the Plains Archaic tradition (5000 BC to the beginning of the first century AD) hunted small game and gathered seeds, tubers, nuts, berries, and other plant foods in season. Most characteristically, however, they hunted bison, wherever conditions permitted. Unlike most native North Americans—whose activities shifted from hunting to a more varied pattern of food-gathering—the Great Plains people switched from hunting big game in general to hunting bison in particular.

NATIONAL MUSEUM OF AMERICAN ART/ART RESOURCE

After the introduction of the horse in the late seventeenth century, Plains people adopted a highly mobile way of life, following the annual migration of the bison herds. This scene, painted by George Catlin in 1832, is entitled *Sioux Encamped on the Upper Missouri, Dressing Buffalo Meat and Robes.*

Without question, the prehorse Plains Indian had developed highly successful ways of procuring adequate supplies of meat thousands of years before the arrival of Spanish explorers in the sixteenth century.

Some evidence suggests that bison were scarce or even absent on the Plains between 5000 BC and 3000 BC, and again between AD 500 and AD 1300. This evidence may simply reflect gaps in the archaeological record, however, rather than the absence of bison. Furthermore, most of this evidence is derived from the southern edge of the Plains, and could be explained by the movement of major herds. In any event, any local shortage of bison would have prompted an exodus from the region, since the native plant foods of the Plains were not diverse enough to support people through the range of seasons.

The Archaic tradition continued into the final centuries of the pre-Christian era, giving rise to a number of locally distinct cultures. Pottery-making was introduced to the Plains, as was mound-building. Sites of the Plains Woodland

TOM MCHUGH/PHOTO RESEARCHERS, INC.

Decorative bison painted on an Arikara (Plains Indian) buffalo hide shield. Such shields were the most sacred possession of Plains warriors.

Painted between 1832 and 1833, this famous work by George Catlin, entitled *Buffalo Hunt under the Wolf-skin Mask*, shows how Plains hunters disguised in wolfskins stalked individual bison. Being accustomed to wolves, the animals took little notice as the hunters crept to within bowshot.

NATIONAL MUSEUM OF AMERICAN ART/ART RESOURCE

THE GRANGER COLLECTION

Indians Hunting the Bison by Karl Bodmer (1844). The arrival of the horse with the Spanish in the seventeenth century revolutionized bison hunting on the Plains, making it possible for hunters to overtake running herds and to kill animals at close range.

A Sioux war shield depicting warriors in battle, both mounted and on foot. Such shields were generally made from the hump of a buffalo, and provided Plains warriors with effective protection over many centuries. They fell into disuse with the introduction of the Winchester, whose bullets could penetrate the tough hide. Lighter-weight shields were made for ceremonial use.
C.M. DIXON

tradition (250 BC to AD 950) are scattered from Oklahoma and Texas to North Dakota, diminishing westwards towards the Rocky Mountains.

It seems likely that these communities subsisted by hunting and gathering along creeks and in valleys. Bone refuse suggests that deer and small mammals were more important than bison in the central Plains (although bison hunting remained important to the north and west). There is evidence that the Hopewellian communities near Kansas City, and possibly in Nebraska, cultivated maize in this period.

In the eastern Plains (from North Dakota to northern Texas) and the western Plains (from Montana to New Mexico), agricultural communities known as the Plains Village tradition (AD 900 to AD 1850) developed. Several variations on this single tradition emerged over much of the Plains between the ninth and eleventh centuries. More sedentary societies developed in eastern South Dakota (and adjoining areas), western Missouri, and eastern Nebraska. Smaller, semi-settled village groups lived in south-central Nebraska and north-central Kansas.

These Plains Village communities shared a number of characteristics. All groups depended on maize and other tropical cultigens (cultivated plants) to a significant extent. They worked the rich, alluvial soils of the Missouri and its tributaries with hoes made of bison shoulder blades. In the eastern Plains, native plant foods and animals (including bison) formed a major part of the diet. Bison became more important in the central and western Plains, a drought-prone area where agriculture was hazardous. As the boundary between long-grass and short-grass prairie shifted eastwards, the bison herds expanded.

Many of these eastern Plains villages were fortified to protect several hundred people. Most sites show evidence of permanent lodges, each occupied by a number of families. These earthen lodges were generally larger and more substantial than the wooden houses of the Woodland peoples, and were occupied throughout most of the year. Dry moats and stockades protected the villages, and there were a number of underground storage pits inside the houses. Groups in the Dakotas built rectangular structures, whereas those in the central Plains lived in smaller houses with four center-post supports. In the west, Plains groups interacted with the Pueblo peoples of the Southwest, and adopted some of their practices. (See the feature *Hunter–Farmer Relationships.*)

Spanish explorers introduced horses to the Plains from the American Southwest towards the end of the seventeenth century. With horses, Plains Indians became much more mobile—a great advantage when hunting bison. But the horse also brought with it new forms of warfare, and the practice of horse-thieving. Not long afterwards, firearms reached the Plains from the east, leading to a progressive migration of some Eastern Woodland groups onto the Plains. Some groups, such as the Omaha, adopted the Plains Village agricultural way of life. Other groups, such as the Sioux, became completely mobile societies, relying entirely on bison hunting and raiding. This way of life was short-lived, however, because the bison herds were progressively driven close to extinction. Many of the village tribes retained their traditional agricultural practices into the eighteenth and nineteenth centuries, only to be gradually undermined by European and indigenous diseases, trade, war, and treaties.

SOME LESSONS FROM THE HUMAN PAST

Smaller-scale human societies—both modern and prehistoric—hardly live up to the romantic images of popular literature; nor are they as "affluent" as the anthropologists of the 1960s led us to believe. Hunger has clearly been at least a seasonal problem for many historic and contemporary groups, and starvation not unknown. Contemporary hunter-gatherers appear to be chronically lean, and occasionally hungry. They take in few kilojoules (calories), partly because most wild foods—both plant and animal—are sparse, and partly because their foods are high in bulk but low in energy value (in contrast to modern-day processed foods). Because they have to compete for living space with more powerful neighbors, contemporary small-scale societies also tend to inhabit impoverished and/or isolated areas.

These realities, however, do not overshadow one fact: there is simply no evidence to show that the development of agricultural technology has reduced the risk of starvation. Every agricultural strategy that attempts to reduce or eliminate food crises generates not only benefits but also costs and risks.

Small-scale cultivation may help to reduce the risk of seasonal hunger; cultivation and protection of plants may reduce the risk of crop failure; food storage may help to protect people against seasonal shortages or crop failure. Each advantage, however, is outweighed by the greater vulnerability of domestic crops to climatic fluctuation and other natural hazards—a vulnerability enhanced by the specialized nature and narrow focus of many agricultural systems. The advantages are also offset by the loss of mobility, the limits and possible failure of primitive storage systems, and the vulnerability of settled communities to political expropriation of their stored food. Although agricultural technology does increase the total amount of available food, there is no evidence that the evolution of a settled, agricultural way of life improves the reliability of the human food supply.

The same is true of infectious diseases. Prehistoric hunter-gatherers were visited by fewer infections and suffered lower overall rates of disease than most other world populations. Moreover, the relatively good nutrition of hunter-gatherers may have buttressed them against those infections they did encounter. Further, if we leave aside the high life expectancies of mid-twentieth-century affluence made possible by the biomedical revolution, it becomes clear that the adoption of agriculture and a sedentary way of life did not increase adult life expectancy. In fact, there is some evidence that it shortened it.

We must rethink both scholarly and popular ideas relating to human progress. We have built our images of human history too exclusively upon the experiences of privileged societies. We must revise our notion that "civilization" represents progress in human wellbeing.

MUSEUM FÜR VÖLKERKUNDE, BERLIN/WERNER FORMAN ARCHIVE

A painted buffalo skull in the Arapaho or Blackfeet style. Decorated buffalo skulls were sometimes used as a central feature of sacred areas associated with various spiritual practices. They were also decorated and piled up in rock shrines made to attract bison herds. The Blackfeet occasionally decorated their sweat houses with a buffalo skull painted with red spots on one side and black on the other; sagebrush was thrust in the nose and eye sockets.

CONSTANTINE MANOS/MAGNUM

Before the arrival of Europeans, maize was the most popular indigenous plant in the Americas, and was critical to daily subsistence and the ceremonial life of native America. Recent research into bone chemistry, however, has shown that a diet based on maize has a decided downside, leading to severe nutritional deficiencies. When it is eaten exclusively or forms a very high proportion of the diet, maize can result in diseases such as anemia and pellagra.

HUNTER–FARMER RELATIONSHIPS

Katherine A. Spielmann

Hunter-gatherers have shared the world with farmers since plants were domesticated about 10,000 years ago. Today, the vast majority of hunter-gatherer populations exist within, and depend on, more powerful, agricultural societies. Modern-day hunter-gatherers often provide animal and forest products and/or labor in return for agricultural produce and manufactured goods. Both their subsistence activities and their settlement systems are usually constrained by agricultural populations. If we look backward in time several thousand years, however, we see that interactions between hunters and farmers were dramatically different. Relationships were more balanced, being voluntary rather than based on coercion.

THE GRANGER COLLECTION

An Assiniboin camp scene painted by Karl Bodmer in 1844. These equestrian hunters followed bison herds across the northern Plains, living in bison-skin tepees.

Although hunter-gatherers and farmers have been in contact with one another for thousands of years, this fact has failed to influence anthropological thought until recently. It has been assumed that prehistoric hunter-gatherers and farmers were separate, independent, and self-sufficient communities, and that agricultural societies expanded in the Old and New Worlds at hunter-gatherers' expense. They either became farmers themselves or, having been displaced by farmers, were forced into remote and inhospitable areas.

Hunter–Farmer Exchange

When we look at early historical records, particularly for North America, it becomes clear that hunter-gatherer and tribal farming communities did not exist in isolation from one another. In fact, there are numerous cases in which they developed very strong economic, social, and religious ties. During the eighteenth century, for example, Cheyenne, Assiniboin, Cree, and Crow hunters on the northern Plains exchanged dried bison meat, fat, hide clothing, and prairie-turnip flour for maize in the villages of Mandan, Hidatsa, and Arikara, along the Missouri River. In the Great Lakes area, seventeenth-century Algonquin hunters exchanged furs, fish, and meat with Huron farmers for maize. Items important for a community's religious ceremonies, such as tobacco and medicine bundles, were also acquired through exchange.

These exchanges usually took place at least annually, when the hunters paid lengthy visits to the farming villages. Intermarriage occasionally cemented already strong individual trade partnerships. During times of crisis, it was not unusual for one group to take refuge with the other, as the Jemez Pueblo Indians did with the Navajo during the Spanish conquest of the North American Southwest.

Mutual Dependence

These interdependent relationships are particularly interesting, because, unlike today, neither group had greater power than the other and so neither could manipulate the relationship to any great degree. Instead, two very different cultural traditions joined forces for mutual benefit.

Archaeological evidence, while not as detailed as historical documents, indicates that hunters and farmers were similarly interdependent in prehistoric times. Often, what is left for the archaeologist to find are the durable gifts, such as knives and arrowheads of exotic stone, jewelry, and ceramics. The quantities of perishable items that were traded, including food and clothing, are difficult to reconstruct from archaeological data. It is possible, however, to model the exchange of perishable items by computer simulation. For example, one can assess the ability of a farming population to produce an annual surplus of corn to trade to hunters.

Plains–Pueblo Exchange

Another example of exchange between hunters and farmers in prehistoric times is provided by the Pueblo farmers of New Mexico and the bison hunters of the southern Plains. This exchange system is mentioned in numerous Spanish documents of the sixteenth and seventeenth centuries, and has been confirmed by archaeological finds at both Plains hunter-gatherer camps and Pueblo villages.

Chroniclers of the first Spanish expeditions to the Southwest, in the

JENNY MILLS

An adobe apartment house in Taos Pueblo, New Mexico. The ladders provided access to the flat rooftops, which people used for work and play.

SCHINDLER COLLECTION, NEW YORK/WERNER FORMAN ARCHIVE

↑ The design on this Navajo rug, depicting *Yeis* (supernatural beings) flanking a ripening maize plant, originated in the sand paintings created during Navajo sings, or curing rituals.

mid-1500s, wrote that hunters from the Plains would arrive at the pueblos on the eastern border of the Southwest region, including Taos, Pecos, and Gran Quivira, and exchange bison meat, fat, and hides for corn, cotton blankets, and ceramics. The loads of bison products were carried to the pueblos on *travois*—conveyances consisting of baskets attached to tent poles, which were pulled along by dogs. Plains bison meat was probably an important source of meat protein for the Pueblo, as the sizeable Pueblo populations had most likely overhunted local species of large game, such as antelope and mule deer.

The hunters usually came around harvest time, and remained camped near the pueblos for several months before returning to the Plains. Pueblo corn made an important contribution to their diet, as wild sources of carbohydrate are not abundant on the southern Plains. Some of these hunters were probably ancestors of the present-day Apache.

It is thought that this exchange system developed about a century before the arrival of the Spanish. This belief is based on the presence of Pueblo ceramics dating from the mid-1400s in Plains hunter-gatherer camp sites, and of bison bone and Plains stone tools of similar and more recent age in Pueblo middens.

Evidence for overhunting has been found in excavations of rubbish middens at the pueblo of Gran Quivira, in New Mexico. Antelope, the most important local large game animal, was hunted near this pueblo in the fourteenth century. (Skeletal remains of antelope found in middens have all been dated to that century.) In the fifteenth century, however, antelopes appear to have been hunted further afield, as the bulkier parts of the carcass were not brought back to the pueblo. Moreover, during this period, there is a dramatic increase in the amount of bison bone, particularly ribs, in the middens. These bones are probably the remains of slabs of dried meat traded by Plains hunters.

Hides may have been just as valuable to the Pueblo farmers as meat. Early Spanish explorers reported that many Pueblo men, as far west as the Hopi, wore robes of bison fur during the winter. By the fifteenth century, substantial quantities of pottery, obsidian, and other craft items were exchanged across the Southwest, and bison hides no doubt formed part of this exchange system.

With the Spanish colonization of the Southwest in 1598, the Plains–Pueblo trade system changed dramatically. The Spaniards wanted to trade with the Plains hunters themselves, and were able to offer them such coveted items as horses and metal. Moreover, drought and tribute payments to the Spaniards reduced the Pueblos' ability to produce a food surplus. The relationship between the two groups never entirely disappeared, however, and some Pueblo and Apache people have strong ties to this day.

VICTORIA AND ALBERT MUSEUM, LONDON/RAINBIRD/ROBERT HARDING PICTURE LIBRARY

THE CLASH OF CULTURES

A D 6 2 0 – T H E P R E S E N T

Demographics and Deadly Quarrels

HENRY F. DOBYNS

FOR THOUSANDS OF YEARS, people from different societies have usually treated each other in one of two ways. When they focused on physical, cultural, or religious differences, they fought. When peace prevailed, they exchanged commodities, ideas, stories, dances, music, foods, and genes. Because both tendencies still operate in today's "global village", we should try to understand why human beings behave in this manner.

Basic differences in ways of life have long been the cause of clashes between peoples. Villagers and townsfolk often had to defend their water, fields, crops, and other property against roving bands with different beliefs. Irrigation farmers in the Middle East have had to defend key oases from bands of nomadic herders, who coveted their cultivated pastures and water. In the Americas, gardeners living a village life were harried by wandering bands of hunters and warriors from remote times until the late nineteenth century.

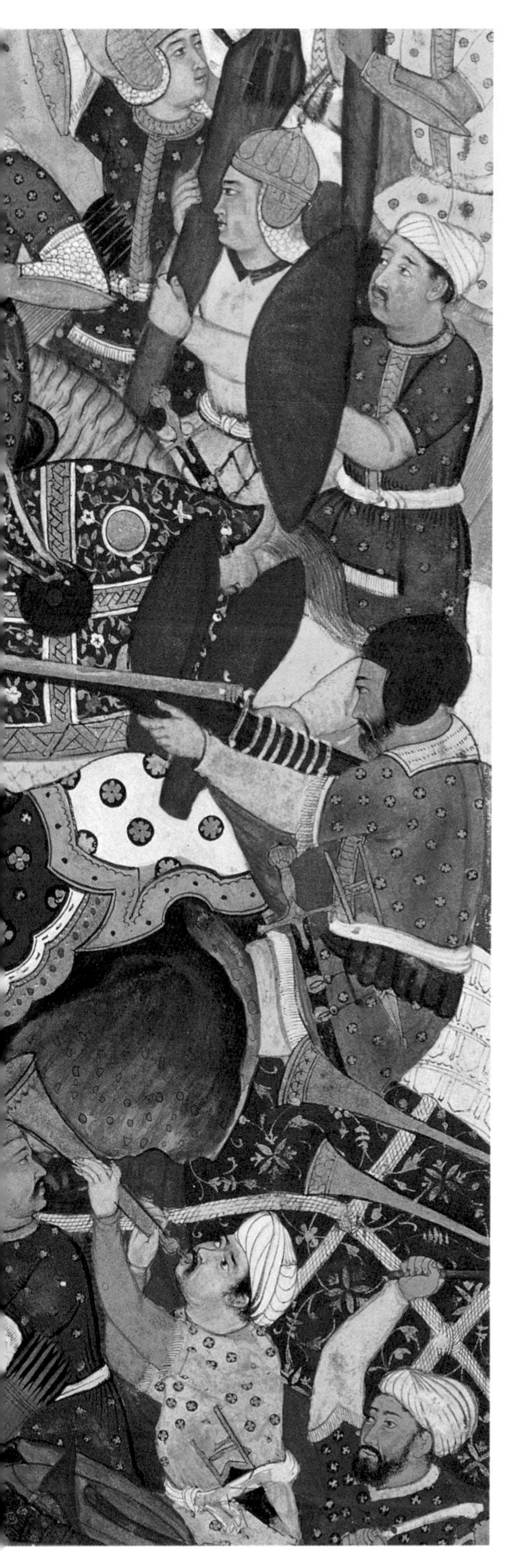

This portrayal of the capture of the ruler Bahadur Khan eloquently conveys the melee-style encounter that was typical of Near Eastern warfare in the sixteenth century. The main tactic was to try to capture the opposition's commander.

A Portuguese map of Brazil dating from 1565. Lacking knowledge of non-coastal terrain, the cartographer filled the interior with a scene depicting a native American family, one of whom is harvesting Brazilwood trees.
THE GRANGER COLLECTION

The scale of clashes between peoples of different cultures escalated about 10,000 years ago in Europe and Asia, and 5,000 years ago in the Americas. Aggressive marauders forced peaceful farmers and gardeners to yield their small surplus of crops. These "warriors" eventually formed a new ruling class, and their leader became a "king". Those men who would rather fight than farm formed armies to fight other armies, and imposed state religions. In this way, a few men came to lead the many who labored to produce food. The ancient Sumerians, Egyptians, Asian Indians, Chinese, Maya, Aztecs, Inka, Greeks, and Romans took this structure of society for granted for thousands of years.

For perhaps as long as armies have existed, disease has played a decisive role in human conflicts. Because early armies were quite evenly matched militarily, wars typically ended in a draw. From time to time, an infectious organism evolved in one society. Once the people of that society had gained immunity to the disease it carried, they had a military advantage over enemies who had not yet been exposed to it. The spread of fatal diseases helped the immune to conquer the non-immune and to annex their territory. (See the feature *The Spread of Infectious Diseases*.)

⇧ A colored line drawing of a Southwest Asian mounted archer dating from about AD 1400.
THE GRANGER COLLECTION

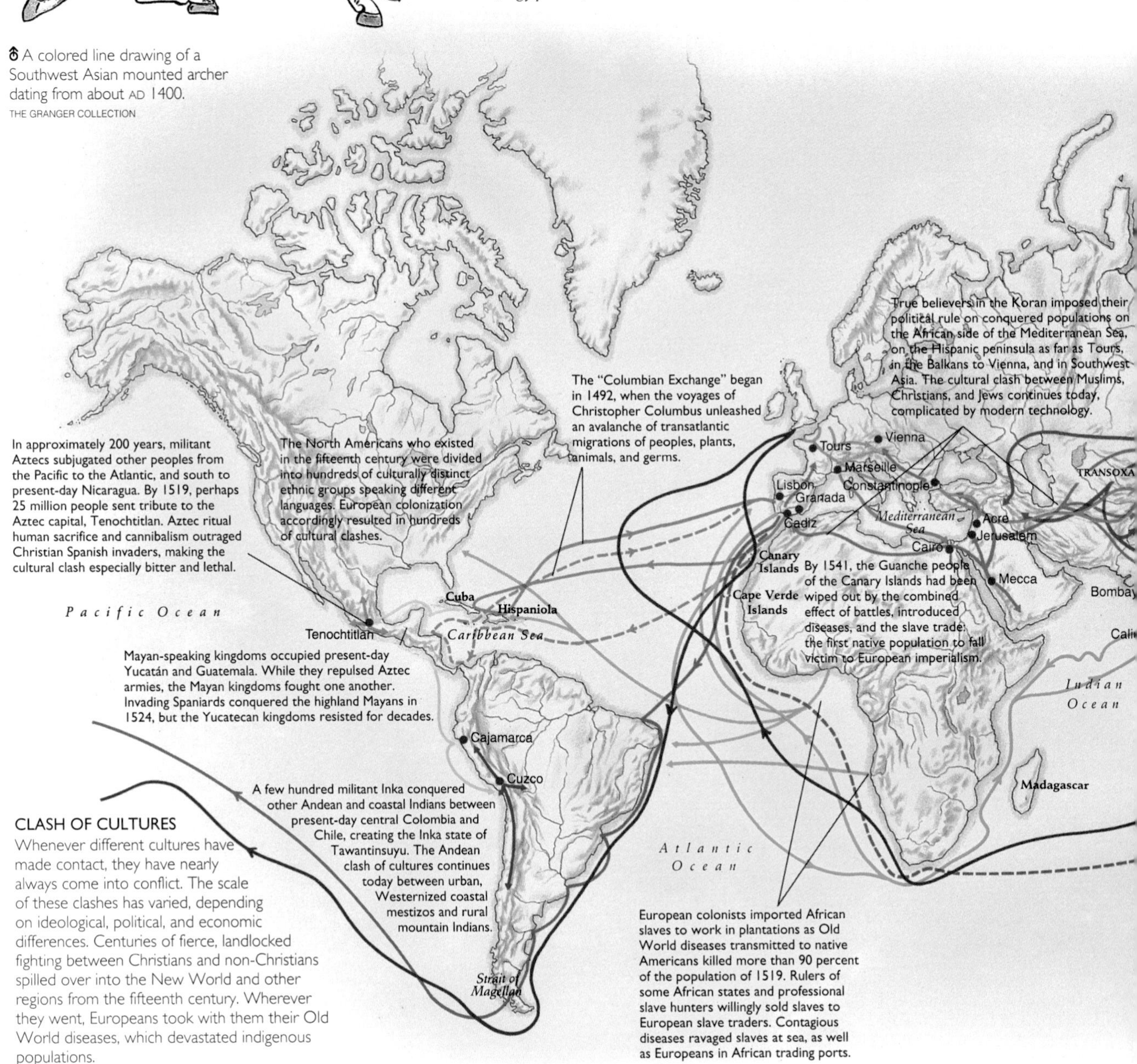

True believers in the Koran imposed their political rule on conquered populations on the African side of the Mediterranean Sea, on the Hispanic peninsula as far as Tours, in the Balkans to Vienna, and in Southwest Asia. The cultural clash between Muslims, Christians, and Jews continues today, complicated by modern technology.
The "Columbian Exchange" began in 1492, when the voyages of Christopher Columbus unleashed an avalanche of transatlantic migrations of peoples, plants, animals, and germs.
In approximately 200 years, militant Aztecs subjugated other peoples from the Pacific to the Atlantic, and south to present-day Nicaragua. By 1519, perhaps 25 million people sent tribute to the Aztec capital, Tenochtitlan. Aztec ritual human sacrifice and cannibalism outraged Christian Spanish invaders, making the cultural clash especially bitter and lethal.
The North Americans who existed in the fifteenth century were divided into hundreds of culturally distinct ethnic groups speaking different languages. European colonization accordingly resulted in hundreds of cultural clashes.
Tours
Vienna
Marseille
TRANSOXA
Lisbon
Constantinople
Granada
Cadiz
Mediterranean Sea
Acre
Jerusalem
Cairo
Canary Islands
By 1541, the Guanche people of the Canary Islands had been wiped out by the combined effect of battles, introduced diseases, and the slave trade: the first native population to fall victim to European imperialism.
Mecca
Cape Verde Islands
Bombay
Pacific Ocean
Cuba
Hispaniola
Tenochtitlan
Caribbean Sea
Cali
Mayan-speaking kingdoms occupied present-day Yucatán and Guatemala. While they repulsed Aztec armies, the Mayan kingdoms fought one another. Invading Spaniards conquered the highland Mayans in 1524, but the Yucatecan kingdoms resisted for decades.
Indian Ocean
Cajamarca
Cuzco
Madagascar
A few hundred militant Inka conquered other Andean and coastal Indians between present-day central Colombia and Chile, creating the Inka state of Tawantinsuyu. The Andean clash of cultures continues today between urban, Westernized coastal mestizos and rural mountain Indians.
Atlantic Ocean
European colonists imported African slaves to work in plantations as Old World diseases transmitted to native Americans killed more than 90 percent of the population of 1519. Rulers of some African states and professional slave hunters willingly sold slaves to European slave traders. Contagious diseases ravaged slaves at sea, as well as Europeans in African trading ports.
Strait of Magellan

CLASH OF CULTURES
Whenever different cultures have made contact, they have nearly always come into conflict. The scale of these clashes has varied, depending on ideological, political, and economic differences. Centuries of fierce, landlocked fighting between Christians and non-Christians spilled over into the New World and other regions from the fifteenth century. Wherever they went, Europeans took with them their Old World diseases, which devastated indigenous populations.
CARTOGRAPHY: RAY SIM/

Traders also spread diseases, especially after horses were domesticated, about 3000 BC, making it possible to travel further and faster. Pilgrims journeying to and from shrines and sacred places also spread diseases. Through centuries of warfare, pilgrimage, and commerce, most Eurasian peoples came to share most of the diseases that evolved in that region. The more isolated peoples of the Americas, Australia, and the Pacific islands did not.

Spreading the Word of God

The scale of clashes between different cultures increased dramatically once religious prophets or priests began to use force in the cause of spreading a specific belief system. The Islamic

VICTORIA AND ALBERT MUSEUM, LONDON/WERNER FORMAN ARCHIVE

The British pushed northwards from Calcutta during the seventeenth century, largely through the initiatives of the British East India Company. Here, an officer of the company rides in procession on an elephant.

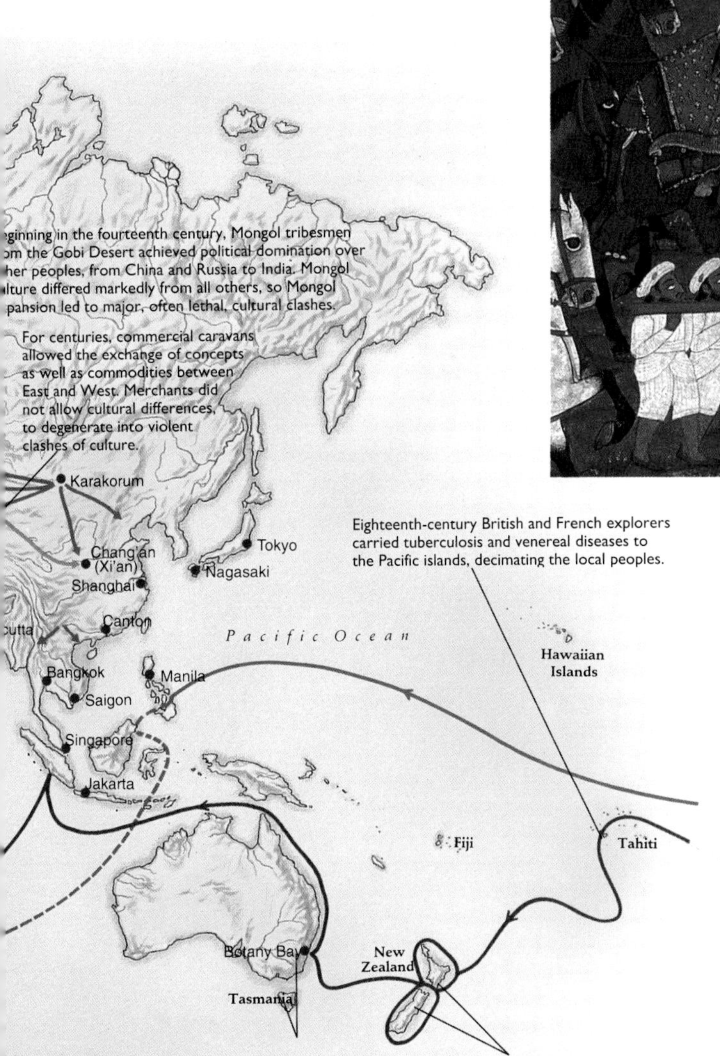

ginning in the fourteenth century, Mongol tribesmen
om the Gobi Desert achieved political domination over
her peoples, from China and Russia to India. Mongol
lture differed markedly from all others, so Mongol
pansion led to major, often lethal, cultural clashes.
For centuries, commercial caravans allowed the exchange of concepts as well as commodities between East and West. Merchants did not allow cultural differences to degenerate into violent clashes of culture.
Karakorum
Chang'an (Xi'an)
Shanghai
Tokyo
Nagasaki
Canton
Bangkok
Manila
Saigon
Singapore
Jakarta
Pacific Ocean
Eighteenth-century British and French explorers carried tuberculosis and venereal diseases to the Pacific islands, decimating the local peoples.
Hawaiian Islands
Fiji
Tahiti
Botany Bay
Tasmania
New Zealand
Aborigines across the continent shared a remarkably similar cultural pattern, and were ill prepared to resist militant European invaders. Nor were they immune to Old World diseases, which killed millions. The introduction of European domestic animals changed the very environment in which Aborigines lived.
Having colonized New Zealand in canoes, the Maori flourished there until Europeans invaded early in the nineteenth century. As Old World diseases depleted their numbers, the Maori military tradition betrayed them into trying to defeat invaders in battle with inferior weapons.
Islamic expansion
First Crusade AD 1095 – AD 1099
Mongol expansion
Caravan trading routes
Aztec empire
Inka empire
Slave trade
Christopher Columbus
First voyage AD 1492 – AD 1493
Fourth voyage AD 1502 – AD 1504
Vasco da Gama AD 1497 – AD 1498
Hernán Cortéz AD 1518 – AD 1519
Ferdinand Magellan AD 1519 – AD 1522
Juan S. del Cano AD 1522
Francisco Pizarro AD 1531 – AD 1532
James Cook AD 1768 – AD 1771
Napoleon Bonaparte AD 1798

THE CLASH OF CULTURES: AD 620 – AD 1945

	EUROPE AND ASIA	THE AMERICAS AND THE PACIFIC	THE ATLANTIC AND AFRICA
1945	Japan surrenders to end Second World War 1945		
	First World War ends 1918		
	Suez Canal opens 1869	Smallpox ravages Australian Aborigines 1829	Christian missionaries penetrate Africa 1800s
	US Navy forces Japan to trade with West 1854	Missionaries colonize New Zealand 1814	
	Britain–China Opium War 1839 – 1842		
1800	Napoleon occupies Egypt 1798	Smallpox ravages Australian Aborigines 1789	
	China expels Christian missionaries 1724	Smallpox ravages native North Americans 1779 – 1781	
	British East India Company authorized to wage war 1661	Smallpox decimates Pacific peoples 1770	
	Japan outlaws Christianity 1606 – 1613	Europeans discover Australia, New Zealand, Hawaiian islands 1769	
		Europeans discover Tahiti 1767	
	European ships reach Japan 1543	Yellow fever introduced to the Americas 1647	
	Portuguese reach Canton 1517	Plague kills native Americans 1545 – 1548	Canary Island natives become extinct 1541
	Portuguese reach India 1498	Spanish conquer Inka, aided by measles and smallpox 1532	Smallpox transmitted to Caribbean island natives 1518
	Muslims expelled from Iberian peninsula 1492	Measles halves New Spain's native population 1531	European ships begin to call at African coastal trading ports; beginning of trade in goods and slaves 1505
	Muslims capture Christian Constantinople 1453	Spanish conquer Maya, aided by smallpox 1524	European Christian assault on Africa halted by African diseases 1500s
	Muslims recapture Acre; last Crusade 1291	Spanish conquer Aztecs, aided by smallpox 1519 – 1520	Portuguese colonize Cape Verde Islands 1460
	Mongols destroy Baghdad 1258	Spanish begin to colonize the Americas 1493	French and Spanish begin Canary Islands conquest; beginning of modern European imperialism 1402
	Mongols destroy Transoxania and Eastern Persia 1220 – 1225		
	Mongols invade China 1211		
	Muslims recapture Jerusalem 1187		
	Chinese defeat Muslim ruler of Persia 1141		
	Crusaders capture Jerusalem from Muslims 1099		
	Crusaders decimated by local diseases 1098		
	First Crusade begins 1095		
1000	Muslims occupy the Punjab 1004		
	Chinese massacre Muslims at Canton 879		
	Sunni Muslim caliph begins persecution of Shiites and non-Muslims 847		
	Muslim naval dominance of the Mediterranean 827		
620	Prophecies of Mohammed 622 – 630		

prophet Mohammed fundamentally altered the course of human affairs in just this way between AD 622 and AD 630. Within 75 years, Islamic armies had conquered the lands along the eastern and southern shores of the Mediterranean Sea, the Iberian peninsula, and the Middle East. Traveling along ancient caravan trading routes, they penetrated Iraq, Iran, and Transoxania, reaching the borders of India and China.

Initially, the clash between Islam and native cultures was minimal. When Islamic forces captured Jerusalem, they guaranteed the inhabitants' lives, property, freedom of religion, and access to churches. Conquered peoples had to pay taxes, however, which financed early Islamic kingdoms. Two centuries after the Prophet, a fanatical Sunni caliph made it official policy between 847 and 861 to persecute Shiites, Jews, and Christians, all of whom had previously been tolerated.

Having seized naval command of the Mediterranean by 827, the Muslims destroyed Europe's profitable trade with the East. Thus, economic as well as ideological factors underlay the violent clash between Muslims and Christians. The Islamic invasion of Europe prompted Christians to give expression to a growing religious intolerance in the defense of their territory. The Muslims, on the other hand, provided Europeans with an example of religious tolerance, along with such cultural and technological advances as large libraries, universities, paved and lighted streets, rice, fruits from western Asia, and canal irrigation.

European Christians pursued two strategies to regain ground from Islam. The "local strategy" was for small kingdoms to battle onwards, almost meter by meter, in an effort to recover lost land. The Christians reclaimed the entire Iberian peninsula between 733 and 1492, when the last Islamic ruler, Mohammad XI (Boabdil), surrendered Granada and retreated to North Africa. The "grand strategy" was to try to reconquer the Christian Holy Land of Palestine. Pope Urban II launched the First Crusade in 1095, and in 1099, Jerusalem, the shrine-city of Christendom, was captured.

Ultimately, the Crusades failed, owing to the hostile environment. The local population harbored diseases, including strains of malaria, to which Europeans were not immune. Crusaders perished from local epidemic and endemic diseases faster than they could be replaced. Even the kingdom of Jerusalem had a peak population of only 100,000. Elsewhere, the Crusaders formed small enclaves within fortified towns or castles. The Muslims recaptured Jerusalem in 1187, after its able young Crusader king, Baldwin IV, died from leprosy. The last Crusade ended when the Muslims recaptured Acre (now Akko) in 1291.

A fifteenth-century drawing showing Christian Crusaders, led by Louis IX, disembarking at Damietta (now Dumyāt), on the sea coast of the Nile delta, on 5 June 1249.

MUSEE CONDE, CHANTILLY/E.T. ARCHIVE/ AUSTRALIAN PICTURE LIBRARY

MUSEUM VOOR SCHONE KUNSTEN/SCALA

MUSEUM OF CATALAN ART, BARCELONA/WERNER FORMAN ARCHIVE

A detail from the fresco known as *The Conquest of Mallorca*, by an unknown Arab artist. Mounted, lightly armored Moors are shown riding under flags of the kind that designated local militia units within Muslim armies.

This painting of the Muslim siege of Jerusalem in 1187 presents an idealized image of sacred architecture, while portraying Muslims as villains. The strong defensive wall that protected Jerusalem for centuries was much thicker than that shown here.

❦ Navigators, astronomers, and astrologers used a range of observation instruments to compute position, direction, and time. This astrolobe, based on a Moorish design, was probably crafted in France in the fourteenth century.

NATIONAL MARITIME MUSEUM, GREENWICH/ WERNER FORMAN ARCHIVE

The Crusaders did learn some lessons from their exploits, which brought about major changes. A Crusader bishop wrote in 1218, for example, that the compass was a necessity for sea voyagers. Having learned on their Chinese frontier how to make paper, the Muslims later passed on the technique to Europeans. Crusaders also returned home with a taste for refined cane sugar, a product previously unknown in Europe.

From Islam's eastern frontier, seafarers crossed the Indian Ocean to trade at Canton (present-day Guangzhou), until the Chinese massacred Canton's Muslims in 879. Nearly 300 years later, in 1141, a refugee from a fallen Chinese dynasty defeated Persia's Islamic ruler. That setback opened the way for Turks and Mongols, who drove both Muslims and Christians westwards for 500 years.

The geographic scale of cultural clashes expanded again when Iberian ships ventured into the Atlantic Ocean. In 1402, French and Spanish adventurers began the conquest of the Guanche people of the Canary Islands. They and their successors tested the techniques and technology of subduing native peoples that Europeans later employed throughout the Americas and the Pacific islands. In the process, the Guanches became the first native people to be exterminated by modern imperialism, having been wiped out by 1541.

The invaders killed the Guanches in battle, infected them with Old World diseases to which they had no resistance, and shipped off large numbers to slavery in Europe. Women were kept as concubines and converted to Christianity. An epidemic in 1495 proved particularly lethal, and the conquest was completed in 1496.

Different peoples have distinctive cultural views as to what constitutes a proper environment. Europeans prefer to see familiar plants and animals wherever they are. So they burned the Canary Islands forests and introduced rabbits, which multiplied until they consumed nearly every native plant that remained. A European entrepreneur started a sugar cane plantation on Gran Canaria in 1484. Drastic ecological changes are typical of the islands Europeans have invaded, because native people, animals, and plants are left with no places of refuge.

Prince Henry the Navigator of Portugal brought the modern world closer when he launched a systematic exploration of the western, Atlantic coast of Africa in the 1420s and 1430s. Portugal colonized the Cape Verde Islands in 1460, and Fernando Bioko and São Tomé in the 1470s. In 1487, Bartholomeu Dias sailed south to modern-day Namibia. Rounding the Cape of Good Hope in 1497, Vasco da Gama sailed on to India the following year, using his ship's cannons to establish a beachhead and to open trade.

Between 1519 and 1522, Spain's Ferdinand Magellan (who died in 1521) and Juan S. del Cano circumnavigated the globe via the Straits of

THE GRANGER COLLECTION

❦ This colored line engraving by a European artist, made about 1585, depicts Ferdinand Magellan, in 1520, sailing through the narrow, cold, windy strait later named after him. The fanciful figures may be viewed as allegories for the strait's treacherous currents.

CHATEAU, VERSAILLES/GIRAUDON

Magellan, Guam, the Philippines, India, and the Cape of Good Hope. European Christians had outflanked the Islamic powers they had failed to defeat on land by sailing around them. The caravan trade that had carried precious commodities between Europe and the East died.

Christians and Muslims skirmished for centuries on the shores of the Mediterranean Sea. Then, the intellectual and military ferment unleashed by the French Revolution led to direct European intervention in the Arab world. In 1798, Napoleon's army easily occupied Egypt, shattering Islam's historic belief in its unchallengeable superiority over Western infidels.

Technological changes altered Islamic as well as Western economics and politics. In 1822, Egypt established the Arab world's first Muslim printing press. Construction of the first railroad in Egypt began in 1851. By 1914, almost 5,000 kilometers (3,000 miles) of track had been laid. The opening of the Suez Canal late in 1869 attracted steamships to Egyptian ports. As freight rates fell, government policies encouraged Nile Valley farmers to grow cotton and sugar cane for export to industrial nations. American maize became Egypt's staple food crop, fueling population growth. Two world wars and yet more technological changes completely shattered traditional Islamic economic structures.

Expansion into Africa

As they outflanked the Islamic peoples, European ships encountered many peoples who were neither Christian nor Muslim. Christians promptly labeled these newly contacted peoples "heathens". Christian dogma held that heathens, like Muslims, were subject to conquest by "just war". The Age of Discovery in the sixteenth century set the world stage for a European effort to convert many heathens to Christianity by force of arms and/or missionary persuasion. Sailing ships equipped with compasses and cannons enabled Europeans to dominate politically divided native peoples living on sea coasts all around the globe.

The diseases that defeated the Crusaders greatly handicapped European Christians in their assault on other Old World societies. Sub-Saharan Africans not only shared most of the diseases Europeans carried, but also had some lethal ones of their own. Dengue, yellow fever, and a virulent strain of malaria made African ports particularly deadly places for Europeans, who usually settled for profitable business arrangements with the rulers of small African coastal states. European ships called at coastal ports to load gold, ivory, and slaves (initially prisoners-of-war) supplied by native rulers. English ships soon entered the trade and expanded it. Africa exported an average of 2,800 slaves annually after 1570, 7,000 after 1603, 15,000 after 1648, and 24,000 after 1670.

Napoleon Bonaparte disembarked his French expedition at Adjmir, in Egypt, on 1 July 1798, and occupied Alexandria the following day. On 13 July, French forces engaged Mameluke cavalry, and on 21 July, Napoleon assembled his infantrymen into square formations and French firepower repulsed the charges of the renowned Mameluke cavalry. Napoleon's French troops won a decisive victory over the Mamelukes, and rapidly went on to establish their domination over the whole of Egypt.

THE SPREAD OF INFECTIOUS DISEASES

Ann F. Ramenofsky

In the late nineteenth century, Europeans justified their expansion beyond continental Europe by Social Darwinist ideas of the "survival of the fittest". Because Europeans viewed themselves as the fittest, it was only natural for them to dominate native populations across the globe. In the late twentieth century, such a simplistic account of the spread and success of European culture is neither accepted nor acceptable.

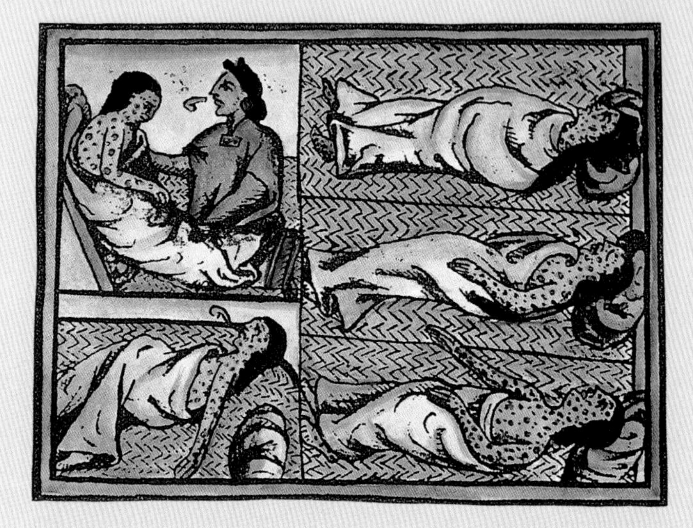

In this sixteenth-century illustration, a medicine man ministers to Aztec Indians infected by smallpox, the deadly legacy of the Spanish invaders.
THE GRANGER COLLECTION

Although there was no single cause of Europeans' success in continents outside Europe, the spread of contagious diseases looms large in contemporary thinking on the issue. Why is this? How do we know that such common childhood diseases as mumps, measles, influenza, and pneumonia contributed to European success?

Epidemic diseases were the constant companions of European explorers and settlers. Wherever Europeans ventured, they carried their parasites as baggage. Consequently, diseases spread whenever Europeans came into contact with native peoples. The result of such contact in one setting was likely to be repeated in others. In 1519, for instance, the Spaniard Hernán Cortéz invaded central Mexico. Even though his force was outnumbered by the Aztecs, the Spaniards prevailed, and the Aztec capital of Tenochtitlan–Tlatelolco came under Spanish control. This was because a microbial, as well as a physical, invasion had taken place. As Cortéz's army invaded the capital, smallpox brought illness and death to the Aztecs.

Hosts and Parasites

The interaction between a parasite and its host is the key to understanding the lethal power of an infectious disease. A microbe is a parasite that seeks to invade a human cell. If the predator cell is successful, the host body will start producing new generations of microbes, and the person may die as a result. If the parasite is repelled, it must either find another victim or die itself.

THE GRANGER COLLECTION

A scene from the Lienzo de Tlaxcala canvas showing Hernán Cortéz and a band of Tlaxcaltecs marching to Tenochtitlan in 1519.

Biochemical immunity boosts the host's chances of repelling a foreign infectious microbe, but this capacity is not always present. Immunity can take one of two forms: it can be active and long-term, developing through previous exposure to, and recovery from, a foreign parasite; or passive and short-term, when an infant obtains a mother's antibodies through breastfeeding. In the case of an infectious disease, the likelihood of developing resistance increases with the frequency of exposure, and with illness and recovery.

The Rise of Epidemic Diseases

With the exception of malaria and yellow fever, most epidemic diseases, including measles, diphtheria, and influenza, originated in Europe or western Asia. Two factors appear to have been essential to this development: the concentration of people in towns or cities, and the presence of herd animals. From the evidence of ovine tuberculosis, bubonic plague, and smallpox, it seems likely that animals were the reservoir of the parasites that spread to humans. We know from the archaeological record that people in western Asia began domesticating herd animals some 8,000 years ago. By 3000 BC, a great many people were living in cities, along with their herd animals. Not surprisingly, descriptions of outbreaks of epidemic diseases appear in cuneiform texts shortly after that date.

The association of large groups of people and herd animals is unique to Eurasia, making the evolution of the major epidemic killers unique to that region. In the Americas, for example, the conditions favorable to the evolution of epidemic diseases were not present. Native populations built cities, but most of the indigenous herd animals had died out at the end of the Pleistocene era—thousands of years before cities evolved. Although other animals had been domesticated by the time Europeans arrived—Muscovy ducks, llamas, and guinea pigs, for

BRITISH MUSEUM/WERNER FORMAN ARCHIVE

The importance of domesticated animals is reflected in this detail from the Standard of Ur, a mosaic from the Sumerian city of Ur, in southern Mesopotamia. Made of lapis lazuli, shell, stones, and mother-of-pearl, this famous mosaic dates from 2500 BC.

example—they were species that were relatively free of diseases.

Epidemic syphilis is the only known infectious disease whose evolution cannot be accounted for in this way. Although older work attributed the origin of this deadly disease to native peoples of the Americas, recent work has reversed that thinking. Epidemic syphilis is one of a group of diseases, including yaws, pinta, and endemic syphilis, caused by the organism treponema. Because treponemal diseases were present in both the New and Old Worlds before 1492, it is likely that epidemic syphilis is a new form of the disease that evolved from the merging of the previously separate forms. Neither Europeans nor native Americans had any immunity to this treponemal form, and both groups were ravaged by it.

Disease and Conquest

Mass death has occurred throughout human history and prehistory whenever Europeans carried a foreign infectious parasite to a population that represented virgin soil. Although archaeologists and historians are still unraveling the complexities of the spread of global diseases, there can be no question that Europeans introduced numerous infectious parasites to native peoples of the Americas and the Pacific Basin. The consequences were nothing short of catastrophic. With native deaths came loss of cultural traditions, which Europeans then rapidly replaced with their own.

It is clear that any consideration of the Social Darwinist account of history must be tempered by the insights we have gained from the modern study of epidemiology. Without such knowledge, it is all too easy to confuse differences in immunity with differences in human abilities, leading to false perceptions of racial superiority.

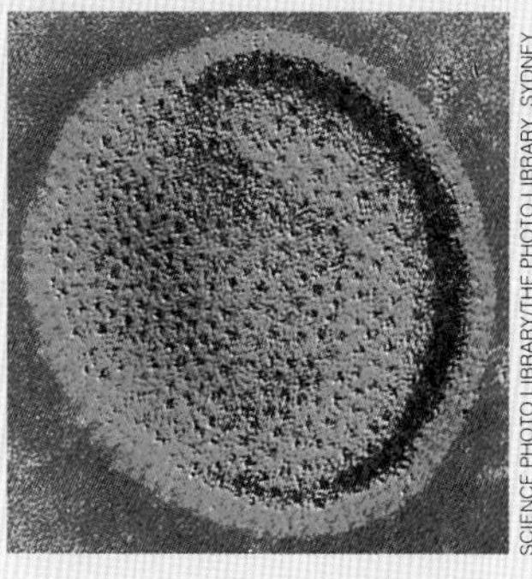

SCIENCE PHOTO LIBRARY/THE PHOTO LIBRARY, SYDNEY

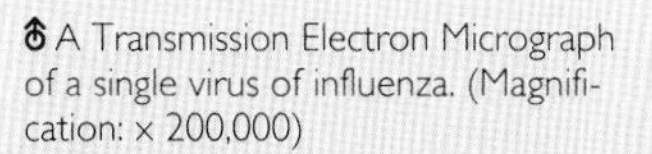

A Transmission Electron Micrograph of a single virus of influenza. (Magnification: × 200,000)

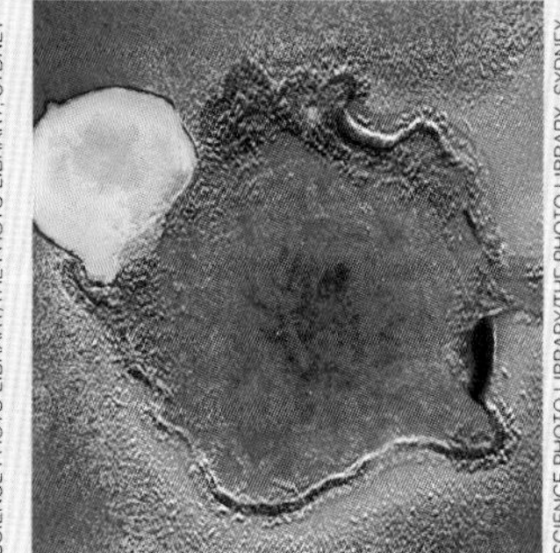

SCIENCE PHOTO LIBRARY/THE PHOTO LIBRARY, SYDNEY

A Transmission Electron Micrograph (TEM) of a single virus particle, or virion, of measles in the process of replicating. (Magnification: × 35,000)

SCIENCE PHOTO LIBRARY/THE PHOTO LIBRARY, SYDNEY

Numerous virions of the polio virus, which causes severe disability in humans. (Magnification: × 7,500)

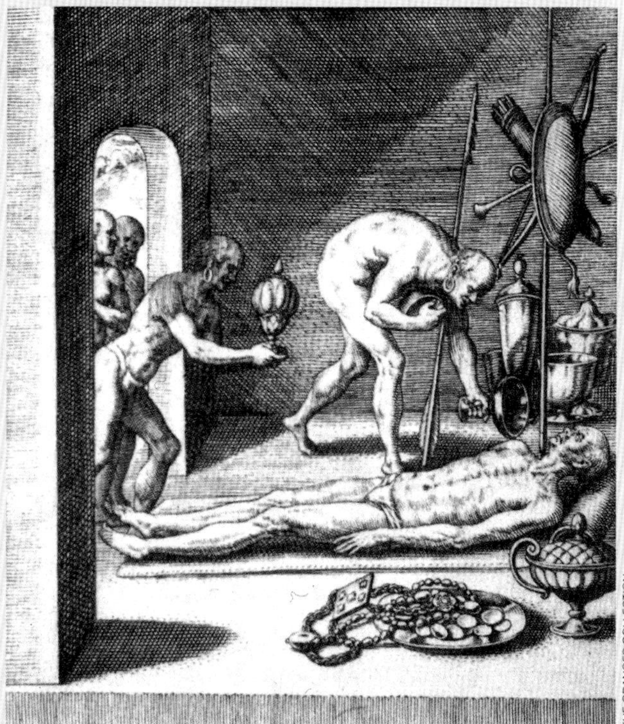

THE GRANGER COLLECTION

A detail from an etching made in 1590 by the Flemish engraver Theodor de Bry, depicting the burial rites of native Americans who died from smallpox.

MUSEO D'ARTE, SAO PAULO/GIRAUDON

An artist's portrayal of a plantation overseer giving orders to heavily burdened native slaves.

Traders probably first planted maize in Africa to provide a supply of easily preserved food to feed slaves during voyages to the Americas. Maize and manioc (cassava) later spread over most of the continent as staple foods. Europeans did not at first attempt to reach the healthier African highlands, which were already densely populated. During the sixteenth century, powerful native kingdoms blocked the way. Christian missionaries led the nineteenth-century European penetration of these areas, increasing sectarian divisions as they made converts. Some African prophets added to the divisiveness by founding new sects that combined Christian ideas with native ones.

But Europe never managed to export enough colonists to the African uplands to create anything more than immigrant enclaves surrounded by far more numerous natives. Consequently, colonial domination of most African peoples ended soon after the Second World War. Populations made up of peoples of different cultures, together with a history of disunity, have kept postcolonial nations in Africa fragile, and unable to prevent periodic violent clashes.

India and the Orient

Europeans fared somewhat better along the densely populated coasts of India, Malaysia, Indonesia, China, and Japan than they did in Africa. Like Africans, however, Asian peoples shared many diseases with Europeans but harbored others, including dysenteries and poxes, to which Europeans were not immune. Spread by Hindu pilgrims, cholera became a significant barrier to European colonization.

This example of Indonesian artistry in batik cloth was made in Java about 1920 for export to the Netherlands. The panel depicts a state coach riding in procession.

PRIVATE COLLECTION PRAGUE/ WERNER FORMAN ARCHIVE

Sixteenth-century Europeans therefore decided to establish only coastal "ports of trade". Some Eastern rulers welcomed trade with Europeans; warships forced others to acquiesce to trading relations. The ports of trade meanwhile grew into major cities—Calcutta, Bombay, Bangkok, Jakarta, Saigon, Manila, Singapore, Canton, Shanghai, Nagasaki, and Tokyo. Because they attracted native merchants, entrepreneurs, and increasing numbers of other natives dissatisfied with the hardships and restrictions of rural life, they grew faster than cities that offered less upward social mobility. Over time, several ports of trade came to dominate their hinterlands both commercially and culturally. The clash of cultures took on a distinctively urban–rural dimension in the populous Orient and on the Indian subcontinent, where rural societies teeming with peasants remained culturally conservative, while ports of trade changed.

When Vasco da Gama reached India in 1498, Muslims and Hindus had been in conflict for almost 500 years—since the time Muslims had occupied the Punjab, in 1004. Europeans added a new dimension to the clash of cultures in India, seeking economic profits rather than religious conversions. The Dutch East India Company, chartered in 1602, seized most of Portugal's routes and trading ports. England's East India Company then displaced the Dutch, after its new charter of 1661 authorized it to wage war and appoint governors. Expanding northwards from Calcutta, the British conquered some native rulers and negotiated protectorates over others. They fostered economic and social unification by building railroads to link various parts of the subcontinent, and by establishing a system of secular education. Hindus adapted faster to secular school instruction than did Islamic ex-rulers, soldiers, and policemen. The formally educated came to regard the uneducated with contempt, compounding the already existing cultural conflict between local communities.

Secular schools, the growth of commerce, and British social and political dominance motivated both Hindus and Muslims to learn the English language. Since numerous native languages were spoken on the subcontinent, it made sense to use English for government and trade once a single administration was in place to ensure orderly commerce. The many native languages remained significant badges of ethnic identity.

By transporting food to where it was scarce, the railroads halted famines, helped by supplies of American maize, manioc, peanuts, and sweet potatoes. So India's population grew from 120 million in 1800 to more than 500 million in 1970.

The British never migrated to India in sufficient numbers to form more than minute enclaves surrounded by native multitudes. European males sexually exploited native women, but the Anglo-Indian population was much too small to make an impact. Most Anglo-Indians worked for the railroads, taking on many characteristics of a Hindu caste.

Britain also introduced the principles and some of the practice of democratic elections contested by political parties. In 1885, Hindus founded the Indian National Congress, and in 1909, Muslims established the Muslim League. Both later sought independence, which Britain granted in 1947.

Opposite page: A European artist's Eurocentric and imaginative depiction of Vasco de Gama's arrival at the Indian port city of Calicut (now Kozhikode) in 1498. The coming of Europeans added an economic as well as a third cultural dimension to the long-standing clash of Muslim and Hindu cultures on the Indian subcontinent.

The giant British East India Company achieved naval superiority over the Chinese government during the First Opium War, which was waged from 1839 to 1842 to force China to open its ports to the profitable trade in opium. One of the results of this war was the cession of Hong Kong to Britain. This contemporary English engraving shows the company's steamship *Nemesis* destroying Chinese war junks under sail on Anson's Bay, on 7 January 1841.

Hindus and Muslims immediately went to war. Both the Congress and the League proved to be more like communal religious movements than secular political parties, and India and Pakistan emerged as new nations. Independent Pakistan has struggled to modernize, despite continued internal clashes between secularism and its Islamic heritage, authoritarian militarism, and historic Anglo-Islamic cultural synthesis.

Sailing east from India, the Portuguese reached Canton (now Guangzhou) in 1517. The inevitable conflict ensued as these European Christians came up against the civilized, Confucian Chinese, whose history of dynastic government extended back to about 2200 BC. China both benefited and suffered as a result. Chinese farmers had double-cropped 60-day rice in irrigated, terraced fields since the eleventh century. By 1570, they had begun to grow American sweet potatoes, maize, and peanuts on formerly unused fields. Now China is the world's largest sweet potato producer and the second largest producer of maize and peanuts. These foods fueled a growth in population from 100 million to 400 million between 1660 and 1900.

Dutch ships reached Canton in 1604, English ships in 1637. In 1680, China began trading with the East India Company, but it expelled Catholic missionaries in 1724, and in 1757, it restricted foreign trade to Canton. Pursuing profits, Britain fought an Opium War with China from 1839 to 1842 to force unrestricted commerce in that drug.

European ships reached feudal Japan in 1543, and missionaries followed six years later. So outraged were the Tokugawa shoguns by their activities that, between 1606 and 1613, they outlawed Christianity, finally expelling the Spaniards in 1624 and the Portuguese in 1638. American potatoes had arrived before these events, and stayed. The sweet potato became a mainstay on Okinawa and the white potato on Hokkaido, reinforcing the staple food of rice.

Japan did allow an enclave of Dutch traders to remain on an artificial island in Nagasaki Harbor. Lacking firearms in 1543, the Japanese established a coastal cannon battery in 1555 and excluded unwanted visitors until steamships replaced sailing ships. In 1854, a United States fleet menaced Tokyo Harbor until the shogunate agreed to trade with the West. Forced into the world market in 1868, Japan decided to industrialize. It has since steadily expanded its share of the market, despite a temporary setback when its venture into military colonialism from 1930 to 1945 ended in defeat.

The New World of the Americas

In the final decade of the fifteenth century, the monarchs of Castile-Aragon and England followed the example of Portugal's Prince Henry the Navigator by subsidizing sailing expeditions into the Atlantic. In 1492, Christopher Columbus, flying Castile's banner, reached the Caribbean islands.

While Europeans explored the Atlantic, warlike peoples in the central Andes and central Mexico were busy conquering their neighbors. The Andean Inka and the Mexican Aztecs forced the people they defeated to pay them economic tribute, to worship their gods, and to change their customs. These actions roused peoples on their borders to resist by consolidating their own military power. As a result, a large number of native kingdoms surrounded the two empires by the late fifteenth century. These groups had been in cultural conflict for more than a hundred years when Columbus arrived in the New World.

The many diseases that afflicted European and Asian peoples at the end of the fifteenth century had evolved since the last glacial period, after the ancestors of native Americans had crossed the Ice Age land bridge from Siberia to Alaska. Native Americans had not, therefore, been exposed to these diseases until Iberian ships crossed the Atlantic. Europeans and Asians soon carried to the Americas more than 20 diseases, which proved to be highly lethal to the native peoples.

In 1493, Columbus set sail again, this time with a fleet of 17 ships, carrying some 1,500 sailors and settlers, together with horses, cattle, sheep, goats, pigs, fruit trees, and crop seeds. Thus began in earnest the ecological invasion of the Americas, initiated by the historic first voyage of 1492: the so-called "Columbian Exchange", which proved to be very unequal.

MARY EVANS PICTURE LIBRARY

↑ Taíno Cacique Caonabó is captured by the Spanish invaders. As this drawing shows, Spanish horses played a vital role in this violent clash of cultures.

The plants the newcomers introduced included wheat for bread; barley for beer; root crops, such as onions, radishes, carrots, and beets; and lettuce, cabbages, brussels sprouts, chickpeas (garbanzo beans), melons, grapevines, dates, citrus fruits, olives, and the increasingly important sugar cane. Horses, cattle, and pigs were kept in unfenced fields and damaged native crops. Spanish sugar cane plantations transformed large areas of the landscape. As American laborers died, colonists replaced them with African slaves, who were more resistant to Old World diseases.

No inhabitant of the New World, except the guinea pig and a few plants, successfully invaded the Old World. The few American domesticated plants that did spread to the Old World—maize, potatoes, tomatoes, and manioc—became indispensable to European and African diets. Like sugar, wheat, and rice, these plant foods furthered the dietary unification of humankind.

Columbus and his companions on his second voyage unwittingly carried with them biological weapons of conquest. Perhaps the pigs and/or horses the Spaniards transported to the Caribbean island of Hispaniola carried an influenza virus that spread to the natives, who had no resistance to it. Coming from the malaria-ridden Mediterranean basin, some Spaniards carried the malarial parasite. These and other Old World diseases the Spaniards carried across the ocean ravaged the native population.

In 1496, Hispaniola's indigenous inhabitants numbered about eight million. Twenty years later, only a few thousand survived. Disease, starvation, overwork, Spanish massacres, and infanticide by native mothers unwilling to have their infants grow up under the colonial yoke had virtually destroyed the native population. A few natives paddled canoes to refuge in Cuba, but some three million Cuban natives suffered a similar fate.

THE GRANGER COLLECTION

↑ An eighteenth-century French line engraving showing black slaves working on a West Indian cotton plantation.

EXPLORER/MARY EVANS PICTURE LIBRARY

← An unknown artist's portrayal of the historic first encounter between Christopher Columbus and insular native Americans in 1492. This meeting between two worlds initiated the so-called "Columbian Exchange" of plants, animals, peoples, and diseases, irrevocably altering the course of world history.

MAIZE: GIFT OF THE NEW WORLD GODS

WENDY J. BUSTARD AND ANN F. RAMENOFSKY

On his fifteenth-century voyages to the New World, Columbus carried with him the cultivated plants of the Old World, returning with a cornucopia of indigenous and (to Europeans) exotic New World plants: papaya, guavas, avocados, pineapples, tomatoes, chilies, cocoa, and tobacco. His bounty also included the more mundane plants destined to become worldwide staples: maize, potatoes, sweet potatoes, and manioc. Almost immediately, domesticated plants from the Old and New Worlds began crisscrossing the oceans in a traffic that has resulted in the dietary unification of humankind.

The New World Staple

Maize is one of the most successful cultivars in terms of its biological development and dispersal. From its beginnings in the tropical lowlands of Mexico more than 7,000 years ago, maize (or corn) has spread across the world. Maize was the most important indigenous grain in the New World. Like wheat and rice in the Old World, it helped to build such ancient and complex civilizations as the Maya, Aztec, and Inka empires. In return, these peoples worshiped corn gods, whom they credited with bringing them this gift. Today, maize is grown in almost all types of environments throughout the world. Although this suggests that maize is easy to cultivate, it is, in fact, a crop that requires a great deal of attention and labor. Given this seeming contradiction, how are we to explain its popularity?

An illustration of a maize plant from Gerarde's *Herball* of 1597.
THE GRANGER COLLECTION

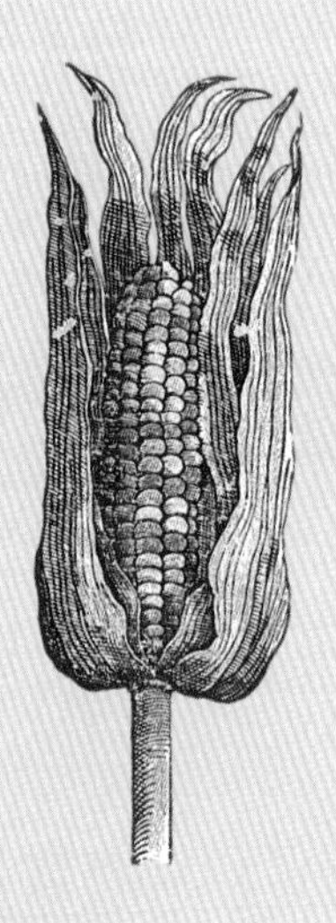

A colored woodcut of an ear of maize from Ramusio's *Navigationi et Viaggi*, published in Venice in 1556.
THE GRANGER COLLECTION

Maize has certain properties that make it a particularly useful source of food. It is an excellent source of essential nutrients, including carbohydrates, sugar, and fat. Because maize mutates very readily, farmers have been able to develop many different hybrid varieties. Maize will grow in soils that are too dry or too wet for rice or wheat, and in mountainous terrain ill-suited to the cultivation of Old World cereals. Moreover, once harvested, maize can be stored almost indefinitely. The Hopi of the American Southwest traditionally store a three-year supply of maize to guard against drought and famine. Maize is also highly productive per unit of land, and having a short growing season, it yields large quantities of food quickly. Finally, maize can be grown without the use of modern technology, making it an important food for growing populations in less industrialized nations.

Climate and Culture

The genetic adaptability of maize accounts for its rapid dispersal around the world. High productivity, ease of storage, and a high nutritional content explain its popularity. But despite its usefulness, maize is not eaten everywhere. It is not popular in England or Ireland, for instance, where, as in other northern European countries, potatoes are the preferred crop. Why have these nations resisted the appeal of maize as a staple food? The answer lies partly in climatic requirements and partly in cultural attitudes.

An Inka ceramic plate with maize cobs.
ARCHAEOLOGICAL MUSEUM, LIMA/E.T. ARCHIVE/ AUSTRALIAN PICTURE LIBRARY

While maize is grown on every continent except Antarctica, it is a tropical and temperate zone crop and so requires a certain number of frost-free days in the growing season, depending on the variety. Parts of northern Europe are simply too cold. But there seems to be a stronger, cultural factor at work, as well. The northern European reluctance to eat maize dates to the contact period. Despite the fact that European settlers in the Americas enthusiastically added maize to their diet, Europeans who stayed at home did not see the culinary virtues of so-called "Indian corn". A cultural bias associating maize with the New World and Africa apparently lay behind this.

Today, maize is more widely distributed in Africa than any other food plant and is a staple food in east and central sub-Saharan Africa.

A Madagascan boy carries a load of maize cobs on his head.
FRANS LANTING/MINDEN PICTURES

Maize was brought to the coasts of West Africa during the early half of the sixteenth century, probably by Portuguese slavers. Its productivity, coupled with its value as a source of carbohydrates, made maize very attractive as a cheap food for slaves. Thus, from the time of European contact, it was associated with both the natives of the New World and the African slaves sent there. These associations probably affected the European view of this food. An early English account complains that maize is hard to digest, a poor substitute for wheat, and more fit for pigs than people.

Despite their reluctance to eat maize themselves, Europeans grow maize as fodder for livestock. Unlike other plants, it can be fed to all types of livestock, and it has greatly enhanced meat and dairy production in Europe and the United States. In such places as Africa, the Middle East, and Asia, however, where there is no cultural bias against it, maize has increased the agricultural productivity of many nations and sustained growing human populations. Whether it is used as food for humans or livestock, maize is a gift of great importance from the Americas to the entire world.

In 1519, Hernán Cortéz led a Spanish expeditionary force to mainland Mexico. Although the Aztec emperor Moctezuma II at first sent troops to oppose the Spaniards, he later welcomed them to Tenochtitlan–Tlatelolco, his capital city. After Cortéz took the emperor captive, Aztec patriots attacked the invaders and drove them from the city. Although the patriots had won a battle, they later lost the war.

Smallpox made the difference. In 1520, a newcomer transmitted the virus to natives of the city of Cholula. From there, the virus spread like wildfire through the dense population of the American highlands, who had no resistance to it. The disease killed Moctezuma II. When Cortéz returned in 1521 and laid siege to the imperial capital, a less able and less experienced royal, Cuitláhuac, had succeeded to the Aztec throne, to lead an army and a populace halved by the epidemic. After about 80 days, he was succeeded by Cuauhtemoc.

The invaders built pinnaces—light schooners equipped with oars—which gave them an advantage over native dugout canoes on the Valley of Mexico's lakes. This was a key factor in the defeat of Tenochtitlan–Tlatelolco. Being built on an island, the city depended on canoes to ferry its supplies. The Spaniards recruited enough native allies from people alienated by Aztec domination and demands for tribute to gain the upper hand. The allies advanced along the causeways connecting the city to the lake shores behind cannons protected by wooden bulwarks. Spanish pugnacity, pinnaces, cannons, and smallpox, aided by native political divisions, produced the final collapse of Aztec resistance in Tenochtitlan–Tlatelolco, bringing an end to the once mighty empire. European Christians replaced the Aztecs as overlords, priests, and collectors of tribute from the diminished imperial population. They treated the conquered Aztecs as the latter had treated the peoples they conquered, destroying their temples, their idols, and their written records. Priests supervised the building of Roman Catholic churches on the ruins, filling them with statues and paintings of saints.

A dozen Franciscan friars initiated mass conversions in New Spain (as colonial Mexico was then called) in 1524, seven years after Martin Luther had begun the Protestant Reformation in Europe. When a native leader converted, so did his followers. In time, native leaders died or colonial rulers usurped their authority, wielding total political power. Villagers grasped a tiny measure of control over their lives by joining brotherhoods or sisterhoods that sponsored and conducted church festivals.

A detail from a seventeenth-century Spanish painting of the final Spanish attack on the Aztec's island-city capital of Tenochtitlan–Tlatelolco, in 1521.

The meeting of the Spanish conquistador Hernán Cortéz and the Aztec ruler Moctezuma II at Tenochtitlan–Tlatelolco in 1519. Cortéz was at first received as a god, but was later driven from the Aztec capital. Returning in 1521, he overthrew the Aztec empire with the help of native allies.

Smallpox spread southwards through Central America to the populous Andean area, weakening these communities in advance of Spanish attack. Death rates on the scale the Aztecs had suffered so weakened Maya kingdoms in southern Mexico and Guatemala that a Spanish army was able to conquer them during a series of hard-fought battles in 1524. The disease killed the Inka emperor and his heir apparent, along with half the officers and men in the imperial army. An illegitimate son of the dead emperor disputed the succession with a legitimate son. The pretender had hardly defeated his rival when the Spaniards invaded the Inka empire, already terminally weakened by a major measles epidemic the invaders had helped to spread southwards along South America's Pacific coast as they sailed from Panama to Peru between 1531 and 1532. The emperor Atawalpa watched helplessly as the imperial forces faded away—even before the Spanish invaders scattered his personal escort with cannon fire and cavalry lances in the public square of Cajamarca.

Old World diseases continued to assault America's native peoples long after the conquests they had helped bring about. Bubonic plague struck at the center of colonial New Spain between 1545 and 1548; and smallpox recurred from 1562 to 1564, plague from 1576 to 1580, measles and smallpox from 1592 to 1593, and plague once more from 1613 to 1617. The indigenous population of this best-documented colonial region fell from some 30 million in 1519 to less than a million in 1620. Native Americans throughout the hemisphere

This Aztec drawing from a codex depicts victims of the smallpox epidemic of 1538. Shrouds cover bodies of the dead; two Aztecs in the throes of death are shown at bottom right.

THE GRANGER COLLECTION

A native Indian ambassador presents gifts to the Spanish conquistador Hernán Cortéz and his berobed female interpreter, Doña Marina, in this scene from an Aztec codex.

E.T. ARCHIVE/AUSTRALIAN PICTURE LIBRARY

suffered the world's most catastrophic epidemic, perhaps as many as 100 million perishing betwee 1493 and 1620.

Some native peoples disappeared altogether, including Florida's Calusa. In the same region, a dozen Timucuan-speaking peoples diminished to a few hundred survivors, whom Spain evacuated in 1764. Lower California's Pericue, Cochimie, and Guaycura peoples perished within 150 years of Jesuit missionaries founding the first Christian mission on the peninsula in 1697.

In the Americas, then, cultures clashed only to the extent that native societies survived the combined onslaughts of disease and both voluntary (in the case of Europeans) and involuntary (in the case of Africans) colonization.

With their dominant social and economic status, many European males took sexual advantage of native American women. These unions diminished native numbers but created a rapidly growing mestizo population, or "New American Race". As this population expanded, it became increasingly common for European, Creole, and mestizo men to take native wives or concubines, who helped to swell mestizo numbers by passing as mestizos. As a result of this process, some indigenous cultures became extinct. Such was the fate of the Opata culture of northwestern Mexico in the nineteenth century.

While natives living in high altitudes from Mexico to Chile were genetically adapted to an environment short in oxygen, Europeans adapted only slowly to these conditions. Men became infertile, and women had great difficulty bearing live babies. For this reason, the mountains remained native strongholds, even though a few European colonists economically exploited the general population over whom they ruled.

The tropical lowlands differed dramatically from the highlands. Malaria, hookworm, and other introduced diseases decimated most of the native inhabitants of these regions. Europeans did not fare much better. With their genetic sickle cell resistance to malaria and their previous exposure to yellow, dengue, and other fevers, Africans proved to be the people best able to survive in this environment, spreading throughout the tropical lowland areas until they eventually outnumbered other groups in coastal Brazil, Venezuela, Colombia, Ecuador, Panama, Costa Rica, Nicaragua, Guatemala, and Belize.

The high European death rate in the lowlands resulted in a loosening of control over African slaves. From early in the sixteenth century, slaves began to escape from plantations, forming free African–American villages beyond colonial frontiers and often kidnapping native women for concubines and wives. Some were of mixed descent, because slave women bore the children of Europeans. Consequently, their descendants also belong to the New American Race, sharing a culture distinctive enough to generate continued clashes with Americans of European descent.

In 1492, the temperate areas were much less densely populated than the tropical highlands. As their inhabitants were struck down by Old World diseases, these zones were left relatively vacant, inviting occupation by newcomer colonists and their livestock. The rapidly industrializing urban populations of the nineteenth century had created an increased demand for meat, and so the Argentine and United States armies drove native big-game hunters from the Pampas and the Great Plains to allow newcomers to establish ranches and grow cereals. Artillery, together with deliberate destruction of the big-game species on which the natives largely depended, completed the conquest. Pampas and Plains became neo-Europes, with European land tenure, export crops, and native enclaves.

The Franciscan missionary Francisco Pareja teaching Christian concepts to Timucuan-speaking native Americans in Florida. This woodcut appeared in Pareja's *Cathecismo En Lengua Castellana y Timuquana*, which was printed in Mexico City in 1612.
THE GRANGER COLLECTION

A mid-nineteenth-century artist's impression of the landing of Roman Catholic missionaries of the Dominican order on the Venezuelan coast at Coro, and their first encounter with the native Americans whom they hoped to convert.
MARY EVANS PICTURE LIBRARY

ROYAL GEOGRAPHICAL SOCIETY/BRIDGEMAN-GIRAUDON

Maori warriors dancing in front of the great *pa* (fortress) of Oinemutu, at Lake Rotorua, in New Zealand. Once they acquired firearms in the 1820s, the warlike Maori decimated themselves in the most devastating military campaigns in the history of New Zealand.

MITCHELL LIBRARY, STATE LIBRARY OF NEW SOUTH WALES

Entitled *Smoking Out the Opossum*, this drawing, published in 1813, shows one of many hunting techniques involving the use of fire that were traditionally employed by Australian Aborigines. Aborigines used controlled burning to manage their environment for thousands of years before the coming of Europeans.

Pacific Exploration

The Treaty of Paris, signed in 1763, ended a world war and freed England and France to dispatch ships to explore the Pacific Ocean. In 1767, Europeans discovered Tahiti, and in 1769, Australia, New Zealand, and the Hawaiian Islands. The English explorer James Cook took to New Zealand the white potato, bred from an Andean ancestor. That crop, plus pigs, transformed food production among the Maori. Ships' crews carried tuberculosis and venereal diseases to the Pacific islands, where they ravaged the native peoples.

Although Australia's native peoples grew no food that the English recognized, the English saw the continent as an ideal dumping ground for convicts. Convict misery did not, however, love Aboriginal company. This cruel fact is best illustrated by the near-extermination of natives of the island of Tasmania. In 1803, the British governor of New South Wales, Philip Gidley King, dispatched 9 soldiers, 3 women, and 21 convicts to establish a European settlement on the island. In 1804, the Aborigines drove kangaroos along an ancient game path running through the site of the colonists' hamlet at Risdon Cove. The soldiers fired two cannons loaded with grapeshot at them. This was the start of a long guerrilla war. When convicts and settlers ran out of fresh meat, they shot out the upland game. Sealers slaughtered coastal mammals, and kidnapped women for their sexual pleasure. Whalers, sealers, and escaped convicts alike slaughtered native men. Sheep ate out Aboriginal food plants. By 1850, Tasmanian Aborigines were officially extinct, although descendants of kidnapped women have kept some of their heritage alive.

Australia's arid central desert became a refuge for Aboriginal people as European livestock depleted coastal and grassland resources. Yet malnutrition, epidemics—smallpox in 1789 and 1829, influenza in 1820 and 1838—venereal diseases, warfare, and interbreeding reduced Aboriginal numbers from more than a million in 1788 to 60,000 by about 1920. By 1991, the population had grown to 180,000. More than 150 "outstation" enclaves manage their own resources in their traditional lands under the Aboriginal Lands Act 1976. Australia became a major neo-Europe, exporting surplus cereal grains and meat.

Church of England missionaries initiated European colonization of New Zealand in 1814. Like other Stone Age native peoples, Maori coveted metal tools. The whalers who occasionally called at the mission stations traded muskets to Maori. In 1820, one chief sailed to England to meet the king, and returned with a suit of armor and several guns. During the following decade, Maori decimated themselves in the most lethal military campaigns in New Zealand's history. Victorious Maori enslaved enemy male survivors and "rented" captive women to crewmen of whaling vessels, further depressing the native birth rate. The Maori population diminished by half between 1800 and 1840. British authorities intervened by imposing a Draconian program of pacification. Then Europeans introduced sheep and European land tenure, and soon converted New Zealand into another neo-Europe.

European overseas colonialism reached a climax in the nineteenth century. As European industrial nations exhausted the natural resources within their borders, they sought replacements in colonies. As factories grew in size and productive capacity, their owners urged national governments to expand colonial markets for manufactured goods. When Germany finally unified, between 1870 and 1871, it copied older colonial powers and set out to conquer wherever it could. European nations raced to conquer Pacific island peoples and inhospitable parts of Africa that had long remained refuge areas, as well as the coasts and interior highlands of the Mediterranean.

At first, Europeans traded with Pacific peoples while basing whaling ships on some islands. Like native Americans, Pacific peoples had no immunity to Old World diseases. After 1770, epidemic Eurasian diseases killed between four and four and a half million natives. By 1900, only some 180,000 Polynesians survived, although Melanesians and Micronesians fared better.

In the nineteenth century, Europeans first plundered scattered groves of sandalwood trees on Pacific island coasts. European colonists then followed Christian missionaries to the islands. Some European powers preserved native land rights, which they had not done elsewhere.

Natives kept 82.5 percent of the Fiji Islands, while Euro-peans took control of the fertile coastal land near harbors to grow cotton and then sugar cane, and finally to build tourist hotels. Plantation owners brought in laborers from southern India. By 1986, their descendants comprised 48.7 percent of the population, and Fijians 46 percent, even though the latter have increased since about 1900. Europeans, Chinese, and others comprised 5.2 percent of the population at that date. Traditional Fijian culture remains at risk.

As soon as Pacific islanders stopped killing strangers, significant numbers of Europeans deserted ship (and culture) to live in native societies. "Beachcomber" genes may be present in up to three-quarters of today's "Polynesian" population. Such is the frustration of island natives with their position of social and political inequality that they have often proved a willing audience for the numerous prophets who have appeared among them to found neo-Christian sects and cults.

The Clash Continues

The global clash between national variants of Western industrial civilization and non-Western nations, peoples, and cultures continues. National politicians, multinational business executives, and scientists have, in recent years, become the primary proponents of industrial civilization. The presidents and prime ministers who have replaced warrior kings periodically send armies great and small into combat, armed with ever more lethal weapons, for mixed ideological and economic motives. While Christian missionaries continue to seek converts, Europe and the neo-Europes have become so secular that Christian dogma is no longer central to the clash of cultures. Indeed, non-Christian Japan has transformed itself into a major industrial nation on the Western model.

Even Islamic fundamentalists resist not so much Christian as scientific—that is, secular—concepts, along with political and economic domination by the Western world. As airplane, automobile, bus, and truck displaced horse, ass, and camel, they changed the face of the Arab, African, and other worlds. How? They made possible the movement of people, goods, and ideas at a pace and on a scale previously unimaginable. Only a century after a United States fleet forced Japan to open its ports to trade, Japanese factories dominated world automobile, bus, and truck production and sales.

The contemporary clash of cultures continues among greater numbers of human beings than ever before. The spread of key food crops—wheat, rice, sugar cane, maize, potato, manioc—has fed millions of people who could not have been fed before the "Columbian Exchange" began in 1492. Improved public health measures have enabled millions more to survive during the nineteenth and twentieth centuries. The world's population continues to increase. Yet disease organisms such as the tuberculosis bacterium are becoming immune to antibiotics and once again threaten humankind, and parasites lethal to human beings, such as the human immunodeficiency retrovirus, continue to evolve and to assault humankind.

In this watercolor painted in 1843, the artist Orlande Norie visualized a scene from the Maori wars in New Zealand. Unlike other native peoples, who minimized their casualties by employing guerrilla tactics against invaders, the Maori engaged British forces and colonists in pitched battles.

SYLVAIN GRANDADAM/EXPLORER/AUSCAPE

REFERENCE

⟲ The front view of the colossal seated figures of Ramses II at the Great Temple of Abu Simbel, in Lower Nubia, Egypt.

GLOSSARY

acropolis
The citadel of an ancient Greek city. The best-known example is the citadel of Athens (the Acropolis), where a number of temples were erected in the fifth century BC.

adze
A heavy, wide-bladed cutting tool which is attached at right angles to a wooden handle. It was used for trimming and smoothing timber and for such tasks as hollowing out a dug-out canoe.

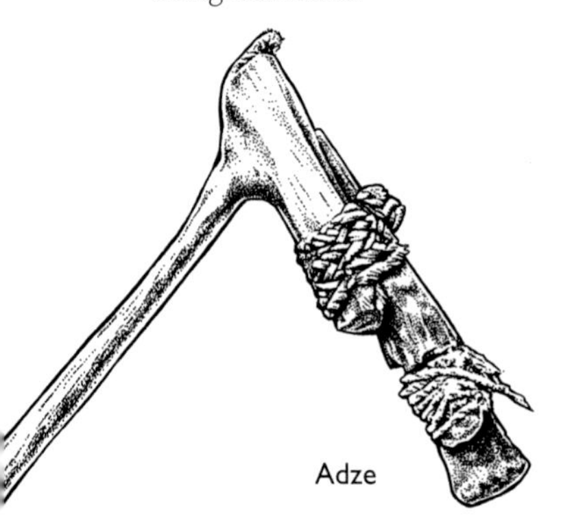

Adze

agora
The public square and marketplace in an ancient Greek city.

amphora
A pottery jar used to hold liquids, especially wine, and to store other substances, such as resin. Amphoras were made in various ovoid shapes throughout the Aegean and eastern Mediterranean regions.

Anasazi
A culture found in southwestern North America in the late prehistoric era (about AD 200 to AD 1600). The Anasazi were agricultural people known for their pueblo-style architecture and finely painted ceramics. Although exact linkages are uncertain, it is clear that modern Pueblo Indian people are descended from Anasazi ancestors. The name Anasazi is derived from a Navajo word meaning "enemy ancestors".

anthropomorphic figure
A figure or object with a human shape or character.

archaeozoology
The study of animal remains, often bones, from the past and of the impact of animals on past economies. Also called zooarchaeology.

arsenical copper
An alloy of copper and arsenic. It was easier to cast than copper, as well as being stronger and harder, and was widely used in the Andes before the introduction of tin bronze. Also called arsenical bronze.

Amphora

Anthromorphic figure

aryballos
A small, one-handled pottery flask, about 5 to 8 centimeters (2 to 3 inches) high, used for scented oil and perfume, and also for some condiments. Originally made at Corinth from about 575 BC, such jars with painted patterns on them were typical for the period until about 550 BC.

Austronesian language family
Austronesian is a major language family to which the languages of Taiwan, martime Southeast Asia, the Pacific (excluding much of New Guinea), Madagascar, and parts of the Southeast Asian mainland belong. Although all Austronesian languages are related, they are not necessarily mutually understandable.

barbican
An outer defense to a fort or settlement, often built as a tower over a gateway.

barrio
In the Andes, a neighborhood or sector of settlement.

be
In ancient Japan, the hereditary occupational groups who provided goods and labor for the Yamato state and nobility between the fifth and seventh centuries AD.

boat grave
A type of burial during the Late Iron Age in which the body or cremated remains were placed in a boat, which was then covered by a mound of earth. Boat graves are found in Scandinavia, and in East Anglia, in Britain. They were particularly common between AD 550 and AD 800.

bracteate
A thin, ornamental dish or plate made of gold or silver.

Brahmin
A member of the highest, or priestly, caste in the Hindu caste system.

Bronze Age
A prehistoric period in the Old World, defined by the use of bronze as a new material for tools, weapons, and ornaments. In Europe, the Bronze Age proper spans the second and early first millennia BC.

calendar round
A ritually and historically important calendar used

throughout Mesoamerica, in which the solar calendar of 365 days ran in parallel with a sacred 260-day ritual calendar. The calendar round is a 52-year cycle, since both calendars begin on the same day only once every 52 years.

caliphate
An Islamic empire ruled by a caliph. The title "caliph" means successor, and was adopted by the rulers of the Islamic world, who were seen as the successors of Mohammed. The caliph was the leader of all Muslims in both spiritual and civic matters.

Canopic vase

canopic vase
A container with a lid in the shape of an animal-headed god, used in ancient Egypt to hold the entrails of an embalmed body.

carnelian
A reddish variety of the semiprecious gemstone chalcedony, much favored in antiquity for jewelry. Carnelian is usually found in volcanic rocks, such as the Deccan Traps of western India (where it is particularly common). Heating improves the color.

Cham
An Austronesian language, closely related to the languages of island Southeast Asia, that was formerly widely spoken in central Vietnam and is still spoken in parts of the Southeast Asian mainland. Cham was probably spoken by the people of Vietnam's Sa-Huynh culture, a late prehistoric Iron Age culture, which formed a series of powerful kingdoms until it was overthrown by the Vietnamese in the fifteenth century AD.

chamber tomb
A type of tomb found in the Aegean region in which the burial place, consisting of one or more room-sized chambers, was at the end of a horizontal or sloping passage cut into the ground, usually into a hillside. Chamber tombs were usually family tombs, and were reused over the generations.

chape
The mounting at the upper end of a scabbard, which has a ring for attaching the scabbard to a belt.

chert
A dark gray or black form of quartz, resembling flint.

chian seed
A grain cultivated in Mesoamerica as a source of food and vegetable oil.

chinampas
A system of cultivation on artificial islands built of vegetation and mud in shallow freshwater lakes. These remarkably fertile fields were created by massive Aztec reclamation projects in the Valley of Mexico.

cinnabar
A naturally occurring ore of mercury, commonly used as a red pigment.

cist grave
A burial place made of large slabs of rock, especially slate, schist, or granite. The name comes from the Greek word *kiste*, meaning chest or box.

city-state
An independent, selfgoverning city. The city-state usually incorporated the territory surrounding the city, as well as smaller towns and villages.

ciudadela
Literally, an apartment or tenement. At the ancient Andean city of Chan Chan, the term has been applied to large, walled enclosures containing courts, storerooms, administrative structures, and platform burials. These enclosures are believed to have been the palaces of the Chimu kings.

Classical Age
The period in history that encompasses the Greek and Roman civilizations.

Codex
A pictorial manuscript. In Mesoamerica, codices were usually painted on bark paper or deerhide.

Commandery
In ancient China, an administrative unit during the Chinese Qin and Han dynasties. The term also refers to the military and administrative outposts established by the Han dynasty in Korea, Vietnam, Tibet, and central Asia.

composite bow
An archer's bow in which the wood of the bow was reinforced on one side by layers of animal sinew and on the other side by animal horn. It was more powerful than a simple bow made of a single piece of wood only.

Confucianism
A system of ethics that follows the teachings of the Chinese philosopher Confucius (Kung Fu-tzu). It emphasizes an idealized human society governed by worthy, educated leaders, in which individuals are loyal to their family and friends, and treat each other as they would like to be treated.

Coptic language
The most recent stage of the language of ancient Egypt. It was used by the Egyptian Christians, and was written in the Greek alphabet with the addition of six letters derived from the Demotic script (the most recent and cursive of the scripts of ancient Egypt).

crater
A large bowl made of pottery or metal. In ancient Greece, craters were used to serve wine, mixed with water in varying proportions, into individual drinking cups—for example, at the all-male drinking parties known as symposia.

crucible smelting
A technique of separating copper from ore by heating

the ore in an open vessel (designed to withstand very high temperatures) rather than in a closed furnace.

cultigen
A variety or species of plant that is known only in cultivation, such as maize, whose wild ancestor is uncertain or unknown.

cultural complex
An assemblage of artifacts and other physical evidence that regularly occur together within a restricted area, and are thought to represent the material remains of a particular group of people, perhaps over several generations.

cuneiform script
A system of writing that developed in Mesopotamia. By means of a square-ended reed, wedge-shaped pictograms were impressed into the smooth surface of wet clay tablets, which were then baked. Cuneiform scripts were used in particular for the Sumerian, Akkadian, Elamite, and Old Persian languages. The oldest examples of developed cuneiform script date from about 2500 BC. The name comes from the Latin word *cuneus,* meaning wedge.

Dasas
The inhabitants of northwestern India at the time of the Indo-European migrations. They are described in the Rig-Veda as having dark faces and snub noses, unintelligible speech, and no religion, but living in fortified cities and being very rich. The Dasas are often identified with the inhabitants of the towns of the Indus Valley culture.

Delphic Oracle
A seer at the Temple of Apollo at Delphi, in Greece. The oracle played an important political role, particularly during the period of Greek colonization from the eighth to sixth century BC.

Dongson drum

diadem
A crown or band of metal worn as a badge of status or office.

DNA
The basic material of chromosomes, which includes the genes. Analysis of the DNA of different primate groups has been used to determine the evolutionary line of modern humans, and DNA techniques have also been used to show for how long the various regional human populations have been separated from each other. DNA analysis of blood residue, both human and animal, on prehistoric tools and weapons may one day provide fresh information on the evolutionary relationships between a range of animal species, and between prehistoric and modern humans.

dolmen
The French term for a megalithic tomb with a single capstone carried by orthostats, or standing stones.

Dongson drum
A type of cast-bronze drum, usually large, made in northern Vietnam and southern China in the first millennium BC and used for warfare and rain-making ceremonies. The drums are named after the site of Dongson, in Than Hoa province, Vietnam, where they were first found in an archaeological context.

Doric order
One of the architectural orders of ancient Greece, characterized in particular by simple columns and a frieze of triglyphs and metopes.

Dravidian language family
Dravidian is a language family spoken in southern India to which the Tamil, Telegu, Malayalam, and Karmada languages belong. It is thought to have been spoken in northern India before the spread of Indo-European languages in the second millennium BC, and was probably the main language of the Harappans.

effigy vessel
A ceramic vessel in the form of an animal or a human. Such vessels were typical artifacts of the Mississippian period in North America (AD 75 to AD 1540).

einkorn
A variety of wheat with pale red kernels, *Triticum monococcum,* which was cultivated in Neolithic times. It probably originated in southeastern Europe and southwestern Asia, and is still grown in mountainous parts of southern Europe as grain for horses.

El Niño
A periodic climatic phenomenon in which tropical waters flow south along the Peruvian coast, causing heavy rains and ecological destruction. In South America, it usually occurs near Christmas —hence the name El Niño, "the (Christ) Child".

emmer
A variety of wheat, *Triticum dicoccum,* which has been cultivated in the Mediterranean region since Neolithic times, and is still grown in the mountainous parts of southern Europe as a cereal crop and livestock food. It is thought to be the ancestor of many other varieties of wheat.

Effigy vessel

epigraphy
The study of texts recorded on durable materials, such as wood, bone, pottery, and stone. Such texts are often the only surviving records of extinct cultures, and chronicle ancient events, beliefs, and lists of kings. Epigraphy encompasses inscriptions from the earliest complex societies to those of modern states.

ethnography
The collecting and study of basic research material, such as artifacts, for analysis of social and cultural structures and processes.

ethnohistory
The anthropological study of historical data on ethnic groups, particularly non-Western peoples.

faience
Bronze Age faience is a primitive form of glass. It is made by baking a mixture of sand and clay to a temperature at which the surface fuses into blue or green glass. Faience beads of Aegean and south-western Asian origin were traded widely in eastern and central Europe, Italy, and the British Isles in the second millennium BC.

feudal system
A hierarchical social system in which the peasantry was ruled by a class of landowners.

fibula
A metal fastener or brooch, used much like a modern safety-pin by many Iron Age and later Europeans, including the Greeks, Etruscans, and Romans. Although primarily functional, fibulas were often also highly decorated items of personal adornment.

freeholder
Members of the peasantry who owned the small plots of land they farmed. Italian freeholders were the main source of recruitment to the Roman army during the period of the Roman Republic.

funerary cult
The ongoing rituals, with their associated offerings, performed for the benefit of the deceased at the tomb or in a funerary temple, by relatives or specially appointed priests.

garrison state
A fortified state established in a strategic position. The garrison states of the Zhou feudalistic network were protected by walled cities, and ruled by the kinsmen and allies through marriage of the Zhou royal house.

geoglyph
An image created on or in the ground. It can be formed by piling up materials on the ground surface or etched into the ground by removing surface materials.

Fibula

Geometric period
A period in Greece between 900 BC and 700 BC, named after a distinctive style of pottery decorated solely with geometric designs, including circles, squares, triangles, meandering lines, zigzags, and rhombic shapes.

glyph
A painted or incised conventionalized sign. Glyphs range from concrete images, such as an animal or a house, to abstractions, such as the use of a footprint to indicate travel, to signs representing the sounds of words.

greave
A piece of armor designed to protect the lower part of the leg.

Hallstatt period
A cultural period of the Late Bronze Age and Early Iron Age in central Europe, divided into four phases, Hallstatt A, B, C, and D. The period of Hallstatt A and B (from about 1200 BC to about 800 BC), also known as the Urnfield period, was characterized by the burial practice of placing the cremated remains of the dead in clay urns, which were then buried. Hallstatt C (from about 800 BC to 600 BC) marks the beginning of the transition from the Bronze Age to the Iron Age. The Hallstatt period is named after a site in Austria. It precedes the La Tène period.

harpoon
A spear-like missile with backward-pointing barbs, loosely hafted, and attached to a line. When hurled at marine mammals, such as seals, the point, if it finds its mark, is separated from the shaft, and the barbs prevent it from being dislodged. The line is used to retrieve the catch.

Glyph

heddle loom
A specialized loom that lifts some of the warp (lengthwise) threads so that the weft (crosswise) threads can be passed through the warp easily and quickly.

Helladic culture
The culture of central and southern mainland Greece in the Bronze Age (3000 BC to 1100 BC).

Hellenistic period
The era between the death of Alexander the Great (323 BC) and the rise of the Roman Empire (27 BC), when a single, uniform civilization, based on Greek traditions, prevailed all over the ancient world, from India, in the east, to Spain, in the west.

helot
A serf or slave in ancient Sparta.

hero cult
In ancient Greece, the worship of a god of partly human and partly divine origin, such as the

Hieroglyphs

worship of the hero Hercules. Hero-cult worship was the forerunner of the worship of living rulers, a feature of Hellenistic and Roman times.

hieroglyphs
The pictographic script used for inscriptions in ancient societies. Many of the symbols consist of a conventionalized picture of the idea or object they represent.

historiography
The writing of history, with particular reference to the examination and evaluation of primary source material. Also, the study of the development of historical method. Here, a term denoting the products of historical writing.

Holocene
The present geological epoch, which began some 10,000 years ago. It falls within the Quaternary period and followed the Pleistocene. The Holocene is marked by rising temperatures throughout the world and the retreat of the ice sheets. During this epoch, agriculture became the common human subsistence practice.

hunter-gatherers
Groups of humans who subsist by gathering wild plants and hunting wild animals. Although many hunter-gatherers regularly move their camp to be near seasonally available wild foods, others remain virtually sedentary throughout the year.

hypostyle
A building in which the roof or ceiling is supported by columns.

iconography
The art of representing or illustrating by means of pictures, images, or figures.

ideogram
A pictorial symbol representing a concept or idea directly, rather than standing for its name or the sequence of sounds that make up its name. Ideograms were often used in early writing systems. (Also known as ideograph).

intaglio
Incised carving (as opposed to relief carving), in which the design is sunk below the surface of hard stone or metal.

Ionic order
One of the architectural orders of ancient Greece, characterized in particular by column heads with spiral coils on each side.

Iron Age
A late prehistoric period in the Old World, defined by the use of iron as the main material for tools and weapons.

Iron-making, direct process
The technique of smelting iron ore in a furnace with charcoal and limestone to produce a spongy, low-carbon form of iron known as a bloom. This is a ductile material, which can then be forged into tools and weapons.

iron-making, indirect process
The technique of smelting iron ore in a furnace at a very high temperature to yield a molten, high-carbon form of iron. Because the high-carbon content makes this material too brittle for most direct uses, it must undergo a secondary process, oxidization, to make it more ductile. It can then be forged into weapons and tools. The indirect process of iron-making was developed in China early in the first millennium BC.

Jainism
An ascetic sect founded in northern India in the sixth century BC in reaction to the rigid Vedic Hindu caste system. Jainism developed alongside Buddhism, with similar doctrines, but emphasized withdrawal from the world.

kana
The Japanese writing system, developed in the ninth century AD from simplified Chinese characters. There are two types of *kana* (*hiragana* and *katakana*), each with symbols for 46 basic sounds. In theory, any sound in Japanese can be written using one of the *kana* systems, but in practice, a combination of the two, together with Chinese characters, is used.

kaolin
A fine white clay formed by the weathering of volcanic rocks. Kaolin is named after the mountain in China that yielded the first clay of this type sent to Europe; it is also known as china clay.

***Karoshti* script**
One of the two main early Indian scripts, used from the fourth century BC to between the third and fourth centuries AD. It may have developed from the Aramaic used by the Achaemenid rulers of northwestern India and was particularly common in that region and along the Ganges Valley as far as Bengal. The name *Karoshti* literally means asses' lips, and is said to refer to the similarity of the highly curvilinear script to the movement of asses' lips.

kava
A narcotic drink prepared by crushing the aromatic roots of the shrub *Piper methysticum* in water. Kava was drunk at ceremonial events in Fiji and other parts of the central Pacific.

Kana

Khmer
An ethnolinguistic group who speak a language that is part of the Mon-Khmer group of Austro-Asiatic languages.

The Khmer are best known for the art and architecture of the ancient city of Angkor, dating from the ninth to the fourteenth centuries AD. Today, the Khmer are found mostly in Cambodia, and in northeastern Thailand and southern Vietnam.

knapping
A technique of striking flakes or blades from a hard, brittle rock, such as flint or obsidian, by means of short, sharp blows delivered with a hammer of stone, bone, or wood. Knapping was used to fashion stone tools and weapons, such as blades and arrowheads, and in the Harappan culture of the Indus Valley was also applied to making beads from agate and carnelian.

kurgan
The Russian term for a burial mound. It is most often used in connection with the nomad cultures of southern Russia and the Ukraine from the fourth millennium BC onwards.

La Tène period
A cultural period of the Iron Age in central Europe lasting from about 500 BC until the Roman conquest of Gaul, in about 50 BC. It is named after a site in Switzerland.

lapis lazuli
A blue-colored semiprecious stone much prized by ancient peoples for use in jewelry and other decorative items. It is found in northern Afghanistan and Iran.

Lapita
A distinctive type of pottery, with finely made bands of decoration in geometric patterns, that appeared throughout much of the western Pacific about 3,000 years ago. In some sites, Lapita pottery is associated with elaborate shell tools and ornaments, the use of obsidian, and long-distance trade, so that it appears to represent a culture, although this is not yet clear.

latifundia
Large agricultural estates owned by the Roman upper classes and usually worked by slaves. The first *latifundia* were created in Italy towards the end of the Roman Republic. They were common throughout the western part of the empire in the early centuries of the first millennium AD.

Linear A script
The system of writing used in Minoan Crete from the early palace period (1900 BC to 1700 BC) until about 1400 BC. A syllabic script, it is found most often inscribed on clay tablets (in the form of economic records) and on religious vessels made of stone.

Linear B script
The system of writing used in Mycenaean Greece. Like Linear A, it is a syllabic script and was probably created in Crete in the late fifteenth century BC by adding many signs to the existing Linear A signs. It is known chiefly from Knossos, on Crete, from Pylos, in Mycenae, and from Tiryns and Thebes, on the Greek mainland. The script is found most often inscribed on clay tablets, but also on terracotta jars that were traded throughout the Aegean region. Linear B was the writing system used for the economic administration of the kingdoms of Mycenae.

loess
A loamy deposit consisting of fine particles of windblown soil, laid down during the Ice Age. Loess forms a fertile and easily worked soil.

logograph
A symbol that represents a frequently recurring word or phrase. Also called a logogram.

lost-wax casting
A method of casting complex forms, such as statuary. The object is modeled in wax and then surrounded by a clay mold. When the clay is heated, the wax melts and drains away, leaving a hollow space that can be filled with molten metal.

macehualli
In the Aztec period, a commoner who cultivated land held by his or her descent group.

magnetite
A magnetic form of iron. In the Mesoamerican region, especially in the Early Formative period (1500 BC to 900 BC), it was commonly mined and polished to make mirrors and compasses.

maguey
The fleshy-leafed agave plant of tropical America. American Indians ate both the flowerhead, which they harvested after it had bloomed, and the heart of the maguey, which they prepared by digging up the entire plant and roasting it in earth ovens for 24 to 72 hours.

Mahavamsa
The most important historical and religious book of Sri Lanka. Written between the second century BC and the first century AD, it records the arrival of the Indo-European-speaking Sihalas in the fifth century BC and the conversion of Sri Lanka to Buddhism in the third century BC.

Mandala

mandala
In Tantric Hinduism and Buddhism, a design, usually circular, symbolizing the universe and used as an aid to religious meditation. Although mandalas are commonly two-dimensional, such as the Tibetan *tanka* (cloth scroll painting), three-dimensional examples also exist, notably the monument of Borobudur, in Indonesia, dating from the ninth century AD.

manioc
Also called cassava, manioc (*Manihot esculenta*) is a starchy

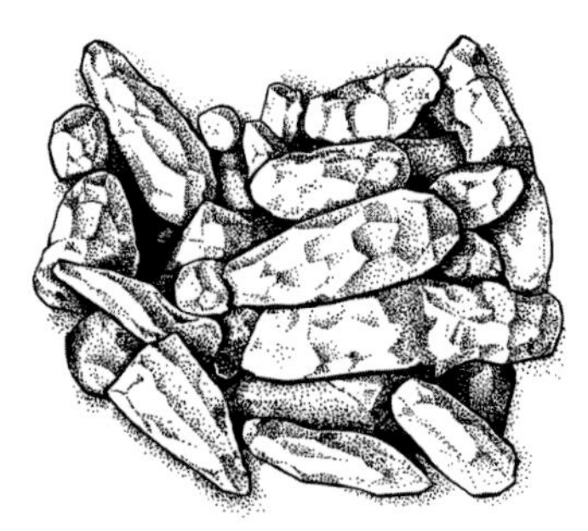

Manioc

root crop that can be processed into an important food. It was the staple diet throughout most of Amazonia and the Caribbean at the time of European contact. Manioc is the source of tapioca.

mano
The Spanish term that is commonly used by American archaeologists for the smoothed, hand-held stone used to grind seeds, pigments, or other relatively soft material against the concave surface of a larger, usually immobile, lower grindstone, or metate. It is also known as an upper grindstone.

mastaba
In ancient Egypt during the Old Kingdom, a flat-roofed, rectangular structure, housing an offering chapel, built over a deep shaft that contained a burial chamber or burial chambers. The word comes from the Arabic for bench, and was used by Egyptian workers during mid-nineteenth-century excavations because of the similarity in appearance of the mastabas to oblong benches.

Megapode (brush turkey)

mausoleum
The original mausoleum was the gigantic tomb of Maussollos, ruler of Caria, in Southwest Asia Minor, from 377 BC to 353 BC. It was considered one of the seven wonders of the ancient world. The word later came to be used for any tomb built on a monumental scale.

mayeque
In the Aztec period, a landless, rural tenant farmer.

megalithic monument
A funerary or commemorative monument built from exceptionally large stones. Its name comes from the Greek words *megas* (large) and *lithos* (stone).

megapode
A member of a family of stocky, medium-sized birds found in Australia and the islands of the southwestern Pacific that build huge mounds of decaying vegetable matter in which to incubate their eggs.

megaron
The architectural unit that forms the main hall of a Mycenaean house or the central block of a Mycenaean palace. It is rectangular in plan and comprises a main room, sometimes with a central circular hearth, that is accessed through one or two outer rooms.

Menhirs

menhir
A standing stone, most often referred to in a megalithic context.

mesquite pod
The edible, bean-like seed vessel harvested from the mesquite tree (genus *Prosopis*) of arid Central America. Native Americans cooked the sugary pods into a syrup; the seeds could also be roasted and eaten.

mestizo
A person of mixed European and American Indian ancestry.

metate
The Spanish term commonly used by American archaeologists for a smoothed, usually immobile, stone with a concave upper surface on which seeds, pigments, or other relatively soft material can be ground with the aid of a hand-held upper grindstone, or mano. It is also known as a lower grindstone, or concave quern.

metope
In the Doric architectural order, the square panel between the triglyphs of the frieze.

midden
An extensive deposit of settlement refuse, which may include the remains of shells, bones, ashes, and discarded implements. Middens are commonly built up over many years and mark the site of previous human habitation.

mitmaq
A Quechua term for a group of people moved from one place to another, frequently over long distances. The Inka used the establishment of colonies as a strategy for breaking up disloyal groups and for placing loyal groups among rebellious ones. *Mitmaq* were also used to colonize newly reclaimed land and to make it productive.

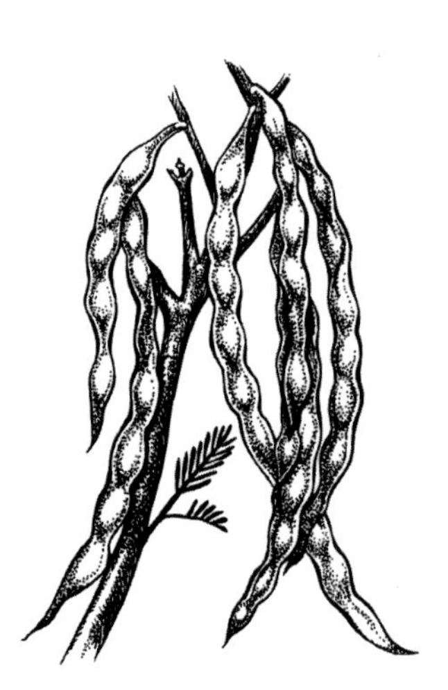

Mesquite pods

mobile
The settlement pattern of social groups who move from place to place within a given territory, building camps at each site.

Mon kingdom
The name often applied to the area of distribution in Burma (Myanmar) and Thailand of the earliest known examples of images of the Buddha. The images, in stone, terracotta, and stucco, date from between the sixth century AD and the thirteenth century AD and share a common style, called Dvaravati. There is little evidence, however, of a unified kingdom corresponding to the geographical spread of Dvaravati objects.

Mongol
The Mongol, or Yuan, dynasty (AD 1279 to AD 1368) was established by Kublai Khan, the grandson of Genghis Khan. Its rule was short, but powerful. In the early years of the dynasty, in the course of a military campaign aimed at bringing southern China under their control, Mongol armies invaded and sacked the Burmese capital at Pagan.

monotheism
The belief or doctrine that there is only one god.

Moriori
The native Polynesian inhabitants of the Chatham Islands, east of New Zealand. The Moriori, who were heavily dependent on marine resources, are thought to have settled the islands from New Zealand about AD 1400. They were conquered, enslaved, and assimilated by Maori immigrants in the mid-1800s.

mound architecture
The use of elevated mounds of stone and earth as the foundation for buildings, platforms, and pyramids, which were often made of adobe (mudbrick).

nation-state
A political unit consisting of a number of diverse cities and their hinterlands, organized into a single state with a unified set of laws and system of government.

Near Oceania
Those islands of the Pacific that can be reached by water-craft without going out of sight of land. Basically, Near Oceania comprises the Indonesian archipelago, the Philippines, New Guinea, and the Solomon Islands.

necropolis
A burial site or cemetery, often near a town.

Neolithic
Literally, the "New Stone Age". The term refers to the final phase of the Stone Age, when farming became an essential part of the economy.

nephrite
A form of jade, whitish to dark green in color, prized as an ornamental stone for carving and jewelry.

New World
The American continents. Also called the western hemisphere.

Noh drama
A form of Japanese theater characterized by stylized movement, music, and chanting, and the use of masks and elaborate costumes. Noh dates from the fourteenth century AD, and was originally patronized by the warrior class.

nomadic
A term used by ethnographers to describe the movements of whole social groups of pastoralists who utilize different parts of a given territory in different seasons, usually summer and winter pastures, and build camps for those periods.

nomarch
In ancient Egypt, a provincial governor.

obsidian
A black, glassy volcanic rock often used to make sharp-edged tools.

Old World
The part of the world known to Europeans before contact with the Americas, comprising Europe, Africa, and Asia. Also called the eastern hemisphere.

oligarchy
A system of government in which the state is ruled by a small clique of wealthy people.

oppidum
A fortified Celtic town that had residential, industrial, market, and administrative functions.

oracle-bone inscriptions
During the Shang dynasty, inscriptions recording predictions, made on dried turtle shell or animal bone. The shells or bones were heated with burning grass to produce patterns of cracks, which were interpreted by a diviner, and the prediction revealed by each pattern inscribed beside it. The writing system used for oracle-bone inscriptions is a prototype of modern written Chinese.

paleobotany
The study of ancient plants from fossil remains and other evidence, such as vegetable materials, preserved by charring, desiccation, or in waterlogged deposits. Paleobotany provides information about the climate and environment and about materials available for food, fuel, tools, and shelter.

Paleoindians
The big-game hunters of the Americas from the earliest known, about 10,000 BC, to about 6,000 BC. Some investigators regard the term as referring to all hunting groups involved with now-extinct mammals, in which case the peoples who hunted the species of bison that became extinct about 4,500 BC would also be classified as Paleoindians.

Paleolithic
Literally, the "Old Stone Age". It began some two million to three million years ago with the emergence of humans and the earliest forms of chipped stone tools, and continued through the Pleistocene Ice Age until the retreat of the glaciers some 12,000 years ago. The Paleolithic is equivalent to the Stone Age in sub-Saharan Africa.

palynology
The analysis of ancient pollen grains and the spores of mosses and lichens to reveal evidence of past environments.

papyrus
A reed, *Cyperus papyrus*, found in the Mediterranean region and northern Africa, especially

Egypt. Its stems, when split open, flattened out, and pasted together in two layers, formed a writing material that was easily made, flexible, and portable. The stems were also bound together to make lightweight fishing skiffs. The fan-shaped flower spray of the papyrus was a popular decorative motif in the art of ancient Egypt.

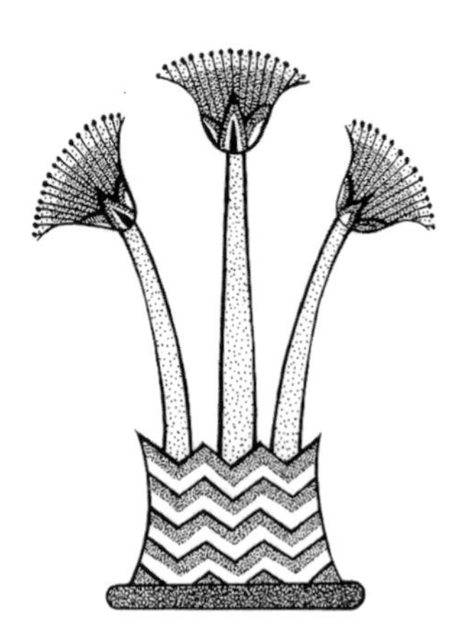

Papyrus

patrician
A member of the highest level of the hereditary aristocracy during the time of the Roman Republic.

petroglyph
A picture or symbol engraved, pecked, or incised into a rock.

pictograph
A picture or symbol that represents a word or group of words. Also called a pictogram.

pit house
A dwelling with the floor dug down below ground level to make it easier to weatherproof against wind. Often, all that remains on an archaeological site is a large, shallow pit.

platform mound
A platform of earth and stone, usually rectangular in shape, that forms a base for the construction of a building, such as a palace or temple.

plaza
An unroofed, but architecturally enclosed, space, around or within which are placed platforms, mounds and their associated buildings, such as palaces and temples.

plebeian
A member of the freeborn, commoner class during the time of the Roman Republic.

Pleistocene
The first epoch of the geological period known as the Quaternary, preceding the Holocene (or present) epoch and beginning some two million years ago. It was marked by the advance of ice sheets across northern Europe and North America. During this epoch, giant mammals existed, and in the Late Pleistocene, modern humans appeared.

Quetzal (male and female)

polis
A city-state in ancient Greece.

pre-Columbian
A term used to describe the period in the Americas before European contact.

Ptolemaic Egypt
Egypt during the Hellenistic era, when it was ruled by the dynasty of the Macedonian general Ptolemy I (323 BC to 283 BC) and his descendants.

pueblo
A Spanish term meaning town or village, and applied by sixteenth-century explorers to the village dwellings of the American Southwest. When capitalized, Pueblo generally refers to a specific Native American group, culture, or site.

quetzal
A bird of Central America, *Pharomachrus mocinno*, whose distinctive and brightly colored plumage was highly valued in Mesoamerica. The Aztec emperor Moctezuma's headdress, given as a gift to the Spanish conquistador Cortéz, was made mainly of brilliant green quetzal feathers. It is the national bird of Guatemala.

quinoa
A nutritious grain, *Chenopodium quinoa*, widely cultivated at high elevations in Andean prehistory.

Remote Oceania
The small islands of the Pacific that can only be reached by sailing out of sight of land. Remote Oceania includes all the islands east of a line stretching from the Philippines to the Solomons.

repoussé
A method of shaping metal artifacts, or of decorating them with patterns in relief, by hammering or pressing on the underside.

rune stone
A memorial stone with inscriptions of runes, a northern European script believed to have been developed in the fourth century AD. Rune stones from the Viking period are found throughout Scandinavia.

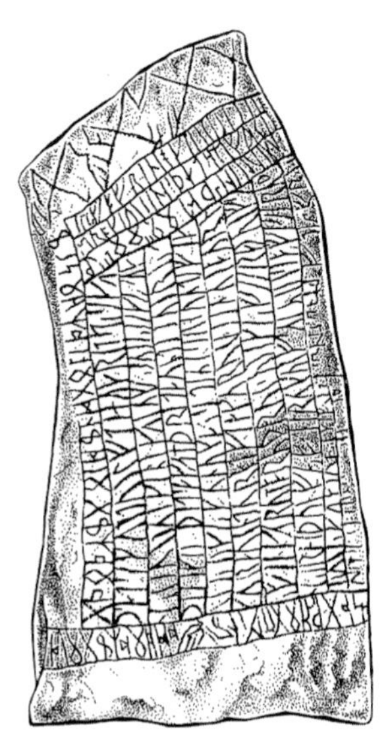

Rune stone

saddle quern
The earliest-known example of milling equipment, invented in Neolithic times. It consisted of a large, slightly concave, lower stone and a smaller upper stone. Grain spread on the surface of the lower stone was ground by being rubbed over with the upper stone.

samurai
A Japanese warrior elite that developed from small, aristocratic warrior bands of the early medieval era to become the ruling class of Japan from about AD 1200 until the late nineteenth century.

Sanskrit
The most important early Indo-European language of northern India. For several centuries, it was the medium for much Hindu and Buddhist religious writing. Sanskrit is related to Greek and Latin.

Sed festival
In ancient Egypt, a festival marking the first 30 years of a king's reign, when the gods of the land, in the form of their cult images, came together in the capital to perform a ritual renewal of the powers of the king. Some elements of the ceremony repeat those of the coronation, others are a test of the king's physical strength.

sedentism
A way of life in which people remain settled in one place throughout the year.

Seleucid
A dynasty of Greek rulers descended from Seleucus I, a general under Alexander the Great, who lived from about 358 BC to 281 BC. From the fourth century BC to the first century BC, the Seleucid dynasty ruled over an area extending from Asia Minor to the Indus River, in present-day Pakistan.

Sherd

Semite
A set of related languages assumed to be associated with an ethnic group who has inhabited portions of Southwest Asia since the time of the first cities. Arabic and Hebrew are surviving examples of Semitic languages.

shaft tomb
A tomb in the form of a rectangular shaft, with a burial chamber at its base. After the burial had been made, the chamber was roofed, and the shaft above it filled in. Elaborate examples, such as the six shaft tombs of Grave Circle A, at Mycenae, consist of stone-lined shafts with stone and wooden roofing covering the burial chambers.

shaman
A person believed to have supernatural powers. In times of sickness, shortage of game, or any other threat to a community's survival, the shaman is called upon to mediate with the spirit world on the community's behalf. The shaman presides over rituals, and may also be responsible for the keeping of laws and the continuity of traditions. Shamanism is the dominant element in the religion of most known arctic and subarctic hunter-gatherers. Most shamans are male.

sherd
A small piece of broken pottery.

Shinto
A Japanese religion, central to which is the veneration of a large number of kami, or deities, which represent all natural things, both animate and inanimate. This feature reflects its dual nature as both a loose system of folk beliefs and, until 1945, a highly structured state religion. Although Shinto is usually regarded as the indigenous religion of mainland Japan, it has a long and complex history, during which it has absorbed influences from the other religious traditions of Japan, including Buddhism, Confucianism, and folk religion.

shogun
One of a line of hereditary military dictators in Japan from about AD 1200 to AD 1867. Originally, the position was that of a general appointed by the emperor, but following the rise to power of the warrior class in the medieval period, the shogun became the real ruler of Japan, and remained so until the restoration of the Meiji emperor in the late nineteenth century.

situla
A bucket-shaped vessel made of metal, often with a swinging handle across the rim.

slash-and-burn agriculture
A method of agriculture in which vegetation is felled, left to dry out, and then burned. Seeds are later planted in holes poked into the ashes.

sodalite
A relatively hard, bright blue mineral commonly used for ornamental purposes. It is often confused with lapis lazuli, which has a similar color.

stele
An upright slab or column of stone, often decorated with carvings or bearing inscriptions.

Stele

stucco
A weather-resistant plaster used as a wall covering and for decorative architectural features such as moldings, friezes, facades, and cornices. The Maya decorated temples and other monumental architecture with stucco masks and figures.

stupa
A dome-shaped monument of earth, brick, or stone, often elaborately decorated with sculpture and railings, housing a relic of the Buddha or of a Buddhist saint.

Stupa

stylus
A sharpened wooden implement shaped like a pen with a wedge-shaped tip. It was used for impressing cuneiform writing into wet clay tablets, which were then baked.

Sumerians
The people who occupied southern Mesopotamia from about 3000 BC to 2000 BC. The Sumerians had their own distinct language, and are credited, among many other innovations, with inventing the world's earliest writing system. Some scholars believe that the Sumerians go back much further and may even have been the first sedentary inhabitants of southern Mesopotamia, from about 5500 BC.

suzerainty
The authority or power that a ruler or state holds over a dependent state, especially the control of its foreign affairs.

sweat welding
A metallurgical technique by which two pieces of metal are bonded together when heat is applied to a small piece of the same metal placed between them.

Taoism
An ancient Chinese system of philosophy that is based on noninterference with the natural world and the leading of a simple, honest life. In the second century AD, a religion with the same name appeared in China in reaction to the growing popularity of Indian-originated Buddhism.

tapa
A paper-like barkcloth of the Pacific islands made by soaking and then beating the inner bark of the paper mulberry tree (*Broussonetia papyrifera*).

taro
The large rootstock of a plant (*Colocasia* sp.) of tropical Asian origin and now found around the world. It is rich in starch and is a staple food in the Pacific islands.

tea ceremony
A traditional Japanese ceremony in which powdered, bitter green tea is prepared, served, and drunk following set rules of etiquette. The simplicity of the setting and utensils, combined with the stylized movements of the ceremony itself, is said to produce a feeling of spiritual tranquillity in the participants. Tea drinking was introduced to Japan from China more than 1,000 years ago and became popular with Zen monks in the late twelfth century. The highly ritualized tea ceremony was developed and refined in the medieval period.

tenoned mosaic
The mosaic design formed when a series of stone sculptures is set into the exterior facade of a masonry building, such as by the Maya at Copán, in Honduras. There, the front of the stone was carved with a face or symbol, while the middle and rear parts formed a long butt, or tenon, that anchored the stone into the interior fill of the building. The mosaic design created by fitting together a number of stones was not only pleasing to the eye but also carried a symbolic message to the viewer.

Tea whisk and chakin cloth

Tenoned mosaic sculpture

teocalli
A Nahuatl (Aztec) term for temple.

tholos tomb
A type of tomb, built of stone and set partly underground, associated with the Mycenaean culture of ancient Greece. It consists of a beehive-shaped chamber with a corbeled roof, accessed through a long passage called a *dromos*. The entrance to the passage is a tall doorway topped by a steep-sided gable.

tlatoani
A Nahuatl (Aztec) term for ruler.

triglyph
In the Doric architectural order, the vertically grooved panel between the two metopes of the frieze.

tuff
A hard rock of volcanic origin, comprised of compacted or cemented volcanic ash and dust.

tuffaceous rock
A soft, porous rock consisting of compacted volcanic ash or dust.

tumulus
A large, circular tomb with an earthen mound on top. Tumuli were used for the burial chambers of Etruscan aristocrats in the Archaic period (from the sixth century BC to the fifth century BC), and the style was later revived by the Roman emperors Augustus and Hadrian.

tussah
A strong, coarse, tan-colored silk obtained from the cocoon of wild silkworms in China. When woven, this silk results in a tougher, shorter-fibered fabric than that made from the silk of the cultivated varieties of silkworm.

'Ubaid period
The period in southern Mesopotamia during which the first villages, and later, the first towns and cities, appeared and many of the characteristics of Sumerian civilization emerged. Objects such as clay tools, a distinctive style of painted pottery, and characteristic buildings help archaeologists identify settlements that were occupied during the 'Ubaid period. It extended for about 2,000 years from about 5500 BC.

Urnfield period
A group of related Late Bronze Age cultures in Europe characterized by the practice of placing the cremated remains of a dead person in a pottery funerary urn, which was then buried in a cemetery of urns. The practice dates from about 1300 BC, when urnfield graves became increasingly common in eastern central Europe; from there, this burial rite spread west, to Italy and Spain, north, across the Rhine to Germany, and east, to the steppes of Russia. Other features of the Urnfield period include copper-mining and sheet-bronze metalworking. The Urnfield period continued until the start of the Iron Age, about 750 BC, when inhumation once again became the dominant form of burial in many areas.

Vedas
The ancient sacred writings of Hinduism, comprising the Rig-Veda, the Yajur-Veda, the Sama-Veda, and the Atharva-Veda. The Rig-Veda records the arrival of Indo-Europeans in India, their struggles with the Dasas, and the establishment of their religious, cultural, and social life. The Vedas are written in Sanskrit and are thought to have been compiled in the late second millennium BC.

Villanova period
An Early Iron Age period in Italy, extending from about 900 BC to about 700 BC, that laid the foundations for the Etruscan culture. It is named after a site near Bologna.

waka
A Quechua term for a sacred place or object. In modern archaeological usage, it usually refers to an archaeological site—in particular, a large adobe mound.

Wei zhi
The official history of the Chinese Wei dynasty (AD 220 to AD 264), compiled in the late third century and containing important early written accounts of the Japanese islands.

wet-rice technology
A type of farming in which rice is grown in specially prepared flooded fields known as paddies. Although rice can also be grown under dry conditions, wet-rice cultivation in paddy fields is much more productive, and has a considerable antiquity in Asia. The paddy fields are surrounded by low embankments, or levees, and must be continually leveled to maintain a constant depth of water, usually about 10 centimeters (4 inches). The fields can be flooded naturally or by irrigation channels, and are kept inundated during the growing season. About a month before harvesting, the water is removed and the field left to dry.

Growing wet rice

Zen
A school of meditative Buddhism that developed in China under Taoist influence in the sixth century AD. It emphasizes simplicity, restraint, and a strictly disciplined way of life as the means to enlightenment. Zen had a profound influence on the religious and artistic life of medieval Japan.

ziggurat
A truncated pyramid of varying height that served as a platform for temples in the early cities of Mesopotamia. The first ziggurats were modest constructions, but by 2000 BC, more imposing examples dominated the great cities of southern Mesopotamia.

Ziggurat

ILLUSTRATIONS: KEN RINKEL

INDEX

C

D

E